CAMELOT AND AVALON

A Distributed Transaction Facility

THE MORGAN KAUFMANN SERIES IN DATA MANAGEMENT SYSTEMS

Series Editor, Jim Gray

Camelot and Avalon: A Distributed Transaction Facility
Edited by Jeffrey L. Eppinger (Transarc Corporation), Lily B. Mummert (Carnegie Mellon University), and Alfred Z. Spector (Transarc Corporation)

Database Modeling and Design: The Entity-Relationship Approach
Toby J. Teorey (University of Michigan)

Readings in Object-Oriented Database Systems
Edited by Stanley B. Zdonik (Brown University) and David Maier (Oregon Graduate Center)

Readings in Database Systems
Edited by Michael Stonebraker (University of California, Berkeley)

Deductive Databases and Logic Programming
Jack Minker (University of Maryland)

CAMELOT AND AVALON

A Distributed Transaction Facility

Edited by

Jeffrey L. Eppinger
Transarc Corporation

Lily B. Mummert
Carnegie Mellon University

Alfred Z. Spector
Transarc Corporation

MORGAN KAUFMANN PUBLISHERS, INC.
SAN MATEO, CA

Sponsoring Editor Bruce Spatz
Production Editor Sharon Montooth
Cover Designer Victoria Ann Philp

Library of Congress Cataloging-in-Publication Data

Camelot and Avalon : a distributed transaction facility / edited by Jeffrey L. Eppinger, Lily B. Mummert, Alfred Z. Spector.
p. cm. -- (The Morgan Kaufmann series in data management systems, ISSN 1046-1698)
Includes bibliographical references and index.
ISBN 1-55860-185-6
1. Distributed data bases. 2. Avalon. 3. Camelot (Computer file)
I. Eppinger, Jeffrey L. II. Mummert, Lily B. III. Spector, Alfred Z. IV. Series.
QA76.9.D3C363 1991
005.75'8--dc20 90-24944
CIP

Morgan Kaufmann Publishers, Inc.
2929 Campus Drive, Suite 260
San Mateo, CA 94403

95 94 93 92 91 5 4 3 2 1 **RRD**

This research was sponsored by IBM and by the Defense Advanced Research Projects Agency (DOD), ARPA Order No. 4976 (Amendment 20), under contract F33615-87-C-1499 monitored by the Avionics Laboratory, Wright Air Force Aeronautical Laboratories, Wright-Patterson Air Force Base. The views and conclusions contained in this document are those of the authors and should not be interpreted as representing the official policies, either expressed or implied, of any of the sponsoring agencies or of the United States Government.

Foreword

Camelot and Avalon are landmark systems – they show how the transaction concept can be layered atop operating system kernels and how transaction semantics can be integrated with conventional programming languages. The result is a transactional execution environment for all applications. With this design, programming languages can easily provide persistent data types; implementors of new types can make the types transactional; and implementors of applications can structure the applications as collections of transactions. It is now widely accepted that transactions are the key to constructing reliable distributed objects and computations. In the past, transactions were used almost exclusively in commercial database applications. Such applications use transactions to get the *ACID* execution properties:

- Atomicity: The transaction consists of a collection of actions. The system provides the all-or-nothing illusion that either all these operations are performed or none of them are performed – the transaction either commits or aborts.

- Consistency: Transactions are assumed to perform correct transformations of the abstract system state. The transaction concept allows the programmer to declare such consistency points and allows the system to validate them by application-supplied checks.

- Isolation: While a transaction is updating shared data, that data may be temporarily inconsistent. Such inconsistent data must not be exposed to other transactions until the updater commits. The system must give each transaction the illusion that it is running in isolation; that is, it appears that all other transactions either ran previous to the start of this transaction or ran subsequent to its commit.

- Durability: Once a transaction commits, its updates must be durable. The new state of all objects it updated will be preserved, even in case of hardware or software failures.

These ACID properties were first used to protect data in centralized database applications. But with the advent of distributed databases, transactional RPC became the key technique for structuring distributed database queries and updates. About a decade ago, researchers began generalizing the transaction concept to the broader context of distributed computations. The Argus project at the Massachusetts Institute of Technology, and the TABS group at Carnegie Mellon University pioneered this work. The MIT group, led by Barbara Liskov, evolved the CLU language to Argus, a persistent programming language that included distributed and nested transactions. The CMU group, led by Alfred Spector, initially focused on integrating a general transaction model with an operating system kernel. Their goal was to structure the transaction manager as an "open" interface which could be used by any programming language and any resource manager. They implemented the

TABS system which provided an open, general-purpose nested-transaction mechanism on top of the Accent kernel. By 1985, both the Argus and TABS systems were operational and both demonstrated the validity of the approach, but both had disappointing performance. The thesis of TABS was that transactions could be efficiently layered on an operating system kernel as a general-purpose facility open to all resource managers (data servers in TABS/Camelot terminology). Camelot, the successor to TABS, corrected many of its performance problems, generalized many of the basic concepts, and demonstrated the original thesis – the Camelot transaction manager was efficient and derived much of its performance, flexibility, and generality from careful use of operating system kernel facilities. Included with Camelot is the Library, a collection of C procedures that ease resource manager (data server) implementation. Several resource managers have been written using the Camelot Library, including the Jack and Jill example in Chapter 5 of this book. The Avalon programming language, a persistent C++, is implemented as a layer on Camelot. Both Avalon and the Camelot Library show how persistent programming languages can be implemented atop an open transaction manager. It is fair to say that Camelot and Avalon have widely influenced other transaction processing systems. They made substantial contributions to algorithms in many areas. Notable examples are:

- transactional virtual memory integrated with the memory manager,
- transactional remote procedure call,
- commit protocols including lazy commit, non-blocking commit, and group commit,
- log replication protocols for a cluster of servers,
- parallel, nested transactions,
- transaction semantics integrated as a C Programming Language library to automate the standard aspects of constructing transactional clients and servers,
- persistent programming language data types, and
- a zero-knowledge approach to authenticating and authorizing clients and servers.

Their solutions in these areas are prototypes for future transaction processing systems. Open recovery managers such as IBM's MVS DBSR, DEC's VMS DECdtm, and X/Open DTP all have this open style, allowing new resource managers to implement new object types with transactional semantics.

This book tells ALL about Camelot and Avalon. It gives the design rationale, explains the key algorithms, and then describes how they are implemented. The presentation should satisfy even the most curious; it includes implementation details down to the C-structures of interfaces and control blocks. In addition, it includes a detailed study of the performance of the resulting system. As such, this is an excellent book for the novice and the guru, alike. It teaches the novice the basic concepts, and exemplifies these concepts with a concrete implementation. It presents the guru with a whole new world: one in which transactional RPC is not a special-purpose database-only technique, but rather a structuring principle for reliable distributed computations. It shows how the transaction mechanism interacts with the operating system kernel, the communication subsystem, and how it is externalized to its resource manager and application clients. In addition, it explains the system's performance and administration.

Jim Gray
Digital Equipment Corporation

Preface

This book presents details of a general-purpose distributed transaction facility. Future thinking information system specialists will find that this book addresses transactions from paradigms for modern programming languages to details of two-phase commitment protocols. Our goal is to provide the reader with a comprehensive view of an experimental distributed transaction facility so that he can develop a good *intuitive* understanding of these vital concepts as distributed systems comes of age.

Camelot and Avalon are research systems built at Carnegie Mellon University. Camelot is a transaction processing facility for C programmers. It is layered on top of the Mach operating system. The Camelot Library provides procedures and macros that naturally extend C for transaction semantics. Avalon is a language for C++ programmers that extends C++ to support transactions and highly concurrent access to shared data. Avalon is implemented as a layer on top of Camelot.

The book is organized into six parts to reflect the different levels of understanding on which the reader might focus:

- **Part I: The Extended Camelot Interface** presents the high-level interface for Camelot programmers. We assume a good understanding of UNIX[1] and C. The first chapters in this part introduce Camelot and Mach. The Camelot chapter also presents a brief introduction to transactions. The Mach chapter includes material on how to create transactional remote procedure call interfaces.

  Subsequent chapters in this part describe the Camelot Library and Node Configuration Application. The Camelot Library provides extensions to the C programming language implemented with macros and calls to library procedures. To help clarify the explanations, we repeatedly refer to an example application (Jack) and data server (Jill) that are distributed with Camelot. Jack provides an interactive interface that is invoked in response to user commands. Jill implements read and write operations on a recoverable array of non-negative integers.

- **Part II: The Primitive Camelot Interface** describes Camelot's low-level message interfaces. These interfaces are hidden by the Camelot Library and the Camelot Node Configuration Application. Chapters in this part describe the interfaces for Mach's message passing and thread of control primitives, as well as interfaces to Camelot's recoverable virtual memory, transaction management, and node management components. The material discussed in these chapters presents Camelot's structure in much greater detail and should aid in debugging Camelot programs. It also provides information needed to write new Camelot libraries.

[1]Registered trademark of AT&T.

- **Part III: Design Rationale** explains how Camelot is organized internally. The first chapter describes the overall design of Camelot. Subsequent chapters describe each of the Camelot components in detail.
- **Part IV: The Avalon Language** presents a new programming language that extends C++ to provide support for transactions. In Avalon, the recoverability attribute for storage is inherited via the type mechanism. The language also supports hybrid atomic transactions to allow highly concurrent access to data.
- **Part V: Advanced Features** presents three research packages that can be used with Camelot. The first package is an experimental version of the Camelot Library for Lisp. The second is the Strongbox security package. The third is the distributed log facility that allows Camelot nodes to spool log data to stable storage that is maintained on other nodes.
- **Part VI: The Appendices** describe how to debug Camelot programs, the Camelot abort codes, the Camelot interface specifications, and the Avalon grammar.

Readers that desire a high-level view of the system should focus on the early chapters in each part as they introduce issues each part addresses. The reader that desires a broad understanding of distributed transactions should read the first and third parts of the book as they present high-level concepts and design decisions of Camelot. Specialists that wish to learn how to implement a distributed transaction facility will find the functional separation of the Camelot components in Parts II and III makes the implementation details easier to grasp. Researchers will find discussions of the many novel aspects of the Camelot and Avalon systems throughout the book.

This document describes Camelot as of release 1.0(84) and Mach as of release 2.5. This book was a collaborative effort of Joshua Bloch, Stewart Clamen, Eric Cooper, Dean Daniels, David Detlefs, Richard Draves, Dan Duchamp, Jeffrey Eppinger, Maurice Herlihy, Elliot Jaffe, Karen Kietzke, Richard Lerner, Su-Yuen Ling, David McDonald, George Michaels, Lily Mummert, Sherri Nichols, Randy Pausch, Alfred Spector, Peter Stout, Dean Thompson, Doug Tygar, Jeannette Wing, and Bennet Yee. Kathryn Swedlow provided editorial assistance. Initially, this book was oriented as a Camelot manual. The focus later shifted to a comprehensive description of Camelot and related software. We thank Jim Gray, Norm Hutchinson, and Domenico Ferrari for their guidance during this refocusing.

The developers of Camelot are deeply indebted to the initial users of the system, who have helped to uncover a number of bugs and design failures. These users are Steven Berman, Gregory Bruell, Mark Hahn, Andrew Hastings, Scott Jones, Toshihiko Kato, Jay Kistler, Puneet Kumar, Maria Okasaki, Mahadev Satyanarayanan, Ellen Siegel, and David Steere. Prose from various Mach Project documents has been incorporated into the text, with permission of the authors (including Mary Thompson and Rick Rashid).

Jeffrey L. Eppinger
Transarc Corporation

Lily B. Mummert
Carnegie Mellon University

Alfred Z. Spector
Transarc Corporation

Contents

List of Figures

List of Tables

Part I

The Extended Camelot Interface

Chapter 1

Introduction to Camelot

Alfred Z. Spector
Jeffrey L. Eppinger

Distributed transactions are an important programming paradigm for simplifying the construction of reliable and available distributed applications, particularly applications that require concurrent access to shared, mutable data. The Camelot[1] distributed transaction facility simplifies the construction of such applications by providing an easy-to-use and efficient implementation of distributed transactions.

1.1 Background

A transaction is a collection of operations bracketed by two markers: `BEGIN_TRANSACTION` and `END_TRANSACTION`. Transactions provide three properties that reduce the attention a programmer must pay to concurrency and failures [39, 107]:

1. **Failure atomicity**: If a transaction's work is interrupted by a failure, any partially completed results will be undone. A programmer or user can then attempt the work again by reissuing the same or a similar transaction.

2. **Permanence**: If a transaction completes successfully, the results of its operations will never be lost, except in the event of a catastrophe. Systems can be designed to reduce the risk of catastrophes to any desired probability.

3. **Serializability**: Transactions are allowed to execute concurrently, but the results will be the same as if the transactions executed serially. Serializability ensures that concurrently executing transactions cannot observe inconsistencies. Therefore, programmers are free to cause temporary inconsistencies during the execution of a transaction knowing that their partial modifications will never be visible.

[1]The name Camelot stands for **Ca**rnegie **Me**llon **Lo**w **O**verhead **T**ransaction Facility.

It is assumed that programmers write transactions so that they will take the database from one consistent state to another. With this consistency assumption and the failure atomicity, permanence, and serializability properties, databases are guaranteed to remain consistent across failures. Frequently, the three transaction properties and the consistency assumption are called the four ACID properties of a transaction: **a**tomicity (failure atomicity), **c**onsistency, **i**solation (serializability), and **d**urability (permanence).

A transaction that performs operations on objects scattered across a distributed system is said to be a *distributed transaction*. The distribution of objects on multiple processing nodes can permit increased performance and system availability due to parallelism and the storage of multiple copies of data. For example, the use of *replicated* objects can permit access to data despite the failure of some of the nodes on which those data reside. As in centralized systems, transactions control the effects of parallelism and failures, thereby making it easier to maintain invariants on shared data. IBM Almaden's R* and Quicksilver, MIT's Argus, and Tandem's NonStop SQL [66, 42, 75, 115] are four of a number of systems that support distributed transactions.

To better support parallelism and limit the effects of failures, transactions can be *nested* [82, 94]. Nested transactions permit a transaction to spawn child transactions that can run in parallel. All children are synchronized so that both they and the parent transaction still exhibit serializability. Because nested transactions are permitted to abort without causing the parent transaction to abort, they can permit parent transactions to tolerate failures. The properties of nested transactions are listed below. For more details on the Camelot nested transaction model, see Chapter 9.

- An outermost (or *top-level*) transaction can initiate multiple nested transactions that can execute in parallel with each other. Nested transactions may in turn spawn other nested transactions. In the model used in Camelot, a parent suspends its operation until all of its children commit or abort.

- A nested transaction may inherit locks that are held by an ancestor, but not those held by a sibling. (Note that an ancestor is suspended while its children operate.)

- When a transaction commits, all of its locks, including those that it inherited, are given to, and then held by, its parent. Hence, all locks are held until the outermost parent commits or aborts, at which time they are dropped. Correspondingly, the effects of a nested transaction are made permanent only when its top-level transaction commits.

- If a failure occurs that causes a nested transaction to abort before it reaches the end of its work, all of its work and the work of its children is undone, all locks that it acquired are either dropped or returned to its parent, and its parent is notified. The parent may then choose to continue processing or abort itself.

1.2 A Transaction Example

Transactions are commonly used in banks' computer systems. The following example describes a highly simplified banking system and demonstrates cases in which failure atomicity, serializability, and permanence are useful. The example is written using Camelot Library primitives, described in Chapter 3.

```
BEGIN_TRANSACTION
  savings_balance = fetch_balance(savings_acct_num);
  if (savings_balance < 100.00) {
    ABORT(ERROR_INSUFFICIENT_FUNDS);
  }

  savings_balance = savings_balance - 100.00;
  store_balance(savings_acct_num, savings_balance);

  checking_balance = fetch_balance(checking_acct_num);
  checking_balance = checking_balance + 100.00;
  store_balance(checking_acct_num, checking_balance);
END_TRANSACTION(status)

if (status == ERROR_INSUFFICIENT_FUNDS) {
  . . .
} else {
  . . .
}
```

Figure 1.1: A transaction to transfer $100 from savings to checking.

Figure 1.1 shows the code an automatic teller machine might use to transfer $100 from a savings account to a checking account. Consider what happens if the system should crash after it stored the reduced savings balance, but before it stored the increased checking balance. In a non-transactional environment, $100 would be lost. But, the transaction model guarantees failure atomicity; the system will undo the withdrawal from the savings account when the system restarts.

Perhaps the bank runs a process at the end of each month to add interest to each savings account. Figure 1.2 illustrates a transaction that could be used to add interest to a single account. It is possible for an "interest" transaction on a given account to run at the same time as a "transfer" transaction involving that same account. Figure 1.3 shows what could happen if these two transactions were allowed to interfere with each other. In that figure, the "transfer" transaction interrupts the "interest" transaction. When the "interest" transaction continues, it overwrites the savings balance and the record of $100 withdrawal is lost. The serializability property of transactions guarantees that transactions cannot interfere with each other in this way.

In any implementation of a transaction system, an account balance cannot be read or written unless it is cached in physical memory. Consider what would happen if $100 were transferred from savings account S_1, to checking account C_1. The account records for S_1 and C_1 are stored on disk pages with records for other accounts.[2] For efficiency, the transaction processing system may delay copying some pages back to non-volatile, secondary storage, even after the "transfer" transaction

[2]The fixed cost of reading data from and writing data to secondary storage is large, but the incremental cost is relatively small. Consequently, data are transferred in large, contiguous chunks called pages or blocks. A typical page might contain tens or hundreds of account records.

```
BEGIN_TRANSACTION
  savings_balance = fetch_balance(savings_acct_num);
  savings_balance = savings_balance * 1.004375;
  store_balance(savings_acct_num, savings_balance);
END_TRANSACTION(status)

if (status != SUCCESS) {
  . . .
} else {
  . . .
}
```

Figure 1.2: A transaction that adds monthly interest to savings account.

```
BEGIN_TRANSACTION
  savings_balance = fetch_balance(savings_acct_num);
  savings_balance = savings_balance * 1.004375;
```

...interest transaction is preempted...

```
BEGIN_TRANSACTION
  savings_balance = fetch_balance(savings_acct_num);
  if (savings_balance < 100.00) {
    ABORT(ERROR_INSUFFICIENT_FUNDS);
  }

  savings_balance = savings_balance - 100.00;
  store_balance(savings_acct_num, savings_balance);

  checking_balance = fetch_balance(checking_acct_num);
  checking_balance = checking_balance + 100.00;
  store_balance(checking_acct_num, checking_balance);
END_TRANSACTION(status)
```

...interest transaction resumes...

```
  store_balance(savings_acct_num, savings_balance);
END_TRANSACTION(status)
```

Figure 1.3: A Non-serializable Schedule

This figure shows an interleaving of transactions that is non-serializable; this results in an unrecorded withdrawal.

has finished. Therefore, if the system should crash soon after the "transfer" transaction has finished, the updated savings or checking balance might be lost. The permanence property guarantees that the effects of a completed transaction will not be lost due to such a failure. Should the system crash, the transaction system will redo any lost updates from the "transfer" transaction when the system restarts.

If the savings and checking balances are kept on different nodes, or if the "transfer" transaction is driven from a remote node, the probability of failure increases as does the potential for concurrency.

1.3 Overview of the Camelot Distributed Transaction Facility

Camelot implements the recovery, synchronization, and communication mechanisms needed to support the execution of distributed transactions and the definition of shared abstract objects. Camelot runs with the underlying support of the UNIX-compatible Mach operating system [93] and its programming tools. Camelot provides flexible support for distributed transactions that access a wide variety of user-defined objects. Internally, Camelot uses many efficient algorithms to reduce the overhead of transaction execution including *write-ahead logging*, careful management of recoverable data, and highly tuned commit protocols.

Camelot is based on the *client-server model*, with both clients and servers implemented as Mach tasks.[3] In particular, long-lived data objects are encapsulated within *data server tasks*, which execute operations in response to remote procedure calls (RPCs). RPCs (or SERVER_CALLs, in the terminology of the Camelot Library) are issued by applications or other data servers located on either local or remote nodes (See Figure 1.4). A transaction may include calls to any number of servers.

Camelot uses standard communication protocols and runs on a general purpose programming environment (Mach) on a variety of computers, including shared-memory multiprocessors. Communication protocols implemented by Camelot and Mach use the Arpanet IP and UDP protocol [86] to simplify use of Camelot in large distributed systems. Mach's UNIX-compatibility makes Camelot easier to use and ensures the availability of good program development tools. Mach provides flexible support for interprocess communication, shared memory, multiple threads of control, multiprocessors, and virtual memory. Mach's machine independence helps to make Camelot more widely useful. Camelot runs on the IBM RT[4] PC, Sun 3s[5] and DEC VAXes[6] of many types, and our experience has been that it is easily portable to other architectures that run Mach.

To further reduce the effort required to construct reliable distributed systems, the Avalon programming language utilizes Camelot facilities to provide linguistic support for reliable applications [49]. Avalon encompasses compatible extensions to C++ and automatically generates calls on Camelot and Mach facilities. Avalon is further described in Part IV of this guide.

---

[3]Mach tasks are similar to UNIX processes.

[4]Trademark of International Business Machines Corporation.

[5]Trademark of Sun Microsystems Incorporated.

[6]Trademark of Digital Equipment Corporation.

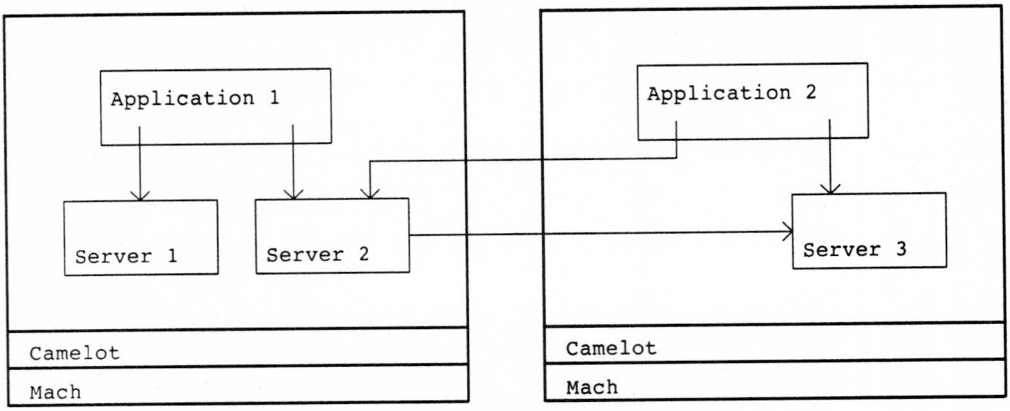

Figure 1.4: Client Server Model in Camelot
This figure illustrates the client-server model as it is used in Camelot. The applications and servers are Mach tasks. The outer boxes represent separate processing nodes. An arrow indicates an RPC issued by a client to invoke an operation on a server. Application 1 calls operations on local Servers 1 and 2. Server 2 calls an operation on remote Server 3 to execute the work requested by Application 1. Application 2 calls operations on remote Server 2 and local Server 3. In the Camelot model, servers encapsulate shared, recoverable data.

1.4 Major Camelot Functions

The basic building blocks for reliable distributed applications are provided by Mach, its communication facilities, and the MIG RPC stub generator [54, 56]. These building blocks include tasks, multiple threads of control within tasks, message passing, and shared virtual memory between tasks. Descriptions of these building blocks are provided in Chapters 2 and 7. Camelot provides the remaining facilities for the support of reliable distributed applications, including mechanisms for system configuration, recoverable storage allocation and use, transaction management, and locking.[7]

1.4.1 Node Configuration

Camelot supports dynamic allocation and deallocation of both new data servers and the *recoverable storage* in which data servers store long-lived objects. At every node, Camelot maintains a collection of configuration data to support this dynamic activity. This configuration data contains a list of the data servers that should be restarted after a crash, the recoverable storage to which they should be attached, and their recoverable storage allocation limits. These configuration data are stored in recoverable storage and may be updated transactionally by properly authorized users, as described in Chapters 4 and 10.

[7]Camelot also supports Avalon's use of hybrid atomicity.

1.4.2 Library Support for Data Servers and Applications

The Camelot Library is composed of routines and macros that allow a user to implement data servers and applications. For servers, it provides a common message handling framework and standard processing functions for system messages. Thus, the task of writing a server is reduced to writing procedures for the operations supported by the server.

The Library provides several categories of support routines to facilitate the task of writing these procedures. Transaction control routines provide the ability to initiate and abort top-level and nested transactions. Data manipulation routines permit the creation and modification of static recoverable objects. Locking routines maintain the serializability of transactions. (Lock inheritance among families of subtransactions is handled automatically.) Critical sections control concurrent access to local objects. Macros facilitate RPCs to other servers.

Applications use a subset of Library facilities. In particular, they use the transaction control routines and server access macros. The Camelot Library is described in Chapters 3 and 12.

1.4.3 Recoverable Storage

Camelot provides data servers with up to 2^{48} bytes of recoverable storage. With the cooperation of Mach, Camelot permits data servers to map that storage into their address spaces, though data servers must call Mach to remap their address space when they exceed their virtual addressing limits. To simplify the allocation of contiguous regions of disk space, Camelot assumes that all allocation and deallocation space requests are coarse (e.g., in tens or hundreds of kilobytes). The Camelot Library provides support for small-grained storage management.

Camelot provides data servers with logging services for recording modifications to objects. These services allow modifications of recoverable storage to be undone or redone after failures so that failure atomicity and permanence guarantees can be met. Camelot automatically coordinates the paging of recoverable storage to maintain the write-ahead log invariant [29].

Camelot's recovery functions include transaction abort and server, node, and media-failure recovery. To support these functions, Camelot provides two forms of write-ahead value logging: one form in which only new values are written to the log, and a second form in which both old values and new values are written. In comparison with old-value/new-value logging, new-value logging requires less log space, but increases paging for long-running transactions. This is because pages can not be written back to their home location until a transaction commits. Camelot assumes that the invoker of a top-level transaction knows the approximate length of the transaction and will accordingly specify the type of logging.

Camelot writes log data to locally duplexed storage or to storage that is replicated on a collection of dedicated network log servers [24]. The latter form of logging is called *distributed logging*. In some environments, the use of a shared network logging facility could have survivability, operational performance, and cost advantages. Survivability is better with a replicated logging facility because it can tolerate the destruction of one or more entire processing nodes. Operational advantages accrue because it is easier to manage high volumes of log data at a small number of logging nodes, rather than at all transaction processing nodes. Performance becomes better because shared facilities can have faster hardware than could be afforded for each processing node. Finally, providing a shared network logging facility is cheaper than dedicating duplexed disks to each processing node, particularly in workstation environments. Distributed logging is described in Chapter 25.

Camelot also provides utilities to save and restore archival dumps of recoverable storage. Archival dumps limit the amount of log space that is needed to recover from media failures.

Use of recoverable storage is described in Chapters 3 and 8.

1.4.4 Transaction Management

Camelot provides facilities for beginning, committing, and aborting new top-level and nested transactions.

- When a top-level transaction is begun, the transaction can be permitted to invoke operations on any number of servers, or it can be restricted to the server that initiates the transaction. In the latter case, the transaction is called *server-based* and it has substantially less overhead.

- When a transaction attempts to commit, a *blocking*, *non-blocking*, or *lazy* commit protocol can be specified. Blocking (two-phase) commit guarantees failure atomicity and permanence, but failures may cause data to remain locked until a coordinator is restarted or a network is repaired. Non-blocking commit, though more expensive in the normal case, reduces the likelihood that a node's data will remain locked until another node or network partition is repaired. Lazy commit is only for transactions that are local to a server and it does not guarantee permanence of effect until another transaction (on the same node) has later committed with either a blocking or non-blocking commit.

- Both the system and users can initiate aborts. Users can abort either the innermost nested transaction or an entire top-level transaction. Abort calls take a status variable as an argument that Camelot will propagate to all sites involved with the transaction.

In addition to these standard transaction management functions, Camelot provides an inquiry facility for determining a transaction's status. This is used to support lock inheritance and hybrid atomicity. Transaction management functions are described in Chapters 3 and 9.

1.4.5 Security and Authentication

Camelot provides an integrated set of tools, collectively called *Strongbox*, that provide end-to-end client/server authentication and encryption. Strongbox provides programmers with strong guarantees as to the privacy and integrity of their data. However, Strongbox does not prevent traffic analysis or denial of service attacks.

Strongbox primitives are very similar to Camelot Library primitives, making them easy to use. For example, a programmer uses the `SERVER_CALL` primitive to make a regular call on a server, and `SEC_SERVER_CALL` to make an authenticated, encrypted call on a server.

Because Strongbox is layered on top of Camelot, programmers are free to choose whether or not they want to use the security facility it provides. The use and design of Strongbox are described in Chapter 24.

1.5 Camelot from a User's Point of View

From an application programmer's perspective, Camelot is very easy to use. The Camelot Library hides most of Camelot's internal structure from the user and automatically calls the appropriate

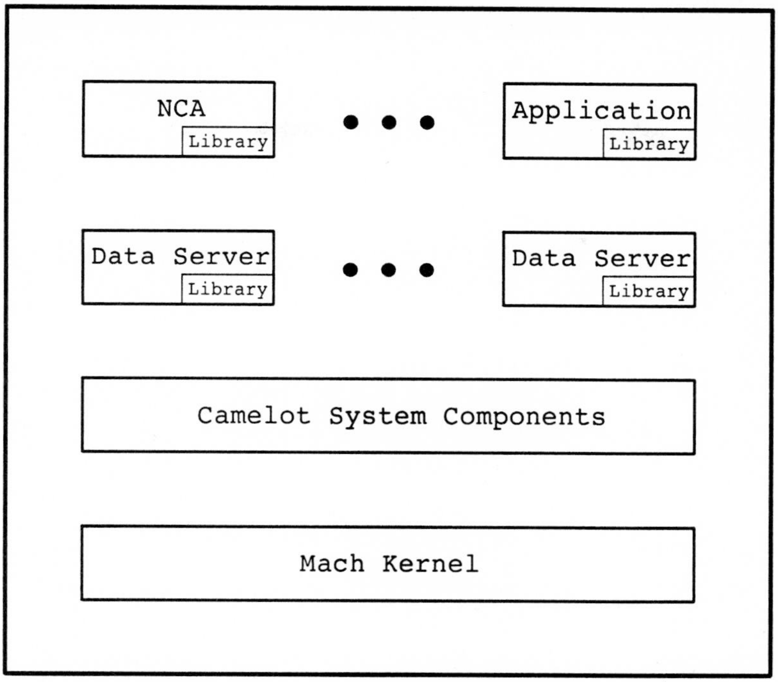

Figure 1.5: A User's View of Camelot
This figure depicts Camelot from the point of view of an application programmer. A collection of applications and data servers run on each Camelot node. Camelot is simply a black box accessed via the Camelot Library loaded in each application and data server. The Node Configuration Application (NCA) is used to administer the node.

lower-level Camelot interfaces. For example, the Camelot Library `MODIFY` macro, which assigns new data to a region of recoverable storage, automatically generates calls on lower-level Camelot interfaces to pin one or more pages in memory and spool log data. (These calls are needed to make write-ahead logging work.) Thus, users of the Camelot Library can view Camelot as a black box running on top of the Mach operating system, as illustrated in Figure 1.5.

Part I of the book presents Camelot from the application programmer's perspective. Chapter 2 gives an introduction to the Mach Operating System. Section 2.4 is particularly important because it describes how to create RPC interfaces for use with Camelot. Chapter 3 describes the Camelot Library extensions for the C programming language. Chapter 4 discusses node configuration and Chapter 5 presents sample code for the Jack application and the Jill server written using the Camelot Library.

Chapter 2

An Introduction to Mach for Camelot Users

Randy Pausch
Dean S. Thompson
Jeffrey L. Eppinger

Mach is a multiprocessor operating system that is binary compatible with Berkeley's UNIX 4.3 Release. The Mach system looks just like UNIX to programmers not using the Mach extensions. Almost all of the databases, text editors, compilers, shells, and other facilities that run on UNIX 4.3 BSD run unchanged under Mach.

The following sections describe several ways in which Mach has extended the standard UNIX process, virtual memory, and communication abstractions. This chapter provides a general background for those who intend to use Camelot through calls on the Camelot Library routines (described in Chapter 3). Users interested in bypassing the Camelot Library and building servers and applications directly on top of Mach and Camelot should read Chapter 7 and Appendix C. In addition, the *Mach Kernel Interface Manual* [8] explains the new features available under Mach.

2.1 Tasks and Threads

The idea of a UNIX process, with a collection of resources and a single thread of control, does not extend well to multi-threaded applications. Typical server implementations under the UNIX operating system use `fork` to create separate processes for each client. This consumes far more resources than are really necessary, and introduces added complexity if these processes must then use pipes or the file system to communicate. To overcome this problem, many application programmers use coroutine packages to manage multiple contexts within a single process. Such packages are inefficient on a multiprocessor because the kernel has no knowledge of these coroutines and therefore cannot schedule them on separate processors. Furthermore, a page fault in one coroutine will cause all coroutines to be suspended.

Mach addresses this problem by dividing the process abstraction into two orthogonal abstractions: the *task* and the *thread*. A task is a collection of system resources, including virtual address space and a set of capabilities. A thread is a unit of scheduling (i.e., a lightweight process), and is the specification of an execution state within a task. A task is generally a high overhead object (much like a process), whereas a thread is a relatively low overhead object.

Multiple threads may execute within a single task. On tightly coupled shared memory multiprocessors, multiple threads within the same task may execute in parallel. Thus, an application can fully exploit the available parallelism with only a modest overhead in the kernel. On a uniprocessor, multiple threads are a convenient structuring mechanism; if one thread takes a page fault, for example, other threads can still execute.

Tasks are manipulated in essentially the same way processes are under the UNIX operating system. The single task that implements a Jill server, for example, is created by Camelot through Mach calls very similar to the UNIX `fork` and `exec` calls. The single task that implements a Jack application is created by a user, probably by typing `jack` to a shell.

To simplify the development of parallel programs, Mach supports a package called C threads that provides multiple threads of control for parallelism, shared variables, mutual exclusion for critical sections, and condition variables for synchronization of threads. This package is described in greater detail in Section 7.3.

2.2 Virtual Memory Management

The Mach virtual memory design allows tasks to:

- allocate regions of virtual memory;
- deallocate regions of virtual memory;
- specify the inheritance of regions of virtual memory;
- set the protection on regions of virtual memory;
- specify a user-level task to handle paging for regions of virtual memory.

Mach allows for both copy-on-write and read/write sharing of memory between tasks. Copy-on-write virtual memory is often the result of fork operations or large message transfers. *Shared memory* is created when tasks permit their children to access parts of their address space. The only restriction Mach imposes is that regions must be aligned on system page boundaries.

When a fork operation is invoked, a new (child) address map is created based on the old (parent) address map's inheritance values. Inheritance for each page may be specified as *shared*, *copy*, or *none*. Pages specified as *shared* are available for read and write access in both the parent and child address maps. Pages specified as *copy* are effectively copied into the child's address space, although for efficiency the data is usually not actually copied until the child modifies it. If the inheritance specification is *none*, the page is not passed to the child at all. In this case, the child's corresponding address is left unallocated. By default, newly allocated memory is given the *copy* inheritance value.

Like inheritance, protection may be specified on a per-page basis. A protection is a combination of read, write, and execute permissions. Protection will be enforced only when the hardware supports it.

When virtual memory is created, special paging tasks, called *external memory managers*, may be specified to handle page faults and page-out requests. The kernel will request data from that task when a page must come in and send data to that task when a page must be written back to disk. A standard pager is provided with Mach to serve as the default for newly allocated memory. The default pager zero fills memory when it is first accessed. The current default pager uses the UNIX file system to store paged-out data, eliminating the need for separate paging partitions. External memory managers are discussed more in Section 7.2.

2.3 Interprocess Communication

Interprocess communication in the UNIX operating system occurs through a variety of mechanisms, including pipes, psuedo terminals, signals, and sockets. Internet domain sockets, the primary mechanism for network communication, have the disadvantage of using global machine specific names without location independence or protection. Data is passed uninterpreted by the kernel as streams of bytes. The Mach interprocess communication facility provides location independence, security, and data type tagging through the use of two abstractions: ports and messages.

The *port* is the basic transport abstraction provided by Mach. A port is a protected kernel object with a finite length message queue, one receiver, and any number of senders. The task that allocates a port through a Mach kernel call is initially the receiver and the only sender. This task can then publish the send access rights by registering the port with a name server. Alternatively, any task with send or receive access to a port can grant the same access to another task by sending port access rights in a message.

To reduce the number of threads in the task and the programming complexity, a task can receive on multiple ports by putting these ports into *port sets*. A port set is allocated and deallocated with special system calls. Other system calls are provided add ports into and remove ports from port sets. Initially Mach supported only one port set per task. There were calls to *enable* (add) or *disable* (remove) ports from this port set. For compatibility, Mach still supports a default port set. An *enabled port* is a port in this port set.

A *message* consists of a fixed length header and a variable size collection of typed data objects, possibly including port capabilities and pointers to out-of-line data. Most Mach users will never need to know exactly how messages are formatted, or how to create or interpret them. Instead, they will use the Mach Interface Generator (MIG) to automatically implement remote procedure calls as described in the next section.

A special user-level task called the *Network Message Server* is responsible for transparently extending interprocess communication across the network. The Network Message Server effectively acts as a local representative for tasks on remote nodes. Messages destined for ports with remote receivers are actually sent to the local network server. The local network server converts the destination port to a network address and port identifier, and forwards the message. The network server at the destination node forwards the message to the corresponding local port using the kernel interprocess communication primitives. Neither the sender nor the receiver can directly determine that they are communicating with a remote node.

Ports are used by tasks to represent services or data structures. For example, the Jill server registers a port that can be considered to represent an integer array. The Jack application requests operations on this array by sending messages to the port that represents it. Ports used this way can be considered capabilities to objects in an object-oriented system.

2.4 Mach Interface Generator

This section describes how to create communication interfaces for Camelot data servers using the Mach Interface Generator (MIG). MIG is a remote procedure call (RPC) stub compiler that is supplied with Mach systems. Section 2.4.2 explains what files MIG uses for input and output. Section 2.4.3 specifies the MIG input language. Information about MIG's advanced features can be found in the MIG Manual [54].

2.4.1 Remote Procedure Calls

A Camelot application or data server invokes an operation on a data server by issuing an RPC. Figure 2.1 shows a more detailed view of the control flow during the execution of an RPC. The calling application or data server is called a *client*.

To issue an RPC, a client first calls a local MIG-generated *stub procedure* that is responsible for executing the RPC. The stub procedure first packs input arguments into a *request message* and then sends the request message to the data server. The stub procedure then waits for the *response message* to come back from the data server.

Camelot data server processes have multiple threads of control waiting to receive incoming requests. This waiting is done within the `START_SERVER` routine, discussed in Section 3.4. When a request message arrives, the server calls a MIG-generated *demux procedure* to decode the message. (A pointer to this procedure is typically used as the `demuxProc` parameter to `START_SERVER` routine.) This demux procedure unpacks the input parameters from the message, determines which of the operations in the server is being called, and executes a local procedure call to invoke that operation. When the operation is finished, the demux procedure packs the output parameters into the response message. The packed message is sent back to the client (typically by the code in `START_SERVER`). The stub procedure on the client side receives the response message, unpacks the output parameters and returns them to the client code that called the local stub procedure.

2.4.2 Using MIG

To use MIG, a programmer creates a `.defs` file which specifies the RPCs that the server accepts. MIG compiles this specification file into three output files containing C code; two of these files are compiled and/or linked into client programs, and the third is compiled and linked into server programs. The programmer typically does not need to examine the contents of the generated files.

In order for Jack, an application, to call Jill, a server, the programmer must first create a file called `jill.defs`. This file must be processed with MIG by typing `mig jill.defs`. MIG will create the files `jill.h`, `jillUser.c`, and `jillServer.c`. The Jack application includes the header file `jill.h`; it contains `extern` and `#include` statements that define the stub procedures and their parameter types (see Section 2.4.3 below). The `.h` files generated by MIG are C++ compatible. The file `jillUser.c` contains the C code for the stub routines; it must be compiled and linked into the Jack application. The file `jillServer.c` contains the C code for the demux routine; it must be compiled and linked into the Jill server. The demux routine will have the name `jill_server`.

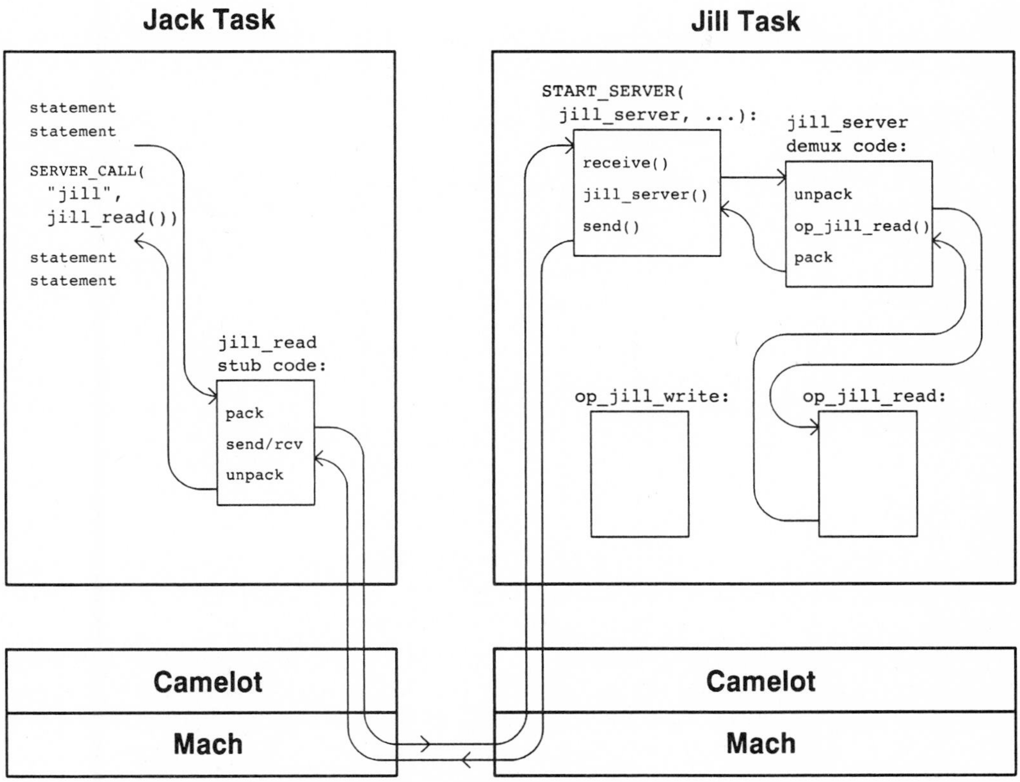

Figure 2.1: The Operation of a Mach Remote Procedure Call

This figure illustrates the control flow of an RPC. The Jill server provides two operations that can be invoked via RPCs: `jill_write` and `jill_read`. The Jack application invokes operation `jill_read` using the `SERVER_CALL` macro (see Section 3.3.3. The stub code for `jill_read` sends the request message to the Jill server. At the server side, the request message is received in the `START_SERVER` routine (see Section 3.4) and routed to the local `op_jill_read` routine by the MIG generated demux code in `jill_server`. The `op_jill_read` routine implements the `jill_read` operation. When this local procedure finishes, it returns the value that is sent back to Jack.

```
subsystem jill 69000;

#include <camelot.defs>

camelotroutine jill_read(
                index                : int;
            OUT value                : int);

camelotroutine jill_write(
                index                : int;
                value                : int);
```

Figure 2.2: The MIG Specification file `jill.defs`

2.4.3 Contents of a MIG Specification File

Programmers must create a MIG specification file for each server. The specification for the Jill server is given in Figure 2.2. This example is discussed in more detail in Chapter 5.

MIG first runs `.defs` files through `/lib/cpp`. This means that C-style comments, macros, and include files can be used in `.defs` files. There are four important sections in a MIG `.defs` file: identification, MIG data types, imported C declarations, and routine definitions.

Identification

The first MIG statement in a `.defs` file is the `subsystem` statement. This statement is used to specify the name of the interface and the message ID base. The subsystem name is used as the prefix for files generated by MIG and as the prefix for the demux routine generated by MIG.

MIG gives each routine an integer identifier. These identifiers are used by the demux routines to determine how to unpack request messages. MIG assigns identifiers starting with the message ID base specified in the `subsystem` statement. MIG assumes that each `.defs` file defines fewer than 100 RPCs, and uses the convention that each message ID base is a multiple of 200. All interfaces that use the same communication channel must have distinct message IDs. Since the Camelot Library uses separate communication channels for Camelot messages, user defined interfaces do not conflict with internal Camelot interfaces.

MIG Data Types

The MIG generated code packs (and unpacks) parameters into (and out of) messages. MIG must be told the size of each parameter type and how to pack it. The file `camelot.defs` defines how to pass many parameter types including `long`, `u_long`, `int`, `u_int`, `short`, `u_short`, `char`, `u_char`, `boolean_t`, `pointer_t` and many types defined in `camelot_types.h`.[1] Because the file `camelot.defs` defines several parameter types which are invisibly passed by `camelotroutines`, it must be included in `.defs` files that define `camelotroutines`.

[1]The Mach Network Message Server performs the necessary translations for these simple data types when passing them across machine types with different representations.

Because the interface to the Jill server uses only `int` parameter types, the data type section in `jill.defs` consists only of the statement `#include <camelot.defs>`. To define other parameter types, use a MIG `type` statement. The simplest way to declare new types is to create an array of some other type. To pass an array of 10 integers, use the following declaration:

```
type my_array_t = array [10] of int;
```

The MIG definition of a structure is less intuitive. It specifies the size of the structure in terms of some previously defined type. For example, to define a structure that contains 10 integers, use the following definition:

```
type my_struct_t = struct [10] of int;
```

The difference between the array and structure definitions is that array parameters are passed as pointers to the RPC stub procedure where as structure parameters are passed by copying the structure onto the stack.[2]

To pass structures that have fields of different types or that contain bit fields, use a structure declaration that is the proper size in bytes and has the proper alignment. The definition of `my_struct_t`, above, is acceptable for any 40 byte structure that is aligned on an `int` boundary (assuming an `int` is four bytes). Unfortunately, when sending these structures across the machine types, the Network Message Server will byte swap the structure as though it contained `int`s. Similarly, if the definition were

```
type my_struct_t = struct [40] of char;
```

the message would not be byte swapped when passed across machine types. There is no good way to pass arbitrary structures across machine types.[3] This is a major deficiency of MIG and Mach IPC.

C strings are passed using a more primitive type construct. A C string type of at most 256 characters would be defined as follows:

```
type my_string_t = (MSG_TYPE_STRING,2048)
```

where the number 2048 is the size in bits (i.e., 2048 = 256 bytes * 8 bits/byte). This method is preferred over the more intuitive method of passing C strings as an array of characters.[4]

---

[2]Structures can be passed as arrays with fewer copies. Just declare the parameter's type to be the appropriate size array and use a pointer to the structure as the argument to the stub procedure.

[3]You can pass the individual field separately. If the structure contains only bit fields, you may be able to use different definitions of the structure for each machine type (and compiler) so that when the structure is passed across machine types, the bits end up in the right places. For example, see the definition of a Camelot transaction identifier in Figure 16.1.

[4]When `MSG_TYPE_STRING` is used, the string is copied into the message with `strncpy` which will stop when a null character is reached. If `my_string_t` were defined as an array of characters, all 256 characters would be copied. This might cause a segmentation violation if there were not 256 bytes allocated to a string which is passed as a parameter.

Imported C Declarations

Types actually need to be defined twice: once so that the C compiler knows the definition of the type, and once so MIG knows how to pass parameters of the type (as shown above). C type declarations must be defined in a `.h` file that you write. The `import` statement is added to the `.defs` file so that MIG will generate `#include` statements in the code it generates. For example, if the C type declaration for `my_struct_t` is defined in the file `my_types.h`, you must add the line

```
import <my_types.h>;
```

to the `.defs` file. The `camelot.defs` file contains `import` statements for all the types it declares. This is why `jill.defs` has no `import` statements.

Routine Definitions

Routines declared in MIG files specify the operations that can be invoked via RPC calls. The word `camelotroutine` must precede the name of each RPC defined in the MIG file. Parameters are specified with a Pascal-like syntax. Parameters may be `IN`, `OUT`, or `INOUT`, meaning that values are sent in the request message, in the response message, or in both messages, respectively. Parameters that are not explicitly defined to be `IN`, `OUT`, or `INOUT` are assumed to be `IN`.[5] `camelotroutines` do not have a return value (i.e., they are `void` functions).

MIG generates a client stub procedure for each routine defined in the `.defs` file. The stub procedures have the same names as the routine names specified in the `camelotroutine` declarations. The MIG generated demux routine calls operation routines in the server. The server must define an operation routine for each `camelotroutine` declared in the `.defs` file. These operation routines must have names that are the same as the names in the declarations except that they have the `op_` prefix.[6]

In our example, the files `jill.h` and `jillUser.c` declare stubs for void two functions:

```
void jill_read(index,valuePtr)          void jill_write(index,value)
    int     index;                          int     index;
    int    *valuePtr;                       int     value;
```

`camelotroutines` must be called with the `SERVER_CALL` macros described in Section 3.3.3.[7]

The file `jillServer.c` declares a demux routine called `jill_server` which may call two operation routines:

```
void op_jill_read(index,valuePtr)       void op_jill_write(index,value)
    int     index;                          int     index;
    int    *valuePtr;                       int     value;
```

---

[5]Forgetting to add these keywords is a fairly typical beginner's mistake; if the keywords are omitted, the incoming or outgoing values of parameters will not be correct.

[6]This prefix is necessary for two reasons. First, this allows data servers to be clients of an interface that they implement. Second, it allows applications and data servers to pass Lint. If they had the same names there would be many Lint conflicts due to the fact that the client stubs actually have extra parameters and return values.

[7]The client stub routines actually take more parameters than are explained here, and actually return a value. This difference is hidden by the `SERVER_CALL` macro.

Chapter 3

The Camelot Library

Joshua J. Bloch

3.1 Introduction

The Camelot primitives described in Part II of this guide are fairly low-level operations, analogous to UNIX system calls. Building Camelot programs directly on top of these primitives would be tedious and, since all Camelot programs use many of the same functions, would involve a great deal of duplicated effort. The Camelot Library is a collection of C functions and macros that facilitate the construction of Camelot programs. The Library's purpose is to provide appropriately high level primitives so that writing Camelot programs is a natural, painless process. These primitives encapsulate the functionality common to all Camelot programs so that programmers need not duplicate each other's efforts, and programs are kept small and readable.

The Camelot Library extends the execution model presented by the C programming language in several ways. We briefly describe the new elements in the execution model below:

- **Servers and Applications** - Two classes of programs, called *servers* and *applications*, can be constructed with the Library. Typically, servers are programs whose function is to process remote procedure calls (RPCs) on a collection of persistent abstract data objects, in a transaction-consistent manner. Servers can declare and manipulate *recoverable objects*, receive RPCs, initiate *transactions*, and perform RPCs on other servers. Applications are programs that can initiate transactions and perform RPCs on servers.

- **Transactions** - Threads of control within servers and applications have a new run-time attribute: the transaction under which they are running. If a thread is not currently running under a transaction, it is said to be *outside the scope of a transaction*. The scoping is dynamic (i.e., the transaction attribute persists across function calls). Server threads inherit the transaction attribute from the calling application (or server) thread. Control flow automatically follows transaction status; if a transaction aborts, program execution continues at the appropriate location in the appropriate thread.

- **Recoverable Objects** - A new storage class is provided for servers, called the *recoverable* *object*. Recoverable objects are like global variables, except that they are *long-lived* and *transaction-consistent*. By *long-lived*, we mean that they maintain their values across server crashes and node crashes. By *transaction-consistent*, we mean that the value of a recoverable object seen by a server thread running in the scope of a transaction reflects only the modifications performed by committed transactions that were serialized before the transaction examining the object.

- **Locks** - In order to ensure that recoverable objects are transaction-consistent, servers must explicitly secure an appropriate *lock* prior to accessing a recoverable object. A *logical locking* facility is provided, whereby locks are held on *lock names*, which the programmer associates with recoverable data objects as he sees fit. To guarantee strict serializability, including repeatable reads, programmers should adhere to the two-phase locking protocol [38], in which all locks are obtained before any locks are released. Locks are automatically dropped when a transaction commits or aborts.

- **Server Calls** - A new type of function call, the *server call*, allows servers and applications to make RPCs on servers.

- **Threads of Control** - Camelot Library programs have multiple lightweight processes or *threads* running concurrently. Servers have multiple *request handler threads* so that multiple incoming RPCs can be processed concurrently. Servers and applications both have invisible *system message handler threads*, which process system messages to perform commit and abort processing and data recovery. Primitives are also provided for programmers to create concurrent threads explicitly.

The remainder of this chapter is organized as follows. Section 3.2 contains instructions for using the Camelot Library. Sections 3.3 and 3.4 introduce sets of Library constructs that are sufficient to write simple applications and servers. These sections should give the reader a broad understanding of the structure of servers and applications. Section 3.5 contains several caveats concerning the use of the Camelot Library. Section 3.6 describes the remaining Library constructs; these constructs are used to implement more complex applications and servers.

3.2 Using the Camelot Library

In order to use the Camelot Library, servers and applications must include the Camelot Library header file in all source files. This is accomplished by putting the line:

```
#include <camlib/camlib.h>
```

at the head of each source file. The Camelot Library header file in turn includes all Camelot and Mach header files that are needed by Camelot Library servers and applications. Servers and applications must be linked with the Camelot, Cam, Threads and Mach libraries. Thus, the command to compile a Camelot Library program `foo.c` would look like this:

```
cc foo.c -lcamlib -lcam -lthreads -lmach
```

3.3 Application Basics

In this section we present a small set of Library constructs that is sufficient to write simple applications. The **Jack** application, found in Section 5.3, uses only these constructs. It is suggested that the reader refer to Section 5.3 as he reads this section, to see how the constructs are used in the context of an actual application.

3.3.1 Structure

An application is essentially a C program that can call servers and initiate transactions. Unlike ordinary C programs, applications have a *system thread* running in the background. The primary purpose of the system thread is to relay news of exogenous aborts of application-initiated transactions to the application. The system thread does its work invisibly, and can be ignored by the programmer, with one small exception: to terminate the execution of an application, the `exit` function must be called explicitly. If the program merely "falls off" the main function, it will hang instead of terminating, as the system thread will continue execution.

An application must call `INITIALIZE_APPLICATION` before it can call servers or begin transactions. This procedure initializes the application's internal data structures and attempts to register the application with the Camelot system. The `INITIALIZE_APPLICATION` call returns `TRUE` if initialization is successful. If Camelot is not running on the node, `INITIALIZE_APPLICATION` returns `FALSE`, indicating that the caller can run only as a *limited application*. Limited applications can call servers but cannot initiate transactions. Limited applications are discussed in Section 3.6.8.

```
boolean_t INITIALIZE_APPLICATION(applName)
char *applName;
```

`applName` Descriptive name used by Camelot to refer to this application in error and informational messages.

3.3.2 Transactions

The basic Library construct to create a transaction is the *transaction block*, delimited by the keywords `BEGIN_TRANSACTION` and `END_TRANSACTION`. Syntactically, the transaction block is a single compound statement. It initiates a transaction, and the code between the delimiters executes under the scope of the transaction. The transaction environment is dynamically scoped: if a function is called from within the scope of a transaction, the thread that called the function is still running under the transaction, even though it is lexically outside the transaction block. Transaction blocks are legal in servers as well as applications.

```
BEGIN_TRANSACTION
    <declarations>
```

```
        <arbitrary C code>

    END_TRANSACTION(status)
```

`status` (`OUT int`) Must be a variable in the scope of the enclosing block. When the transaction has completed, the variable will contain a value specifying the outcome of the transaction. Status will be 0 if the transaction committed. Codes between 1 and $2^{16} - 1$ (inclusive) are voluntary abort codes, and other values are system abort codes.

`END_TRANSACTION` takes a single parameter: a status variable. After the transaction block completes execution, this variable can be examined to determine the outcome of the transaction. A value of zero indicates that the transaction committed. Values in between one and $2^{16} - 1$ (inclusive) indicate that the transaction was voluntarily aborted via a call to `ABORT` (or `ABORT_TOP_LEVEL`) with the given status. Other values are system abort codes, described in Appendix B.

A function called `ABORT_CODE_TO_STR` is provided to translate a system abort code into a printable character string describing the condition that caused the abort. If `ABORT_CODE_TO_STR` is passed a status code that is not a valid system abort code, it returns a short string describing the abort code as best it can. (e.g., "Transaction Committed Successfully" or "User abort code: 43"). However, `ABORT_CODE_TO_STR` is typically used only when it has been determined that a status code is indeed a system abort code, as the function cannot produce detailed error messages for user abort codes, which are specific to a server or application.

```
char *ABORT_CODE_TO_STR(status)
int status;

printf("%s\n", ABORT_CODE_TO_STR(status));
```

`status` Transaction status code.

A nested transaction results if one transaction block occurs within the (dynamic) scope of another. (See Section 9.1 for a discussion of nested transactions.) If a transaction block is executed outside the scope of a transaction, a new top-level transaction is created. The transaction type of the new transaction family defaults to *new value logging, standard*. (See Sections 3.6.1 and 9.2.1 for information on transaction types.) The commit protocol defaults to *two-phased*. (See Chapter 9 and Section 3.6.1, **Commit Protocols**, for information on commit protocols.) These defaults can be overridden using an alternate form of the top-level transaction block construct, described in Section 3.6.1, **Top-Level Transactions**.

The `ABORT` primitive aborts the transaction in whose scope the primitive occurs. If it occurs in the scope of a nested transaction, only the innermost nested transaction is aborted. Execution of the primitive causes immediate transfer of control to the statement following the end of the (dynamically) enclosing transaction block. `ABORT` takes a single argument, an integer status code to be returned in the status variable of the `END_TRANSACTION` delimiter of the enclosing transaction block. The `ABORT` primitive is illegal outside the scope of a transaction. The primitive can be used by servers as well as applications.

ABORT_TOP_LEVEL aborts the enclosing top-level transaction (i.e., it aborts the entire family of the transaction in whose scope it occurs). Like ABORT, it takes a status code, causes immediate transfer of control, and can be used by servers as well as applications.

```
ABORT(status);
ABORT_TOP_LEVEL(status);
```

status (int) Status code to be returned. The status code must be between 1 and $2^{16} - 1$. If the status code is out of range, the system abort code ACC_ILLEGAL_USER_ABORT_CODE will be returned.

3.3.3 Calling Servers

The *server call* construct allows applications (and servers) to perform RPCs on servers. The RPC runs under the scope of the transaction in whose scope the server call occurs. Server calls are only legal within the scope of a transaction. Note that the parameters to the call may be evaluated twice, so they should contain no side effects.

```
SERVER_CALL(serverName, call);
```

serverName (char *) The name of the server, as specified in the INITIALIZE_SERVER call.

call The actual call. The arguments to the call must be preceded by the keyword ARGS, unless the call has no arguments, in which case the keyword NOARGS must be used. (These keywords cause hidden system arguments to be passed.)

```
Examples:
    SERVER_CALL("Jill", jill_write(ARGS index, value));
    SERVER_CALL("Jill", jill_reset(NOARGS));
```

If the RPC does not return within sixty seconds, the transaction on whose behalf the RPC was made aborts with status ACC_SERVER_CALL_TIMEOUT. An alternate form of the server call construct, described in Section 3.6.8, allows the programmer to specify the timeout interval explicitly.

A server call can be made to a server on a specific remote site by appending "@<site name>" to the server's name in the server call construct. The programmer may not always know or care on which site a server resides: sometimes he may wish to perform a call on a server with a given name at *any* site where such a server is running. This effect can be achieved with the server call construct by appending the characters "@*" to the server's name.

3.4 Server Basics

In this section we present a small set of Library constructs that is sufficient to write simple servers. The **Jill** server, found in Section 5.4, uses only these constructs. It is suggested that the reader refer to Section 5.4 as he reads this section, to see how the constructs are used in the context of an actual server.

3.4.1 Structure

The function of a server is to receive *requests* (RPCs) from clients, service them by performing the specified operation, and send the results back to the client. It can take arbitrarily long to perform an operation. (e.g., operations may wait for locks on shared data objects.) To achieve reasonable performance, it is imperative that servers concurrently handle multiple requests. Therefore, servers have multiple *request handler* threads, which are dedicated to processing requests.

To run within the Camelot system, servers must perform numerous housekeeping tasks. Servers must establish and maintain communication channels with various system tasks, handle recovery procedures in the event of transaction abort or server crash, and participate in commit and abort protocols. In order to perform all of these hidden functions, the server must maintain records of all the transactions in which it participates, the transaction families to which they belong, the locks they hold, and so forth. Some of the hidden functions are accomplished by receiving and processing *system messages* from the various tasks that comprise the Camelot system. A server must respond quickly to system messages even when it is busy servicing other system messages. Therefore, servers have multiple *system message handler* threads, which are dedicated to processing system messages.

The Library primitives to create a server are `INITIALIZE_SERVER` and `START_SERVER`. From the programmer's point of view, `INITIALIZE_SERVER` identifies the program as a server and initializes it, and `START_SERVER` causes the server to start processing RPCs.

Before a server can start processing RPCs, it must perform various initializations. If the server is being restarted after a crash, it must restore recoverable storage to a transaction consistent state. The server must initialize the tables used to keep track of its internal state, establish communication with various system tasks, and register its name with the name server. System message handler threads must be started. All of these initializations are performed by `INITIALIZE_SERVER`.

`INITIALIZE_SERVER` allows the programmer to specify an initialization procedure that is executed only once, the first time the server is successfully started. This procedure, `initProc`, will generally be used to perform server-specific initialization of recoverable data objects. It runs under a transaction. The server will not start operating until this transaction has committed.[1] The use of an `initProc` is optional: a value of `NULL` for `initProc` indicates that no initialization procedure is to be used.

`INITIALIZE_SERVER` will register the server's name and "address" (port) with the system-wide name server unless the programmer specifies that the server is *unlisted*, by setting the `unlisted` parameter to `TRUE`. If a server is not unlisted, any server or application that knows the server's name can perform RPCs on the server. Making a server unlisted allows the server to maintain strict access control by only revealing its address to trusted allies. More information on writing unlisted servers can be found in Section 3.6.8.

[1] Thus, a voluntary abort from within `initProc` would prevent a server from operating.

```
INITIALIZE_SERVER(initProc, unlisted, name);
```

`initProc` (`void (*)()`) Procedure (no arguments) called once when the server is first brought up. Generally, this procedure will initialize the server's recoverable storage. It runs as a top level transaction, and we guarantee that it will be executed to completion before the server starts operation. (Optional parameter; may be `NULL`.)

`unlisted` (`boolean_t`) Flag to indicate whether this is an **unlisted server**. Unlisted servers do not automatically publicize their service with the system name server, thus strict control over access rights can be maintained.

`name` (`char *`) The server's name. If unlisted is `FALSE`, the service will be publicized under this name.

The `START_SERVER` primitive causes a server to commence servicing requests, by starting the server's request handler threads. The `START_SERVER` function never returns, so any statements after the call to `START_SERVER` are "dead code", and will never be executed.

```
void START_SERVER(demuxProc, maxMpl, transTimeOut)
    boolean_t        (*demuxProc)();
    u_int            maxMpl;
    u_int            transTimeOut;
```

`demuxProc` A function, typically generated by MIG, that checks to see if a message represents an RPC to this server, and if so, executes the appropriate operation procedure with the arguments contained in the message. The `demuxProc` must return `TRUE` if and only if the message was recognized and processed.

`maxMpl` Maximum multiprogramming level for serving requests. New threads will be allocated in response to demand, up to this level. Specifying a maximum multiprogramming level less than two causes a maximum of two threads to be enforced.

`transTimeOut` The amount of time that a transaction family is allowed to remain uncommitted at the server, in seconds. If this interval elapses and the family has not committed or aborted, the family will be aborted by the server. The interval is measured from the time that a server call on behalf of the family arrives at the server, or a new family is created at the server. Each additional server call on behalf of a family causes the family's interval timer to be reset. A value of zero for `transTimeOut` indicates that no time limit should be enforced.

Ideally, the programmer would label certain functions in his server as *operation procedures*, and the server would automatically accept RPCs for these functions when `START_SERVER` was called.

Unfortunately, this is not feasible in a Library implementation. Thus we require the programmer to specify the external interface to his server with a Mach Interface Generator (MIG) definitions file, as described in Section 2.4.2. MIG translates the definitions file into a set of server stubs, and provides a function that demultiplexes an incoming message to the appropriate operation procedure via the appropriate server stub. The programmer passes the MIG-generated demultiplexor function to `START_SERVER` in the `demuxProc` argument. The MIG-generated demultiplexor function is generally called <Server Name>`Server`. Note that operation procedures must have the prefix `op_` at the beginning of their names. The prefix is *not* used in server calls nor in the MIG definition file.

The two remaining parameters to `START_SERVER` allow the programmer to specify resource usage limitations on the server. Initially, two threads are allocated to handle RPCs. The number of request handler threads will increase dynamically in response to demand. If there were no upper limit on the number of threads, a broken or malicious application could cripple the node on which the server resided by sending a large number of blocking requests, each of which consumed a thread. Therefore, the parameter, `maxMpl`, is provided to specify the maximum number of threads that can be allocated to handle RPCs. (`Mpl` stands for MultiProgramming Level.) Setting this value too low can cause transactions to deadlock unnecessarily.

As a transaction executes, it acquires locks on the recoverable objects it accesses. This prevents concurrent transactions from viewing intermediate results of the transaction, or interfering with it. If concurrent transactions desire access to the same objects, they must wait until this transaction commits or aborts. If transactions were allowed to remain uncommitted indefinitely, they could prevent other transactions from proceeding. Therefore, the `transTimeOut` parameter is provided to allow the programmer to specify the maximum length of time that a transaction family can remain uncommitted at a server. After this timeout interval elapses, the server can abort the family. The time interval is measured from the time the server receives an RPC on behalf of the family, or the family is created at the server. The interval timer is reset each time the server receives an RPC from the family.

The transaction timeout facility is intended to prevent excessive resource usage in a server by runaway operations or by clients that have gone dormant during an active transaction. This facility does not, however, address the problem of runaway clients that repeatedly call a server at close intervals.

The main program for a server will typically consist of a single call to `INITIALIZE_SERVER` followed by a single call to `START_SERVER`. In between these two calls, the programmer may place initialization code to be executed each time the server is restarted. This code will not be automatically enclosed in a transaction, but the programmer can explicitly enclose code in a transaction if he desires. (e.g., He may wish to modify recoverable objects.) The call to `INITIALIZE_SERVER` may be preceded by code to interpret the command line arguments (`argc` and `argv`). In this fashion, the command line arguments can be used to affect the parameters to `INITIALIZE_SERVER`, or to affect the behavior of the initialization procedure. It is not legal to begin a transaction or invoke any other Library construct until `INITIALIZE_SERVER` has been called.

When a client performs an RPC, the operation procedure at the server runs in the scope of the same transaction in whose scope the server call was made. If the server aborts this transaction, automatic transfer of control occurs in the client. Voluntarily aborting the transaction with the `ABORT` primitive can be used as a powerful cross-machine exception reporting mechanism. The abort codes that a server is capable of generating are thus part of the interface that it exports. If an operation procedure performs some activity that can cause an abort (e.g., it does a "nested" server call), the programmer may wish to "intercept" any abort caused by the activity rather than letting it abort the enclosing transaction at the client. This effect is achieved by enclosing the abort-prone activity in a nested transaction. If the nested transaction aborts, the server can, for instance, retry the operation by some alternative means.

3.4.2 Recoverable Objects

The Camelot system provides servers with *recoverable storage*, which is long-lived and transaction-consistent. (Recoverable storage is described in Chapter 8.) The Camelot Library makes recoverable storage available to programmers in the form of *recoverable objects*, which are long-lived, transaction-consistent global variables. In this section, we present Library constructs to declare, access, modify and lock recoverable objects.

Declaration

The *recoverable object declaration block* is used to declare recoverable objects in a server. There are no constraints on the data type of a recoverable object; any legal C object declaration can occur in this construct. No initializers are permitted in the declarations, but recoverable objects are automatically initialized to zero (or all zeros, in the case of multi-word objects).[2]

```
BEGIN_RECOVERABLE_DECLARATIONS

    <Zero or more C declarations>

END_RECOVERABLE_DECLARATIONS
```

All servers must have a recoverable object declaration block. If a server uses no recoverable objects, its recoverable object declaration block can be empty. The recoverable object declaration block must be visible in all files that access recoverable objects, and the file containing the call to `INITIALIZE_SERVER`. It is critical that the declarations be identical in all the files comprising a server, as the declarations define a template for interpreting the recoverable segment. If different modules have different ideas about how objects are mapped into the segment, chaos will result. In order to enforce a unique interpretation of the recoverable segment, it is highly recommended that the recoverable object declarations be placed in a `.h` file that is included in all server source files.

The recoverable declarations should not be changed once a server has been started, as recoverable objects persist even if a server is stopped, modified, and restarted. Of course, the recoverable declarations can be changed if the server is deleted (Section 4.1), as deleting the server causes the recoverable segment to be destroyed. While the Library does not enforce the restriction that the declarations not be changed, it does enforce that the total size of the declared recoverable objects remain constant. Thus, new recoverable objects can be "added" to a server without destroying the existing recoverable objects, by declaring an array of integers (or characters) for future expansion. When the programmer wants to add a recoverable object, he must replace a part of the expansion

[2]For efficiency, the initialization is done lazily: each page of the recoverable segment is zeroed the first time it is referenced.

area with the new object. It is critical that the layout of the recoverable segment not change. A simple way to ensure this is to place the declaration for the expansion area at the end of the recoverable object declaration block. To add a new object, a declaration is placed in between the last "real" declaration and the expansion area declaration, and the size of the expansion area is reduced appropriately.

Access

To access all or part of a recoverable object, the `REC` macro is applied to the object name, as declared in the recoverable object declaration block.

```
b = REC(name);
c = REC(name[43]);
d = REC(name[27].foo);
ptr = &REC(name[45]);
```

`name` Name of the object to be accessed. Can be all or part of any object declared in a recoverable object declaration block.

Recoverable objects can only be accessed from within the scope of a transaction. An attempt to reference a recoverable object outside the scope of a transaction may not be flagged by the server, but the results will be indeterminate.

Recoverable objects can also be accessed by dereferencing pointers to them. Pointers to recoverable objects are generated by applying the `&` operator to the `REC` macro. Pointers to recoverable objects can be passed to functions, pointer arithmetic works properly on them, and so forth. Recoverable objects are guaranteed not to move in recoverable memory, even if the server crashes, so pointers to recoverable objects can be stored in recoverable objects to create recoverable linked data structures.

Modification

The *recoverable assignment* construct is used to modify all or part of a recoverable object.

```
MODIFY(object, newValue);
```

`object` The recoverable object to be modified. Must be of a type that can be used on the left side of an assignment. (A syntax error will result if object is an array, but array elements or structures are fine.)

`newValue` The new value to be stored in object.

```
Examples:
   MODIFY(REC(name), newValue);
   MODIFY(*ptr, newValue);
```

The recoverable assignment construct is a precise analogue for recoverable objects of the C assignment statement. The construct can be thought of as the assignment statement:

```
object = newValue;
```

Type coercion and compile-time type checking are performed as they would be in the corresponding assignment statement. Note that an ordinary assignment statement ***must not*** be substituted for a recoverable assignment, as modifying a recoverable object involves much more than merely changing the contents of the memory representing the object. Neither the compiler nor the runtime system will catch this error, but it will cause erroneous behavior. Note that the first argument ("left hand side") of the recoverable assignment is evaluated twice, so it should have no side effects. Needless to say, the recoverable assignment construct is legal only within the scope of a transaction.

It is illegal to perform any Library calls (other than `REC`) from within a recoverable assignment (i.e., no Library calls may result from the evaluation of the arguments to the construct). Attempts to violate this restriction will result in the server halting with an appropriate error message printed in the system log.

Locking

Earlier we said that recoverable objects were transaction-consistent. In fact, this is only true if appropriate locks are secured prior to accessing the objects. It would have been possible for the Library to automatically obtain locks when recoverable objects were read or written, rendering locks invisible to the programmer. However, this approach would have decreased concurrency and increased locking overhead to an intolerable level. Only the programmer has sufficient knowledge to determine the appropriate granularity for locking, and the appropriate type of lock to seek prior to performing a given operation. Thus, we provide *logical locking* facilities, whereby the programmer obtains locks on *lock names*, which he can associate with recoverable objects as he sees fit. The `LOCK` call is the basic Library primitive for obtaining a lock.

```
LOCK(name, nameSpace, mode);
```

`name` (`u_int`) Name on which the lock is sought.
`nameSpace` (`u_int`) The name space pertaining to the name.
`mode` (`camlib_lock_mode_t`) Mode of lock sought.

The lock mode can be either `LOCK_MODE_READ` (shared) or `LOCK_MODE_WRITE` (exclusive). Locks names are drawn from the set of 32-bit integers. In addition to a lock name, the programmer must provide a *lock name space*, also drawn from the set of 32-bit integers. Locks only conflict with locks of the same name in the same space. Lock name spaces must be allocated explicitly, with the exception of `LOCK_SPACE_PRIMARY`. The use of allocated name spaces is discussed in Section 3.6.7. Simple servers should just use `LOCK_SPACE_PRIMARY`.

The programmer must ensure that lock names are used consistently. A straightforward scheme is to use the address of a recoverable object as the name of the lock governing access to the object. The `LOCK_NAME` primitive is provided to generate names of this type.

```
LOCK_NAME(object, nameSpace, mode))
```

`object` The recoverable object for which a lock name is desired.

```
Example:
   LOCK(LOCK_NAME(REC(object)), nameSpace, mode))
```

If the LOCK_NAME construct is used to generate any lock names in a given lock space, it should be used to generate all of the names in that lock space. Otherwise, names generated with LOCK_NAME might conflict with names specified explicitly.

The programmer must ensure that no two lock names refer to intersecting objects. For instance, using the LOCK_NAME primitive, it is possible for one transaction to get a write lock on a structure and a concurrent transaction to get a write lock on some component of the structure. If this happens, serializability can be lost, and the integrity of the data can be destroyed.

A typical call to LOCK follows:

```
LOCK(LOCK_NAME(REC(c)), LOCK_SPACE_PRIMARY, LOCK_MODE_READ);
```

If the lock sought is not available at the time LOCK is called, the calling thread blocks until the lock is available. If a transaction holding a read lock on a name seeks a write lock on the name, the read lock will be promoted to a write lock as soon as the write lock can be granted. If a transaction seeks a lock that it already possesses, or a transaction with a write lock on a name seeks a read lock on the name, LOCK returns immediately without granting any new lock to the calling transaction. Lock inheritance within a transaction family is handled automatically: if a transaction seeks a lock while a conflicting lock is held by a concurrent family member, the calling thread blocks until the transaction can *inherit* the lock. (See Section 9.1 for a discussion of lock inheritance in nested transactions.) All locks granted to a transaction by LOCK are automatically dropped when the transaction aborts or the transaction family commits. In this manner, strict two-phase locking is enforced.

3.4.3 Summary

To create a simple server, perform the following steps:

1. Write a header file containing a recoverable object declaration block for the recoverable objects used by the server.

2. Write operation procedures to implement each operation supported by the server.

3. Write a MIG definitions file for the operation procedures, as described in Section 2.4, and run it through MIG.

4. If recoverable objects requires initialization beyond automatic zeroing, write an `initProc`.

5. Write a main program (`main()`) consisting of a call to INITIALIZE_SERVER followed by a call to START_SERVER.

6. Compile the server with the MIG output server stubs and the libraries listed in Section 3.2.

3.5 Caveats

3.5.1 Static Variables in Servers

Global and other static variables should generally be avoided in servers, as no mechanism exists in the Library for synchronizing concurrent access to these variables. Furthermore, it is difficult to maintain invariants on static data structures, as static variables are not recovered if a transaction aborts after modifying them. If threads need to communicate, they should generally do so through recoverable memory. Proper use of the Library's locking facility will assure synchronization. No synchronization problem exists with automatic variables, as each thread has its own copy of any automatic variables in its scope.

Occasionally, efficiency concerns may dictate that global variables be used. In such cases, synchronization can be accomplished by using the Cthreads library mutex and condition variable facilities directly. However, this requires *great* care. A thread should not make any Library calls (other than REC) while in possession of a mutex, as Library calls can cause the thread to "notice" an abort and transfer control out of the aborted transaction. If a thread transfers control while in possession of a mutex, it will never relinquish the mutex, unless special action is taken via an abort procedure. Thus, no thread will ever be able to lock the mutex again. An attempt by a thread to lock the "lost" mutex will cause the thread to block forever. The only way to free such a blocked thread is to kill the server. If the blocked thread is running on behalf of a transaction, the server will be killed automatically when the transaction times out and the server aborts it.

3.5.2 Direct Use of Low-Level Facilities

Direct use of low-level Camelot and Cthreads primitives, described in Part II of this guide, is prohibited in Camelot Library servers and applications. There are several exceptions to this rule, such as judicious use of the Cthreads mutex facility as described above. But in general, the direct use of low-level calls will cause unpredictable and incorrect behavior on the part of servers and applications. For instance, it is always wrong to create additional threads via direct use of Cthreads primitives. These threads lack the data structures necessary to use the Library primitives. At best, attempts to use the Library primitives from within these threads will cause segmentation violations. At worst, such attempts will cause random behavior and corruption of data.

It should almost always be possible to achieve a desired effect without resorting to direct use of low-level Camelot and Cthreads facilities. But if the programmer must use a low-level facility in a manner not explicitly described in this chapter, he is advised to examine relevant portions of the Library source code first. In order to use a low-level facility correctly, the programmer must fully understand the interactions of his use of the facility with the Library's.

3.5.3 Transfer of Control

Transfer of control into or out of the body of a transaction block via *goto*, *longjmp*, function return, *break* or *continue* is strictly prohibited. Unpredictable behavior will generally result. The only legitimate way to forcibly exit the scope of a transaction is to abort it. It is legal to kill a server or application from within the scope of a transaction, which aborts the transaction, as well as any others in progress at the server or application. Transfer of control into or out of the body of a cofor or cobegin block (described in Section 3.6.2) is prohibited and will produce undefined results.

3.5.4 Standard I/O From Servers

Servers are not attached to any particular tty when they run, so their standard input, standard output and standard error file pointers are cleared by Camelot. Thus, `printfs`, `scanfs` and the like cannot be used in a server unless the server resets its standard file pointers. Standard output and standard error might be connected to a disk file that serves as a log for recording the operation of the server. For most servers, we do not envision a use for standard input.

3.5.5 Runaway Transactions at Servers

A transaction cannot be aborted while there are still threads operating on its behalf at a server. If an attempt to abort a transaction blocks for a sufficiently long period because there are still threads operating on behalf of the transaction at a server, Camelot will be forced to kill the server in order to abort the transaction. Killing a server is extremely expensive, causing all transactions in progress at the server to abort, and requiring the server to go through a lengthy recovery procedure before it can begin operation anew.

When an abort begins, all servers that participated in the transaction are informed that it is aborting. Camelot Library servers record this fact in a table, causing threads operating on behalf of the transaction to cease operation on behalf of the transaction if they subsequently execute any Library operation other than REC. When the last thread operating on behalf of the transaction ceases operation, the server informs the system, allowing the abort to proceed. Thus, a server should not perform long computations that contain no Library operations other than REC while it is operating on behalf of a transaction, lest it subject itself to being killed by the system.

We provide a function called ABORT_CHECK that causes a server thread to cease operation on behalf of the current transaction immediately if the transaction is aborting. ABORT_CHECK is the same function called by other Library operations prior to execution. This function should be called occasionally from computations that might otherwise prevent servers from responding quickly to abort attempts. It executes very quickly (several machine instructions) so there is no performance penalty for calling it from time to time.

```
ABORT_CHECK();
```

ABORT_CHECK can also be called from applications. It causes an application thread to transfer control immediately if its transaction has been aborted. It is not as important to call ABORT_CHECK from applications as from servers, as the system will not kill an application if its threads continue to operate on behalf of an aborting transaction. But typically, all computation done by an application on behalf of an aborted transaction is wasted. Thus it is advantageous from a performance standpoint to pepper long computations that contain no other Library calls with occasional calls to ABORT_CHECK. There is nothing to be gained by calling ABORT_CHECK from outside of the scope of a transaction, although it will cause no harm.

3.6 Advanced Constructs

The constructs described in this section may be used in combination with those previously described to write more complex servers and applications. All of the constructs in the Camelot Library that have not already been introduced are described in this section, which is divided into functional groups.

3.6.1 Transactions

The constructs presented in this section allow added flexibility in creating and aborting transactions. All of these constructs can be used in both servers and applications.

Top-Level Transactions

The *top-level transaction block*, delimited by the keywords `BEGIN_TOP_LEVEL_TRANSACTION` and `END_TOP_LEVEL_TRANSACTION`, initiates a top-level transaction. When it occurs outside the scope of a transaction, it is identical in function to a transaction block. When it occurs inside the scope of a transaction, it creates a new top-level transaction, and the code inside the top-level transaction block runs under the scope of the new transaction. When the new transaction completes (commits or aborts), the thread continues executing on behalf of the transaction it was executing when it encountered the top-level transaction block. All of the locks held by the new transaction family will be freed as soon as it commits or aborts, and any changes it made to recoverable objects will immediately be observable to the outside world. (A call to `ABORT_TOP_LEVEL` from within a top-level transaction block aborts only the innermost nested top-level transaction.)

`END_TOP_LEVEL_TRANSACTION` takes a status variable, which can be examined to determine whether the new transaction family committed or aborted. Its interpretation is identical to the status variable in an ordinary transaction block. The top-level transaction block construct is syntactically a single compound statement.

```
BEGIN_TOP_LEVEL_TRANSACTION
    <declarations>

    <arbitrary C code>

END_TOP_LEVEL_TRANSACTION(status)
```

`status` `(OUT int)` Must be a variable in the scope of the enclosing block. When the transaction has completed, the variable will contain a value specifying the outcome of the transaction. Status will be 0 if the transaction committed. Codes between 1 and $2^{16}-1$ are voluntary abort codes, and other values are system abort codes.

The transaction type of the new transaction family defaults to *new value logging, standard* (see below). The commit protocol defaults to two-phased. These defaults can be circumvented by use of the following alternate form of the top-level transaction block:

```
BEGIN_TOP_LEVEL_TRANSACTION_2(transType)
    <declarations>

    <arbitrary C code>

END_TOP_LEVEL_TRANSACTION_2(commitProt, status)
```

`transType` (`transaction_type_t`) The transaction type.
`commitProt` (`protocol_type_t`) The commit protocol.
`status` (`OUT int`) Must be a variable in the scope of the enclosing block. When the transaction has completed, the variable will contain a value specifying the outcome of the transaction. Status will be 0 if the transaction committed. Codes between 1 and $2^{16} - 1$ (inclusive) are voluntary abort codes, and other values are system abort codes.

Transaction Types

Transaction types are chosen from the list below:

- `TRAN_OVNV_HYBRIDATOMIC` - Old value/new value logging, hybrid atomic.
- `TRAN_OVNV_STANDARD` - Old value/new value logging, standard.
- `TRAN_NV_HYBRIDATOMIC` - New value logging, hybrid atomic.
- `TRAN_NV_STANDARD` - New value logging, standard.
- `TRAN_OVNV_SERVER_BASED` - Old value/new value logging, server-based.
- `TRAN_NV_SERVER_BASED` - New value logging, server-based.

New value logging uses roughly half the log space of old value/new value logging, but prevents modified portions of recoverable objects from being paged out to disk until the transaction family that modified the objects commits. Thus, the use of new value logging for long running transactions can cause data to be *pinned* for long periods of time, which in turn can cause excessive paging activity.

Hybrid-atomic transactions differ from standard transactions only in that a timestamp is presented to the prepare procedure in hybrid atomic transactions. (See Section 3.6.9 for a discussion of prepare procedures.) The key property of these timestamps is that the ordering of transactions' timestamps is consistent with the order in which the transactions are serialized. Researchers are investigating the use of hybrid-atomic transactions to implement highly concurrent data objects [47].

Server-based transactions are a special class of transactions that run substantially faster than other transactions, but do not permit the full range of operations normally available from within transactions. Specifically, it is illegal to do server calls or begin subtransactions from within a server-based transaction. As the name implies, server-based transactions can only be initiated by servers, not applications.

Commit Protocols

Commit protocols are chosen from the list below.

- `PROT_TWO_PHASED` - Two-phased commit protocol.
- `PROT_NON_BLOCKING` - Nonblocking commit protocol.
- `PROT_LAZY` - Lazy commit. (server-based transactions only.)

The commit protocols are described in depth in Chapter 16. We briefly summarize them here. The two-phased commit protocol is the standard protocol. If the node on which a transaction was begun (the *coordinator*) crashes during the prepare phase of the two phase protocol, servers that voted to commit the transaction must hold all of the transaction's locks until the coordinator has recovered. This will impede the progress of other transactions that wish to access the locked data at the server. Normally, this should not be a problem, as the "window of vulnerability" during which a node crash can cause this situation to occur will be very short. If, however, prepare procedures (see Section 3.6.9) take a long time to execute, the window of vulnerability will be lengthened.

The nonblocking commit protocol is a slower, three phase protocol that avoids the problem described in the previous paragraph. It should be used in situations where the increased availability is judged to be worth the added cost.

The lazy commit protocol is only legal for server-based transactions. It is extremely fast, but it must be used with care, as transactions committed with this protocol (*lazy transactions*) do not possess the same basic properties as other transactions. While lazy transactions *are* failure atomic and serializable, they do not become permanent until a subsequent, non-lazy non-read-only transaction commits at the same server.[3] Note that if lazy transactions are "nested" within a non-lazy transaction, and the non-lazy transaction modifies a recoverable object (or obtains a write lock) and commits, it is guaranteed that the nested lazy transactions have become permanent.

Transaction Identifiers

All transactions have unique identifiers, as described in Section 16.2.2, **Transaction Identifier**. When writing Camelot Library servers and applications, programmers usually ignore transaction identifiers (TIDs). However, it is sometimes desirable for a server or an application to know the TID of the transaction under whose scope it is currently running. The `THIS_TID` primitive returns the TID of the current transaction or `CAM_TID_NULL` if it is called from outside the scope of a transaction.

```
cam_tid_t tid;

tid = THIS_TID;
```

[3]In fact, lazy transactions become permanent when the next log force occurs on the same node. Committing a non-lazy non-read-only transaction ensures a log force.

Aborting Transactions

Sometimes a server (or application) may wish to abort a transaction other than the one under which it is currently running. A procedure called ABORT_NAMED_TRANSACTION is provided for this purpose. The transaction to be aborted is specified by its TID, and the abort code is specified as in ABORT and ABORT_TOP_LEVEL.

```
boolean_t ABORT_NAMED_TRANSACTION(tid, status)
cam_tid_t        tid;
int              status;
```

`tid` The TID of the transaction to be aborted.

`status` The status code to pass on to the transaction enclosing the given transaction.

Since the transaction in whose scope a call to ABORT_NAMED_TRANSACTION occurs is not necessarily the transaction being aborted, the programmer generally has no assurance that the transaction has not already committed or aborted. If the transaction to be aborted is not top-level, has already committed, and its top-level ancestor hasn't yet committed, its nearest uncommitted ancestor is aborted. In this case, the system abort code AC_COMMITTED_CHILD_ABORTED is used instead of the given user abort code. ABORT_NAMED_TRANSACTION returns TRUE if the indicated transaction (or its ancestor) is aborted successfully. If the top-level ancestor has already committed or aborted, the call has no effect and FALSE is returned.

Generally, the thread calling ABORT_NAMED_TRANSACTION will not be running under the transaction being aborted. If, however, this is the case, an immediate transfer of control will occur as if ABORT or ABORT_TOP_LEVEL had been called. Normally, transfer of control will occur at the appropriate thread(s) as soon as they try to perform a Camelot Library operation. Note that ABORT_NAMED_TRANSACTION will succeed in aborting a transaction only if the transaction was active at the server or application containing the call.

3.6.2 Concurrent Nested Transactions

The transaction block constructs described thus far allow only a single nested transaction to run at a time. One of the major advantages of nested transactions is that they allow parallelism within a transaction family with serializability and failure independence among the parallel operations. In this section, we describe two constructs that create multiple concurrent subtransactions. The *cobegin block* runs a fixed number of subtransactions, and the *cofor block* runs a variable number, determined at runtime. If either of these constructs occurs outside the scope of a transaction, top-level transactions are created. Syntactically, both of these constructs are compound statements. Control flow does not proceed beyond a cobegin or cofor block until all of the transactions created by the block have completed (committed or aborted). These constructs can be used in servers and applications.

The cobegin block is delimited by the keywords COBEGIN and COEND, and contains a call to TRANS for each subtransaction to be created. No other statements are permitted between the delimiters. The calls to TRANS have three arguments. The first is a pointer to a function to be called in the transaction. The second is an argument to be passed to the function. Only a single, pointer-sized parameter can be passed to the function. The third argument is a status variable, whose interpretation is identical to the status variable in a transaction block. The status variables for all of the transactions in the cobegin block can be examined after the block finishes execution.

```
COBEGIN
    TRANS(proc1, arg1, status1);
    TRANS(proc2, arg2, status2);
              .
              .
              .
    TRANS(procN, argN, statusN);
COEND
```

or:

```
COBEGIN
    TRANS_2(proc1, arg1, status1, transType1, commitProt1);
    TRANS_2(proc2, arg2, status2, transType2, commitProt2);
              .
              .
              .
    TRANS_2(procN, argN, statusN, transTypeN, commitProtN);
COEND
```

`proc` (`void (*)()`) The procedure to be executed as a transaction. The procedure can take at most one argument, and it must be passable as a pointer.

`arg` (`Any type that can be cast to a pointer`) The argument to pass to `proc`. If `proc` doesn't take an argument, this parameter is ignored.

`status` (`OUT int`) Must be a variable in the scope of the enclosing block. When the transaction has completed, the variable will contain a value specifying the outcome of the transaction. Status will be 0 if the transaction committed. 1 through $2^{16} - 1$ are voluntary abort codes, and other values are system abort codes.

`transType` (`transaction_type_t`) The transaction type.

`commitProt` (`protocol_type_t`) The commit protocol.

If a cobegin or cofor block occurs outside the scope of a transaction, top-level transactions are created. If the `TRANS` macro is used, the transaction type of the new transactions will default to new value, standard, and the commit protocols will default to two-phased. These defaults can be overridden by using the `TRANS_2` macro in place of `TRANS`. The use of `TRANS_2` in place of `TRANS` will have no effect if the cobegin block occurs within the scope of a transaction; nested transactions inherit their parent's transaction type, and have no commit protocol.

The cofor block runs a variable number of subtransactions, determined at runtime. This construct is essentially a 'for loop', with each iteration spawning a concurrent subtransaction. The cofor block has a loop variable, which ranges from zero to the number of subtransactions to be generated minus one. It contains a single call to `TRANS`, which spawns one subtransaction for each value the loop variable takes on.

```
COFOR(loopVar, numThreads)
   TRANS(proc, arg, status);
COEND
```

or:

```
COFOR(loopVar, numThreads)
   TRANS_2(proc, arg, status, transType, commitProt);
COEND
```

`loopVar` (`OUT int`) `loopVar` must be an integer variable in the scope of the block containing the `COFOR`. It loops from zero to `numThreads-1`.

`numThreads` (`int`) The number of threads to be run by the `COFOR`. (This expression will be evaluated once, at the top of the loop.)

`status` (`OUT int`) Must be a variable in the scope of the enclosing block. When the block has completed, the variable will contain a value specifying the outcome of the transaction. Status will be 0 if the transaction committed. 1 through $2^{16} - 1$ are voluntary abort codes, and other values are system abort codes. This parameter can refer to the loop variable (*e.g.*, as an array index) so that a different status variable is used for each transaction.

`proc` (`void (*)()`) The procedure to be executed as a transaction. The procedure can take at most one argument, and it must be passable as a pointer. This parameter can refer to the loop variable so that it evaluates differently for each transaction.

`arg` (`any type that can be cast to a pointer`) The argument to pass to `proc`. If `proc` doesn't take an argument, this parameter is ignored. This parameter can refer to the loop variable so that it evaluates differently for each transaction.

`transType` (`transaction_type_t`) The transaction type.

`commitProt` (`protocol_type_t`) The commit protocol.

Note that only a single, integer-sized parameter can be passed to the function run in each subtransaction of a cofor or cobegin block. While somewhat inelegant, this does not represent a real restriction on the power of the constructs. An arbitrary number of parameters can be transmitted by passing a pointer to an "argument block" structure. In Figure 3.1, we show how a cofor block might be used to perform simultaneous reads of N replicas of an object. Note the use of the loop variable

```
/*
 * arg_block_t -- Argument block for 'thread procedure' replica_opr,
 * which performs an operation on a replica server.
 */
typedef struct arg_block
{
    char    *server;       /* Name of server on which to do operation */
    opr_t   opr;           /* The operation (OP_READ or OP_WRITE) */
    obj_t   value;         /* The value read, or the value to write */
    int     version;       /* The version number read, or to write */
} arg_block_t;

/*
 * replica_opr - Procedure to perform a read or write operation on a
 * replica of an object.
 */
void replica_opr(p)
arg_block_t *p;
{
        ...
}

main()
{
    int i, status[N];
    char *server[N];
    arg_block_t arg_block[N];
        ...

    /* Set up argument blocks for concurrent read subtransactions */
    for (i=0; i<N; i++)
    {
        arg_block[i].server = server[i];
        arg_block[i].opr = OP_READ;
    }

    /* Perform the concurrent reads */
    COFOR(i, N)
        TRANS(replica_opr, &arg_block[i], status[i]);
    COEND

    /* The values read and their version numbers will be in
     * argBlock[i].value and arg_block[i].version.  The abort codes
     * for the subtransactions will be in status[i], which will be
     * zero for the subtransactions that succeeded. */

        ...
}
```

Figure 3.1: COFOR **Example**

to pass a different argument block to each subtransaction. Note also that values can be returned in the argument block.

3.6.3 Concurrent Threads

It is sometimes desirable to create multiple threads running concurrently on behalf of the same transaction. This practice is dangerous, as locking is no longer sufficient to ensure serializability. However, there may be situations where the cost of creating subtransactions is intolerable. The `THREAD` macro is provided for use in these situations. It is used in place of `TRANS` in a cobegin or cofor block, and causes the newly created thread(s) to execute under the same transactional scope as the cobegin or cofor block. If the block runs in the scope of a transaction, the newly created threads will run in the scope of the same transaction. While it is legal to mix calls to `THREAD` and `TRANS` in the same cobegin block, it is ungainly, and should be avoided.

```
COBEGIN
   THREAD(proc1, arg1);
   THREAD(proc2, arg2);
              .
              .
              .
   THREAD(procN, argN);
COEND
```

or:

```
COFOR(loopVar, numThreads)
   THREAD(proc, arg);
COEND
```

`proc` `(void (*)())` The procedure to be executed by the thread. The procedure can take at most one argument, and it must be passable as a pointer.

`arg` `(any type that can be cast to a pointer)` The argument to pass to `proc`. If `proc` doesn't take an argument, this parameter is ignored.

Locking behavior can be *extremely* unpredictable when the `THREAD` construct is used. If two threads are running on behalf of the same transaction, and they seek to obtain conflicting locks (e.g., write locks on the same object), both threads will succeed; locks are held by transactions, not threads, and a transaction cannot conflict with itself. A similar problem results if one thread is running on behalf of a transaction and a concurrent thread is running on behalf of a descendant transaction. A more subtle problem concerns descendants of a transaction that are running in multiple concurrent threads. If two subtransactions of a given transaction are created concurrently at different sites, and threads operating on behalf of these two subtransactions seek a conflicting lock at a server, both threads will succeed in obtaining the lock. This is due to the vagaries of the FPI optimization, which is described in Section 12.2.3, **Locking**, and Section 16.3.5.

As a rule, the *only* safe use of the THREAD construct is to create threads, each of which accesses data disjoint from the data accessed by the other threads created in the same operation.[4] This rule applies not only to data accessed directly by each thread, but to data accessed by server calls from the thread, by subtransactions created in the thread, by additional threads created from the thread, etc. One should never count on locking to serialize the actions of threads resulting from use of the THREAD primitive. The THREAD macro should always be used with great care.

3.6.4 Asynchronous Threads

The concurrent constructs presented thus far run *synchronously*. That is, the calling thread waits for all of the newly created threads to finish before resuming execution. A primitive called CONCURRENT_THREAD is provided to start a new thread running and return immediately, so that the new thread and the calling thread run concurrently. CONCURRENT_THREAD takes two arguments, a function to run in the new thread, and an argument to be passed to the function. The new thread vanishes when (and if) the procedure to be called returns.

```
void CONCURRENT_THREAD(proc, arg)
    void            (*proc)();
    any_t           arg;
```

proc The procedure that runs in the new thread. May take up to one argument, of any type that can be passed as a pointer.

arg The argument to be passed to proc. (Ignored if proc has no argument.) arg should not point to an automatic (stack) object, as such an object can easily be deallocated while the concurrent thread is still running.

Regardless of what transactional scope the CONCURRENT_THREAD construct occurs in, the thread that is created initially runs outside the scope of a transaction. Once created, the thread is free to initiate new top-level transactions. By design, the Camelot library does *not* provide a construct that creates a concurrent thread that runs under the scope of the enclosing transaction. Such a construct would unacceptably compromise the Camelot library's transaction scoping model.

3.6.5 Recoverable Objects

Modification

The *recoverable assignment* construct is the analogue of the C assignment statement for recoverable objects. Like the C assignment statement, the recoverable assignment performs compile time type checking, and type coercion. Sometimes, the programmer may wish to suppress type checking and

[4]This rule applies only if the cobegin or cofor block occurs within the scope of a transaction. Outside the scope of a transaction, the THREAD construct merely creates additional threads running outside the scope of a transaction, which do not represent a safety problem.

type coercion, and perform a "byte copy" into a recoverable object. A macro called MODIFY_BYTES is provided for this purpose. It is the recoverable analogue of the bcopy function in the C library.

```
MODIFY_BYTES(objectPtr, newValuePtr, length);
```

objectPtr A pointer to the recoverable object to be modified.
newValuePtr A pointer to the new value to be stored in object.
length The length, in bytes, of the object to be modified.

```
Example:
   MODIFY_BYTES(&REC(name), newValuePtr, sizeof(REC(name)));
```

Dynamic Allocation

Camelot Library servers divide their recoverable segments into three parts. The recoverable objects declared by the programmer comprise the *external static area*. The Library maintains several recoverable objects for its own use, invisible to the programmer, in the *internal static area*. The remainder of the recoverable segment is the *recoverable heap*. The Library provides a recoverable dynamic storage allocator to allocate and free objects from the recoverable heap at runtime. It is used to implement recoverable dynamic data structures, in the same manner as the C library's storage allocator is used to implement ordinary dynamic data structures.

The REC_MALLOC primitive is used to allocate a word-aligned block of recoverable storage. It is the recoverable analogue of the malloc function in the C library. Like other constructs that manipulate recoverable storage, REC_MALLOC can only be called from within the scope of a transaction. If the transaction aborts, the allocated piece of recoverable memory is returned to the heap. Unlike malloc, REC_MALLOC does not return a null pointer if insufficient memory exists on the heap to fill the request. Instead, it aborts the enclosing transaction, with abort code ACC_MALLOC_OUT_OF_MEMORY.

```
char *ptr;

ptr = REC_MALLOC(size);
```

size (int) The size, in bytes, of the memory block desired.

The REC_NEW primitive is used to allocate a single object of a given type. It returns a typed pointer to the object. It is just a piece of syntactic sugar that calls REC_MALLOC, hiding the cast and the sizeof operation from the programmer.

```
type *fp;

fp = REC_NEW(type);
```

`type` The type of the new object to be allocated.

When an object is allocated using REC_MALLOC (or REC_NEW) a pointer to the object should be stored in a recoverable object by the same transaction that allocates the object. This guarantees that, if the transaction succeeds and the object is actually allocated, a pointer to the object exists, so that the object can be accessed in the future, and eventually deallocated. Failure to follow this advice will cause a recoverable storage leak.

The REC_FREE procedure is used to return a piece of storage allocated with REC_MALLOC (or REC_NEW). If the transaction from which REC_FREE was called aborts, the object remains allocated and its contents are unaffected.

```
REC_FREE(ptr);
```

`ptr` `(char *)` Pointer to a block returned by REC_MALLOC.

REC_FREE attempts to verify that its argument is a valid pointer to a piece of memory allocated with REC_MALLOC. If the argument is found to be invalid, an error message is printed and the server is halted. However, the check is not perfect, and a REC_FREE of an invalid pointer can corrupt the recoverable heap. The check is sufficient to catch most common errors, like freeing the same object twice, freeing a null pointer and freeing a garbage pointer that points outside the recoverable heap.

Optimizing Access

The primitives presented in this section are used to optimize access to recoverable objects on the basis of prior knowledge of likely access patterns. They are only recommended for large databases where paging activity is substantial. They can be ignored by most programmers. The recoverable segment is implemented in virtual memory. (See Chapter 14 for details.) All of the primitives in this section modify the caching behavior of the virtual memory system in order to optimize for known access patterns.

The PREFETCH primitive returns immediately and causes the pages containing a given object to be fetched into main memory from the backing store, asynchronously. If PREFETCH is called sufficiently in advance of access to the object, the object will be in main memory when it is needed, eliminating the latency that would normally be present. PREFETCH can be used to interleave the manipulation of recoverable objects with the fetching of objects that will be needed in the near future. An alternate version of PREFETCH is provided wherein the portion of memory to be prefetched is described by a pointer and a length.

```
PREFETCH(object);
PREFETCH_BYTES(ptr, length);
```

`object` The recoverable object to be fetched from disk.
`ptr` A pointer to the area of recoverable memory to be fetched from disk.
`length` The length of the area in bytes.

```
Example:
   PREFETCH(REC(name));
```

The PREFLUSH primitive returns immediately and causes the pages containing the given object to be flushed from main memory to the backing store, asynchronously. PREFLUSH is used to free pages in main memory once it is determined that a recoverable object will no longer be needed in the foreseeable future. Like PREFETCH, PREFLUSH takes a recoverable object as its argument. An alternate version of PREFLUSH is provided wherein the portion of memory to be preflushed is described by a pointer and a length, as in PREFETCH_BYTES.

```
PREFLUSH(object);
PREFLUSH_BYTES(ptr, length);
```

The ZERO_FILL primitive causes the given recoverable object to be filled with zeros. This call reduces the cost of subsequent modifies if old value/new value logging is being used. It is only worthwhile for large objects, greater that 200 K bytes in length. The ZERO_FILL primitive has the semantics of a top-level transaction: it executes atomically, and once it returns, the object has been cleared, and will remain cleared even if the enclosing transaction aborts. An alternate version of ZERO_FILL is provided wherein the portion memory to be preflushed is described by a pointer and a length.

```
ZERO_FILL(object);
ZERO_FILL_BYTES(ptr, length);
```

Note that the current implementations of ZERO_FILL and ZERO_FILL_BYTES are temporary. They are semantically equivalent to the architected implementation, but they are much less efficient. In the temporary implementation, a server-based transaction is created, and the object is zeroed with multiple calls to MODIFY_BYTES.

3.6.6 Recoverable Libraries

The basic Camelot Library construct for exporting a recoverable abstraction is the server. An alternative vehicle is a library, which the programmer links in with his server. Such a library contains functions to manipulate recoverable abstract data objects of some type. In addition, the library may provide functions to dynamically create and destroy objects. The create function typically allocates space for the object with REC_MALLOC and returns a pointer that the server must save in recoverable storage to retain access to the object. Alternatively, the library's header file may define a macro to be invoked within the server's recoverable object declaration block that statically allocates space for an object. Note that these two options are not mutually exclusive: a single library can support dynamic and static objects.

The use of such a library saves the cost of an RPC per operation that would be required if a separate server were used to implement the abstraction. The RPC is typically the most expensive part of performing an operation on a Camelot server. Thus it is advantageous for programmers to use such libraries in place of separate servers where practical. Note that libraries of this sort do not require any special Camelot Library constructs; they are merely collections of functions written with the Camelot Library, designed for inclusion into multiple servers.

3.6.7 Locking

Lock Name Spaces

If programmers could arbitrarily associate any lock name with any object, lock names would constitute a global name space at a server. The programmer could manage the name space if he wrote all of the code that obtained locks at a server himself. However, it is desirable that programmers be able to share reusable packages that implement recoverable abstract data objects. Each package needs to obtain locks in order to perform operations on the objects it implements. If locks from one package-object conflicted with locks from another, concurrency would be reduced, deadlocks could occur, and incorrect program behavior might result. In order to prevent this situation, locks are drawn from *lock name spaces*, and locks only conflict with other locks held on the same name in the same name space. Name spaces are identified by 32-bit integers. The Library provides a primitive, `ALLOC_LOCK_SPACE`, that returns a lock name space identifier, guaranteed to be distinct from all other name spaces allocated at the server.

```
u_int newLockSpace;

newLockSpace = ALLOC_LOCK_SPACE();
```

A typical usage pattern for `ALLOC_LOCK_SPACE` is as follows. A package will contain one or more primitives to create recoverable abstract data objects. When such a primitive is executed, a new lock space is allocated with `ALLOC_LOCK_SPACE` and stored in recoverable memory in a header for the object. The package will also contain several primitives to manipulate the recoverable objects it implements. Each time one of these primitives is called on an object, the package obtains all of its locks from the lock space stored in the header for the object.

`LOCK_SPACE_PRIMARY`, introduced in Section 3.4.2, **Locking**, is distinct from all spaces returned by `ALLOC_LOCK_SPACE`. Typically `LOCK_SPACE_PRIMARY` will be used as the sole lock space in simple servers that implement a single object. Using `LOCK_SPACE_PRIMARY` in a package designed for inclusion in multiple servers would be extremely bad form.

A companion primitive to `ALLOC_LOCK_SPACE`, called `FREE_LOCK_SPACE`, is provided to return a lock space to the pool so that it can be reused. Currently, `FREE_LOCK_SPACE` is a no-op, as each server has 2^{32} lock spaces, so no server is likely to run out of lock spaces in the foreseeable future. However, a server would be disabled if it had no more lock spaces to give out, so it may someday be prudent to implement `FREE_LOCK_SPACE`.

```
u_int lockSpace;

FREE_LOCK_SPACE(lockSpace);
```

Nonblocking Lock Requests

The LOCK primitive, introduced in Section 3.4.2, **Locking**, is a *blocking* primitive: if the desired lock is not immediately available, it waits until the lock is available. A nonblocking primitive, called TRY_LOCK, obtains the specified lock only if it is immediately available. In this case it returns the value TRUE. Otherwise, it returns immediately with the value FALSE, but unlike LOCK, it never waits.

```
if (TRY_LOCK(name, nameSpace, mode))
    ...;
else
    ...;
```

name (u_int) Name on which the lock is sought.
nameSpace (u_int) The name space pertaining to the name.
mode (camlib_lock_mode_t) Mode of lock sought.

Releasing and Demoting Locks

Ordinarily, the programmer does not release locks explicitly: they are automatically released by the Library when the transaction holding the lock commits or aborts. In this manner, strict two-phase locking is enforced. However, primitives exist for servers to release locks manually, or demote write locks to read locks. These primitives must be used with extreme caution, especially on write locks, as they make it very easy to violate serializability. Judicious use of these primitives can, however, greatly increase concurrency.

The UNLOCK primitive causes a transaction to return a lock prematurely.

```
UNLOCK(name, nameSpace);
```

name (u_int) Name on which the lock is sought.
nameSpace (u_int) The name space pertaining to the name.

The DEMOTE_LOCK primitive causes a write lock held by a transaction to be demoted to a read lock.

```
DEMOTE_LOCK(name, nameSpace);
```

name (u_int) Name on which the lock is sought.
nameSpace (u_int) The name space pertaining to the name.

The semantics of the UNLOCK and DEMOTE_LOCK primitives are fairly subtle. As originally implemented, the UNLOCK operation dropped a lock outright. The typical use of the UNLOCK operation is to undo the effects of *a particular call* to LOCK: a procedure obtains a lock, examines some data, and decides that it doesn't really need the lock, so it does an UNLOCK. But suppose a transaction obtains a lock and then calls a procedure that obtains the same lock and proceeds to unlock it. With our original semantics, this procedure call would have the unintended side effect of dropping the lock that was held prior to the call.

To rectify this problem, we use *multiple possession semantics*, whereby a *read count* and a *write count* are maintained for every transaction holding a lock on a given name. These counts represent the *multiplicity* with which a transaction holds read and write locks on a name: the number of times the transaction has locked the name and not subsequently unlocked it. If a transaction already holds a lock on a name, the LOCK operation merely increments the appropriate count. Instead of dropping or demoting a lock outright, the UNLOCK and DEMOTE_LOCK operations adjust the relevant counts. The lock is dropped or demoted only if a count is decremented to zero.

There is an unfortunate glitch in the interface provided by the UNLOCK operation in combination with multiple possession semantics. If a transaction holds a lock with nonzero read and write counts, and issues an UNLOCK on it, the Library "doesn't know" whether to decrement the read or write count. The read count must be decremented so that a write lock is not inadvertently dropped, allowing other transactions to view uncommitted results. If the programmer actually wants to drop a write lock, he can reliably achieve this effect by first doing a DEMOTE_LOCK and then an UNLOCK. The net effect of this sequence of operations is to decrement the write multiplicity.

Note that the UNLOCK and DEMOTE_LOCK primitives must be called from the same transaction that acquired the lock; once a nested transaction commits, the locks it held cannot be released or demoted until its family commits or aborts.

As currently implemented, UNLOCK and DEMOTE_LOCK are not effective for resolving preexisting lock conflicts within a family. If a thread seeking a lock is blocked due to a conflict with another transaction in the same family, and the transaction holding the lock unlocks or demotes it, the blocked thread will *not* be awakened. It will remain blocked until the transaction that held the lock commits up to the *least common ancestor* of the two transactions.

3.6.8 Calling Servers

Controlling Timeout Interval

The SERVER_CALL_2 primitive is identical to the SERVER_CALL primitive (Section 3.3.3), except that it allows the programmer to set the timeout interval. If the server call has not completed after this interval elapses, the enclosing transaction aborts with status ACC_SERVER_CALL_TIMEOUT.

```
SERVER_CALL_2(serverName, call, timeOut);
```

serverName (char *) The name of the server, as specified in the INITIALIZE_SERVER call.

call The actual call. The arguments to the call must be preceded by the keyword ARGS, unless the call has no arguments, in which case the keyword NOARGS must be used. (These keywords cause hidden system arguments to be passed.)

timeOut (u_int) Timeout interval in milliseconds. A value of zero indicates that the largest possible timeout value should be used. (Approximately 50 days.)

```
Examples:
   SERVER_CALL_2("Jill", jill_write(ARGS index, value), 1000);
   SERVER_CALL_2("Jill", jill_reset(NOARGS), 1000);
```

Wrapped Server Calls

As mentioned in Section 3.3, Camelot supports *limited applications*, applications on nodes where Camelot is not running. Limited applications cannot initiate transactions. Ordinary server calls, made with the SERVER_CALL and SERVER_CALL_2 primitives, are only legal within the scope of a transaction, so they cannot be used in limited applications. Limited applications must use *wrapped server calls*, which cause an operation to be automatically "wrapped" in a top-level transaction at the called server. The WRAP_SERVER_CALL and WRAP_SERVER_CALL_2 primitives are used to perform wrapped server calls.

If an ordinary server call fails, control transfers to the end of the enclosing transaction block at the client, and the status variable of the transaction indicates the failure. In a wrapped server call, the programmer has no way of examining the status variable directly, as the enclosing transaction runs at the called server. Thus, a status parameter is added to the WRAP_SERVER_CALL primitive to indicate the final status of the transaction that was created at the server to perform the operation.

There is one important case where the interpretation of the WRAP_SERVER_CALL status value differs from that of the transaction status variable. If an ordinary server call times out, the enclosing transaction is automatically aborted by the client. If a wrapped server call times out, the client has no way of aborting the transaction, which exists only at the server. In fact, the transaction may already have committed when the timeout occurs. Thus, a status return of ACC_SERVER_CALL_TIMEOUT from a wrapped server call does not imply that the operation failed. In general, it cannot be determined if a timed out wrapped server call succeeded or failed. The best one can do is to make another RPC to the same server, whose result can be used to determine whether the first call was successful.

Note that the parameters to the call may be evaluated twice, so they should contain no side effects.

```
WRAP_SERVER_CALL(serverName, call, status);
```

serverName (char *) Name of the server.

call The actual call. The arguments to the call must be preceded by the keyword ARGS, unless the call has no arguments, in which case the keyword NOARGS must be used. (These keywords cause hidden system arguments to be passed.)

`status` (int) A variable in which the status of the remote transaction will be placed. (Must be in the scope of the block containing the call.)

```
Examples:
   WRAP_SERVER_CALL("Jill", jill_write(ARGS index, value),
                    status);
   WRAP_SERVER_CALL("Jill", jill_reset(NOARGS), status);
```

When WRAP_SERVER_CALL is used, the transaction type of the transaction created at the server defaults to new value, standard. The commit protocol defaults to two-phased. The time-out value for the call defaults to 60 seconds. All of these defaults can be overridden with the WRAP_SERVER_CALL_2 primitive.

```
WRAP_SERVER_CALL_2(serverName, call, status,
                   transType, commitProt, timeOut)
```

`serverName` ((char *) Name of the server.
`call` The actual call. The arguments to the call must be preceded by the keyword ARGS, unless the call has no arguments, in which case the keyword NOARGS must be used. (These keywords cause hidden system arguments to be passed.)
`status` (int) A variable in which the status of the remote transaction will be placed. (Must be in the scope of the block containing the call.)
`transType` (transaction_type_t) The transaction type.
`commitProt` (protocol_type_t) The commit protocol.
`timeOut` (u_int) Timeout interval in milliseconds. A value of zero indicates that the largest possible timeout value should be used. (Approximately 50 days.)

```
Examples:
   WRAP_SERVER_CALL_2("Jill", jill_write(ARGS index, value),
                      status, TRAN_NV_STANDARD,
                      PROT_TWO_PHASED, 1000);
   WRAP_SERVER_CALL_2("Jill", jill_reset(NOARGS),
                      status, TRAN_NV_STANDARD,
                      PROT_TWO_PHASED, 1000);
```

Although the primary purpose of wrapped server calls is to support limited applications, wrapped server calls are also legal within the scope of a transaction.

Unlisted Servers

As mentioned in Section 3.4, the programmer can choose whether or not to list a server with the system name server. In this section, we discuss the use of *unlisted servers*.

The START_SERVER procedure causes a number of *request handler* threads to wait for incoming RPCs. These threads are waiting for messages arriving on any *enabled* port. In listed servers, the INITIALIZE_SERVER call allocates and enables a port, and publicizes the name by registering the port with the system name server. Listed servers typically will not have receive rights on any enabled ports other than the one allocated by INITIALIZE_SERVER.

Unlisted servers must allocate and enable one or more ports using appropriate Mach calls, and pass the ports, directly or through an intermediary, to their potential clients. To call the server, the clients use any of the four server call primitives described previously, with the macro invocation UNLISTED_SERVER(port) in place of the server name.

```
UNLISTED_SERVER(port)
```

port The port on which the RPC will be sent to the unlisted server.

```
Examples:
    SERVER_CALL(UNLISTED_SERVER(port),
                jill_write(ARGS index, value));
    SERVER_CALL_2(UNLISTED_SERVER(port),
                  jill_write(ARGS index, value), 1000);
    WRAP_SERVER_CALL(UNLISTED_SERVER(port),
                     jill_write(ARGS index, value), status);
    WRAP_SERVER_CALL_2(UNLISTED_SERVER(port),
                       jill_write(ARGS index, value),
                       status, TRAN_NV_STANDARD,
                       PROT_TWO_PHASED, 1000);
or:
    NOARGS form of any of the above calls.
```

Servers, listed as well as unlisted, can provide varying levels of service to different clients using the following technique. A port is allocated and enabled for each service level (i.e., privilege group). Clients in each privilege group are given a different port on which to send RPCs to the server. To determine whether a given operation is legal for a given client, the server checks whether the port on which the RPC came in indicates an appropriate privilege group. In order to do this, the server must be able to identify the port on which an RPC arrived. This is accomplished using the THIS_PORT primitive.

```
port_t port;

port = THIS_PORT;
```

Note that THIS_PORT should only be called from the thread chosen by a server to process an RPC; the receiving port will *not* be passed down to "sub-threads" created with cobegin blocks, cofor blocks, or the CONCURRENT_THREAD primitive.

3.6.9 Server Operation

Prepare, Commit and Abort Procedures

Once a server joins a transaction, it will be included in the commit or abort protocol for the transaction's family. (See Chapter 9 for a discussion of commit and abort protocols.) The programmer may wish to execute server specific procedures whenever a transaction that ran at a server is asked to prepare, commit, or abort at the server. An alternate form of `INITIALIZE_SERVER`, called `INITIALIZE_SERVER_2` allows the programmer to specify procedures to be called when these events occur.

```
INITIALIZE_SERVER_2(initProc, unlisted, name,
                    prepareProc, commitProc, abortProc);
```

`initProc` `(void (*)())` Procedure (no arguments) called once when the server is first brought up. Generally, this procedure will initialize the server's recoverable storage. It runs as a top level transaction, and we guarantee that it will be executed to completion before the server starts operation. (Optional parameter; may be `NULL`.)

`unlisted` `(boolean_t)` Flag to indicate whether this is an *unlisted* server. Unlisted servers do not automatically publicize their service with the system name server, thus strict control over access rights can be maintained.

`name` `(char *)` The server's name. If unlisted is `FALSE`, the service will be publicized under this name.

`prepareProc` `(boolean_t (*)())` This procedure will be executed each time a transaction family that called the server is asked to prepare. It is passed two arguments, the TID of the top level transaction in the family and the serialization timestamp for the family. The timestamp will only be meaningful if the family was hybrid atomic. Otherwise it will be null. The prepare proc must return a boolean value, indicating how the server is to vote in the commit protocol. (`TRUE`:Commit, `FALSE`:Abort.) (Optional parameter; may be `NULL`.)

`commitProc` `(void (*)())` This procedure is executed after a family that called the server commits. It is passed one argument, the TID of the top level transaction in the family. No guarantees are made that the commit proc will be executed if the server crashes. (Optional parameter; may be `NULL`.)

`abortProc` `(void (*)())` Analogous to `CommitProc` for aborts, except that the abort proc is called on a per transaction basis rather than a per family basis. The abort proc is given one argument, the TID of the aborting transaction. No guarantees are made that the abort proc will be executed if the server crashes. (Optional parameter; may be `NULL`.)

Unlike commit and abort procedures, the prepare procedure must return a boolean value. If `FALSE` is returned, the server will vote to abort the transaction, ensuring that it does not commit.

Note that a server will not execute the commit or abort procedure for a transaction family if it votes read-only in the prepare phase of the family's commit protocol. If the programmer desires to ensure that a server executes the commit or abort procedure for a family, he must ensure that the server does not vote read-only for that family. This is accomplished by doing a dummy `MODIFY`, or just securing a write lock, from within a transaction in the family. Prepare, commit and abort procedures are never executed for server based transactions. No guarantees are made that prepare, commit or abort procedures will be executed at a server if it crashes.

Uses of Prepare, Commit and Abort Procedures

Prepare, commit and abort procedures can be used for many purposes. In the paragraphs below we briefly describe several uses. This list is not intended to be comprehensive; rather it attempts to give the flavor of the things that can be done with these procedures. It is still a research problem to determine what these procedures are useful for and which uses are practical. Many programmers will have no need for them.

Commit procedures can be used to delay some events until after a transaction commits. For instance, a display monitoring the internal state of a server could be updated to reflect the effects of a transaction after it commits. Abort procedures can be used to undo the effects of top-level transactions spawned by a server while executing RPCs for the transaction being aborted. Commit and abort procedures might conceivably be used to implement some alternative type of recoverable storage to the recoverable objects offered by the Camelot Library.

Prepare procedures give servers a last chance to abort transactions they were involved in. Thus a server could respond quickly to certain requests and attempt to service them at its own pace. If the server had not yet succeeded in servicing all such requests pertaining to a transaction being prepared, it could cause the transaction to be aborted by voting 'no' with a prepare procedure.

Killing Servers

The `TERMINATE_SERVER` procedure causes a server to halt execution. The given error message is printed on the system log. `TERMINATE_SERVER` should be called when an error is detected that indicates that the server's operation is impaired and continued operation would be useless or harmful.

```
void TERMINATE_SERVER(message)
    char *message;
```

`message` The message to be printed in the system log.

3.6.10 Status Reports

Camelot Library applications and servers contain a facility to produce status reports summarizing the contents of their internal data structures. These reports contain a list of the families and transactions active at a server or application. In addition, server status reports contain a list of locks held by each transaction. Many other tidbits are included, not all of which will be meaningful to the average programmer. Status reports are produced in response to a "Camelot signal" of **systat**. (See Section A.2.5 for information on the Camelot signal facility.) Sending the appropriate signal is accomplished by typing the following command to the shell:

```
camsignal <PID of server of application> systat
```

Applications print their status reports on the controlling tty. Servers direct their status reports to the system log.

3.6.11 Modifying Camelot Library Behavior

Occasionally the programmer may wish to modify or examine various internal Camelot Library parameters. The variables and macros described in this section have been made available for this purpose. External declarations for the variables described below are included by `camlib.h`. The facilities described in this section are not really a part of the primary interface provided by the Camelot Library. We believe that very few programmers will need to use them.

Handling Port Deaths

Whenever a port on which a Mach process has *receive rights* dies, the process is sent a *port death message* on its *notify port*. In Camelot Library servers, system threads normally intercept these messages. If the programmer wants a server to perform some action upon the death of a port, he can write a *port death procedure*, which will be called each time a port death message is received. The dead port will be passed to the function as its only argument. To install a port death procedure, merely store a pointer to the function in `camlibPortDeathProc`.

```
void (*camlibPortDeathProc)() ;
```

One potential use of the port death procedure is to allow a server to take some action each time an application (or server) that performed RPCs on the server dies. The death of an application causes all of its ports to be deallocated, which in turn causes port death messages to be sent to all of the servers it called.

Changing the Port on which Servers Receive RPCs

Normally, server request handler threads wait for RPCs on all enabled ports. Occasionally, the programmer may wish to have one or more request handler threads wait for requests on a specific port. The `CamlibSetRpcReceivePort` function is provided for this purpose. This function sets the port on which the calling thread will henceforth wait for RPCs. It has no effect if it is called from any thread other than a request handler thread.

```
CamlibSetRpcReceivePort(port);
```

`port` (`port_t`) The port on which the calling thread is to wait for requests.

The `CamlibSetRpcReceivePort` is typically used to make server threads that handle only a special class of requests. This ensures that a thread will always be available to handle requests of this class even if the server is bombarded with ordinary requests.

Determining Recoverable Segment Location

All of a server's recoverable objects, as well as its recoverable heap and its internal (Library) recoverable data are stored in a single contiguous region of (virtual) memory. The variables `camlibRecSegLow` and `camlibRecSegHigh`, both `u_ints`, can be examined to determine the start and end addresses of this region. The variables are set by `INITIALIZE_SERVER`.

Suppressing Transaction Timeout

Normally, servers abort transactions that have remained uncommitted longer than a timeout interval specified to `INITIALIZE_SERVER`. (See Section 3.4.) The `CamlibSuppressTransTimeout` function is provided to suppress this behavior on a per-transaction basis. When this function is called from a server thread, the transaction family under whose scope the call occurs is exempted from being aborted due to transaction timeout.

```
CamlibSuppressTransTimeout();
```

Once `CamlibSuppressTransTimeout` has been called, the transaction family in question is allowed to remain at the server indefinitely, with the following exception: If all of the transactions in the family that have done work at a server abort, the server will purge all records of the family. If a future RPC causes the family to reappear at the server, it will again be subject to transaction timeout, unless `CamlibSuppressTransTimeout` is called again.

Chapter 4

Camelot Node Configuration

Jeffrey L. Eppinger
George Michaels

This chapter discusses the Camelot Node Configuration Application (NCA). Camelot users can run the NCA to specify the following configuration information: which data servers to run, when to restart data servers, data server storage quotas, desired node recovery time, the granularity of allocation for recoverable segment backing store, which Camelot users are allowed to create data servers, and which Camelot users are allowed to create new Camelot user accounts.

This configuration information is stored in the recoverable storage maintained by a special data server called the Node Server. The Node Server interface is described in Chapter 10. The NCA accepts commands from a user and issues remote procedure calls (RPCs) to the Node Server to query or update the Node Server's database. Server and account maintenance are described in Sections 4.1 and 4.2, respectively. Section 4.3 tells how to update configuration information on remote nodes. Section 4.4 gives general information about the Node Server database. Finally, section 4.5 lists all the commands that the NCA provides.

The NCA is an ordinary application program that can be executed from the shell. After the NCA is started, the user must enter a login ID and password.[1] The user is then prompted for commands.

4.1 Server Maintenance

The most common use of the NCA is to set up, start, and stop data servers. Unlike most programs, Camelot data servers cannot simply be run from the shell. They must be started by the Disk Manager, so that they can inherit shared memory regions and ports to communicate with the Camelot system components. Also, the Disk Manager must be able to start servers automatically at times to run recovery on their recoverable segments. To start a server, the Disk Manager needs to know what command line to execute, how much recoverable storage the server is allowed, and the name of the

---

[1] When Camelot is initialized on a node, a single user is created with login ID `admin` and password `admin`. The password to the `admin` account should be changed or the account deleted since the Node Server can be accessed via the network. See Section 4.3.

server and its recoverable segment. All of this information is maintained in recoverable storage by the Node Server, and can be updated by users through the NCA. In addition, the NCA allows users to request that servers be started, stopped, and deleted.

Backing store for recoverable storage is allocated in large fixed-size units called *chunks*. The chunk size determines the granularity of backing store allocation between data servers. Perhaps more importantly, the chunk size is the unit of granularity of sparse usage of backing store within a single server's address space. Each server's recoverable storage is statically partitioned into chunk-sized regions, and physical storage is allocated for a chunk when any of its pages is first flushed to disk. Using a smaller chunk size reduces the amount of space that is wasted when servers use their recoverable address space sparsely. However, the total cost of allocating a new chunk is a few tens of thousands of instructions, so using of a large chunk size reduces the total overhead of chunk allocation. Also, the total number of chunks that can be allocated is fixed (currently at 38,000 chunks), so a large enough chunk size must be chosen to address the available physical storage. Typical chunk sizes are two to sixteen pages.

Below is a sample session for the server in `/usr/ralph/src/srv/accounts`. In this example, and in those that follow, user entries are in italics:

```
login: admin
password: admin
```

The account, `admin`, is an example; each node maintains its own list of users and privileges. To add the server, the command `addserver`, or simply `as`, is used. After the `nca>` prompt is presented, the user might type:

```
nca> AddServer
  server id (0 = next available):[0]
  owner: [admin]
  auto restart (y,n):[n]
  command line: /usr/ralph/src/srv/accounts
  segment id (0 = for next available):[0]
  quota (in chunks, each chunk is 8192 bytes):[1] 2
    server: 13 owner: admin auto-restart: no
    segment: 13 quota: 16384 bytes
    cmdline: /usr/ralph/src/srv/accounts
```

The server has just been successfully added to the database. This does not mean that the server is running, only that the Node Server knows of its existence. To run the server, the user must type,

```
nca> StartServer 13
```

Notice that the server number of 13 was assigned when the server was added.

4.2 Account Maintenance

Another important use of the NCA is to maintain a Camelot user database for each node. Any user with administrative privileges is able to create and destroy user accounts, and to modify passwords and privileges.

Let us imagine that a node administrator wishes to create an account for a new user, Ralph Jones. In order to add an account, the administrator must be logged into the NCA using an account with *admin* privileges. Ralph is to be added as a user with *user* privileges. This provides Ralph with the ability to create his own servers, start them, and modify them. He will not have the right to modify other users' servers or accounts. The administrator creates Ralph's account as follows:

```
nca> AddUser
  new user: jones
  privilege (n,u,a):[n]  u
    new password: twinky
  retype new password: twinky
```

4.3 Accessing a Remote Node Server

The NCA accepts one argument on its command line, which is interpreted as the name of a remote node. The NCA then connects to the Node Server on that node. For example, the login that follows would be on the Node Server database at the Internet node "scotland":

```
% nca scotland.camelot.cs.cmu.edu
login:
```

4.4 The Node Server Database

The Node Server maintains a database that includes the following information about the node:

- a list of users who may access the Node Server database,
- a list of servers, server owners, and server restart parameters,
- a list of servers that are up,
- a table mapping chunks of recoverable storage to physical disk locations,
- the desired node and server recovery time, and
- the size in bytes for each chunk (unit of recoverable storage allocation).

The database also includes other node-specific information that must survive crashes of the node. The NCA provides an interactive interface to this database, using RPCs to the Node Server where the data is actually stored. The Node Server (described in Chapter 10) uses Camelot to update this data transactionally like other Camelot servers.

All nodes are initialized with an administrative account whose username and password are `admin`. To start the NCA, issue the `nca` command to the shell[2] and login.

[2]The Camelot `bin` directory must be in the shell's `PATH` environment variable.

The first time the default administrative account is used, its password should be changed using the `PassWord` command. This is especially important because the node configuration information is accessible via the network. To access the database on a remote workstation, use the remote node's name as the first argument on the NCA command line.

Each account has one of three privilege levels: *admin*, *user*, and *none*, abbreviated `a`, `u`, and `n`. Privilege level *admin* provides complete rights to node configuration functions; privilege level *user* only allows a user to create, delete, and manipulate his own servers; and privilege level *none* only permits information to be listed.

The NCA commands are listed below. The command parser expects characters in lower case. Commands need not be spelled out in full as long as they are uniquely specified; they may also be abbreviated as indicated below (in parentheses). Command arguments can often be typed after the command at the `nca>` prompt. If arguments are omitted, the NCA will prompt the user for them individually. In order to specify the command line for a server in a case where there are arguments, the command lines should be delimited by `'` or `"`. Thus, the above example that shows how to add a server could have been typed as follows:

```
nca>  as 0 admin n '/usr/ralph/src/srv/accounts' 0 2
      server: 13 owner: admin auto-restart: no
      segment: 13 quota: 16384 bytes
      cmdline: /usr/ralph/src/srv/accounts
```

Defaults, if available, are shown delimited by square brackets. The user may accept a default value by just pressing return.

4.5 Commands Listed

Accounts with *admin* privileges may issue the following commands:

`AddUser (au)` This command is used to create a new user account. You must specify a username, a password, and a privilege.

`DeleteUser (du)` This command is used to delete a user account. You must specify a username.

`SetChunkSize (scs)` This command sets the chunk size in bytes on this node. The chunk size must be a power of 2. Other values will not be accepted. (Chunks are the unit of allocation for recoverable backing storage.)

`SetPrivilege (sp)` This command is used to change a user's privileges. You must specify a username and a privilege level.

`SetRecoveryTime (srt)` This command is used to specify a target recovery time, which is the maximum desirable time for server recovery or node failure recovery. Camelot times each recovery pass and counts the number of records read. This information is used along with the target recovery time to determine how often to perform checkpoints and when to abort long-running transactions. Appendix 18 discusses the trade-offs between recovery time and forward processing speed that can be obtained from changing this parameter.

`SetRestartPolicy (srp)` This command is used to specify how often auto-restart servers that have died should be automatically recovered. You must specify a time period in minutes, and the number of restarts allowed in that interval. The purpose of limiting restarts is to avoid severely loading the system with repeated attempts to recover a server that dies every time it is recovered. When an auto-restart server dies, the system will attempt to recover it no more than the specified number of times. Then it will wait for the specified interval before attempting further restarts of the same server.

`Shutdown` This command immediately shuts down Camelot and all servers on the node.

Accounts with *admin* or *user* privileges may issue the following commands:

`AddServer (as)` This command is used to create a new data server (or a new instance of a data server). You must specify a server ID, the name (including path) of an executable binary to be run, the username of the owner, an auto-restart flag, and a list of segment ids and segment quotas. The auto-restart flag indicates whether the data server should be restarted after it dies or the node crashes.

`DeleteServer (ds)` This command is used to delete data servers (or an instance of a data server). You must specify a server ID, or you can specify a list of server ID's on the command line. If you do not have admin privileges, you must be the owner of the data servers.

`KillServer (ks)` This command tells the Node Server to bring down a data server. You must specify a server ID, or you can specify a list of server ID's on the command line. If you do not have admin privileges, you must be the owner of the data servers.

`SetAutorestart (sa)` This command allows you to set or clear the data server's auto-restart flag. You must specify a server ID and an auto-restart flag. The auto-restart flag indicates that the data server should be restarted after a node failure. If you do not have admin privileges, you must be the owner of the server.

`StartServer (ss)` This command tells the Node Server to bring up a data server. You must specify a server ID, or you can specify a list of server ID's on the command line. If you do not have admin privileges, you must be the owner of the data servers.

`SetCommandline (sc)` This command allows you to change the command line of a server. You must specify a server ID, and a new command line. If you do not have admin privileges, you must be the owner of the server.

`SetQuota (sq)` This command allows you to change a segment's quota of recoverable storage. You must specify a server ID, a segment ID and a quota in chunks. If you do not have *admin* privileges, you must be the owner of the server.

All accounts may issue the following commands:

`Help (?)` This command shows information about how to use the NCA.

`ListLogins (ll)` This command shows the users who are currently logged in.

`ListServers (ls)` This command shows information about all servers. A server ID or list of server IDs may be optionally specified to limit the output to those servers.

`ListUsers (lu)` This command shows information about all users.

`PassWord (pw)` This command is used to change a user's password. If you do not have admin privileges, you may only change your own password.

`Quit (q)` This command logs the user out of the NCA.

`Statistics (s)` This command displays the chunk size in bytes for this node, the target recovery time in seconds, the current checkpoint interval in number of records (as determined by the system from the target recovery time and the measured elapsed time of earlier recoveries), and the current server restart policy.

`Uptime (u)` This command shows how long Camelot has been up on this node.

Chapter 5

A Sample Camelot Application and Server

Joshua J. Bloch

5.1 Introduction

In this chapter, we present a sample Camelot application and server, called *Jack* and *Jill*, respectively. The basic purpose of this chapter is to demonstrate the use of the extended Camelot interface, and in particular, the Camelot Library. The material in this chapter, in combination with the other chapters in this part, should provide a good basis for a working knowledge of the Camelot system.

The Jill server implements a recoverable array of positive integers. The Jack application allows the user to interactively construct and execute nested transactions that perform operations on the Jill server. Jill supports two operations: *read*, which takes an array index and returns the value stored at the location specified by the index, and *write*, which takes an index and a positive integer value, and stores the value at the specified location. All of the array locations are initially set to -1 to indicate that they have not been written by the client.

The remainder of this chapter is organized as follows. In Section 5.2, we present a sample user interaction with Jack.[1] In Sections 5.3 and 5.4, we present the source code for Jack and Jill with explanatory notes. In Section 5.5, we describe the procedures for compiling Jack and Jill, and for installing and starting Jill.

5.2 Sample Execution

In this section, we present an annotated typescript of a user's interaction with the Jack application. The interaction shows how the Jack application is used to manipulate the recoverable array implemented by the Jill server. It demonstrates some of the basic properties of transactions, nested transactions, and locks.

[1]This example was originally written by Jeannette Wing for the Avalon version of Jack and Jill.

We assume that a Jill server has already been installed on the user's node and started. The procedures for doing these things are illustrated in Section 5.5. To start Jack (after making sure that the directory containing the `jack` executable is on our search path), we type:

```
% jack
```

The Jack application starts a transaction and responds with:

```
Type ? for a list of commands.
Jack[1]
```

`Jack[1]` is the prompt. The "1" indicates the current transaction nesting level. If we type "?", we get the following list of commands:

```
Commands are:
    r   Read array element.
    w   Write array element.
    b   Begin nested transaction.
    c   Commit innermost transaction.
    a   Abort innermost transaction.
    A   Abort top level transaction.
    q   Abort top level transaction and quit program.

Jack[1]
```

Let's say that we want to read what is stored at location 7 of the array:

```
Jack[1] r
Location to read: 7
Location 7 is uninitialized.
Jack[1]
```

As we can see, we have not yet given location 7 a value. Let's do so:

```
Jack[1] w
Location to write: 7
Value to write: 44
Write succeeded.
Jack[1] r
Location to read: 7
Value at location 7 is 44.
Jack[1]
```

Now we can begin a subtransaction, using the "b" command. In this transaction, we first read the value in location 7, and then give it a new value:

```
Jack[1] b
Jack[2] r
Location to read: 7
Value at location 7 is 44.
Jack[2] w
Location to write: 7
```

```
Value to write: 69
Write succeeded.
Jack[2] r
Location to read: 7
Value at location 7 is 69.
Jack[2]
```

Note that the prompt has changed to indicate the transaction nesting level. Let's continue with another nested transaction:

```
Jack[2] b
Jack[3] r
Location to read: 7
Value at location 7 is 69.
Jack[3] w
Location to write: 7
Value to write: 100
Write succeeded.
Jack[3] r
Location to read: 7
Value at location 7 is 100.
Jack[3]
```

If we commit this subtransaction, then we return to its parent, with its effects visible:

```
Jack[3] c
Transaction committed.
Jack[2] r
Location to read: 7
Value at location 7 is 100.
Jack[2]
```

If, however, we now abort the second-level transaction, we return to the top-level transaction, and none of the effects of the aborted transaction (or its descendants) are visible.

```
Jack[2] a
Transaction aborted as per request.
Jack[1] r
Location to read: 7
Value at location 7 is 44.
Jack[1]
```

Now, suppose we start up another instance of `jack` (in another window, perhaps). In this Jack, we start a transaction, and write into location 10. Then we attempt to read the value we previously wrote into location 7.

```
% jack
Type ? for a list of commands.
Jack[1] w
Location to write: 10
Value to write: 10
Write succeeded.
Jack[1] r
Location to read: 7
```

The second Jack ("Jack B") does not immediately return an answer. This is because the first Jack ("Jack A") has a *write lock* on location 7. This lock excludes other transactions from observing the value written there. This is needed to ensure serializability: Jack A's transaction may either commit or abort. If it commits, then Jack B's query should return 44; if it aborts, then Jack B should inform the user that location 7 is still uninitialized. Thus, Jack B cannot return anything until Jack A's top-level transaction terminates. Let's commit Jack A's transaction:

```
Jack[1] c
Transaction committed.
(Transaction was top level.)            Value at location 7 is 44.
Jack[1]                                 Jack[1]
```

Committing Jack A's transaction allowed Jack B's transaction to proceed with the completion of the read operation.

Jack A automatically starts a new top-level transaction when it commits the top-level transaction. If we attempt to read the value in location 7 from Jack A's new transaction, we succeed even though the transaction running in Jack B already has a *read lock* on location 7.

```
Jack[1] r
Location to read: 7
Value at location 7 is 44.
```

Thus, we see that multiple transactions are allowed to possess read locks on an object simultaneously: concurrent reads do not violate serializability.

If, however, we attempt to write a new value into location 7 from this transaction, Jack A is suspended:

```
Jack[1] w
Location to write: 7
Value to write: 70
```

Jack A cannot write into location 7 because Jack B's transaction has already observed a value there. Jack A must wait for Jack B's transaction to terminate before it can invalidate this observation. Let's terminate Jack B's transaction with an abort:

```
                                        Jack[1] a
                                        Transaction aborted as per request.
Write succeeded.                        (Transaction was top level.)
Jack[1] r                               Jack[1]
Location to read: 7
Value at location 7 is 70.
Jack[1]
```

Note that even if Jack B had committed, Jack A would still read 70 from location 7 since Jack A's write would still be serialized after Jack B's read.

5.3 The Application

The Jack application consists of a single source file, which we break into four pieces for presentation in this section. The head of the source file and the main procedure are illustrated in Figure 5.1. The source file `#includes` four header files: two standard UNIX header files, `stdio.h`, and `ctype.h`; the Camelot Library header file `camlib.h`; and a header file for the Jill server, `jill_client.h`. The file `ctype.h` contains character classification macros that we use to parse user input. The file `jill_client.h` is presented in Section 5.4.

We define `USER_REQUESTED_ABORT`, a user abort code generated by Jack, to be 100. We could have chosen any integer value that does not conflict with the user abort codes returned by Jill. This restriction illustrates the fact that the user abort codes generated by a server are an important part of the interface that it exports.

Jack's main procedure is fairly straightforward. It initializes Jack as a Camelot Library application and repeatedly calls `jill_transaction`. This function interactively constructs and executes a nested transaction that operates on the Jill server.

The `jill_transaction` function, illustrated in Figures 5.2 and 5.3, is the heart of the Jack application. It creates a transaction and enters a command loop. Each iteration of the command loop prompts the user for a command and executes it on behalf of the transaction.

```
/*
 * jack.c -- A simple application to exercise the Jill server.
 */
#include <stdio.h>
#include <ctype.h>
#include <camlib/camlib.h>
#include <jill_client.h>

#define USER_REQUESTED_ABORT    100

main()
{
    if(!INITIALIZE_APPLICATION("Jack"))
    {
        printf("Camelot is not running on this node!\n");
        exit(1);
    }

    printf("Type ? for a list of commands.\n");

    while(TRUE)
    {
        jill_transaction(1);
        printf("(Transaction was top level.)\n");
    }
}
```

Figure 5.1: Jack - Main Procedure

```
/*
 * jill_transaction -- Interactively construct and perform a transaction
 * utilizing the jill server.  Can be called recursively to construct nested
 * transactions.  Nesting depth is passed in level so it can be printed
 * in prompts.
 */
jill_transaction(level)
int level;
{
    int status;

    BEGIN_TRANSACTION
        char cmd;

        do
        {
            printf("Jack[%d] ", level);
            do
                cmd = getchar();
            while(isspace(cmd));

            switch(cmd)
            {
              case 'r':     /* Read an array element */
                do_jill_read();
                break;
              case 'w':     /* Write an array element */
                do_jill_write();
                break;
              case 'b':     /* Begin a subtransaction */
                jill_transaction(level+1);
                break;
              case 'c':     /* Commit this transaction */
                break;
              case 'a':     /* Abort this transaction */
                ABORT(USER_REQUESTED_ABORT);
              case 'A':     /* Abort top level transaction */
                ABORT_TOP_LEVEL(USER_REQUESTED_ABORT);
              case 'q':     /* Abort top level transaction and quit */
                exit(0);
              case '?':     /* Print short help message */
                print_help();
                break;
              default:
               printf("Unknown command. Type ? for a list of commands.\n");
            }
        } while(cmd != 'c');
    END_TRANSACTION(status)
```

Figure 5.2: Jack - `jill_transaction` Function

```
    switch(status)
    {
      case 0:
        printf("Transaction committed.\n");
        break;
      case USER_REQUESTED_ABORT:
        printf("Transaction aborted as per request.\n");
        break;
      case INDEX_OUT_OF_BOUNDS:
        printf("Transaction aborted: Array index out of bounds.\n");
        break;
      case ILLEGAL_VALUE:
        printf("Transaction aborted:  Attempt to write a negative value.\n");
        break;
      default:
        printf("%s\n", ABORT_CODE_TO_STR(status));
    }
}
```

Figure 5.3: Jack - `jill_transaction` Function

The "r" command reads an element from the Jill array, and the "w" command writes an element to the Jill array. The functions to perform these operations are illustrated in Figure 5.4. Notice that if the `SERVER_CALL` fails (e.g., because of an index out of bounds), Jill aborts the transaction and control returns to the `jill_transaction` function.

The most interesting aspect of the `jill_transaction` function is the manner in which it creates nested transactions. When `jill_transaction` is called from outside the scope of a transaction, as in Figure 5.1, it creates a new top-level transaction. When the "b" command is invoked, `jill_transaction` calls itself recursively to create a nested transaction. The current nesting level is incremented and passed to the recursive invocation of `jill_transaction`, so the nesting level can be included in prompts to the user. When `jill_transaction` is called from `main`, the constant 1 is passed to indicate that a top-level transaction is being created.

The "c" command commits the current transaction. It causes the program to exit the command loop, where it encounters the end of the transaction block. This causes the Library to attempt to commit the transaction. The status code returned in `status` indicates whether the transaction committed successfully.

The "a" and "A" commands abort the current and top-level transaction, respectively, by calling the appropriate Camelot Library abort primitive. We have omitted the traditional `break` statement in these cases to emphasize the fact that `ABORT` and `ABORT_TOP_LEVEL` cause immediate, unconditional transfer of control.

The switch statement following the transaction block prints a message describing the outcome of the transaction (Figure 5.3). The switch statement checks if the status is zero, indicating success, or if it is any of the user abort codes that Jack and Jill can generate. If the switch statement falls through to the default case, the status must be a Camelot system abort code; it is passed on to the `ABORT_CODE_TO_STR` function to generate an appropriate message.

```
/*
 * do_jill_read -- Query the user for an index and read that location from
 * the Jill recoverable array server.
 */
do_jill_read()
{
    int index, value;

    printf("Location to read: ");
    scanf("%d", &index);
    putchar('\n');

    SERVER_CALL("jill", jill_read(ARGS index, &value));

    if (value == -1)
        printf("Location %d is uninitialized.\n", index);
    else
        printf("Value at location %d is %d.\n", index, value);
}


/*
 * do_jill_write -- Query the user for an index and value, and the Jill
 * recoverable array server write the value to the location.
 */
do_jill_write()
{
    int index, value;

    printf("Location to write: ");
    scanf("%d", &index);
    printf("Value to write: ");
    scanf("%d", &value);
    putchar('\n');

    SERVER_CALL("jill", jill_write(ARGS index, value));

    printf("Write succeeded.\n");
}
```

Figure 5.4: Jack - Read and Write Functions

```
/*
 * print_help -- Prints the commands.
 */
print_help()
{
    printf("\n\
Commands are: \n\
    r   Read array element.\n\
    w   Write array element.\n\
    b   Begin nested transaction.\n\
    c   Commit innermost transaction.\n\
    a   Abort innermost transaction.\n\
    A   Abort top level transaction.\n\
    q   Abort top level transaction and quit program.\n\n");
}
```

Figure 5.5: Jack - Help Function

The "q" command quits the Jack application. Note that we do not bother explicitly aborting the transaction(s) in progress; instead we rely on the Camelot system to notice that the application that started the transaction(s) has died, and abort them.

The "?" command prints a list of the commands that Jack understands. The function is illustrated in Figure 5.5.

5.4 The Server

The Jill server consists of one source file, two header files and a MIG interface description file. The MIG interface description file, illustrated in Figure 5.6, contains MIG declarations for the functions exported by the Jill server. From this file, MIG generates server stubs, client stubs, a demultiplexor function for the server stubs, and a header file for the client stubs. The use of MIG, including the construction of interface description files, is described in detail in Section 2.4.

The client header file, `jill_client.h`, is illustrated in Figure 5.7. This file contains the external declarations and constant definitions required to use the Jill server. It is `#included` by all clients of the Jill server. The client header file in turn `#includes jill.h`, which is automatically generated by MIG from `jill.defs`. `jill.h` contains external declarations for the client stubs of the functions exported by Jill. The client header file also defines the abort codes exported by Jill.

The internal header file for Jill, called `jill_internal.h`, is illustrated in Figure 5.8. This file contains the declarations shared by Jill's source files. In fact, Jill has only a single source file, and the contents of `jill_internal.h` could appear directly in this file. For pedagogical reasons, however, we provide an internal header file to show which definitions would be shared if Jill had multiple source files.

The file `jill_internal.h` contains Jill's recoverable object declaration block and a constant definition for the size of the Jill array. As discussed in Section 3.4.2, a server's recoverable object

```
/*
 *  jill.defs -- MIG interface for the jill server, which implements
 *  a recoverable array.
 */

subsystem camelot jill 69000;

#include <camelot.defs>

camelotroutine jill_read(
                index           : int;
            OUT value           : int);

camelotroutine jill_write(
                index           : int;
                value           : int);
```

Figure 5.6: Jill - MIG Interface Description File

```
/*
 * jill_client.h -- External header file for the Jill server.  Definitions
 * shared by Jill and its clients.
 */

#include "jill.h"

/*
 * User abort codes exported by Jill
 */

#define INDEX_OUT_OF_BOUNDS 1    /* Attempt to access a location out of bounds */
#define ILLEGAL_VALUE       2    /* Attempt to insert a negative number */
```

Figure 5.7: Jill - Client Header File

```
/*
 * jill_internal.h -- Internal header file for the Jill server.
 */

/*
 * System Constant(s)
 */
#define ARRAY_SIZE  1000    /* Number of cells in the array */


/*
 * Recoverable Object Declarations
 */
BEGIN_RECOVERABLE_DECLARATIONS
    struct jill_array_struct
    {
        int data[ARRAY_SIZE];
    } jill_array;
END_RECOVERABLE_DECLARATIONS
```

Figure 5.8: Jill - Internal Header File

declaration block should always be in a header file. Jill has only a single recoverable object, the array whose operations it exports. Note that the array is declared inside a structure; this allows the entire array to be changed with a single `MODIFY` statement.

We present the Jill server source file in three parts. The main procedure is illustrated in Figure 5.9. Note that the client header file is `#included` as well as the internal header file. This gives Jill access to the definitions of the user abort codes that it exports. Jill shares these definitions with its clients.

The main procedure is straightforward. It consists of a call to `INITIALIZE_SERVER` followed by a call to `START_SERVER`. The `FALSE` in the second argument to `INITIALIZE_SERVER` causes Jill to be a *listed* server, so that Jill's clients can address Jill by name. The demultiplexor function `jill_server`, passed in the first argument to `START_SERVER`, is automatically generated by MIG from `jill.defs`. The `10` in the second argument causes Jill to enforce a maximum of ten concurrent requests. The `0` in the third argument causes Jill to disable transaction timeouts. This is important because Jill has interactive clients, like Jack. Transactions involving Jill can last for long periods of time, and it would be a great annoyance to users of interactive applications if their transactions timed out while they were deciding what to do next.

The first argument to `INITIALIZE_SERVER`, `jill_init`, is an *initialization procedure*, executed only once, the first time Jill is successfully started. The procedure, illustrated in Figure 5.10, initializes the array to contain -1 in every location. For efficiency, this is accomplished with a single call to `MODIFY`, rather than one call for each location in the array. (Each call to `MODIFY` takes about 1 ms on a 3 MIPS workstation.) In fact, the (one-time) cost of a thousand modifies when the server is first started is negligible. We use a single `MODIFY`, however, to illustrate the point that multiple `MODIFYs` should be combined when feasible.

The operation procedures for the two operations exported by Jill are illustrated in Figure 5.11.

```
/*
 * jill.c -- A simple Camelot server that implements a recoverable array.
 */

#include <stdio.h>
#include <camlib/camlib.h>
#include "jill_internal.h"
#include "jill_client.h"

void jill_init();
int jill_server();


main()
{
    extern boolean_t jill_server();

    INITIALIZE_SERVER(jill_init, FALSE, "jill");
    START_SERVER(jill_server, 10, 0);
}
```

Figure 5.9: Jill - Main Procedure

```
/*
 * jill_init -- Initialization procedure for the jill server.  Initializes
 * the data array to contain all -1's, to indicate that the cells have
 * not yet been written.
 */
void jill_init()
{
    struct jill_array_struct temp;
    int i;

    /* Load up a temporary copy of the array with -1's */
    for (i=0; i < ARRAY_SIZE; i++)
        temp.data[i] = -1;

    MODIFY(REC(jill_array), temp);
}
```

Figure 5.10: Jill - Initialization Procedure

```
/*
 * Operation Procedures
 */

/*
 * op_jill_read -- Return in *valPtr the positive integer stored at the given
 * index in the recoverable array.  -1 is returned if the cell has not yet
 * been written to.  Transaction is aborted with code INDEX_OUT_OF_BOUNDS
 * if index is out of bounds.
 */
void op_jill_read(index, valPtr)
int index, *valPtr;
{
    /* If index is out of bounds, return an error code */
    if (index < 0 || index >= ARRAY_SIZE)
        ABORT(INDEX_OUT_OF_BOUNDS);

    LOCK((unsigned) index, LOCK_SPACE_PRIMARY, LOCK_MODE_READ);
    *valPtr = REC(jill_array.data[index]);
    return;
}

/*
 * op_jill_write -- Store value at location index in the recoverable array.
 * Abort occurs if index is out of bounds (INDEX_OUT_OF_BOUNDS) or value
 * is negative (ILLEGAL_VALUE).
 */
void op_jill_write(index, value)
int index, value;
{
    /* If index is out of bounds, return an error code */
    if (index < 0 || index >= ARRAY_SIZE)
        ABORT(INDEX_OUT_OF_BOUNDS);

    /* If value is negative, return an error code */
    if (value < 0)
        ABORT(ILLEGAL_VALUE);

    LOCK((unsigned) index, LOCK_SPACE_PRIMARY, LOCK_MODE_WRITE);
    MODIFY(REC(jill_array.data[index]), value);

    return;
}
```

Figure 5.11: Jill - Operation Procedures

Both operation procedures perform three steps. First, they check that their input parameters are in range; if their input parameters are out of range, they abort the calling transaction with the appropriate user abort code. Second, they get the appropriate lock. Finally, they perform the operation on the Jill array with REC or MODIFY.

Note that the ABORT operation transfers control in the server as well as in the application. In an abstract sense, it can be thought of as transferring control from the server *to* the appropriate location in the application.

Locks are obtained on the array index pertaining to an operation. It would have been possible to use the LOCK_NAME macro to generate lock names, but it was simpler to use array indices directly. If Jill maintained multiple arrays, the direct use of array indices as lock names would have caused artificial concurrency restrictions; each index would refer to multiple locations, one in each array. Under these circumstances, it would be appropriate to use the LOCK_NAME facility.

All of the locks used by Jill are drawn from Jill's *primary lock name space*. This is appropriate, as Jill is a server unto itself, not a library that is linked into other servers.

5.5 Installation

Before compiling Jack or Jill, the MIG interface description for Jill must be processed. This accomplished with the following command:

```
mig -r jill.defs
```

This produces three files: jillServer.c contains server stubs and a demultiplexor function, jillUser.c contains client stubs, and jill.h contains external declarations for the client stubs.

The following command is used to compile Jack:

```
cc -o jack jack.c jillClient.o -lcamlib -lthreads -lcam -lmach
```

The following command is used to compile Jill:

```
cc -o jill jill.c jillServer.o -lcamlib -lthreads -lcam -lmach
```

To install the Jill server, the user must run the Node Configuration Application (NCA), described in Chapter 4. A sample NCA session in which the user installs and starts the Jill server is illustrated below. It is assumed that Camelot is already running.

To run the NCA, we type "nca" in response to the shell prompt, and enter a Camelot user ID and password:

```
% nca
login: admin
Password:

  connected users: admin
nca>
```

If we type "?" in response to the NCA's prompt, we get the following list of commands:

```
The following commands are available:

  ADMIN:   AddUser (au)
           DeleteUser (du)
           SetChunkSize (scs)
           SetPrivilege (sp)
           SetRecoveryTime (srt)
           SetRestartPolicy (srp)
           Shutdown

  USER:    AddServer (as)
           DeleteServer (ds)
           KillServer (ks)
           SetAutorestart (sa)
           SetCommandline (sc)
           SetQuota (sq)
           StartServer (ss)

  OTHER:   Help (?)
           ListLogins (ll)
           ListServers (ls)
           ListUsers (lu)
           PassWord (pw)
           Quit (q)
           Statistics (s)
           Uptime (u)
```

To add a server, we type "as". The NCA responds by prompting us for various information about the server to be added. Some prompts are followed by a default value in brackets. To select the default value, just hit return.

The server ID, owner, and segment ID parameters are of no concern to most users. It is generally advisable to accept the default values for these parameters. A positive response ("y") to the "auto-restart" prompt indicates that Camelot should automatically restart the server if it crashes. This is appropriate for fully debugged servers that are expected to remain available at all times. If we are debugging a server, or just bringing it up for a single, short-term use, a negative response ("n") is appropriate.

The command line is the pathname for the server executable, followed by any command line arguments that the server expects. The pathname need not be fully specified; the NCA examines the normal search path as if the command line had been typed to the shell.

The quota is the total size of the server's recoverable segment in chunks. (A chunk is generally 8K bytes.) The quota must be large enough for all of the server's recoverable objects. This includes the static recoverable objects in the server's recoverable object declaration block, a small area for Library use (currently 128 bytes), and all of the storage eventually consumed by `REC_MALLOC`s. If the quota is set too low for the static recoverable objects, the server will not start. If the server runs out of storage on a `REC_MALLOC`, the enclosing transaction will abort with the appropriate system abort code.

We accept the default values for all parameters except the command line:

```
nca> as
  server id (0 = next available): [0]
```

```
owner: [admin]
auto restart (y,n): [n]
command line: jill
segment id (0 = for next available): [0]
quota (in chunks): [1]
```

When we respond to the last parameter prompt, the NCA attempts to find the server executable and creates an entry for the server in its database. If the NCA fails to find the server, or some other error occurs, it prints an appropriate error message and creates no entry in its database. Otherwise, it summarizes the entry to indicate success:

```
server: 2     owner: admin      auto-restart: no
segment: 2        quota: 16384 bytes
cmdline: /usr/camelot/bin/jill
```

Now we enter the "ss" command to start the server. We choose to type the server ID (2) on the command line, although we do not have to; the NCA would prompt us for it if we did not provide it. The NCA responds immediately and starts the server asynchronously. We wait a few seconds for the server to start, and type "ls" to get a list of the servers that Camelot knows about:

```
nca> ss 2
nca> ls

    server: 2     owner: admin      auto-restart: no    state: up
    segment: 2
    chunk quota: 1           (16384       bytes)
    chunks used: 0           (0           bytes)

    command line: /usr/camelot/bin/jill
```

We see that Jill is now up and running. To quit the NCA, we type "q":

```
nca> q

Logged out.

%
```

Once Jill is running, the user is free to start one or more Jack processes, as illustrated in Section 5.2.

Part II

The Primitive Camelot Interface

Chapter 6

The Structure of Camelot

Jeffrey L. Eppinger

From the point of view of an application programmer, Camelot is a black box accessed via the Camelot Library. The Camelot Library accesses Camelot using a collection of interfaces that implement recoverable virtual memory, transaction management, and node management. Figure 6.1 depicts the Camelot system from the point of the Camelot Library.

This part of the book provides additional background on the Mach operating system and describes the primitive interfaces used by the Camelot Library. Section 6.1 of this chapter presents the Camelot architecture in more detail and Section 6.2 shows the interaction among the Camelot system components when transactions are executed by showing the message flow for a simple Jack and Jill transaction. This example gives perspective about the interaction of the component processes.

Many interfaces of the component processes will be described in subsequent chapters in this part. Chapter 7 describes the communication, threading, and external memory management facilities that Mach provides. Chapter 8 explains the Camelot support for recoverable virtual memory. Chapter 9 describes the interface to the Transaction Manager. Chapter 10 describes the interface to the Node Server.

6.1 The Camelot Architecture

The structure of a Camelot node is depicted in Figure 6.2. It is unfortunate that at this point readers must understand so much of the internal structure of Camelot, but this system is most easily explained from the point of view of the system components. Part III presents the rationale for the internal design of Camelot.

Camelot runs on top of the Mach kernel. Users view the collection of tasks that comprise Camelot as a layer on top of the operating system. Camelot users write *data servers* and *applications*.

- **Data servers** maintain permanent data in recoverable virtual memory and/or by calling other data servers.

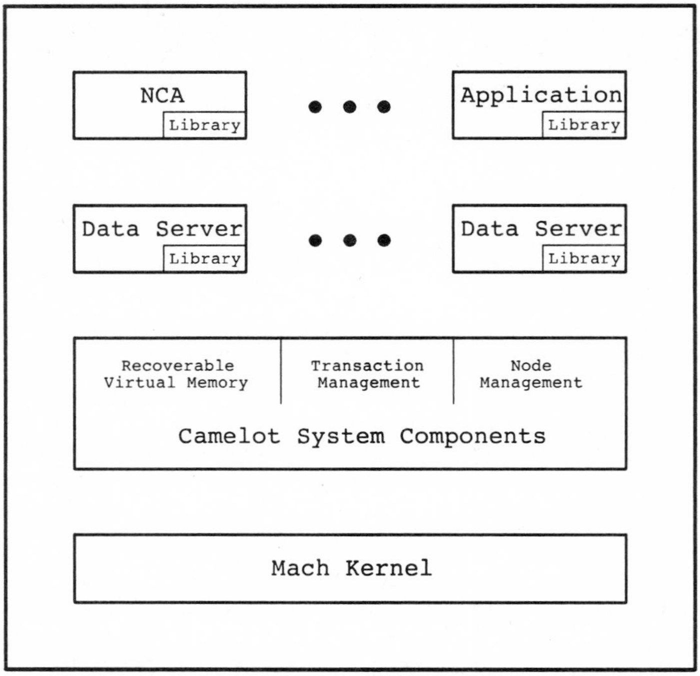

Figure 6.1: Interfaces to Camelot
Data servers and applications are written by Camelot users, typically using the interface provided by the Camelot Library. This figure depicts the interfaces to the Camelot system used by the Camelot Library. Camelot provides interfaces for managing recoverable virtual memory, transactions, and the node.

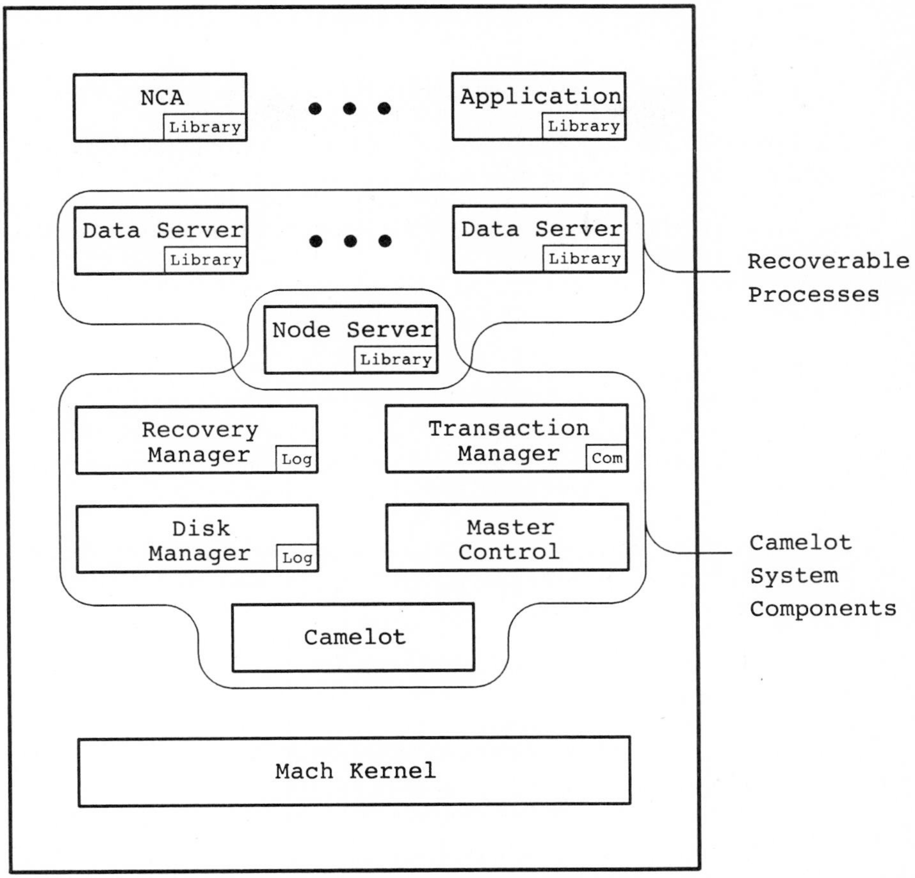

Figure 6.2: The Structure of a Camelot Node

This figure depicts the structure of a Camelot node. Data servers and applications are written by Camelot users. Data servers maintain permanent data in recoverable virtual memory. Applications begin and end transactions that invoke operations on data servers by executing remote procedure calls (RPCs). The Camelot layer is composed of several processes: the Transaction Manager, the Recovery Manager, the Disk Manager, and the Camelot and Master Control tasks. A write-ahead log is supported by the Log Manager, which for performance is embedded in the Disk and Recovery Managers. Distributed transactions are supported by the Communication Manager which is embedded in the Transaction Manager. The Node Server is a distinguished data server used to store configuration information.

- **Applications** begin and end transactions that invoke operations on data servers by executing RPCs. Data servers can act as applications, initiating transactions.

The Camelot layer is composed of the following components:

- The **Node Server** is a distinguished data server used to store configuration information.
- The **Transaction Manager** guarantees consensus among a transaction's participants as to whether the transaction commits or aborts.
- The **Recovery Manager** is responsible for restoring a transaction-consistent state after a failure.
- The **Disk Manager** is responsible for buffer management and maintaining the common log.
- The **Communication Manager** is responsible for transparently extending communications across the network. It interacts with the Transaction Manager to piggy-back data on RPCs to track the spread of transactions to other nodes. The Communication Manager is also responsible for providing a name service so applications can locate data servers. For efficiency, the Communication Manager is linked with the Transaction Manager.
- The **Log Manager** writes and reads records in stable storage. For efficiency, the Log Manager is loaded in both the Disk Manager and the Recovery Manager. The copy in the Recovery Manager only allows read access.
- The **Camelot** and **Master Control** processes facilitate system initialization and serialize debugging output.

Each data server does its own lock management so that it can take advantage of type specific and/or timestamp-based locking schemes.

As mentioned above, the Communication Manager is loaded with the Transaction Manager and the Log Manager is loaded with both the Disk Manager and the Recovery Manager. Interactions between components are still specified by RPC interfaces, however local procedure calls are used to invoke the operations. The specification of these RPC interfaces is provided in Appendix C.

The primitive interface to Camelot is somewhat complex. However, the Camelot Library provides an easy-to-use interface that exports macros such as `BEGIN_TRANSACTION`, `LOCK`, *etc.* These macros interface with other threads executing in the Library to handle correctly transaction commitment and abort and to access recoverable virtual memory. See Chapter 3.

6.2 An Example Message Flow

To illustrate how the Camelot architecture works, consider the Jack and Jill example. All of the interfaces described in this example will be discussed in the subsequent chapters of this book. This example is a narrative that provides the reader with perspective about the interaction among the Camelot components during the execution of a transaction.

Jill provides access to a recoverable array of integers. Jack might run the following transaction:

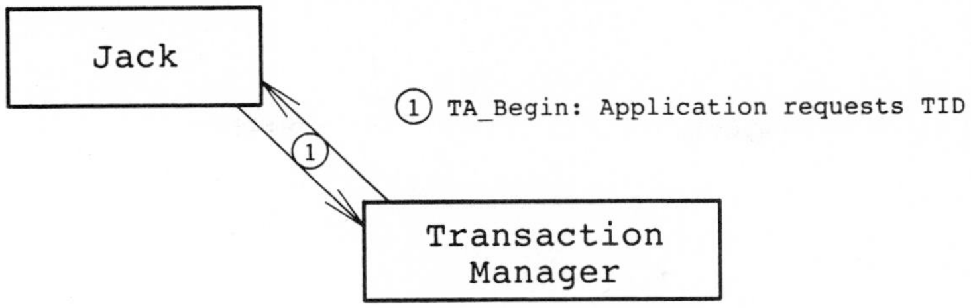

Figure 6.3: Messages for the BEGIN_TRANSACTION Statement

```
BEGIN_TRANSACTION
    ...
    SERVER_CALL('Jill', jill_read(ARGS index, &value));
    ...
    SERVER_CALL('Jill', jill_write(ARGS index, value));
    ...
END_TRANSACTION(status)
```

When the BEGIN_TRANSACTION statement is executed, Jack executes a TA_Begin[1] RPC to the Transaction Manager requesting a transaction identifier (TID). This is illustrated in Figure 6.3.

When the first SERVER_CALL statement is executed, the application issues a CA_Lookup RPC to the Communication Manager to get a communications port for Jill. This communications port is then cached for future use. Using this port, Jack sends the jill_read RPC. The SERVER_CALL macro implicitly passes the TID in the jill_read RPC. If Jill is on the same node as the application, the messages go directly to Jill. The case when Jill is on a different node is discussed below. When the request arrives, Jill joins the transaction by notifying the Transaction Manager with the TS_Join RPC. Jill does the requested work: in this case Jill must lock the specified integer for read access by the transaction, read it from recoverable storage and return it to Jack. If the page of recoverable storage containing the integer is not currently cached in a physical memory buffer, Jill page faults. The kernel determines that the region of memory on which Jill is faulting is managed by an external memory manager, namely, the Disk Manager. The kernel then forwards the request to the Disk Manager via the external memory management interface. The Disk Manager receives a memory_object_data_request message from the kernel. The Disk Manager finds the missing page in non-volatile disk storage and sends the page to the kernel so the fault can be cleared. After

[1] Camelot RPCs (and asynchronous one-way messages) use a two-letter prefix as a naming convention. The first letter identifies the server that will process the request. The second letter identifies the client. The following letters are used:

- A - A generic application
- C - Communication Manager
- D - Disk Manager
- M - Master Control
- N - Node Server
- R - Recovery Manager
- S - A generic data server
- T - Transaction Manager

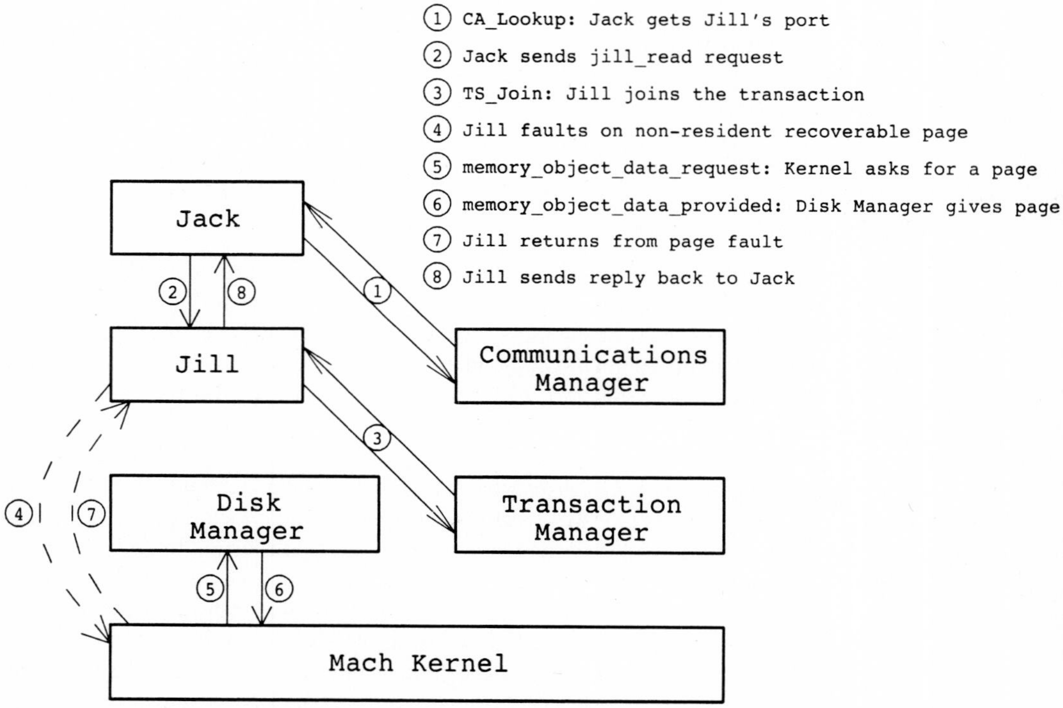
① CA_Lookup: Jack gets Jill's port
② Jack sends jill_read request
③ TS_Join: Jill joins the transaction
④ Jill faults on non-resident recoverable page
⑤ memory_object_data_request: Kernel asks for a page
⑥ memory_object_data_provided: Disk Manager gives page
⑦ Jill returns from page fault
⑧ Jill sends reply back to Jack
Jack
Jill
Communications Manager
Disk Manager
Transaction Manager
Mach Kernel
1
2
3
4
5
6
7
8

Figure 6.4: Messages for the `jill_read` Server Call

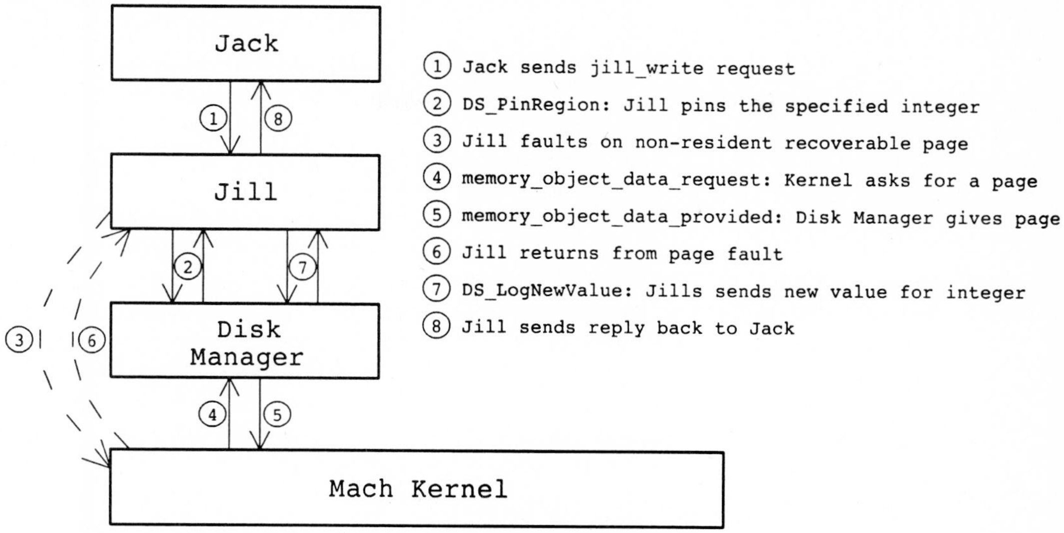

Figure 6.5: Messages for the `jill_write` Server Call

reading the integer, Jill packs it in the reply and sends it back to Jack. This is illustrated in Figure 6.4. If there is an error (e.g., the `index` is out of range), Jill aborts the transaction.

Once Jack receives the reply it can continue. When the second `SERVER_CALL` statement is executed, the communications port for Jill is found in Jack's port cache. Using this port, Jack sends the `jill_write` RPC to Jill. Since Jill has already joined the transaction, another `TS_Join` RPC is not sent to the Transaction Manager. Jill processes the request: in this case Jill must lock the specified integer for write access by the transaction and set it to have the new value. To write recoverable virtual memory, the "pin-update-log" sequence is used. Before modifying the integer, Jill sends a `DS_PinRegion` RPC to the Disk Manager. Then Jill writes the integer in virtual memory. If the integer is on a page of recoverable virtual memory that is not currently cached in a physical memory buffer, Jill page faults. The page fault is handled as described above. Finally, Jill sends the `DS_LogNewValue` (or `DS_LogOldValueNewValue`) RPC to the Disk Manager to spool a description of the change. This is illustrated in Figure 6.5. Optimizations to this protocol are discussed in Chapter 8.

When the `END_TRANSACTION` statement is executed, Jack sends a `TA_End` RPC to the Transaction Manager requesting that the transaction be committed. Since the only participating server, Jill, is local to the initiating application, Jack, an optimized local protocol is used. The Transaction Manager sends an `ST_Vote` RPC to Jill asking if it wishes to allow the transaction to commit. If Jill responds affirmatively, the Transaction Manager executes a `DT_SmallLogWrite` RPC to the Disk Manager requesting that a commit record be written (forced) to the log. After the log record is written, the Transaction Manager responds to the Jack's request to commit the transaction and notifies Jill that the transaction has committed using an `ST_Commit` message. Upon receiving the commit notification, Jill can drop the locks held by the transaction. This is illustrated in Figure 6.6. If Jill responds negatively to the `ST_Vote`, the transaction will abort. Abort cases are described below.

If Jack and Jill are on different nodes, a surrogate port for Jill is obtained by issuing the `CA_Lookup` call when executing the first `SERVER_CALL` statement. Messages sent to the surrogate port go to the local Communication Manager. The local Communication Manager obtains transaction-related data from the local Transaction Manager using the `TC_SendingRequest` RPC. Transaction-related data includes the genealogy of the transaction making the request, and other information that the local Transaction Manager wishes to forward to the remote Transaction Manager. The local Communication Manager then forwards the request and transaction-related data to the remote Communication Manager. Upon receipt of the request, the remote Communication Manager gives the transaction-related data to the remote Transaction Manager using the `TC_ReceivedRequest` RPC, and forwards the request to Jill. The reply is sent analogously: the `TC_SendingReply` and `TC_ReceivedReply` RPCs are used to piggyback Transaction Manager data on the reply, and the Communication Manager employs a similar forwarding mechanism. This is illustrated in Figure 6.7. Should Jill page fault, the Disk Manager on Jill's node will handle it.

When Jack and Jill are on different nodes, the local Transaction Manager employs a two-phased commitment protocol. The local Transaction Manager knows a transaction is distributed because it received a `TC_SendingRequest` RPC. Using the site specified in this RPC, the local Transaction Manager maintains a list of sites to which the transaction has spread. In this case the list contains one site. The local Transaction Manager then contacts the remote Transaction Manager and asks it to prepare itself to commit the transaction. The remote Transaction Manager sends `ST_Vote`

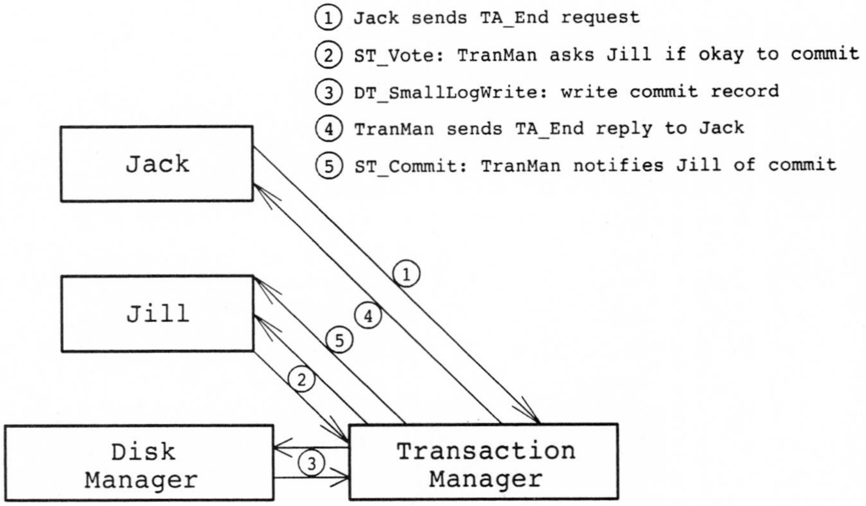
1 Jack sends TA_End request
2 ST_Vote: TranMan asks Jill if okay to commit
3 DT_SmallLogWrite: write commit record
4 TranMan sends TA_End reply to Jack
5 ST_Commit: TranMan notifies Jill of commit
Jack
Jill
Disk Manager
Transaction Manager
1
4
5
2
3

Figure 6.6: Messages for the `END_TRANSACTION` Statement
This diagram depicts the messages sent during the local commitment protocol, when the transaction successfully commits.

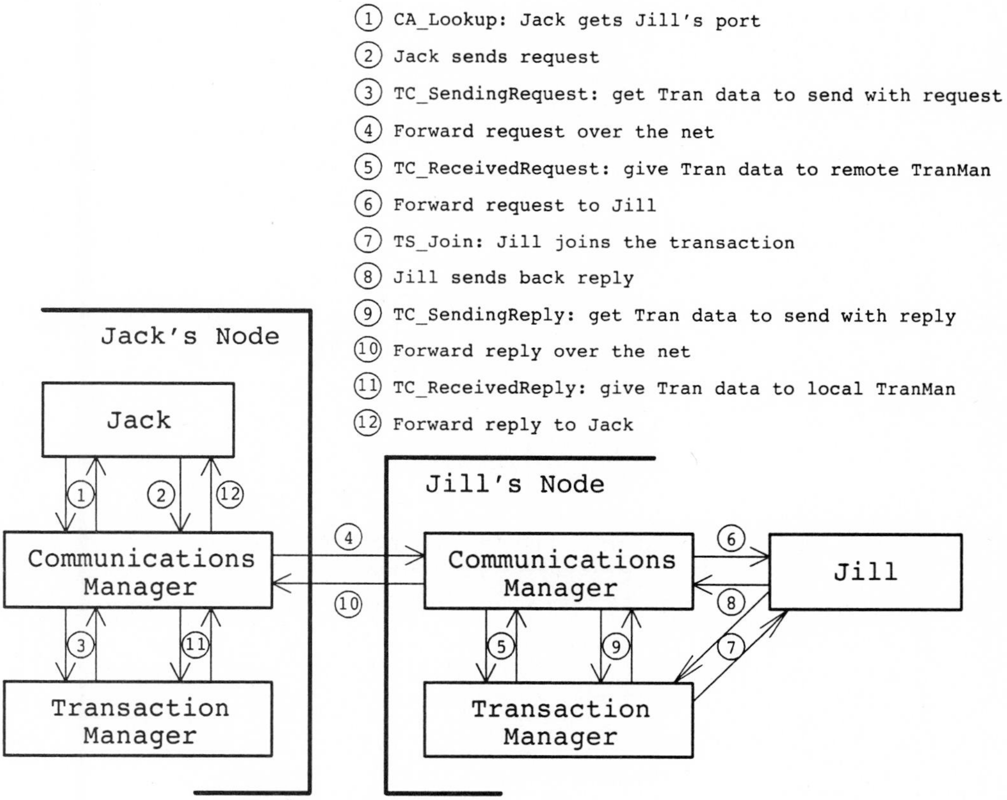

① CA_Lookup: Jack gets Jill's port
② Jack sends request
③ TC_SendingRequest: get Tran data to send with request
④ Forward request over the net
⑤ TC_ReceivedRequest: give Tran data to remote TranMan
⑥ Forward request to Jill
⑦ TS_Join: Jill joins the transaction
⑧ Jill sends back reply
⑨ TC_SendingReply: get Tran data to send with reply
⑩ Forward reply over the net
⑪ TC_ReceivedReply: give Tran data to local TranMan
⑫ Forward reply to Jack
Jack's Node
Jack
Communications Manager
Transaction Manager
Jill's Node
Communications Manager
Jill
Transaction Manager

Figure 6.7: Messages for a Network Server Call

This diagram depicts the messages sent during the first network RPC to a remote server. Subsequent SERVER_CALL to the same Jill server will result in fewer local messages because the various processes cache information. In particular, the CA_Lookup and TS_Join messages would not be sent during a subsequent call.

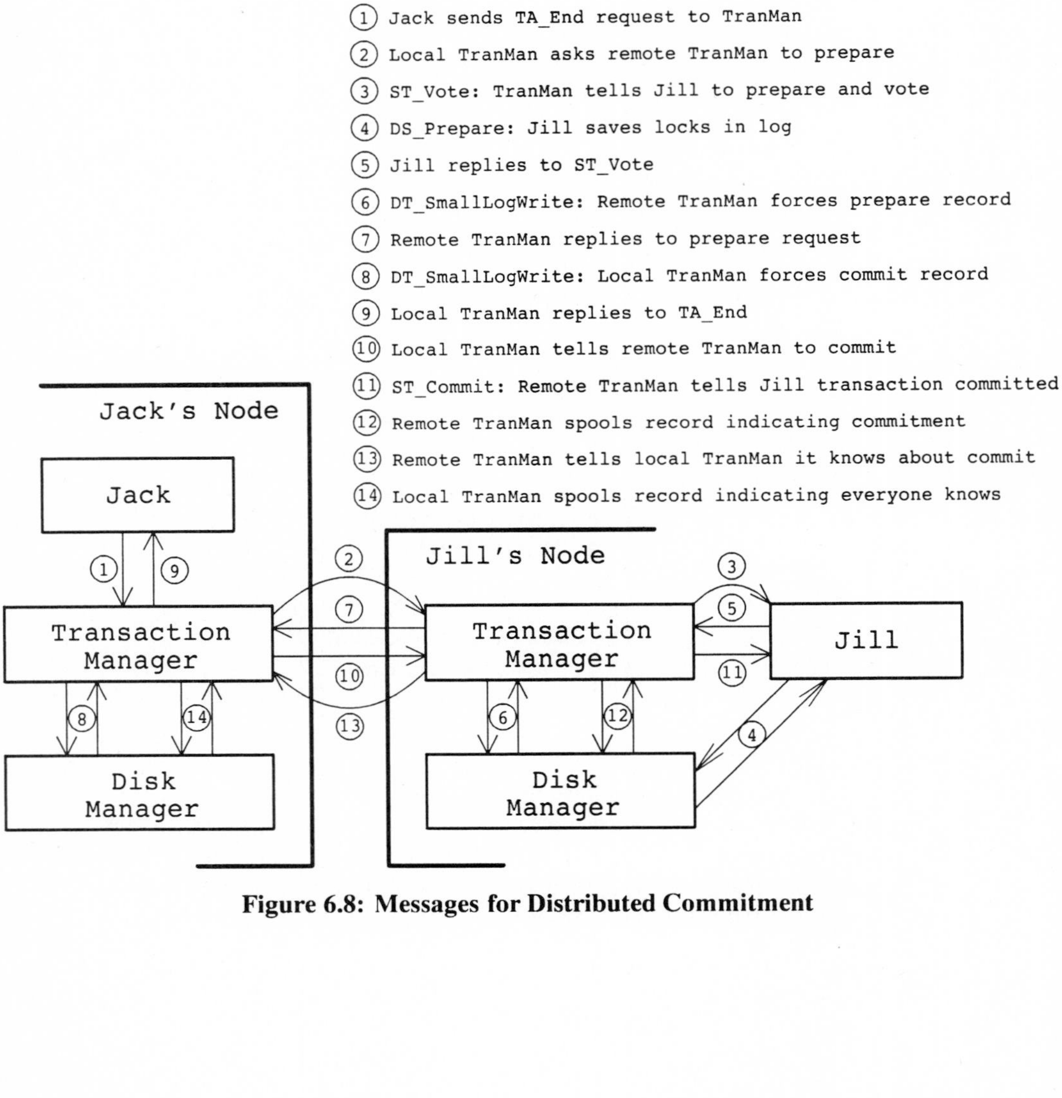
(1) Jack sends TA_End request to TranMan
(2) Local TranMan asks remote TranMan to prepare
(3) ST_Vote: TranMan tells Jill to prepare and vote
(4) DS_Prepare: Jill saves locks in log
(5) Jill replies to ST_Vote
(6) DT_SmallLogWrite: Remote TranMan forces prepare record
(7) Remote TranMan replies to prepare request
(8) DT_SmallLogWrite: Local TranMan forces commit record
(9) Local TranMan replies to TA_End
(10) Local TranMan tells remote TranMan to commit
(11) ST_Commit: Remote TranMan tells Jill transaction committed
(12) Remote TranMan spools record indicating commitment
(13) Remote TranMan tells local TranMan it knows about commit
(14) Local TranMan spools record indicating everyone knows
Jack's Node
Jack
Transaction Manager
Disk Manager
Jill's Node
Transaction Manager
Jill
Disk Manager

Figure 6.8: Messages for Distributed Commitment

messages to all the servers on that node asking if each is willing to commit the transaction and telling each server to prepare. The servers, in this case only Jill, prepare by saving lock information in the log using the DS_Prepare RPC. If the servers vote affirmatively, the remote Transaction Manager tells the remote Disk Manager to write a record to the log (using the DT_SmallLogWrite RPC) indicating this decision. The remote Transaction Manager tells the local Transaction Manager that the remote site is prepared. The local Transaction Manager then tells the local Disk Manager to write a commit record to the log (again, using DT_SmallLogWrite). After the commit record is written, the local Transaction Manager notifies the application, Jack, and remote Transaction Manager which in turn notifies Jill that the transaction has committed. The remote Transaction Manager spools a commit record to its log. After this record is written, the remote Transaction Manager tells the local Transaction Manager that it knows the transaction committed; it tells the remote Communication Manager to forget about the transaction and removes information about this transaction from its data structures. Once the local Transaction Manager knows that the remote Transaction Manager has recorded the fact that the transaction committed, it spools a record to the log indicating that everyone knows the transaction has committed. Then the local Transaction Manager tells the local Communication Manager to forget about this transaction and removes information about this transaction from its data structures. This is illustrated in Figure 6.8.

The transaction control messages for beginning, joining, and ending transactions are carefully designed so that the transaction can be aborted any time before it is prepared. Any task participating in a transaction can send a TA_Kill RPC to its Transaction Manager to kill the transaction.[2] Data servers can also abort a transaction by voting no in response to an ST_Vote message during the commit protocol. Camelot components may abort a transaction for reasons of network failure, timeout, protocol error, or resource utilization. If a transaction is aborted, the Transaction Manager sends an ST_Suspend RPC to all the participating data servers and sends an AT_TransactionHasDied message to the application that started the transaction. These messages allow data servers and the application to stop all threads of control executing on behalf of the transaction and determine how to proceed.[3] Once the servers participating in the transaction on a site have replied to the ST_Suspend RPC, the Transaction Manager on that site sends an RT_Abort RPC to the Recovery Manager on that site. The Recovery Manager reads log records and other implementation specific information from the Disk Manager. The Recovery Manager determines which data and operations must be undone and which must be redone. The Recovery Manager tells the data servers on the node to perform the changes with SR_RestoreBatch calls. To make the changes, the data server does only the "pin-update" part of the "pin-update-log" sequence. Page faults are handled in the usual way. The Recovery Manager updates some implementation specific information in the Disk Manager, again, described below. The Recovery Manager replies to the RT_Abort call. The Transaction Manager spools an abort record to the log. Finally, the Transaction Manager sends ST_Abort messages to the data servers notifying them that the transaction has aborted and that they can drop the transaction's locks. This is illustrated in Figure 6.9.

[2] If the transaction is prepared, TA_Kill returns a suitable error code.

[3] For example, the Camelot Library stops all threads working on behalf of the transaction, and flow of control continues at the application's END_TRANSACTION statement with the status variable indicating that the transaction has aborted and gives a code describing the problem.

1. AT_TransactionHasDied: TranMan notifies Jack
2. ST_Suspend: Jill must stop processing this transaction
3. RT_Abort: TranMan tells RecMan to abort the transaction
4. RecMan gets log and other data
5. SR_RestoreBatch: RecMan tells Jill to undo and redo
6. DS_PinRegion: Jill pins regions before modifying
7. memory_object_data_request: Kernel asks for a page
8. memory_object_data_provided: Disk Manager gives a page
9. RecMan updates recovery information in DiskMan
10. RecMan replies to RT_Abort call
11. DT_SmallLogWrite: TranMan spools abort record
12. ST_Abort: TranMan notifies Jill that transaction aborted

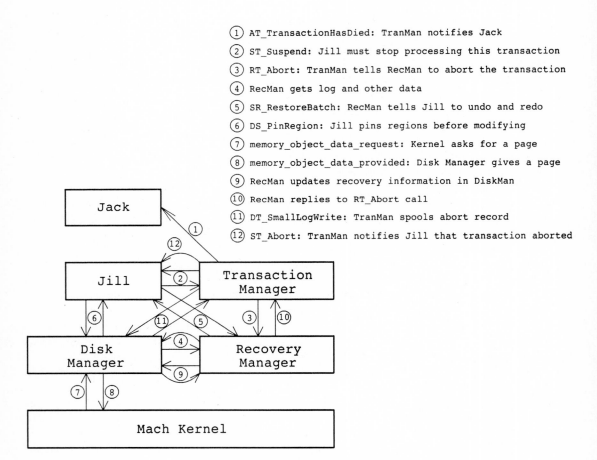

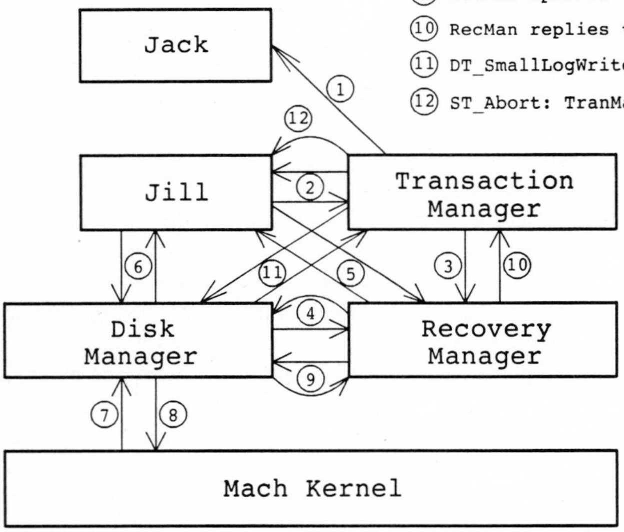

Figure 6.9: Messages for Abort
This figure depicts the message flow for a local abort of a (top-level) transaction. If the transaction is distributed, this local abort protocol is followed on each node that participated in the transaction.

Chapter 7

Mach for Camelot Implementors

Peter D. Stout, Eric C. Cooper,
Richard P. Draves, and Dean S. Thompson

This chapter discusses facilities provided under Mach that were used in building Camelot. These facilities are also used by the Camelot Library, in conjunction with Camelot's lower-level interfaces. The following sections discuss the details of interprocess communication, the Mach external memory management interface, and the C Threads package. It is assumed that the reader is familiar with the material presented in Chapter 2.

7.1 Interprocess Communication

Interprocess communication in Mach is based on two abstractions: ports and messages. This section discusses these abstractions in detail, and introduces primitives that manipulate them. For additional information on these primitives, the interested reader is directed to the *Mach Kernel Interface Manual* [8]. This section also discusses extensions to the communication facility provided by Camelot.

7.1.1 Ports

Ports are protected kernel objects to which messages may be sent and queued until reception. Access rights to a port consist of the ability to send to or receive from that port. A task may hold either send or send and receive rights. Threads within a task may only refer to ports to which that task has been given access. When a new port is created within a task, that task is given all access rights to that port.

The port access rights are operationally defined as follows. *Send access* to a port implies that a message can be sent to that port. If the port is destroyed during the time a task has send access, a message will be sent from the kernel to that task saying that the port has disappeared. *Receive access* to a port implies send rights to a port and allows a message to be dequeued from that port.

Only one task may have receive access for a given port at a time; however, more than one thread within that task may concurrently attempt to receive messages from a given port.

Port access rights are passed in messages, are interpreted by the kernel, and are transferred from the sender to the kernel upon message transmission and to the receiver upon message receipt. Send rights are kept by the original task as well as being transmitted to the receiver task, but receive rights are removed from the original task at the time of the send, and appear in the user task when the receive is done. During the time between the send and receive, the kernel holds the rights and any messages sent to the port will be queued awaiting a new task to receive on the port. If the task that was intended to receive the rights dies before it does the receive, the rights are handled as though the receive had been done before the task died.

7.1.2 Messages

Messages are ordered collections of typed data consisting of a fixed size message header and a variable size message body. The C type definition for the message header is as follows:

```
typedef struct {
        unsigned int    msg_unused : 24,
                        msg_simple : 8;
        msg_size_t      msg_size;
        int             msg_type;
        port_t          msg_local_port;
        port_t          msg_remote_port;
        int             msg_id;
} msg_header_t;
```

The `msg_local_port` and `msg_remote_port` fields are used to name the ports on which a message is to be received or sent. The `msg_size` field is used to describe the size of the message to be sent or the maximum size of the message which can be received. The `msg_simple` field is used to indicate that no ports or out-of-line data is contained in the body (see below). The `msg_id` field may be used by user programs to identify the meaning of this message to the intended recipient.

The variable data part of a message consists of an array of data descriptors and data. Each data descriptor is of the following form:

```
typedef struct  {
        unsigned int    msg_type_name : 8,
                        msg_type_size : 8,
                        msg_type_number : 12,
                        msg_type_inline : 1,
                        msg_type_longform : 1,
                        msg_type_deallocate : 1,
                        msg_type_unused : 1;
} msg_type_t;
```

The `msg_type_name` field identifies what type of data is being sent. The `msg_type_size` and `msg_type_number` fields specify the size of the data item (in bits) and the number of items, respectively. The `msg_type_inline` field indicates that the actual data follows the type descriptor, otherwise (in the case of *out-of-line* data) it is a pointer to the data. The `msg_type_longform` field is an escape mechanism for sending more or larger items than can be described by a msg_type_t. If this bit is set, then this type descriptor is actually the first part of a msg_type_long_t. The msg_type_deallocate field is only used if the data item is a port or out-of-line data, in which case it tells the kernel to deallocate the port right or memory when the message is sent.

A data item or a pointer to data follows each data descriptor. If the data is any type of integer being passed across the network between machines with different byte ordering conventions, the Mach Network Message server swaps the bytes as appropriate. If the data is a pointer and the send is local, it is transferred into the recipient's address space (this is done efficiently as a virtual transfer with copy-on-write). If the send goes across the network, the data is copied and then mapped into the recipient's address space. Port rights are handled by the kernel as described above.

7.1.3 Primitives

This section lists the primitive calls Mach provides for message and port manipulation and gives brief descriptions.

The msg_send system call transmits a message from the current task to the remote port specified in the message header field (msg_remote_port).

```
msg_return_t msg_send(header, option, timeout)
                msg_header_t     *header;
                msg_option_t     option;
                msg_timeout_t    timeout;
```

*header A pointer to the message header. The message consists of its header, followed by a variable number of data descriptors and data items.

option Usually either MSG_OPTION_NONE or SEND_TIMEOUT if the timeout parameter is meaningful.

timeout The number of milliseconds to wait on a blocked port.

The msg_receive system call retrieves the next message from a port specified in the msg_local_port field of the specified message header. A task can receive on a port set simply by using the port set name in place of the port name in the msg_local_port field. In this case, the message that is received will be from a port that is a member of the port set and the msg_local_port field will be set to the port on which the message was found.

```
msg_return_t    msg_receive(header, option, timeout)
                msg_header_t     *header;
                msg_option_t     option;
                msg_timeout_t    timeout;
```

*header A pointer to the message header. Space for body of the message must be left after the message header.

option Usually either MSG_OPTION_NONE or RCV_TIMEOUT if the timeout parameter is meaningful.

timeout The number of milliseconds to wait to receive a message.

The `msg_rpc` system call is a hybrid call which performs a `msg_send` followed by a `msg_receive`, using the same message buffer.

```
msg_return_t msg_rpc(header, option, rcv_size,
                    send_timeout, rcv_timeout)
                msg_header_t    *header;
                msg_option_t    option;
                msg_size_t      rcv_size;
                msg_timeout_t   send_timeout;
                msg_timeout_t   rcv_timeout;
```

`*header` A pointer to the message header. The body of the message to be sent must follow the header. Sufficient space for body of the message to be received must be left after the message header. The local copy of the message sent will be destroyed.

`option` Either `MSG_OPTION_NONE`, `RCV_TIMEOUT`, `SEND_TIMEOUT`, or the logical or of `RCV_TIMEOUT` and `SEND_TIMEOUT`.

`timeout` The number of milliseconds to wait to send or receive a message.

The `port_allocate` system call creates a new port for the specified task. The target task initially has both send and receive rights to the port.

```
routine port_allocate(
                task            : task_t;
            OUT port_name       : port_name_t);
```

`task` The port on which the kernel receives requests for the target task.

`port_name` The newly created port.

The `port_deallocate` system call removes the target task's access to a port. If the target task is the port's receiver, then the port is destroyed and all other tasks with send access are notified of the port's destruction.

```
routine port_deallocate(
                task            : task_t;
                port_name       : port_name_t);
```

`task` The port on which the kernel receives requests for the target task.

`port_name` The port to be deallocated.

The `port_set_allocate` system call creates a new port set for this task. The port set is initially empty.

```
routine port_set_allocate(
                task            : task_t;
            OUT set_name        : port_set_name_t);
```

`task` The port on which the kernel receives requests for the target task.

`set_name` The port representing the newly created port set.

The `port_set_deallocate` system call destroys a port set. If the port set is not empty, all members will be removed first.

```
routine port_set_deallocate(
                task            : task_t;
                set_name        : port_set_name_t);
```

`task` The port on which the kernel receives requests for the target task.
`set_name` The port representing the port set that will be deallocated.

The `port_set_add` system call adds a port to a port set. If the port is already a member of another port set, it is first removed from that other port set.

```
routine port_set_add(
                task            : task_t;
                set_name        : port_set_name_t;
                port_name       : port_name_t);
```

`task` The port on which the kernel receives requests for the target task.
`set_name` The port set.
`port_name` The port to be added to the port set.

The `port_set_remove` system call removes a port from whichever port set it may be in.

```
routine port_set_remove(
                task            : task_t;
                port_name       : port_name_t);
```

`task` The port on which the kernel receives requests for the target task.
`port_name` The port to be removed from a port set.

7.1.4 Camelot Extensions

To support distributed transactions, Camelot has a Communication Manager task which provides a distributed name service and monitors the spread of transactions between sites. Like the Mach Network Message Server, the actions of the Communication Manager are invisible to the Camelot servers and applications.

The Camelot name server allows applications and data servers to transparently locate service ports for data servers. To use the name service, clients must first look it up with the Mach Network Message Server. Most clients, data servers and full applications, will be able to use the name server on their local machine. Limited applications, however, will need to look up a Camelot name server on a machine where Camelot is running, typically the machine on which the server they are using is located.

The name service interface is described in Sections C.2 and C.3. Transaction monitoring and the design of the Camelot Communication Manager are presented in Chapter 17.

7.2 The External Memory Management Interface

The Mach external memory management interface is a novel feature that allows user-level processes to back virtual memory [124]. This flexible interface allows user-level file systems to provide mapped files and allows network-shared virtual memory [64]. Camelot uses this interface to provide recoverable virtual memory.

In Camelot, the Disk Manager is the external memory manager that backs a server's recoverable virtual memory. It enforces the write-ahead log protocol on the external memory objects it backs. The spooling of log records is synchronized with updates to recoverable virtual memory using a "pin-update-log" protocol described in Section 8.4.

To use the external memory management interface, a client task (e.g., a Camelot server) maps an external memory object into its address space using the `vm_map` kernel call. The external memory object is represented by a port that is obtained from the external memory manager task. The first time a client task maps an external memory object into its address space,[1] the kernel sends a `memory_object_init` message to the port representing the object (i.e., to the external memory manager). This is illustrated in Figure 7.1. The initialization message contains a port to which the external memory manager can send messages to respond to kernel data requests or to request that the kernel flush certain pages.

When a thread in the client task first reads a page of its address space to which the external object has been mapped, the thread takes a page fault. The kernel requests data for the page by sending a `memory_object_data_request` message to the port representing the object. The external memory manager task receives the request, finds the data and returns it to the kernel with the `memory_object_data_provided` call. The kernel puts the page into the client task's address space and resumes the thread. This procedure is illustrated in Figure 7.2. Subsequent accesses to the page will not incur page faults until the page is reclaimed.

The kernel manages a buffer pool of physical memory. If all of the physical memory buffers are in use, and more are needed, the kernel will reclaim some buffers. Clean buffers are simply removed from task address spaces and reused. Subsequent access to those virtual pages will cause page faults. Dirty pages must be written out to backing storage before the physical memory buffers can be reused. When the physical memory buffer is caching a page from an external memory object, the kernel sends the dirty page to the external memory manager with the `memory_object_data_write` message. The external memory manager must write this page out to backing storage and deallocate the page from its address space with the `vm_deallocate` message. Once the kernel sends such a page to an external memory manager, it is backed by the kernel. If the page is again selected for replacement, the kernel will use its own backing storage to clean the page. This means that a slow external memory manager will cause double paging.

7.3 C Threads

This section describes the package that supports multiple threads of control, usable from within the C language. The package provides multiple threads of control for parallelism, shared variables, mutual exclusion for critical sections, and condition variables for synchronization of threads. The facilities provided are similar to those found in Mesa [62] and Modula-2+ [96].

[1] In Camelot, this is done by the Library during server initialization.

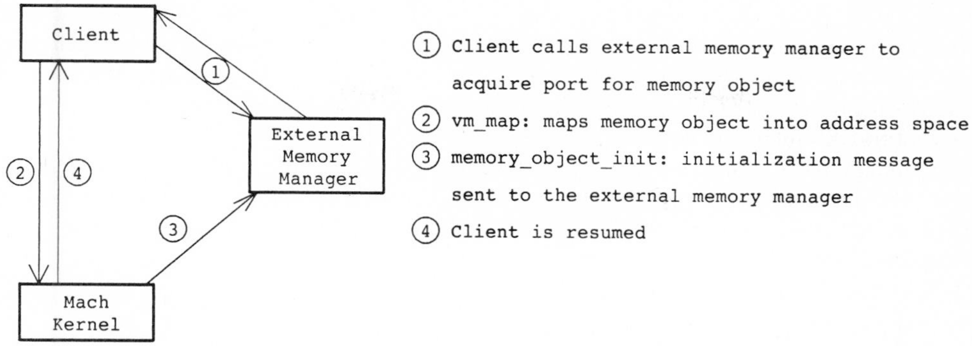

Figure 7.1: Mapping an External Memory Object
The client maps an external memory object into its address space. The external memory manager holds receive rights on a port that represents the external memory object. The kernel sends an initialization message to the port. The external memory manager task receives the message.

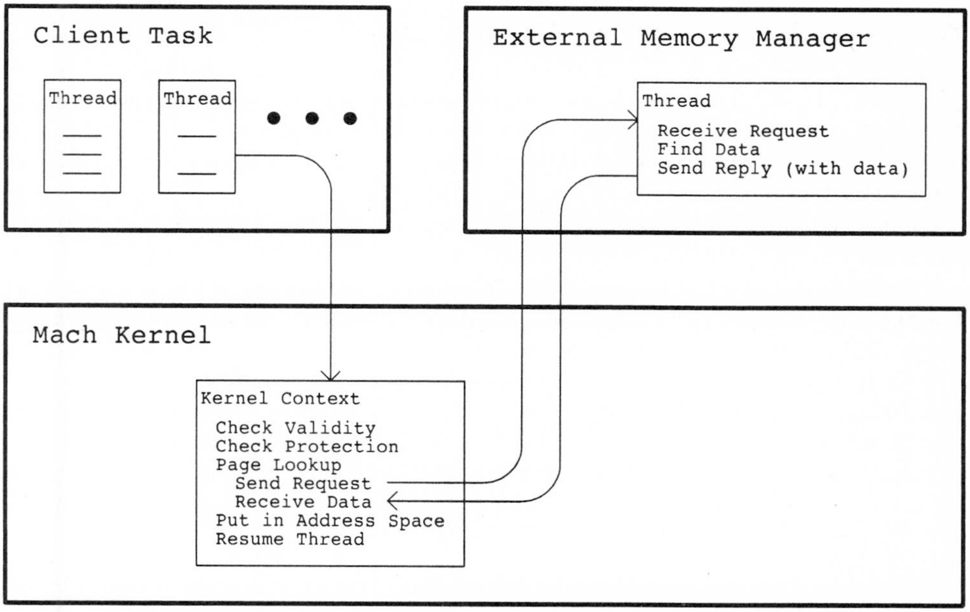

Figure 7.2: A Page Fault an External Memory Object
A client thread takes a page fault on a page to which an external memory object has been mapped. The kernel requests the page from the external memory manager, puts the page into the client task's address space, and resumes the client thread.

The Camelot Library, as described in Chapter 12, makes use of the multiprocessing and locking primitives discussed in this chapter. For example, multi-threading enables the Camelot Library to handle system messages independent of the server's processing of client remote procedure calls. The material presented in this chapter will primarily be of interest to programmers writing servers that will be handling multiple asynchronous events. In simple servers and applications the Camelot Library's `THREAD` interface will most likely be sufficient.

An attempt has been made to use a consistent style of naming for the abstractions implemented by the C Threads package. All types, macros, and functions implementing a given abstract data type are prefixed with the type name and an underscore. The name of the type itself is suffixed with `_t` and is defined via a C `typedef`.

7.3.1 Threads of Control

When a C program starts, it contains a single thread of control, the one executing `main()`. The thread of control is an active entity, moving from statement to statement, calling and returning from procedures. New threads are created by *fork* operations.

```
cthread_t cthread_fork(func, arg)
        any_t (*func)();
        any_t arg;
```

The `any_t` type (`typedef ... any_t;`) represents a pointer to any C type. The `cthread_t` type (`typedef ... cthread_t;`) is an abstract "handle" that uniquely identifies a thread of control.[2] Values of type `cthread_t` will be referred to as thread identifiers.

The `cthread_fork()` procedure creates a new thread of control in which `func(arg)` is executed concurrently with the caller's thread. This is the sole means of creating new threads. Arguments larger than a pointer must be passed by reference. Similarly, multiple arguments must be simulated by passing a pointer to a structure containing several components.[3] The call to `cthread_fork()` returns a thread identifier that can be passed to `cthread_join()` or `cthread_detach()` (see below). Every thread *must* be either joined or detached exactly once.

Forking a new thread of control is similar to calling a procedure, except that the caller does not wait for the procedure to return. Instead, the caller continues to execute in parallel with the execution of the procedure in the newly forked thread. At some later time, the caller may rendezvous with the thread and retrieve its result (if any) by means of a *join* operation, or the caller may *detach* the newly created thread to assert that no thread will ever be interested in joining it.

A thread terminates when it returns from the top-level procedure it was executing.[4] If the thread has not been detached, it remains in limbo until another thread either joins it or detaches it; if it has been detached, no such rendezvous is necessary.

---

[2]Uniqueness is guaranteed only for the lifetime of the thread. When a thread exits, the implementation is free to re-use its handle.

[3]Common errors that programmers make are storing the argument block in the calling thread's stack or in dynamically allocated storage, which the calling thread deallocates without having joined the new thread. See Section 7.3.3 for additional discussion of shared variables.

[4]The Mach version of the C start-up code also arranges for this to be true of the initial thread executing `main()`: a call to `cthread_exit()` occurs when `main()` returns, allowing detached threads to continue executing. The programmer may explicitly call `exit()` to terminate all threads in the program.

```
void cthread_exit(result)
        any_t result;
```

This procedure causes termination of the calling thread. An implicit `cthread_exit()` occurs when the top-level function of a thread returns, but it may also be called explicitly. The result will be passed to the thread that joins the caller, or discarded if the caller is detached.

```
any_t cthread_join(t)
        cthread_t t;
```

This function suspends the caller until the thread `t` terminates. The caller receives either the result of `t`'s top-level function or the argument with which `t` explicitly called `cthread_exit()`.

```
void cthread_detach(t)
        cthread_t t;
```

The detach operation is used to indicate that the given thread will never be joined. This is usually known at the time the thread is forked, so the most efficient usage is the following:

```
        cthread_detach(cthread_fork(procedure, argument));
```

A thread may, however, be detached at any time after it is forked, as long as no other attempt is made to join it or detach it.

```
void cthread_yield()
```

This procedure is a hint to the scheduler, suggesting that this would be a convenient point to schedule another thread to run on the current processor. Calls to `cthread_yield()` are unnecessary in an implementation with preemptive scheduling, but may be required to avoid starvation in a coroutine-based implementation.

```
cthread_t cthread_self()
```

This function returns the caller's own thread identifier, which is the same value that was returned by `cthread_fork()` to the creator of the thread. The thread identifier uniquely identifies the thread, and hence may be used as a key in data structures that associate user data with individual threads. Since thread identifiers may be re-used by the underlying implementation, the programmer should be careful to clean up such associations when threads exit.

```
void cthread_set_data(t, data)
        cthread_t t;
        any_t data;

any_t cthread_data(t)
        cthread_t t;
```

These functions allow the user to associate arbitrary data with a thread, providing a simple form of thread-specific "global" variable. More elaborate mechanisms, such as per-thread property lists or hash tables, can then be built with these primitives.

After a thread exits, any attempt to get or set its associated data is illegal, so any deallocation or other cleanup of the data must be done before the thread exits. It is always safe to access the data associated with the caller's own thread (`cthread_self()`), or with a thread that has not yet been joined or detached.

7.3.2 Synchronization

This section describes mutual exclusion and synchronization primitives, called *mutexes* and *condition variables*. In general, these primitives are used to constrain the possible interleavings of thread execution streams. They separate the two most common uses of Dijkstra's `P()` and `V()` operations into distinct facilities. This approach basically implements monitors [51, 62] without the syntactic sugar.

Mutually exclusive access to mutable data is necessary to guarantee consistency of that data. As an example, consider concurrent attempts to update a simple counter. Suppose two threads each read the current value into a (thread-local) register, increment it, and write the value back in some order. The counter will only be incremented once, so the work of one of the threads will be lost. A mutex solves this problem (called a *race condition*) by making the read-increment-write action *atomic* — indivisible with respect to the execution of other threads. Before reading a counter, a thread locks the associated mutex. After depositing a new value, the thread unlocks the mutex. If another thread tries to use the counter while the mutex is held, its attempt to lock the mutex will not succeed until the first thread releases it. If several threads try to lock the mutex at the same time, the C Threads package guarantees that exactly one will succeed; the rest will block.

In general, mutex variables allow the programmer to protect *critical regions* — operations on shared data that must be performed indivisibly. This is sufficient to prevent competing threads from conflicting with one another, but threads do more than just compete: presumably, they also cooperate in a larger computation. In a typical multi-threaded application, one thread will rely on the results produced by another. When these results take the form of updates to a shared data structure, the problem of thread synchronization arises.

The condition variables provided by the C Threads package allow one or more threads to wait until another has finished updating a shared data structure. The definition of when an update is finished depends on the application; it typically requires the computation of some boolean-valued function of the shared data, which we will call its *status*. (The simplest example is a boolean variable whose status is simply its value.) As before, the shared data must be protected by a mutex, so that the update and the status computation exclude one another. For example, an update of a complicated linked structure might temporarily introduce cycles or invalid pointers. A status computation that traverses the structure could fail horribly if it observes such an inconsistent state.

Condition variables are used to indicate that the status of some shared data structure has changed. The application is responsible for maintaining the association between the condition variable and this status change. A thread waits for a status change by performing a `condition_wait()` operation on the associated condition variable. Whenever a thread changes the status of the shared data, it signals the associated condition to wake up any thread waiting for that status change. Unlike Hoare's original monitors [51], there is no guarantee that the awakened thread is the first to execute after the condition is signaled. As soon as the signaling thread releases the mutex, other threads may modify the data. A waiting thread must always check the status of the shared data after being awakened, and wait again if necessary.

Special care must be taken with data structures that are dynamically allocated and deallocated. In particular, if the mutex that is controlling access to a dynamically allocated record is itself part of the record, one must be sure that no thread is waiting for the mutex before freeing the record.

Attempting to lock a mutex that one already holds is another common error. The offending thread will block waiting for itself. This can happen when a thread is traversing a complicated data structure, locking as it goes, and reaches the same data by different paths. Another instance of the problem occurs when a thread is locking pairs of elements in an array and fails to check for the special case of the elements being identical.

In general, one must be very careful to avoid *deadlock*, in which one or more threads are permanently blocked waiting for one another. The above scenarios are special cases of deadlock. The easiest way to avoid deadlock with mutexes is to impose a total ordering on them, and then ensure that they are locked in increasing order only.

The programmer must decide what granularity to use in protecting shared data with mutexes and conditions. At one extreme, one can use a single mutex protecting all shared memory, and one condition that signifies any change to that shared memory. At the other extreme, one can associate every object with its own mutex and its own condition variables, one for each possible change in the status of that object. Finer granularity normally increases the possible parallelism, because fewer threads are waiting for mutexes or conditions at any time, but it also increases the overhead due to mutual exclusion and synchronization, and increases the possibility of deadlock.

The C Thread synchronization primitives can be used to build custom locking packages. A custom lock would consist of a mutex and a collection of variables to maintain the necessary state of the lock. A simple example would be a "safe" mutex, which keeps a thread from deadlocking with itself, by associating the thread ID of the locker with the lock. A more complicated example, similar to Camelot's read/write locking package, is given in Section 7.3.6.

Management of Synchronization Variables

A mutex or condition variable can be allocated dynamically from the heap, or the programmer can take an object of the referent type, initialize it appropriately, and then use its address. Before deallocating such an object, the programmer must guarantee that no other thread will reference it. In particular, a thread blocked in `mutex_lock()` or `condition_wait()` should be viewed as referencing the object continually, so freeing the object "out from under" such a thread is erroneous, and can result in bugs that are extremely difficult to track down.

Operations on Mutexes

```
typedef struct mutex {...} *mutex_t;

void mutex_lock(m)
        mutex_t m;

int mutex_try_lock(m)
```

```
        mutex_t m;

void mutex_unlock(m)
        mutex_t m;
```

The mutex_lock() procedure attempts to lock the mutex m and blocks until it succeeds. If several threads attempt to lock the same mutex concurrently, one will succeed, and the others will block until m is unlocked. The case of a thread attempting to lock a mutex it has already locked is *not* treated specially; deadlock will result.

The mutex_try_lock() function attempts to lock the mutex m, like mutex_lock(), and returns TRUE if it succeeds. If m is already locked, however, mutex_try_lock() immediately returns FALSE rather than blocking. This function is especially useful for increasing concurrency when accessing multiple identical resources. Starting with a random resource, the mutex associated with each resource can be tried in turn.

The mutex_unlock() procedure unlocks mutex m, giving other threads a chance to lock it.

Operations on Condition Variables

```
typedef struct condition {...} *condition_t;

void condition_wait(c, m)
        condition_t c;
        mutex_t m;

void condition_signal(c)
        condition_t c;

void condition_broadcast(c)
        condition_t c;
```

The condition_wait() procedure unlocks m and suspends the calling thread. The caller will be awakened if c is signaled by another thread. condition_wait() will then lock m before returning. Since other threads may execute between the time that c is signaled and the time that the caller re-acquires m, the caller should check that the shared data is in the desired state, see Section 7.3.6 for an example. The application should guarantee that the status change associated with c can only occur while m is locked.

The condition_signal() procedure should be called when one thread wishes to indicate that the status change represented by the condition variable has occurred. If any other threads are waiting (via condition_wait()), then at least one of them will be awakened. If no threads are waiting, then nothing happens. The condition_broadcast() procedure is similar to condition_signal(), except that it awakens *all* threads waiting for the condition, not just one of them.

7.3.3 Shared Variables

All global and static variables are shared among all threads: if one thread modifies such a variable, all other threads will observe the new value. In addition, a variable reachable from a pointer is shared among all threads that can dereference that pointer. This includes objects pointed to by shared variables of pointer type, as well as arguments passed by reference in `cthread_fork()`.

When pointers are shared, some care is required to avoid dangling reference problems. The programmer must ensure that the lifetime of the object pointed to is long enough to allow the other threads to dereference the pointer. Since there is no bound on the relative execution speed of threads, the simplest solution is to share pointers to global or heap-allocated objects only. If a pointer to a local variable is shared, the procedure in which that variable is defined must remain active until it can be guaranteed that the pointer will no longer be dereferenced by other threads. The synchronization functions can be used to ensure this.

Unless a subroutine library has been designed to work in the presence of multiple threads, and specifies that fact in its interface, the programmer must assume that the operations provided by the library make unprotected use of shared data. Subroutines that are documented as returning pointers to static data areas are obvious culprits, but other routines may share data privately and so be equally guilty. The programmer must therefore use a mutex that is locked before every library call (or sequence of library calls) and unlocked afterwards.

Dynamic allocation and freeing of user-defined data structures is typically accomplished with the standard C functions `malloc()` and `free()`. The C Threads package provides versions of these functions that work correctly in the presence of multiple threads. Safe versions of the standard C library are provided with the Mach distribution.

7.3.4 Using the C Threads Package

All of the functions described have been implemented for the Mach operating system. To compile a program that uses C Threads, the user must include the file `cthreads.h`. The standard way to link a program that uses C Threads is to specify the `-lthreads` library, described below, followed by the `-lmach` library on the `cc` command line. The run-time initialization of the package is handled by the Mach version of the C start up code.

There are two other C Threads implementations available. One, `-ltask_threads`, uses one Mach task (UNIX process) per thread, and uses the Mach virtual memory primitives to share memory between threads. This model could easily be ported to other shared memory systems. The other, `-lco_threads`, uses coroutines within a single Mach task (UNIX process). The coroutine scheduling is non-preemptive, hence `cthread_yield()` should be called within loops that do not otherwise call synchronization procedures. This version is primarily intended for debugging purposes. See [21] for additional details about these implementations.

The Mach Thread Implementation

The `-lthreads` library uses one Mach thread per C thread. These threads are preemptively scheduled, and may execute in parallel on a multiprocessor. This is the implementation of choice for the production version of a C Threads program.

The current version of the `-lthreads` implementation affords the programmer limited control over how threads wait for mutex and condition variables. The `mutex_spin_limit` variable controls the number of iterations of busy waiting before a thread begins to yield the processor when waiting for a mutex. The `condition_spin_limit` and `condition_yield_limit` variables control the number of iterations of busy waiting and processor yielding, respectively, before a thread suspends itself when waiting for a condition.

A thread suspends itself via a Mach `msg_receive()` on a per-thread synchronization port; another thread wakes it up using a Mach `msg_send()` to the suspended thread's synchronization port. Allowing each synchronization port to buffer one message eliminates the need for a wakeup-waiting indication.

Controlling Thread Stack Sizes

All C thread stacks are the same size, which is determined by `cthread_init()` based on the value of the UNIX stack resource limit. Since resource limits are inherited, the easiest way to change the thread stack size is to use the shell's `limit` command before running the multi-threaded application, either interactively or in a "wrapper" shell script.

Thread stacks are created full-size, not grown incrementally. The implementations rely on the Mach virtual memory system to allocate physical memory only as needed by the thread, and to manage the resulting sparsely populated address space efficiently.

7.3.5 Debugging

Most debuggers available under Mach cannot yet be used on programs linked with `-lthreads`, although an enhanced version of *gdb* for Mach threads is available [10]. Furthermore, the very act of turning on tracing or adding print statements may perturb programs that incorrectly depend on thread execution speed. One technique that is useful in such cases is to vary the granularity of locking and synchronization used in the program, making sure that the program works with coarse-grained synchronization before refining it further.

Camelot provides a number of debugging tools, including tracing macros, conditionally executed print statements, and routines to gather locking statistics. The tracing macros use a circular in-memory buffer in order to minimize their impact on thread execution speed. Appendix A describes these tools in greater detail. For information about the low-level debugging of multi-threaded programs see the C Threads manual [21].

7.3.6 Example

This section presents a simple shared/exclusive locking package for C Threads. When a writer is waiting for the lock, no further readers will get the lock so that writers are not starved by readers. Readers can be starved by writers, but in the common case of many readers and few writers this is the correct behavior.

```
#include <cthreads.h>

/*
 * rw_lock_t -- The structure used to represent a lock and the
 * corresponding pointer type.
 */
```

```
typedef struct rw_lock
{
    struct mutex latch;           /* Short term latch to sync. lock ops */
    struct condition read_free;   /* Indicates lock is free for readers */
    int nreaders;                 /* Number of read locks held */
    struct condition write_free;  /* Indicates lock is free for writers */
    int write;                    /* Flag to indicate write lock held */
    int nwrite_waiters;           /* Number of threads waiting for write lock */
} *rw_lock_t;

/*
 * Rw_LockInit -- Initialize a lock.
 */

void Rw_LockInit(lockPtr)
    rw_lock_t      *lockPtr;
{
    mutex_init(&lockPtr->latch);
    condition_init(&lockPtr->read_free);
    lockPtr->nreaders = 0;
    condition_init(&lockPtr->write_free);
    lockPtr->write = FALSE;
    lockPtr->nwrite_waiters = 0;

    return;
}

/*
 * Rw_LockAlloc -- Allocates and initializes a new lock variable.
 * Returns a pointer to the new lock.
 */

rw_lock_t *Rw_LockAlloc()
{
    rw_lock_t  *newLockPtr;

    newLockPtr = (rw_lock_t *) malloc(sizeof(rw_lock_t));
    ASSERT(newLockPtr != (rw_lock_t *) 0);
    Rw_LockInit(newLockPtr);

    return(newLockPtr);
}


/*
 * Rw_LockFree -- Free a lock allocated with Rw_LockAlloc.
 */

void Rw_LockFree(lockPtr)
    rw_lock_t  *lockPtr;
{
    (void) free((char *) lockPtr);
    return;
}
```

```
/*
 * Rw_ReadLock -- Obtain a shared lock on the given lock variable.
 * If the lock is unavailable, the calling thread will block until
 * the lock becomes available.
 */

void Rw_ReadLock(lockPtr)
    rw_lock_t  *lockPtr;
{
    mutex_lock(&lockPtr->latch);
    while (lockPtr->write || lockPtr->nwrite_waiters != 0) {
        condition_wait(&lockPtr->read_free, &lockPtr->latch);
    }
    lockPtr->nreaders++;
    mutex_unlock(&lockPtr->latch);

    return;
}


/*
 * Rw_WriteLock -- Obtain an exclusive lock on the given lock variable.
 * If the lock is unavailable, the calling thread will block until the
 * lock becomes available.
 */

void Rw_WriteLock(lockPtr)
    rw_lock_t  *lockPtr;
{
    mutex_lock(&lockPtr->latch);
    lockPtr->nwrite_waiters++;
    while (lockPtr->nreaders != 0 || lockPtr->write) {
        condition_wait(&lockPtr->write_free, &lockPtr->latch);
    }
    lockPtr->nwrite_waiters--;
    lockPtr->write = TRUE;
    mutex_unlock(&lockPtr->latch);

    return;
}


/*
 * Rw_TryReadLock -- Obtain a shared lock on the given lock variable,
 * if it's immediately available.  Returns TRUE iff the lock was
 * obtained else FALSE.
 */

boolean_t Rw_TryReadLock(lockPtr)
    rw_lock_t  *lockPtr
{
    boolean_t   gotLock;
```

```
    mutex_lock(&lockPtr->latch);
    if (lockPtr->write || lockPtr->nwrite_waiters != 0) {
        gotLock = FALSE;
    } else {
        lockPtr->nreaders++;
        gotLock = TRUE;
    }
    mutex_unlock(&lockPtr->latch);

    return(gotLock);
}

/*
 * Rw_TryWriteLock -- Obtain a shared lock on the given lock variable, if
 * it's immediately available. Returns TRUE iff the lock was obtained
 * else FALSE.
 */

boolean_t Rw_TryWriteLock(lockPtr)
    rw_lock_t  *lockPtr;
{
    boolean_t   gotLock;

    mutex_lock(&lockPtr->latch);
    if (lockPtr->nreaders != 0 || lockPtr->write) {
        gotLock = FALSE;
    } else {
        lockPtr->write = TRUE;
        gotLock = TRUE;
    }
    mutex_unlock(&lockPtr->latch);

    return(gotLock);
}


/*
 * Rw_Unlock -- Releases the lock previously obtained via Rw_Lock (or
 * Rw_TryLock).  It is crucial that this procedure be called only if
 * the lock is actually held.
 */

void Rw_Unlock(lockPtr)
    rw_lock_t  *lockPtr;
{
    mutex_lock(&lockPtr->latch);
    if (lockPtr->write)
        lockPtr->write = FALSE;
    else
        lockPtr->nreaders--;
    if (lockPtr->nreaders == 0)
        if (lockPtr->nwrite_waiters != 0)
            condition_signal(&lockPtr->write_free);
```

```
        else
            condition_broadcast(&lockPtr->read_free);
    mutex_unlock(&lockPtr->latch);

    return;
}
```

Chapter 8

Recoverable Storage Management in Camelot

Jeffrey L. Eppinger
Sherri Menees Nichols

Camelot provides a recoverable virtual memory abstraction. Data servers map their recoverable storage into their virtual address spaces. Camelot provides the necessary primitives to transactionally read and write recoverable virtual memory. This chapter describes how a data server that does not use the Camelot Library would use Camelot to manage recoverable storage. In general, other styles of transactional language support could be constructed on Camelot and these libraries would manage recoverable storage using the facilities described in this chapter.

Section 8.1 introduces recoverable segments and region pointers. Section 8.2 describes data server initialization. Section 8.3 explains how to map recoverable storage into a data server's address space. Section 8.4 explains how to modify recoverable storage. Section 8.5 describes the interface to the shared memory queues. Section 8.6 explains the messages sent to data servers during recovery.

8.1 Recoverable Segments and Regions

Each data server in the Camelot environment has one or more segments of recoverable storage associated with it. This recoverable storage can be mapped into a data server's address space and modified transactionally, as described below. The data server learns how many recoverable segments it has been allocated and the sizes of these segments from the segment descriptor list returned in the `DS_Initialize` call (see Section 8.2). The segment descriptor is shown in Figure 8.1.

In calls to Camelot, regions within a segment are referenced by a region pointer and a length in bytes. Regions must be smaller than 2^{32} bytes in length. A region pointer, shown in Figure 8.2, consists of a 16-bit segment identifier and a 48-bit offset. The segment identifier is a field in the segment descriptor returned from the `DS_Initialize` call (see Section 8.2).

Because of the limitations of some virtual memory hardware, sparse utilization of virtual memory can be expensive. For example, this is a problem on the VAX. The VAX has two page

```
typedef struct cam_segment_desc {
        cam_server_id_t      serverId;
        cam_segment_id_t     segmentId;
        u_short              unused;
        unsigned short       highSize;       /* upper 16 bits of size */
        unsigned int         lowSize;        /* lower 32 bits of size */
} cam_segment_desc_t;

typedef         cam_segment_desc_t  *cam_segment_desc_list_t;
```

Figure 8.1: Camelot Segment Descriptor

```
typedef struct cam_regptr {
        cam_segment_id_t        segmentId;
        unsigned short          highOffset;      /* high 16 bits of offset */
        unsigned int            lowOffset;       /* low 32 bits */
} cam_regptr_t;

typedef cam_regptr_t            *cam_regptr_list_t;
```

Figure 8.2: Camelot Region Pointer

tables per user-level process. One page table is intended for access to the code, static data, and heap region that grows up from the bottom of the user's address space. The other page table is intended for access to the stack region of the that grows down from the top of the user's address space. The page tables are of variable length; the problem is that if a program accesses a page in the middle of its address space, one of the page tables will grow very large.

Constraints on VAX page tables have a significant impact on data server writers because a common practice for a data server writer is to map a large recoverable segment entirely into his address space and then to use this segment densely. The Camelot Library maps the segment into the same place every time so that virtual addresses can be stored in recoverable storage. If the data server maps the recoverable segment into space allocated from the heap region, additional heap space will have to be allocated around the recoverable segment. Now the recoverable segment can be used densely growing up from bottom of the segment, but when the heap allocates space above the segment, the lower page table will grow very large.

Since Mach provides multiple threads, each thread has its own stack. These stacks are of a small, bounded size and are allocated from the heap. This leaves the upper page table unused on a VAX. For this reason, recoverable storage grows down. This allows the Camelot Library (and data server writers) to map recoverable storage into the top of the address space and use it growing down. The VAX page tables efficiently handle this configuration. Paging hardware designed to handle sparse access to address spaces work well with this scheme, yet it does not preclude efficient sparse access to recoverable storage.

Offsets are decreasing values. The offset of the highest byte in a recoverable segment is`0xffffffffffff`(i.e., `highOffset=0xffff` and `lowOffset=0xffffffff`). The lowest byte in the segment has offset `0xffffffffffff - segmentDesc.size + 1`. When the segment size is smaller than 2^{32}, the `highOffset` is `0xffff` and the `lowOffset` is conveniently `-segmentDesc.lowSize` (on twos-complement machines). The segment size is given in the segment descriptor returned from the `DS_Initialize` call (see Section 8.2).

8.2 Initialization

When a data server process is started, it uses the `DS_Initialize` call to get its resource allocation information from the Disk Manager.

```
routine DS_Initialize(
            dsPort           : port_t;
        OUT serverId         : cam_server_id_t;
        OUT recoveryOnly     : boolean_t;
        OUT tsPort           : port_t;
        OUT mPort            : port_t;
        OUT sPort            : port_t
                   = (MSG_TYPE_PORT_ALL, 32);
        OUT sharedMemAddr    : vm_address_t;
        OUT segDescList      : cam_segment_desc_list_t;
        OUT segPortList      : port_array_t);
```

`dsPort` The port on which the Disk Manager receives requests from this server.

`serverId` The ID of this server. This value is informational. For security reasons, data servers never provide IDs in requests to Camelot. The data server's ID is derived from the port in which the request is made. It is conceivable that a data server might use its ID in the NA interface to ask the Node Server to give it information about itself, or to change its resource allocations.

`recoveryOnly` A flag is set to `TRUE` if the server is expected to just recover and exit. Otherwise the server will recover and make itself available for use.

`tsPort` The port used in calls to the Transaction Manager for beginning, joining, and killing transactions.

`mPort` The port used to send debugging information to the MCP.

`sPort` The port used to receive requests from Camelot system components. These requests indicate that transactions have prepared, committed, or aborted. During transaction abort and recovery, these messages describe changes which must be made to recoverable storage. Upon receiving the reply to the `DS_Initialize` message, the data server will get receive and ownership rights on the `sPort`.

`sharedMemAddr` The address of the shared memory queue. This queue is used to efficiently pin regions and spool log records.

`segDescList` A list of this server's segment descriptors.

`segPortList` A list of ports used in the `vm_allocate_pager` call to map recoverable storage into a data server's address space.

8.3 Mapping

The server is responsible for mapping recoverable segments into its address space. This mapping is done using the `vm_map` kernel call, described in Section 7.2. The `DS_Initialize` call returns the paging ports (in `segPortList`) and sizes (in the segment descriptors in the `segDescList`) required by `vm_map` call. If a segment is larger than 2^{32} bytes, a separate paging port will be used for each 2^{32} byte region. The server can specify where in its address space to map the segment. The amount of an address space that can be used for mapping recoverable storage is limited only by hardware/operating systems on the address space and the size of the data server's code, static data, heap and stacks. The whole segment need not be mapped in to the data server's address space. Different parts of a segment can be mapped into different places in the server's address space.

```
routine vm_map(
                target_task      : task;
          INOUT address          : vm_offset_t;
                size             : vm_size_t;
                mask             : vm_offset_t;
                anywhere         : boolean_t;
                memory_object    : memory_object_t;
                offset           : vm_offset_t;
                copy             : boolean_t;
                cur_protection   : vm_prot_t;
                max_protection   : vm_prot_t;
                inheritance      : vm_inherit_t);
```

`target_task` Task to be affected.

`address` Starting address. If the anywhere option is used, this address is ignored. The address actually allocated will be returned in `address`.

`size` Number of bytes to allocate (rounded by the system in a machine dependent way).

`mask` Alignment restriction. Bits asserted in this mask must not be asserted in the address returned.

`anywhere` If set, the kernel should find and allocate any region of the specified size, and return the address of the resulting region in `address`

`memory_object` Port that represents the memory object: used by user tasks in `vm_map`; used by the make requests for data or other management actions. If this port is `MEMORY_OBJECT_NULL`, then zero-filled memory is allocated instead.

`offset` An offset within a memory object, in bytes. The kernel does not page align this offset.

`copy` If set, the range of the memory object should be copied to the target task, rather than mapped read-write.

Most servers do not have more data than will fit into their address space. Such a server typically maps its recoverable data into its virtual address space. The current implementation of the Camelot Library only supports one recoverable segment which must fit into the server's address space. Further, the Library uses compiled-in knowledge about the layout of each machine's address space to map the recoverable segment into the same place in the server's address space every time the server starts. This affords Library clients the convenience of storing (in recoverable storage) virtual memory pointers to other parts of recoverable storage.

8.4 Forward Processing

As soon as the server starts, it will begin receiving calls on its `sPort`. These calls will be from the Camelot Recovery Manager describing changes necessary to bring the server's recoverable storage back to a transaction consistent state. Section 8.6 describes these calls and how they are processed. For now, assume the server is coming up for the first time. No changes to its recoverable storage are necessary. The first message it receives will be `SR_RecoveryComplete`. The data server is now ready to begin work.

```
simpleroutine SR_RecoveryComplete(
                    sPort              : port_t);
```

`sPort` The port on which a data server receives requests from Camelot components.

When a data server starts for the first time, its recoverable storage is all zero-filled. If a data server's recoverable storage needs to be initialized to values other than zeros, it should initialize the recoverable storage after receiving the `SR_RecoveryComplete` message. The server must make these changes transactionally, as described below. There should be some way for the server to detect that the initialization has been done so that subsequent restarts will not initialize recoverable storage, again. This is typically done by setting a boolean variable in recoverable storage which is transactionally initialized with the other data.

Transactions are identified by transaction identifiers (TIDs), which may be obtained from the Transaction Manager (see Section 9.2.1, **Creating Transactions**) or arrive in requests from client applications.

Data servers use their recoverable storage by transactionally reading and updating regions within it. To read a region in recoverable storage, the data server simply reads virtual memory. A TID is not necessary for reading, but is typically used for locking. Writing a region in recoverable storage is more complicated.

Before modifying a region in recoverable storage, the region must be *pinned* in virtual memory so the page (or pages) on which it resides will not be written back to non-volatile storage in an inconsistent state. This is necessary to enforce the write-ahead log protocol that Camelot uses to ensure consistency. The pinning is accomplished with `DS_PinRegion`.

```
routine DS_PinRegion(
                    dsPort             : port_t;
                    tid                : cam_tid_t;
```

```
                    regptr              : cam_regptr_t;
                    size                : u_int);
```

`dsPort` The port on which the Disk Manager receives requests from this server.
`tid` The identifier of the transaction pinning this region.
`regptr` The pointer to the region being pinned.
`size` The size of the region being pinned.

After the region is pinned, the data server modifies the region in virtual memory and then spools a log record describing the change. If the transaction is a new-value transaction, the `DS_LogNewValue` call is used. This call spools a log record containing the new value of the region into the log. The page (or pages) on which the region resides cannot be written back to non-volatile storage until the transaction commits because the log record does not contain an old value which can be used to undo the modification. Therefore, upon receiving a `DS_LogNewValue` call, the Disk Manager sets up the unpin for the region so that it is unpinned after the transaction completes. If the transaction is long running (leaving pages pinned too long), the Disk Manager aborts the transaction.

```
routine DS_LogNewValue(
                    dsPort              : port_t;
                    tid                 : cam_tid_t;
                    regptr              : cam_regptr_t;
                    newValue            : pointer_t);
```

`dsPort` The port on which the Disk Manager receives requests from this server.
`tid` The identifier of the transaction pinning this region.
`regptr` The pointer to the region being pinned.
`newValue` The new value of this region, sent out of line.

If the transaction is an old-value/new-value transaction, the `DS_LogOldValueNewValue` call is used. This call takes both an old value and a new value. This means that the page (or pages) on which the region resides can now be written back to backing storage (if the system desires), because the old value in the log record will allow the modification to be undone. Therefore, upon receiving a `DS_LogOldValueNewValue` call, the Disk Manager unpins the region.

```
routine DS_LogOldValueNewValue(
                    dsPort              : port_t;
                    tid                 : cam_tid_t;
                    regptr              : cam_regptr_t;
                    oldValue            : pointer_t;
                    newValue            : pointer_t);
```

`dsPort` The port on which the Disk Manager receives requests from this server.

`tid` The identifier of the transaction pinning this region.
`regptr` The pointer to the region being pinned.
`oldValue` The old value of this region, sent out of line.
`newValue` The new value of this region, sent out of line.

An important caveat for the server designer is the Camelot recovery algorithm's assumption that transactions modify regions in accordance with the nested transaction model described in Section 9.1. This model states that if one transaction modifies a region, the region cannot be modified by another transaction unless that transaction is an active descendant of original transaction or the original transaction completes. The Camelot Library provides read and write locks to facilitate this, but the designer of a data server is free to use other means, such as hybrid atomicity [120], to prevent such *comodification*. If comodification does occur, no guarantees concerning data integrity are given.

When a transaction attempts to commit, the Transaction Manager sends an `ST_Vote` message to each data server involved in the transaction (see Section 9.3.2). If the transaction is distributed, the `ST_Vote` call indicates that the data server must *prepare*. At this point the server must save lock (and any other) information about this transaction using the `DS_Prepare` call. This call stores the server's data in the log. In the case of a server failure, this information will be returned to the server in using the `SR_RePrepare` call (see Section 8.6).

```
routine DS_Prepare(
                dsPort          : port_t;
                famId           : cam_fam_id_t;
                prepareData     : pointer_t);
```

`dsPort` The port on which the Disk Manager receives requests from this server.
`famId` The ID of the transaction family.
`prepareData` The data to be stored in the prepare record, sent out of line.

8.5 The Shared Memory Queues

To reduce the cost of issuing calls during forward processing, each data server has its own (private) shared memory queue with the Disk Manager. Internally the Camelot Library uses routines which provide the same function as the `DS` calls, except that they use the shared memory queue when possible. If there is not enough room in the shared memory queue, the corresponding `DS` calls are used. The Disk Manager processes requests in the shared memory queue before it processes an incoming message so that requests are processed in the proper order.

```
void Dsq_Init(shMemAddr)
    vm_address_t    shMemAddr;
```

`shMemAddr` The virtual address of the shared memory queue. This value is provided by the `DS_Initialize` call.

```
kern_return_t Dsq_PinRegion(dsPort,tidPtr,regptr,
                                          sizeInBytes)
    port_t           dsPort;
    cam_tid_t       *tidPtr;
    cam_regptr_t     regptr;
    u_int            sizeInBytes;
```

`dsPort` The `dsPort` provided in the `DS_Initialize` call.
`tidPtr` A pointer to the transaction ID of the transaction on behalf of which the modification is being done.
`regptr` The region pointer for the region being modified.
`sizeInBytes` The length in bytes of the region.

```
kern_return_t Dsq_LogOldValueNewValue(dsPort,tidPtr,
                regptr,oldValuePtr,newValuePtr,sizeInBytes)
    port_t           dsPort;
    cam_tid_t       *tidPtr;
    cam_regptr_t     regptr;
    pointer_t        oldValuePtr;
    pointer_t        newValuePtr;
    u_int            sizeInBytes;
```

`dsPort` The `dsPort` provided in the `DS_Initialize` call.
`tidPtr` A pointer to the transaction ID of the transaction on behalf of which the modification is being done.
`regptr` The region pointer for the region being modified.
`oldValuePtr` A pointer to the old value.
`newValuePtr` A pointer to the new value.
`sizeInBytes` The length in bytes of the region.

```
kern_return_t Dsq_LogNewValue(dsPort,tidPtr,regptr,
                          newValuePtr,sizeInBytes)
    port_t           dsPort;
    cam_tid_t       *tidPtr;
    cam_regptr_t     regptr;
    pointer_t        newValuePtr;
    u_int            sizeInBytes;
```

`dsPort` The `dsPort` provided in the `DS_Initialize` call.
`tidPtr` A pointer to the transaction ID of the transaction on behalf of which the modification is being done.
`regptr` The region pointer for the region being modified.
`newValuePtr` A pointer to the new value.
`sizeInBytes` The length in bytes of the region.

```
kern_return_t Dsq_Prepare(dsPort,famIdPtr,dataPtr,
                                        sizeInBytes)
    port_t           dsPort;
    cam_fam_id_t    *famIdPtr;
    pointer_t        dataPtr;
    u_int            sizeInBytes;
```

`dsPort` The `dsPort` provided in the `DS_Initialize` call.
`famIdPtr` A pointer to the top (family) part of transaction ID of the transaction which is being prepared.
`dataPtr` A pointer to the prepare data.
`sizeInBytes` The length in bytes of the prepare data.

The interface for prefetching, preflushing, and zero-filling is also provided through the shared memory interface.

```
kern_return_t Dsq_Prefetch(dsPort,regptr,sizeInBytes)
    port_t           dsPort;
    cam_regptr_t     regptr;
    u_int            sizeInBytes;
```

`dsPort` The `dsPort` provided in the `DS_Initialize` call.
`regptr` The region pointer for the region being prefetched.
`sizeInBytes` The length in bytes of the region.

```
kern_return_t Dsq_Preflush(dsPort,regptr,sizeInBytes)
    port_t           dsPort;
    cam_regptr_t     regptr;
    u_int            sizeInBytes;
```

`dsPort` The `dsPort` provided in the `DS_Initialize` call.
`regptr` The region pointer for the region being preflushed.
`sizeInBytes` The length in bytes of the region.

```
kern_return_t Dsq_ZeroFill(dsPort,regptr,sizeInBytes)
    port_t           dsPort;
    cam_regptr_t     regptr;
    u_int            sizeInBytes;
```

`dsPort` The `dsPort` provided in the `DS_Initialize` call.
`regptr` The region pointer for the region being zero filled.
`sizeInBytes` The length in bytes of the region.

8.6 Recovery Processing

Recovery processing is done when a server comes up or when a transaction aborts (but the server does not crash). During recovery processing, the Recovery Manager uses information in the log and sometimes information in non-volatile storage to restore a data server's storage to a correct, consistent state. The details of the recovery algorithm are explained in Chapter 15.

The Recovery Manager sends `SR_RestoreObject` calls to the data server instructing the server to change the state of its recoverable storage.

```
routine SR_RestoreObject(
                    sPort             : port_t;
                    regptr            : cam_regptr_t;
                    value             : pointer_t);
```

`regptr` A pointer to the region being restored.
`value` The value to restore to region, sent out of line.

If the server crashed during commit processing for a distributed transaction, and the transaction has not yet committed or aborted, the server will get a `SR_RePrepare` call from the Recovery Manager.

```
routine SR_RePrepare(
                    sPort             : port_t;
                    famId             : cam_fam_id_t;
                    prepareData       : pointer_t);
```

`sPort` The port on which a data server receives requests from Camelot components.
`famId` The ID of the transaction prepared family.
`prepareData` The data written in the `DS_Prepare` call.

To reduce the cost of sending a large number of `SR_RestoreObject` calls, the Recovery Manager may use the `SR_RestoreBatch` call.

```
routine SR_RestoreBatch(
                    sPort             : port_t;
                    dataPtr           : pointer_t);
```

`sPort` The port on which a data server receives requests from Camelot components.
`data` The data sent contains one or more occurrences of: `cam_reg_ptr` region pointer, `u_int` length, data filled to next `int` word.

Chapter 9

Transaction Management in Camelot

Lily B. Mummert
Dan Duchamp

This chapter describes how data servers and applications interact with the Transaction Manager. The Transaction Manager is a process on each Camelot node that communicates with applications and data servers to keep track of the progress of every active transaction. By using this information and communicating with Transaction Managers on other Camelot nodes, it ensures that all sites involved in the transaction agree on its outcome. Applications and data servers can start transactions and request that they be committed or aborted. Servers must cooperate with the Transaction Manager in executing the protocols for committing and aborting transactions.

Section 9.1 describes the transaction model used by Camelot and introduces terminology. Sections 9.2 and 9.3 describe transaction management services for applications and servers, respectively.

9.1 The Nested Transaction Model

Under the nesting model specified by Moss [82], transactions behave as follows:

- A transaction (*parent*) can spawn one or more nested transactions (*children*). Any number of children may be active simultaneously. A parent is prohibited from accessing any of its locked data so long as any active child exists. A transaction with no parent is called a *top-level* transaction. A top-level transaction and all of its *descendants* (the generalization of child) are a *transaction family*.
- A descendant can *inherit* locks held by an *ancestor*. A lock obtained by inheritance is in no way different from a lock obtained normally.
- When a child commits, its locks (both inherited and newly acquired) are given (*anti-inherited*) to the parent.
- When a child aborts, its newly acquired locks are dropped, and its inherited locks are anti-inherited.

- The effects of a committed child are made permanent only when the top-level transaction commits. The sole effect of the commitment of a nested transaction is to anti-inherit its locks.

- A failure (e.g., node or server crash) after the commitment of a child and before the attempted commit of the top-level transaction results in the abort of the entire transaction family.

An additional restriction is that a parent may not commit until all of its children are finished (i.e., committed or aborted). There is no such restriction on a parent aborting. This restriction is illustrated in Figure 9.1.

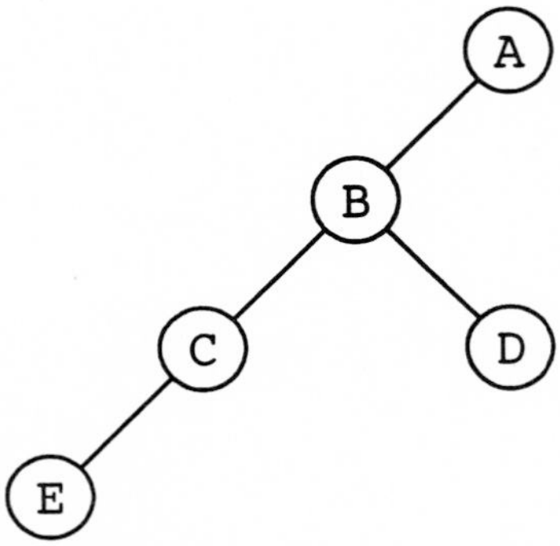

Figure 9.1: Example Family of Transactions
A is the parent of B. B is the parent of C and D. C is the parent of E. Only D and E are active. Transaction E must be finished before transaction C can commit. Similarly, transactions C and D must both be finished before transaction B can commit, and B must be finished before A can commit.

9.2 Transaction Services for Applications

An application process obtains transaction management services through calls in the TA interface. The calls permit an application to register itself to receive transaction management services, and then to create, commit and abort transactions. The AT interface consists of messages that an application may receive from the Transaction Manager. There is one call in this interface, used to notify an application that a transaction has aborted. The interaction between an application and the Transaction Manager for a particular transaction (family) is shown in Figure 9.2.

9.2.1 The TA Interface

A variety of error codes are returned by calls to the Transaction Manager. Table 9.1 lists the error codes returned by each call in the TA and TS interfaces. Noteworthy return codes are discussed in the interface specifications.

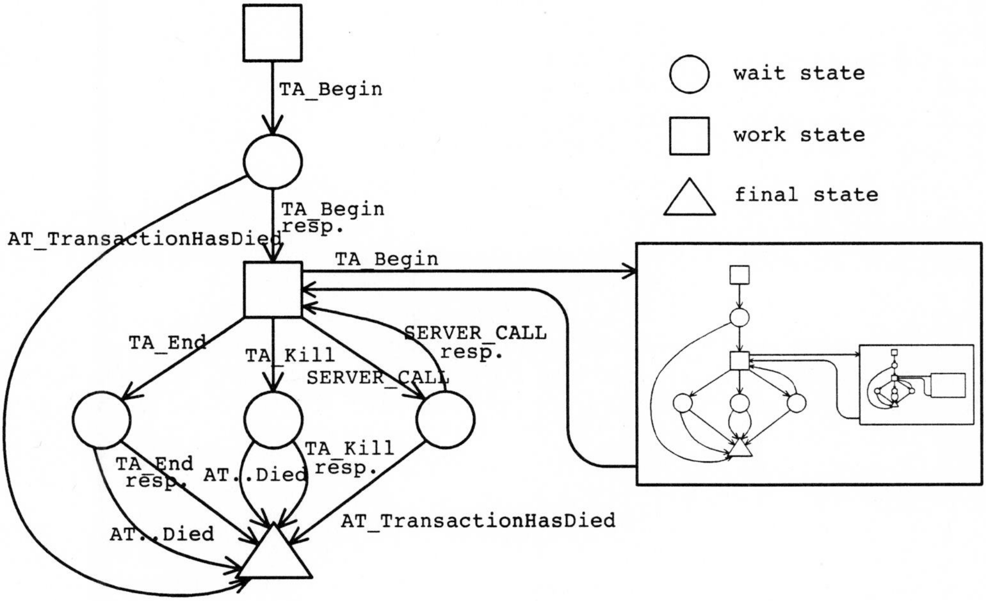

Figure 9.2: Applications and the Transaction Manager

An arc from a work state to a wait state represents a message sent from the application to the Transaction Manager. An arc from a wait state to a work state represents a message sent from the Transaction Manager to the application. It is assumed that `TA_AddApplication` has already been called. If a timeout occurs during a server call, the application may abort the transaction. The application may be notified that the transaction has aborted at any point after it is begun. An `AT_TransactionHasDied` message for a nested transaction causes control to be returned to the parent.

Event	Return Code	Used by
success	CAM_ER_SUCCESS	all
garbage transaction identifier	CAM_ER_BAD_TID	all
bad transaction type	CAM_ER_BAD_TRANS_TYPE	TA_Begin, TA_GetTids
bad protocol	CAM_ER_BAD_PROTOCOL	TA_End
application not found	CAM_ER_APPL_NOT_FOUND	all TA calls
server not found	CAM_ER_SERVER_NOT_FOUND	all TS calls
transaction (or family) not found	CAM_ER_TRANS_NOT_FOUND	all
already aborted	CAM_ER_TRANS_ALREADY_ABORTED	TA_Kill
bad transaction state	CAM_ER_CALL_NOT_ALLOWED	all
children not all terminated	CAM_ER_ACTIVE_CHILDREN	TA_End
not beginner	CAM_ER_NOT_BEGINNER	TA_End
too many transactions wanted	CAM_ER_TOO_MANY_TIDS	TA_GetTids
internal failure	CAM_ER_TRANMAN_ERROR	all

Table 9.1: Transaction Manager Return Codes

Registering an Application

Before using transaction management services, an application must first register itself with the Transaction Manager to exchange ports that will be used in subsequent calls.[1] This is done by calling `TA_AddApplication`. The application can obtain the Transaction Manager's port for this call from the local name server. Once an application is registered, it is free to use the transaction management calls in the TA interface.

```
routine TA_AddApplication(
                tPort              : port_t;
                atPort             : port_t;
                applName           : camelot_string_t;
            OUT applicationID      : cam_application_id_t;
            OUT taPort             : port_t);
```

`tPort` is a special port registered at the name server (under the name `TranPort`) by the Transaction Manager. The Transaction Manager listens only for `TA_AddApplication` calls on this port.

`atPort` is the port to which messages in the AT interface will be sent.

`applName` is a string containing the name of the application.

`applicationID` is an integer unique among applications at this site.

`taPort` is the port to which the application should send its future `TA_` calls.

The `applName` argument is used largely for debugging in Camelot, but it could be used along with a password for authentication.

An application identifier is an integer guaranteed to be unique at a node as long as Camelot remains running on that node. When Camelot is restarted, identifiers are allocated anew starting at

[1] This is done so that the `atPort` does not have to be shipped in subsequent calls.

1. The purpose of the application identifier is to provide a way that an application can identify itself in output statements or displays. Use of this identifier is voluntary.

Each application is given its own `taPort`, so that there is no need for including the identity of the caller in any call to the TA interface. Messages received by the Transaction Manager on a particular port are assumed to come from the application to which the port was given, so the application should be careful about giving another process send rights to its `taPort`.

Creating Transactions

An application creates transactions using `TA_Begin` or `TA_GetTids`. `TA_GetTids`, an optimization of `TA_Begin`, has the effect of creating a group of transactions at once. Applications which use many transactions may use `TA_GetTids` instead of calling `TA_Begin` for each one.

The result of using these calls successfully is one or more *transaction identifiers*, or TIDs. A TID is a capability – it proves the application has started a transaction. Holders of a TID may make server calls on behalf of the transaction it represents, or abort the work done by that transaction. Therefore an application should be careful about giving TIDs to other processes. The format and contents of the TID is discussed in detail in Section 16.2.2, **Transaction Identifier**.

```
routine TA_Begin(
                taPort          : port_t;
                parentTid       : cam_tid_t;
                transType       : cam_transaction_type_t;
            OUT newTid          : cam_tid_t);
```

`taPort` is the port returned by the `TA_AddApplication` call.

`parentTid` specifies whether to start a top-level or nested transaction. When it is all 0's (`CAM_NULL_TID`), a new top-level transaction is begun. If it already exists, a nested transaction is begun as its child.

`transType` specifies what kind of transaction to begin. The six possibilities are the cross product of the commit class (standard, hybrid atomic, or server-based), and the logging method (new value or old value/new value). Nested transactions are automatically coerced to the parent's type if the types do not match.

`newTid` is an out parameter containing the TID of the new transaction.

```
routine TA_GetTids(
                taPort          : port_t;
                parentTid       : cam_tid_t;
                transType       : cam_transaction_type_t;
                numRequested    : u_int;
            OUT newTidArray     : cam_tid_array_t);
```

`taPort` The port returned from the `TA_AddApplication` call.

`parentTid` The identifier of the parent of the new transactions.

`transType` The type of transaction to begin.

`numRequested` The number of TIDs requested.
`newTidArray` An array of new TIDs, returned out-of-line.

The `transType` argument specifies which of six types of transaction to create. The transaction type argument is meaningful only on top-level transactions. The type of a child transaction is coerced to be that of its parent. The options `TRAN_OVNV_HYBRIDATOMIC` and `TRAN_NV_HYBRIDATOMIC` specify hybrid-atomic transactions employing old-value/new-value logging and new-value-only logging, respectively. The options `TRAN_OVNV_STANDARD` and `TRAN_NV_STANDARD` specify "regular" transactions without hybrid atomicity. The options `TRAN_OVNV_SERVERBASED` and `TRAN_NV_SERVERBASED` specify server-based transactions. A server-based transaction is one which is initiated by a server, makes no server calls, and creates no children. It is an optimization for what we expect to be a common case. The Transaction Manager is not notified of server-based transactions unless they abort.

The choice of logging method should be made by estimating how long the transaction will run. Logging only new values produces less logging activity, but reduces the effective size of real memory because the pages of all modified objects are required to stay pinned throughout the duration of the transaction. It is not meaningful to have transactions in the same family use different logging methods, and the Transaction Manager will coerce a nested transaction to be of the same logging type as its top-level parent. Server-based transactions are meaningful only as top-level transactions. An attempt to begin a nested server-based transaction will result in failure.

Ending Transactions

The `TA_End` call requests that a transaction be committed. Two restrictions apply to its use. The first is that the end call for a transaction must be from the same process (identified by `taPort`) as the earlier begin call. The second restriction is that every nested transaction must be ended (committed or aborted) before the parent transaction is allowed to end.

```
routine TA_End(
                taPort          : port_t;
                tid             : cam_tid_t;
                protocolType    : cam_protocol_type_t;
            OUT timestamp       : cam_timestamp_t;
            OUT status          : int);
```

`taPort` from the `TA_AddApplication` call. This port must be the same as the port of the caller of `TA_Begin`.

`tid` is the TID of the transaction to be committed. All of its children must be committed or aborted at the time of this call.

`protocolType` is the type of commit protocol to be used, either two-phase or non-blocking.

`timestamp` is the commit timestamp. This is returned non-null for hybrid atomic transactions.

`status` indicates whether the transaction committed successfully. It is 0 if the transaction committed, and `CAM_AC_COMMIT_FAILED` if the commit failed. If there were uncompleted nested transactions at the time of the call, it contains CAM_ER_ACTIVE_CHILDREN. If the transaction was already aborted, it contains the abort code.

When TA_End is called with a top-level transaction as the argument, Camelot executes a protocol that tries to commit all of the operations performed by the top-level transaction and all of its committed descendants. For nested transactions, "commitment" is simply an indication that its locks should be anti-inherited. The changes performed by nested transactions are not permanent until the top-level transaction commits.

The protocolType argument specifies which of two commitment protocols to use for distributed transactions. The protocol type is important only for top-level transactions; its value is ignored when nested transactions end. Two-phase commit is the default. The non-blocking commit protocol permits commitment to proceed as long as a majority of the nodes involved in the transaction are able to communicate. Two-phase commit is a faster protocol, but is vulnerable to *blocking* if the application's node should crash at an inopportune moment. Commitment protocols are discussed in detail in Chapter 16.

When a top-level transaction is reported to be committed, it means that its effects are guaranteed to be permanent, and that *eventually* all its locks will be dropped. It does *not* mean that the locks held by the transaction have been dropped, either at the local node or at remote nodes. Fortunately, "eventually" almost always means "very soon."

Aborting Transactions

The TA_Kill call allows an application to attempt to abort a transaction. Killing a transaction eventually results in the death of all transactions nested within it. It does not mean that the locks held by the transaction or its descendants have been dropped, either at the local node or at remote nodes. Eventually this will happen, and "eventually" almost always means "very soon."

```
routine TA_Kill(
                taPort          : port_t;
                tid             : cam_tid_t;
                status          : int);
```

taPort from the TA_AddApplication call.
tid is the identifier of the transaction to be aborted.
status is the abort code describing the cause of the abort.

Getting Timestamps

Camelot provides a logical clock [60] to allow servers to timestamp data and operations. In particular, this allows experimentation with hybrid-atomic locking techniques, which entail comparison of timestamps for serialization. (In this case, the timestamp would be used in conjunction with the hybrid-atomic transaction type.) A server may obtain a timestamp by using the TA_GetTimeStamp call.

```
routine TA_GetTimeStamp(
                taPort          : port_t;
            OUT timestamp       : cam_timestamp_t);
```

`tsPort` is the port on which the Transaction Manager receives calls from servers.
`timestamp` is the current timestamp.

More information on timestamps may be found in Section 16.2.2, **Timestamps and Lamport Clock**.

9.2.2 The AT Interface

The AT interface consists of one call–the asynchronous message `AT_TransactionHasDied`.

Abort Notification

The Transaction Manager sends the `AT_TransactionHasDied` message to an application when a transaction aborts for a reason other than the application having called `TA_Kill`. The port to which this message is sent is the `atPort` given by the application in the `TA_AddApplication` call. If a top-level transaction aborts, the `AT_TransactionHasDied` message is sent for the top-level transaction only. Otherwise, a message is sent for each descendant as well. The order in which the messages are sent is undefined.

```
simpleroutine AT_TransactionHasDied(
                atPort          : port_t;
                tid             : cam_tid_t;
                status          : int);
```

`atPort` the port on which the application receives messages from the Transaction Manager.
`tid` the transaction that is dying.
`status` a description of the cause of the abort.

Port Death

An application has no responsibility with regard to port death, although it may want to exit if it receives a port death notice for its `tPort`. If an application receives notice of the death of a server port, Camelot will abort all of its transactions that used the dead server. The application will receive an `AT_TransactionHasDied` message for each of these transactions that it started.

The Transaction Manager concludes that an application is dead if it receives a port death notice for the `atPort` that was given to the application by the `TA_AddApplication` call. When that port dies, the Transaction Manager aborts all transactions begun by that process. This means that an application that finds itself confused can rely on the mechanism of deallocating the `atPort` in order to reset to the very simple state wherein no transactions exist. After doing so, it must reissue the `TA_AddApplication` call before using any other calls in the TA interface.

Timeout

If an application times out while waiting for an operation to reply, then it is obligated to abort the current transaction. Calling `TA_End` after a timeout would commit an ill-defined transaction, because it would not be known whether the operation was performed.

9.3 Transaction Services for Servers

A server process obtains transaction management services through the calls of the TA and TS interfaces. The types of service are beginning and ending transactions, joining existing transactions, and resolving lock conflicts. To begin, end, and abort transactions, servers should use the appropriate calls in the TA interface. The interaction between a server and the Transaction Manager is illustrated in Figures 9.3 and 9.4.

9.3.1 The TS Interface

Registering Servers

The Transaction Manager must be aware of the presence of each data server at its site so that a specialized port can be allocated for communication with it. Just as with the TA interface, the dependence upon an authenticated port eliminates one argument (the server ID) from each procedure in the TS interface. Server authentication is handled automatically by the Disk Manager in cooperation with the Node Server, and the call that registers a server with the Transaction Manager is made by the Disk Manager (`TD_AddDataServer`). The Disk Manager is involved with server creation for security reasons. Like the `TA_AddApplication` call, one port is passed in and one is passed out. The in port is used by the Transaction Manager to make ST interface calls, and the out port is the authenticated port for TS interface calls by that server. Unlike `TA_AddApplication`, however, a server identifier is passed *in*. This ID is permanent and unique among all servers at a site.

```
routine TD_AddDataServer(
                tdPort          : port_t;
                serverId        : cam_server_id_t;
                sendPort        : port_t;
            OUT rcvPort         : port_t);
```

`tdPort` is the port on which the Transaction Manager receives messages from the Disk Manager.
`serverId` is the permanent ID of the server.
`sendPort` is the port to which Transaction Manager sends messages to servers.
`rcvPort` is the port to which the server sends messages to the Transaction Manager.

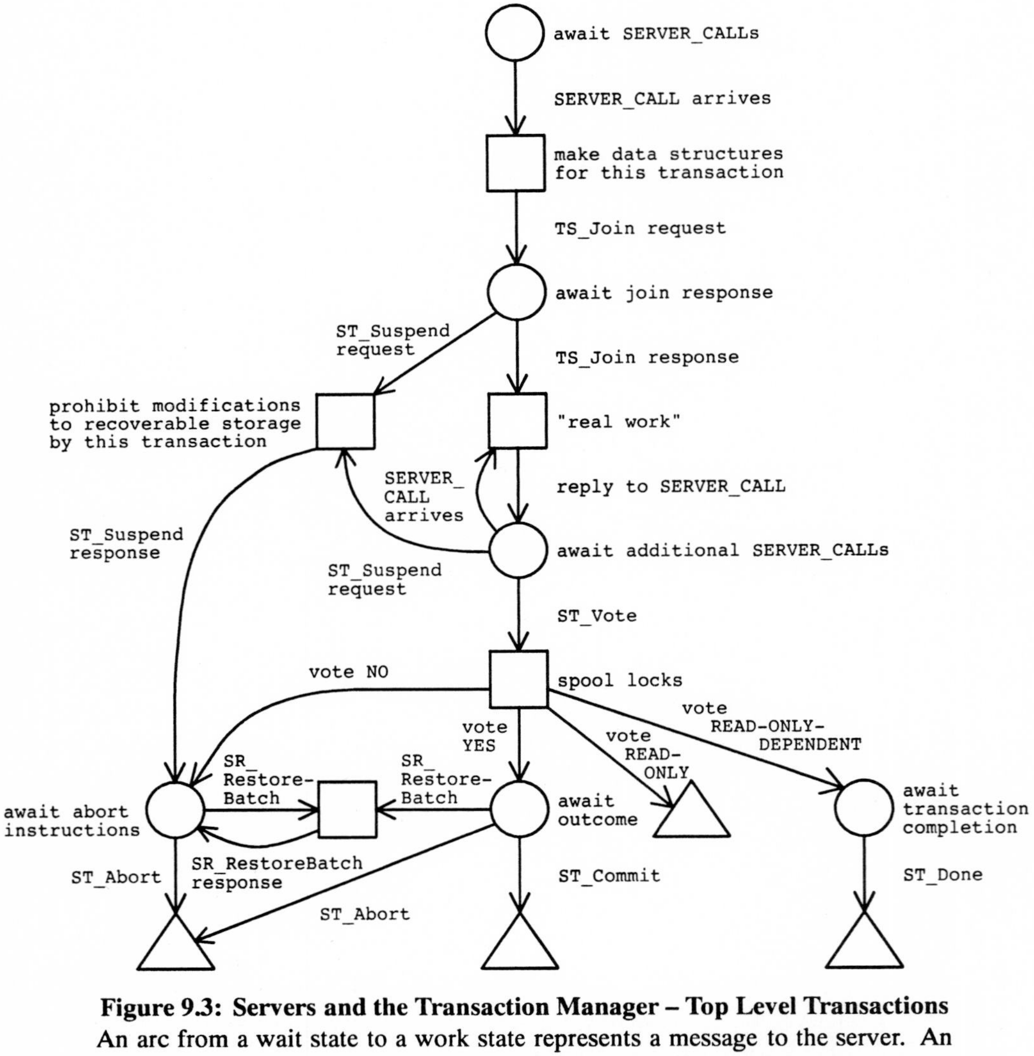

Figure 9.3: Servers and the Transaction Manager – Top Level Transactions
An arc from a wait state to a work state represents a message to the server. An arc from a work state to a wait state represents an outgoing server message. "Real work" may include locking, unlocking, and modifying data, making server calls, beginning, ending and aborting transactions, and resolving lock conflicts.

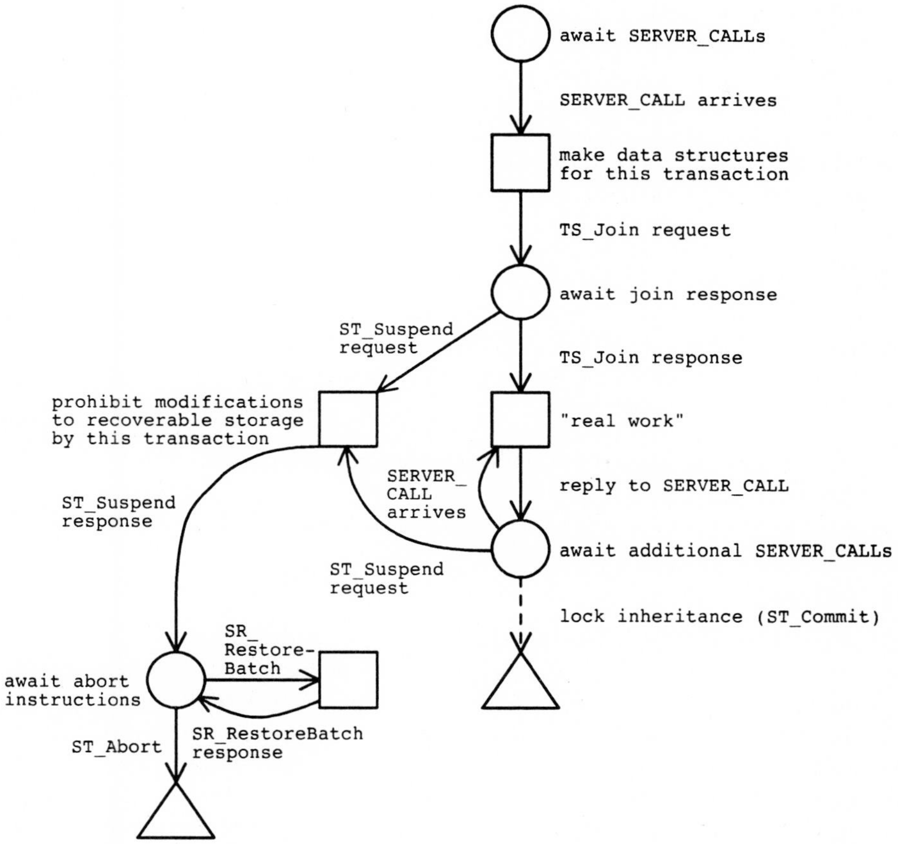

Figure 9.4: Servers and the Transaction Manager – Nested Transactions
Server states are as in Figure 9.3. When `TA_End` is called on a nested transaction, the Transaction Manager marks it as committed, but does not execute a commit protocol. Therefore, an `ST_Commit` message is not sent to the server, and locks on behalf of the nested transaction are not dropped. If there is a conflict on a lock by a transaction in the same family, the lock inheritance protocol will be executed and the committed nested transaction will anti-inherit the lock.

Joining Transactions

A server must make the `TS_Join` call before the first time that it performs an operation for a transaction. The call need not be made before later operations for the same transaction. If the server cannot join a particular transaction, then it must refuse to do any work on behalf of that transaction.

The purpose of joining is two-fold: first, to inform the Transaction Manager which servers must be included in the commitment protocol, and second, to prevent a server from doing an operation for a transaction that is already aborted or in the process of aborting. The possibility of server operations being simultaneous with abort arises if one server aborts a transaction while the application sends an operation request to another (previously unused) server. If the operation were to be performed, the server would be holding locks for a transaction that is already finished at its site.

Because servers may be multi-threaded, some mechanism must be used to prevent concurrent threads running on behalf of the same transaction from making multiple `TS_Join` requests. The Camelot Library implementation uses a "join lock" to delay subsequent threads until the join is completed.

```
routine TS_Join(
                        tsPort              : port_t;
                        tid                 : cam_tid_t);
```

`tsPort` is the port on which the Transaction Manager receives calls from servers.

`tid` is the identifier of the transaction that the caller wants to join.

Resolving Lock Conflicts

Nested transactions may inherit and anti-inherit locks from their parents. One way to implement locking for nested transactions would be to associate a stack of transactions with each lock. The top transaction is the current holder of the lock. To inherit is to push. To anti-inherit is to pop. A naive method for doing anti-inheritance is to inform every server at the time a nested transaction commits, so that it may pop the committed transaction from all of its lock stacks. This method of lock anti-inheritance, called *eager evaluation*, ensures that every lock entry is always up to date, but requires the sending of many messages, some of which may travel between nodes. Something like this method is used in both Locus [83] and ERMS [88], with the result that both implementations are quite slow [121, 87].

To circumvent the performance problem, Camelot uses *lazy-evaluation* anti-inheritance [73]: when a nested transaction commits, no effort is made to update lock entries that list the committed nested transaction as the holder until the top-level transaction commits or until another transaction tries to obtain the lock. No laziness is employed when a nested transaction aborts: its effects are undone and its locks dropped immediately. Figure 9.5 compares lazy versus eager evaluation.

Two cases of lock conflicts can be distinguished: when the two transactions are members of the same family, and when they are not. When a conflict occurs between two transactions from different families, the resolution is obvious: the lock cannot be broken. When a conflict occurs between two transactions in the same family (*relatives*), it is necessary to determine the pedigrees of the nominal holder and the requester and to determine if the nominal holder is *committed up to* their *least common ancestor*. Referring to Figure 9.1, the least common ancestor of D and E is B, so

Eager Evaluation

1. Transaction E commits;
2. A message is sent to S saying that locks held by E are now held by C;
3. Transaction C commits;
4. A message is sent to S saying that locks held by C are now held by B;
5. Transaction D requests L;
6. Server S must determine whether D is a descendant of B. If so, the lock should be granted to D.

Lazy Evaluation

1. Transaction E commits. No message is sent;
2. Transaction C commits. No message is sent;
3. Transaction D requests L;
4. Server S must determine that C is the least common ancestor of D and E.
5. The server must find out if C is committed. If so, the lock should be granted to D.

Figure 9.5: Alternatives for Lock Anti-Inheritance

Suppose that data server S holds lock L for transaction E of the family pictured in Figure 9.1. Indicated above are the steps that would be taken by eager evaluation and lazy evaluation methods in the case that E then C commit, and then transaction D requests L.

a lock that is still listed as being held by transaction E can be granted to D only if C is committed.[2] If E is committed but C is not, the lock remains held (by C) and D must wait.

The Transaction Manager provides two calls that answer the question of whether the lock can be inherited: `TS_IsLockInheritable` and `TS_WaitBeforeInheritingLock`. The former returns `true` if the lock holder has committed with respect to the least common ancestor of it and the lock requester or if the holder has aborted. The latter, a blocking call, returns only when the lock holder has so committed or when the lock holder or lock requester aborts.

```
routine TS_IsLockInheritable(
                    tsPort          : port_t;
                    holdingTrans    : cam_tid_t;
                    requestingTrans : cam_tid_t;
              OUT   answer          : boolean_t);
```

`tsPort` is the Transaction Manager's port for the server.
`holdingTrans` is the transaction that is the nominal holder.
`requestingTrans` is the transaction requesting the lock.
`answer` indicates whether or not the lock may be inherited. It will be true if the requestor and the holder are committed up to their least common ancestor, or if the holder cannot be found.

[2]According to the model, if C is committed then E was committed earlier.

```
routine TS_WaitBeforeInheritingLock(
                tsPort          : port_t;
                holdingTrans    : cam_tid_t;
                requestingTrans: cam_tid_t);
```

`tsPort` is the Transaction Manager's port for the server.
`holdingTrans` is the transaction that is the nominal holder.
`requestingTrans` is the transaction requesting the lock.

The Camelot Library has the ability to resolve most intra-familial lock conflicts internally using an optimization called the *family position indicator* or FPI. Thus the Library rarely issues `TS_IsLockInheritable` and `TS_WaitBeforeInheritingLock` calls. Family position indicators are discussed in detail in Chapter 16.

9.3.2 The ST Interface

Servers are required to handle the calls in this interface. They can be split into two small groups:

1. The `ST_Suspend` and `ST_Abort` calls, used during abort.

2. The `ST_Vote`, `ST_Commit`, `ST_Done`, and `ST_Abort` calls, used during commitment.

Implementing the Abort Protocol

From a server's viewpoint, the abort protocol begins when the synchronous `ST_Suspend` call is received. This call instructs servers to stop serving a transaction which is being aborted. A server must not respond to the call until it is certain that no threads will operate on behalf of this transaction ever again. This includes reading or modifying recoverable storage (see Section 16.3.4, **Orphans and Consistency**). If a tree of transactions is aborting, an `ST_Suspend` will be sent for each one.

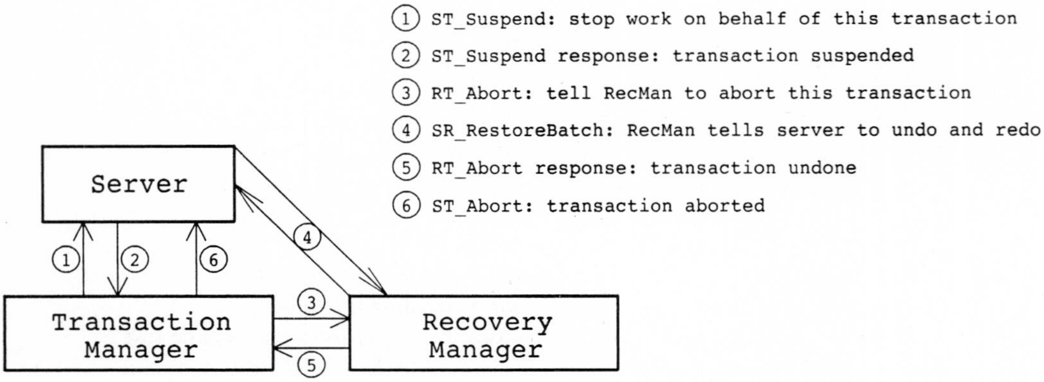

(1) ST_Suspend: stop work on behalf of this transaction
(2) ST_Suspend response: transaction suspended
(3) RT_Abort: tell RecMan to abort this transaction
(4) SR_RestoreBatch: RecMan tells server to undo and redo
(5) RT_Abort response: transaction undone
(6) ST_Abort: transaction aborted
Server
Transaction Manager
Recovery Manager
1
2
6
3
4
5

Figure 9.6: Abort Protocol
Only one `SR_RestoreObject` call is shown, but any number may occur.

```
routine ST_Suspend(
                sPort               : port_t;
                tid                 : cam_tid_t;
                status              : int);
```

`sPort` is the port on which the server receives messages from the Transaction Manager.
`tid` is the identifier of the transaction being aborted.
`status` is a code for the cause of the abort.

Once this is done and the server responds to `ST_Suspend`, it may receive a series of `SR_RestoreBatch` calls sent by the Recovery Manager, which uses the contents of the log as the specification of how to undo the transaction. Once every object has been returned to the value it had before the transaction started, the Transaction Manager will make the asynchronous `ST_Abort` call:

```
simpleroutine ST_Abort(
                sPort               : port_t;
                tid                 : cam_tid_t);
```

`sPort` is the port on which the server receives messages from the Transaction Manager.
`tid` is the identifier of the transaction that aborted.

Receipt of this call is a signal to drop all locks held by the transaction and to expunge any data structures allocated for it. The sequence of calls received during abort is illustrated in Figure 9.6.

If many transactions are aborting (e.g., transactions B, C, D, and E in Figure 9.1), then this abort procedure is carried out for every transaction, one after another, from the bottom of the "aborting tree" up to the top. Referring to the example, the order of abort would be: E, C, D, B.

Implementing the Commit Protocol

From the viewpoint of a server, the commit protocol begins when the `ST_Vote` call is received. This call instructs servers to suspend and then vote on the transaction.

```
routine ST_Vote(
                sPort               : port_t;
                famId               : cam_fam_id_t;
                timestamp           : cam_timestamp_t;
                prepare             : boolean_t;
            OUT result              : cam_vote_t);
```

`sPort` is the port on which the server receives messages from the Transaction Manager.
`famId` is identifier of the transaction family.
`timestamp` is the commit timestamp.

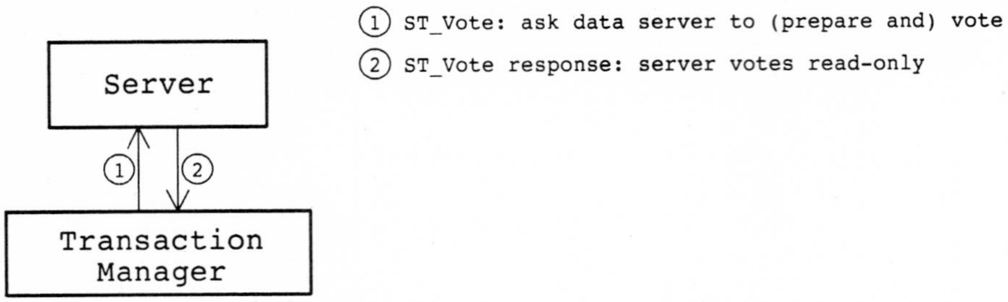

Figure 9.7: Commitment Protocol – Read-only Independent Vote

`prepare` if TRUE, the server should log its locks before responding. This will be the case only at subordinate sites.
`result` is the server's vote.

The commitment protocol is executed only for top-level transactions. When an `ST_Vote` call is received, the server must no longer distinguish among transactions in the family, but rather treat the effects of the entire family as if a single transaction had performed them all. To service the `ST_Vote` call, a server should perform the following steps:

1. Drop read locks.
2. If the transaction family is hybrid-atomic, use the timestamp as needed.
3. Decide how to vote. There are four ways to vote: yes, no, read-only independent, and read-only dependent.
4. If the server has decided to vote yes, and if the prepared argument is `TRUE`, then place the transaction's locks into the log by calling `DS_Prepare`.
5. Return the vote.

The *yes* vote indicates that the transaction has modified data, and that the server wishes to commit. The *no vote* indicates that some event has happened that makes commit impossible or undesirable, and that the transaction should be aborted. Casting a no vote ensures that the transaction will abort. The *read-only independent vote* is cast in the case that a transaction has acquired only read locks. A server that votes read-only will be dropped from the commit protocol and will receive no further messages about that transaction, so after voting read-only the server should drop locks and expunge data structures allocated to the transaction. This is illustrated in Figure 9.7. Like the independent read-only vote, the *read-only dependent vote* is cast if a transaction has acquired only read locks. But this vote indicates that the transaction depends on a previous lazily committed transaction. The Transaction Manager must ensure the permanence of the lazy transaction before allowing the read-only dependent transaction to commit. This is illustrated in Figure 9.8. If the vote call times out, the Transaction Manager will assume a no vote on behalf of the server.

Those servers that voted yes eventually receive either an `ST_Commit` or an `ST_Abort` message, indicating whether or not commit was successful. Those that voted no will receive an `ST_Abort`.

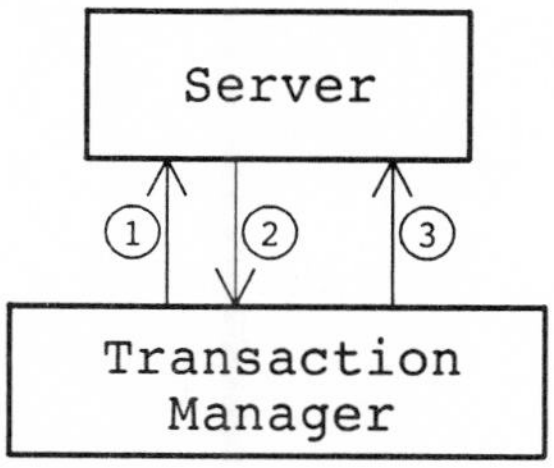

(1) ST_Vote: ask data server to (prepare and) vote
(2) ST_Vote response: server votes read-only-dependent
(3) ST_Done: transaction completed

Figure 9.8: Commitment Protocol – Read-only Dependent Vote

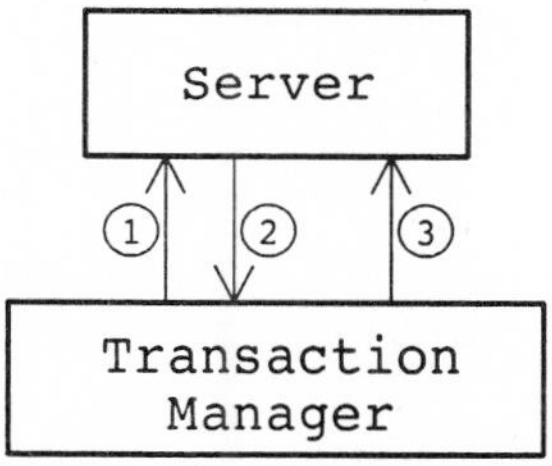

(1) ST_Vote: ask data server to (prepare and) vote
(2) ST_Vote response: server votes yes
(3) ST_Commit: transaction committed

Figure 9.9: Commitment Protocol – Yes Vote, Successful Commit

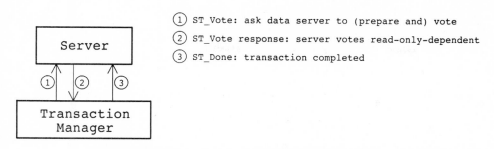

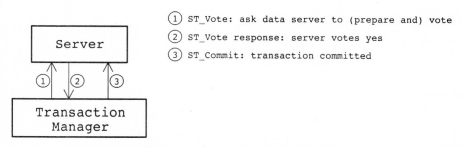

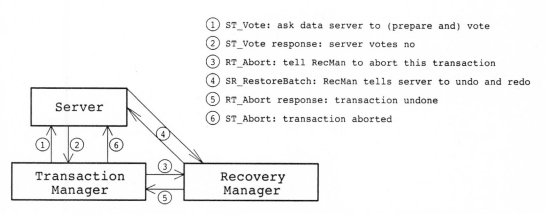

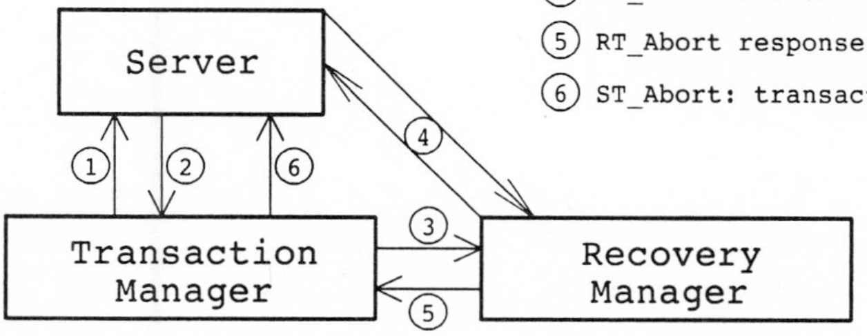

(1) ST_Vote: ask data server to (prepare and) vote
(2) ST_Vote response: server votes no
(3) RT_Abort: tell RecMan to abort this transaction
(4) SR_RestoreBatch: RecMan tells server to undo and redo
(5) RT_Abort response: transaction undone
(6) ST_Abort: transaction aborted

Figure 9.10: Commitment Protocol – Yes or No Vote, Abort During Commit

Those that voted read-only dependent will receive an `ST_Done`. In any case, the server should perform whatever operations are relevant to that case and then drop its locks.

```
simpleroutine ST_Commit(
                    sPort           : port_t;
                    famId           : cam_fam_id_t);
```

`sPort` is the port on which the server receives messages from the Transaction Manager.
`famId` is the identifier of the family that committed.

```
simpleroutine ST_Abort(
                    sPort           : port_t;
                    tid             : cam_tid_t);
```

`sPort` is the port on which the server receives messages from the Transaction Manager.
`tid` is the identifier of the transaction that aborted.

```
simpleroutine ST_Done(
                    sPort           : port_t;
                    famId           : cam_fam_id_t);
```

`sPort` is the port on which the server receives messages from the Transaction Manager.
`famId` is the identifier of the family that completed.

If the Transaction Manager times out on a read-only server, the server will receive an `ST_Abort`. Therefore, the server should do something reasonable when it receives this message for a transaction it does not know about. Figures 9.9 and 9.10 indicate the sequence of messages exchanged between Transaction Manager and data server in successful and unsuccessful commit.

Like `ST_Vote`, `ST_Commit` and `ST_Done` specify only the family identifier; conversely, `ST_Abort` specifies the TID. In retrospect, there should have been two interface calls in place of `ST_Abort`. One would indicate that an abort has completed, and specify a TID. The other would serve as a commit outcome, and specify a family identifier.

Chapter 10

Camelot Node Management

Dean Thompson
George Michaels

The Node Server is structured like an ordinary data server. It makes straightforward use of the Camelot Library described in Chapter 3 to implement a simple locking strategy and statically allocated recoverable storage. The Node Server has a unique position in the Camelot system, however, because of its close relationship with one very powerful client: the Disk Manager. The Node Server provides the Disk Manager with the recoverable storage needed to permanently map recoverable virtual memory addresses into physical backing store. The Node Server also keeps track of server configuration data, and is permitted to make calls on the Disk Manager to bring data servers up and down.

Like any other Camelot data server, the Node Server maintains a database in recoverable virtual memory and exports controlled access to that data through a remote procedure call (RPC) interface. For the most part, the Node Server structures its data as a very simple relational database. One relation associates a name, password, and privilege level with each authorized user of the Node Server. Another relation stores a command line, owner name, and recoverable storage quota for each server configured to run on the node. Two relations cooperate to recoverably map locations in each server's recoverable virtual memory to physical offsets in backing store. The Node Server also maintains some data that is not relational. It uses recoverable variables to store configuration parameters such as the number of sectors per chunk of recoverable storage and the server restart policy parameters. And, in addition to providing access to its recoverable data, the Node Server exports access to a volatile *server state* maintained by the Disk Manager.

This chapter describes two interfaces to the Node Server: the application interface and the Disk Manager's interface. The application interface is used primarily by the Node Configuration Application (the NCA), an interactive program described in Chapter 4. It can also be used by other applications and data servers to dynamically create and destroy data servers, to change their configuration, and to bring them up and down. The Disk Manager's interface to the Node Server cannot be called by any other program, but it is included in this chapter because it helps explain the Node Server's purpose and design.

10.1 The NA interface

The application interface to the Node Server provides calls to read and modify the Node Server user and server databases, to determine the current state of a server, and to bring servers up and down. It also provides calls to read and update the recoverable variables that store node configuration parameters such as the target recovery time, the recoverable storage allocation granularity, and the server restart policy parameters. Many of the calls in the NA interface correspond exactly to commands accepted by the Node Configuration Application discussed in Chapter 4. That chapter should be consulted for additional information about call arguments.

Each Node Server request is executed in its own top-level transaction, and therefore is permanent and retains no locks. This makes the interface simpler and more consistent, since some Node Server operations (such as server recovery) involve real-world events and others must drop locks immediately to avoid blocking the Disk Manager. The Node Server also uses the "house-cleaner" provided by the Camelot Library to abort transactions that stay active at the Node Server for more than about fifteen seconds.

10.1.1 Node Server Logins

Before a client (other than the Disk Manager) can make requests of the Node Server, the client must volunteer its user name and password in a call to `NA_Login`. If these are valid, the Node Server will return a *key* as an out parameter. This key must be included by the client in all additional requests as a way of establishing the client's identity.

```
camelotroutine NA_Login(
                userName          : user_name_t;
                password          : password_t;
            OUT key               : cam_tid_t);
```

`userName` The user name of the person logging in.
`password` The password of the user logging in.
`key` A token to identify the caller in subsequent calls.

The `NA_Login` call must be made within the scope of a transaction. The key that it returns is valid until this login transaction commits or aborts. The client can cancel the login by explicitly ending the login transaction. Otherwise, the login will eventually expire because the client will exit and the transaction will automatically be aborted by Camelot. If the client makes other use of the login transaction (such as RPCs or modifications of recoverable storage), then it is responsible for handling any possible abort and establishing a new login if necessary. In particular, it is important to remember that the Disk Manager routinely aborts transactions as necessary to reclaim log space. This is guaranteed not to happen to a transaction unless it modifies recoverable storage, and the `NA_Login` routine is careful not to modify recoverable storage on behalf of the login transaction.

Many of the Node Server routines abort the calling transaction when they encounter an error. Also, any Node Server routine other than `NA_Login` may modify recoverable storage on behalf of the calling transaction, leaving it vulnerable to abort by the Disk Manager. For these reasons, it is often best not to use the login transaction for calls to the Node Server after `NA_Login`. One simple approach is to begin a new top-level transaction within the scope of the login transaction.

The NA_ListLogins call provides access to the list of users who are currently logged in.

```
camelotroutine NA_ListLogins(
                    key               : cam_tid_t;
                OUT userNameList      : user_name_list_t);
```

key The key identifies the caller.
userNameList This is the list of users currently logged in.

Any user with more than one active login transaction will appear more than once in the list.

10.1.2 Node Server Users

When the Node Server initializes its database, it creates an entry for one privileged user called admin, with password admin. This user is in the highest of the three privilege categories: ADMIN, USER, and NONE. The password of this automatically created user should be changed the first time it is used.

Any user with ADMIN privileges can use the NA_AddUser and NA_DeleteUser functions to add and delete other users.

```
camelotroutine NA_AddUser(
                    key               : cam_tid_t;
                    userName          : user_name_t;
                    password          : password_t;
                    privilege         : privilege_t);
```

key The key identifies the caller.
userName This is the new user name.
password This is the password for the new user.
privilege The privilege to be allowed to the new user.

```
camelotroutine NA_DeleteUser(
                    key               : cam_tid_t;
                    userName          : user_name_t);
```

key The key identifies the caller.
userName This is the name of the user to be deleted from the system.

A user's privilege level must be specified using one of NA_PRIV_ADMIN, NA_PRIV_USER, or NA_PRIV_NONE. Users with active login transaction and users that own servers cannot be deleted.

The application interface also permits a user with ADMIN privileges to change another user's password or privilege level, and permits a user to change its own password.

```
camelotroutine NA_SetPrivilege(
                    key               : cam_tid_t;
                    userName          : user_name_t;
                    privilege         : privilege_t);
```

`key` The key identifies the caller.
`userName` The name of the user whose privileges are being changed.
`privilege` The new privilege that the specified user will be permited.

```
camelotroutine NA_SetPassword(
                    key                 : cam_tid_t;
                    userName            : user_name_t;
                    password            : password_t);
```

`key` The key identifies the caller.
`userName` This is the name of the user whose password is being changed.
`password` This is the new password for the user.

Any logged-in user can call `NA_ListUsers` to list the users of a node or `NA_ShowUser` to see a user's privilege level.

```
camelotroutine NA_ListUsers(
                    key                 : cam_tid_t;
                OUT userlist            : user_name_list_t);
```

`key` The key identifies the caller.
`userName` This is the list of the authorized users of Camelot on this system.

```
camelotroutine NA_ShowUser(
                    key                 : cam_tid_t;
                    userName            : user_name_t;
                OUT privilege           : privilege_t);
```

`key` The key identifies the caller.
`userName` This the user about whom the information is requested.
`privilege` This is the privilege of the specifed user.

10.1.3 Server Configuration

Any user with ADMIN or USER privileges can insert servers in the Node Server database with `NA_AddServer`.

```
camelotroutine NA_AddServer(
                    key                 : cam_tid_t;
              INOUT serverID            : cam_server_id_t;
                    owner               : user_name_t;
                    autoRestart         : boolean_t;
                    commandLine         : camelot_string_t;
              INOUT segmentID           : cam_segment_id_t;
                    quotaChunks         : u_int);
```

`key` The key identifies the caller.
`serverID` This is the server identifier that will be assigned to the new server.
`owner` This the name of the user that owns the server.
`autoRestart` This is true if the server should be restarted whenever Camelot is restarted.
`commandLine` This is the command line that will be used to start the server.
`segmentID` This is the segment identifier for the recoverable segment that the server will use.
`quotaChunks` This is the size of the server's recoverable segment in chunks.

If the `serverID` parameter is `nullServerId`, the Node Server returns an unused server ID. Similarly, if the `segmentID` parameter is `nullSegmentId`, the Node Server returns an unused segment ID.

When a server is added to the Node Server's database, its state is `CAM_SS_DOWN_CLEAN` by default. Later, when it is started, it progresses through `CAM_SS_RECOVERING` to `CAM_SS_UP`. If it is automatically started for recovery only (to reclaim log space) then it is placed in the `CAM_SS_RECOVERING_ONLY` state during recovery. When a data server is explicitly killed through the Node Server application interface, it passes through `CAM_SS_RECOVERING_KILLED`, `CAM_SS_RECOVERING_ONLY_KILLED`, or `CAM_SS_UP_KILLED` as appropriate. Once the data server is down, it is in one of four states depending on whether it is in a transaction-consistent state (whether it is "clean") and whether it is involved in prepared transactions. These four possible states for down servers are `CAM_SS_DOWN_CLEAN`, `CAM_SS_DOWN_DIRTY`, `CAM_SS_DOWN_PREPARED`, and `CAM_SS_DOWN_DIRTY_PREPARED`. A server must be in one of the down states in order to be restarted or deleted.

After a server is inserted in the database, it is owned by the user who inserted it. That user, or any user with ADMIN privileges, can later use other Node Server application interface calls to change the characteristics of the server.

`NA_SetAutoRestart` changes the setting of the server's auto-restart flag.

```
camelotroutine NA_SetAutoRestart(
                key              : cam_tid_t;
                serverID         : cam_server_id_t;
                autoRestart      : boolean_t);
```

`key` The key identifies the caller.
`serverID` This identifies the server to be affected.
`autoRestart` This indicates whether or not the server should be restarted when Camelot restarts on this node.

`NA_SetCommandLine` changes a server's command line.

```
camelotroutine NA_SetCommandLine(
                key              : cam_tid_t;
```

```
                     serverID          : cam_server_id_t;
                     commandLine       : camelot_string_t);
```

`key` The key identifies the caller.
`serverID` This identifies the server whose command is to be changed.
`commandLine` The new command to be used to start the server.

The command line is the path and file name of the server program followed by switches and arguments.

`NA_SetQuota` changes a segment's quota.

```
camelotroutine NA_SetQuota(
                     key               : cam_tid_t;
                     segmentID         : cam_segment_id_t;
                     quotaChunks       : int);
```

`key` The key identifies the caller.
`segmentID` This identifies the segment whose quota is being changed.
`quotaChunks` This is the new quota, in chunks, for the segment.

A quota is the number of chunks allocated for backing the server's recoverable storage. The number of chunks allocated for a segment may only be increased, never decreased.

A server's owner, or any user with ADMIN privileges, can use `NA_DeleteServer` to delete the server from the Node Server's database. This permanently destroys the server's recoverable data and returns its backing storage for reallocation.

```
camelotroutine NA_DeleteServer(
                     key               : cam_tid_t;
                     serverID          : cam_server_id_t);
```

`key` The key identifies the caller.
`serverID` The identifier of the server to be deleted.

Any user can use `NA_ListServers` to list the servers on a node and call `NA_ShowServer` see the configuration of a server.

```
camelotroutine NA_ListServers(
                     key               : cam_tid_t;
                 OUT serverlist        : cam_server_id_list_t);
```

`key` The key identifies the caller.
`serverList` This is the ids of the Camelot servers registered with the Node Server.

```
camelotroutine NA_ShowServer(
                     key               : cam_tid_t;
                     serverID          : cam_server_id_t;
```

```
                OUT owner           : user_name_t;
                OUT autoRestart     : boolean_t;
                OUT commandLine     : camelot_string_t;
                OUT segDescList     : cam_segment_desc_list_t;
                OUT chunksUsedList  : cam_size_list_t;
                OUT state           : cam_server_state_t);
```

`key` The key identifies the caller.

`serverId` This is the identifier of the server that the caller wants information about.

`owner` The name of user that owns the server.

`autoRestart` This is true, if the server should automatically be restarted when Camelot is restarted.

`commandLine` This is the command used to start the server.

`segDescList` This is an array of descriptors describing the recoverable segments associated with the server.

`chucksUsedList` This array lists the number of chunks used by the server in each of its recoverable segments.

`state` This is the current state of the server.

10.1.4 Node Configuration

Any user with ADMIN privileges can change the recoverable configuration variables that parameterize the behavior of the node. These include the chunk size (unit of recoverable storage allocation), the desired average server recovery time, and the server restart policy parameters. Any logged-in user can examine the configuration variables.

The chunk size can be changed with `NA_SetChunkSize`. This call must be made when there are currently no servers in the Node Server's database. The chunk size must be specified in two ways. The first is the size in bytes of each chunk. This is for use by the Node Server itself. The other is the number of bits wide the chunk size is. This is effectively the base two log of the size in bytes. The chunk size for a node can only be modified when there are no servers configured on the node.

```
camelotroutine NA_SetChunkSize(
                    key             : cam_tid_t;
                    chunkBytes      : u_int;
                    chunkBits       : u_int);
```

`key` The key identifies the caller.

`chunkBytes` This is the size, in bytes, of a chunk of recoverable storage.

`chunkBits` This is the base two log of `chunkBytes`.

Any logged-in user can examine the chunk size using `NA_ShowChunkSize`.

```
camelotroutine NA_ShowChunkSize(
                    key             : cam_tid_t;
                OUT chunkBytes      : u_int);
```

`key` The key identifies the caller.
`chunkBytes` This is the current size, in bytes, of a chunk of recoverable storage.

The target recovery time can be set with `NA_SetRecTime`. This is the amount of time Camelot should plan to spend on server or node recovery. The Node Server maintains a short list of recently observed recovery times and provides this data to the Disk Manager on request. The Disk Manager attempts to meet the target recovery time by flushing pages and aborting long-running transactions.

```
camelotroutine NA_SetRecTime(
                    key                : cam_tid_t;
                    minutes            : u_int);
```

`key` The key identifies the caller.
`minutes` This is the maximum duration of node recovery that the user will tolerate. Camelot will calculate how often it needs to write checkpoint records so that it can perform node recovery within this time limit.

The `NA_ListRecTime` call allows applications to examine the current target recovery time.

```
camelotroutine NA_ListRecTime(
                    key                : cam_tid_t;
          OUT       minutes            : u_int);
```

`key` The key identifies the caller.
`minutes` This is the current maximum time allowed for node recovery. See the description of `NA_SetRecTime` for more information.

The `NA_SetRestartPolicy` call sets the restart policy parameters. Servers will not be auto-restarted more than `limit` times every `interval` minutes.

```
camelotroutine NA_SetRestartPolicy(
                    key                : cam_tid_t;
                    limit              : u_int;
                    interval           : u_int);
```

`key` The key identifies the caller.
`limit` The number of times a server may be restarted during the given interval.
`interval` This is the length of the restart interval in minutes.

Another call, `NA_ListRestartPolicy`, is provided to allow applications to examine the current restart policy parameters.

```
camelotroutine NA_ListRestartPolicy(
                    key                : cam_tid_t;
          OUT       limit              : u_int;
          OUT       interval           : u_int);
```

`key` The key identifies the caller.
`limit` The number of times a server may be restarted during the listed interval.
`interval` This is the length of the restart interval in minutes.

10.1.5 System State

In addition to providing controlled access to Node Server recoverable storage, the Node Server application interface provides some access to volatile system state. It allows appropriately authorized clients to examine the current checkpoint interval, to determine how long the system has been up, to bring servers up and down, and even to shut down Camelot itself.

The `NA_ListCheckpointInterval` call gets the current checkpoint interval from the Node Server, which gets it from the Disk Manager. The checkpoint interval is computed from the target recovery time and other information.

```
camelotroutine NA_ListCheckpointInterval(
                   key                 : cam_tid_t;
               OUT interval            : u_int);
```

`key` The key identifies the caller.
`interval` This is the current size of the checkpoint interval in records.

Any logged-in client can determine how long Camelot has been running by issuing the `NA_GetUpTime` call.

```
camelotroutine NA_GetUpTime(
          OUT      upTime : u_int);
```

`upTime` The current uptime in seconds.

A server can be started by its owner, or by any user with ADMIN privileges, using the `NA_StartServer` call.

```
camelotroutine NA_StartServers(
                   key                 : cam_tid_t;
                   serverID            : cam_server_id_list_t);
```

`key` The key identifies the caller.
`serverID` The identifier of the server to be started.

Similarly, a server can be shut down with `NA_ShutdownServer`.

```
camelotroutine NA_ShutdownServer(
                   key                 : cam_tid_t;
                   serverID            : cam_server_id_t;
                   cleanLevel          : clean_level_t);
```

`key` The key identifies the caller.

`serverID` The identifier of the server to be killed.

`cleanLevel` An indication of whether to attempt to shut the server down cleanly, allowing current transactions to finish. This parameter is currently unused.

The Node Server forwards this request to the Disk Manager, which immediately sends a signal to the server.

Any user with ADMIN privileges can shut down Camelot using the `NA_ShutdownCamelot` call.

```
camelotroutine NA_ShutdownCamelot(key : cam_tid_t);
```

`key` The key identifies the caller.

Part III

Design Rationale

Chapter 11

The Design of Camelot

Alfred Z. Spector

Camelot is implemented by several components that work together to provide an easy-to-use, general-purpose distributed transaction facility. This part of the book describes the rationale for these components and the internal designs of each of the major components. This chapter presents an overview of the design of Camelot. Chapter 12 describes the implementation of the Camelot Library. The designs of the major internal components, the Log Manager, the Disk Manager, the Recovery Manager, the Transaction Manager, and the Communication Manager are given in Chapters 13–17. The final chapter of this part, Chapter 18, is a performance analysis of Camelot.

11.1 Introduction

Most computer systems projects have a simple, central goal. However, systems designers must then balance particular (lower-level) functional and performance goals (or specifications) against the constraints that govern a system's development and operation.

Our central goal in the Camelot Project was to develop a system embodying innovative techniques for simplifying the development of reliable distributed programs. There was no doubt that Camelot would utilize transaction technology.

Initially, the project needed to specify the precise collection of functions that Camelot would support; Also, performance specifications had to be developed. Fortunately, these jobs were made easier since many intended uses for the Camelot system were known.

Early on, the development and target computing environments were constrained to be Mach and C. There was the possibility of influencing the personnel and funding levels, as the funding proposal was being developed simultaneously with the design. Important constraints to take into account were the career requirements of faculty, students, and staff involved in the project.

Because most project members had built a similar system, there was a crucial head start in understanding the complexity and performance of different collections of potential functions. It was quickly realized that Camelot would require the development of 50,000 to 100,000 lines of new computer code, so great care had to be exercised to keep the complexity to a minimum.

This chapter will explore further the design and implementation of Camelot. This section continues to explain in more detail the functional and performance goals of Camelot and the constraints the implementors accepted. Then, Section 11.2 describes the top-level design of Camelot and the rationale for that design. Section 11.3 lists the major algorithms used in Camelot and provides references to more detailed descriptions of them in the subsequent chapters. Section 11.4 describes the systems work that most influenced the top-level design of Camelot. Finally, Section 11.5 provides a partial critique of Camelot from the perspective of a developer, and discusses interesting additional projects for Camelot or a similar facility.

11.1.1 Functional Goals

Camelot's design supports secure, authenticated inter-node communication; control of parallelism on a node, including the use of shared-memory multiprocessors; inter-transaction synchronization; and transaction recovery after transaction, server, node, and media failures. The following list describes these functions in more detail.

- **Distributed transactions.** Transactions simplify the maintenance of invariants on shared data and are particularly useful in distributed environments that require recovery from partial failures.
- **Nested transactions.** Nested transactions simplify handling concurrency within transactions and partial failures.
- **Transactions on both small and large quantities of data.** Supporting many types of transactions provides flexibility for a wide variety of applications.
- **Transactions on user-defined, shared objects.** Supporting user-defined objects provides flexible, high performance access to shared data. (This is similar to the goals of researchers who are developing extensible database management systems [65, 113]. However, those researchers have systems that have a more complex and functional data model.)
- **Transactions with non-blocking commit protocols.** Non-blocking commit protocols reduce the likelihood that access to data will be delayed due to node or network failures.
- **Support for relatively large data objects.** Large (multi-gigabyte) data objects are necessary to support many databases. Each Camelot server can store up to a few gigabytes, and there can be many servers per node.
- **Easily constructed applications and servers.** An easy-to-use library of powerful primitives makes it easy for UNIX/C programmers to develop clients and servers. Applications and servers are easy to write because programmers can declare and access recoverable data objects in ways very similar to normal C practice. They need only handle issues of locking, which Camelot assumes are best done by the server designer. Easily used remote procedure calls (RPCs) make accessing servers almost as easy as local procedure calls. An easy-to-use library is part-way between full linguistic support, as in Argus or Avalon [75, 49], and raw system calls.
- **Automatic management of threads.** Thread management, using Mach supplied threads of control simplifies the development of clients and servers and reduces machine dependencies in user code.

- **Support for flexible synchronization.** Logical locks, implemented within servers, and support for hybrid atomicity provide the possibility of high concurrency.

- **Flexible logging support.** In addition to local logging, Camelot provides distributed logging that permits the use of Camelot in environments where high data integrity is required and/or there is no local stable storage.

- **Simplified node configuration.** An easy-to-use node configuration application permits authorized users, whether local or across a network, to install servers on nodes, crash and recover servers, set quotas, and the like.

- **Node autonomy.** Node autonomy results from the fact that nodes can abort transactions at almost any time. There is little likelihood that a node's data can be unavailable due to a remote failure, particularly when non-blocking commitment is used.

- **Support for multiple servers per node.** Multiple servers makes possible cleanly supporting separate data abstractions and partitioning data into multiple servers. Separate servers can be installed, can crash, and can be restarted independently during normal system operation.

- **Support for multiple disks per node.** Supporting multiple disks makes possible storing large amounts of data and higher disk bandwidth.

- **Machine independent execution.** Execution on all the hardware running the Mach operating system, including shared memory multiprocessors, permits developers to purchase hardware having the lowest cost/MIPS, and to allocate the right types and sizes of processors to servers.

- **Protection from erroneous clients and servers.** A transaction processing facility should not fail due to erroneous clients or servers. At worst, a client should be able to corrupt the integrity of only the servers to which it has access and a server should only corrupt data it supports and not Camelot as a whole.

- **Support for authentication and protection.** A transaction processing facility must not only make data easy to share, but it must also provide primitives to control the use and modification of that data. Authentication and encryption facilities are the minimum facilities required. Protection against traffic analysis and denial of service attacks is also desirable, though Camelot Release 1 does not attempt to do this.

- **Appropriate documentation.** By virtue of the need to disseminate information to the technical community and to provide useful, prototype services, Camelot required both detailed technical documentation (in the form of this book and various Ph.D. theses), as well as a number of survey papers.

To varying degrees, Camelot has met all of these objectives. A somewhat detailed critique follows in Section 11.5.1.

11.1.2 Performance Goals

Camelot's performance goals apply to both normal operation and recovery after failures. The performance goals for transactions that eventually commit are as follows:

- **I/O of recoverable data.** Camelot should not add appreciably to the cost of normal I/O, and should permit servers to supply knowledge of data access patterns, thereby permitting even more efficient I/O. Additionally, Camelot must be able to perform parallel I/O to disks, up to the limits of the underlying operating system.

- **Transaction execution.** The per-transaction overhead of top-level transactions should be sufficiently low to make even short transactions feasible. The per-transaction overhead of nested-transactions should be a small constant that does not preclude their wide use.

- **Operation calls.** Camelot should not add appreciable overhead to normal RPCs.

- **Synchronization.** The cost of obtaining a free or shared logical lock should be very low: less than a thousand instructions. Access to locks previously held by other transactions may be much higher, particularly if they have been held by transactions within the same transaction family.

- **Operation on multiprocessors.** Camelot should not have bottlenecks that preclude the efficient use of shared memory multiprocessors.

- **Checkpointing.** Camelot should be able to perform checkpoints and the associated flushing of dirty pages efficiently, so as to reduce the number of log records that need to be considered during node recovery.

In all instances, Camelot should provide maximal throughput by permitting overlapped use of I/O devices, processors, and networks.

Additionally, Camelot should perform well relative to other systems on standard transaction processing benchmarks, such as ET-1 [6]. This benchmark was repeatedly run during development to test the design and implementation of the system.

Camelot's recovery processing performance goals are the following:

- **Transaction abort.** Camelot's processing of aborts should require roughly the same time as the Camelot system time in forward processing. Importantly, nodes should never have to wait for other nodes to recover before finishing an abort. (This latter goal is related to the functional goal of node autonomy, above.)

- **Node failure.** Recovery after node failure should require 10% to 100% of the cost of forward processing. The 100% cost should occur only when forward processing is doing little else but streaming log records at full speed. With checkpoint and hot-page flushing reasonably occurring every 10 minutes or so, node recovery should require between 1 and 10 minutes.

- **Media failure.** Media failure recovery should require only the time to transfer the archival dump file plus at most 10% of the execution time since the most recent archival dump was written. This could be on the order of an hour for heavily-used databases with nightly dumps.

- **Continued forward processing.** Forward processing should continue during transaction abort processing. Forward processing on operational servers should be possible during node or media recovery of other servers.

To varying degrees, Camelot meets these performance goals; see Chapter 18 for performance details and Section 11.5.1 for some specific performance criticisms.

11.1.3 Constraints

The design and implementation of Camelot were heavily influenced by the design, implementation, and schedule of Mach. The latter affected Camelot since some features of Mach were developed only as Camelot matured.

- The feature of both UNIX and Mach that most influenced Camelot is the necessity of implementing separate protected components as separate tasks. The high cost of context switching implied that Camelot had to be designed to minimize the number of times that RPCs are used to cross subsystem boundaries. On Mach, calling one local subsystem from another via RPC is about 100 to 1000 times slower than issuing a local procedure call. Sometimes Camelot's design or implementation combines two logically separate functions into one task to reduce inter-task communication. In some instances, Camelot also uses Mach's shared memory for communication.

- Calling one subsystem from another non-local subsystem is 1000 to 10000 times slower than issuing a local procedure call. This influenced Camelot to reduce the number of non-local RPCs to the minimum and to use UDP datagrams in the Transaction Manager and the distributed Log Manager (see Chapter 25).

- Control of paging I/O on Mach requires the addition of an external memory manager task [124]. I/O to secondary storage must ultimately be done using the UNIX file system calls, to either the raw or buffered file system.

- The use of Camelot had to be natural for UNIX C programmers.

There were a number of other constraints on Camelot's design, arising from the fact that it was done in a university environment. These constraints include the following:

- There had to be identifiable research that could lead to Ph.D. theses for the 5 senior graduate students on the project.

- There were roughly 15 man-years available from the beginning of the design of Camelot to its alpha-test release. This included time for designing, coding, testing, and documenting.

- Camelot's design had to be modular enough to accommodate change during implementation.

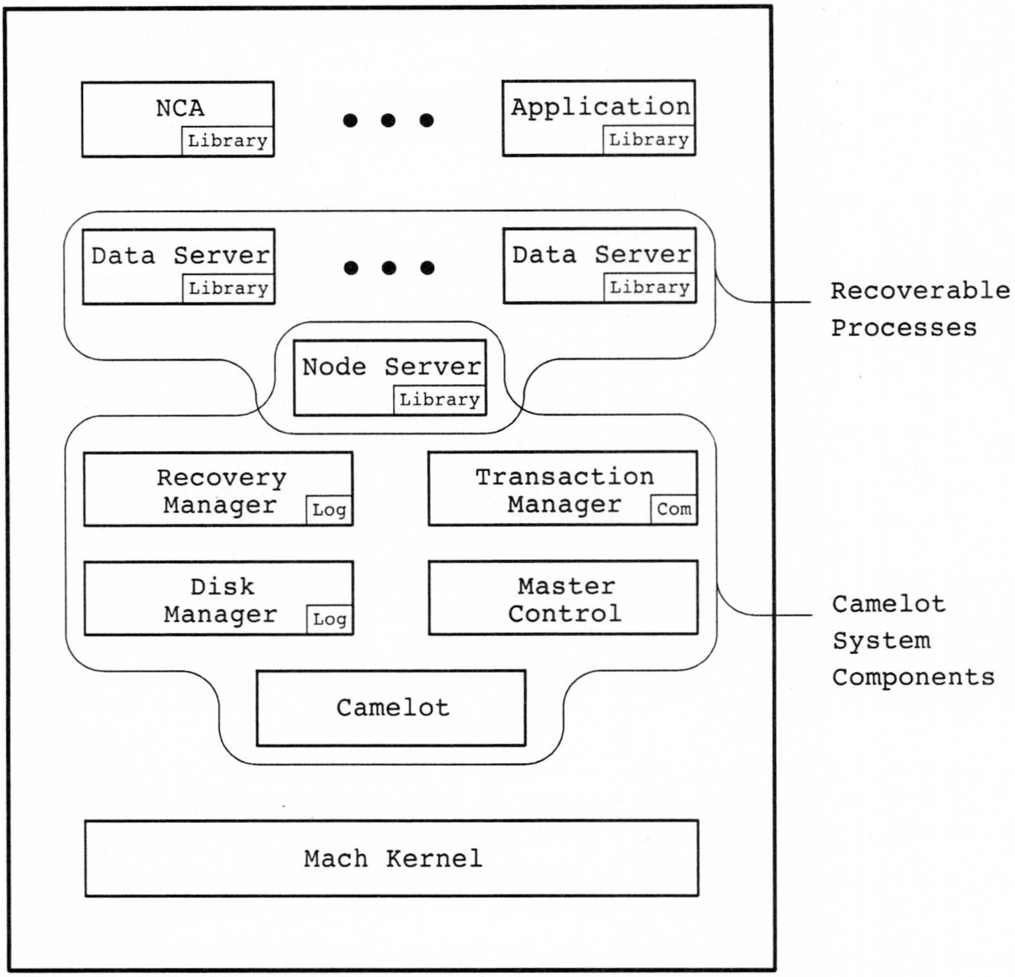

Figure 11.1: Tasks in Camelot

This figure depicts the structure of a Camelot node. The Node Server is both a part of Camelot and a Camelot data server because it is the repository of essential configuration data. The Node Configuration Application (NCA) permits users to exercise control over a node's configuration. Other data servers and applications use the facilities of Camelot and Mach.

11.2 Architecture

11.2.1 Architectural Summary

Camelot consists of nine components which run on each Camelot processing node and the Camelot Library, which is used by programmers writing applications and servers. For performance reasons, the Log Manager is loaded into the Disk and Recovery Managers. Similarly, the Communication Manager is loaded into the Transaction Manager. In addition, the distributed logging component uses one task on each log server node. As was summarized in Chapter 1 and shown in Figure 11.1, the components running on each Camelot processing node are as follows:

- **Camelot.** The Camelot task restarts Camelot after a crash using configuration data stored in the file system or interactively supplied by a user. The Camelot task calls the Master control task and passes it a collection of switches.

- **Master Control.** This task processes command line switches, and redirects failure output to an error log. It is not normally involved in the execution of Camelot, and its design is not described in this guide.

- **Disk Manager.** The Disk Manager allocates and deallocates recoverable storage, accepts and writes log records locally, and adheres to the write-ahead log protocol. The Disk Manager writes pages to or reads pages from the disk when Mach needs to service page faults on recoverable storage or to clean primary memory. It performs checkpoints to limit the amount of work required during recovery and works closely with the Recovery Manager when failures are being processed. To write log records, the Disk Manager makes calls to a copy of the Log Manager that is loaded with Disk Manager. Chapter 14 describes the design of the Disk Manager.

- **Recovery Manager.** The Recovery Manager is responsible for transaction abort, server recovery, node recovery, and media-failure recovery. Server and node recovery require one and two backward passes over the log, respectively. To access the log efficiently during recovery, a read-only copy of the Log Manager is loaded with the Recovery Manager. Chapter 15 describes the design of the Recovery Manager.

- **Log Manager.** The Log Manager writes and reads records in stable storage. For efficiency, the Log Manager is loaded in both the Disk Manager and the Recovery Manager. The copy in the Recovery Manager only allows read access. Chapter 13 describes the design of the local Log Manager.

- **Transaction Manager.** The Transaction Manager coordinates the initiation, commit, and abort of local and distributed transactions. It fully supports nested transactions. The Transaction Manager is also responsible for providing logical clock services. For efficiency, the Communications Manager is loaded with the Transaction Manager. Chapter 16 describes the design of the Transaction Manager.

- **Communication Manager.** The Communication Manager forwards inter-node Mach messages. It interacts with the Transaction Manager to piggyback data on RPCs to track the spread of transactions to other nodes. The Communication Manager also provides a name service that creates communication channels to named servers. (The Transaction Manager and distributed logging service use IP datagrams, thereby bypassing the Communication Manager.) For efficiency, the Communication Manager is loaded with the Transaction Manager. Chapter 17 describes the design of the Communication Manager.

- **Node Server.** The Node Server is the repository of configuration data necessary for restarting the node, including the mapping of recoverable segments to disk addresses. It stores its data in recoverable storage and is recovered before other servers. Portions of the design of the Node Server are described in Chapters 10 and 14.

- **Node Configuration Application.** The Node Configuration Application (NCA) permits Camelot's users to update data in the Node Server and to crash and restart servers. The NCA is a very simple Camelot application built using the Camelot Library. Its interface was described in Chapter 4.

In addition to these basic system tasks, Camelot provides an easy-to-use extension to the C programming language known as the Camelot Library. The design of the Camelot Library is described in Chapter 12.

11.2.2 Architectural Rationale

As mentioned above, a major goal of the top-level architecture of Camelot is to reduce the number of times that messages need to be exchanged between Mach tasks. This leads to a decomposition in which commonly performed functions are performed by the Camelot Library without the need to send messages. (In particular, servers may lock and modify objects without sending messages.) It also leads to the merging of the local Log Manager and Disk Manager into one task.

Shared memory could be used more extensively in Camelot if the correctness of applications and data servers were assumed. However, because Camelot must protect itself and its clients, it must execute in protected address spaces.

Code modularity was the second most important goal, and this led to the division of the Recovery Manager, Transaction Manager, and Disk Manager into separate tasks. The Recovery Manager is not active and hence rarely communicates with any task, so it was an obvious candidate to become a separate task. The Transaction Manager and Disk Manager communicate only once or twice for write transactions. The Transaction Manager and Communication Manager communicate frequently and have to maintain much shared state, so we ultimately determined that the two should be combined into one address space. The Camelot Project decided that the benefits of being able to more easily develop separate tasks outweighed the slight performance benefits that would have accrued from having a single, large task.

11.3 Algorithms

This section contains a list of some of the key algorithms used by Camelot and references to the chapters that describe them:

- Chapter 12 describes the thread management and runtime data structures and algorithms used in the Camelot Library.

- Chapter 13 describes the algorithms for manipulating the log, including how the group commit optimization is done.
- Chapters 14 and 15 describe the common log, recoverable virtual memory, and write-ahead logging algorithms.
- Chapter 16 describes the intra-family locking, two-phase commit, non-blocking commit, and transaction abort processing algorithms.
- Chapter 17 describes the technique used to track the spread of distributed transactions.

11.4 Related Systems Work

A number of systems projects have had an influence on Camelot. Two with a major impact are IMS and R* [53, 122], both of which have transaction processing components designed to support a particular database model. Internally, portions of Camelot's synchronization, recovery, and commit algorithms are direct descendants of those in IMS or R*. TMF and CICS [52, 44] are early commercial systems that also substantially influenced the collection of functions that we decided to incorporate in Camelot.

A number of transactional file systems have been built: The Locus transactional file system [121] and the Alpine system [16] are two of the more complete ones. These influenced Camelot somewhat less than the systems described above, mostly because their transaction implementation was developed for a somewhat restrictive data type (the file).

Argus [75], TABS [105, 106], CPR [18], and Quicksilver [42] are four other systems with goals similar to those of Camelot. The details vary in a number of ways such as the attention paid to ease of use, practicality, security, performance, machine independence, etc. Camelot benefited primarily from Argus and TABS, as information on CPR and Quicksilver became available only after Camelot was designed.

11.4.1 R*

Camelot is similar in a number of ways to R*. R* is a distributed database management system, developed at IBM San Jose Research, that supports transactions on relational database servers [66]. The transaction facility of R* is implemented by a combination of the underlying operating system, CICS [52] and a component called TM*. Together these components permit data servers to register themselves and their operations when they are ready to receive requests, and they perform routing of operation requests to local data servers. Data servers create a local context for each client, and additional requests are routed to the appropriate context. The facility also issues transaction identifiers, oversees transaction commitment and abortion, and does deadlock detection.

Data servers in R* have two types of interfaces. The first type includes operations specific to a data server. (These would be defined in Camelot as MIG `camelotroutines`.) The second type includes operations required for transaction management, deadlock detection/resolution, and remote access by other data servers. (These latter operations are similar to those in Camelot's data server-Transaction Manager, Transaction Manager-data server, and data server-Recovery Manager interfaces described in Part II.) In R*, requests are never directly issued to remote data servers. Instead, they are passed to local data servers, which then interact with remote ones.

Though Camelot and R* both provide transaction facilities to applications and data servers, they differ in many ways. For example, Camelot, its applications, and its data servers are implemented as a collection of processes that communicate via messages, rather than via the protected procedure calls, which R* uses. Camelot can invoke remote data servers directly in a transparent fashion. Also, Camelot data servers use both a common log and recovery algorithms provided by the system, while data servers in R* must provide for their own recovery. Internally, Camelot data servers can use any Mach-supplied thread of control to process an operation, while R* requires operations from a transaction to continually reuse the same CICS-supplied thread. Camelot provides substantial linguistic support for writing data servers, via the Camelot and Strongbox Libraries. Camelot was intended to support many data servers and data types while R* was intended primarily to support distributed relational databases.

11.4.2 Argus

Argus is a programming language developed at the MIT Laboratory for Computer Science that supports transactions and user-defined types on which transactions can operate [69, 70, 72, 75].

Internally, Argus contains many facilities that are analogous to those of Camelot and R*. However, it also provides a programming language, similar to CLU [71], with which to use these facilities. Some objects can be implemented without the type implementor having to consider synchronization or recovery issues. However, types needing highly concurrent access require explicit attention to synchronization and recovery. For these high concurrency types, synchronization and recovery are done with the aid of a specialized object, called a *mutex*, rather than via explicit locking and logging.

Data servers may request exclusive access to a mutex, release exclusive access to a mutex, and temporarily release access to a mutex. In the latter case, they are reawakened by the system after a certain interval has passed. Inter-transaction synchronization is done with a data server first gaining access to a mutex and then evaluating a predicate on (permanent) stored data. From this predicate, a data server can determine if it can proceed or if it must pause and await another transaction's commitment. In the latter case, the data server can temporarily release access to the mutex and re-apply the predicate after it been awakened by the system. Argus achieves permanence of effect because it guarantees that mutex objects will be written to stable storage before the transaction that has modified them commits.

Argus makes it easier to program certain types of reliable applications than does Camelot. Camelot always requires the use of locks and special macros for accessing recoverable objects. Argus also has a programming model that makes it more difficult for the programmer to make subtle mistakes. Camelot's advantages lie with some of its implementation techniques (e.g., attention paid to machine independence, write-ahead logging, support for very large objects, etc.) and the flexibility of its programming interface. While programmers can get themselves into trouble, the extended and primitive interfaces can support a very wide variety of data servers, and even permit implementors to provide entirely new programming interfaces. Further, Camelot provides the support necessary to implement high-level languages such as Avalon as described in Part IV.

11.5 Conclusions

11.5.1 Design and Implementation Weaknesses

Camelot's design goals have proven to be reasonable. However, Camelot would be more useful if it met some additional requirements:

- **An open log.** The Camelot Log Manager permits use only by the Camelot Disk Manager, Recovery Manager, and Transaction Manager. While recoverable storage can obviate the need for other recovery mechanisms, servers may nonetheless wish to implement their own recovery techniques using a private buffer pool and recovery algorithm. Having interfaces to permit them to read from and write to the common log would be valuable to them.

- **Better portability and interoperability.** Many Camelot components (e.g., the Transaction Manager) could have been implemented more portably, increasing the utility of the Camelot code base. Camelot would be more useful if it supported access to transaction services on other platforms.

- **More flexible locking.** A locking mechanism that better supported intention locks [38] would be a useful addition to the Library.

In retrospect, the choice of algorithms for Camelot seems to have been reasonable. Despite the fact that the Camelot team did not understand the complexity of efficient checkpointing, distributed abort, and communication until near the end of the Camelot implementation effort, the resultant algorithms appear to work satisfactorily and to be reasonably close to what is needed.

However, there are a number of implementation details that did not turn out well. For example, the recoverable storage allocator has too much overhead, and a simpler storage allocation algorithm should be used. Insufficient attention was paid to the performance of recovery, so it can be slow under some circumstances. Many Camelot components are overly complicated and should be rewritten to simplify them, and enhance their reliability. For example, the Transaction Manager should be rewritten to be table driven. Overall, the system is not reliable, and an enormous amount of additional work would be required to make it so.

The performance evaluation of Camelot has many gaps in it, despite the substantial amount of work that has been done. For example, when running the ET-1 benchmark, there are occasional transactions that become delayed for a second or so, and the reason is still unclear. Also, there has been little evaluation of the use of Camelot on multiprocessors. Camelot is designed to effectively use multiple CPUs per node, but this aspect of the design has hardly been tested.

Perhaps the greatest weakness of Camelot was the lack of component testing as the system was developed. Due to a lack of formal code review and testing processes, too many bugs were found via the stress testing of the complete system. Because of the complexity of a system like Camelot, this lack of a sufficiently careful development methodology will prevent Camelot from achieving the reliability required for production systems.

11.5.2 Future Work

There are many interesting features and algorithms to add to a system such as Camelot. As discussed above, an open log could be provided, and Camelot could be made to be more portable and interoperable. Listed below are some other interesting projects. Some of them are good research problems; others are straightforward.

- Operation (or transition) logging, to permit higher concurrency and reduced log space requirements, would be a benefit for many applications.

- Support for transaction priorities and deadlock detection might make the system more useful in environments with more critical response time requirements. Deadlock detection involving arbitrary abstract types in a large environment (e.g., the Internet) may be difficult and possibly impractical.

- A recoverable abstract data type library would simplify the job of building servers. For example, an ISAM or VSAM package would make it much easier to write database-like applications.

- Recoverable segments that can be shared by (e.g., mapped into) multiple servers *simultaneously* would provide another strategy for gaining parallelism on loosely coupled systems. This *data sharing* model would be a major addition and it would permit Camelot to be the basis for closely coupled multiprocessing, as well as distributed systems. Work on appropriate locking to support this model has just been completed [43].

- A system like Camelot should contain tools that simplify performance measurement and testing. A data capture tool would collect performance data and permit clients to gauge critical performance metrics such as the number of messages, page faults, deadlocks, and transactions per second. A workload distributing component would distribute applications (or synthetic workloads) to multiple nodes on the system to provide the loading needed for performance evaluation and testing. A fault insertion component would permit simulated faults to be inserted according to a pre-specified distribution. This component is crucial for understanding the behavior of both Camelot and applications running on it.

Overall, Camelot's designers believe that Camelot has achieved its goal of demonstrating a coherent design for a general purpose transaction facility for UNIX-like environments. While there are some flaws in both Camelot's design and implementation, Camelot is a workable prototype that is useful both for elucidating certain concepts in distributed systems and as a basis for experimentation.

Chapter 12

The Design of the Camelot Library

Joshua J. Bloch

12.1 Introduction

The basic purpose of the Camelot Library is to facilitate the construction of Camelot servers and applications by C programmers. The primitive Camelot interface, described in Part II of this guide, is very powerful but inconvenient to use directly. In order to use the primitive Camelot interface, the programmer must involve himself in numerous low level protocols; he must pin and log changes to recoverable objects, process recovery requests in the event of an abort or server crash, and create, join, commit, and abort transactions. The commit and abort protocols are themselves complex multistage operations. The programmer must concern himself with numerous low level data objects like communication ports, transaction ID's, object descriptors and semaphores. In addition, the programmer must implement several necessary functions that are not provided by the primitive interface, like lock management for recoverable objects and thread management for concurrent operations.

It is our contention that the great majority of the low level detail in the primitive interface is of no concern to the average programmer. With the Camelot Library, we aim to provide a much higher level model of the services offered by the Camelot system that enables the programmer to take advantage of the power offered by Camelot, while ignoring the bulk of its complexity. We also aim to implement the functionality required by most servers and applications that is not implemented by the primitive interface.

12.1.1 Functional Goals

Broadly, the functional goals of the Camelot Library were to provide a Camelot interface for C programmers with the following properties:

- **Ease of Use** - The process of creating servers and applications should be natural and straightforward; the programmer should not have to bend over backwards to achieve desired effects.
- **Elegance** - Source programs should be terse, readable and esthetically pleasing.

- **Simplicity** - The facility should be easy to learn.
- **Power** - It should be possible to create a very wide variety of servers and applications using the facility.

Most servers and applications require various functions that are not implemented by the modules comprising the Camelot system. Our goals of elegance, ease of use and simplicity dictated that the Library should implement these functions. The major new functions implemented by the Library are listed below:

- **Message Dispatching** - Servers must open a communication channel and monitor it for incoming requests. Multiple threads must be available to service requests, in order to prevent concurrent transactions from deadlocking and to increase throughput. Both servers and applications must monitor communication channels for system messages. Again, multithreading is essential to ensure liveness. The Library implements a multithreaded message dispatcher which serves as the basic framework for servers and applications.
- **System Message Processing** - Both servers and applications must process and respond to system messages from the Transaction Manager and, in the case of servers, the Recovery Manager. The Library performs this function invisibly. In order to do so, it must maintain a database of information about all transactions in progress.
- **Lock Management** - The protocols specified by the primitive Camelot interface ensure atomicity and permanence of transactions, but it is primarily the responsibility of the server to ensure serializability. The Library provides a shared/exclusive mode lock manager for this purpose.
- **Explicit Concurrency** - The primitive Camelot interface allows servers and applications to run multiple concurrent subtransactions. It is the responsibility of the server or application to allocate threads with which to execute the subtransactions and to ensure that the threads do not interfere with one another. The Library primitives for concurrent subtransactions perform these functions.
- **Execution Control** - When a transaction aborts, the Camelot system ensures that all servers and applications participating in the transaction are made aware of the abort and ensures that any changes to recoverable objects made by the aborted transaction are undone. But it does not ensure that program threads operating on behalf of the transaction are handled appropriately, allowing the servers and applications to get on with their work. This task is the responsibility of the servers and applications. It is complicated by the fact that threads may be waiting for responses to server calls, or for locks to break. The Library handles this task in a fully automatic, invisible fashion, so that the server or application appears to continue execution immediately after the end of the block corresponding to the aborted transaction.
- **Exception Reporting** - The Library integrates an exception reporting mechanism into its execution control mechanism. When execution resumes after a transaction aborts, a status code is returned, which allows the program to determine the cause of the abort and handle the exception as the programmer sees fit.

In addition to the essential functions listed above, the Library implements several other facilities useful to many servers. One such facility is a recoverable storage allocator, which allows servers to manipulate dynamic recoverable data objects. Another such facility is a "house cleaner", which aborts transactions that remain uncommitted at a server for an excessive period of time. This frees the locks and other resources that were tied up at the server by the long-running transaction. The programmer specifies how long transactions can remain uncommitted at a server before they are automatically aborted.

12.1.2 Performance Goals

The primary performance goal for the Camelot Library was that servers and applications written with the Library should run almost as fast as well written hand coded servers and applications written directly on top of the primitive Camelot interface.

12.1.3 Constraints

The greatest constraint on the Camelot Library was that it had to be quick to design and implement. A single programmer was available for the task. Project scheduling constraints dictated that the Library achieve limited functionality within a few months of initial design, and full functionality within a year.

12.2 Architecture

In this section, we discuss the architecture of the Camelot Library. The section is divided into three parts. In the first part, we discuss the implementation architecture of the Library itself. In the second part, we discuss the interface presented by the Library from a linguistic design standpoint. In the third part, we discuss the internal structure of servers and applications constructed with the Library.

12.2.1 Implementation

As its name implies, the Camelot Library is implemented as an ordinary C library: a collection of functions and a header file to go with them. However, it is very different in character from the typical C library in that it exports many macros and significantly extends the syntax and semantics of the C language. Thus, it can be considered an *embedded language*. Such embedded languages are common in the Lisp community.

Implementing the Camelot programming facility as a library has advantages and disadvantages. Other possible implementations included a new compiler, modifications to an existing C compiler, and a preprocessor to be run prior to C compilation.

The greatest advantage of the embedded language implementation is the speed with which it can be created. Much of the time-consuming effort involved in writing a compiler capable of generating reasonable quality code is avoided by inheriting this facility from a pre-existing C compiler. Another major advantage of this approach is that it allows the programmer to use many existing support tools designed for C programs, like Lint, the program checker, and various source level debuggers. The effectiveness of these tools is reduced somewhat by the fact that the information they generate can refer to C code in macro expansions of Library constructs. This information will not always be meaningful to the programmer.

The greatest disadvantage of the embedded language implementation is the set of restrictions that it places on the syntax and semantics of the language. This problem is exacerbated by the well known shortcomings of the C macro preprocessor (CPP). Another disadvantage of the embedded language implementation is that syntax errors can cause confusing compiler error messages, which can refer to C code generated by the macro preprocessor, one step removed from the actual source code. For example, an attempt to modify an undeclared recoverable object, x, will yield four identical error messages, "x: Unrecognizable field name." A more pernicious form of the same problem is that misuse of Library constructs can generate syntactically valid C code that is totally incorrect. The compiler has no way of detecting this, since it does not know about the new constructs at a sufficiently high level.

While writing a new compiler allows complete flexibility in defining the syntax and semantics of the language, and permits construction of a complete error checking facility, it was clearly out of the question due to manpower and time constraints. Modifying an existing C compiler has similar advantages to writing a new one, without such great implementation costs. But both of these approaches share two major disadvantages that precluded their use. First, adopting either approach would have placed us in the position of maintaining a portable C compiler and related support tools. This would have required far more manpower than we had available, and conflicted with our project goals. Second, these approaches would have forced us to use the same compiler on every machine that runs Camelot. With the embedded language approach, we can use the C compiler best suited to each machine. This is particularly important for novel processor architectures, where the compiler does machine specific optimizations like register allocation, for a RISC machine, or instruction scheduling, for a pipelined architecture.

The preprocessor approach is actually quite similar to the embedded language approach. Both rely on a library of C functions for runtime support. The only difference is that writing a special purpose preprocessor allows greater flexibility in defining the syntax of the language. In exchange for this flexibility, several disadvantages are incurred. Writing a preprocessor can be quite a large undertaking, depending on how powerful it is. Syntax error messages for any errors that are not caught by the preprocessor can be extremely cryptic, as the messages are generated on the basis of C code that is two preprocessing stages removed from the source program. It is, at best, extremely inconvenient to use pre-existing C language support tools, as these tools must be applied to the preprocessor output, which may bear little textual resemblance to the original source code. A final disadvantage of the preprocessor approach is that the additional preprocessing phase can add significantly to compilation times.

The main advantage of a preprocessor implementation over an embedded language, greater flexibility in defining the syntax of the language, is a mixed blessing. While it would have allowed us to avoid awkward syntax, it would also have allowed us to produce a language that was very different from C. Since it was our goal to make a facility that was easy for C programmers to learn and use, we wanted to keep our language as close as possible to C. Specifically, we wished only to extend C, not to change it, and to keep our extensions in the spirit of C. While a preprocessor implementation would not have precluded this goal, it would have required great care and restraint in designing the interface in order to achieve the goal. On balance, we felt that the advantages of an embedded language implementation over a preprocessor implementation outweighed the disadvantages.

12.2.2 Interface

In designing the interface presented by the Camelot Library, we pursued the goals outlined in Section 12.1.1. In doing so, we found several basic design principles emerging. In this section, we outline these principles and discuss our interface in terms of them.

Design Principles

A basic underlying principle we followed in designing our interface was that it should be as small as possible. Specifically, the number of new constructs should be kept to a minimum, and the number of arguments to each new construct should be kept to a minimum. Each argument to a new construct should express some real information that the Library needs *from the programmer* in order to perform its function. The programmer should never have to pass information from one Library construct to another if the Library could keep track of this information automatically. For example, the Camelot primitive to initialize a server returns a number of ports (communication channels) that the server must use to communicate with the various Camelot system tasks. The Library never passes these ports on to the programmer, but uses the appropriate port invisibly whenever a message needs to be sent to one of the components.

If the Library could guess the value of an argument to a construct correctly, the programmer should not have to specify this argument, except in cases where the Library's guess would be wrong. In other words, the argument should default to its usual value if it is unspecified. Unfortunately, C does not provide any good mechanism for implementing default argument values. The approach we have taken is to provide two versions of constructs for which we would like to have default argument values. The simple version always uses the default(s). The extended version allows the programmer to specify the values of the arguments in question. The extended version always has the name of the simple version followed by the characters "_2". While this approach increases the number of constructs in the Library, it greatly reduces the number of arguments in frequently used constructs. The net result is that programmers generally have fewer arguments to worry about and programs are much neater.

The "minimalist" principles outlined in the preceding paragraphs advance our goals of ease of use, elegance and simplicity. Unfortunately, these three goals conflict with our fourth goal, that our language be powerful. This is one of the basic problems that face language designers. All languages represent a tradeoff among our four goals. If a language consists of a small number of low level primitives, it may be simple and powerful, but programs will be long and difficult to write (e.g., pure Lisp). If a language consists of a small number of high level primitives, programs may be short and easy to write, but the language will be limited in terms of the range of programs that can be written without using the constructs in unreasonable and inefficient ways (e.g., special purpose languages like RPG II). If a language consists of many high level primitives, it will be difficult to learn and compilers will be difficult to construct (e.g., Ada).

Our approach to the tradeoff was to first design a core of fairly high level primitives according to the minimalist principles described above. This core is powerful enough to construct a large class of servers and applications, while retaining simplicity, elegance and ease of use. Then we extended the core with some lower level primitives that allow programmers with special needs to construct more complex servers and applications.

For example, our core language makes no reference to ports, and the average programmer can completely ignore their existence. Occasionally, a programmer may wish to have a server issue ports to clients, and have the clients use them explicitly, for purposes of authentication (i.e., use them as *capabilities*). For this programmer, we provide the `UNLISTED_SERVER` and `THIS_PORT` constructs. These constructs allow a client to explicitly specify a send port when doing a remote procedure call (RPC), and allow a server to determine the port on which the RPC arrived.

While the added lower level primitives increase the size and the difficulty of the language, they can be ignored until (and unless) the programmer feels a need for them. In effect, they produce a "bi-level" language, which gives the average programmer the advantages of a high level language while allowing the exceptional programmer the full power of the underlying low level language.

Care was taken to ensure that the added low level primitives interact well with the high level core. For instance, the `UNLISTED_SERVER` construct takes the place of the server name parameter in the standard `SERVER_CALL` primitive. The syntactic change to the call neatly mirrors the semantic change: instead of addressing the server by its name, the programmer addresses it by its port.

Designing a language *extension* that is simple, elegant and easy to use requires special care. The base language, in this case C, presents the programmer with a model of his environment. When we add a new construct to the language, we should think in terms of how it affects that model. New constructs should exploit the paradigms already implicit in the programmer's model of the base language. In this way, the programmer does not have to learn the new constructs from scratch. He merely observes that some element of the extended model is like some element of the base model. Once he has made this observation, he should be able to use the all of the relevant new constructs by analogy. New constructs should interact with the base language in a predictable fashion.

For example, we wanted to give servers the ability to manipulate recoverable memory. The C paradigm for memory is the variable. C programmers know that variables have a type and a value, and can be declared, read, modified, passed to functions and so forth. By the principles outlined in the previous paragraph, the best way to give servers the ability to manipulate recoverable memory is to add to the language a new storage class with all of these same properties. This is exactly the approach we took.

From the programmer's standpoint, recoverable objects are like C global variables with several exceptions. Only servers can have recoverable objects. They are transaction consistent (assuming appropriate locks are secured prior to access), and persist across server crashes. They must be declared, accessed and modified using only the appropriate Library constructs. Beyond these few exceptions, recoverable objects are just like any other C variables. They can be passed to functions. Pointers can be taken to them, or to components of them. Pointer arithmetic on these pointers works properly, and so forth. Thus, the programmer's previous knowledge of C allows him to manipulate recoverable objects with little effort.

Interface Design Summary

We summarize the design of our interface in terms of the design principles outlined above. Library constructs are broken into six groups, corresponding to the six major elements that the Library adds to the model presented by the C language. We make note of design decisions that shaped our interface.

The first addition to the C model consists of the two classes of programs that can be written with the Library, *servers* and *applications*. Typically, servers are programs whose function is to process RPCs on a collection of abstract data objects, in a transaction-consistent manner. Servers can declare and manipulate recoverable objects, process RPCs, create transactions, and perform RPCs to other servers. The primitives to create a server are INITIALIZE_SERVER and START_SERVER. From the programmer's standpoint, INITIALIZE_SERVER identifies the program as a server, and START_SERVER causes the server to start processing RPCs.

Ideally, the programmer would merely label certain functions in his server as external, and the server would automatically accept RPCs for these functions. Unfortunately, this is not feasible in a library implementation. Thus we require the programmer to specify the external interface to his server using MIG (see Section 2.4.2). MIG translates the interface specification into a set of server stubs, and provides a function that demultiplexes an incoming message to the appropriate external function via the appropriate server stub. The programmer passes the MIG-generated demultiplexor function on to the Library as the first argument of the START_SERVER construct.

The Library automatically handles the commit and abort protocols for transactions with which the server is involved, so the average programmer can ignore the existence of these protocols. However, the exceptional programmer may want a server to take special actions at various phases in the commit and abort processing of transactions. An extended version of INITIALIZE_SERVER is provided that allows the programmer to specify functions to be executed at critical points in the commit and abort protocols.

Applications are merely C programs that can create transactions and perform RPCs to servers. The Library construct to create an application is INITIALIZE_APPLICATION. This construct returns a boolean value indicating whether or not Camelot is running on the application's node.

If Camelot is not running, the program cannot create transactions, but is allowed to perform RPCs to remote servers at nodes where Camelot is running. The program is said to run as a *limited application*. The programmer must take special care if he desires to write a program that can run as a limited application, as an attempt to start a transaction from within a limited application will cause the program to die.

The second addition to the C model is the new runtime environment, the *transaction*. It is here that we most aggressively pursued our minimalist design principles. In the primitive interface, a *transaction identifier* (TID) is issued by the Transaction Manager when a transaction is begun, and must be passed explicitly each time the program wishes to take action on behalf of the transaction. A single thread of control can begin multiple transactions with several calls to TA_Begin (or a single call to TA_GetTids), and act on behalf of any of these transactions. We felt that our goals of ease of use and elegance would be best advanced by restricting each thread to operate on behalf of a single transaction at any given time. This restriction permits the Library to hide the TID from the programmer, using it as necessary, so that the programmer need not be aware of its existence. In essence, the current transaction becomes a hidden attribute of a thread. The THIS_TID primitive is provided for the exceptional programmer who needs to know the TID under which a thread is running, but this primitive is definitely a low level component in our bi-level taxonomy. The average programmer need not be aware that TIDs exist.

The basic Library construct to create a transaction is the *transaction block*, delimited by the keywords BEGIN_TRANSACTION and END_TRANSACTION. The *transaction block* is a scoped environment, syntactically and semantically similar to C's curly braces block. The transaction environment is dynamically scoped: if a function is called from within the scope of a transaction, the thread that called the function is still running under the transaction, even though it is lexically outside the transaction block. We briefly considered lexical scoping for ease of implementation, but quickly abandoned the idea because the resulting construct was inelegant. Lexical scoping would have prevented transactions from making proper use of C's basic construct for structured programming, the function call. When transaction blocks are (dynamically) nested, nested transactions result.

The *top-level transaction block* construct is provided to create a new top-level transaction from within the scope of another transaction. When a new transaction family is created with the *transaction block* or *top-level transaction block* construct, the transaction type for new family defaults to *new value logging, standard*, and the commit protocol defaults to *two phased*. An extended version of the top-level transaction block construct is provided that allows the programmer to specify the transaction type and commit protocol for the new family. We anticipate that many programmers will be able to use the basic calls without worrying about the concepts of transaction type and commit protocol.

Two basic primitives are provided to abort transactions. The `ABORT` primitive aborts the (innermost) enclosing transaction, and the `ABORT_TOP_LEVEL` primitive aborts the top-level enclosing transaction (i.e., the entire family of the transaction under which the calling thread is currently running). It is not possible to abort an intermediate level transaction using these primitives. We feel that this is something that programmers will rarely, if ever, want to do. However, in keeping with our bi-level design philosophy, the exceptional programmer who desires this effect can achieve it with the `ABORT_NAMED_TRANSACTION` primitive, which takes a TID argument in addition to an abort code.

The abort primitives allow the programmer to pass an abort code to the status variable in the `END_TRANSACTION` delimiter of the aborted transaction. This produces a powerful exception reporting mechanism, whereby any thread executing on behalf of a transaction can "raise an exception" by aborting the transaction with a code expressing the reason for the abort. The thread issuing the abort need not be running on the same node as the thread that created the transaction; the abort will propagate across machine boundaries as necessary, and the thread that created the transaction will continue execution immediately following the transaction block representing the aborted transaction. The thread that created the transaction can examine the status code for the abort, and handle the exception as the programmer sees fit.

The third addition to the C model is a new storage class, the *recoverable object*. As discussed in **Design Principles**, above, recoverable objects are long lived, transaction consistent analogues of C's global variables. Unlike global variables, all of a server's recoverable objects must be declared in a single declaration block. Our interface might have been more elegant if programmers could declare recoverable objects separately in each file, or even declare recoverable objects whose scope was restricted to arbitrary code blocks (analogous to C's static storage class). However, this would not have been feasible to implement. Even if we were not restricted by a library implementation, it would be difficult to come up with reasonable semantics, given that recoverable objects persist while programs change over time. With a single recoverable object declaration block, we merely prevent the user from changing the total size of the variables declared in the block, and trust him not to change the layout of the block. No obvious analogue to this policy exists if multiple declarations are allowed.

The `REC` and `MODIFY` constructs (defined in Section 3.4.2) are not necessary from an interface design standpoint. Their existence is an unfortunate consequence of the fact that we chose to do a library implementation. A compiler or preprocessor could automatically recognize uses of recoverable static variables and execute the proper procedure to examine or modify them. The `REC` and `MODIFY` constructs are representative of the syntactic penalty we paid for choosing a library implementation. They don't reduce the power of the language, or even make it much more difficult to use. They just make it a bit less pretty, in a fairly superficial sense.

Recoverable analogues of the `malloc` and `free` calls are provided to allow programmers to construct dynamic recoverable objects. This facility is very useful, as all of a server's static recoverable objects must be known at compile time, but it is desirable that servers be able to create new recoverable objects in response to RPCs.

Advanced calls are provided that allow programmers with prior knowledge of data access patterns to increase the performance of the underlying virtual memory system by prefetching recoverable objects from disk prior to use, or flushing them out to disk when they are no longer needed. Use of this facility is only warranted when large amounts of recoverable data are being accessed.

The fourth addition to the C model is a new abstract data object, the *lock*. A major design decision regarding locks was that they should be visible to the programmer. It would have been possible for the Library to automatically obtain locks prior to reading and writing recoverable objects, allowing the programmer to ignore their existence. We liked this approach for its simplicity, but felt that it represented an excessive restriction on the power of our language. While automatic locking ensures serializability of transactions, it can decrease concurrency, increase locking overhead and cause transactions to deadlock. Only the programmer has sufficient knowledge to determine the appropriate granularity for locking, and the appropriate type of lock to seek prior to performing an operation.

We provide blocking and nonblocking primitives for obtaining locks. Ordinarily, the programmer does not release locks explicitly: they are automatically released by the Library when transactions commit or abort. In this manner, strict two-phase locking is enforced. Occasionally, the programmer may wish to release a lock early, when he knows that it is safe to do so, in order to increase concurrency. The `UNLOCK` primitive is provided for this purpose. In a similar vein, the `DEMOTE_LOCK` primitive allows the programmer to demote write locks to read locks. Lock inheritance among transactions in the same family is handled automatically by the Library.

Another design decision concerning the locking portion of our interface was the choice of the space of objects on which locks are held. One possibility was the recoverable objects themselves. However, it would have been difficult to deal properly with the fact that objects can intersect one another arbitrarily.[1] We chose instead to implement a *logical locking* facility, wherein locks are held on names, which the programmer associates with recoverable objects as he sees fit. In order to prevent the set of lock names from being a shared global name space, lock names are qualified with a *lock name space*, as described in Section 3.6.7. Lock names are chosen from the set of 32-bit integers. In the common case wherein recoverable objects do not intersect, it is trivial to generate a 32-bit integer for an object that results in correct locking behavior. We provide a macro (`LOCK_NAME`) for this purpose. The integers also serve as a convenient name space for a wide variety of logical locking schemes. For example, array indices can be used as lock names for array elements. Finally, the use of integers as lock names works out well from an implementation perspective, since lock names must be hashed frequently, and integers can be hashed very quickly.

The fifth addition to the C model consists of two new types of function calls, *server calls* and *wrapped server calls*. These constructs allow applications and servers to make RPCs to servers. A server call can only be made from within the scope of a transaction, and the call executes in the same transactional scope at the server. A wrapped server call differs from a server call in that it

[1] *Range locking* [102] solves this problem, but it is much more complex to implement than traditional locking disciplines.

can be made outside of the scope of a transaction, and the call is "wrapped" in a new top-level transaction at the server. Wrapped server calls are thus legal from limited applications, which cannot create transactions. The ARGS and NOARGS keywords required in the SERVER_CALL and WRAP_SERVER_CALL constructs serve no real purpose in our interface. They are workarounds for a shortcoming in the C preprocessor.[2]

The sixth and final addition to the C model is a computational entity, the *thread*. Multiple threads of control execute concurrently in Camelot Library programs. These threads fall into three broad categories. Servers use multiple threads to service RPCs concurrently, in order to prevent deadlock and yield adequate throughput. All Camelot Library programs have *system threads*, which run in the background to perform transaction processing and other essential system functions. Finally, various constructs are provided that allow Camelot Library programs to create concurrent threads explicitly. These primitives are typically used to perform concurrent RPCs on multiple servers, and less commonly, to utilize a multiprocessor effectively.

The processing of system messages is fairly routine. By our minimalist design principles, the programmer should not have to concern himself with this task, or even be aware of the system messages' existence. Thus the threads that perform this task should be completely invisible to the programmer. But it would be an unacceptable restriction on the power of our interface if the exceptional programmer who wished to take special action on receipt of system messages were unable to do so. Thus we provide an alternate version of INITIALIZE_SERVER that allows the programmer to supply *prepare*, *commit* and *abort procedures*, which are executed on receipt of the appropriate system message.

The basic constructs for explicit concurrency are the *cobegin block* and the *cofor block*. In their normal form, they create subtransactions of the current transaction, and the thread running on behalf of the current transaction pauses until the subtransactions complete. This discipline ensures that normal locking procedures are sufficient to enforce serializability, so the programmer does not have to worry about the effects of concurrency. Unfortunately, there is some cost associated with creating the subtransactions. Generally the cost should not be prohibitive, but occasionally a programmer may wish to use concurrency in a performance-critical application where the cost would be intolerable. The THREAD construct is provided for these situations. Use of this construct requires extreme caution, as locking is no longer sufficient to prevent co-modification, or viewing of inconsistent data.

In the cofor and cobegin blocks, only a single pointer-sized argument can be passed to the functions that run in the new threads. This is a necessary consequence of the Library implementation. While it is somewhat inelegant, it does not represent a real restriction on the power of the constructs. An arbitrary number of parameters can be transmitted by passing a pointer to an argument block structure, as described in Section 3.6.2.

The cofor and cobegin block constructs are *synchronous*; they do not allow programs to create "background threads" that runs concurrently with the thread that created them. The primitive CONCURRENT_THREAD is provided for this purpose. The new thread created by this primitive initially runs outside the scope of a transaction. It is a conscious omission that no primitive is provided to create a background thread that runs under the scope of the calling transaction. While such a primitive would increase the power of our language, it would fundamentally change its character, making it far less structured. As it stands, the programmer is guaranteed that when

[2]The technical term for this technique is "ugly hack".

a thread reaches the end of a transaction block, all unaborted work undertaken on behalf of the transaction and its descendants has completed. Such a primitive would destroy this guarantee. Additionally, it would create serializability problems like those of the `THREAD` primitive, made more severe by the fact that the calling thread would generally have no way of knowing when the background thread had completed.

12.2.3 Server and Application Structure

In this section, we describe the internal workings of servers and applications built with the Camelot Library. The section is divided into three parts. In the first part, we discuss process structure. In the second part, we discuss data structures. In the third part, we discuss algorithms.

Process Structure

Camelot Library servers and applications are Mach tasks, which support multiple threads of control. Initially, all C programs are created with a single thread. The Camelot Library creates additional threads at various points in the lifetimes of servers and applications, using the primitives provided by the C Threads Library (Chapter 7.3).

When a server's initial thread executes the `INITIALIZE_SERVER` primitive, three additional threads are created. Two of these threads are *system message handlers*. They wait on a port for messages from the Transaction Manager and the Recovery Manager. When a message comes in on this port, one of the system message handlers receives the message, performs the appropriate function, sends a reply message if required, and waits on the port for another message. In other words, these threads invisibly handle the server's part of the commit, abort and recovery protocols. The third thread created by `INITIALIZE_SERVER`, the *notify handler*, is relatively unimportant. Whenever a port on which the server has receive rights dies, Mach automatically sends an *emergency message* on the server's *notify port*. The notify handler waits on this port, and if a port death message corresponding to a port that is critical to the server's operation arrives, the notify handler prints an appropriate error message and kills the server.

When a system message handler receives a message, it checks to see if any other system message handlers are free (i.e., waiting for incoming system messages). If all of the other system message handlers are busy, the handler that received the message creates an additional system message handler before it processes the message. In this way, the server ensures that there will always be at least one system message handler free to handle an incoming system message. This property is critical to proper server operation. Extra threads created in response to demand are never terminated, as they consume virtually no more resources waiting on a port than they would if they were terminated. If the extra threads are ever needed again, they are ready and waiting.

When a server's initial thread executes the `START_SERVER` primitive, two additional threads are created. These threads are called *request handlers*. They wait on all enabled ports for RPCs from the server's clients. When a message comes in on an enabled port, one of the request handlers receives the message, passes it on to the appropriate function, sends a reply message, and continues waiting for RPCs. After creating the request handlers, `START_SERVER` terminates the thread in which it is executing, the server's initial thread.

Like system message handlers, request handlers reproduce when necessary to ensure that there is always a free request handler available. However, request handlers will not reproduce beyond the maximum number specified by the programmer as the maxMpl parameter to the START_SERVER construct. This limits resource consumption by the server, to prevent a broken or malicious application from crippling the server's node. It is permissible to limit the number of request handlers, as it is *not* critical to a server's operation that all RPCs are handled promptly. At worst, some server calls will time out, causing the enclosing transactions to abort.

START_SERVER can also create a third thread, called the *house cleaner*. This thread is responsible for aborting transactions that remain too long at the server, which prevents excessive resource usage by long-running transactions. The transTimeOut parameter to START_SERVER indicates how long a transaction can remain at the server before it can be aborted. A zero value for this parameter indicates that the server should never abort transactions for staying too long. In this case, no house cleaner thread is created.

When an application's initial thread executes the INITIALIZE_APPLICATION primitive, one *application system message handler* thread is created. This thread is similar in function to a server's system message handler, but much simpler. Applications receive no messages from the Recovery Manager, and only a single type of message from the Transaction Manager. Messages of this type, indicating that a transaction initiated by the server has died, require no reply. There is no need for more than one application system message handler, so the handler does not reproduce. After creating the application system message handler, the INITIALIZE_APPLICATION primitive returns, allowing the application's initial thread to continue execution.

Additional threads are also created in response to CONCURRENT_THREAD constructs, cobegin blocks, and cofor blocks. Unlike the various system threads, these threads are visible to the programmer, and vanish when they have finished executing the function for which they were created.

Data Structures

In this section, we discuss briefly the major internal data structures in Camelot Library programs. Some of these data structures exist only in servers and others exist in different forms in servers and applications, as indicated in the descriptions below. Discussion of some parts of the data structures is deferred to the **Techniques** section, below, to simplify exposition.

Thread Data Blocks Camelot Library programs have multiple threads that can run user level code: request handlers, system message handlers (which can run prepare procedures, commit procedures and abort procedures), main threads, and threads created to handle explicit concurrency. The C Threads library allows programs to associate a word of data with each thread. The Camelot Library allocates a *thread data block* each time a new thread that can run user level code is created, and associates a pointer to this block with the thread.

The main use of the thread data block is to store the hidden state associated with a thread: primarily, the TID of the transaction under which the thread is running and a setjmp/longjmp buffer indicating the location to which the thread should transfer control in the event of an abort. A pointer to the current transaction's *transaction data block* is cached in the thread data block for quick access. Another important piece of state stored in the thread data block is the *modify-in-progress* flag, which is set while a thread is doing a MODIFY operation. This flag is used to enforce the restriction that no other Library operations are permitted while a MODIFY is in progress. A final piece of state is the *transactional mutex stack* associated with this thread. Transactional mutexes are internally-used mutexes that are automatically dropped when a thread exits the scope of a transaction.[3]

The thread data block is also used as a way to pass an extra argument to a procedure. This is how we are able to use the same primitive to perform server calls on listed and unlisted servers. The `UNLISTED` macro places its port argument in a field in the thread data block and returns a constant value. The `SERVER_CALL` primitive checks its server name argument against this constant, and if they match, it knows that the call is for an unlisted server whose port is in the thread data block.

Transaction Table and Family Table Each server maintains a hash table of *transaction data blocks* and a hash table of *family data blocks*. Transaction data blocks are maintained for transactions that have made RPCs to the server, or were created by it, and family data blocks are maintained for the families to which the transactions belong. The tables contain the information that enables the server to automatically respond to system messages concerning the transactions and families. The tables are also used whenever the Library needs information about a transaction or family in order to perform a Library function. The information in the tables is updated when Library functions are executed, and in response to system messages.

The transaction table is indexed by TID and the family table is indexed by *family identifier* (FID). (The family identifier is a component of the transaction identifier that uniquely identifies the family to which a transaction belongs.) The transaction data blocks for the transactions in a family that have done work at the server are linked together to form a list. The head pointer for the list is stored in the relevant family data block. Each transaction data block contains a "back-pointer" to the family data block, to save on hashing costs.

The transaction data block contains an abort code, which is set when the transaction is suspended; an abort flag, which is set when the transaction is aborted; a shared/exclusive mode latch used to delay the response to the `ST_Suspend` call (defined in Section 9.3.2, **Implementing the Abort Protocol**) until all threads have ceased operating on behalf of the aborting transaction; a list of names on which the transaction holds locks; a flag indicating whether the transaction is *read-only*; and a flag indicating whether the transaction has used the recoverable heap. The transaction data block also contains the *on-call list* and the *lock-wait list* for the family, described below.

The family data block contains a status field used to store the current status of the family (e.g., active, prepared, committed, aborted) and a set of three reference counts that, in combination with the status, enable the Library to determine when it is safe to purge the data blocks for the family. Note that all of the transaction data blocks and the family data block for the family are purged at the same time, rather than purging individual transaction data blocks as soon as possible. This simplifies bookkeeping and locking.

Applications have a family table that is similar in function to servers'. It contains far fewer fields, as applications have fewer hidden functions to perform. Applications do not have an explicit transaction table, but they do have a linked list of transaction blocks for the transactions associated with each family, linked to the appropriate family data block. As is the case for servers, reference counts are maintained in family data blocks and abort codes are stored in transaction data blocks.

The transaction table and the family table, as well as all other hash tables in the Camelot Library are implemented with a generic macro package that implements a set of hash table functions given

[3] We considered exporting transactional mutexes as part of our interface, but we were not convinced that they were a good user-level construct.

a data type, key type, hash function, etc. The package is specifically designed for hash tables in concurrent use by multiple threads. Each hash bucket has a mutex associated with it, and various latching options may be specified.

Accessed Server Table Although the SERVER_CALL construct allows servers to be specified by name, internally a port is required to send an RPC. Mach provides a name service whereby a server can associate a port with its name. (Camelot Library servers check in their names when INITIALIZE_SERVER is called.) The first time a client performs an RPC on a server, the Library must query the name server for the port associated with the server's name. This operation requires a task switch, therefore it is desirable that clients cache the port to avoid the expense of a name server lookup on successive calls to the same server. The cache is maintained in a hash table indexed by server name, called the *accessed server table.*

Concurrent Operation Data Blocks Servers and applications maintain a *concurrent operation data block* for each *concurrent operation* (cobegin or cofor block) in progress. This data block is used to keep track of how many threads associated with the operation are still running, so that the last thread to complete can signal the parent thread to continue execution. The concurrent operation data block contains the number of uncompleted child threads and a condition variable on which the parent thread waits.

Multiprogramming Data Blocks Servers must keep track of how many system message handlers and request handlers are running, and how many of them are currently free to accept incoming messages. This information enables servers to produce new threads as necessary, subject to appropriate limits. The information is stored in two *multiprogramming data blocks*, one for system message handlers and one for request handlers.

Lock Table Servers maintain a hash table of all locks in use at the server, indexed by lock name. Each lock contains a list of *lock-holder records*, one for each transaction currently holding the lock, and a list of *lock-waiter records*, one for each thread currently waiting for the lock. Lock-holder records contain the TID of the holder and a *read-count* and *write-count* expressing the multiplicity with which the transaction holds the lock. (Multiple possession semantics are described in Section 3.6.7.) Lock-waiter records contain the TID of the transaction seeking the lock and the condition variable on which the thread is waiting. The information in the lock table is used to decide if a request for a lock can be granted, and to signal threads waiting for locks when lock conflicts are resolved.

Recoverable Segment Servers maintain recoverable segments. Recoverable segments are divided into three parts. Two of these parts are externally visible: the static recoverable area, consisting of the recoverable objects that the programmer has declared explicitly, and the recoverable heap, accessed via REC_MALLOC and REC_FREE. In addition, there is a hidden part of the recoverable segment called the *internal recoverable segment.* This part consists of the recoverable objects used internally by the Library.

Five objects are stored in the internal recoverable segment. A flag is stored that indicates whether the server has been started before. This flag is used to decide whether to run the initialization procedure when the server is starting up. The size of the static recoverable area is stored to ensure that the programmer does not attempt to change this size once the server has been started. Two counters are stored, one of which is used to generate lock space names, and one of which is used to generate TIDs for server-based transactions. Finally, the header for the recoverable heap is stored in the internal recoverable segment.

Algorithms

In this section we briefly describe some of the more important algorithms used by the Camelot Library. Brevity demands that we omit a lot of detail from these descriptions, but we try to convey the important ideas.

Execution Control From the programmer's standpoint, Camelot Library program threads automatically transfer control in response to transaction aborts. Various internal mechanisms cooperate to achieve this effect. Threads are never pre-emptively "shot down" via Mach thread manipulation primitives. Instead, threads "notice" that their transactions have been aborted (or, in the case of server threads, suspended) and autonomously transfer control. Threads check to see if their transaction has been aborted each time they execute a Camelot Library primitive. This check is accomplished with an internal Library function called `CamlibAbortCheck`.

Since programs call `CamlibAbortCheck` very frequently, it is critical from a performance standpoint that it run extremely fast in the common (i.e., non-abort) case. The function must check the abort code entry in the relevant transaction data block to see if the transaction has been suspended or aborted. To eliminate the hashing and searching that would otherwise be required to find the data block, a pointer to the transaction data block is cached in the thread data block. Locking the transaction data block is unnecessary; writing the (single word) abort code is an atomic operation for all known architectures, and reference counting in the family data block guarantees that the transaction data block will not to be deallocated. Thus, `CamlibAbortCheck` requires only a few machine instructions in the common case.

In the remainder of this section, we distinguish the actions that a thread takes when it discovers that its transaction has been suspended from those it takes when its transaction has been aborted. This distinction applies only to servers; applications are not informed when transactions are suspended. When `CamlibAbortCheck` discovers that the current transaction has been suspended, it looks up the top-level transaction to see if it too has been suspended. If so, it waits for the top-level transaction to abort and then transfers control to the top-level abort location stored in the thread data block. Otherwise, it waits for the current transaction to abort and transfers control to the current transaction abort location, also stored in the thread data block. Transfers of control are via `longjmp`.[4]

The simplified code for a transaction block in Figure 12.1 shows how `CamlibAbortCheck` causes the thread to continue execution at the correct point with the correct thread data block contents. Several features of transaction block implementation in Figure 12.1 should be noted. Storing the current thread data block in a local variable (`savedBlock`) prior to modification has the effect of using the thread's built in stack to keep track of the thread data blocks for all of the ancestors of the current transaction. This saves the Library the trouble of maintaining its own stack for every

[4]In fact, the _setjmp and _longjmp functions are used, to avoid the overhead of the system call in setjmp that retrieves the interrupt mask.

```
{
    thread_data_block_t *ptr, savedBlock;

    ptr = our_thread_data_block_ptr();
    savedBlock = *ptr;
    Do the Camelot system call to begin a new transaction;
    ptr->tid = TID of new transaction;
    status = setjmp(&ptr->abortLoc);

    if (status == 0)
    {
        /* Programmer's code goes here */
                    .
                    .
                    .

        Do the Camelot system call to commit the transaction;
        if (the commit fails)
            set status to the appropriate abort code;
    }

    *ptr = savedBlock;      /* Restore thread data block */
    CamlibAbortCheck();     /* Catch higher level abort */
}
```

Figure 12.1: Simplified Expansion of a Transaction Block

thread. Note that whenever `CamlibAbortCheck` transfers control, `CamlibAbortCheck` will be called again after the thread data block is restored. If multiple ancestors have aborted, this has the effect of unwinding the stack up to the nearest unaborted ancestor. When `CamlibAbortCheck` transfers control via `longjmp`, it passes back the abort code for the aborted transaction. When control passes to the statement after the "outermost" aborted transaction block, the local variable `status` will contain the abort code for the outermost aborted transaction.

The mechanism described in the previous paragraphs causes appropriate transfer of control to take place in any thread that executes a Camelot Library primitive after the thread's transaction has been suspended. It does not handle threads that are waiting for RPCs or locks on behalf of the aborted transaction. Separate mechanisms are required for these cases.

After a thread sends an RPC, it waits on a *reply port* for a response. If the calling transaction is suspended at the server before the server sends a response, the server thread processing the RPC may notice the suspend and cease work on behalf of the suspended transaction. If no special action were taken, the thread that sent the RPC would wait until the server call timeout interval expired. This delay would be intolerable from a performance standpoint. Therefore, the thread making the server call places its reply port on an *on-call list* in the relevant transaction data block before sending the RPC. If an `ST_Abort` (or `AT_TransactionHasDied`) comes in while the thread is still waiting for a reply, the system message handler sends special messages, called *death pills* to all of the ports on the on-call list in the transaction data block. When the thread performing the RPC receives a death pill, it calls `CamlibAbortCheck` to effect proper transfer of control.[5]

The technique used to handle threads waiting for lock conflicts to be resolved is very similar to the technique for RPCs. Threads waiting for a lock conflict to be resolved are actually waiting on a condition variable. Before waiting, a thread places this condition variable in a *lock-wait list* in the relevant transaction data block. If an abort comes in, the system message handler broadcasts to each condition variable on the lock-wait list in the transaction data block for the aborted transaction. Whenever a thread waiting for a lock is signaled, it calls `CamlibAbortCheck` before attempting to get the lock. If an abort caused the signal, the thread senses the abort and transfers control appropriately.

A thread waiting for a concurrent operation (cobegin or cofor block) to complete is *not* awakened explicitly when the enclosing transaction aborts. In the case of servers, it would be superfluous to do so, as the fact that the transaction has aborted implies that the child threads in the concurrent operation have already completed, as described below. The last child thread to complete signals the parent, and the parent thread calls `CamlibAbortCheck` upon being signaled, causing proper transfer of control to occur. In the case of applications it would have been possible to wake the parent thread immediately when the enclosing transaction aborted, allowing the child threads to continue operating as *orphans*. While this policy would cause the parent thread to notice the abort and get on with its work more quickly, it would have extremely undesirable consequences.

Child threads in a concurrent operation are passed an argument by the parent. The argument can contain pointers to objects on the parent's stack. Once the parent transfers control, these objects might no longer exist. Furthermore, the same virtual memory can be reused for new automatic variables as the parent thread continues execution. If an orphaned child thread alters an object addressed by a pointer into the parent thread's stack, the parent thread, which is *not* an orphan, will observe random changes its automatic variables. Thus, it is essential for parent threads in concurrent operations to wait until all child threads have completed before transferring control in response to an abort.

While the techniques described above generally prevent threads from operating on behalf of aborted transactions, they do not *guarantee* that orphan threads will never execute a Camelot Library operation. When a server responds to a suspend message, it is *promising* the Transaction Manager that there are no more threads operating on behalf of the suspended transaction. Stronger techniques are required to ensure that this promise is kept. Each transaction has its own *suspend lock*, a shared/exclusive mode lock stored in the transaction data block. Each thread operating on behalf of a transaction obtains the suspend lock in shared mode prior to commencing operation. After the lock is obtained, a check is made to see that the transaction has not been suspended, and the lock is held until the thread ceases operation on behalf of the transaction. When a suspend message is received, the lock is obtained in exclusive mode before responding to the message. This ensures that no threads remain operating on behalf of the transaction when the suspend response is sent.

If a thread is operating on behalf of a transaction when a suspend message is received for the transaction, the thread will cease execution when it "notices" the suspend (i.e., performs a Library operation other that `REC`). If the thread is in the middle of a long computation and does not call any Library operations other that `REC`, the thread will continue operating on behalf of the transaction. This will cause the system message handler thread that received the suspend message to block when

[5]The reply port must be deallocated once a death pill is sent on it, in case the actual response arrives later, or "sneaks in" before the death pill.

it attempts to obtain the suspend lock in exclusive mode. If the system message handler thread remains blocked for sufficiently long, the Transaction Manager will time out on the ST_Suspend call, and then kill the server task in order to abort the transaction. Killing a server is extremely expensive, causing all transactions in progress at the server to abort, and requiring the server to go through a lengthy recovery procedure before it can begin operation anew. But it should happen rarely, if ever, assuming that servers are written with an eye to avoiding long computations that do not call a Library operation from time to time. The CamlibAbortCheck function is exported to the programmer, as ABORT_CHECK, so that it can be called from computations that might otherwise prevent servers from responding quickly to suspends.

The Library must take several precautions to make suspend locking work properly. The TA_Kill call does not respond until the specified transaction has been suspended and aborted. Thus the Library ABORT procedure must drop the suspend lock before calling TA_Kill, to prevent a deadlock from forming. The SERVER_CALL and LOCK operations and their relatives may block for long periods of time. When any Library call is about to enter a wait, it drops the suspend lock. When the wait completes, the Library re-obtains the suspend lock and checks to make sure the transaction has not been suspended. This allows the server to respond promptly to a suspend even if threads are waiting on behalf of the suspended transaction.

When a thread operating on behalf of one transaction enters the scope of a different transaction (by entering a nested transaction block), it drops the suspend lock for the first transaction before obtaining one for the second. When the thread re-enters the scope of the first transaction, it re-obtains the suspend lock for the first transaction and checks to see that it hasn't been suspended. In this way, each thread is responsible for a single suspend lock at a time: threads only have to drop one suspend lock in order to do an abort or a wait. Note that deadlocks would occur when transaction families aborted if threads held suspend locks for enclosing transactional scopes while waiting for a suspended subtransaction to abort.

One more topic remains to be discussed that falls loosely under the heading of execution control. If, in the course of carrying out any of its duties, the Library discovers that a server or application is unsound, it prints out a message detailing the nature of the problem and halts the server or application. For example, if a server tries to perform an illegal operation, like a MODIFY of a recoverable object that would lie outside of its recoverable segment, the server is clearly broken. Since Camelot servers and applications are supposed to be fail-fast, it would be wrong to continue operating a broken server or application.

Locking The procedure for obtaining a lock is illustrated coarsely in Figure 12.2. Lock conflicts can be divided into two groups: conflicts with transactions in another family, termed *outside conflicts*, and conflicts with other transactions in the same family, termed *family conflicts*. The detection and resolution of conflicts is handled very differently for the two groups.

The existence of a conflicting lock-holder record for a transaction from a different family *always* indicates an outside conflict. When an outside conflict is detected, the thread seeking the lock places a lock-waiter record in the lock structure. The lock-waiter record contains the TID of the transaction seeking the lock, and a condition variable on which the thread waits for the conflict to be resolved. Outside conflicts are not resolved until the conflicting transaction's family commits, or the conflicting transaction aborts. In either case, the server is notified by the Transaction Manager as part of the commit or abort protocol. When a lock is dropped as a result of a commit or abort message (or an explicit UNLOCK operation), the server deletes the relevant lock-holder record from

```
void LOCK(name, mode)
{
    obtain mutex on lock structure for given lock name;
    if (no lock structure for this name exists in lock table)
    {
        create lock structure for name;
        insert lock structure into lock table;
    }

    do{
        if (no conflict exists)
            grant lock to transaction;
        else
        {
            drop mutex;
            wait for conflict to be resolved;
            obtain mutex;
        }
    } while (lock not granted);

    drop mutex;
}
```

Figure 12.2: Simplified Locking Procedure

the lock structure and checks to see if any outside conflicts have been resolved by this action. If so, the waiting threads are signaled, and they try again to obtain the desired lock.

Family conflicts, on the other hand, cannot be detected without assistance from the Transaction Manager. If a transaction in the same family as the lock seeker has a lock-holder record for a conflicting lock, a real conflict may or may not exist. A conflict exists only if the transaction holding the lock has not yet committed up to the *least common ancestor* of itself and the transaction seeking the lock. Since subtransaction commits are handled locally, the server will not be informed when this happens.[6]

Usually, it is possible to tell that a conflicting lock-holder record does *not* represent a potential family conflict without consulting the Transaction Manager. TIDs contain a field called the *Family Position Indicator* (FPI), which contains approximate genealogical information about the transaction. If FPI comparison indicates that the lock holder has committed with respect to the lock seeker, then it is safe to assume that no family conflict exists. (FPIs are described in more detail in Section 16.3.5, **Family Position Indicator**.) Only if FPI comparison indicates that the holder has not committed with respect to the seeker does a potential family conflict exist. In this case, the Library asks the Transaction Manager if the conflict is real via the `TS_IsLockInheritable` call. If the Transaction Manager indicates that a family conflict does exist, the thread seeking the lock waits until the conflicting transaction commits to the appropriate level (or aborts), with the

[6]This is a consequence of the particular transaction management protocols adopted by Camelot. Other systems might choose to inform all participating servers when a subtransaction commits, giving rise to an *eager* lock inheritance discipline, instead of the *lazy* discipline employed by Camelot.

TS_WaitBeforeInheritingLock call.

Note that UNLOCK and DEMOTE_LOCK calls that resolve family conflicts will *not* cause the threads waiting for the resolved family conflicts to wake up. A thread remains inactive after calling TS_WaitBeforeInheritingLock until the conflicting transaction commits to the appropriate level or aborts, or the waiting transaction aborts. It would be possible to remedy this deficiency by placing a *family conflict wait record*, containing the *reply port* on which the thread was waiting, in the lock structure prior to calling TS_WaitBeforeInheritingLock. However, this would add to the complexity of the lock manager, and we did not deem it essential.

Also note that the technique described in **Execution Control**, above, for ensuring correct transfer of control on abort in threads waiting for locks does not apply to threads waiting for family conflicts to be resolved. These threads are waiting for responses from the Transaction Manager to TS_WaitBeforeInheritingLock calls. When the Transaction Manager finds out that a transaction has aborted, it sends special error responses to any TS_WaitBeforeInheritingLock calls made on behalf of the aborted transaction that are still outstanding. When a thread receives such an error response, it calls CamlibAbortCheck to effect proper transfer of control.

The family conflict detection scheme described above has a major performance deficiency. When a family conflict is resolved, the thread seeking a lock must again check for family conflicts. All potential family conflicts must again be checked with the Transaction Manager. If no preventive measures were taken, the conflict that was just resolved, and any others that had already been eliminated would be checked again. The checks are very expensive. They require a context switch to the Transaction Manager and sometimes, additional messages to remote Transaction Managers. Therefore, we implemented an optimization to prevent this redundant checking.

A sequence number is associated with each lock possession (i.e., with each lock holder record). The Library checks potential family conflicts with the Transaction Manager in order of ascending sequence number of the holder records representing potential conflicts. When an actual conflict is found, the sequence number is returned to the thread, which then waits for the conflict to be resolved. When the conflict is resolved, the thread again checks for outside and family conflicts. However, the thread knows that it need not ask the Transaction Manager about any potential conflicts with sequence numbers less than or equal to the previously returned sequence number. This ensures that each potential family conflict is checked only once.

Server Calls The server call mechanism is straightforward. Server names are translated into send ports, as described in **Accessed Server Table**, above. Three hidden system parameters that must be included in all server calls are inserted at the head of the argument list by the ARGS or NOARGS keyword: the send port, the TID of the enclosing transaction, and the timeout interval after which the transaction should abort. If the timeout interval elapses and no reply to the request message comes, Mach returns an error code, and the Library aborts the transaction. The MIG generated stub in the client automatically deallocates the reply port, so that a reply message arriving after the timeout cannot disrupt a future RPC.

For wrapped server calls, the Library translates the transaction type and commit protocol specified by the programmer into a special TID. This special TID is passed to the server in the TID field. The server recognizes the special TID as indicating a wrapped server call, decodes it back into a transaction type and a commit protocol, and begins a transaction of the type specified. Note that the Library creates the transaction with the BEGIN_TRANSACTION_2 - END_TRANSACTION_2

```
void HouseCleaner()
{
    while(TRUE)
    {
        clock++;
        sleep for the transTimeOut period;

        get mutex;

        for each family on the active list
            if (time associated with family < clock)
                abort family;

        drop mutex;
    }
}
```

Figure 12.3: Simplified House Cleaning Procedure

construct. This is an instance of the design principle that the Library should use itself wherever possible to keep the Library source files short and readable.

Aborting Long-Running Transactions The house cleaner thread is responsible for aborting transactions that have remained at a server for an excessive amount of time, as specified by the programmer in the `transTimeOut` parameter to `START_SERVER`. The house cleaner maintains two pieces of static data, a "clock" and a list of transaction families active at the server, and a mutex controlling access to the list. Whenever the server joins a new transaction family, the family data block is linked onto the house cleaner's active list and the current value of the clock is recorded in the data block. Thus, the active list associates a rough timestamp with each active family. Successive requests on behalf of the family cause the timestamp associated with the family to be reset to the current value of house cleaner's clock. When a family commits or aborts, its data block is removed from the active list. The house cleaner thread periodically scans the list and aborts long-running transactions. A simplified version of the procedure executed by the house cleaner thread is shown in Figure 12.3.

Our primary design goal for the house cleaner was low overhead. One potential trouble spot was system calls required to measure the timeout intervals. The clock in our design has a resolution equal to the transaction timeout period, hence transactions may be allowed to remain at the server up to twice the timeout period before they are aborted. This represents a conscious tradeoff of precision in favor of decreased overhead. In order to make the house cleaner abort transactions promptly when the timeout interval elapses, the server would have to make a system call each time an RPC arrived to determine the real time. This would be prohibitively expensive if the server were used heavily, and would provide little, if any, benefit.

While the overhead of the procedure in Figure 12.3 does not increase significantly when the server is used heavily, it does not vanish when the server is unused for long periods. The house cleaner corrects this deficiency by going dormant if the active list remains empty for a number of periods. (The number is specified as a compile time constant, initially 10.) Each time a family is placed on the active list, the server checks a flag to see if the house cleaner is dormant. If so, it is awakened by signaling a condition variable.

Our design avoids the expense of locking each family data block each time its timestamp is checked, by using a single mutex for the entire active list and "peeking" at the timestamp without locking the data block. The list is locked each time a family is added or deleted, but need not be locked when a timestamp is updated, as timestamps are 32 bit integers, which are atomically writable. In order to reduce the contention on the mutex, the house cleaner does not issue abort calls while holding the mutex. Instead, it compiles a list of families to be aborted, drops the mutex, and then aborts the families.

Dynamic Allocation of Recoverable Storage The recoverable storage allocator is a two layered system. The bottom layer is a fairly traditional storage allocator (like `malloc` in the C library) that allocates storage off of the recoverable heap. Free storage is organized into lists of equally sized blocks. Block sizes are always a power of two. If the appropriate list for a "basic malloc" request is empty, a new page is allocated off the recoverable heap. The requested block is taken from the new page, and the remainder of the page is placed on the list from which the block would have come.

The recoverable storage allocator is built on top of the basic storage allocator using a simple form of operation logging. The allocator maintains in recoverable storage a log of operations (`REC_MALLOC`s and `REC_FREE`s) performed by transactions in progress. When a transaction calls `REC_MALLOC`, a flag is set in the transaction's data block to indicate that the transaction has used the recoverable storage allocator. Then a new top-level transaction is run that allocates the requested storage using the basic storage allocator, and associates the operation with the calling transaction in the storage allocator's operation log. Finally, a flag is set in the operation log record from within the scope of the calling transaction. This flag is used in crash recovery, as described below. `REC_FREE` is performed exactly like `REC_MALLOC`, except that the new top-level transaction merely inserts the operation record in the log, and does *not* call the basic storage allocator. The top-level transactions created by the allocator are server-based, and use the lazy commit protocol, for efficiency.

When a commit message arrives, the server checks the flags in the transaction data blocks for the committing family to see if any of the transactions used the recoverable storage allocator. If so, the server runs a lazy, server-based transaction that *finalizes* all of the operations done by the transactions. For `REC_MALLOC`s, this consists merely of removing the operation records from the log. For `REC_FREE`s, it consists of actually returning the freed blocks to the storage pool with the basic storage allocator's free operation, as well as removing the operation records from the log.

When an abort message arrives, the server checks the flag in the transaction's data block to see if it used the recoverable storage allocator. If so, the server runs a lazy, server-based transaction that *undoes* all of the operations done by the transactions. For `REC_MALLOC`s, this consists of freeing the allocated data blocks using the low level storage allocator and removing the operation records from the log. For `REC_FREE`s, it consists merely of removing the operation records from the log.

When a server is recovering from a crash, it processes messages from the Recovery Manager, resetting recoverable storage to a transaction-consistent state and creating family data blocks for transaction families that are in the prepared state. When normal recovery is complete, the server calls the storage allocator's recovery procedure. This procedure combs the allocator's operation log. For each transaction in the log, the procedure checks the flag that was set from within the scope of the transaction. If the flag is clear, the transaction aborted, so the undo operation is applied to all of the transaction's operation records. If the flag is set, the routine checks whether a family data block exists for the transaction's family. If so, the transaction is currently prepared, and no action is taken. If no data block exists, the transaction committed, and the finalize operation is applied to the transaction's operation records.

Voting for Read-Only Transactions When a server is asked to prepare a transaction for which it performed no `MODIFYs` and obtained no write locks, it votes either *read-only independent* or *read-only dependent*. It is the server's responsibility to vote read-only dependent if the transaction being prepared might have accessed recoverable data written by a lazy transaction that has not yet been forced out to stable storage. Otherwise the server votes read-only independent. A vote of read-only dependent causes the Transaction Manager to do a log force as part of the commit protocol, to ensure that all of the updates to recoverable storage visible to the read-only transaction are forced to stable storage before the transaction is allowed to commit. This protocol is explained in more detail in Section 9.3.2.

In order to make the determination whether to vote read-only independent or read-only dependent, servers maintain two static variables: `LazySeq` is a counter used to assign a sequence number to each lazy transaction, and `LazyForced` is a variable used to keep track of the highest sequence numbered lazy transaction whose effects have already been forced to stable storage. Each time a lazy transaction that is not itself read-only commits, `LazySeq` is incremented prior to dropping the transaction's locks. This implicitly assigns the new `LazySeq` value to the committing transaction, although the assignment is not recorded anywhere. Each time the server knows that a log force has occurred, it sets `LazyForced` to the highest value that `LazySeq` is known to have attained *before* the log force occurred. If this assignment would cause the value of `LazyForced` to be reduced (i.e., `LazyForced` has been set to a higher value in the meantime) the assignment is suppressed.

When it comes time to determine how to vote on a read-only transaction, the server compares the current values of `LazySeq` and `LazyForced`. If they are equal, the server knows that any data that the transaction could have accessed has already been forced, so it votes read-only independent. Otherwise, it votes read-only dependent.

12.3 Related Work

Other languages for programming transaction systems include Argus [75] and Avalon (Part IV). Both Argus and Avalon are substantially higher level languages than the Camelot Library. They provide more powerful data abstraction facilities but do not permit as much flexibility in directly accessing the underlying transaction system. Argus is a self-contained general purpose programming language and Avalon is an extension to C++. Avalon is implemented on top of the Camelot Library using a preprocessor and run time support software.

12.4 Conclusions

12.4.1 Critique

Roughly ten programmers have used the Camelot Library at Carnegie Mellon University. Roughly forty servers and applications comprising sixty thousand lines of code have thus far been written.

The programs range in complexity from toys like Jack and Jill (Chapter 5) to substantial system programs like Camelot's Node Configuration Application (Chapter 4) and Node Server (Chapter 10). The Camelot Library has been used to build several libraries implementing higher level recoverable data types like hash tables and queues. (This type of library is describe in Section 3.6.6.) A security package called Strongbox (Section 24) and a Common Lisp interface (Section 23) have been implemented on top of the Library. A high level language, Avalon, has been implemented that generates Camelot Library programs as intermediate code (Part IV).

Programmer response to the Camelot Library has been very positive, although there have been a few complaints about the lexical and syntactic dissimilarity between Library constructs and native C constructs.[7] C programmers familiar with transaction system concepts have had little difficulty learning to use the Camelot Library.

Toy servers and applications like Jack and Jill are written quickly and easily, and the source programs have the flavor of introductory programming exercises in a high level language. Yet the Library has proven powerful and efficient enough to handle the complexity and performance requirements of large system programs. Thus, the Library appears to succeed as a "bi-level language".

An advantage of our decision to remove as many details as possible from our interface is that no operating system dependent data objects, like ports, remain in the core of the interface. Thus, most Camelot Library source programs will not have to be modified if Camelot is ported to other operating systems. The Library interface makes a good basis for the design of programming interfaces for other transaction systems, as it hides the details of Camelot. With appropriate modifications, the interface is applicable to base languages other than C. The Common Lisp interface described in Chapter 23 is based on the Library.

The decision to implement the facility as an embedded language has generally fulfilled our expectations in terms of advantages and disadvantages. The entire library consists of approximately 12,000 lines of source code, including substantial internal documentation. A single programmer designed and implemented the entire library, with the exception of the recoverable storage allocator, in roughly a year and a half. The syntax restrictions caused by the embedded language implementation are real, but not severe enough to annoy programmers in practice. The Library has proven extremely portable. It has been used with five C compilers on four processor architectures. Lint, and other tools designed for C source programs have proven effective when applied to Camelot Library programs, though the correspondence between the output and the source programs is not perfect.

It is difficult to quantify the performance of the Library, as virtually no Camelot programs have been written that do not use it, either directly or as part of a layered system. In particular, there are no programs that run directly on top of the primitive interface. Thus, we have no baseline figures with which to compare Library performance. However, we think it is safe to say that the Library is very efficient. We estimate that programs written on top of the Library are no more than five percent slower than programs carefully hand-coded directly on top of the primitive interface, with several exceptions discussed in the following section. The Library is fast enough that the Camelot developers had no qualms about using performance data from Camelot Library programs to describe the performance of the underlying system.

In summary, the Camelot Library has, for the most part, satisfied our initial goal: to create a Camelot interface for C programmers that is easy to use, elegant, simple, powerful and highly efficient. We have demonstrated that it is possible to add transactions to a preexisting language,

[7] Specific objections included long, upper-case keywords and lack of explicit brackets in block constructs.

producing a unified transactional variant of the language. The Library approach allowed for quick development, easy portability, and did not prove unduly restrictive to the syntax of our interface. Our extensions to C provide a compact, high level model of the services offered by a general purpose distributed transaction system. The model makes a good basis for creating transactional variants of other base languages.

12.4.2 Directions for Further Work

Interface Shortcomings

The locking facilities provided by the Library are somewhat limited, providing only shared/exclusive mode locking. It is very cumbersome to implement variable granularity locking schemes on top of these facilities. Commercial systems solve this problem by providing *intention locking* [38]. Additional flexibility could be gained by allowing the programmer to create locks with arbitrary *lock-compatibility matrices*. Another useful facility that could be provided by the lock manager is *range locking* [102]. Range locks provide great flexibility in implementing variable granularity locking.

The `UNLOCK` call should really take another argument, the mode of the lock to be released. As it stands, the programmer must make a fairly inelegant sequence of calls, described in Section 3.6.7, in order to release a write lock. Another deficiency in the semantics provided by the `UNLOCK` and `DEMOTE` calls is that it is impossible to release or demote a lock held by a subtransaction once it has committed. Obvious solutions to this problem suffer from the defect that the `UNLOCK` operation is not idempotent. If a nested transaction containing an `UNLOCK` for a lock obtained by another transaction aborts and is retried, the repeated unlock can compromise serializability. One solution to this problem, devised by Dean Thompson and the author, is the use of *lock handles*. A lock handle is returned by every successful lock request, and serves as an umambiguous name for the lock possession resulting from the the request. The `UNLOCK` call takes a lock handle in place of a lock name and mode. This technique guarantees the idempotence of the `UNLOCK` operation.

Rather than exporting `REC_MALLOC` and `REC_FREE` directly, the Library should export an "sbreak-level" recoverable storage allocator. This allocator would be characterized by a large minimum allocation, high storage efficiency, little or no concurrency, and possibly, low speed. The Library should support the current `REC_MALLOC/REC_FREE` interface, reimplemented on top of the sbreak-level allocator. This would allow users with special needs to write special purpose allocators that could coexist in the same server with the standard allocator and with one another.

A weakness that the Library interface inherits from Camelot concerns the abort code abstraction. The set of user abort codes that can be generated by a "package" (server or subroutine library) constitutes a part of its interface. If two packages use the same (numerical) user abort code, and both packages are called from within the same transaction, it will be impossible to tell which package generated the abort if the ambiguous error code is returned. Thus, user abort codes constitute a type of shared global name space.

One solution to this problem is to nest in a subtransaction each call to a package capable of generating user abort codes. The subtransaction will "catch" an abort generated by the call, allowing the abort code to be interpreted unambiguously. But this will only work if the package does not use the `ABORT_TOP_LEVEL` construct. This suggests that perhaps the Library should not provide the `ABORT_TOP_LEVEL` call, which is seldom used in practice. A more serious problem with this solution is that it is undesirable from a performance standpoint, as nested transactions are costly.

Another weakness that the Library inherits from Camelot is the lack of a facility for performing work on behalf of a transaction at prepare time. This functionality could be used to defer work until prepare time, minimizing the amount of time that locks were held and increasing concurrency. This technique is not without its drawbacks. Doing work at prepare time increases the "window of vulnerability", during which a crash of the transaction coordinator causes resources to be tied up for extended periods at all prepared sites. (See Section 16.3.2, **Operation in the Presence of Failures**, for a description of this phenomenon.) Under many circumstances, however, the concurrency gains outweigh the potential for blockage; this technique is used heavily in commercial systems where highly concurrent access to a shared resource is required.

Implementation Shortcomings

The recoverable dynamic storage allocation package in the Camelot Library is very slow. Its concurrency derives from the use of separate top-level transactions within each call to `REC_MALLOC` and `REC_FREE`, and additional top-level transactions at commit or abort time. This turns out to be too expensive, even when lazy server-based transactions are used. As an alternative to the library's recoverable storage allocator, we implemented a very fast special purpose allocator based on "scatter" techniques. The basic idea is that storage pools are divided into multiple "lanes", and transactions choose which lane to allocate from by hashing their family ID. Allocation (or deallocation) locks a lane for the duration of the transaction, but concurrent transactions are free to allocate from other lanes in the pool. Hashing on the family ID disperses requests across the lanes in a pool, while concentrating multiple requests from one family into a single lane. Non-blocking lock requests are used so that alternate lanes can be tried if the chosen lane is unavailable. We conjecture that similar techniques could be used to build a fast general purpose recoverable storage allocator.

While the Library is generally quite fast, it would benefit from additional performance tuning. The totally uncontested locking path has been optimized somewhat, but it could be further optimized. The family conflict detection logic in the lock manager uses a fairly brute-force approach, which could easily be improved. But it is not clear whether this code is called frequently enough to make such improvements worthwhile.

The lock manager component of the Library makes no attempt to do deadlock detection. Deadlocks are allowed to form, and remain until one of the deadlocked transactions times out and is aborted. This results in unnecessary delays. It would be simple to provide local deadlock detection facilities, wherein the lock manager detected locking requests that would result in deadlocks, and aborted one of the deadlocking transactions. It would be more difficult to implement distributed deadlock detection facilities that detected deadlocks involving multiple servers.

Software Tools

Since Camelot Library programs are actually C programs, many software tools designed for use with C are effective on Camelot Library programs as well. However, some tools, like pretty-printers and syntax editors, will not operate properly on Camelot Library programs. Versions of these tools could be written specifically for Camelot Library programs. One tool that might be useful is a lint-like program that would search for common misuses of Camelot Library constructs not detectable by lint itself.

Chapter 13

The Design of the Camelot Local Log Manager

Dean Thompson
Elliot Jaffe

13.1 Introduction

A Camelot node can be configured to write log data across the network (see Chapter 25) or to local disk storage. The local Log Manager implements the storage of log data in regular disk files or raw partitions on the local machine.

Logging to regular files is no less correct than logging to raw disk partitions.[1] The Log Manager cares only that data can be forced to disk on request. This is accomplished in Mach/UNIX via the `fsync` system call. Logging onto a raw partition is appreciably faster since no additional system call must be made to assure that data is forced to disk. The structures and algorithms used are exactly the same regardless of which type of storage is used. In the remainder of this chapter, the word "file" is used to mean either a regular file or a raw partition.

Log data can be written to one file (*simplex* logging) or in parallel to two files (*duplex* logging). Simplex logging and duplex logging are semantically equivalent. Duplex logging maintains two identical copies of the log, so that no single disk failure (in the log or in the database) can prevent recovery of the database. With simplex logging, damage to the log can cause recoverable data to be corrupted or permanently lost. For this reason, simplex logging should be used only when it is worth paying for improved performance by allowing data to be lost when a disk fails.

Duplex logging is a straightforward extension of the simplex algorithm. Data is written to the second log file by a parallel thread and is read from either copy. Since this is the only difference between the two styles of logging, the rest of this chapter describes only simplex logging.

---

[1]Actually, a log on a raw partition is slightly more robust than one in most file systems. This is because file system data structures may be corrupted during a crash, causing the file to be truncated or lost.

13.2 Architecture

The Log Manager implementation makes the following assumptions concerning the log file:

- There are three possible outcomes of an attempted disk write: the disk write succeeds, the Log Manager crashes, or the Log Manager remains up but detects a failure. If the Log Manager detects a failure, it immediately crashes.

- A failed write operation may successfully write some number of contiguous sectors beginning with the first, detectably corrupt some number after that, and leave some sectors at the end of the span untouched.

- The file used for logging is divided into sectors of a known size. Each disk write is aligned on a sector boundary, and spans some number of contiguous sectors.

We assume that there is one other way disk storage can fail. Any number of sectors may, at any random time, go bad. This type of failure is very rare. It is almost always the result of a hardware error, while the others are quite likely to happen whenever a node goes down due to power failure, hardware failure, or a kernel crash. We assume the likelihood of a random failure destroying the same sector in two copies of the log is so low that duplex logging is an adequate safeguard.[2]

Each log record is stored by the Log Manager as an uninterpreted byte string. When each log record is written, the Log Manager returns a key (called a `log sequence number` or LSN) that can later be used to access that record. Because the Log Manager is able to choose the key, it can include enough information to make later access to that data very easy.

The log is limited to a fixed-size file. It is structured as a circular buffer. The Disk Manager periodically informs the Log Manager how much of the log is still needed for recovery by giving it the LSN of the oldest record that could possibly be read again. The Log Manager uses this LSN to decide which records in the log are no longer needed. The log is said to be *truncated* at this point. Any data before this LSN can be overwritten. When space is low, the Log Manager informs the Disk Manager, which can then flush pages and take measures to reduce log space requirements. The Log Manager will crash Camelot if necessary to avoid overwriting data that is not truncated out of the log.

The Log Manager provides two interfaces for writing data to the log. Records can be *spooled* or *forced*. Forced records are guaranteed to reside permanently on the disk when the call to the Log Manager completes. Spooled records have no such guarantee, but a subsequent force call is guaranteed to force all previously spooled records to disk. These guarantees allow the Camelot system to recover from a node or system crash. The time required to write records to disk, called the *force latency*, should be as short as possible. Writing the log data should be done with the minimum possible overhead. With most existing devices, this means that the log data should be written sequentially. Writing data randomly in the log, or both writing the data and updating a separate index, would be unacceptably slow. The requirement that force latency be minimized strongly constrains the choice of an organization for the log.

When the Log Manager recovers from a shutdown, site crash, or system crash, it must be able to find the *end* of the log. The end of the log is defined to be the last complete record written to the

[2]For extremely critical applications, the log can be stored on any number of log servers physically remote from the logging node. See Chapter 25.

log. To allow the end of the log to be recognized, the Log Manager records the *pass number* in a special field (referred to here as passNbr) in each sector. Initially, every sector has passNbr set to zero. When a sector is written for the first time, passNbr is set to one. When the Log Manager cycles back and writes the same sector again, it sets passNbr to two, and so on. When the Log Manager comes up after a crash, it uses binary search on the sectors in the log to find the last sector written.

Once the Log Manager has found the last sector written before a crash, it must still find the last complete record. To this end, another field in each sector (referred to here as last) contains the offset of the last log record (if any) that begins in the sector. The algorithm for using this information to find the last record is described in the next section. It is more complex than intuition immediately suggests.

We have just described the two extra fields that are added to each sector. There are also two extra fields added to each log record. The first contains the length of the record, and the second gives an offset to the previous record. The record length is needed during recovery of the log after a crash. The offset to the previous record is used to construct the preceding LSN during backward scans of the log (see Chapter 15).

During crash recovery it is necessary to reconstruct not only the end of the log, but also the beginning of the log. The beginning of the log is equivalent to the LSN that is used for truncation. It is the initial point beyond which we cannot write new records. We keep this data in two reserved sectors at the beginning of the log file. Each sector contains a counter, a record of the lowest required sector in the log, and a record of the pass number of the oldest required sector.

13.3 Algorithms

This following sections describe the algorithms that are used for manipulating the log.

13.3.1 Initializing the Log

Before a log is used for the first time, at least the passNbr field in every sector must be set to zero. Since it is impossible to write less than a sector, this means that the Log Manager zeroes the entire log. This is a relatively expensive initialization. It is necessary because to recover from a crash (see Section 13.3.4) the Log Manager must determine exactly which sector was written last. It must do this using information in the sectors themselves. The Log Manager cannot use the information in the special sectors since those sectors are only written at truncation time. To update the special sectors after every data write would unacceptably increase the latency and expense of a force.

13.3.2 Writing a Record

When log records are spooled, they are kept in a write buffer until either an entire track has been buffered or the Disk Manager requests that a record be forced. When a new buffer sector is started, passNbr is set as appropriate and last is set to zero (meaning no record starts in the sector). A record is spooled by buffering its length, the difference between its LSN and the LSN of the previous record, and finally the record data itself. The last field for the sector in which the new record begins is set to the offset from the beginning of the sector to the first byte of the record length.

The Log Manager is responsible for assigning a 64 bit LSN to each log record when it is spooled. Unlike the replicated, distributed Log Manager described in Chapter 25, the local Log Manager is free to choose LSNs so that access is as easy as possible. The local Log Manager creates each 64 bit LSN by concatenating the record's 32 bit pass number and its 32 bit physical offset from the beginning of the log.

Multiple Threads

To make the most efficient use of a file, multiple spool data requests should be processed concurrently with writes. The current local Log Manager implementation supports concurrent processing of a single spool call and multiple force calls.[3]

The main data structure used to spool and write data to a file is a memory resident circular buffer. The Log Manager logically divides the buffer into three sections.

- **Spooled Data:** Data is spooled to this append only region of the buffer. The region grows as data is spooled.
- **Written Data:** Data here is currently being written to disk (via a *write* system call). When the write call completes successfully, this region is appended to the empty buffer region, below.
- **Empty buffer:** The region encompasses all unused space in the circular buffer. The spooled data region is taken from the tail of this region. The written data region is inserted at the head.

Spool data requests are queued until the spooled data region is not busy. Each spool request incrementally adds data to the spooled data region and removes data from the empty region. If the empty region becomes empty, the Log Manager queues a force request for the spooled data region. When the force request is completed, the spooled data region will be empty, and spooling will continue.

Force requests first check to determine whether the data has already been forced. If the data has been forced, then the call returns successfully. If the data is currently in the written data region, then the call waits until the thread currently writing that region completes, at which point the call returns successfully. If the data is in the spooled data region, this thread waits until any current disk writes are completed, and then renames the spooled data region to be the written data region. The thread then starts to write the written data region to the file. When the data has successfully been written, the call returns.

Group Commit

As a result of the threading algorithm, the Log Manager is able to implement *group commit*. The main barrier to transaction commit speed is the need to force a commit record to the file. Typically, this limits a transaction system to no more than 30 transactions per second. Group Commit refers to a technique where many transactions are committed with a single disk force. The current Log Manager design implements this in a very straightforward manner. If a transaction needs to write a commit record and there is no I/O in progress, then the commit record is forced immediately. If a

[3] The interface supports concurrent processing of spool calls, but the implementation does not, and thus serializes them.

log I/O completes and there are other transactions waiting to commit, then all of the records for the waiting transactions are written with a single I/O.

As the graph (Figure 13.1) shows, as more threads compete to write log data and force records, the total number of I/O calls decreases. This decrease reflects multiple force calls being satisfied by single writes. When using Mach in a multiprocessor environment, only one designated processor is allowed to do I/O. This restriction causes the VAX 8200 with 4 processors to be slower than a uniprocessor Sun 3/60 because each thread that request an I/O function must be swapped to run on the one designated processor.

Another interesting result from the group commit experiments was the interaction between processor scheduling and the condition signal and broadcast primitives (see Section 7.3.2). The current implementation of the condition broadcast primitive causes at least as many context swaps to occur as there are waiting threads. Although a context swap is reasonably cheap, there are enough of them to cause an appreciable performance degradation. In fact, our tests showed that as the number of threads increase, the latency of the test actually increased. Once we found the problem, we were able to implement our own version of conditions that were less fair, but required only a single context swap to allow a thread to continue execution after a condition broadcast.

13.3.3 Reading a Record

The Recovery Manager specifies an LSN whenever it reads a record.[4] The Log Manager uses the physical offset contained in the LSN to determine in which sector the record starts. The Log Manager then checks the write buffer and two one-track read buffers to determine if the sector is in memory. If not, it uses the least-recently-used read buffer to load the appropriate track.

Once the first sector that contains part of the record is in memory, the Log Manager checks its `passNbr` field to make sure it agrees with the pass number contained in the LSN that was specified. If the sector's pass number is too low, the given LSN has not been written yet and the Log Manager returns an error indication. If it is too high, the given LSN was in the log but has been overwritten, which is also an error.

If the pass number found in the first sector is correct, the Log Manager reads the record length and the offset to the previous record. It subtracts this offset from the LSN it is reading to obtain an LSN for the next oldest record in the log. It then reads as many sectors as necessary to piece together the entire log record, and returns it to the Recovery Manager.

13.3.4 Recovering from a Node Crash

The physical location of the log and its size are available to Camelot after a crash as part of the node configuration information. Camelot passes this data to the Log Manager, which must reinitialize itself using only this information and the data in the log.

The algorithm described above for reading log records does not require any information other than the location and size of the log. The algorithm for writing a log record, however, requires the location of the oldest record that must be kept in the log (so as not to overwrite it), the LSN of the newest record still in the log, and the physical location of the first free sector.

[4] In Camelot, the Disk Manager writes the log and the Recovery Manager reads the log, but the two are separate processes. To make this work, state (including the current write buffer) is transferred from the Disk Manager to the Recovery Manager when recovery processing begins. In describing the algorithm, it is simplest to ignore this fact.

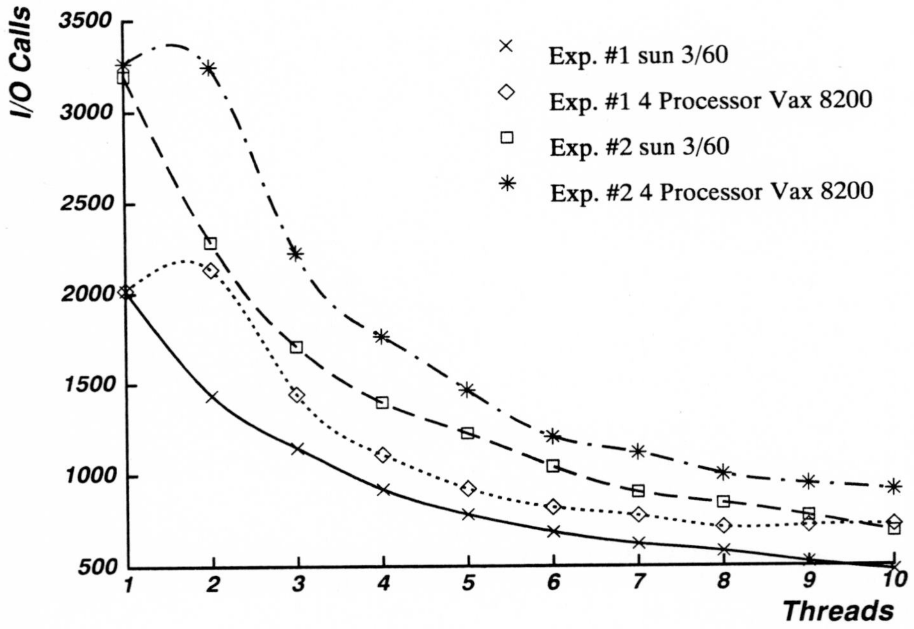

Figure 13.1: Threads vs. I/O calls

The lines represents the number of I/O calls made by the Log Manager for each experiment. Two experimental results are shown. In experiment #1, each thread did 10 log spools of 80 bytes each followed by a single log force. The total number of log spools was 10000 and the total number of log forces was 1000. In experiment #2, each thread did a variable number of log spools (from 0 to 20) followed by a force. In addition, each log spool varied in size from 0 to 160 bytes. The total number of log spools was 10000, and the average number of log forces was 1000.

The location of the oldest record in the log is immediately available from the special sectors described in Section 13.2. The LSN of the newest record and the location of the first free sector are found using the algorithm described below in psuedocode. To avoid cluttering the algorithm with many unimportant details, this code ignores the fact that the log is circular. It also ignores the possibility that there may not be any records at all in the log. The code fragment completes with NEXT_SECTOR_FREE and HIGH_LSN_WRITTEN set to the appropriate values.

```
Read both special sectors;
Let mostRecentSpecial be the special sector with the higher ticker;
currentPassNumber := mostRecentSpecial.currentPassNumber;
Use a binary search to set
    highSectorWritten := the highest sector in the log such
                         that (sector.passNbr = currentPassNumber);

(* We may skip more sectors than absolutely necessary when we set *)
(* NEXT_SECTOR_FREE in the next line, but it is not important.    *)

NEXT_SECTOR_FREE := highSectorWritten + 1;

highSector := highSectorWritten;
While highSector.last = 0
    highSector := highSector - 1;

highSectorNeeded := the highest sector that would have been used
                    when writing the log record at highSector.last;

If highSectorNeeded <= highSectorWritten then

    (* The log record beginning at highSector.last is complete. *)
    (* It is the last complete record in the log.               *)
    HIGH_LSN_WRITTEN := the LSN corresponding to highSector.last;

else

    (* The log record beginning at highSector.last is incomplete. *)
    (* Every log record, however, is preceded by an offset to the *)
    (* (necessarily complete) record that logically precedes it.  *)
    HIGH_LSN_WRITTEN := the LSN corresponding to the record
                        preceding the one at highSector.last;
```

13.4 Related Work

Group commit algorithms have been in use for a number of years [35]. One study of group commit in the Tandem Transaction Monitoring Facility [45] discusses the relative merits of timer values for group commit. In their system, the log consisted only of commit records. The Tandem group made a distinction between a zero-wait timer, such as is implemented in the current Camelot local Log Manager, and a wait timer that forces transaction commit records every *n* milliseconds. They were able to show that in an optimal situation a wait timer will show better system throughput and response in a loaded system. We feel that the zero-wait timer implementation is sufficient for the Camelot system. Furthermore, the wait timer becomes an issue only under very heavy loads. Such loads would most likely be affected not by log latency, but by CPU load in the workstation environment in which Camelot was designed and implemented.

13.5 Conclusions

There are at least three refinements that could be made to this logging algorithm. One is a more sophisticated buffering strategy for satisfying log reads. The use of two track buffers as described here is quite satisfactory, and is very near optimal for some specific uses (such as Camelot server recovery), but could be improved. Currently, for instance, we allow an abort to temporarily preempt server recovery. The abort is likely to reuse both track buffers, and when server recovery resumes, they must be reloaded from disk.

Another refinement is to directly support relocation of bad sectors when duplex logging is used. We currently assume that it is acceptable for the Log Manager to report a disk error and let the system administrator redirect it using the bad block table built into the format of the affected disk partition. The damaged replica of the log can then be reconstructed by copying data from the good replica. This works, but is a bit inconvenient and keeps the node down unnecessarily.

The third refinement that we have considered is the use of "ping-pong buffers". A ping-pong algorithm is one that uses several alternate disk locations (and usually heads) for writing sectors that need to be forced before they are full. This avoids the waste of space caused by repeatedly forcing small disk records using the algorithm described here. Without ping-pong buffers, each log force must round the amount of data that actually needs to be written up to the next even multiple of a sector size. For a ping-pong algorithm to be fast, however, more disk heads must be used than are usually available on a workstation, which is our primary target environment.

The main advantages of the logging algorithm described here are efficiency and ease of implementation. This algorithm streams log data sequentially to disk and moves the disk head as infrequently as possible when writing the log. It allows simple recovery of Log Manager state after a node failure. It also uses a minimum amount of overhead to support scanning the log backward, record by record, during recovery.

Chapter 14

The Design of the Camelot Disk Manager

Jeffrey L. Eppinger

14.1 Introduction

Recoverable virtual memory is implemented by the Camelot Disk Manager. The Disk Manager manages the backing store for recoverable data and coordinates access to the stable storage log. The sections below listing functional goals, performance goals, and constraints are organized and labelled in a hierarchical form. This allows the subsequent section on the Disk Manager's architecture to reference the goals or constraints that are satisfied by each design decision.

14.1.1 Functional Goals

The Camelot Library provides a very easy-to-use interface to Camelot. It can do this, in part, because of the functional goals specified here.

F1. **Manage the backing store for recoverable virtual memory, allowing:**

(a) **Large regions.** We do not want to place any restriction on the sizes of regions the data server can manipulate.

(b) **Large amounts of data.** Many databases contain millions of entries. We must allow a data server to access gigabytes of data.

(c) **Overlapping regions.** For simplicity, some recovery algorithms do not allow regions to overlap. This is a significant restriction on language support. Such a restriction would make it difficult to allow field access to records or to implement a dynamic storage allocator.

F2. **Data servers may access recoverable data by mapping them into their address spaces.** This makes it easier (and faster) to access data. Address translation is done by the operating system. (The operating system can make use of virtual memory hardware to do address translation.) Regions that span page boundaries are easily accessed. Data servers no longer need to determine which data are in the cache. Data transfer between volatile and non-volatile storage may be more efficient.

F3. **Data servers may access more data than fit into their virtual address spaces.** There are databases that contain more that 2^{32} bytes (or words) of data.

F4. **Control the stable storage log:**

(a) **Process requests to write to and read from the stable storage log.** The Disk Manager processes log access requests from data servers, the Transaction Manager, and the Recovery Manager. This allows us to maintain a common log (see Section 14.1.3).

(b) **Initiate checkpoints.** Checkpoints limit recovery time.

(c) **Initiate log truncation.** This helps reduce the amount of data kept in the stable storage log.

(d) **Periodically flush hot pages.** Hot pages must be periodically written to non-volatile storage to allow log truncation.

(e) **Allow long-running transactions.** Log records for long-running (or prepared) transactions can also prevent log truncation. These records must be copied forward.

F5. **Allocate disk storage transactionally.** We do lazy disk allocation to data servers. This allocation must tolerate the same failures that Camelot tolerates. We use Camelot to allocate disk storage for data servers transactionally.

F6. **Allocate disk storage contiguously.** This reduces disk arm motion on sequential data access.

F7. **Update disk storage in place.** This does not scatter the (sequentially accessed) data.

F8. **Transactional administration database.** Each node must keep track of which servers to run, when to take dumps, how frequently to take checkpoints. Camelot keeps this information in a Camelot data server that is accessed transactionally.

F9. **Protect unrelated data servers from accessing each other's data.** Camelot is provided as a node-wide resource. Users must be protected from each other.

F10. **Support failure recovery.** When transactions abort, the Recovery Manager asks the Disk Manager for information. The Disk Manager must maintain this information, provide it to the Recovery Manager on demand, and allow the Recovery Manager to update the information during recoveries.

14.1.2 Performance Goals

P1. **Low overhead per page.** Paging is a major expense in large systems. Some transaction systems could incur double paging costs because they use virtual memory for their buffer pools. Camelot must have a low overhead per page.

P2. **Low overhead on log writes.** A major expense in transaction processing systems is the cost of writing data to the log. We do not want Camelot to add a lot of overhead to this expense.

P3. **Low overhead on log reads.** A less significant expense in transaction processing systems is the cost of reading data from the log. This cost may become significant when log reads slow down the log writes because the disk heads are moved out of position. We address the cost of reading data from the log in Camelot.

P4. **Global LRU page replacement algorithm.** We would like a page replacement algorithm which takes into account total system load, not just the load imposed by Camelot data servers. If the rest of the system is idle, Camelot should use all the available memory. If Camelot is idle, it should not consume vital system resources.

P5. **Prefetching and preflushing of pages.** Data servers (or data server writers) have knowledge about data access patterns. For example, data may be accessed sequentially and performance would benefit from prefetching or preflushing data.

P6. **Zero-fill pages.** Data servers (or data server writers) have knowledge about data access patterns. For example, data may be primarily append-only and performance would benefit from having portions of recoverable storage marked so that they would be zero-filled upon access.

P7. **Efficiently utilize multiple disks.** Large systems have multiple disks. We must be able to use them in parallel.

14.1.3 Constraints

The design of the Camelot Disk Manager was subject to the following constraints imposed by the global architecture of Mach and Camelot.

C1. **Must use messages sparingly.** Messages are orders of magnitude more expensive than a procedure call. Care must be taken to avoid the use of messages when implementing common operations, such as updating recoverable virtual memory.

C2. **Must use multiple threads to get good performance on multiprocessors.**

C3. **Must use UNIX device drivers.** At least, we must use UNIX device drivers initially.

C4. **Must support a common log.** During forward processing, log records are asynchronously spooled to stable storage. A common log allows several performance benefits (see Section 14.2.8).

14.2 Architecture

This section discusses the Disk Manager design in terms of the goals listed in Section 14.1. When a design goal is satisfied, its number is given in parentheses.

14.2.1 The External Memory Management Interface

The Camelot Disk Manager uses the Mach external memory management interface, introduced in Section 7.2. External memory managers allow user-level processes to back virtual memory. The Disk Manager backs recoverable storage for all data servers. Using external memory managers enables data servers to map their recoverable storage into their address spaces (F2). Using external memory managers also prevents double paging (P1). Paging now requires sending several messages. This may be a performance problem, but the Mach project is committed to making external memory managers work efficiently.

The Mach kernel uses a global LRU algorithm (P4). The external memory management interface allows the Disk Manager to put pages into the operating system's primary memory buffer pool before a data server faults on the page and to get pages out of the buffer pool before they are least recently used. This enables the Disk Manager to provide calls to let data servers prefetch and preflush pages (P5).

14.2.2 Region Storage and Specification

Recoverable regions are stored in recoverable segments. A recoverable segment can store up to 2^{48} bytes of storage. A data server can access its recoverable segments by mapping them into its address space, as described above.

Regions can be as large as 2^{32} bytes. This allows large regions (F1a). A data server can have several segments. Regions are specified by a region pointer and a length in bytes. A region pointer is a 16 bit segment identifier and a 48 bit offset. This allows a large number of regions and allows them to overlap (F1b and F1c). Data servers that have more data than fit into their address spaces can remap their address spaces accordingly (F3).

14.2.3 Threads of Control

Mach tasks can have multiple threads of control. This allows the Disk Manager to run several disks and write log records locally or over the network without reducing throughput. (P7 and C2).

14.2.4 Shared Memory Interfaces

The Disk Manager has an asynchronous shared memory interface with each data server. This helps reduce the number of messages sent during write transactions (C1).

14.2.5 Raw Disk I/O

Camelot backs recoverable storage (and the local log) in raw disk partitions (C3). Because the UNIX interface for the raw disk partitions is the same as for buffered files, the UNIX file system can be used for debugging. Performance using buffered files is not as good as that of raw disk partitions because an additional system call must be made to flush the operating system buffers after each write.

14.2.6 The Node Server Database

Camelot provides a distinguished data server called the Node Server. The Node Server is an actual data server that manipulates recoverable data using transactions. All disk mappings, server information and other node configuration information is kept by this server. This allows disk mappings and node configuration information to be kept transactionally (F5 and F8). Disk storage is allocated in large chunks to help keep recoverable pages contiguous on disk (F6). The Disk Manager also uses this configuration information to prevent one data server from accessing another data server's recoverable data by mapping it into its address space (F9).

The Disk Manager supports a special call to zero portions of recoverable storage by removing disk mappings. This causes these pages to be zero-filled when accessed allowing append-only data to be efficiently written (P6).

14.2.7 A Write-ahead Log

The Disk Manager uses write-ahead logging to store recovery information [85, 101]. Write-ahead logging uses an append-only log, structured as a sequence of variable-length records. The log is maintained in non-volatile, or stable, storage. Updates to a data object are made by modifying a copy of the object cached in volatile storage and by spooling one or more records to the log. These records contain an undo component that permits the effects of aborted transactions to be undone, and a redo component, that permits the effects of committed transactions to be redone. Special care must be taken when copying a modified object's pages back to non-volatile storage; the pages cannot be copied back to non-volatile storage until all spooled log records pertaining to those pages have been written to the log. When a cached page is copied back to non-volatile storage, it is copied back to the page from which it was previously read (F7).

14.2.8 A Common Log

The Disk Manager coordinates the use of a common log (C4). All requests to write records to and read records from the log are sent to the Disk Manager. Whenever possible, several log records are written together to stable storage to reduce overhead. However, the write-ahead log protocol requires that relevant log records must be safely stored in stable storage before the volatile representation of an object is copied to non-volatile storage and before transactions commit. This requirement can cause as few as one log record to be synchronously written to stable storage. These expensive, synchronous writes are termed *log forces*.

Maintaining a common log for all data servers results in substantially fewer log forces (P2). The traditional alternative is for each data server and the Transaction Manager to maintain their own logs. In this case, a transaction involving multiple data servers would require a log force at each data server and the Transaction Manager during commitment.[1] In Camelot, the Disk Manager buffers records spooled by data servers so that when the Transaction Manager instructs it to force the log, all the records can be forced at once.

To minimize the cost of reading the log during node recovery we provide a batch read call (P3).

There are several advantages to having the Disk Manager coordinate the use of a common log.

[1]The Transaction Manager would effectively execute a distributed commitment protocol with each local data server. See Section 16.3.2 for information on when log forces are performed during distributed commitment.

- The Disk Manager knows which data server log records have been written into the log. The Disk Manager needs this information to verify that it is safe to copy pages back to non-volatile storage.
- The Disk Manager already has a shared memory interface to each data server. This eliminates the complication of having another shared memory interface between each data server and a logging process.
- There are fewer context swaps.

Descriptions of the records the Disk Manager writes into the log are presented in Section 14.3.3. The Disk Manager uses the local or distributed Log Managers to write log records to the log.

Since the Disk Manager coordinates the common log, it can process requests to write to and read from the log (F4a). The Disk Manager has all the information needed to initiate checkpoints (F4b), initiate log truncation (F4c), flush hot pages (F4d), and copy forward the records of long-running (prepared) transactions (F4e).

The Disk Manager keeps lists of the log records that each transaction has written and lists of log records that describe modifications to each page. This allows the Disk Manager to respond to requests from the Recovery Manager with appropriate information at recovery time (F10).

14.3 Algorithms and Data Structures

Chapter 8 presented the data server's interface for accessing recoverable virtual memory. This section discusses the implementation of that interface. This section may be too detailed for some readers.

Recoverable virtual memory is primarily implemented by the Disk Manager, but the other Camelot components also participate. Section 14.3.1 describes the structure of the shared memory queues. Section 14.3.2 presents the interface that the Log Managers implement (and the Disk Manager uses). Section 14.3.3 describes the different records written into the log. Section 14.3.4 presents the grid, which is the main data structure the Disk Manager uses to keep track of records in the log. The last sections, 14.3.5, 14.3.6, and 14.3.7 discuss node configuration, media failure, and internal concurrency control.

14.3.1 Shared Memory Queues

To spool pin information and log records efficiently, each data server has a private shared memory queue which is shared with the Disk Manager. A data server has access to its own shared memory queue, but not to the queues for any other data server. The shared memory queue is used to send asynchronous messages to the Disk Manager. In addition to pin information and log data, prefetch, preflush, and lazy server-based commit messages may be sent this way.

Traditional latching primitives cannot be used to synchronize the shared memory queue because a server could stop the Disk Manager by holding the latch. Instead, the synchronization takes advantage of the fact that the Disk Manager is the consumer of queue elements and the data server is the producer. This means that only one task writes the head or tail of the queue. This synchronization depends on the fact that reading or writing a pointer is atomic.

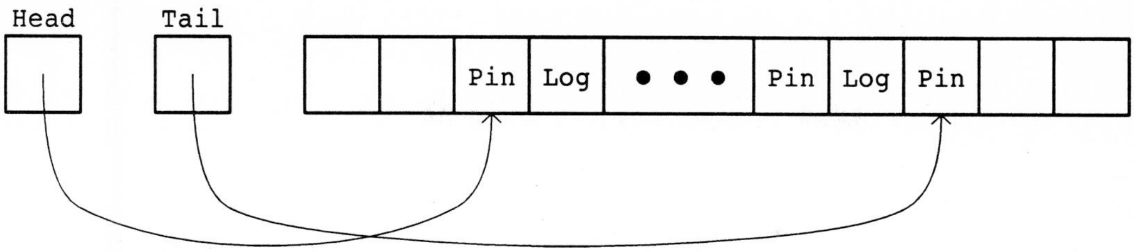

Figure 14.1: A Shared Memory Queue

Consider the queue depicted Figure 14.1. The `Head` is read and written by the data server, but only read by the Disk Manager to determine if the queue is empty. The `Tail` is read and written by the Disk Manager, but only read by the data server to determine if the queue is full. If the queue is full, the data server sends the next request synchronously to the Disk Manager using an RPC. After receiving the request, the Disk Manager processes the contents the queue before processing the request from the data server.

When writing log records, the Transaction Manager tells the Disk Manager which servers are involved. This way, the Disk Manager knows to process these servers' shared memory queues before writing the Transaction Manager's log records. Similarly, the Disk Manager checks the shared memory queue for the appropriate data server before processing `memory_object_data_write` requests from the kernel. Except for the time at which they are processed, requests sent via shared memory and via RPCs are processed identically.

There are several subtle points involved in synchronizing the shared memory queue:

1. There can be no latch to synchronize the data server and the Disk Manager. The Disk Manager cannot wait on such a latch. A malicious server could hold the latch and stop the Disk Manager.

2. The Disk Manager must be careful to copy important data out of the shared memory queue, rather than passing them by reference. This is because the data server could change the data in the shared memory queue after the Disk Manager has checked the validity of the data.

3. The code for queuing and dequeuing data must be very carefully written. Updates to the `Head` and `Tail` may need to be in separate routines so that an optimizing compiler does not move critical stores.

14.3.2 Log Management

The Disk Manager controls access to the stable storage log. For reasons of efficiency, the log service is provided as a module loaded into the Disk Manager at link time, but the interface allows the log service to be provided as an external server. Different implementations of the log module provide a stable storage local log, a non-volatile storage local log (one copy), and a stable storage remote log. Descriptions of these implementations may be found in Chapters 13 and 25.

To write a log record, the `LD_Write` call may be used.[2] A log record is provided in the `recPtr` field. A log sequence number (LSN) is returned in the `lsn` field.

```
routine LD_Write(
                 ldPort              : port_t;
                 recPtr              : pointer_t;
                 forceWhenFull       : boolean_t;
                 newTruncPoint       : cam_lsn_t;
             OUT lsn                 : cam_lsn_t;
             OUT bufferSent          : boolean_t;
             OUT reqTruncPoint       : cam_lsn_t);
```

`ldPort` The port on which the Log Manager receives messages from the Disk Manager. If the Log Manager is loaded into the Disk Manager, this parameter is `PORT_NULL`.

`recPtr` The pointer to the log record, which is sent out of line.

`forceWhenFull` A flag indicating that a force is to be done when this buffer is full.

`newTruncPoint` The LSN of the new truncation point.

`lsn` The LSN of the newly written log record.

`bufferSent` A flag indicating whether or not this log record caused a buffer to be sent to disk. This does not mean that (all of) this log record was sent to disk.

`reqTruncPoint` The LSN that the Log Manager would like to be the new truncation point.

Two LSNs may be compared to determine which is greater or if they are equal. If one LSN is greater than another, the log record to which the greater LSN refers is spooled after the log record to which the lesser LSN refers. The Disk and Recovery Managers may not obtain a meaningful number by subtracting LSNs. Arithmetic operations are only meaningful to the specific Log Manager being used.

The LSN returned by the `LD_Write` call may be presented to the `LD_Read` call to read a record.

```
routine LD_Read(
                 ldPort              : port_t;
                 lsn                 : cam_lsn_t;
             OUT prevLsn             : cam_lsn_t;
             OUT recPtr              : pointer_t);
```

`ldPort` The port on which the Log Manager receives messages from the Disk Manager. If the Log Manager is loaded into the Disk Manager, this parameter is `PORT_NULL`.

[2]A vector gather version of this call, `LD_GatherWrite`, is also provided. The parameters are the same, except that a vector of pointers and lengths is used to pass the record. Using a vector can save the Disk Manager from copying all the fields in a log record into contiguous storage just to give it to the Log Manager, which will copy the record again into the log. By passing a vector pointing to the fields, the Log Manager can gather the fields when it copies the log record into the log, or the network buffer, etc.

`lsn` The LSN of the log record we wish to read.
`prevLsn` The LSN of the log record that precedes the one requested.
`recPtr` A pointer to the record, which is returned out of line.

The LSN returned by the `LD_Write` call may be presented to the `LD_ForceLsn` call to force the log up to the record to which the LSN refers.

```
routine LD_ForceLsn(
            ldPort              : port_t;
            lsn                 : cam_lsn_t);
```

`ldPort` The port on which the Log Manager receives messages from the Disk Manager. If the Log Manager is loaded into the Disk Manager, this parameter is `PORT_NULL`.
`lsn` The LSN of the log record up to which we force.

14.3.3 Log Records

The Disk Manager writes several kinds of records into the log. The first field in each log record indicates the kind of record it is. Log records are divided into the following categories:

- **Modify records** are spooled on behalf of data servers to describe the modifications they make to recoverable regions. Each modify record contains the TID of the transaction that did the modification, a region pointer that specifies the beginning of the region and a length that specifies the region's size. The "first-family" bit indicates that this is the modify record with the lowest LSN for a particular transaction family. The "first-subtransaction" bit indicates that this is the modify record with the lowest LSN for a particular subtransaction. The "first-family" and "first-subtransaction" bits are used by the Recovery Manager to allow early termination of recovery processing. The modify record also contains the new value of the region and, if old-value/new-value logging is used, the old value of the region. A bit in the TID specifies which of new-value or old-value/new-value logging is being used.

- **Prepare records** are spooled by data servers when the Transaction Manager requests that a data server prepare a transaction. The prepare record contains the server ID of the data server and the TID of the preparing transaction. The data server provides the "prepare-data" that is written into the prepare record. Only the data server can interpret the "prepare-data."

- **Fetch records** are spooled by the Disk Manager to denote that a page of recoverable storage has been dirtied. During recovery, the Recovery Manager stops looking for changes to the page when it encounters this record. The first region pinned in a page causes a fetch record to be spooled for that page. No other fetch records will be spooled for the page until an end-write record has been written for this page (see below). The fetch record contains the server ID of the server to which the recoverable storage has been allocated, the region pointer that corresponds to the page of recoverable virtual memory, and the size of the page.

- **End-write records** are spooled after a dirty page has been copied back to non-volatile storage. End-write records have the same fields as fetch records.

- **End-write proposal records** are spooled by the Disk Manager when a page goes into "hot mode" (see Section 14.3.4, **Hot Pages**). End-write proposal records have the same fields as fetch and end-write records.

- **End-write confirmation records** are spooled by the Disk Manager when a page in "hot mode" is finally flushed (see Section 14.3.4, **Hot Pages**). In addition to the fields in fetch and other end-write records, the end-write confirmation record contains the LSN of the end-write proposal record it confirms.

- **Checkpoint records** are written by the Disk Manager. The checkpoint record contains a list of servers that have not yet been recovered, a list of active transaction families, a list of active recoverable segment IDs, a list of active server IDs, a list of active pages, and some data from the Transaction Manager. The Recovery Manager interprets the contents of the record to determine when recovery stops. The Transaction Manager stores information about the states of distributed transactions in the checkpoint record. Only the Transaction Manager can interpret the data it provides for the checkpoint record.

- **Server delete records** are spooled by the Disk Manager to indicate that the preceding log records that pertain to the deleted server should be ignored. The server delete record contains the server ID of the deleted server.

- In response to messages from the Recovery Manager, the Disk Manager spools records describing the Recovery Manager's progress in transaction abort, server recovery, and node recovery. For more details on these records see Chapter 15.

- In response to messages from the Transaction Manager, the Disk Manager writes records describing the state of transactions. For more details on these records see Chapter 16.

Additional bits may be added to the headers of log records to indicate which compressions have been applied. For example, there may be a bit to indicate that all the transaction identifiers (TIDs) are local and the `ipaddress` fields have been removed.

14.3.4 The Grid

The major data structure in the Disk Manager is the grid, which is used to keep track of records in the log. The grid is a natural extension of the two hash tables required to do write-ahead logging: one hash table for the active pages, one for the active transactions. Keeping such careful track of log records is required to support new-value logging.

The grid, depicted in Figure 14.2, is a virtual memory data structure. One axis of the grid is a hash table entry for each active page. The other axis of the grid is a hash table entry for each active transaction. There is an auxiliary hash table with an entry for each subtransaction that points to the transaction record. The definition of the subtransaction record (`sub_tran_record_t`) is not given here. The definitions of the page and transaction records are shown in Figures 14.3 and 14.4, respectively.

Whenever the Disk Manager spools a log record, the Log Manager returns an LSN. After the log record is spooled, the Disk Manager allocates a grid record, inserts the LSN into it, and links the grid record into the grid. If the log record pertains to a particular transaction, the grid record

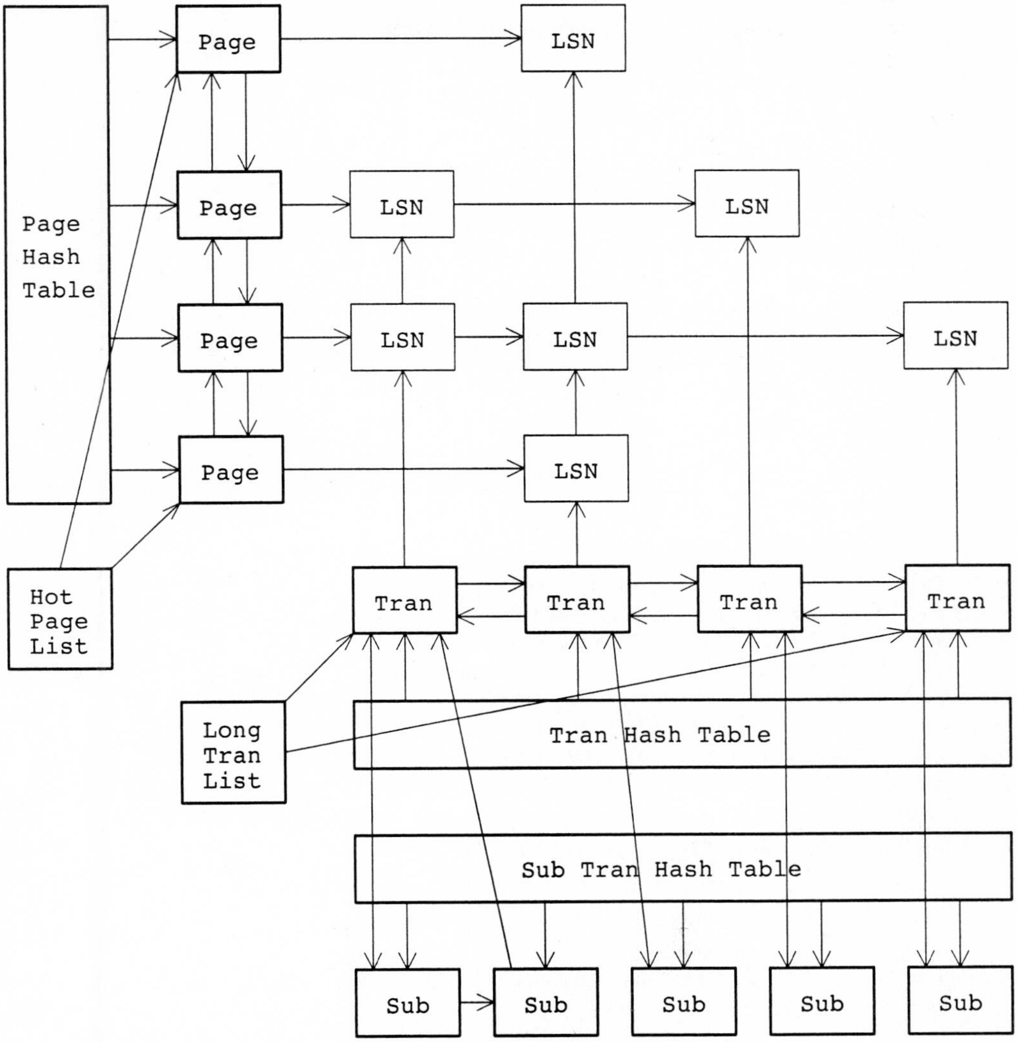

Figure 14.2: The Grid Tracks Records in the Log

The grid is the major data structure in the Disk Manager. The grid is a natural extension of the two hash tables required to do write-ahead logging: one hash table for the active pages, one for the active transactions. One axis of the grid is a hash table entry for each active page. The other axis of the grid is a hash table entry for each active transaction. There is an auxiliary hash table with an entry for each subtransaction. Each active page has a page record in the hash table for pages. Each active transaction has a transaction record in the hash table for transactions.

```
typedef struct page_record {
    cam_rptr_t                    pageId;
    boolean_t                     everPinned;
    u_int                         pinCount;
    boolean_t                     flushing;
    lsn_t                         ewLsn;
    u_int                         ewRecNbr;
    s_record_t                   *serverPtr;
    struct grid_record           *pageGridNewest;
    struct grid_record           *pageGridOldest;
    struct patch_record          *pagePatchNewest;
    struct patch_record          *pagePatchOldest;
    struct page_record       *hotPageNewer;
    struct page_record       *hotPageOlder;
    struct page_record       *lruMoreRecent;
    struct page_record       *lruLessRecent;
    cam_cht_link_t                pageHashLink;
    pointer_t                     data;
} page_record_t;
```

`pageId` The region pointer for (the beginning of) the page.

`everPinned` A boolean that tells if the page was ever pinned. Used at checkpoint after recovery to get rid of pages for which backlinks but no restores were done.

`pinCount` The count of the number of outstanding "pins" on a page.

`flushing` A boolean that is `TRUE` when the page is being copied back to non-volatile storage.

`ewLsn` When flushing a hot page, this will be the LSN of end-write record.

`ewRecNbr` When flushing a hot page, this will be the record number of the end-write record.

`serverPtr` A pointer to the record describing the state of the server that owns the recoverable segment.

`pageGridNewest` The head of the doubly linked list of grid records for this page. Grid records are used to keep track of records in the log.

`pageGridOldest` The tail of the doubly linked list of grid records for this page. Grid records are used to keep track of records in the log.

`pagePatchNewest` The head of the doubly linked list of patch records for this page. Patch records are used to track updates to the page when it is hot.

`pagePatchOldest` The tail of the doubly linked list of patch records for this page. Patch records are used to track updates to the page when it is hot.

`hotPageNewer` The forward link for the hot page list that tracks which page is hottest.

`hotPageOlder` The backward link for the hot page list that tracks which page is hottest.

`lruMoreRecent` The forward links for the LRU chain, which is used when simulating a buffer pool for test purposes.

`lruLessRecent` The backward links for the LRU chain, which is used when simulating a buffer pool for test purposes.

`pageHashLink` The link to the next page record in this hash bucket.

`data` A pointer to a copy of the page. This field only points to data when the page is hot.

Figure 14.3: Page Record

```
typedef struct tran_record {
    cam_fam_id_t              famId;
    boolean_t                 killing;
    boolean_t                 copyingForward;
    boolean_t                 backstopped;
    struct ghost_record      *ghostList;
    struct grid_record       *tranGridNewest;
    struct grid_record       *tranGridOldest;
    struct patch_record      *tranPatchNewest;
    struct patch_record      *tranPatchOldest;
    struct sub_tran_record   *subTranHead;
    struct tran_record       *longTranNewer;
    struct tran_record       *longTranOlder;
    cam_cht_link_t            tranHashLink;
} tran_record_t;
```

`famId` The transaction family identifier.

`killing` A boolean that is `TRUE` when this transaction is a long-running transaction that the Disk Manager is attempting to abort.

`copyingForward` A boolean that is `TRUE` when this transaction is a prepared, long-running transaction that the Disk Manager is copying forward in the log.

`backstopped` A boolean that is `TRUE` when this transaction is a prepared, long-running, new-value transaction that the Disk Manager has backstopped.

`ghostList` A list of servers that have participated in the transaction and have crashed. There will only be entries on this list if the transaction is prepared.

`tranGridNewest` The head of the doubly linked list of grid records for this transaction. Grid records are used to keep track of records in the log.

`tranGridOldest` The tail of the doubly linked list of grid records for this transaction.

`tranPatchNewest` The head of the doubly linked list of patch records for this transaction. Patch records are used to track updates to hot pages that the transaction has modified.

`tranPatchOldest` The tail of the doubly linked list of patch records for this transaction. Patch records are used to track updates to hot pages that the transaction has modified.

`subTranHead` The head of a list of the records for active subtransactions in this family.

`longTranNewer` The forward link for the long-running transaction list that tracks which transaction has run the longest.

`longTranOlder` The backward link for the long-running transaction list that tracks which transaction has run the longest.

`tranHashLink` The link to the next transaction record in this hash bucket.

Figure 14.4: Transaction Record

```
typedef struct grid_record {
    lsn_t                    lsn;
    unsigned int
            unpin            : 1,
            recNbr           : 31;
    struct tran_record      *tranRecPtr;
    struct page_record      *pageRecPtr;
    struct grid_record      *tranGridOlder;
    struct grid_record      *pageGridOlder;
} grid_record_t;
```

`lsn` The LSN of the log record to which the grid record corresponds.
`unpin` A boolean that indicates that the page to which this grid record points should be unpinned when the transaction commits (i.e., this is a new-value modify record).
`recNbr` The Disk Manager internal record number for this log record.
`tranRecPtr` The pointer to the transaction record for this grid record.
`pageRecPtr` The pointer to the page record for this grid record.
`tranGridOlder` The pointer to the next (older) grid record for this transaction.
`pageGridOlder` The pointer to the next (older) grid record for this page.

Figure 14.5: Grid Record

is inserted at the head of the list of grid records for the transaction. If the log record pertains to a particular page, the grid record is inserted at the head of the list of grid records for the page.[3] The format of the grid record is shown in Figure 14.5.

Several algorithms described below need to know how long ago a record was spooled to the log. Since LSNs are only comparable and may not be subtracted to yield a meaningful number, the Disk Manager keeps a count of the number of records spooled since Camelot has started. The volatile record number for this record is stored in the `recNbr` field of each grid record.

The page records are threaded into a doubly-linked list, called the *hot page list*, ordered by oldest log record for that page. The transaction records are threaded into a doubly-linked list, called the *long-running transaction list*, also ordered by oldest log record. As we will see below, page and transaction records are created when the first log record is spooled for the page or transaction. By inserting the page record or the transaction record at the tail of the hot page or long-running transaction list when the record is created, the list will be ordered by oldest log record for page and transaction. The head of each list shows the hottest page and the longest-running transaction. The hot page and long-running transaction lists are used to compute the truncation point (see **Truncation**, below) and to detect hot pages (see **Hot Pages**, below) and long-running transactions (see **Long-Running Transactions**, below).

Pin Requests

When the Disk Manager receives a `DS_PinRegion` request (described in Section 8.4), it looks up each page that contains part of the region in the hash table for active pages. If no page record is

[3] If a record describes a change that spans more than one page, a separate grid record is used for each page.

found, the Disk Manager allocates a page record, initializes it, inserts it into the hash table, spools a fetch record for the page, inserts a grid record for the fetch record into the grid and finally sets the pin count to one.

Log Requests

When the Disk Manager receives a `DS_LogOldValueNewValue` request (described in Section 8.4), it looks up each page and the subtransaction in the appropriate hash tables.[4] It is an error if a page is not pinned. If there is no record for the subtransaction, a `sub_tran_record_t` is created and the `first_sub` bit is set in the modify record. If no `tran_record_t` is found for the transaction family, one is created and the `first_fam` bit is set. The log record is spooled. A grid record is allocated (for each page) and linked into the grid. Because this is an old-value/new-value transaction, the `unpin` field in the grid record is set to zero, and the pin counts are decremented in each page record.

A `DS_LogNewValue` request is handled just as a `DS_LogOldValueNewValue` request except that the `unpin` field is set and the pin counts are not decremented in the page records.

The Transaction Manager uses two calls to write log records. The `DT_LargeLogWrite` call lets the Transaction Manager send an arbitrary amount of data in each list.

```
routine DT_LargeLogWrite(
                    dtPort           : port_t;
                    unsed            : u_int;
                    data             : pointer_t;
                    serverListPtr    : cam_server_id_list_t;
                    completeTrans    : cam_tid_list_t);
```

`dtPort` The port on which the Disk Manager receives messages from the Transaction Manager.

`unused` This parameter is ignored.

`data` The data contains the records, one after another, each record preceded by its length. The length is an aligned `u_int`.

`serverListPtr` A list of servers that should have their shared memory queues processed before the data are processed.

`completeTrans` A list of complete transactions. This list is piggy-backed with these messages so that the Disk Manager can clean its data structures.

The `DT_SmallLogWrite` call allows a fixed maximum amount of data to be sent in each list. The `DT_SmallLogWrite` call is preferred if the data will fit, because fixed sized Mach messages are much cheaper than variable size messages. Except for the amount of data and the cost of the messages, these calls are interchangeable.

```
routine DT_SmallLogWrite(
                dtPort           : port_t;
```

[4]Even a top-level transaction will have an entry in the subtransaction hash table.

```
unused          : u_int;
dataLength      : u_int;
data            : cam_short_log_record_t;
serverCount     : u_int;
serverList      : cam_short_server_id_list_t;
completeLength  : u_int;
completeTrans   : cam_short_tid_list_t);
```

`dtPort` The port on which the Disk Manager receives messages from the Transaction Manager.

`unused` This parameter is ignored.

`dataLength` The length of the data.

`data` The data contains the records, one after another, each record preceded by its length. The length is an aligned `u_int`.

`serverCount` The number of servers in the `serverList`.

`serverList` A list of servers that should have their shared memory queues processed before the data are processed.

`completeLength` The number of TIDs in the `completeList`.

`completeTrans` A list of complete transactions. This list is piggy-backed with these messages so that the Disk Manager can clean its data structures.

When the Disk Manager gets a request from the Transaction Manager to write log records, it first processes the shared memory queues for the servers listed in the `serverList`. Then, the Disk Manager writes the Transaction Manager's log records and forces the log. Finally, the Disk Manager processes the `completeTrans` list. For each transaction on the `completeTrans` list, the Disk Manager looks up the transaction in the transaction hash table. If the transaction is not found, it is assumed to be read-only. If the transaction is found, the Disk Manager cleans up the grid records for the transaction. For each grid record, the Disk Manager checks the `unpin` bit. If it is set, it decrements the pin count in the page record indicating the page is pinned by one fewer transaction. Then, the Disk Manager checks to determine whether the grid record has been freed in the page link direction.[5] If so, the Disk Manager frees the grid record. If not, the Disk Manager marks the grid record as free in the transaction link direction. After the grid records are processed, the transaction record is removed from the hash table and is freed.

Page Out

When the Disk Manager gets a `memory_object_data_write` message from the kernel, it looks up the page in the page hash table. If the page is not found, the data server has not been using the "pin-update-log" protocol. The data server is killed and a diagnostic message is issued. If the page is found in the hash table, the Disk Manager checks the pin count. If the pin count is non-zero, the page's data is saved by setting the `data` field of the page record to point to a copy of the page, and the page is handled as if it were hot (see **Hot Pages**, below). If the pin count is zero, the Disk Manager

[5] A grid record is free in the page or transaction direction if the page or transaction link is set to a special value; in this case, -1 is used.

gets the LSN out of the most recent grid record for this page and forces the log to this LSN. Then the Disk Manager writes the page out to non-volatile storage, allocating disk storage if necessary (see Section 14.3.5, **Disk Allocation**), and then processes the grid records for this page. For each grid record, the Disk Manager checks to determine whether the record is free in the transaction link direction. If not, it marks the record free in the page direction. If so, it frees the grid record. After all the grid records have been processed, the Disk Manager frees the page record.

Most `memory_object_data_write` messages will ask the Disk Manager to write out pages that are least-recently-used or pages that the data server has requested be preflushed. Such pages would only be pinned if the data server should happen to access the page just as it was selected for page out. In this rare case, the kernel will soon ask the Disk Manager for the page back, because there is a data server thread taking a fault on the page.

Before flushing each page, the Disk Manager must check to determine whether it needs to force to the log any spooled records that describe changes to the page. The log force will only be necessary if the page has been modified by a long-running old-value/new-value transaction.[6] In most cases, the commit of a transaction that modified the page will cause the log records to be forced.

Page In

When the Disk Manager receives a `memory_object_data_request` message from the kernel, the Disk Manager looks up the page in the page hash table. If the page record is found and the `data` field points to the page, the Disk Manager has been trying to page out the page, but it was pinned. The Disk Manager will then return a copy of the page to the kernel with the `memory_object_data_provided` message. See **Hot Pages**, below, for an explanation of how the Disk Manager handles page out of pinned pages. If the record is not found or the `data` field does not point to the page, the Disk Manager reads the page from non-volatile storage and returns it to the kernel with the `memory_object_data_provided` message.

Recovery Support

The grid is used to provide information to the Recovery Manager during transaction abort. When a transaction aborts, the Recovery Manager issues a `DR_GetTranLsns` RPC to the Disk Manager. The `tidList` contains a list of subtransactions in the same family. The Disk Manager looks up each TID in the subtransaction hash table. Each transaction that is not in the table is assumed to be read-only (at this site). The Disk Manager returns the number of read-only subtransactions in the `readOnlyCnt` field so that subtransaction abort can stop early, and it returns the list of LSNs in the grid records for this transaction family in the `lsnList` field. The `cachePtr` is used to ship log information from the Disk Manager's logging component to the Recovery Manager's logging component.

```
routine DR_GetTranLsns(
                drPort          : port_t;
                tidList         : cam_tid_list_t;
            OUT lsnList         : cam_lsn_list_t;
```

[6]Forces are not necessary for pages modified by new-value transactions, because new-value transactions keep pages pinned until commit time.

```
                OUT readOnlyCnt      : u_int;
                OUT cachePtr         : pointer_t);
```

`drPort` The port on which the Disk Manager receives requests from the Recovery Manager.

`tidList` the list of transactions in which the Recovory Manager is interested.

`lsnList` The list of the LSNs spooled on behalf of this family. The list is in decreasing order (from newest to oldest). The Disk Manager may not truncate these log records until it gets a `DR_DoneWithLsns` message (see below).

`readOnlyCnt` The count of the number of the given transactions that are read-only.

`cachePtr` refers to the data that must be transferred from the version of Log Manager being used by the Disk Manager to the (read-only) version used by the Recovery Manager to make them consistent.

When the Disk Manager receives a `DR_GetObjectLsns` request from the Recovery Manager, the Disk Manager looks up each page for each region that the Recovery Manager listed in the page hash table. For each such page, the Disk Manager collects the LSNs in the grid records. The Disk Manager constructs a sorted list of these LSNs and returns them to the Recovery Manager in the `lsnList` field.

```
routine DR_GetObjectLsns(
                drPort              : port_t;
                rptrList            : cam_regptr_list_t;
                sizeList            : cam_size_list_t;
            OUT lsnList             : cam_lsn_list_t);
```

`drPort` The port on which the Disk Manager receives requests from the Recovery Manager.

`rptrList` the list of regions in which the Recovery Manager is interested.

`sizeList` the size of the list of regions in the `rptrList`.

`lsnList` The list of the LSNs spooled on behalf of this family. The list is in decreasing order (from newest to oldest). The Disk Manager may not truncate these log records until it gets a DR_DoneWithLsns message (see below).

Checkpoint

To satisfy the recovery algorithm (see Section 15.2.1) and the truncation algorithm (see below), the Disk Manager must write a checkpoint record into the log at regular intervals. The computation of the checkpoint interval is discussed below in **Checkpoint Interval Computation**. The checkpoint interval is a number of records. The Disk Manager keeps track of the number of records written since the last checkpoint. After each message request is processed, the Disk Manager checks to determine whether or not it is time to write a checkpoint record. If it is time, the Disk Manager will write a checkpoint record containing the list of servers that are not recovered (see Section 14.3.5, **Down Servers**), the list of active transaction families (from the transaction hash table), the list of active pages (written as regions, from the page hash table), the list of active segments (and the list of servers that use each segment), and finally, any data the Transaction Manager would like to put into the checkpoint record.

Truncation

The *truncation point* is the earliest record in the log (the record with the lowest LSN) that the Recovery Manager will need to run node, server, or transaction recovery. The Disk Manager gives this LSN to the Log Manager with every log write call. The Log Manager uses this parameter to truncate the log. In a non-volatile Log Manager, records with LSNs lower than the truncation point can be discarded. In a stable storage Log Manager, the truncation point is used to determine the records that can be stored in slow remote storage. The truncation point is also used to approximate the amount of time it will take to recover a node after a crash (see **Hot Pages** and **Long-Running Transactions**, below).

To recover a node (or a server or a transaction), the Recovery Manager may read any log record (with an LSN in a grid record) in the grid. The recovery algorithm always scans back to at least one checkpoint. The truncation point is therefore the minimum LSN of all the grid records in the grid and the LSN of the most recent checkpoint (and the `minRecLsn`, see below).

The Recovery Manager may be aborting a transaction while the truncation point is being computed. The Recovery Manager cannot read a log record with an LSN earlier than the truncation point. For this reason, the Disk Manager keeps track of the LSN for the earliest log record that the Recovery Manager may read in the `minRecLsn` variable. Every time the Disk Manager sends a list of LSNs to the Recovery Manager in a `DR_GetTranLsns` or a `DR_GetObjectLsns` call, the Disk Manager checks to determine whether the lowest LSN is lower than the `minRecLsn`. If so, the Disk Manager sets the `minRecLsn` to this new lowest value. When the Recovery Manager is finished using a list of LSNs, it uses the `DR_DoneWithLsns` call to tell the Disk Manager what the new minimum should be. The `minRecLsn` is also used in the "minimum" computation when computing the truncation point.

```
routine DR_DoneWithLsns(
                    drPort          : port_t;
                    lsn             : cam_lsn_t);
```

`drPort` The port on which the Disk Manager receives requests from the Recovery Manager.

`lsn` The lowest LSN that the Recovery Manager still cares about.

The minimum LSN of all the records in the grid is just the minimum LSN of the hottest page and the longest-running transaction. These LSNs are found simply by chasing two pointers. The truncation point is the minimum of these four LSNs shown below. (Names are taken from the code to show how simple this is.)

```
hotPageOldest->pageGridOldest->lsn
longTranOldest->tranGridOldest->lsn
```

```
l_LastCheckpointLsn
l_MinRecLsn
```

Log records describing data server modifications can be quite large. This means that a checkpoint interval in records is not always sufficient to keep from running out of log space. For this reason, the Log Manager can request a particular truncation point by setting the `reqTruncPoint`. If the last checkpoint's LSN is less than the `reqTruncPoint`, a checkpoint will be taken. The `reqTruncPoint` can also force hot pages to be flushed and long transactions to be aborted.

Hot Pages

A *hot page* is a page that is frequently accessed. Hot pages therefore never become least-recently-used. This means that the kernel will not issue a `memory_object_data_write` call without being asked. If active pages are not regularly written to non-volatile storage, the truncation point will not increase and recovery time will increase. For this reason, hot pages must be flushed at regular intervals. The interval that is chosen is the checkpoint interval. The reason for this choice is discussed below in **Checkpoint Interval Computation**.

After each message request is processed, the Disk Manager checks for hot pages. The Disk Manager knows which page is hottest by looking at the head of the hot page list. By comparing the `recNbr` field of that page's oldest grid record with the record number of the last log record written, the Disk Manager can tell when the hottest page has been in memory longer than a checkpoint interval.[7] If the hottest page has been in memory too long, the Disk Manager sets the `flushing` flag in the page record and asks the Mach kernel to flush the page by using the `memory_object_lock_request` call. This call is used to ask the kernel to flush, clean, or change the protection of a memory object's physical memory pages.

```
simpleroutine memory_object_lock_request(
            paging_request_port        : port_t;
            offset                     : vm_offset_t
            size                       : vm_size_t;
            should_clean               : boolean_t;
            should_flush               : boolean_t;
            lock_value                 : vm_prot_t;
            reply_to                   : port_t);
```

`paging_object_port` The port the kernel provides to service requests about this memory object.

`offset` The offset in the object at which the request begins.

`size` The size in bytes of the region of the object to which the request pertains.

`should_clean` A boolean value that indicates the page(s) should be cleaned by sending a `memory_object_data_provided` message.

[7] If the Log Manager is running out of log space, it requests a truncation point by setting the `reqTruncPoint` parameter in the `LD_Write` call. If the truncation point is greater than the LSN in the oldest grid record for this page, the page is considered hot.

`should_flush` A boolean value that indicates the page(s) should be removed from physical memory.

`lock_value` The access permissions that are denied (read, write, and/or execute.

`reply_to` A port to which a message should be sent when the request has been processed. This parameter can be `PORT_NULL` if no reply is desired.

Flushing hot pages is tricky because pages cannot be written if they are pinned, as they are very likely to be.[8] Since the page is frequently used, the kernel soon asks for the page with a `memory_object_data_request` call. If the Disk Manager just gives the page back to the kernel, it have the same problem as before: the hot page will not be written back. We have considered several algorithms for flushing hot pages:

1. The Disk Manager can delay responding to the kernel's request for the page and wait for the page to become unpinned. This solution does not work. With a multi-threaded server, it is easy to construct a sequence of "pin-update-log" operations that never leaves the page unpinned.

2. The Disk Manager can construct a "can't pin list" for each data server and wait for the page to become unpinned. Once a page is on the "can't pin list" subsequent pin attempts will result in messages to the Disk Manager (rather than using the shared memory queue). The Disk Manager can delay responding to the pin requests until the page is written. This solution does not work either. In the case of new-value logging, the pages modified by a new-value transaction stay pinned until the new-value transaction completes. By not replying to the kernel's request for the page, some data server threads will remain suspended. These threads may be working on behalf of a transaction that has the page pinned. We can send messages to the data server telling it not to allow any new transactions to access this page, but this may stop a nested top-level transaction that is doing work for a transaction that has the page pinned.[9]

3. The Disk Manager can stop all subsequent pins to the page and abort all transactions that have a hot page pinned. This is very expensive. We have not spent very much time optimizing abort and this would make aborts occur with much greater frequency.

4. We can copy the records describing changes to a hot page forward in the log. This would be about as expensive as aborting the transactions because reading the log is very expensive.

---

[8] If the machine on which Camelot is run has lots of memory and the checkpoint interval is small, the Disk Manager may ask for unused pages to be flushed before the kernel detects that they have become LRU. This is because the kernel is not running low on physical buffer pages. This is sensible because if the Disk Manager waited for the kernel to flush these pages, the recovery time constraints would not be met. In such a case, all pages will become hot before they are detected as LRU. When the `memory_object_data_write` request arrives, the page will not be pinned and it will simply be flushed.

[9] This also imposes a restriction on both old-value/new-value and new-value logging implementations. One implementation of the "pin-update-log" sequence is to provide a macro, such as the Camelot Library's `MODIFY` macro. When expanded, this macro first spools a pin request, saves the old value, then executes a C assignment statement to update the region in virtual memory, and finally spools a log request using the saved old value and the new value from virtual memory. The problem is that the right-hand side of the C assignment statement can have side effects. In particular, the right-hand side of the assignment might execute a function call that can execute another `MODIFY` macro. This can lead to a deadlock similar to the multi-threaded deadlock described above.

The actual solution is much cheaper. The Disk Manager does give the page back to the kernel allowing forward progress to continue, however the Disk Manager keeps a copy of the page and writes it when *the copy* becomes unpinned. When the Disk Manager is holding a copy of a page, the page is said to be in "hot mode."

To ensure that a page in hot mode becomes unpinned, the Disk Manager queues new modifications to the page. A new modification is not applied to the Disk Manager's copy of the page until the transaction that did the modify commits.[10] This means that the pin count on the Disk Manager's copy of the page does not go up. Eventually, the transactions that have the page pinned will complete and the pin count will drop to zero. In terms of recovery, the page is considered to have been written as of the time the kernel originally sent it to the Disk Manager. However, the contents of the page will reflect additional committed changes.

The Disk Manager tracks updates to each page in hot mode, applying them to the copy of the page as transactions commit. Updates are tracked in an auxiliary layer in the grid, above the grid records. See Figure 14.6. The rest of this section describes the implementation details of flushing hot pages.

When a page is in hot mode, pin, log, transaction commit, page in, and page out requests manipulate patch records. (This additional function of the grid was not explained above for simplicity.) The structure of a patch record is shown in Figure 14.7.

When a `DS_PinRegion` request arrives, the Disk Manager looks up each page in the page hash table. If the `data` field for a page is not null, the page is in hot mode. Instead of incrementing the pin count, the Disk Manager creates a patch record, sets the `offset` and `length` fields to describe the offset and length of the modification to this page, and links the patch record into the patch grid. The `gridRecPtr` is set to null to indicate that the pin has been done, but not the log.

When a `DS_LogNewValue` or `DS_LogOldValueNewValue` request arrives, the Disk Manager looks up each page in the page hash table. If the page is in hot mode, the Disk Manager looks for a patch record for the previous pin request. If such a patch record is not found, the pin is assumed to have been processed before the page went into hot mode and the log request is processed in the usual manner. If the patch record is found, the grid record is created and the log record is spooled in the usual manner, but the `gridRecPtr` link is set to point to the new grid record. The new value is copied into the patch record.

When a transaction commits, the Disk Manager applies the patch records for the transaction. This simply involves copying the new values out of the patch records into the Disk Manager's copy of the page.

When the page finally becomes unpinned, Disk Manager will write it to disk. All remaining patch records for the page will be processed as follows:

1. Any patch records that represent pin requests but not log requests (i.e., patch records that have a null `gridRecPtr`) will cause the pin count to be incremented.

2. Any patch records for new-value transactions will cause the pin count to be incremented and the `unpin` bit in the corresponding grid record to be set.

3. The patch records for the page will be deleted.

---

[10]Modifications to the kernel's copy of the page are applied immediately in the usual fashion.

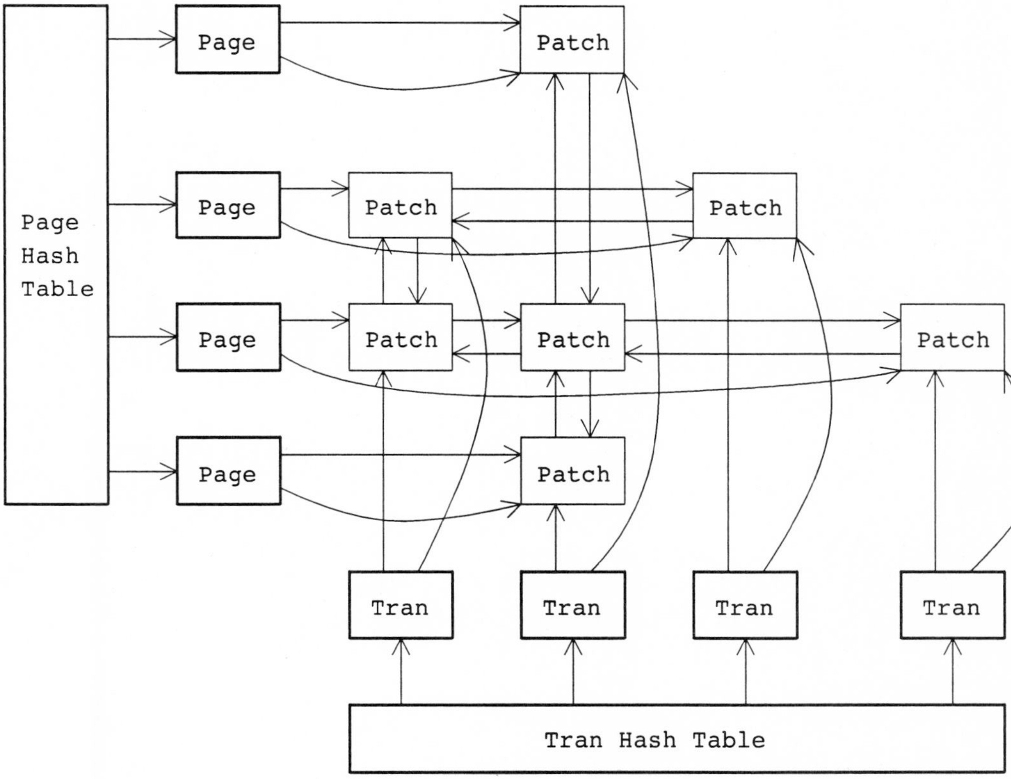

Figure 14.6: Patch Records in the Grid
When a page is in hot mode, patch records are created for each new modification to the page. A patch record is linked into a doubly-linked list of patch records for the page modified and into a doubly-linked list of patch records for the transaction on behalf of which the modification was made.

```
typedef struct patch_record {
    unsigned short          offset;
    unsigned short          length;
    struct grid_record     *gridRecPtr;
    struct tran_record     *tranRecPtr;
    struct page_record     *pageRecPtr;
    struct patch_record    *tranPatchNewer;
    struct patch_record    *tranPatchOlder;
    struct patch_record    *pagePatchNewer;
    struct patch_record    *pagePatchOlder;
    /* the data will be here. */
} patch_record_t;
```

`offset` The offset of the object within the page.
`length` The length of the object.
`gridRecPtr` The pointer to the grid record that this patch record shadows.
`tranRecPtr` The pointer to the transaction record for this patch record.
`pageRecPtr` The pointer to the page record for this patch record.
`tranPatchNewer` The pointer to the previous (newer) patch record for this transaction.
`tranPatchOlder` The pointer to the next (older) patch record for this transaction.
`pagePatchNewer` The pointer to the previous (newer) patch record for this page.
`pagePatchOlder` The pointer to the next (older) patch record for this page.

Figure 14.7: Patch Record

When a page is in hot mode, pin and log requests are queued in patch records. In other words, the pin count will not go up for such a page. As transactions that had the page pinned before it went into hot mode commit, the pin count will go to zero. This allows the page to be written as of the time that it went into hot mode. The page may reflect updates that had not occurred as of the time the page went into hot mode, but these updates will be part of committed transactions.

In very rare circumstances, a page in hot mode may become LRU and the kernel will send it to the Disk Manager requesting that it be flushed. The Disk Manager keeps this page in an auxiliary page table. If the kernel subsequently requests the page, a copy of the page in the auxiliary page table is given to the kernel. If the kernel subsequently flushes a page that is already in the auxiliary page table, the old page in the table is deleted and the more recent page inserted. Once the Disk Manager's copy of the page in hot mode becomes unpinned and is flushed, the page from the auxiliary page table is removed from the table and put into the grid (in hot mode).

Long-Running Transactions

New-value logging was developed for short transactions. New-value transactions keep pages pinned for the duration of the transaction. If the new-value transaction runs longer than a checkpoint interval, the pages it modifies will be detected as hot by the hot page code. The Disk Manager will put the page in hot mode and wait for it to become unpinned. The new-value transaction may not finish for a long time because either the transaction is slow, does a lot of processing, or is prepared and waiting for the coordinator.

The Disk Manager can detect long-running new-value transactions by checking the head of the long-running transaction list. A new-value transaction that runs longer than a checkpoint interval is considered to have run too long. It is aborted using the `TD_Kill` call to the Transaction Manager. If the Transaction Manager reports that the transaction is prepared, the new-value transaction is backstopped and copied forward (see **Copy Forward** and **Backstopping**, below).

If the Log Manager is running out of space in the log, it notifies the Disk Manager by setting the `reqTruncPoint` field in the `LD_Write` call to the LSN at which the Log Manager would like the Disk Manager to truncate. The Disk Manager will abort any transaction that has log records with LSNs less than this truncation point using the `TD_Kill` call to the Transaction Manager. This is how long-running old-value/new-value transactions are aborted. If the Transaction Manager responds by saying that the transaction is prepared, the Disk Manager will copy the records for this transaction forward in the log. (See **Copy Forward**, below.)

Copy Forward

When the Disk Manager attempts to kill a long-running transaction, but it is told by the Transaction Manager that the transaction is prepared, the Disk Manager copies the transaction's records forward in the log. By looking at this transaction's grid records, the Disk Manager knows which log records have been spooled. The Disk Manager (in a separate thread) reads each log record, starting with the oldest, and spools it into the log, again, setting the `isCopyForward` bit. The Disk Manager constructs a list of the LSNs for these new records as it is spooling the new records. The last record to be copied forward is the transaction's prepare record. After the prepare record has been copied forward, the Disk Manager forces the log and changes all the transaction's grid records to have the LSNs of the new records.

The Recovery Manager will not be confused if there is a failure while a transaction is being copied forward. The Recovery Manager uses a backwards scan to process the log, starting with the most recently written records. If the Recovery Manager encounters modify records for a transaction with the `isCopyForward` bit set before it reads a prepare record with the `isCopyForward` bit on, it knows to ignore these records.

Backstopping

Before the Disk Manager attempts to copy forward a prepared new-value transaction, it must backstop it. Backstopping effectively converts the new-value transaction into an old-value/new-value transaction by going through the motions of aborting the transaction and then writing the old values into *backstop records*. Backstop records are linked into the grid for the new-value transaction. After the transaction has been backstopped, the Disk Manager will unpin the pages modified by the new-value transaction. This transaction may now be copied forward.

Checkpoint Interval Computation

The checkpoint interval is dynamically computed. The node administrator tells the Node Server how much time node recovery should take: call this time *r* seconds. Using the `ND_RecoveryStats` call, the Disk Manager passes to the Node Server the number of records processed during the recovery pass and the elapsed time of the recovery pass in milliseconds.

```
camelotroutine ND_RecoveryStats(
                numRecords        : u_int;
                numMsecs          : u_int);
```

`numRecords` The number of records processed in the last recovery pass.

`numMsecs` The number of milliseconds of elapsed time used to do the last recovery pass.

The Node Server keeps statistics from the last 5 recovery passes in its recoverable virtual memory. For each recovery pass, the elapsed time in milliseconds, t_i, and the number of records processed, n_i, are kept. The average time in milliseconds to process a record during recovery is approximately

$$\frac{\sum_{i=1}^{5} t_i}{\sum_{i=1}^{5} n_i}$$

The number of records that are processed in r seconds is

$$\frac{1000r\sum_{i=1}^{5} n_i}{\sum_{i=1}^{5} t_i}$$

Using this formula, the Node Server computes the number of records that should be scanned during a recovery and sends it to the Disk Manager using the `DN_SetRecoveryTime` call.

```
routine DN_SetRecoveryTime(
                dnPort            : port_t;
                maxRecords        : u_int);
```

`dnPort` The port on which the Disk Manager receives requests from the Node Server.

`maxRecords` The maximum number of records to be scanned during recovery.

When the Disk Manager receives a `DN_SetRecoveryTime` request, it sets the checkpoint interval to half `maxRecords` because node recovery takes two recovery passes: one to recover the Node Server and one to recover all the other servers.

The checkpoint interval is used as the hot page flushing interval as well. The reason is that the recovery algorithm will scan back to the truncation point. The truncation point is the minimum LSN of all the LSNs in the grid and the LSN of the last checkpoint (and the `minRecLsn`). If a page remains dirty while more than the checkpoint interval number of log records are written, the page will cause the truncation point to be longer than the checkpoint interval and this may cause node recovery to take longer than the node administrator requested. To prevent this, the hot page flushing interval is the same as the checkpoint interval.

The checkpoint interval is also used as the maximum time that a new-value transaction should run. The reason is that new-value transactions keep pages pinned until they commit. If a new-value transaction runs longer than the checkpoint interval, it will prevent hot pages from being flushed. For this reason, the Disk Manager will kill new-value transactions that run for longer than a checkpoint interval number of records. Long-running transactions should be old-value/new-value.

14.3.5 Node Configuration

The Node Server is a distinguished data server that is used to maintain node configuration information. The Node Server maintains this information in recoverable virtual memory. At system startup, the Disk Manager starts the Node Server by executing a `DN_StartDataServers` call. The Recovery Manager runs a recovery pass just to recover the Node Server's recoverable segment. After the Node Server has been recovered, it has all the information needed in its recoverable virtual memory to start other servers.

The Node Server exports the NA interface to allow client applications to manipulate the Node Server database using Camelot transactions. The NA interface allows users to log in and, if they have the appropriate privileges, to add, delete, and start servers, set the recovery time, set disk allocations, and query the database. The NA interface is described in Chapter 10.

The Node Server exports the ND interface, which is used by the Disk Manager to notify the Node Server about changes in server status and to allocate disk backing storage for data servers dynamically.

Starting Servers

To start a data server, the Node Server sends the `DN_StartDataServers` RPC to the Disk Manager.

```
routine DN_StartDataServers(
                dnPort          : port_t;
                serverIds       : cam_server_id_list_t);
```

`dnPort` The port on which the Disk Manager receives requests from the Node Server.
`serverIds` A list of data servers to be started.

When the Disk Manager receives a `DN_StartDataServers` request, it starts the specified data servers. For each data server, the Disk Manager allocates a server record (`s_record_t`) for bookkeeping, a shared memory queue, and a port that Camelot processes use to communicate with the data server. The format of the server record is shown in Figure 14.8.

The Disk Manager executes a `TD_AddDataServer` RPC to give send rights on the `sPort` to the Transaction Manager and get the data server's `tsPort`.

```
routine TD_AddDataServer(
                tdPort          : port_t;
                serverId        : cam_server_id_t;
                sendPort        : port_t;
            OUT rcvPort         : port_t);
```

`tdPort` is the port on which the Transaction Manager receives messages from the Disk Manager.
`serverId` is the permanent ID of the server.
`sendPort` is the port to which Transaction Manager sends messages to servers.

```
typedef struct s_record {
    cam_server_id_t          serverId;
    struct rw_lock           serverLatch;
    int                      pid;
    port_t                   dsPort;
    port_t                   tsPort;
    port_t                   sPort;
    port_t                   pagingPort;
    port_t                   requestPort;
    cam_segment_desc_t       segDesc;
    s_state_t                state;
    cam_ds_queue_t          *shMemQueuePtr;
    struct mutex             shMemQueueLatch;
    u_int                    preparedTrans;
    cam_cht_link_t           idLink;
    cam_cht_link_t           pidLink;
    cam_cht_link_t           dsLink;
    cam_cht_link_t           sLink;
    cam_cht_link_t           pLink;
    cam_cht_link_t           segLink;
} s_record_t;
```

`serverId` The identifier for the data server.

`serverLatch` A latch that protects access to this record. Server records are never deleted; a server's state is just set to `S_DOWN`. This means that latch chaining need not be done on server records.

`pid` The process ID for this data server, if it is running.

`dsPort` The port the data server used to send messages to the Disk Manager.

`tsPort` The port the data server used to send messages to the Transaction Manager.

`sPort` The port Camelot uses to send messages to the data server.

`pagingPort` The port the kernel uses to send the Disk Manager paging requests for this data server's recoverable virtual memory segment.

`requestPort` The port the Disk Manager uses to send the kernel requests to manipulate this data server's recoverable virtual memory segment.

`segDesc` The segment descriptor for this data server's recoverable virtual memory segment.

`shMemQueuePtr` The pointer to this data server's shared memory queue.

`shMemQueueLatch` The latch that prevents multiple threads in the Disk Manager from concurrently servicing this data server's shared memory queue.

`preparedTrans` If the server is down but has some prepared transactions, this is the number of prepared transactions in which it is participating. As these prepared transactions complete, this number falls to zero and the Disk Manager will know to run surrogate recovery on this server.

`idLink` The link to the next server in the same `id`-hash-table hash bucket.

`pidLink` The link to the next server in the same `pid`-hash-table hash bucket.

`dsLink` The link to the next server in the same `dsPort`-hash-table hash bucket.

`sLink` The link to the next server in the same `sPort`-hash-table hash bucket.

`pLink` The link to the next server in the same `pagingPort`-hash-table hash bucket.

`segLink` The link to the next server in the same `segmentId`-hash-table hash bucket.

Figure 14.8: Server Record

`rcvPort` is the port to which the server sends messages to the Transaction Manager.

The Disk Manager executes the `MD_AddDataServer` call to get the data server's `msPort`. Rights on these ports are later given to the data server in the `DS_Initialize` message.

```
routine MD_AddDataServer(
                mPort           : port_t;
                serverId        : cam_server_id_t;
            OUT msPort          : port_t);
```

`mPort` is the port to the Master Control Program.
`serverId` is the ID of the server.
`msPort` is the port that the server can use to send debugging output.

The Disk Manager then forks and loads the data server's address space. After all data servers have been started, the Disk Manager tells the Recovery Manager to recover the servers using the `RD_RecoverServers` calls.

```
routine RD_RecoverServers(
                rdPort          : port_t;
                serverIDs       : cam_server_id_list_t;
                segDescList     : cam_segment_desc_list_t;
                srPorts         : port_array_t;
                highRecNbr      : u_int;
                cachePtr        : pointer_t =
                ^ array [] of (MSG_TYPE_CHAR, 8, dealloc);
            OUT nbrRecordsProcessed : u_int;
            OUT milliseconds    : u_int);
```

`rdPort` the port on which the Recovery Manager receives messages from the Disk Manager.
`serverIds` the list of servers of be recovered.
`segDescList` is the list of segments used by the servers being recovered.
`srPorts` is the list of ports to be used by the Recovery Manager to perform recovery.
`highRecNbr` is the record number assigned (internally by the Disk Manager) to the last record currently in the log. As the Recovery Manager reads the log, it decrements this record number so that when it backlinks old records into the grid, it can indicate to the Disk Manager exactly how far back they are in the log. The Disk Manager uses this information to control page flush (and potentially other) strategies.
`cachePtr` refers to the data that must be transferred from the version of Log Manager being used by the Disk Manager to the (read-only) version used by the Recovery Manager to make them consistent.
`nbrRecordsProcessed` and `milliseconds` are given to the Node Server by the Disk Manager for use in setting parameters that will affect recovery time.

Server States

When a server changes state and the new state is CAM_SS_DOWN_CLEAN, CAM_SS_DOWN_DIRTY, CAM_SS_DOWN_PREPARED, or CAM_SS_DOWN_DIRTY_PREPARED, the Disk Manager calls the Node Server with the ND_GetRestartAdvice call to ask whether the server should be restarted, and to get needed data if so. The Disk Manager also makes this call after the Node Server asks that a server be started.

```
camelotroutine ND_GetRestartAdvice(
                    serverId          : cam_server_id_t;
                    atYourRequest     : boolean_t;
                    oldState          : cam_server_state_t;
                    newState          : cam_server_state_t;
                OUT shouldRestart     : boolean_t;
                OUT recoveryOnly      : boolean_t;
                OUT commandLine       : pointer_t;
                OUT segDescList       : cam_segment_desc_list_t;
                OUT chunkDescList     : cam_chunk_desc_list_t);
```

serverId The ID of the server about which we inquire.

atYourRequest A flag that, if TRUE, means the Node Server has already requested the server be started and should supply the necessary information. If the atYourRequest flag is FALSE, it means the server has transitioned to a new down state, and the Node Server has the option of restarting it. The Disk Manager describes the transition, and is told whether to restart the server.

oldState The previous state of the data server.

newState The new state of the data server.

shouldRestart A boolean specifying whether the server should be restarted at all.

recoveryOnly A boolean specifying whether the server should just run recovery and exit or should actually stay up. Not meaningful if shouldRestart is FALSE.

commandLine The command line that should be executed to start the server. Not meaningful if shouldRestart is FALSE.

segDescList A list of segment descriptors for the server. Not meaningful if shouldRestart is FALSE.

chunkDescList A list of disk mappings for the server. Not meaningful if shouldRestart is FALSE.

This call returns the following items:

1. shouldRestart is a boolean specifying whether the server should be restarted at all. All other OUT parameters are irrelevant if this one is FALSE.

2. recoveryOnly is a boolean specifying whether the server should just run recovery and exit or should actually stay up.

3. `commandLine` is the command line that should be executed to start the server.

4. `segDescList` is a list of segment descriptors for the server.

5. `chunkDescList` is a list of disk mappings for the server.

If the `atYourRequest` flag is `FALSE`, the data server has transitioned to a new down state, and the Node Server has the option of restarting it. The Disk Manager describes the transition, and is told whether to restart the server.

If the `atYourRequest` flag is `TRUE`, it means that the Node Server has already requested the server be started, and should supply the necessary information. The `oldState` and `newState` fields are irrelevant in this case. (The Node Server cannot send the information to the Disk Manager using the `DN_StartDataServers` call because the Node Server never holds locks while calling the Disk Manager, and the information could become stale if locks are not held.) The Node Server can still decline to do the restart in this case, by returning with `shouldRestart` set to `FALSE`.

Down Servers

Whenever a data server crashes (but the node stays up), the Disk Manager, the Transaction Manager, the Recovery Manager, the Node Server, and the Master Control Program are all notified by the kernel because they all have send rights on the data server's `sPort`. The Node Server sets the server's state to "cleaning." The Transaction Manager aborts any active transactions in which the server is participating and then sends the `DT_ServerCleanupComplete` message to the Disk Manager.

The `DT_ServerCleanupComplete` message contains a list of prepared transactions in which the server is participating. The Disk Manager adds the data server to the `ghostList` in the transaction record for each of the prepared transactions. After the Disk Manager processes the prepared transaction list in the `DT_ServerCleanupComplete` message, it removes all the data server's page records from the grid. It then notifies the Node Server as to the state of the data server using the `ND_ServerDown` message. If there are no prepared transactions in the `DT_ServerCleanupComplete` message and the data server had no page records in the grid, the data server is said to have come down "clean." Otherwise the data server is said to have come down "prepared" and/or "dirty".

When a data server crashes, it may leave records in the common log. Since the data server is down, the existence of these log records will not be reflected in the grid, so the truncation algorithm may truncate them out of the log. After each recovery pass, the Recovery Manager tells the Disk Manager about data servers for which it encountered log records but did not recover. This list is called the `nrList` (i.e., the not recovered list). The Disk Manager gets the `nrList` from the Recovery Manager after the first recovery pass. The Disk Manager then maintains the list itself ignoring `nrLists` from the Recovery Manager produced by subsequent recovery passes.

If a data server comes down "dirty" or "prepared," it is added to the `nrList`. If there are any data servers on the `nrList`, the Disk Manager will not compute a new truncation point. Whenever the Node Server is told that a data server came down "dirty," it runs surrogate recovery on the data server. Surrogate recovery is run by starting a special surrogate data server with the "dirty" data server's recoverable segments. The surrogate data server goes through recovery processing and then asks the Disk Manager to flush its pages using the `DS_FlushAllPages` call. When a prepared

```
typedef struct cam_chunk_desc {
        cam_segment_id_t     segmentId;      /* 2 bytes */
        unsigned short       lowSectAlloc;
        unsigned int         chunkNumber;
        unsigned int         highSectAlloc          : 7,
                             reverseAllocate        : 1,
                             offsetInChunks         : 24;
} cam_chunk_desc_t;

typedef cam_chunk_desc_t *cam_chunk_desc_list_t;
```

Figure 14.9: Camelot Chunk Descriptor

transaction completes, the Disk Manager tells the Node Server to run surrogate recovery using the `ND_RunSurrogate` message.

```
routine DS_FlushAllPages(
                dsPort          : port_t);
```

`dsPort` The port on which the Disk Manager receives requests from this server.

Disk Allocation

Backing storage is allocated lazily during page out. This allows the node administrator to over-allocate storage to servers if desired, and it allows the operating system to page out contiguous pages together.

Storage is allocated on the disk in units called chunks. The chunk size is set on a per disk basis. The chunk size must be a power of 2 bytes and greater than the page size. This restriction allows fast internal computation. All pages within a chunk will be contiguously allocated on the disk. The Node Server maintains a database of chunk to disk mappings in recoverable storage. The Disk Manager caches the active parts of the database.

The cached database in the Disk Manager is simply a hash table of chunk descriptor records (`chunk_desc_t`). A chunk descriptor contains a segment ID, the offset in chunks within the segment, a disk number, the offset in chunks on the disk, the number of disk sectors allocated within that chunk, and a bit indicating whether the sectors are being allocated from the beginning or the end of the chunk. The format of the chunk descriptor is shown in Figure 14.9.

When the Disk Manager has to read a page from a recoverable segment, it looks up the page's `chunk_desc` record in the chunk hash table. If the entry is found, the Disk Manager checks to determine whether the sectors for the page have been allocated. If so, the Disk Manager reads the page from the proper location on the disk. If the sectors have not been allocated or the `chunk_desc` record was not found, the Disk Manager returns a zeroed page.

Disk allocation is done transactionally. When the Disk Manager needs to write a page to non-volatile storage, it looks up the page's chunk in the chunk hash table. If the `chunk_desc` record does not exist, the Disk Manager executes a ND_ChunkAllocate RPC to the Node Server to get one and inserts the chunk_desc that is returned in the chunk hash table. The ND_ChunkAllocate call is a Camelot RPC. The Disk Manager specifies that this RPC should run as a transaction initiated and committed by the Node Server. The transaction is initiated by the Node Server when it receives the request and committed by the Node Server before it returns the reply.

```
camelotroutine ND_ChunkAllocate(
                   segmentId        : cam_segment_id_t;
                   offsetInChunks   : u_int;
                   reverseAllocate  : boolean_t;
               OUT chunkDesc        : cam_chunk_desc_t);
```

`segmentId` The ID of the segment to which we are allocating.
`offsetInChucks` The offset within the segment.
`reverseAllocate` A flag indicating that allocation should take place from the top of the segment down.
`chuckDesc` The new chunk descriptor.

Once the proper chunk_desc record is found, the Disk Manager writes the page out to disk.[11] Then the Disk Manager checks to determine whether the sectors within the chunk for the page must be allocated. If the sectors for the page have not been allocated, the Disk Manager makes a ND_ChunkUpdate call to the Node Server. This RPC runs transactionally just as the ND_ChunkAllocate call does.

```
camelotroutine ND_ChunkUpdate(
                   chunkDesc        : cam_chunk_desc_t;
                   chunkForPart     : u_int;
               OUT chunkNumber      : u_int);
```

`chunkDesc` A valid chunk descriptor that contains a new value for the sectorsAllocated field. Valid chunk_desc_t's are returned by ND_ChunkAllocate or are constructed using a chunkNumber parameter returned by a previous call to ND_ChunkUpdate.
`chunkForPart` A parameter to request a pre-allocated chunk for the specified disk partition. If zero is specified, no pre-allocation will be done.
`chunkNumber` The pre-allocated chunk number.

The Node Server runs the ND_ChunkAllocate and ND_ChunkUpdate transactions as lazy, server-based transactions. A server-based transaction is a transaction that can only execute in the server that began it. A lazy transaction is a transaction that guarantees failure atomicity, but not necessarily permanence. (A lazy transaction's commit record is spooled, not forced, to the log.) Should the node crash before the commit record is written into stable storage, the lazy transaction

[11] If the sectors have not been allocated, the Disk Manager must write the page out to disk before the allocation is recorded. If the allocation was recorded first, and the Disk Manager crashed after the allocation committed but before the page was written to disk, the Disk Manager would read a garbage page off the disk when it came back up.

will abort, even if the `END_TRANSACTION` statement has returned. Only server-based transactions may be lazy. Lazy, server-based transactions are very fast because a synchronous log force is not needed to commit them.

Use of lazy, server-based transactions for disk allocation is correct. After a page is written to non-volatile storage, an `end_write` log record is spooled to the log. If storage allocation is done, the lazy commit record will be spooled to the log before the end_write.

If there is a failure, the log will be in one of three states:

1. The log contains neither the lazy commit record nor the end_write record. The Disk Manager will zero-fill the page when it is read. In this case, the Recovery Manager will not know if the page has been written out. It will undo and redo operations accordingly.

2. The log contains the lazy commit record but not the end_write record. In this case, the Disk Manager will read the page from non-volatile storage, but the Recovery Manager will not know if the page has been written out. It will undo and redo operations accordingly.

3. The log contains both the lazy commit record and the end_write record. In this case, the Disk Manager will read the page from non-volatile storage and the Recovery Manager will know that the page has been written out. It will undo and redo operations accordingly.

The Node Server gets a fixed amount of disk storage at the beginning of the first disk (currently 512K bytes). When the Disk Manager needs to read and write pages for the Node Server, it does not consult the chunk hash table. The location of Node Server chunks is hard-coded into the Disk Manager's code.

The Disk Manager makes several synchronous calls to the Node Server. These up-level calls must be carefully considered when designing the internal synchronization techniques because of the possibility of deadlocks. See Section 14.3.7 for details.

14.3.6 Media Failure

We considered several ways to address the problem of media failure in Camelot:

1. Use stable storage for both the log and backing storage for recoverable virtual memory. Using this approach, media failures will be masked by low-level I/O code. The high level algorithms need no further development to handle media failure.

2. Implement an archival mechanism that dumps the non-volatile backing storage before truncating the log.

   - The archival mechanism can be a "stop-and-copy" scheme in which the system stops once a night and copies the non-volatile storage to an archive area, truncates the log and deletes the previous archive.
   - The archival mechanism can be implemented as a "fuzzy dump" scheme in which a dump of non-volatile storage is taken while the system is running. After the fuzzy dump is saved and the log is truncated, the previous dump is deleted. The advantage of fuzzy dumping is that the system does not stop during dumps, but the disadvantage is that it complicates the recovery code.

We chose the "stop-and-copy" scheme because of its simplicity. The Camelot startup program takes a run-time switch that allows the log and paging partitions to be dumped to a UNIX file (or tape) for backup purposes. In case of media failure, this backup can be restored.

14.3.7 Internal Concurrency Control

The Mach kernel provides multiple threads of control per task. The Disk Manager is implemented in one Mach task and uses multiple threads of control for three reasons:

1. **Concurrent disk I/O.** Multiple threads allow the Disk Manager to concurrently access multiple disks in a duplex log and multiple disks for backing recoverable virtual memory.
2. **Utilization of Multiprocessors.** Multiple threads can execute in parallel on a multiprocessor. By using separate threads to handle requests for different servers and/or transactions, the Disk Manager can process requests in parallel.
3. **Convenient Structure.** Multiple threads are a convenient structuring mechanism. If one thread waits on a latch, executes a synchronous RPC, or executes a synchronous kernel call, other threads can still execute. This is particularly important when making up-level calls to the Node Server, because an up-level call to the Node Server can result in the Node Server making requests to the Disk Manager.

Using multiple threads requires careful synchronization to keep the threads from interfering with one another and to keep threads from deadlocking with each other. Each data structure has one or more exclusive or shared/exclusive mode latches to control access by multiple threads.

- Server records (`s_record_ts`) keep track of information about each data server. Each server record has a read/write latch allowing multiple readers or one writer. Server records are linked into several hash tables. The hash table keys include: data server process ID (`pid`), data server's request port to the Disk Manager (`dsPort`), Disk Manager's request port to the data server (`sPort`), and the recoverable segment's paging port (`pagingPort`). The hash tables have exclusive latches on each bucket. Server records are never deleted. This means that pointers to server records can be saved in other Disk Manager data structures without reference counting and that the hash bucket latch only needs to be held while reading or inserting into the hash bucket.
- Each data server's shared memory queue has an exclusive mode latch. The latch must be held while requests in the queue are processed because it is not always possible to reorder requests (e.g., two requests from the same thread cannot be reordered). The fact that requests in a shared memory queue cannot be processed concurrently will be a performance bottleneck on a large multiprocessor. The bottleneck is easily avoided by sending messages instead of using the shared memory queue.
- The entire grid is protected by a shared/exclusive mode latch. Three rare types of access use the exclusive mode: checkpoint, copy forward cleanup, and data server death.[12] All other accesses to the grid use shared mode.

[12]It is possible to take checkpoints without holding an exclusive mode latch on the grid, but this greatly complicates the recovery algorithm and holding this latch has not resulted in a performance bottleneck.

- Page records (`page_record_ts`) keep track of active pages in the grid. Page records are linked into the page hash table. There is an exclusive mode latch for each bucket. The latch is held whenever the page record is being accessed.

- Transaction records (`tran_record_ts`) keep track of active transactions in the grid. Transaction records are linked into the transaction hash table. There is an exclusive mode latch for each bucket. The latch is held whenever the transaction record is being accessed.

- Subtransaction records (`sub_tran_record_ts`) keep track of subtransaction state information. These records are linked into the subtransaction hash table. This is an exclusive mode latch for each bucket. The latch is held whenever the subtransaction record is being accessed.

- Grid records (`grid_record_ts`) are used to keep track of records in the log. Grid records are linked into the list of grid records for the page and/or transaction that the log record represents.[13] To read a grid record, a thread must hold the exclusive mode latch on either its page or transaction record. To modify a grid record, a thread must hold the latch for both its page and transaction records (if it is on both a page record's and a transaction record's grid record lists).

- Patch records (`patch_record_ts`) are used to track updates to pages that are in hot mode. Patch records are linked into the list of patch records for the page to which the update occurred and into the list of patch records for the transaction on behalf of which the update occurred.[14] To read a patch record, a thread must hold the exclusive mode latch on either its page or its transaction record. To modify a patch record, a thread must hold the latch for both its page and transaction records.

- Several lists are maintained by the Disk Manager. Each list has an exclusive mode latch to control access by concurrent threads.
  - The hot page (`hotPage`) list keeps track of active pages. This list is maintained in order of first dirtied.
  - The long transaction (`longTran`) list keeps track of active transactions. This list is maintained in order of first modification on this node.
  - The not recovered (`nr`) list keeps track of servers that need to be recovered.
  - The segment (`seg`) list keeps track of active segments and their corresponding servers.

- Each disk used for backing recoverable virtual memory has an exclusive mode latch.

To avoid deadlock among threads in the Disk Manager, there is a hierarchy among the latches. All latches are obtained in a canonical order. This guarantees there will be no deadlocks. If a thread is holding a latch numbered n it may not attempt to get a latch numbered less than n. A partial list of latches is given below. A complete list is generated by the Camelot lock precedence checker.

1. The `serverLatches` are shared/exclusive mode latches that guard access to server records.

[13] If a log record describes changes to multiple pages, a grid record will be created for each page.

[14] If an update modifies multiple pages, a patch record will be created for each page.

2. The `shMemQueueLatches` are exclusive mode latches that guard access to the shared memory queues.

3. The `G_GRID` shared/exclusive mode latch guards access to the grid.

4. The `G_PAGE` latches are exclusive mode latches on the hash buckets for pages in the grid. Since a "pin" or "log" request may modify more than one page, latches are obtained in ascending page order. If a log request modifies more than n pages, an exclusive mode `G_GRID` is obtained instead of the `G_PAGE` latches. The hash function guarantees that any n adjacent pages hash to different locations in the hash table. If the size of the hash table for pages is s, this means that $\frac{s-1}{n}$ threads can use this convention to concurrently access the hash table without deadlocking. (Currently, $n = 5$ and $s = 8192$).

5. The `ioLocks` are exclusive mode latches for each disk that is used to back recoverable virtual memory.

6. The `descLocks` are exclusive mode latches for each disk's chunk descriptor hash tables.

7. The `G_TRAN` latches are exclusive mode latches on the hash buckets for transactions in the grid. When cleaning up after a transaction completes, it is necessary to scan the grid in the transaction direction. In this case, we have obtained the `G_TRAN` latch for the transaction, but we need to get a `G_PAGE` latch for each page. If the latch on a page is busy, the Disk Manager releases the `G_TRAN` latch and waits on the `G_PAGE` latch. When the `G_PAGE` latch becomes available, the Disk Manager then tries to get the `G_TRAN` latch again, waiting if necessary. This technique usually obtains the `G_PAGE` latches without waiting, but follows the latch precedence rules to guarantee that there will be no deadlocks.

8. The `G_SUB_TRAN` latches are exclusive mode latches on the hash buckets for subtransactions in the grid.

9. The `hotPageLatch` is the exclusive mode latch on the hot page list.

10. The `longTranLatch` is the exclusive mode latch on the long transaction list.

11. The `l_VarLatch` is the exclusive mode latch on the log state variables.

12. The `nr_Lock` is the exclusive mode latch on the `nrList`.

The Disk Manager makes up-level calls to the Node Server for server death and disk allocation. The Disk Manager allocates a special thread to handle requests from the Node Server and a special thread to handle paging requests from the kernel for the Node Server's recoverable segment. The Node Server has a special thread to handle requests from the Disk Manager. This means that there will always be a thread available to handle Disk Manager requests in the Node Server, and Node Server requests in the Disk Manager. To make sure that the threads used to handle Node Server requests in the Disk Manager are not stuck trying to obtain a latch, we must examine the locks held during up-level requests to the Node Server.

- When notifying the Node Server about server death (`ND_ServerDown`), no latches are held.

- When doing disk allocation (`ND_ChunkAllocation` and `ND_ChuckUpdate`), latches on page hash table buckets are held. For this reason, a separate hash table is used for the Node Server's recoverable segment's active pages.

14.4 Related Work

Many people have considered providing an operating system (OS) managed buffer pool for transaction processing systems. An OS managed buffer pool seems particularly attractive when it is integrated with a file system or with virtual memory. As far as we are aware, the first printed statement about providing an OS managed buffer pool was in 1977 in Jim Gray's notes [38]:

> Buffer manager: maps the data "pages" on secondary storage to primary storage buffer pool. If the operating system provided a really fancy page manager (virtual memory) then the buffer manager might not be needed. But, issues such as double buffering of sequential I/O, Write Ahead Log protocol, checkpoint, and locking seem to argue against using the page managers of existing systems. If you are looking for a hard problem, here is one: define an interface to page management which is usable by data management in lieu of buffer management.

In 1981, Stonebraker published a paper complaining that operating systems do not provide appropriate support for database systems [111]. In 1982, Traiger discussed virtual memory support for database systems in the context of using either the System R shadow paging recovery scheme or write-ahead logging [117]. In 1984, Stonebraker proposed operating system support for transaction management [112]. His choice of a few simple primitives (begin transaction, end transaction, abort transaction) leaves his operating system with many problems due to page-level locking and logging.

All database systems maintain recoverable or persistent data. The Argus programming language and run-time system support recoverable data [70]. The main emphasis of this implementation is language support for persistent data. The CPR system used specialized hardware support to provide a system that maintained recoverable data [18]. The CPR system does hardware-level locking and logging. A modified version of Multics uses transactions internally for the file system [109]. These recent systems have begun to provide recoverable virtual memory.

The prefetch and preflush primitives are provided because least recently used replacement algorithms are not always appropriate [111, 97, 27, 77]. Extensive analyses of double paging rates as a function of buffer pool sizes have been done [103, 15].

14.5 Discussion

This chapter described the implementation of recoverable virtual memory in Camelot. The implementation was affected by several research goals and implementation decisions of the Camelot Project.

The Camelot Project wanted to experiment with new-value recovery. The choice of recovery schemes is basically orthogonal to evaluation of recoverable virtual memory, but it greatly complicates the support the Disk Manager must provide for recovery.

Grid records were necessary to support new-value logging. The decision to maintain grid records in the Disk Manager's virtual memory has been a subject of great debate. The alternative would be to maintain the grid by threading records in the log. The cost of the virtual memory data structure is very cheap. A special storage allocator is used to allocate and free the fixed size grid records. Also, the virtual memory data structure allows fast unpinning of pages when new-value transactions commit.

Key among the implementation decisions was the use of Mach. Local RPCs in Mach are reasonably fast (approximately 1.5 milliseconds on the RT APC), but they are slow enough that their use must be avoided when implementing common operations. For this reason, shared memory queues are used for fast communication between data servers and the Disk Manager.

The Mach philosophy is to provide a basic kernel with a small number of powerful abstractions (tasks, threads, virtual memory, IPC). Everything else should be implemented outside the kernel. The Camelot implementation is consistent with this philosophy. The external memory management interface allows the implementation of recoverable virtual memory without modifying the kernel. It also allowed rapid development of the Camelot Disk Manager.

Chapter 15

The Design of the Camelot Recovery Manager

Dean Thompson

15.1 Introduction

Camelot is designed to protect the data that servers keep in recoverable storage from certain hardware and software failures. It is impossible for any system to protect against all possible failures. It is also unreasonable to pay a heavy price during normal processing just to make recovery from rare failures inexpensive. The designers of a fault-tolerant system must make assumptions about what types of failures will occur and how common each will be. Section 15.1.1 discusses the types of failures against which Camelot protects.

Camelot implements recoverable storage from three types of storage having different access times, reliability, and cost per byte. The first two types of storage, *volatile* and *nonvolatile*, are typically represented by semiconductor RAM and magnetic disk. Volatile storage ("memory") can be accessed and modified very quickly, but its contents are easily corrupted and are lost when the node crashes, and it is relatively expensive. Nonvolatile storage ("disk") is hundreds or thousands of times slower to access or modify than volatile storage, but it is cheaper and does not normally lose its contents when the node crashes. Like most operating systems, Camelot uses memory as a cache for information that resides primarily on disk. When a server attempts to modify a region of recoverable storage that is not already in memory, the Mach kernel sends a message to the Disk Manager asking that one or more fixed-size *pages* be copied in from disk. The actual modification is then done in memory by the server. Eventually, Mach and the Disk Manager cooperate to write the page back to disk so that portion of memory can be reused.

The third type of storage, *stable* storage, is less familiar. Stable storage has about the same access time as a disk, but is assumed to be completely reliable. It is typically implemented as two or more copies of the same data on magnetic or optical disks. Lampson discusses the concept and implementation of stable storage [61] in more detail. Camelot implements stable storage using either two local raw disk partitions (see Chapter 13) or two or more specialized remote nodes called *log servers* (see Chapter 25 or the paper by Daniels [24] for a complete discussion.) The only data structure Camelot keeps in stable storage is a single append-only log file for each node. Because the log is append-only, it is relatively easy to implement with write-once storage such as optical disk. It is also easier than random-access storage to protect from software problems, because it can be designed so that most or all software errors will just append garbage to the log and not damage good data written earlier.

During normal processing, Camelot system components and servers record all modifications to recoverable storage, movements of pages between disk and memory, and outcomes of completed transactions in the log. Section 14.3.3 describes each possible log record in detail. Section 15.2.1 discusses them briefly from the Recovery Manager's point of view.

When any system component detects a failure, it notifies the Recovery Manager, which must read the log and undo or redo the effects of transactions as appropriate. The Recovery Manager also sends information from the log to servers and to the other Camelot components to allow them to restore their internal data structures.

15.1.1 Functional Goals

The purpose of the Recovery Manager is to return recoverable storage to a transaction-consistent state after a failure, and to restore the state of the other Camelot components. A fault-tolerant system like Camelot must always assume some particular *failure model.* A failure model specifies what types of failures are possible and approximately how often they are expected to occur. Some real failures are always outside the model. For example, an undetected disk read error falls outside the Camelot failure model.

Within the Camelot model, failures are classified as either recoverable or catastrophic. The list of recoverable failures includes common ones such as communication problems, node crashes, and deadlocks. It also includes less common failures such as the loss of a disk. Catastrophic failures can be made arbitrarily improbable. For example, in Camelot, the loss of all copies of any part of the log is a catastrophic failure from which no recovery is possible. For most applications, the risk of losing the log is made acceptably low by keeping two copies of the log on the processing node. To protect very critical data, however, it may be worth keeping two or even three copies of the log on physically separate nodes. This does not eliminate the possibility of losing the log, but does reduce it enormously.

Recoverable failures can be divided into three categories:

1. **Transaction abort.** Transactions abort because communication links time out, because participating servers or entire nodes crash, and because of deadlocks, user intervention, and system resource limitations. A transaction may also be aborted by an application or server that detects an inconsistency and does not wish to proceed.

2. **Server crash.** Server crashes can be caused by node failures, software errors in the server, or user intervention. A server may go down voluntarily when it detects an inconsistency in its own state, or involuntarily when Camelot or the Mach kernel determines that it has violated resource-usage or security policies.

3. **Media Failure.** Disks can fail randomly and lose small amounts of data, or they can be destroyed completely by fire or other mishap.

For more discussion of failure types and failure models, see the lecture notes by Lampson [61] and Gray [38].

The Recovery Manager does not support recovery from media failure. It uses the write-ahead log maintained by the Disk Manager (see Chapter 14) to support recovery from from transaction abort and server crash. Camelot supports only *value logging*. When recoverable storage is updated, the *new value* of the modified region is written into a log record called a *modify record*. Depending on the transaction type, the *old value* of the region may also be written into the log.[1] Camelot permits different operations to modify arbitrarily overlapping regions in recoverable storage so long as there is no *comodification* by concurrent transactions. That is, once one transaction has modified a byte, no other transaction may modify the same byte until the first has either committed or aborted.

Most commercial transaction systems implement *operation logging* in addition to, or in place of, value logging. Operation logging involves writing to the log an indication of what operation was done (such as 'insert A in table X' or 'increment integer X') rather than copies of old and new values for the affected data. This can save log space. It also increases concurrency, because the restriction against comodification of the same physical bytes is removed. However, operation logging makes heavier demands of its client and does not mesh as neatly as value logging with recoverable virtual memory. Operation logging requires its client to specify where logical operations begin and end, and to implement a logical inverse for each operation. Fully general operation logging also requires two levels of locking – physical locking within an operation and logical locking between operations – and arbitrary lock conflict matrices. Value logging only requires its client to obtain physical read/write locks and to specify which physical assignments are to recoverable virtual storage. Assignments to recoverable storage can be detected at the language level, leaving only read/write locking as a burden on the client.

When a Camelot server or application begins a transaction, it specifies whether the transaction should be *old-value/new-value* or *new-value-only*. The distinction lies in what values are copied to the log when some region in recoverable storage is modified. The *old value* is the value of the region *before* it is modified. This value will be used to undo the transaction's effects if it does not commit. The *new value* is the contents of the region *after* it has been modified. It will be used if the transaction commits, but if a node or server crashes before the transaction's updates have been written back to disk.

When old-value/new-value logging is used, both values are written into the log every time a region is modified. If new-value-only logging is specified, the new value alone is recorded. In that case, if the transaction fails to commit, the old values must be recovered from the log or from backing storage on disk. To ensure that old values can always be found if needed, the Disk Manager prevents pages from being written back to disk after they have been modified by a new-value-only transaction until that transaction commits.

15.1.2 Performance Goals

In every system, certain failures are very common, and must be handled smoothly and cheaply. On a given Camelot node, for instance, transactions are assumed to abort as often as several times

[1] What we call a *new value* is sometimes referred to as an *after-image*. Similarly, an *old value* is sometimes called a *before-image*.

per minute. As a rule, aborting a transaction should involve about as much system overhead as successfully committing one.

Other failures are less common, but may occur every few hours or days. We expect, for example, that bugs or routine maintenance will cause servers or entire nodes to go down about this often. Server or node recovery can reasonably take from a few minutes up to ten or fifteen minutes, depending on how active the node or server was in the period just before it crashed and how often checkpoints are being done.

Disks fail only several times a year to once every several years, so it is acceptable for media failure recovery to take an hour or more.

15.1.3 Constraints

A fundamental constraint in the design of the Recovery Manager was the decision, made very early on, to use a log rather than shadowing as the primary recovery mechanism. Shadowing is a technique in which, whenever a transaction begins to modify an object, the object is copied and only the copy is changed. All of the objects modified by a transaction replace their predecessors simultaneously, through an atomic pointer swap, when the transaction commits. If a transaction fails to commit, the pointer swap is never done, and the new copies are thrown away. Shadowing is an elegant technique, but it is inefficient when used on large databases. For a transaction to commit permanently, new copies of the objects it has modified must be written back to disk. They cannot be written over the old copies, in case the node fails while writing is in progress, so they must be written to newly allocated storage. If the new storage is allocated close to the old storage for each object, committing the transaction is expensive because widely separated disk sectors must be updated. If not, the contiguity of related objects is broken, and a price will be paid the next time the objects are accessed.

Given that a log is to be used for recovery, the most far-reaching constraint is the requirement that the log must be append-only, and that it must almost always be read sequentially. Existing data in the log cannot be changed, and reading the log in random order is extremely expensive. So long as the log is read sequentially, the expense of recovery is determined almost entirely by how much log data must be read. The recovery algorithm is designed to use as little log data as possible (without unacceptably slowing forward processing) and to make only one pass over the log. Also, since physical memory is limited and paging is expensive, the recovery algorithm is designed with careful attention to the size of data structures that must be maintained during recovery.

To simplify coding and debugging, the Recovery Manager was isolated in its own Mach task (like the Disk Manager and the Transaction Manager). It communicates with servers and with other Camelot tasks through Mach messages. This type of communication is three orders of magnitude more expensive than a local procedure call. Separating the Disk Manager and Recovery Manager into separate processes may have been a bad decision; see section 15.5.

15.2 Architecture

The Recovery Manager is essentially single-threaded: it has multiple threads waiting for requests, but it allows only one server recovery, media recovery, or abort thread to do work at a time. If a media recovery request is received while server recovery is in progress, or visa versa, the request waits. Both media recovery and server recovery wait until any currently active abort operation completes. Abort requests are allowed to interrupt media or server recovery, but only when recovery voluntarily yields control.

This is the most efficient scheduling algorithm on most systems because multiple recovery operations executing in parallel would cause excessive motion of the log head. Conveniently, it is also a very easy scheduling algorithm to implement and analyze. In the few cases where data is shared between two recovery threads, only interleaved operations on the data structures involved need to be considered, not concurrent ones.

The only data structure that the Recovery Manager maintains between recovery operations is a hash table of ports indexed by server ID. When the Disk Manager requests that a server be recovered, the server's port is entered into this hash table. If any call from the Recovery Manager to a server times out or otherwise fails, the Recovery Manager uses a synchronous call to the Disk Manager (`DR_KillServer`) to make sure the server is actually down, and if it is down, the Recovery Manager deletes that server's port from the table.

Regardless of where log records originate, they are actually written into the log by the Disk Manager. When local logging is used, however, log records are read directly by the Recovery Manager. To make this possible, the Disk Manager passes the Recovery Manager a block of out-of-line data that contains the entire state of the Log Manager. This block of Log Manager state is replaced every time a new recovery operation begins. The Recovery Manager can begin with this Log Manager state and read records correctly while the Disk Manager continues to write the log. When server or media recovery is preempted by an abort and then resumed, it begins reading records where it left off but with a Log Manager state that has been updated by the abort thread.

The server port hash table and the Log Manager state are the only two data structures that are ever shared between two recovery operations, concurrent or otherwise. Each individual recovery operation uses its own set of hash tables and a ***region tree*** as described in Section 15.2.2.

15.2.1 The Log

The log is more than just another copy of recoverable storage. It contains information about the state of every transaction that is recent enough to be of interest. It also lists the modifications that each transaction has made to recoverable storage, so that transactional consistency can be restored after a node crash, server crash, or transaction abort. The log contains records written by the Transaction Manager (see Chapter 16) that allow the local node to resume participation in commit protocols with other nodes after it crashes and restarts. The log holds lists of locks held at each server by transactions that are in the 'prepared' state, so that these locks can be reinstated if the server crashes and restarts. The log also contains information about the movement of pages between memory and backing store. This section describes the records in the log, omitting some details that are not important to the Recovery Manager.

The following records are written into the log during forward processing:

- **Modify** records are written when recoverable storage is modified. Each modify record contains a copy of the new value of the modified region. Each old-value/new-value modify record also contains a copy of the region before it was modified. Modify records have the following fields:

  - `version` A version number identifying the format of the record.

- `isFirstTopTran` A flag, set to `TRUE` if this is the first modify record for this transaction family.
- `isFirstSubTran` A flag, set to `TRUE` if this is the first modify for this subtransaction.
- `serverId` A unique identifier for the server whose recoverable storage is being modified.
- `transactionId` A unique identifier for the transaction.
- `regptr` A region pointer referring to the beginning of the modified region.
- `valueLength` The length of the region being modified.
- `newValue` The value of the region after it is modified.
- `oldValue` The value of the region before it was modified (not used for new-value-only transactions).

- **Server-prepare** records list locks held at a given server by transactions in the prepare phase of the commit protocol.

- **Tran-prepare** records are written by the Transaction Manager when transaction families prepare. They contain information needed by the Transaction Manager to resume participation in commit protocols after a crash. They are also used by the Recovery Manager along with Tran-commit and Tran-abort records to determine the states of transactions after a crash.

- **Tran-commit** records are written by the Transaction Manager when transaction families commit.

- **Tran-abort** records are written by the Transaction Manager when transaction families abort.

- **Fetch** records are written by the Disk Manager when pages of recoverable storage are brought in from disk. A fetch record allows the Recovery Manager, which is scanning the log backward at recovery time, to clear its data structures for the page.

- **End-write** records are written by the Disk Manager after pages have been successfully written back to disk. During its backward pass through the log, the Recovery Manager uses end-write records to know that upcoming modifications to the same page are safely on disk.[2]

- **Checkpoint** records are written by the Disk Manager during forward processing to give the Recovery Manager information it must have in order to terminate recovery before reading the entire log. Each checkpoint record contains the following lists:
  - *Inactive servers.* Includes all servers that have records in the log, but that do not own segments or regions included in the active segment or active region lists.
  - *Active transaction families.* Includes all transaction families that have modified data at the node and not completed.

[2]Note that end-write records are only useful for determining that certain updates *did* get written back to disk. Because end-write records are written after pages go out, the Recovery Manager can *never* safely assume that any update did *not* get written.

- *Active segments.* Includes all segments for which modify records may be found in the log and whose servers are not listed as inactive. Each segment's entry includes the identifier of the server that owns it.
- *Active regions.* Lists all regions of recoverable storage for which modifications have not yet been written back to disk, if the servers to whom they belong are not listed as inactive.

The following records are added to the log during recovery (including transaction abort):

- **Rec-abort** records list individual new-value-only transactions that have aborted. All rec-abort records in the log are chained together.
- **Undomodify** records contain the old values from old-value/new-value modify records written on behalf of transactions that have been aborted.
- **Backstop** records contain old values collected for new-value-only transactions that remain prepared for long periods of time.

As each log record is written, the Log Manager assigns it a unique log sequence number (LSN) that the Recovery Manager can use to refer to the log record when reading it.

The Disk Manager adheres to the *write-ahead log* protocol, meaning that modify records are always confirmed to be in stable storage before any pages to which they refer are copied back to disk. (For more detail see Gray's notes [38] or the paper by Traiger [117]). Otherwise, if a node crash occurred after a page with uncommitted modifications had gone out but before the corresponding modify records had made it to the log, the Recovery Manager would not be able to tell that the data on disk was wrong.

15.2.2 The Region Tree

To efficiently record the state of arbitrarily overlapping regions of recoverable storage, the Recovery Manager uses a data structure that we call a *region tree.* Every byte of recoverable storage on a node can be addressed by a 64 bit *region pointer.* The upper 16 bits of a region pointer specify the *segment,* and the lower 48 are a byte address within that segment. The region tree is a balanced binary tree of consecutive ranges of region pointers, or 'regions'. Each region in the tree has some data associated with it. This data is typically several flags and a server ID; its exact contents depend on the type of recovery being done. If the data associated with two adjacent regions is identical, then the two regions may be collapsed together and one set of data may be thrown away.

Besides creation and destruction, there is only one operation on a region tree:

```
ForEachCase(IN low, high, regionProc, INOUT treePtr, contextPtr)
```

The arguments to `ForEachCase` are as follows:

- `low, high` Pointers to the beginning and end of a region of recoverable storage.
- `regionProc` Pointer to a procedure defined by the user.
- `treePtr` Pointer to the region tree itself.
- `contextPtr` Pointer to whatever additional arguments the user of the package would like to pass in to `regionProc`.

`ForEachCase` first splits any region in the tree that overlaps a boundary of the specified range. Then, it descends the tree to `low` and begins an inorder walk to `high`. During the walk, it constructs a list of regions (entries in the tree) and gaps (spaces between entries) that cover the range. For every region and gap on the list, it calls `regionProc`. It passes as arguments the low and high region pointers of the region or gap, a pointer to the data associated with the region or `NULL` for a gap, and the pointer to additional arguments that was supplied by the caller of `ForEachCase()`. `regionProc` is permitted to modify the data passed to it and return the same pointer it was given. Or, it can allocate a new block of data and return a pointer to that. To delete a region, `regionProc` can return `NULL` as its result.

The region tree package makes it easy to ignore the existence of overlapping regions when implementing recovery algorithms. An easy way to reason about these algorithms is to imagine that each byte of recoverable storage is dealt with separately. When a log record refers to a range of bytes, an algorithm conceptually iterates through the bytes and refers to state information associated with each one. The region tree is an optimization used to break the range into intervals such that all bytes within an interval have the same state and can be processed together.

15.3 Algorithms

The Camelot Recovery Manager implements three distinct recovery algorithms: old-value/new-value abort, new-value-only abort and server recovery. The following sections sketch these algorithms. A final section discusses a hypothetical media recovery algorithm. The media recovery algorithm is included to indicate how media recovery could be integrated into Camelot. It has interesting similarities to new-value-only abort and to server recovery.

The old-value/new-value abort algorithm is extremely simple. When an old-value/new-value transaction aborts, the Recovery Manager reads all records written by that transaction in reverse order, restoring each old value from the log.

The other algorithms are more complex but have a great deal in common. They each involve one scan that begins at the end of the log and proceeds backwards, from newer records to older ones, until recovery is complete.[3] They each use several hash tables and one region tree to record all information needed to process each log record as it is encountered. They never restore any region more than once. They always use the last good value in the log for a given region. This is the first value encountered in a backward recovery scan.

The algorithms used for new-value-only abort, server recovery, and media recovery differ primarily in which log records they can use and which they must ignore, and in the conditions that must be satisfied before they terminate. The new-value-only abort algorithm uses lists of log sequence numbers obtained from the Disk Manager to avoid reading many irrelevant records. It also uses these lists to decide when to terminate. The server recovery algorithm must analyze every log record it encounters, and has its own complex set of rules for termination. The media recovery algorithm discards values for regions other than the ones it is recovering. It must also ignore all

[3]This is not quite true for new-value-only abort. It actually uses one pass to read all modify records written by the transactions being aborted and another to find updates to the same regions by other transactions. This is an artifact introduced because the Disk Manager and the Recovery Manager are in separate processes and must communicate through a narrow channel. In practice, the extra pass is not a performance problem. Since new-value-only transactions are required to be short, the first pass is always short. Also, the two passes usually overlap only a small amount if at all, so normal buffering of log data effectively combines the two passes into one.

end-write records up to the point where the regions to which they refer were archived. It can terminate only when it has restored all of the regions it is recovering.

15.3.1 Old-value/new-value Abort

Old-value/new-value abort is invoked by the Transaction Manager, which calls `RT_Abort` to pass the Recovery Manager a list of transactions to be aborted. The transactions on this list must comprise some entire branch of a transaction family that is currently active. That is, the list must include exactly one active transaction and all of that transaction's active or committed descendants. An exception is made for the abort of an entire family, which can occur after the Transaction Manager has forgotten the list of descendants. In this case, the abort list contains only the top-level member of the family.

The essence of the old-value/new-value abort algorithm is extremely simple. The Recovery Manager first obtains from the Disk Manager a list of all modify records written on behalf of the family that contains the aborting transaction branch. It then reads these records in the reverse of the order they were written. It checks each modify record to determine if it was written by the aborting branch. If it was, the Recovery Manager uses `SR_RestoreBatch` to send the old value of the modified region to the appropriate server. The Recovery Manager also calls `DR_UndoOvnv` to write a compensating undomodify record.

As is all too often the case, performance concerns and other practical complications make the actual implementation much more complex. Many of these complications also apply to the other recovery algorithms. Since old-value/new-value abort is the simplest algorithm, this is a good opportunity to describe the practical complications in detail.

After being invoked by the Transaction Manager, the Recovery Manager checks the abort list to determine whether the family being aborted is old-value/new-value or new-value-only. Because all members of a family have the same transaction type, the Recovery Manager can just check a flag in the first transaction on the list. Based on this test, the Recovery Manager selects the algorithm described in this section or the new-value-only algorithm described in the next one.

The next step is to synchronize with the server recovery thread. The abort thread latches a mutex and checks a global variable to determine whether server recovery is in progress. If there is no server recovery in progress, the abort thread immediately sets a flag indicating that an abort is in progress and drops the mutex. Otherwise, the abort thread waits until server recovery pauses. Then it sets the flag to indicate an active abort, drops the mutex, and deallocates the block of Log Manager state (see Section 15.2) that was being used by the server recovery thread.

The Recovery Manager then initializes two hash tables. One hash table, `lsnsAlreadySeen`, will be used to avoid processing log records twice when there are duplicates in the list obtained from the Disk Manager. It initializes another hash table called `lsnsUndoneEarlier`, which will be used to avoid undoing modifications of recoverable storage that were undone in some earlier abort or server recovery.

The Recovery Manager next does a `DR_GetTranLsns` call to the Disk Manager. It passes in the list of aborting transactions that it received from the Transaction Manager. It receives a list of log records written by the aborting family, a count of how many of the aborting transactions are read-only, and a new state block for the Log Manager. It makes a call to the Log Manager to install the new state block. Then it zeroes a counter called `firstModifyCnt`; this counter will be incremented each time the first modify in some aborting transaction is processed, and the abort will be terminated when the counter is equal to the number of transactions in the aborting branch.

If the list of log records is not empty, at least one of the aborting transactions is not read-only. The Recovery Manager loops through the list of log records, processing each one. First, it inserts the log record's LSN into the `lsnsAlreadySeen` hash table. Then it checks the record type. If the record is an undomodify record, it just extracts the LSN of the modify this record undid and inserts it into the `lsnsUndoneEarlier` hash table.

If the record is a modify, the Recovery Manager first checks the `lsnsUndoneEarlier` hash table to find out if it has processed a corresponding undomodify. If so, it skips this record. If not, it checks to determine if this record is part of the aborting branch.

If the record is a modify written by the aborting branch, the Recovery Manager checks the `isFirstSubTran` flag to determine if this is the first modify written by some subtransaction. If so, it increments `firstModifyCnt`. In any case, it extracts the modify record's old value and places it, along with its length and address, into a queue associated with the server that wrote the record.

When all log records in the list acquired from the Disk Manager have been processed, or when `firstModifyCnt` is equal to the number of transactions in the aborting branch, the Recovery Manager knows that all log records have been processed. It then iterates through the servers that were involved, processing their queues of modify records to be undone. It packs all of the old values for each server into one buffer and calls `SR_RestoreBatch` to send them to the server. This is much more efficient than it would have been to send them each individually. When the server processes the call, it pins each region and restores it to its old value. When the call returns, the Recovery Manager does a `DR_UndoModify` call to the Disk Manager for each old value to unpin the region and write an undomodify record.

Finally, the Recovery Manager calls `DR_DoneWithLsns` in the Disk Manager to inform it that the log records whose LSNs it obtained are no longer needed in the log to support this abort. The Recovery Manager clears the two hash tables, `lsnsAlreadySeen` and `lsnsUndoneEarlier`, and, if no server recovery is in progress, it deallocates the block of Log Manager state. It locks the mutex that is used for synchronization between abort and server recovery, resets the flag that had indicated an abort in progress, and drops the mutex. Then it returns to the Transaction Manager.

15.3.2 New-value-only Abort

The Transaction Manager invokes new-value-only abort in exactly the same manner as old-value/new-value. The Recovery Manager distinguishes between the two by examining the transaction type field in the transaction identifier. New-value-only abort is substantially more complex than old-value/new-value abort. To keep the description simple, this section omits details that are roughly the same in both algorithms.

New-value-only abort involves two major phases. First, the Recovery Manager calls the Disk Manager using `DR_GetTranLsns` to obtain a list of all modify records written on behalf of the transaction family that contains the transactions being aborted. It scans these records as it would for old-value/new-value abort, except that this time there are no old values from which to restore. The Recovery Manager just marks each modified region in a region tree to indicate that it needs to be restored. It also records the LSNs of all records that are read during this phase in a hash table called `lsnsAlreadySeen`.

When new-value-only transactions are aborted, no undomodify records are written in the log. Instead, the aborting transaction identifiers (TIDs) are listed in rec-abort records. This means that the Recovery Manager must process rec-abort records instead of undomodify records to determine which modify records have already been aborted.

To begin the second phase, the Recovery Manager walks the region tree to obtain a list of regions that were modified by the aborting transaction. It passes this list to the Disk Manager in a call to `DR_GetObjectLsns`. The Disk Manager uses the list of modified regions to produce a list of modified pages. It then returns to the Recovery Manager a list of LSNs for all log records that describe modifications to those pages since they were last read from disk.[4]

The Recovery Manager reads the records whose LSNs were returned by the Disk Manager, in the reverse of the order they were written. It examines these records to find the first (most recently written) good value for each region modified by the aborting branch. It restores each region to the correct value and sets a flag in the region tree to prevent the region from being restored again. During this pass, the Recovery Manager reads records written by both new-value-only and old-value/new-value transactions. It processes both rec-abort records and undomodify records to avoid using values from transactions that have aborted. During this pass the Recovery Manager also reads records written by the aborting transaction family itself. This is essential, because the most recent good value for a region modified by an aborting subtransaction may well be a value written by a committed subtransaction in the same family. However, the Recovery Manager uses the `lsnsAlreadySeen` hash table to avoid restoring regions from modify records written by the aborting transaction branch.

15.3.3 Server Recovery

When the Disk Manager restarts a server, it invokes the Recovery Manager to restore the server's recoverable storage to a transaction-consistent state. Many modifications to recoverable storage may have been made in memory on behalf of committed (or prepared) transactions but not yet written to disk. The Recovery Manager must redo these modifications before normal processing can begin. Other modifications may have been made on behalf of transactions that were still active at the time of the crash, or that had not yet been completely aborted. It is impossible to tell for sure from the log whether normal paging activity had caused these modifications to be written to disk or not, so they must be undone.[5] The Recovery Manager must also reinstate locks held by prepared transactions. It must rebuild the data structures that are maintained by the Disk Manager to support aborts that occur once the server is running. And it must supply the Transaction Manager with information about transaction state.

During server recovery, the Recovery Manager uses a region tree to maintain the following flags for each region of recoverable storage:

- It sets the `done` flag after restoring the region.
- It sets the `safe` flag when it learns from an end-write record that the page containing this region was safely written to disk.

[4]This algorithm may return irrelevant LSNs, but it will never omit needed LSNs.

[5]Actually, if a server goes down without the entire node crashing, all active transactions that had involved the server will be aborted immediately. They will be considered "aborted", rather than "active", when the server is later recovered. If the entire node crashes, however, transactions will be left in the "active" state.

- It sets the `unsafe` flag when it learns from a checkpoint record that the page containing this region was in memory at the time of the crash.

All of these flags are initialized to `FALSE`. The Recovery Manager also keeps the following lists and hash tables:

- The `brList` lists servers the servers that are being recovered.
- The `nrList` lists servers that are not being recovered, but for which the Recovery Manager has seen records in the log.
- The `tranState` table records the final state of each transaction whose outcome the Recovery Manager is able to determine. The Recovery Manager updates this state information by observing transaction management records in the log.
- The `tidsAbortedEarlier` table contains TIDs for new-value-only transactions that aborted.

The `brList` is initialized with the list of data servers provided by the Disk Manager when it invoked server recovery. The other list and tables are initially empty.

During server recovery, the Recovery Manager processes all log records, beginning with the most recent one and proceeding toward older records. It stops processing records when it has read at least one checkpoint record, when it has no more regions flagged as unsafe and no more transactions listed as incomplete, and it did not encounter any of the servers it is recovering in the last checkpoint's `nrList`. It ignores records for servers not being recovered, or for deleted servers after the point in the log where they were deleted. Otherwise, it processes each record as follows:

- It checks each **Modify**, **undomodify**, and **backstop** record to determine whether or not it contains data that should be restored. If the transaction that wrote the record is listed in `tidsAbortedEarlier`, meaning that an abort record was seen for it earlier in recovery, the Recovery Manager ignores the record. Otherwise, it restores each region that is not `safe` or `done` from the data in the record and sets each newly-restored region to `done`. If the record is an old-value/new-value modify whose state in the `tranState` table is aborted, the Recovery Manager restores each region from the old value rather than the new value.
- It ignores a **Server-prepare** record if it has not seen a tran-prepare record for the same transaction, or if it has seen an abort or commit record for the transaction. Otherwise, it replays the server-prepare record to the server that wrote it so the server can restore its locks for that transaction.
- It checks the state of each **Tran-prepare** record's transaction to determine if that transaction has a known outcome. If it doesn't, then it is still prepared. The Recovery Manager replays the record to the Transaction Manager and sets the transaction state to prepared.
- It replays each **tran-commit** record that refers to a distributed transaction to the Transaction Manager. It sets the state of the transaction that wrote the record to "committed".
- It replays each **tran-abort** record that refers to a distributed transaction to the Transaction Manager. It sets the state of the transaction that wrote the record to "aborted".

- When it reads a **fetch** record, The Recovery Manager clears its data structures for the page. Because the Recovery Manager is processing records in the reverse of the order they were written, the fetch record, which was written when the page was brought into memory, indicates that all modifications to the page that could possibly have been lost in the crash have been processed.

- When it reads an **end-write** record, the Recovery Manager marks all regions in the corresponding page as `safe`. The end-write record indicates that upcoming updates to the page were safely written to disk before the crash.

- When it encounters a **rec-abort** record, the Recovery Manager adds the transaction recorded in the record to the `tidsAbortededEarlier` hash table.

- When it reads a **checkpoint** record, the Recovery Manager processes each of the lists the record contains. It adds inactive servers to its `nrList`. If any server on the `brList` is listed as inactive, the Recovery Manager sets a flag to indicate that it cannot terminate recovery until it reads another checkpoint record.

  If this is the first checkpoint record encountered in a recovery pass, the Recovery Manager adds servers that have segments listed as active, but that are not up and are not being recovered to its `nrList`.

  The Recovery Manager sets the state of transactions that are listed in the checkpoint and whose outcome it does not already know to "aborted". It can treat these transactions as "aborted" and not "active" because their modifications were undone by the recovery pass that wrote the checkpoint record.

  The Recovery Manager also recomputes its list of unsafe regions based on the entries in the active region list. Any region that is listed as active but not already flagged as `safe` must now be considered `unsafe`.

The Recovery Manager deals with many complications beyond this basic algorithm. It checks the version number of each log record to be sure it is current. It accumulates for the Disk Manager a list of servers that are not being recovered but whose records it has seen. It calls the Disk Manager using `DR_BackLinkPage` to link all records written by pages that were active at the time of the crash into the page lines of the Disk Manager's grid (see Chapter 14). During the first server recovery pass after Camelot is brought up, the Recovery Manager calls the Disk Manager to link all records written by prepared transactions into the transaction lines of the grid.

The Recovery Manager must also handle transactions that were copied forward in the log by the Disk Manager. A `copyForward` bit in each record indicates whether it was written as its transaction was being copied forward. Only prepared transactions are ever copied forward (other incomplete transactions are aborted), so the existence of a prepare record with the copy forward bit set indicates to the Recovery Manager that the transaction was successfully copied forward in its entirety. In this case, the Recovery Manager processes the records for this transaction that have `copyForward` set and ignores the redundant older copies. Transactions that do not have a `copyForward` prepare in the log were not completely copied forward. The Recovery Manager ignores any `copyForward` records for these transactions and reads the original records instead.

15.4 Related Work

We are not aware of any system which has separated recovery from the related processing done during forward processing. The functionality of the Camelot Recovery Manager and the Camelot Disk Manager are normally combined into one module. For a discussion of work related to this area, see 14.4.

15.5 Conclusions

We have implemented a thorough, flexible recovery algorithm that requires only one pass to recover any given set of servers. To bring up a node and then bring up a set of servers we use two passes; the first must recover the Node Server so mappings of recoverable storage to disk are available when the other servers are recovered. It would be very simple to eliminate this extra pass by keeping a small separate log for the Node Server database.

When Camelot was being designed on paper, we worried that handling arbitrarily overlapping regions during recovery might turn out to be difficult. The "region tree" module described earlier in this chapter isolates all of the difficulties with overlapping regions in one efficient package based on a standard AVL tree [1]. This greatly simplified the rest of the Recovery Manager implementation. However, it still requires a great deal of computation. Processing a modify record or any other record that affects a specific region of recoverable storage involves descending the tree at the low point of the region, splitting any existing region that straddles that point, walking the tree up to the high point, and splitting any existing region that straddles the high point. The expense depends greatly on the shape of the tree, but seems to average over a thousand instructions per record. This would be a strong motivation to use an algorithm that avoids this expense by processing the log forward (replaying history), rather than searching for the last good update. The ARIES algorithm [80] is a good algorithm of this kind.

We initially believed that to isolate errors during the implementation process, it was important to use a separate process for each major component of the system. Restricting the Recovery Manager to a separate process proved to be exceedingly difficult. More than once we spent several weeks devising a simpler interface between the Recovery Manager and some other component when that interface had become too complicated and inefficient. At times we felt that the discipline imposed by the remote procedure call (RPC) interface was forcing us to improve the modularity of the system. However, the expense of the RPC interface forced us to make some changes that are obviously artificial. For example, before each recovery operation we transfer a large cache from the Disk Manager's instance of the Log Manager to the Recovery Manager so that we don't have to go to the expense of reading each record through an RPC interface. If we were designing the system again we would avoid such a complete separation between the recovery logic and the logic used during forward processing to support recovery.

Chapter 16

The Design of the Camelot Transaction Manager

Lily B. Mummert
Dan Duchamp
Peter D. Stout

16.1 Introduction

This chapter motivates and describes the inner workings of the Transaction Manager. The purpose of the Transaction Manager is to maintain the state of transaction families and guarantee the consistency of such state. To facilitate this, the Transaction Manager makes use of the following protocols:

1. **Local commitment.** This service, as well as the next two, is available through the `TA_End` call.

2. **Distributed two-phase commitment.**

3. **Distributed non-blocking commitment.**

4. **Abort Processing.** This service is available through the `TA_Kill` call.

5. **Lock Inheritance.** This service is available through the `TS_IsLockInheritable` and `TS_WaitBeforeInheritingLock` calls.

The Transaction Manager also gathers enough information to detect crashes, creates and distributes transaction identifiers (TIDs), and maintains a node's logical clock.

The operation of each of the above protocols is described in Section 16.3. Except for local commitment, each of these is a distributed protocol that is intended to operate among processes on several nodes. The commitment protocols operate only for top-level transactions; the only effect of "committing" a nested transaction is for the local Transaction Manager to remember that it happened.

The purpose of the commitment and abort protocols is to provide agreement among a group of servers. In principle, these protocols could be implemented by having the servers communicate among themselves directly, without the intervention of the Transaction Manager. Argus [73] works this way. Camelot employs a separate transaction management process in order to simplify the construction of servers and to reduce the number of inter-node messages needed to execute the protocols.

16.1.1 Functional Goals

One of the main goals of Camelot is to provide an expansive notion of what a transaction can do. Each of the transaction management protocols helps in some way to support a rich transaction model without compromising performance. Two distributed commitment protocols and an abort protocol operate for transactions that are arbitrarily distributed. The commitment protocols provide for commitment of nested transactions with minimal overhead, and still allow commitment of a whole family of transactions to be accomplished with no more messages than those strictly needed. The abort protocol permits clean abortion of child transactions so that parents and siblings may still commit. The lock inheritance protocol resolves the situation wherein two or more members of the same transaction family contend to obtain the same lock. Timestamps needed for servers to maintain hybrid atomic data are embedded in the messages of the commitment protocols.

Another primary goal of Camelot is to provide the tools with which highly available applications may be built. Both the non-blocking commitment and abort protocols are designed to continue in spite of any single failure.

16.1.2 Performance Goals

The Transaction Manager has two primary performance goals. First, it should only be invoked to begin or end transactions (i.e., there should be no incremental costs associated with operations within the transaction). Second, the service should have low overhead per transaction. Unfortunately, these goals can be contradictory: for example, the implementation of nested transactions can carry significant overhead. For this reason, we have traded off the first goal in favor of the second, and have strived to optimize common cases. We believe the common cases are top-level transactions, concurrent nested transactions with no sharing, and serial nested transactions (for failure isolation).

16.1.3 Constraints

External influences upon the design of the Transaction Manager are imposed by the failure model and the network environment provided by Mach, MIG, and the Network Message Server. The failure model is as follows:

- Any Camelot application or server may fail at any time.
- Node failures, due to hardware failures or Camelot or Mach malfunction, may also occur at any time.
- Processes and nodes *fail fast*, meaning that a failure results in the node or process halting immediately, then losing its volatile memory.
- The network may partition arbitrarily.

The underlying Mach/MIG/Network Message Server environment provides no reliable mechanism for rapidly detecting the crash of a remote node or the failure of any process on a remote node. Since port death messages can be delayed or lost, a node may only notice that a remote node has crashed upon its next transmission to a port on that node.

16.2 Architecture

This section describes the architecture of the Transaction Manager in terms of the goals and constraints outlined above. The main functional goal is to support a variety of transaction types, while the main performance goal is to do this without sacrificing performance in common cases. The implementation of these goals is constrained by the failure model.

Function

Some of the complexity of the Transaction Manager stems from supporting nested transactions. Data structures are more complex because nesting forces a separation between a transaction and a transaction family. Different functions apply to each object – for example, the commitment protocols operate on families, while the abort and lock inheritance protocols operate chiefly on transactions. In addition, the TID is larger. Half of the Camelot TID is devoted to nested transactions.

A significant amount of additional information must be collected to support distributed transactions. In the distributed case, the Camelot Transaction Manager collects the following information:

- Node accumulation on a family basis. The Transaction Manager monitors the spread of transactions to sites just as it monitors contact with servers. It keeps track of all the nodes that have been visited by a particular transaction family. This list of nodes is used by the commitment and abort protocols.

- Node accumulation on a transaction basis. The abort protocol requires knowledge of the nodes visited by a particular transaction, rather than by the entire family.

- Notice of migration. The Transaction Manager must be apprised when a transaction first leaves the node, so that it knows to ask for a list of nodes when committing or aborting.

- Notice of arrival. In order to prevent the forging of TIDs, the Transaction Manager must be aware of every legitimate transaction active at its node. By being notified the first time a transaction migrates to its node, the Transaction Manager knows that every true TID was either created locally or arrived in a remote procedure call (RPC) from another node.

- Timestamps. The logical time at which a transaction family first visits a node is recorded. This is used to detect sites that have crashed and recovered during the lifetime of the family.

To support hybrid-atomic transactions, timestamps are included in the messages and log records of the commitment protocols.

Performance

The Transaction Manager is heavily optimized for top-level transactions. Most of the overhead is associated with committing the transaction. The two-phase commitment implementation uses all known optimizations. Non-blocking commitment is achieved using three message phases, which is minimal [104]. Local transactions are optimized to write fewer log records than their distributed counterparts. Server-based (local, single-server) transactions are implemented such that there are no RPCs to the Transaction Manager. Lazy server-based transactions are further optimized to eliminate messages to the Disk Manager and reduce disk latency.

End transaction processing overhead is practically eliminated for nested transactions through a lazy commitment strategy. The nesting model used by Camelot allows locks to be passed between members of the same family if they are committed with respect to their least common ancestor. Since the Transaction Manager sends no messages to participating servers to commit such transactions, locks are not anti-inherited at commitment time. In the case of a lock conflict, the Transaction Manager must determine the genealogy and states of the transactions in question. If the transactions are distributed, their genealogies are shipped to remote sites on their first visit. States are not shipped, as the cost of maintaining them would be prohibitive. The distributed lock inheritance protocol contacts the creation site of the transaction for this information if needed.

We believe that concurrent nested transactions will rarely experience lock conflicts. The cost of lock conflict resolution is still an issue for serial nested transactions, however, we expect that these transactions will not be deeply nested. In this case, use of an optimization called the *family position indicator* (see Section 16.3.5) greatly reduces the likelihood that the Transaction Manager will have to be contacted to resolve lock conflicts.

Another consequence of using a lazy commitment protocol is the requirement for a unanimous distributed abort protocol. All nodes must be notified of a nested abort to prevent commitment of inconsistent work when the family commits. For example, consider a transaction created at node A, with a child that does work on nodes A and B. If node B aborts the child and does not notify node A, then when the top-level transaction commits, it will commit the partial work of its child.

Constraints

The failure model is the major constraint under which the Transaction Manager must operate. A server or application failure is detected by the Transaction Manager when it receives the port death message for the process. The Transaction Manager then aborts all transactions that were involved with that process. A node failure during a distributed transaction is detected when an RPC times out. The Camelot Library aborts the transaction using the `TA_Kill` call. If the transaction is in the process of committing, it will commit or abort everywhere depending on when the failure occurred (before or after prepare time). If there is a nested abort in progress, the top-level transaction will abort. Information on prepared and committed transactions is stored in the log; when the node restarts, the log is consulted to determine state. Partitions are interpreted as node failures, and are handled as described above. The Transaction Manager uses a *low-water mark* [67] technique to detect that a node has crashed and recovered since the last time a particular transaction visited it. This is discussed in Section 16.3.6.

16.2.1 Use of Multiple Threads

The Transaction Manager is a service process that contains multiple threads of control. These include a timer thread, signal thread, and multiple service threads. The timer thread signals timeouts in the distributed communication protocols. The signal thread provides debugging information in response to messages from Camelot developers. Service threads respond to request messages from applications, servers, or other Camelot components. When idle, these threads are waiting to receive a message (e.g., a `TA_End` call) on one of the Transaction Manager's service ports.

A service request may result in the sending and receiving of other messages (e.g., the inter-node datagrams of the distributed commitment protocol). If so, then the response to the service request is delayed and not sent until the proper moment. Multi-threading allows such requests to run concurrently on shared memory multiprocessors.

Data structures within the Transaction Manager are locked such that only one request for a transaction family may be serviced at a time. Subsequent requests on behalf of that family block until the request in progress completes. If a service requiring an exchange of network messages is requested, then family data structures are unlocked while the exchange is in progress.

16.2.2 Exported Data Types

Exported types maintained by the Transaction Manager are presented in this section.

Transaction Identifier

The format and management of the transaction identifier is one of the most important design decisions in a transaction management system. No data type permeates the system as does this one. The content of the TID is influenced by the following considerations:

- local vs. distributed
- nested vs. top-level
- fixed vs. variable length
- uniqueness
- genealogy
- relation to other family members
- security, forgeability

The Camelot transaction identifier, presented in Figure 16.1, is a six word quantity composed of a family identifier and the subtransaction identifier. The family identifier contains forty bits of counters for local uniqueness and a node ID to identify the creation site and to ensure global uniqueness. The counter is initialized from the log. If the log is reinitialized the counter is started at 0. Other fields in the family identifier include transaction type indicators and checksum bits to reduce the chances that a TID may be forged. The subtransaction identifier contains a node ID to identify the creator site, a counter for uniqueness within a family, and a hint about the position of the subtransaction relative to other family members (see Section 16.3.5, **Family Position Indicator**).

A consequence of fixing the length of the TID is that there must be some mechanism for discovering the complete genealogies of two transactions that conflict over a lock. In principle, a complete transaction genealogy is unbounded in length. Genealogy data (a list of subtransaction identifiers) is distributed by piggybacking it onto RPC requests.

```
typedef struct cam_fam_id {
        cam_node_id_t       nodeId;
        unsigned int
                                highTicker   : 8,
                                randomBits   : 16,
                                reserved     : 4,
                                wrapCode     : 1,
                                hybridAtomic: 1,
                                serverBased : 1,
                                ovnv         : 1,
                                lowTicker    : 32;
} cam_fam_id_t;

typedef struct cam_sub_id {
    cam_node_id_t   nodeId;
    u_int      ticker;
    cam_fpi_t          fpi;
} cam_sub_id_t;

typedef struct cam_tid {
    cam_fam_id_t    famId;
    cam_sub_id_t    subId;
} cam_tid_t;
```

Figure 16.1: Camelot Transaction Identifier

The Transaction Manager is the sole creator of TIDs. TIDs are not explicitly destroyed; they become obsolete after the transaction they represent has completed. Since any process that knows a TID can abort the transaction it represents (provided the abort is requested on a site that the transaction has visited), security of TIDs involves restricting the flow of TIDs and ensuring that they are difficult to forge. The Transaction Manager creating the transaction sets the `randomBits` of the family identifier for this purpose. Unfortunately, this field is overloaded; for server-based transactions `randomBits` holds the server ID instead.

Timestamps and Lamport Clocks

A Lamport clock is a logical clock [60]; its value bears no relationship to the actual time of day. However, it does provide a logical analog of the flow of time, because it guarantees the following two properties: its value increases strictly monotonically, so that on a given node every timestamp is later than its predecessor; and the reception of a message on one node occurs logically after the sending from another node. To maintain the first invariant, the clock in incremented every time it is read. To maintain the second invariant, every transactional RPC is timestamped when it leaves, and the clock at the recipient site is updated upon its arrival.

The timestamp, presented in Figure 16.2, is a 96-bit number that contains a Lamport clock value in the high 64 bits, and a node ID (IP address) in the low 32 bits. The Lamport clock value provides the time ordering, and the node ID makes timestamps unique.

Timestamps are exported by Camelot, but maintenance of the clock and timestamp generation

```
typedef struct cam_lamport_clock {
        unsigned int high;
        unsigned int low;
} cam_lamport_clock_t;

typedef struct cam_timestamp {
        cam_lamport_clock_t time;
        cam_node_id_t nodeId;
} cam_timestamp_t;
```

Figure 16.2: Timestamps in Camelot

is handled by the Transaction Manager. Camelot uses timestamps for sequencing hybrid-atomic transactions and for crash detection (see Section 16.3.6).

16.2.3 Internal Data Structures

In this section, the major data structures of the Transaction Manager are presented.

Family and Transaction Data Structures

The Transaction Manager keeps a table of *family records*, hashed by TID. The family record includes the family ID, state, a list of sites visited by transactions in the family, a list of servers involved with transactions in the family, and status fields used by the commitment and abort protocols (such as the number of vote responses that are being awaited). The family record also contains a hash table for its members. *Transaction records* include the TID, state, a list of sites visited by the transaction, a list of servers involved with the transaction, and status fields used by the abort and lock inheritance protocols.

In addition to the links between transaction records in a bucket, a tree structure is superimposed upon the transaction records in a family using parent, child, and sibling links.

Family and associated transaction records are deleted when the family either commits or aborts. Information on committed and aborted nested transactions is retained for lock inheritance purposes.

Locking is done at the family level. There is a lock on each family hash table bucket and each family record. To access a family or transaction, a thread obtains the bucket lock, then the record lock. Locks are released in the same order.

Servers

A list of all servers known to Camelot is kept in a table hashed by server ID. The Transaction Manager adds a server to the table when it receives a `TD_AddDataServer` message from the Disk Manager. The *server record* includes the server ID, state, and ports for communication to and from the Transaction Manager. Records are updated when servers crash or recover. Server IDs are reused, so server records are never explicitly deleted from the table.

Records in the server tables are referenced from server records kept in the family and transaction records, to reduce duplication of information. The family server record contains additional

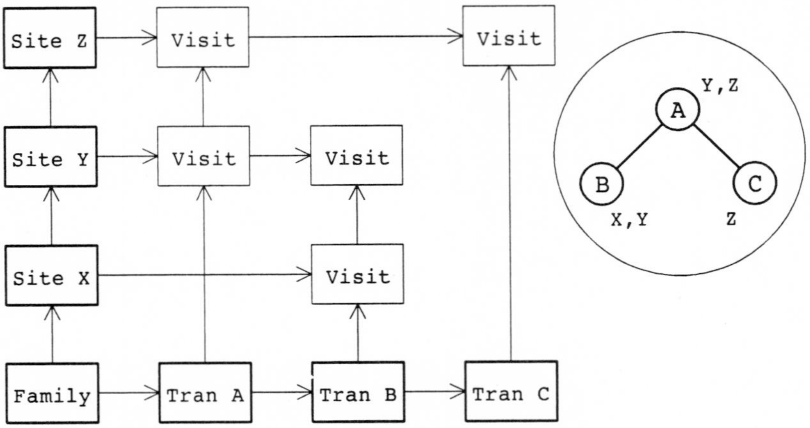

Figure 16.3: Site Grid for a Transaction Family
Transaction A has visited sites Y and Z. Child B has visited sites X and Y. Child C has visited site Z.

information about servers involved with its members, such as the number of members with which it is involved, and a field for storing the server vote during the commitment protocol.

Sites

Site information is kept in both the family and transaction records. Each family record has associated with it a list of all sites visited by its members. The family *site record* includes a timestamp, the site state, and fields to assist in packing site information for inclusion into transactional RPCs.

To indicate which members of a family have visited a site, a grid of *visit records* is kept between the family site list and the transaction list. An example is shown in Figure 16.3. This structure is similar to the grid maintained by the Disk Manager, presented in Chapter 14.

To make crash detection possible, a site remains in the family site list even if all of the work on behalf on the family at that site has been aborted. In this case, no transaction will reference it in the grid. This is discussed further in Section 16.3.6.

16.2.4 Messages

The Transaction Manager uses 20 kinds of datagrams. All messages contain a message type, version, and a TID. The type, additional content, and use of each message is listed below.

1. vote (two-phase) – commit timestamp, list of dangerous sites (see below). Sent by the coordinator during the prepare phase of the two-phase commitment protocol.
2. vote response (two-phase) – vote. Sent by subordinates during the prepare phase of the two-phase commitment protocol.
3. vote (non-blocking) – commit timestamp, list of sites and states, list of dangerous sites.

4. vote response (non-blocking) – vote, list of sites and states
5. join quorum – list of sites and states. Used in non-blocking commitment.
6. in quorum – quorum selection (commit or abort), list of sites and states. Used in non-blocking commitment.
7. outcome (two-phase) – outcome of the transaction (commit or abort). Sent by the coordinator during the outcome phase of the two-phase commitment protocol.
8. outcome response (two-phase) Sent by subordinates during the outcome phase of the two-phase commitment protocol.
9. outcome (non-blocking) – outcome of transaction, list of sites and states.
10. outcome response (non-blocking) – list of sites and states.
11. outcome query. Used by subordinates in both commitment protocols when an outcome message is overdue.
12. kill – abort code. Used in the abort protocol; upon receipt, the local effects of the specified transaction are undone.
13. kill response. In nested abort, used to indicate that the effects of the specified transaction have been undone at the sending node and all nodes to which the transaction spread from the sending node.
14. died – abort initiation site, abort code. Sent when a transaction is aborted at a node other than the node on which it was created.
15. died response. Used to indicate that a distributed nested abort has completed.
16. danger – dangerous site. Used in nested abort; the dangerous site is a site that could not be reached by the abort protocol and may contain unaborted work.
17. danger response.
18. transaction status request (immediate). Used in the lock inheritance protocol to determine if a transaction has completed (and can anti-inherit locks).
19. transaction status request (wait). Same as above, except the receiving thread waits until the transaction has completed.
20. transaction status response – committed and completed indicators. Contains the state of a transaction; used for lock inheritance.

16.2.5 Log Records

The Transaction Manager writes 19 kinds of log records. Every record begins with a version number, a record type indicator, and a family identifier. After this standard prelude follows the record-specific data:

1. TID – counters from the family identifier. Written periodically to indicate the value of the last TID issued. After a crash, a delta is added to the value in the last TID record in the log to ensure that TIDs do not repeat.
2. checkpoint – This is an amalgam of possibly many committed coordinator records and one TID record. The Transaction Manager uses this record to store information that it needs to save across crashes.
3. prepared (two-phase) – Contains address of coordinator, number of local servers, server IDs.
4. prepared (non-blocking) – Contents include that of the two-phase prepare record, the number of subordinates, and the IP addresses and states of other subordinates.

5. committed (local) – Contains a timestamp for hybrid atomicity.
6. committed coordinator – Used in two-phase commitment. Contains a timestamp (for hybrid atomicity), the number of subordinates and the IP addresses of subordinates.
7. committed subordinate – Used in two-phase commitment. No extra data.
8. committed (non-blocking) – Contains the number of subordinates, and the IP addresses and states of subordinates.
9. commit done (two-phased) – No extra data.
10. commit done (non-blocking) – No extra data.
11. commit quorum – Used in non-blocking commitment. Contains the number of subordinates and a list of IP addresses and states of other subordinates.
12. aborted (abort) – Used by the abort protocol when a top-level transaction aborts.
13. aborted (local) – Used for a local commitment time abort. No extra data.
14. aborted coordinator – Used for a two-phase commitment time abort. No extra data.
15. aborted subordinate – Used for a two-phase commitment time abort. No extra data.
16. aborted (non-blocking) – Extra data same as abort quorum record.
17. abort done (two-phase) – No extra data.
18. abort done (non-blocking) – No extra data.
19. abort quorum – Used in non-blocking commitment. Extra data same as commit quorum record.

16.3 Algorithms

The major transaction management algorithms are distributed *protocols*, which involve an exchange of messages between one or more processes. Protocols drive processes from one state into another with the goal of each of them ending up in one of a number of final states.

Each of the four major Transaction Manager protocols (the three commitment protocols and the abort protocol) is explained in three sections: one to describe the usual, error-free operation of the protocol; one to describe what happens in case of errors at other nodes, and one to describe how to recover the local node if it crashed while executing the protocol.

16.3.1 Local Commitment Protocol

The protocol for local commitment is a simple version of two-phase commitment [38]. Local commitment without failures is illustrated in Figure 16.4.

Normal Operation

The sequence of events in an attempt to commit locally is:

1. The application calls `TA_End` and blocks until it receives the response.

2. The Transaction Manager makes the synchronous `ST_Vote` call sequentially to each server involved in the transaction. The `prepare` argument is `FALSE`, indicating that the server needs not write its locks to the log.

```
(1) Application sends TA_End request
(2) ST_Vote: TranMan gets vote from Server 1.   (Vote is Yes)
(3) ST_Vote: TranMan gets vote from Server 2.   (Vote is Read-only dependent)
(4) ST_Vote: TranMan gets vote from Server 3.   (Vote is Read-only)
(5) DT_SmallLogWrite: write commit record
(6) TranMan sends TA_End reply to application
(7) ST_Commit: TranMan notifies Server 1 of commit
(8) ST_Done: TranMan notifies Server 2 of transaction completion
```

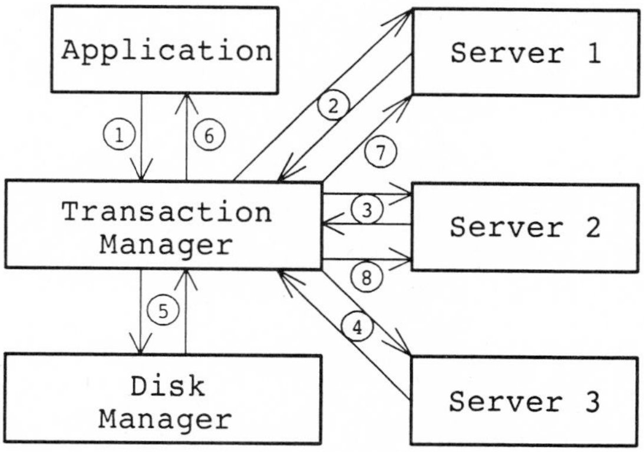

Figure 16.4: Local Commitment Protocol

3. Upon receiving ST_Vote, each server decides to vote yes, no, read-only, or read-only dependent. (See Section 9.3.2 for the meaning of the server vote.) The vote is returned in response to the ST_Vote call. Any server that votes read-only can immediately drop its locks and forget about the transaction, meaning that it may purge its data structures; it will receive no further protocol messages pertaining to this transaction. Those servers that vote otherwise can drop read locks, but must maintain write locks.

4. The Transaction Manager tallies the votes.

   - If all votes are read-only, the protocol can end early: the Transaction Manager sends the reply to TA_End, and expunges its data structures and forgets about the transaction.
   - If any vote is no, the Transaction Manager decides to abort, invokes the recovery process by calling RT_Abort, and then forces an abort record into the log.
   - If all votes are read-only or read-only dependent and at least one is read-only dependent, the Transaction Manager forces the log to ensure the permanence of the previous lazily committed transaction.
   - If all votes are yes, read-only or read-only dependent and at least one is yes, then the Transaction Manager forces into the log an indication that the transaction is committed.

5. The Transaction Manager sends the reply to `TA_End`, informing the application program of the outcome of its attempt to commit.

6. Depending upon the outcome, the Transaction Manager sends either an `ST_Commit`, an `ST_Abort`, or an `ST_Done` message to all servers that voted yes, no, or read-only dependent. No messages are sent to those that voted read-only.

7. Once one of the above messages is received, a server drops its write locks and forgets the transaction.

8. The Transaction Manager forgets the transaction.

Operation in the Presence of Failures

Local commitment is considerably simpler than distributed commitment because having all involved processes (i.e., the Transaction Manager and the servers) on the same node reduces the trouble caused by failures. Specifically, no message is ever lost, and the possibility that a server might crash is of no consequence: the state to which it recovers is determined by the presence or absence of a commitment record in the local log. In distributed commitment, a server must prepare itself to either commit or abort depending on an instruction from another node. If a transaction is local, a server need not prepare because it will be automatically recovered into the correct state.

Recovery

Recovery of an interrupted execution of the local commitment protocol is simple. If the log contains a commit record, then the transaction is committed and the Recovery Manager is thereby instructed to redo its effects. If there is no commit record, the transaction is aborted and its effects are undone.

16.3.2 Distributed Two Phase Commitment Protocol

Distributed commitment is more complicated than local commitment because the decision to commit or abort is made at a single designated node, and the other nodes must prepare themselves for either outcome. The node that makes the decision is that on which the application process resides, and is called the *coordinator*. All other nodes are called *subordinates*. The coordinator knows the identity of all subordinates; each subordinate knows the identity of the coordinator, but not of the other subordinates.

Normal Operation

Listed below is the sequence of events in the commitment of a top-level transaction. Figure 16.5 depicts each event in the case of successful commitment.

1. The application calls `TA_End` and blocks until it receives the response.

2. The coordinator sends `ST_Vote` (`prepare` argument `FALSE`) to all local servers that are involved in the transaction and sends a vote message to all subordinate Transaction Managers.

After receiving the vote message, each subordinate Transaction Manager makes an `ST_Vote` (`prepare` argument `TRUE`) call on all the appropriate servers at its node.

3. After receiving `ST_Vote`, each server votes yes, no, read-only, or read-only dependent. If a server at a subordinate node decides to vote yes, then it must spool into the log the list of locks held by that transaction before it can return its vote. The servers at the coordinator's node do not need to write their lock list into the log; they simply vote. Just as with local commitment, any server that votes read-only can immediately forget about the transaction.

4. If all servers at a subordinate node have voted yes or read-only and if at least one has voted yes, then the Transaction Manager at that node forces a *prepare* record into the log (indicating that the transaction is irrevocably prepared to commit at that node), and sends a message to the coordinator indicating that all the servers at its node have voted to commit. If all servers at a node vote read-only, then no prepare record is written and the node votes read-only. If all servers vote read-only or read-only dependent, then the Transaction Manager at that node flushes the log (to guarantee the permanence of the lazily committed transaction on which the read-only transaction depends), and an `ST_Done` to servers that voted read-only dependent. The node then votes read-only. If any server has voted no, then no prepare record is forced and the node votes no. The prepare record contains the identity of the coordinator. There are two reasons to force a prepare record. One is to record the fact that the node has forfeited the right to abort the transaction: it must wait for the coordinator to tell it whether to commit or abort. The second is to ensure that the locks spooled earlier by the servers are placed into the log before the node returns its vote. Once the prepare record is forced, the subordinate sends a vote response message to the coordinator indicating that it is prepared.

5. The coordinator waits for a certain period of time, retransmitting vote messages up to some fixed number of times[1]. At the end of this period, if any subordinate node or local server has not yet voted, the coordinator assumes a no vote on behalf of that node and aborts the transaction. If all votes are in on time, the coordinator tallies them. If there are any no votes, the coordinator will decide to abort. If all votes are yes, read-only, or read-only dependent (from a local server), the coordinator decides to commit.

6. To commit, the coordinator forces into the log an indication that the transaction is committed. The commit record must include the identity of the subordinates so that, after recovery, the coordinator will be able to determine whether every subordinate knows the outcome of the transaction. The coordinator can forget the transaction only once every subordinate is aware of its outcome. To abort, `RT_Abort` is called and then an abort log record is forced. In either case, after the log record is written, the `TA_End` response is sent.

7. The coordinator sends an `ST_Commit` (or `ST_Abort`) message to all local servers that did not vote read-only, and an `ST_Done` message to each local server that voted read-only dependent. It also sends an outcome message (commit or abort) to each subordinate that did not vote read-only. Messages are not sent to servers or nodes that voted read-only, since they have already forgotten about the transaction. The `ST_Commit` (`ST_Abort`) message serves to notify a server to drop its write locks.

[1]This number is specified to the Transaction Manager as a command line argument.

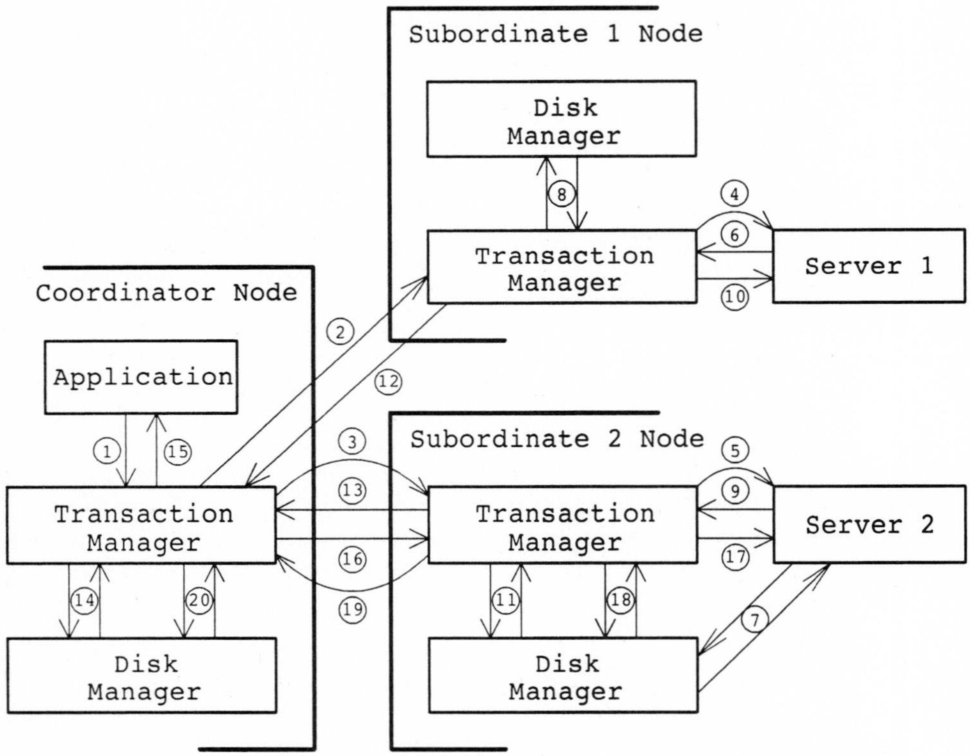

Figure 16.5: Distributed Two-Phase Commitment without Errors

(1) Application sends TA_End request to Coordinator TranMan

(2) Coordinator TranMan asks Subordinate 1 TranMan to vote

(3) Coordinator TranMan asks Subordinate 2 TranMan to vote

(4) ST_Vote: Subordinate 1 TranMan tells Server 1 to vote

(5) ST_Vote: Subordinate 2 TranMan tells Server 2 to vote

(6) Server 1 votes read-only dependent

(7) DS_Prepare: Server 2 saves locks in log

(8) DT_SmallLogWrite: Subordinate 1 TranMan forces the log

(9) Server 2 votes yes

(10) ST_Done: Subordinate 1 TranMan tells Server 1 to drop locks and clean up

(11) DT_SmallLogWrite: Subordinate 2 TranMan forces prepare record

(12) Subordinate 1 TranMan votes read-only

(13) Subordinate 2 TranMan votes yes

(14) DT_SmallLogWrite: Coordinator TranMan forces commit record

(15) Coordinator TranMan replies to TA_End

(16) Coordinator TranMan tells Subordinate 2 TranMan that the transaction committed

(17) ST_Commit: Subordinate 2 TranMan tells Server 2 that the transaction committed

(18) Subordinate 2 TranMan spools record indicating commitment

(19) Subordinate 2 TranMan acknowledges transaction commitment

(20) Coordinator TranMan spools done record

8. A subordinate that receives an outcome message sends ST_Commit (ST_Abort) to all servers that did not vote read-only or read-only dependent, and then spools a log record that indicates the outcome of the transaction. Once a server receives the ST_Commit (ST_Abort) message, it drops its locks and forgets the transaction.

9. Once the subordinate's log record is eventually forced, the subordinate Transaction Manager sends an outcome response message to the coordinator, and forgets about the transaction. There are two purposes for writing a commit record at a subordinate node: to allow the node to recover the transaction after a crash without having to communicate with the coordinator and to allow the coordinator to forget about the transaction. If it were the case that recovering subordinates always had to ask the coordinator for the outcome, then the coordinator could never forget.

10. The coordinator spools a *done* record, and forgets about the transaction. The purpose of the done record is to record the fact that all subordinates are aware of the outcome, and that the coordinating Transaction Manager will never again be asked about the transaction. The done record can be spooled and not forced because its function is purely advisory. Should the coordinator crash before the done record is in the log, then the only consequence is for it to re-send an extra commit message when it recovers, to verify that it can spool another done record.

Operation in the Presence of Failures

Occasionally, messages will be lost. Because the datagram loss rate is relatively low (typically around 2% in our large local network environment), retransmitting once or twice almost always serves to transmit a message.

If, after performing retransmissions, the coordinator fails to hear from a subordinate during the vote phase, then the coordinator must assume that the subordinate has failed and impute a no vote to that subordinate. Once the coordinator decides the outcome of the transaction, it retransmits the outcome message until it is acknowledged.[2] A backoff strategy is necessary for these repeated retransmissions.

A prepared subordinate has no choice but to wait for the outcome message from the coordinator. While waiting, it is said to be *blocked*. If the coordinator crashes after a subordinate sends its vote response, but before it receives an outcome message, it could wait indefinitely. This "window of vulnerability" is the weakness of distributed two-phase commitment. The action to take when a message is missing is summarized in Table 16.1.

Recovery

The action to take upon recovery is summarized in Table 16.2.

[2]The abort outcome message does not require an acknowledgment. If the coordinator were to finish processing a transaction without abort acknowledgments, and were asked about the outcome afterwards, the coordinator would presume the transaction aborted.

Missing Message	Action
Prepare response	Resend Prepare a small number of times, then assume a no vote.
Commit	Ask the coordinator the outcome of the transaction.
Abort	Ask the coordinator the outcome of the transaction.
Commit-ack	Resend commit.
Abort-ack	Resend abort.

Table 16.1: Coping with Missing Messages in Two Phase Commit

Last Record In Log	Action
Prepared	Ask the coordinator the outcome of the transaction.
Committed Subordinate	Send commit-ack to the coordinator, because it may be waiting for it.
Aborted Subordinate	Send abort-ack to the coordinator, because it may be waiting for it.
Committed Coordinator	Send commit to all subordinates, because some may still be prepared.
Aborted Coordinator	Send abort to all subordinates, because some may still be prepared.
Done Coordinator	Forget the transaction.

Table 16.2: Recovering from Two Phase Commit

16.3.3 Non-blocking Commitment Protocol

The weakness of distributed two-phase commitment is that there exists a point at which all the votes needed to make the commit/abort decision are concentrated at one node (the coordinator). If this node is lost, then the other nodes must wait for it to return.

The non-blocking commitment (NBC) protocol ensures that at least one site will not block in the event of a single failure by making the following changes to two-phase commit:

- The prepare message contains the list of sites involved in the transaction.
- A subordinate that times out on a commit/abort notice may become a coordinator and finish the transaction.
- There is an additional phase inserted into the middle of the protocol during which subordinates learn about how other subordinates voted.

The remainder of this section provides a brief description of the non-blocking commitment protocol used by Camelot. For a more detailed treatment, the interested reader is urged to see Duchamp [26].

Normal Operation

Listed below is the sequence of events for the commitment of a top-level transaction using the non-blocking protocol.

1. The application calls `TA_End` and blocks until it receives the response.
2. The coordinator sends `ST_Vote` (`prepare` argument `TRUE`) to all local servers that are involved in the transaction. Servers vote as described in the distributed two-phase commitment protocol (Section 16.3.2).

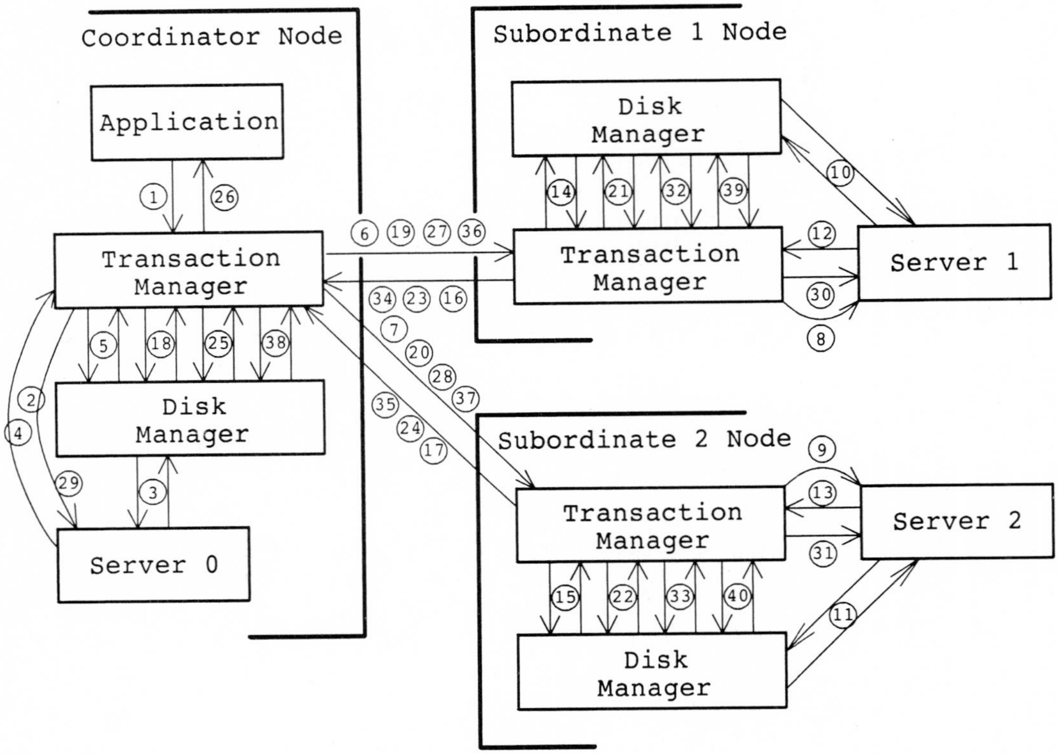

(1) Application sends TA_End request to Coordinator TranMan

(2) ST_Vote: Coordinator TranMan tells Server 0 to vote

(3) DS_Prepare: Server 0 saves locks in log

(4) Server 0 votes yes

(5) Coordinator TranMan forces prepare record

(6) Coordinator TranMan asks Subordinate 1 TranMan to vote

(7) Coordinator TranMan asks Subordinate 2 TranMan to vote

Figure 16.6: Non-blocking Commitment without Errors

(8) ST_Vote: Subordinate 1 TranMan tells Server 1 to vote

(9) ST_Vote: Subordinate 2 TranMan tells Server 2 to vote

(10) DS_Prepare: Server 1 saves locks in log

(11) DS_Prepare: Server 2 saves locks in log

(12) Server 1 votes yes

(13) Server 2 votes yes

(14) DT_SmallLogWrite: Subordinate 1 TranMan forces prepare record

(15) DT_SmallLogWrite: Subordinate 2 TranMan forces prepare record

(16) Subordinate 1 TranMan votes yes

(17) Subordinate 2 TranMan votes yes

(18) Coordinator TranMan spools commit quorum record

(19) Coordinator TranMan tells Subordinate 1 TranMan to join commit quorum

(20) Coordinator TranMan tells Subordinate 2 TranMan to join commit quorum

(21) DT_SmallLogWrite: Subordinate 1 TranMan forces commit quorum record

(22) DT_SmallLogWrite: Subordinate 2 TranMan forces commit quorum record

(23) Subordinate 1 TranMan acknowledges join quorum

(24) Subordinate 2 TranMan acknowledges join quorum

(25) DT_SmallLogWrite: Coordinator TranMan forces commit record

(26) Coordinator TranMan replies to TA_End

(27) Coordinator TranMan tells Subordinate 1 TranMan that the transaction committed

(28) Coordinator TranMan tells Subordinate 2 TranMan that the transaction committed

(29) ST_Commit: Coordinator TranMan tells Server 0 that the transaction committed

(30) ST_Commit: Subordinate 1 TranMan tells Server 1 that the transaction committed

(31) ST_Commit: Subordinate 2 TranMan tells Server 2 that the transaction committed

(32) Subordinate 1 TranMan spools record indicating commitment

(33) Subordinate 2 TranMan spools record indicating commitment

(34) Subordinate 1 TranMan acknowledges transaction commitment

(35) Subordinate 2 TranMan acknowledges transaction commitment

(36) Coordinator TranMan tells Subordinate 1 TranMan to forget

(37) Coordinator TranMan tells Subordinate 2 TranMan to forget

(38) Coordinator TranMan spools done record and forgets

(39) Subordinate 1 TranMan spools done record and forgets

(40) Subordinate 2 TranMan spools done record and forgets

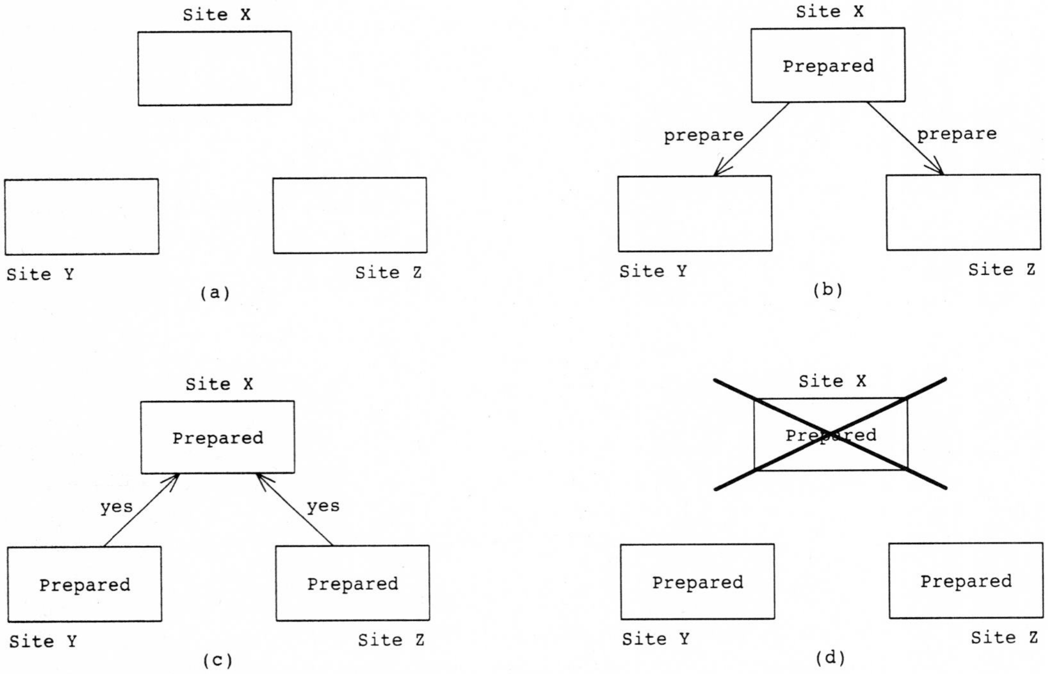

Figure 16.7: Non-blocking Commitment with Coordinator Crash
Part (a) depicts a transaction in progress at sites X, Y, and Z. The transaction originated at site X. The transaction ends in part (b), which initiates the commitment protocol. In part (c), the transaction is prepared. The coordinator crashes in part (d). Site Y times out on the join quorum message in part (e), and becomes the coordinator. According to its site information, site Z may still be active (i.e., the last update to its site information occurred when it processed the prepare message, which listed only site X as prepared). Since site Z is already prepared, it responds immediately in part (f). Since no servers on its site voted no, site Y joins the commit group in part (g). Likewise, site Z joins the commit group in part (h). Having achieved a commit quorum, site Y commits the transaction in part (i) and notifies all sites of the outcome. Since by part (j) site X has not responded, site Y will continue to send the outcome message to site X until it recovers. Only the originating site can instruct other sites to forget the transaction, so the forget phase of the protocol will not occur until site X recovers.

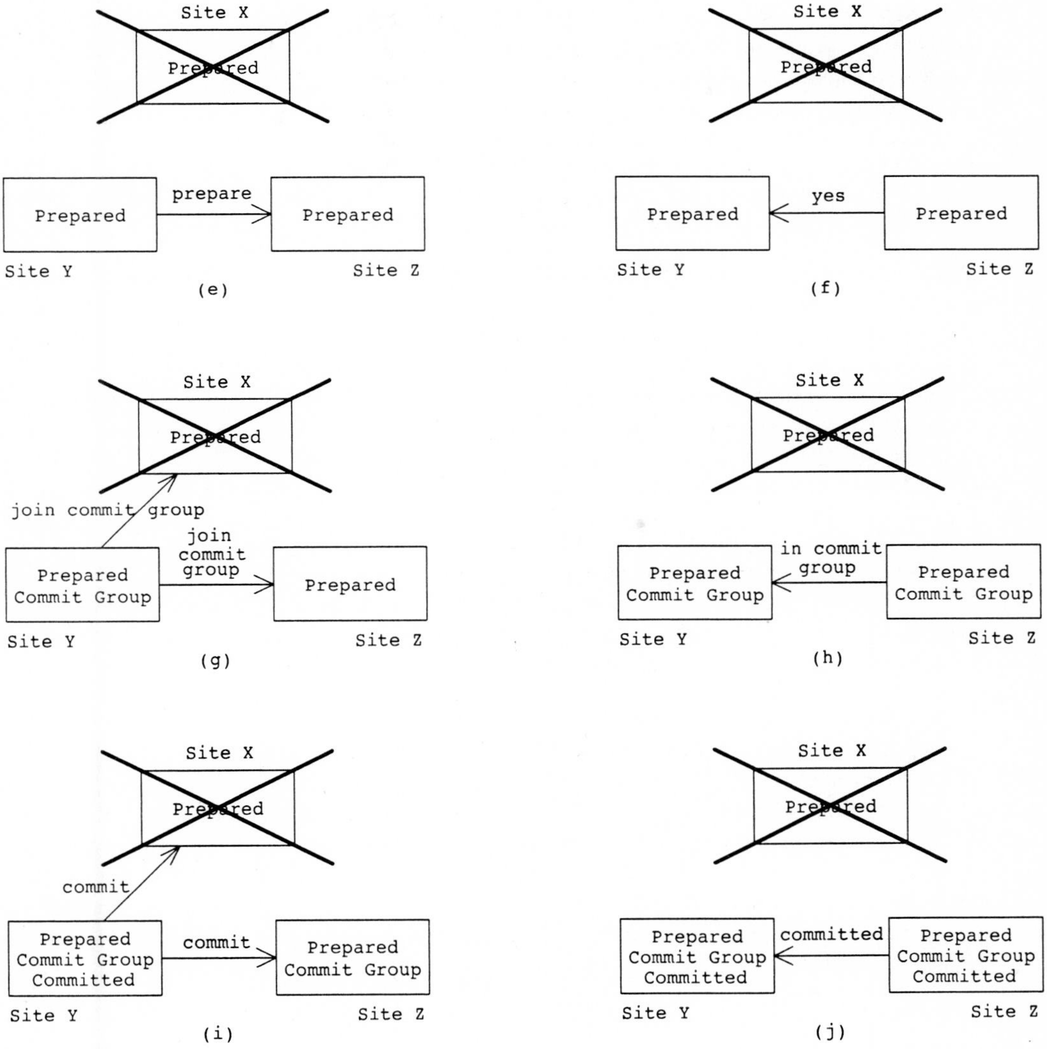
Site X
Prepared
prepare
Prepared
Prepared
Site Y
Site Z
(e)
Site X
Prepared
yes
Prepared
Prepared
Site Y
Site Z
(f)
Site X
Prepared
join commit group
join commit group
Prepared Commit Group
Prepared
Site Y
Site Z
(g)
Site X
Prepared
in commit group
Prepared Commit Group
Prepared Commit Group
Site Y
Site Z
(h)
Site X
Prepared
commit
commit
Prepared Commit Group Committed
Prepared Commit Group
Site Y
Site Z
(i)
Site X
Prepared
committed
Prepared Commit Group Committed
Prepared Commit Group Committed
Site Y
Site Z
(j)

3. The coordinator examines the server votes. If votes are yes, read-only or read-only dependent and at least one is yes, the coordinator forces a prepare record to the log. Preparing locally before sending vote messages to the other sites involved in the transaction makes commit more likely. If there is a no vote, the protocol ends early. The coordinator aborts the transaction, forces an abort record into the log, and sends an abort outcome message to all sites involved in the transaction. If all votes are read-only or read-only dependent and at least one is read-only dependent, coordinator flushes the log and sends an `ST_Done` message to each server that voted read-only dependent. In this case, flushing the log allows the coordinator to treat the transaction as a read-only transaction. If all votes are read-only, then we go to the next step.

4. The coordinator sends a vote message to all the sites involved in the transaction. Unlike in distributed two-phase commit, the NBC vote message contains a list of all sites involved in the transaction, but no indication of who the coordinator is.

5. After receiving the vote message, each subordinate Transaction Manager makes an `ST_Vote` (`prepare` argument `TRUE`) call on all the appropriate servers at its node. If all servers at a subordinate node have voted yes or read-only and if at least one has voted yes, then the Transaction Manager at that node forces a prepare record into the log and sends a message back to the coordinator indicating that all the servers at its node have voted to commit. If all servers at a node vote read-only, then no prepare record is written and the node votes read-only. If all servers vote read-only or read-only dependent, then the Transaction Manager at that node flushes the log, and sends an `ST_Done` to servers that voted read-only dependent. The node then votes read-only. If any server has voted no, then no prepare record is forced and the node votes no.

6. The coordinator waits for a certain period of time, retransmitting vote messages up to some fixed number of times. At the end of this period, if any subordinate node has not yet voted, the coordinator assumes a no vote on behalf of that node.

7. The coordinator examines the votes. If all sites voted yes, read-only, or read-only dependent and at least one voted yes, then the coordinator joins the *commit quorum* and spools a commit quorum record to the log. This records the fact that all sites are prepared. If any site voted no, then it joins the *abort quorum* and spools an abort quorum record to the log. This records the belief that some sites are not prepared. If all sites voted read-only the protocol ends early – the coordinator broadcasts a forget message, spools a record indicating that the protocol has completed (the done record), sends a `TA_End` response, and forgets the transaction. Upon receiving the forget message, each subordinate spools a done record and forgets the transaction.

8. The coordinator sends a *join quorum* message to each subordinate. The purpose of this message is to find out if enough sites believe the transaction should commit (or abort). The join quorum message contains a list of sites and their states, which reflect how they voted. Subordinates use this information to update the information they already have from the prepare message.

9. Subordinates receive join quorum messages. If no server on this site has voted no, and a site has joined the commit quorum, then the subordinate joins the commit quorum. Otherwise, it

joins the abort quorum. The subordinate forces a record to the log indicating which quorum it joined.

10. The coordinator collects join quorum responses. If the responses constitute a quorum, the coordinator forces a log record indicating the outcome, sends the TA_End response, and then broadcasts the outcome to the subordinates.

11. Subordinates receive outcome messages. Each subordinate spools an outcome record. Once the record is written, it sends an outcome response.

12. The coordinator collects outcome responses. Once they are in, it broadcasts a forget message, spools a record to the log indicating that the protocol has completed (the done record), and then forgets the transaction. Upon receiving this message, subordinates spool the done record to the log and forget the transaction.

Figure 16.6 illustrates the execution of the non-blocking protocol with no failures. Using the same example, Figure 16.7 illustrates the execution of the protocol in the case of a coordinator failure. Notice that in this latter scenario the two-phase protocol would block.

Operation in the Presence of Failures

A failure is always manifested as an inability to communicate. Whether the cause of the failure is a lost message, process crash, node crash, or network partition cannot be determined. The most pernicious failure is partition, since if the commitment protocol is designed with insufficient care, different groups of nodes may decide to reach opposite outcomes. The purpose for having a majority vote determine transaction outcome is to allow at most one group of nodes to terminate the transaction in the event of a partition [104].

Just as in two-phase commitment, the loss of a subordinate is tolerable. The coordinator either counts the subordinate as a no vote (if the protocol is in the vote phase), or continues to resend to that node. This strategy is indicated in Table 16.3. Unlike two-phase commit, if too many subordinates are lost, this protocol may block – there may not be enough sites left to form a quorum of either type.

The resend strategy for subordinates is indicated in Table 16.4. If the coordinator is lost, one or more subordinates may become coordinators. Where a new coordinator picks up the protocol depends on its state. If it was a subordinate waiting for a join quorum message, it begins by ensuring that all other sites on its list are prepared (sending prepare messages to any non-prepared sites), and then broadcasting a join quorum message. If it was waiting for an outcome message, then it checks to see if there is a quorum (resending join quorum messages if necessary) and then broadcasts an outcome. While the presence of multiple coordinators may be confusing, it is not a problem. For more details on dealing with multiple coordinators, see Duchamp [26].

Recovery

The action to take upon recovery is summarized in Table 16.5. Note that the recovered node assumes the role of a coordinator.

Missing Message	Action
Prepare response	Resend Prepare a small number of times, then assume a no vote.
Have-joined-quorum	Resend Join quorum.
Outcome response	Resend Outcome.

Table 16.3: Coping with a Missing Message from a Subordinate in Non-blocking Commit

Missing Message	Action
Join-quorum	Broadcast prepare.
Outcome	Broadcast Join-quorum.
Forget	Send Outcome response to the coordinator.

Table 16.4: Coping with a Missing Message from the Coordinator in Non-blocking Commit

Last Record In Log	Action
Prepared	Send prepare to all nodes.
In-(Commit/Abort)-quorum	Send Join-quorum to all nodes.
Commit/Abort	Send Outcome to all nodes.

Table 16.5: Recovering from Non-blocking Commit

16.3.4 Abort Protocol

Aborting a transaction that may be both distributed and nested is a tricky problem for which there are no traditional solutions like two-phase commitment. Unlike a commitment protocol, an abort protocol must "hit a moving target": the transaction to be aborted can be spreading at the same time that the abort protocol is attempting to track it down. This is because any process involved in the transaction (not just the application) can order it to be aborted. The goals of an abort protocol are (in order of importance):

- Atomicity: ensure that all nodes agree about whether the transaction commits or aborts.
- Autonomy: never require a node to communicate with another in order to abort (also called *unilateral abort*).
- Usefulness: insofar as possible, allow a parent to commit after a child has aborted.
- Speed: return from abort call and/or drop locks as fast as possible.
- Cleanliness: insofar as possible, reduce the occurrence of orphans.

Obviously, it is very difficult (at least) to completely satisfy each requirement. The constraints placed upon the design are (in no particular order):

- The performance of common operations (RPCs, commitment) must not be degraded: there can be no increase in the number of log writes or messages in order to facilitate abort. In addition, it is forbidden to specify messages whose size is proportional to the number of transactions executed in a family.

- There can be no alteration to the essential features of the commitment protocol: messages are sent only for top-level transactions and only between coordinator and subordinates.
- In order for the Recovery Manager to correctly undo aborted work, it is necessary either for a single `RT_Abort` call to specify all transactions (in a family) that have modified the same data, or for those transactions to be undone one-by-one "bottom up" from descendant to ancestor.
- The protocol cannot block in case of failure.
- The abbreviated TID format cannot be altered.
- A transaction cannot end (`TA_End`) until all of its children are either ended (`TA_End`) or killed (`TA_Kill`).
- There is no underlying crash detection mechanism that can be relied upon to provide a rapid notification of a crash. That is, a node can crash, recover, and locally abort a transaction without any other node knowing that this has happened.

The abort call (i.e., `TA_Kill`) is a synchronous call that invokes an abort protocol that tracks down and kills all work, unless a failure (crash, partition) prevents communication between nodes. In the absence of failure, the protocol is orphan-free. Another pleasant consequence of tracking down all work before returning is that (if there are no failures) after `TA_Kill` returns, commitment of the parent can begin knowing that it is the only termination activity in progress. The disadvantage of having a synchronous call is that it is slower to return than an asynchronous call would be.

There are several ways to initiate an abort:

- A kill call made by the application (`TA_Kill`).
- A kill call made by a process other than the application.
- A message received from another node with notification that a transaction has aborted. This is called a *died message*.
- A message received from another node with the instruction to abort locally, then spread the abort notice to all nodes to which the transaction migrated. This is called a *kill message*.

The Transaction Manager uses two abort protocols: one for top-level transactions, and one for nested transactions. The top-level abort protocol is unilateral. Strictly speaking, the nested abort protocol is not unilateral, but if failures occur during nested abort processing, the Transaction Manager may resort to the unilateral protocol to abort the family.

Before describing the protocols, it is necessary to introduce some terminology. A transaction's *abort group* is the set of all transactions whose death is implied by the death of that transaction. This set includes all transactions that are descendants of the specified transaction. If the transaction is nested and committed, the abort group is its closest active ancestor and all of its descendants. The *abort root* is the topmost node in the tree formed by the abort group.

The *local abort protocol* is the procedure used to undo any changes made by an abort group on a single node involved with any member of that group. From the Transaction Manager's point of view, a local abort consists of the following steps:

1. Call `ST_Suspend` for each server involved in the abort group. This tells each server to stop processing on behalf of transactions in the abort group.
2. Call `RT_Abort` for the abort group. This tells the Recovery Manager to undo the changes made by transactions in the abort group.
3. Spool a log record indicating that the transactions in the abort group have aborted.
4. Call `ST_Abort` for suspended servers. This notifies the servers that the transactions have been aborted.
5. Call `AT_TransactionHasDied` for any applications that need to be notified of the deaths of any transactions in the abort group.

Figure 6.9 illustrates the local abort procedure.

In a distributed transaction, the node on which an abort begins (i.e. the node on which the `TA_Kill` is received) is called the *abort initiator*. The node on which an aborting transaction was created is the *abort source*. In the top-level case, the abort source is the coordinator. All other nodes involved with the aborting transaction or its descendants are *intermediate nodes*.

Top-level Abort Protocol

The procedure for the top-level abort protocol is as follows:

1. A `TA_Kill` request arrives at the abort initiator.
2. If the abort source is the same as the abort initiator, skip to the next step. Otherwise, send a message to the abort source to notify it of the abort. This message is a *died message*.
3. Perform a local abort at the abort initiator.
4. Without waiting for notice to percolate from the home node, inform the nodes to which the abort group has spread to that they should abort. This is done by sending a *kill message*. When a node receives a kill message, it immediately executes the local abort procedure for the transaction indicated.
5. Send `AT_TransactionHasDied` to applications involved with the transaction.
6. Respond to the `TA_Kill`.
7. Forget the transaction.

This approach allows a node to abort unilaterally. The purpose of informing the home node is to allow notice of the abort to spread from the home node outward (eventually) to all nodes that the transaction has visited. The list of nodes to which a transaction has spread is kept in virtual memory by the Transaction Manager, and so is lost if a node crashes. Thus, the abort protocol cannot be sure to have reached all nodes if some node is unreachable (and assumed to be down).

Notice that in the top-level protocol no acknowledgments are expected for kill and died messages. The idea behind this protocol is to notify as many nodes as possible of the abort, and perform a local abort to prevent the transaction from committing. An example of the top-level abort protocol is shown in Figure 16.8.

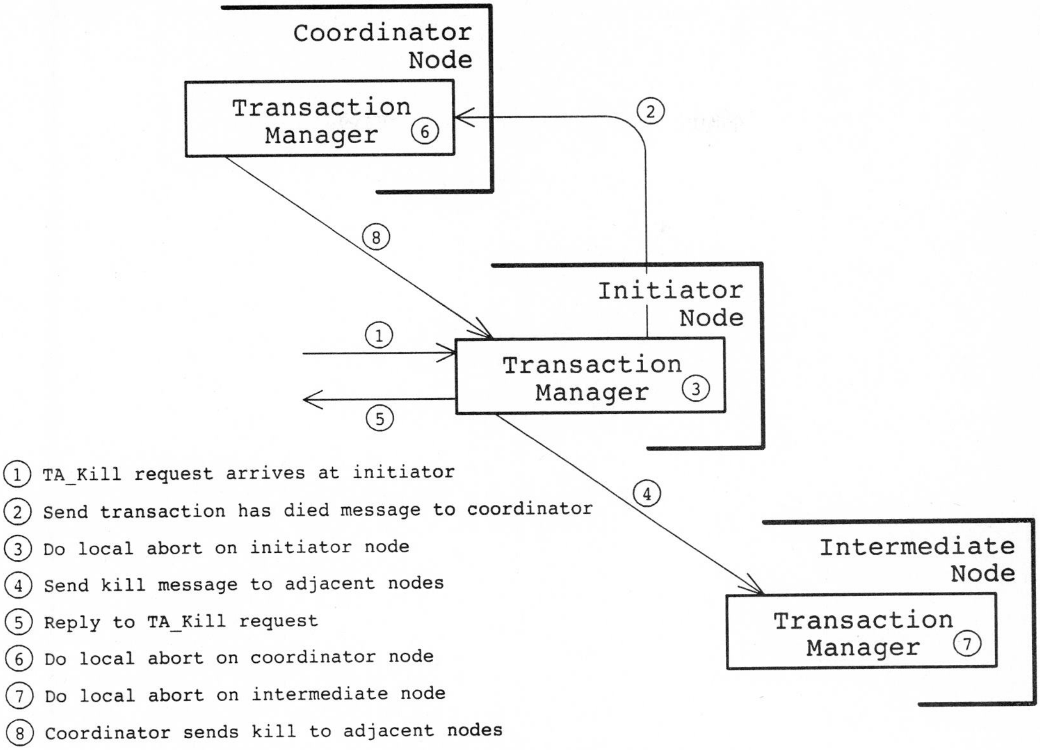
Coordinator Node
Transaction Manager 6
2
8
Initiator Node
1
Transaction Manager 3
5
4
Intermediate Node
Transaction Manager 7
1 TA_Kill request arrives at initiator
2 Send transaction has died message to coordinator
3 Do local abort on initiator node
4 Send kill message to adjacent nodes
5 Reply to TA_Kill request
6 Do local abort on coordinator node
7 Do local abort on intermediate node
8 Coordinator sends kill to adjacent nodes

Figure 16.8: Distributed abort of a top-level transaction

Nested Abort Protocol

It is more difficult to ensure atomicity for an aborting distributed nested transaction because it may be aborted at any site to which it traveled, and achieving failure isolation greatly increases the number of failure cases that must be tolerated.

Below is the normal procedure for nested abort. Since the roles of the abort source, initiator, and intermediate nodes are all different, we explain the procedure for each one separately. Note that the abort source and the abort initiator may be the same node, and there may be no intermediate sites. These cases are covered in the lists below.

The normal procedure for distributed nested abort at the abort initiator is:

1. A `TA_Kill` arrives.

2. Send a died message to the abort source.

3. Wait for a kill message.

4. A kill message arrives.

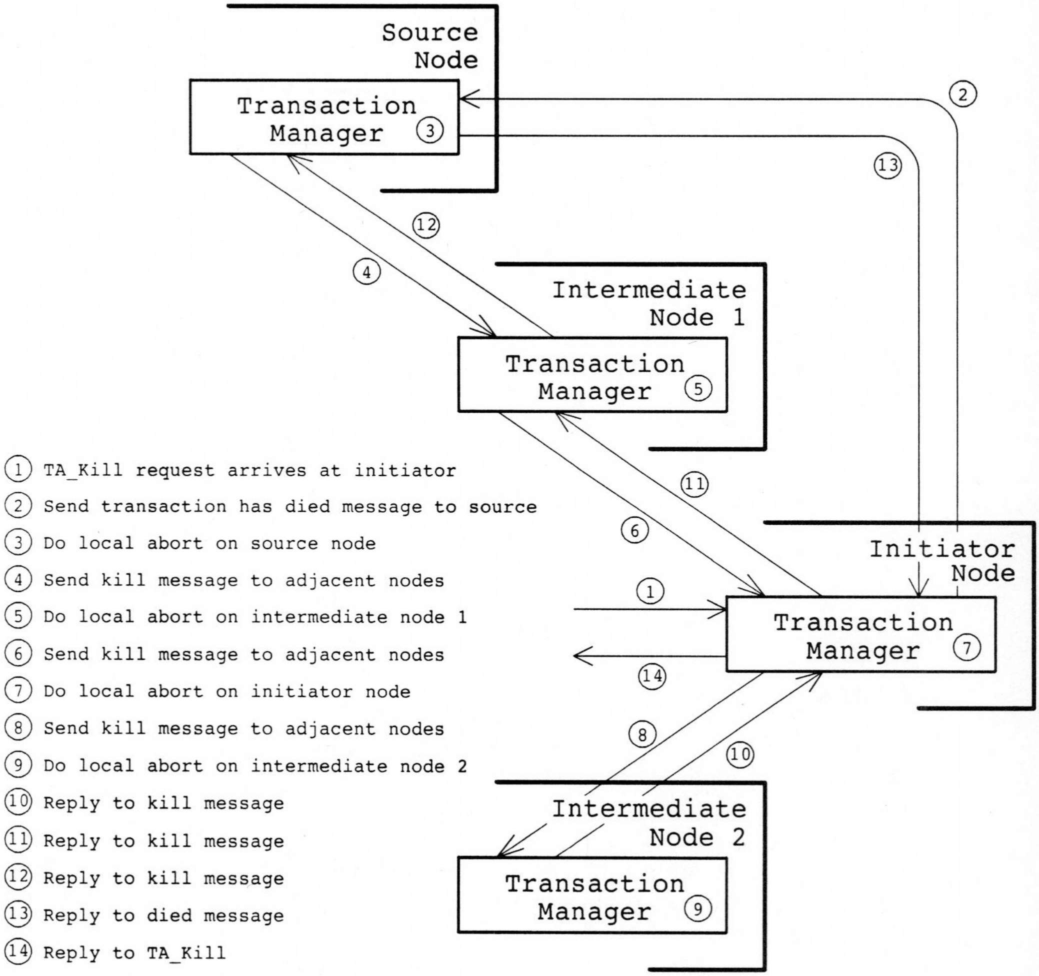
Source
Node
Transaction
Manager ③
②
⑬
⑫
④
Intermediate
Node 1
Transaction
Manager ⑤
⑪
⑥
Initiator
Node
①
Transaction
Manager ⑦
⑭
⑧
⑩
Intermediate
Node 2
Transaction
Manager ⑨
① TA_Kill request arrives at initiator
② Send transaction has died message to source
③ Do local abort on source node
④ Send kill message to adjacent nodes
⑤ Do local abort on intermediate node 1
⑥ Send kill message to adjacent nodes
⑦ Do local abort on initiator node
⑧ Send kill message to adjacent nodes
⑨ Do local abort on intermediate node 2
⑩ Reply to kill message
⑪ Reply to kill message
⑫ Reply to kill message
⑬ Reply to died message
⑭ Reply to TA_Kill

Figure 16.9: Distributed abort of an active nested transaction

5. Perform a local abort.
6. Send an `AT_TransactionHasDied` to applications involved with the transaction.
7. If the transaction has spread from this node, then send a kill message to nodes to which the transaction has spread. Otherwise, send a kill-response to the sender of the kill. (Note that the sender of the kill does not have to be the abort source.)
8. Wait for a died-response message from the abort source.
9. Died-response message arrives.
10. Respond to the `TA_Kill`.

The normal procedure for distributed nested abort at the abort source is:

1. A died message arrives.
2. Find an active abort root. Since nested commits are lazy, this transaction may have already committed without the initiator knowing about it. If it is committed, then find and abort the closest active ancestor. If the closest active ancestor was created elsewhere, this node sends a died message to the ancestor's creator, and the remote node becomes the abort source.
3. Perform a local abort.
4. Send an `AT_TransactionHasDied` to applications involved with the transaction.
5. If the transaction has spread from this node, then send a kill message to nodes to which the transaction has spread. Otherwise, the abort is done. Send a died-response message to the abort initiator.
6. Wait for kill-response messages.
7. All kill-responses arrive.
8. Send the died response to the abort initiator.

For all other nodes, the abort procedure is:

1. A kill message arrives.
2. Perform a local abort.
3. Send an `AT_TransactionHasDied` to applications involved with the transaction.
4. If the transaction has spread from this node, then send a kill message to nodes to which the transaction has spread. Otherwise, the procedure is done. Send a kill-response to the sender of the kill.
5. Wait for kill-response messages.
6. All kill-responses arrive. Propagate the kill response back to the sender of the kill.

If the abort source and the abort initiator are the same (i.e. the `TA_Kill` received is for a locally created transaction), then the abort source executes steps 3 to 7 of its procedure, and then sends the `TA_Kill` response.

An example of an abort of an active, distributed, nested transaction is shown in Figure 16.9.

Orphans and Consistency

It is an unfortunate fact of life in distributed transaction systems that, under certain circumstances, a thread can continue to run on behalf of a transaction after the transaction has aborted. Such threads are called *orphans*. During a distributed abort, an attempt is made to detect and exterminate orphans, but it is nearly impossible to prevent orphans entirely. For example, suppose a partition occurs and a transaction spanning the partition aborts: it may take some time for the news of the abort to cross the partition. Orphans could be prevented by using a "two-phase abort" protocol, analogous to the two-phase commit protocol, but this would introduce intolerable delays into the abort operation.

The serializability property implies that a transaction observes recoverable objects in a consistent state: it sees only the effects of committed transactions that were serialized before it. It is fairly straightforward to enforce this property in transactions that eventually commit; it is much more difficult to ensure that orphans never observe inconsistency. One might think that no harm could come of an orphan observing an inconsistency, as any modifications that an orphan makes will be undone when news of the abort reaches the server, and any objects that the orphan modifies remain locked until that time. Unfortunately, this is not sufficient to insure that no damage is done to the server. For example, suppose all transactions preserve the invariant that some recoverable integer represents a valid array index. If an orphan were to observe an inconsistent value for this integer, and use the value as the index for a write operation to a volatile or recoverable array, arbitrary damage to the server could result.

Ideally, a transaction system should prevent orphans from observing any inconsistencies. It is fairly straightforward to insure that orphans do not observe any *local inconsistencies* (i.e., violations of invariants pertaining to the recoverable data at a single server). The system merely insures that abort recovery does not begin at a server while threads are still operating at the server on behalf of the aborting transaction. In Camelot, this is accomplished with the `ST_Suspend` call. See Section 12.2.3, **Techniques, Execution of Control,** for a discussion of how the Camelot Library enforces the suspend protocol.

Unfortunately, all known algorithms for insuring that orphans never observe distributed inconsistency are prohibitively expensive [74]. The expense, chiefly added communication costs, is not limited to transactions that abort, but affects all transactions. Neither Camelot nor any other distributed transaction system of which we are aware has implemented a protocol that prevents orphans from observing distributed inconsistencies. We conjecture that it is feasible to write reliable programs even if orphans may observe distributed inconsistencies by following a few simple guidelines. To the best of our knowledge, no one has yet attempted to codify these guidelines.

Operation in the Presence of Failures

If a node is unable to communicate a kill or died message to another node, it is possible that the destination node is down and that its crash has left orphaned work on other nodes. In the worst case, this node has also done work for committed members of the same family. If the `TA_Kill` call were to return at this point, a top-level commitment could be executed, and inconsistent work would be committed. To avoid this, a node that fails to communicate with another sends a *danger message* to the coordinator node of the transaction family, indicating that the destination could not be contacted and may have orphaned work. When the coordinator initiates commitment, it will include in the prepare message a list of *dangerous sites* that were unreachable during the earlier abort. A node receiving the prepare checks if it has communicated with any dangerous site, and if so it votes no to commitment. In the case of a set of nested transactions each performing an RPC to a separate node, the dangerous node will not be used by any other transaction in the family, and the family will be able to commit. Though a failure detected during the abort protocol does not block the protocol, this scheme is conservative in that it may result in an unnecessary failure of the attempt to commit the family.

Recovery

It does not matter if a node crashes while executing the abort protocol. When the node recovers, the transaction will be undone whether or not there is an abort record in the log.

16.3.5 Lock Inheritance

Lock inheritance is possible between two transactions in the same family when the lock holder is committed up to the least common ancestor of the lock holder and the lock requester. In this case, we say the lock holder is *committed with respect to* the lock requester. The Transaction Manager provides a service through the `TS_IsLockInheritable` and `TS_WaitBeforeInheritingLock` calls that enables the requester of a lock to find out whether the lock is inheritable or alternatively, to wait until the lock becomes inheritable. Camelot provides an optimization called the *family position indicator*, or FPI, that enables the lock manager component of the Camelot Library to resolve most lock conflicts internally.[3] The Transaction Manager service is used only when the FPI does not yield the required information. Both techniques are discussed below.

Family Position Indicator

The family position indicator is a field in the TID that indicates the position of the transaction in its family tree. An FPI comparison macro is provided to allow a server to determine whether one transaction has committed with respect to another, given the FPIs of the two transactions. Since transactions may spawn any number of subtransactions, and may be nested to any depth, the family position of an arbitrary transaction cannot be described exactly in a fixed amount of space. The FPI, however, occupies a single 32 bit word in the TID (itself a fixed size object); if a transaction has too many siblings or is nested too deeply, the FPI can describe its position only approximately. Under these circumstances, the FPI comparison macro sometimes errs, but always on the side of caution, causing the server to ask the Transaction Manager if the lock is inheritable. For the great majority of lock inheritances, however, the FPI saves the cost of the `TS_IsLockInheritable` RPC.

The internal structure of the FPI is illustrated in Figure 16.10. The FPI consists of four *(sequence-number, serial-number)* pairs. The number of pairs used in a transaction's FPI is equal to the nesting depth of the transaction, up to a maximum of 4. An unused pair is indicated by a sequence number of 0.

When a transaction is begun, its FPI is assigned by Transaction Manager as follows. All top-level transactions have the same FPI, a word of zeros. A transaction "inherits" its parent's FPI, with one additional *(sequence-number, serial-number)* pair appended after the last pair used in the parent's FPI. If the parent's nesting depth is already 4 or higher, the child gets the same FPI as the

[3] This idea is due to Joshua Bloch.

```
typedef struct {
    unsigned int
        seq1 : 4, ser1 : 4,
        seq2 : 4, ser2 : 4,
        seq3 : 4, ser3 : 4,
        seq4 : 4, ser4 : 4,
} fpi_t;
```

Figure 16.10: FPI Internal Structure

```
    if (transaction is parent's first child)
    {
        sequence = pseudorandom number between 1 and 15;
        serial = 0;
    }
    else
    {
        if (any siblings of this transaction are currently active)
        {
            sequence = previous sibling's sequence number;
            serial = Min(previous sibling's serial number + 1, 15);
        }
        else
        {
            sequence = (previous sibling's sequence number % 15) + 1;
            serial = 0;
        }
    }
```

Figure 16.11: Procedure for Assigning New Serial-Sequence Pair in FPI

parent. The new pair in a child's FPI is set by the Transaction Manager according to the procedure shown in Figure 16.11. In essence, this procedure divides the children of each transaction into groups of concurrent siblings. Each group has a different sequence number and children in the same group have different serial numbers. Sequence numbers wrap around at 15, and serial numbers for a given group stick at 15.

The FPI comparison macro is illustrated in Figure 16.12. It is fairly straightforward to show that this macro returns FALSE if the two transactions whose FPIs it is passed are descendants of two distinct concurrent children of some transaction. In this case, the Transaction Manager must be consulted to determine whether the first transaction has committed with respect to the second. If the two transactions are not descendants of two distinct concurrent children of some transaction, it is safe to assume that the first transaction has committed with respect to the second. In this case, the macro will generally return TRUE, though it may return FALSE if the transactions are too deeply nested, or if an ancestor of either transaction had too many concurrent siblings. The sizes of sequence and serial numbers at each level can be tuned based on observed family structures to

```
/*
 * FPI_CWRT -- Takes two family position indicators (FPIs) as arguments.
 * Returns TRUE if the first transaction is committed with respect to the
 * second, FALSE if it cannot be determined from the FPIs.  (The FPIs must
 * come from transactions in the same family.)
 */

#define FPI_CWRT(f1, f2)                                                    \
  ((f1).seq1 != (f2).seq1 ? TRUE :                                          \
   ((f1).ser1 !=  (f2).ser1 ||  (f1).ser1 == 15 ? FALSE :                   \
                                                                            \
    ((f1).seq2 != (f2).seq2 || (f1).seq2 == 0 ? TRUE :                      \
     ((f1).ser2 !=  (f2).ser2 ||  (f1).ser2 == 15 ? FALSE :                 \
                                                                            \
      ((f1).seq3 != (f2).seq3 || (f1).seq3 == 0 ? TRUE :                    \
       ((f1).ser3 !=  (f2).ser3 ||  (f1).ser3 == 15 ? FALSE :               \
                                                                            \
        ((f1).seq4 != (f2).seq4 || (f1).seq4 == 0 ? TRUE : FALSE)))))))
```

Figure 16.12: FPI Comparison Macro

reduce false negatives.

Lock Inheritance Protocol

The `TS_IsLockInheritable` and `TS_WaitBeforeInheritingLock` calls invoke a simple, possibly distributed protocol whose object is to find out whether or not the lock holder and the lock requester are committed up to their least common ancestor. The protocol works as follows:

1. `TS_IsLockInheritable` (or `TS_WaitBeforeInheritingLock`) is called. The holder and requester should be in the same family.

2. Find the *least common ancestor minus one*, or the ancestor of the holder that is the child of the least common ancestor. The pair is committed up to the least common ancestor if this transaction is committed. If this transaction is locally created, the state of the transaction yields the answer. If the transaction is remotely created, then an inquiry message must be sent to the creation site to determine its state.

3. If `TS_IsLockInheritable` was called, a response is returned as soon as possible. Otherwise, the response is delayed until the state of the least common ancestor minus one changes to committed or aborted.

Implicit in this description is the assumption that the genealogy of a transaction is available at any site that the transaction has visited. When a transaction leaves a site, the Transaction Manager piggybacks its genealogy onto the outgoing RPC. The remote Transaction Manager unpacks the genealogy and constructs records as necessary to maintain the same tree structure for the branch down to the transaction.

16.3.6 Crash Detection

The Transaction Manager uses timestamps as low-water marks to detect sites that have crashed and recovered during the life of a transaction. Low-water marks indicate the logical time at which a transaction family first visited a site.

When a transaction family is created, a site record is created for the local site containing the current Lamport clock value. When a transaction leaves a site, the Transaction Manager piggybacks the timestamps from all family site records on the outgoing RPC request. If the site list indicates that the remote site has not previously been visited by a member of this family, then a null timestamp for the remote site is sent as well. The Lamport clock is updated when the RPC leaves, and this value is piggybacked on the request. At the remote node, the Lamport clock is updated to be greater than the current local time and the RPC timestamp. If there was a null timestamp for this node in the site list, the updated clock value replaces the null timestamp. When the transaction returns from the remote node, the site list is piggybacked on the RPC response. New information is used to update the family site records at the originating node. On all subsequent calls to a given node, the data for the local and remote nodes remains the same.

To guarantee that timestamps are not inadvertently reused after a node crash, a time record containing a logical clock value is periodically written to the log. In effect, this record serves to

RPC	Site List in RPC
2|W	1|W,0|X
3|W	1|W,0|X,0|Y
4|X	1|W,3|X,0|Z
6|Z	1|W,3|X,5|Z
8|X	1|W,3|X,5|Z
5|Y	1|W,0|X,4|Y,0|Z
1002|Z	1|W,0|X,4|Y,1001|Z
1004|Y	1|W,0|X,4|Y,1001|Z

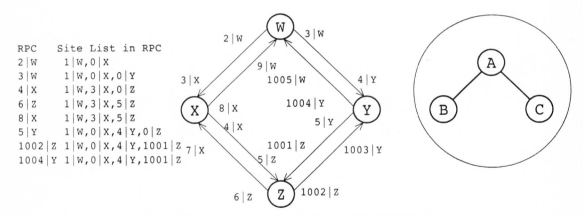

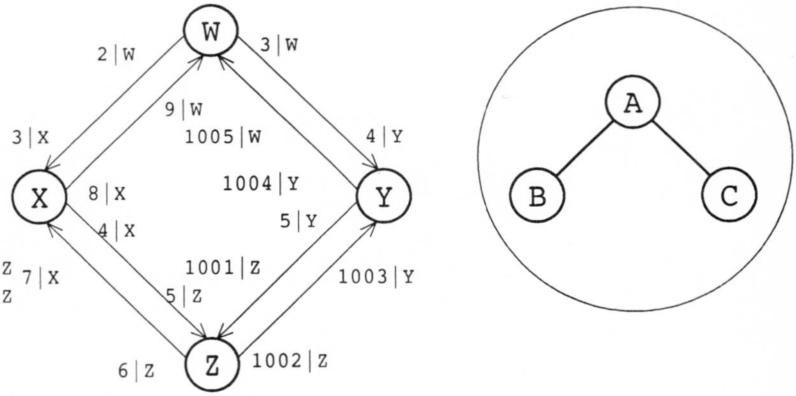

Figure 16.13: Using Timestamps for Crash Detection
Transaction A is created at site W. The local site record is timestamped with 1|W. Transaction 1 creates two concurrent children, B and C. Transaction B spreads to site X (at time 2|W) and is timestamped on arrival with 3|X. Transaction C leaves site W at logical time 3|W, arriving at site Y at 4|Y. Transaction B leaves site X at time 4|X, and arrives at site Z at 5|Z. At time 6|Z it returns to site X, arriving at 7|X. Then at 8|X it returns to site W, arriving at 9|W. Now site Z crashes. Transaction C spreads to site Z at time 5|Y and is timestamped on arrival with 1001|Z. It leaves site Z at 1002|Z, returning through site Y, and arrives back at site W at time 1005|W. Since the transaction family now has two different first visit timestamps for site Z (5 and 1001), site W deduces that site Z crashed.

preallocate a block of timestamps; the value is an upper limit on the timestamps that will be generated before another time record is written to the log. If the node crashes, upon recovery the clock is set to no less than the value in the most recent time record in the log.

If a remote node crashes during the lifetime of a transaction family, and members of the family visit it before and after the crash, the timestamps returned by the crashed node in the site list on the RPC responses after the crash will be greater than the timestamps in the site list on RPC responses before the crash. This will cause the Transaction Manager to abort the transaction. An example of such a scenario is in Figure 16.13.

For the crash detection strategy to work, the time at which a family first visited a site must not be forgotten until the family has either committed or aborted, even if all work at the site has been aborted. If such a site were purged from the site list, subsequent visits to the site by the family would appear to have occurred after a non-existent crash.

16.4 Related Work

A number of organizations and individuals have made contributions to efficient commitment protocols. The read-only and presumed abort optimizations to two-phase commitment were invented by the IBM R* project [81]. The Camelot optimization of not forcing commit records on subordinates is similar to the optimization to two-phase commitment in DeWitt, et. al. [31]. Camelot's non-blocking commitment protocol is unique, but rests upon the theoretical groundwork laid by Skeen [104].

The idea of lock inheritance was written about by Moss [82] and used in Argus [73]; their implementation is quite different, being based upon doing lazy abort plus orphan detection.

16.5 Conclusions

Both local and distributed transactions have been tested using a facility that creates transactions of random type and nesting level, and commits or aborts them randomly. While this simulated workload provides a good test of various Camelot functions, it does not provide information on the relative utility of such functions.

Much of the Transaction Manager has been implemented twice. In general, the first implementation of the commitment protocols was satisfactory. The abort protocol, however, was a much more difficult problem. The first design attempted to achieve unilateral abort for nested transactions. We found that allowing unilateral nested abort greatly increased the chances that the transaction family would abort at commit time. This was contrary to our expected use for nested transactions, namely, for failure isolation.

The existing abort protocol implementation uses dangerous sites, which are nodes that have not responded to certain messages during the abort protocol and therefore may have orphaned work. In retrospect, we feel that dangerous sites are too conservative. A site is labeled dangerous regardless of which subtransactions traveled through it, and retains this label even if the failure is resolved. A more selective approach, which was considered but not implemented, is to attach the "dangerous" label to a transaction instead of a site. The genealogy of the dangerous transaction is then piggybacked on all RPC requests and responses. A Transaction Manager that receives dangerous transaction data checks to determine if the transaction is known at its site. If not, it creates the appropriate data structures from the genealogy and marks the transaction aborted. If the transaction is known and active, then it is orphaned work and is aborted. A newly arrived transaction is not allowed to perform work on a site on which it or any of its ancestors are marked as aborted. The advantage of dangerous transactions is that only truly orphaned work is aborted, and therefore the top-level transaction has a much greater chance of committing. The drawback of this method is that it requires sending genealogies, which could potentially be very large. But since the dangerous transaction list would usually be small, the finer abort granularity and intuitive appeal of this approach outweigh this drawback.

The lock inheritance protocol was reimplemented after the decision was made to ship genealogies off site. Before this, the lock inheritance protocol included a protocol to find the genealogy of a transaction by traveling through the sites that it had visited as it gathered ancestor TIDs. Besides the intolerable performance this yielded, the complexity of the protocol outweighed the benefit of not having to ship genealogy data.

Locking of transaction and family records was reimplemented after a failed attempt at locking on a transaction basis. This was just one symptom of confusion about the distinction between a transaction and a family, which became apparent when the single threaded implementation of the Transaction Manager was converted to make use of multiple threads. Locking at the family level has proven to be much cleaner, easier to implement, and easier to debug. There are some operations, however, which might benefit from transaction-level locking, such as abort, nested commit, and lock inheritance. Currently these operations require holding a family lock, thus removing concurrency.

Communication between Transaction Managers was influenced by the decision to use datagrams instead of connections. A datagram interface was selected at design time because datagrams held a clear performance advantage, and the commitment protocols already handled retransmission and duplicate detection. At that time, MIG did not support communication with datagrams, which meant the Transaction Manager would not have a stub-generated Transaction Manager-to-Transaction Manager ("TT") interface. Since then, the performance of connection based communication in Mach has improved. Connection based communication holds several advantages over datagrams. Development and debugging time is decreased considerably since support for message packing and crash detection is provided, and there is only one communication mechanism to support. In addition, support for authentication and encryption is generally available. Because of these advantages and the lack of a significant performance difference between datagrams and connections, in our environment, connection-based communication would now be preferable.

Approximately 20% of the code in the Transaction Manager involves support for nested transactions. Nesting was intended for failure isolation, such as for applications that make use of replicated data. We expected in this case that a subtransaction would be used for each replica, although Bloch [11] used a subtransaction for an entire operation, as that was the granularity of failure. Nesting is useful for abstractions involving the use of RPC. Typically transactions are shallowly nested with sequential children. Because of this, FPIs have eliminated the great majority of calls to the Transaction Manager to resolve lock conflicts. FPIs are ineffective when concurrent siblings access the same data; we have not observed this behavior except in contrived test cases.

Chapter 17

The Design of the Camelot Communication Manager

Peter D. Stout

17.1 Introduction

The Camelot Communication Manager provides a name service for Camelot servers and support for distributed transactional remote procedure calls (RPCs). The name service is used by applications to find data servers. The name service dispenses surrogate local ports for network ports so that all distributed transactional RPCs pass through the Communication Manager. A more detailed discussion of the architecture is provided in Section 17.2. Algorithms are presented in Section 17.3, related work in Section 17.4, and conclusions in Section 17.5.

17.2 Architecture

The Communication Manager is an independent component of Camelot that is designed to operate either as a library linked into the Transaction Manager or as a separate process. It is multi-threaded to better support its many clients. Idle threads block waiting to receive a message on the Communication Manager's service port. The Communication Manager uses port sets to allow it to wait for messages on a collection of ports. To insure prompt service, there is always at least one thread waiting for new messages to arrive.

Incoming messages will be either a name service request or a transactional RPC that needs to be forwarded. There is a special message type that allows Camelot to quickly identify transactional RPCs. All other messages are given to the name service module.

The Communication Manager stores server names and ports in a grid structure. One edge of the grid is indexed by the server names and the other by the nodes in the network. Each entry in the grid (i.e., each *(name, node)* pair) has two ports associated with it: the first is for local communication; the second is used for network communication. The mapping between local port and network port and back again is supported by two hash tables. The Communication Manager uses these mappings when it is forwarding transactional RPCs.

Each node record contains the IP address of that site and a list of reply ports that are used in forwarding RPCs. For security reasons, these ports are only used for Communication Manager to Communication Manager messages. These ports are reused to amortize the cost of allocating (reply) ports across many RPCs. It also turns out that deallocating a network port is extremely expensive, since the Network Message Server uses broadcast to implement port death notification. Since each node may have multiple names associated with it, the Communication Manager maintains a hash-table of host names with each entry pointing to the appropriate node record.

17.3 Algorithms

The design of the name service module is dependent on the needs of the message monitoring module. To correctly inform the Transaction Manager of the spread of all transactions the Communication Manager needs to see all transactional RPCs. With this constraint in mind, Section 17.3.1 describes how the Camelot name server is implemented. Section 17.3.2 describes what the Communication Manager does when it forwards a transactional RPC.

17.3.1 Name Service

As mentioned in Section 7.1.4 Camelot data servers use `CS_SignIn` to register a service port with the Camelot name server. The port passed in that call is stored as the local port in the name service's grid. When the Communication Manager processes the `CS_SignIn`, it automatically allocates a *network* port[1] to be used for remote communication. This dual port mechanism allows local communication to be fast, while guaranteeing that the Communication Manager will see all network communication. The Communication Manager needs to see remote transactional RPCs so that it can inform the Transaction Manager of the transaction spread. This will be described in greater detail in Section 17.3.2.

When a `CA_Lookup` or a `CS_Lookup` request is received, the Communication Manager returns the local port for any server on the local site. If the server is on a different machine, the name server uses an internal Communication Manager-to-Communication Manager interface to retrieve the port for the remote server. This call returns the server's network port (i.e., the port allocated by the remote Communication Manager). The local Communication Manager then allocates a local port that it will pass to the client.

When a server dies or calls `CS_SignOut`, the Communication Manager deallocates its network port. This will cause the Network Message Server to send port death notifications to all the remote Communication Managers that have looked up that server. This distributed port death notification is neither timely nor guaranteed.

[1] The distinction between local and network port types is currently only an arbitrary one maintained by the Communication Manager. Both are implemented as ports. This may not be true in all future implementations (e.g., the Nectar version proposed in Section 17.5).

17.3.2 Remote Server Calls

This section describes the path of a server call, or transactional RPC, from the client to the server and back. The Camelot Communication Manager uses a special Mach message type, MSG_TYPE_CAMELOT, to identify messages that are part of a transactional RPC. During the course of the example, consider the RPC to be operating on behalf of transaction *T*. All Communication Manager - Transaction Manager communications are between process on the same node.

When a request message arrives on a local port,[2] the Communication Manager looks up the corresponding network port. At the same time, the destination site, *S*, of the message is determined. The Transaction Manager is then notified that a request message is being sent to site *S* on behalf of *T*.[3] The Transaction Manager sends the Communication Manager a block of data that is to be piggybacked on the request message. Depending on the size of the client's message, this data is either appended to the message or sent out-of-line. The first method is preferred, when possible, because sending out-of-line data is expensive. The Communication Manager then forwards the message via the Network Message Server to the remote site.

When the request message arrives on *S*, the Communication Manager on *S* passes the piggybacked data to the Transaction Manager. If the Transaction Manager allows, the Communication Manager looks up the local port that corresponds to the network port on which the message arrived and forwards the message to the server. The thread handling the request blocks waiting for the server to reply. To protect clients from malicious servers, a reply port is allocated for each RPC. If the Communication Manager were to use the same reply port while communicating with different servers, then any of those servers would be able to send a message to that port. As a result, a client would have to trust all of the servers on any node to which it talked, rather than those servers that it used.[4]

When the server replies to the server call, the Communication Manager notifies the Transaction Manager that a reply message is being sent. The block of data that the Transaction Manager returns is piggybacked onto the reply portion of the RPC. The message is then sent back to the originating Communication Manager, which has a thread waiting for it. The piggybacked information is given to the Transaction Manager, and if the Transaction Manager permits, the reply is returned to the client.

If a remote node crashes, it is necessary to awaken the threads that are waiting for replies from that site. A Communication Manager detects that a remote site has crashed when it receives a port death notice for the remote Communication Manager's service port. When this occurs, the Communication Manager deallocates all of the reply ports that were used in communicating with that site. If there are threads waiting on any of those ports, they are first sent special messages indicating that the remote node crashed.

---

[2]The Communication Manager distinguishes between messages from local clients and remote Communication Managers by checking whether or not the MSG_TYPE_RPC bit is set. If it is set, then the message must be a local one, since the Network Message Server always resets this bit.

[3]The Communication Manager detects a WRAP_SERVER_CALL and does not notify the Transaction Manager in this case.

[4]To avoid the overhead of allocating and deallocating a reply port for each RPC, it would be possible to have a pool of reply ports associated with each server, similar to what is done for each remote Communication Manager. Future versions of the Mach Operating System will support the notion of a send-once right for a port. This mechanism allows the recipient of a message to send one message (i.e., a reply) to the specified port. This is the ideal solution since it avoids the allocation overhead without requiring that the Communication Manager manage pools of reply ports.

17.3.3 Piggyback Data

The information piggybacked on messages includes a Camelot timestamp (see Section 16.2.2), specifying when the message was sent, the genealogy of *T*, a list of all the sites visited by members of *T*'s family, and a list indicating which of those sites *T* has visited. The timestamp is used to maintain the Lamport clocks on the two nodes. The first thing that the Transaction Manager on *S* does as it processes the piggybacked information is to compare the message's originating time with its own current notion of the time, updating its clock as appropriate. This will guarantee that all work done on *S* will occur at a time that is logically later than the time when the message was sent. *T*'s genealogy allows the Transaction Manager on *S* to insert *T* into the correct place in its family tree. Each entry in the site list is a Camelot timestamp indicating when the transaction family first arrived at the specified site. These low-water marks are used to detect crashes of entire Camelot nodes.

17.4 Related Work

The basic architecture of the Camelot Communication Manager was inspired by the architecture of the Mach Network Message Server [40]. The Network Message Server provides a name service. Whenever a lookup is done on a remote server, the Network Message Server hands out a surrogate local port. Messages sent to the local port are received by the Network Message Server and are forwarded to the remote Network Message Server on the node where the remote server is actually running. The remote Network Message Server will use local Mach communication to send the message to the remote server.

17.5 Conclusions

Like most parts of Camelot, the Communication Manager has evolved over the course of the project. This evolution has been slower than that of the rest of the system for two reasons. First, local transactions had to run correctly before distributed ones could be tested. Second, there was a lack of understanding of the difficulties involved with distributed transactions. The remainder of this section discusses and evaluates the various implementations of the Communication Manager and suggests future areas of work.

The Communication Manager was initially implemented as a special addition to the Network Message Server. In processing network messages, the Network Message Server would check for the `MSG_TYPE_CAMELOT` bit. If the message was a Camelot message, the Network Message Server would pass it to the Communication Manager for processing before it was forwarded. The Communication Manager maintained information about the state of each transaction that it believed to be active. The Communication Manager would notify the Transaction Manager the first time a transaction left or arrived at a site. The Transaction Manager would inform the Communication Manager whenever a distributed transaction changed state (e.g., active to aborting).

The advantage of this implementation was that it required fewer additional messages (i.e., only when the transaction first left or arrived at a site) than any of the later implementations. At the time that Camelot was using this version of the Communication Manager, the Mach group was working on an secure version of the Network Message Server [98]. The Camelot group abandoned this version because of the difficulties this parallel development created.

When the Communication Manager was removed from the Network Message Server, it was moved into its own process. However, the basic interface was not changed. As Camelot development proceeded, it was discovered that this interface had a fundamental flaw. The interface required the Communication Manager and the Transaction Manager to maintain parallel data structures. There were several situations in which the two process could end up in a deadlock because of the locking required to synchronize access to individual transaction records. The current implementation uses a new interface which does not require the Communication Manager to maintain any data structures about transactions.

The major cost of having the Communication Manager in a separate process is the overhead of the additional local RPC on each of the nodes. Camelot currently runs with the Communication Manager linked into the Transaction Manager due to the overhead of using local RPCs to pass the piggybacked data back and forth. One solution that has not yet been explored would be to remove Camelot's dependence on the Network Message Server (i.e., have the Communication Manager put messages directly on to the network). This would require that the Communication Manager handle several jobs that are currently handled by the Network Message Server, such as type conversion and passing out-of-line data. that are currently handled by the Network Message Server. This solution would eliminate the extra RPCs and have the side benefit of making Camelot more portable. Work in this area will probably be done as part of the port to the Nectar network [7].

In the current implementation, each transactional RPC that is forwarded ties up a thread in each of the Communication Managers involved.[5] This is a waste of system resources and ultimately puts a limit on the number of outstanding messages. The designer felt, given the facilities available at the time, that tying up a thread greatly simplified the design of message forwarding module. With the development of port sets in Mach, this is no longer true. It would now be possible to divide the current port set up into four smaller sets: local request ports, network request ports, local reply ports, and network reply ports. Two additional hash tables would be needed to map between local and network reply ports. This design would also be easier to port to an environment where the local and network communication links were different. It would also make it easier to separate the name service and message forwarding modules.

There is a major type of communication that is currently not handled by the Camelot Communication Manager and that is Transaction Manager-to-Transaction Manager communication. As discussed in Section 16.2.4, Camelot uses datagrams to implement the various commit and abort protocols. Camelot's use of two transport mechanisms would make porting it to a third different transport mechanism more difficult. If the Communication Manager were redesigned as suggested above, the Transaction Manager should also be modified to send all transactional network communication through the Communication Manager, including commitment protocols. The result of these modifications would be a Camelot that could be readily ported to other network interfaces.

In the near future, Camelot will be ported to a high speed network being developed by the Nectar project at Carnegie Mellon University. Each host in Nectar network has its own communications co-processor. Among the things that we are interested in studying with this port is the possibility of running the Camelot Communication Manager on this co-processor. As part of this port, the previously described modifications to the Communication Manager may be implemented.

---

[5]The threads are blocked, waiting for the reply, in `msg_rpc`.

Chapter 18

Performance of Select Camelot Functions

Peter D. Stout
Elliot D. Jaffe
Alfred Z. Spector

It is necessary for users to understand Camelot's performance in order to successfully develop high performance applications and servers. Unlike sequential programming language primitives whose resource usage is fairly clear, Camelot's primitives use many resources (CPU as well as disk I/O, log I/O, log bandwidth, and network bandwidth), and they use them in quantities that are more difficult to comprehend. In addition, Camelot presents the following complications that do not occur in most sequential programs:

- **Parallelism in the consumption of resources.** Camelot uses resources both synchronously and asynchronously. For example, long transactions write most of their log data *asynchronously*, but they write one log record *synchronously* at the end.

- **The large number of options for configuring and using Camelot.** For example, the performance of logging varies substantially depending on whether a node is using simplex or duplex local logging (either with raw or Unix file system partitions), or distributed logging.

- **The variety of computers on which Camelot executes.** Because of Camelot's diverse resource usage, extrapolation from one machine to another is difficult. Understanding Camelot's performance on shared-memory multiprocessors is even more difficult.

In spite of these difficulties, this chapter aims at helping a user to understand Camelot's performance. Its emphasis is on uniprocessors.

Section 18.1 lists the various resources that Camelot uses and the units in which they are measured. It also describes the hardware on which the measurements were made. Section 18.2 presents the costs of the major Camelot Library primitives in terms of these metrics. Distributed elapsed time measurements were made on only one machine architecture and local elapsed time measurements on two architectures. We regret that the reader may have a difficult job extrapolating to other machine architectures. Some metrics are machine independent. Section 18.3 then presents the costs of accessing Camelot recoverable data. Section 18.4 discusses the performance of transaction abort, server recovery, and node recovery. Additional analyses of Camelot performance can be found in several Ph.D. theses[11, 22, 26, 28].

18.1 Performance Metrics

There are three performance metrics considered in this section:

1. **Elapsed Time**, in milliseconds, abbreviated *Elapsed*. Elapsed time is needed to determine if applications will meet response requirements and to estimate the duration that locks will be held. Two flavors of elapsed time are presented: *Elapsed RT* is the time taken on an IBM RT/APC, and *Elapsed DS* is the time taken on a DECstation 5000/200. Times for the DECstation are only provided for local tests.

2. **Log data written**, in bytes, abbreviated *LogData*. Knowing the amount of log data written permits an estimate of the load at which the logging device(s) will saturate. Furthermore, *LogData* permits a programmer to estimate the rate at which the log will fill. If duplexing is in use, two copies are written.

3. **Log forces**, in the number of forces, abbreviated *Forces*. Knowing the number of log forces permits an estimate of the load at which the logging device(s) will saturate. If duplexing is in use, two copies are written.

The numbers reported in the following tables are accurate to two significant digits. We assume no contention on any resources Camelot consumes (i.e., we assume no other network traffic, no other disk activity, no other transactions being executed, etc.). The reader will note that not all Camelot features have been measured; for example, there are no measurements of group commit or the `COBEGIN...COEND` constructs. In general, constructs that have very variable performance or involve substantial local parallelism have not been included.

18.2 Library Costs

The section describes the performance of remote procedure call (RPC) primitives, synchronization primitives, and transaction management primitives.

Methodology

Performance numbers presented in the tables were obtained by measuring individual operations, rather than measuring many operations as a group and dividing by the group size. This was necessary because certain operations, such as `BEGIN_TRANSACTION`, cannot be performed many times without being mixed with other time-consuming operations (in this case `END_TRANSACTION`).

Unfortunately, we do not have access to a hardware clock that is fast and accurate enough to measure most Camelot operations.[1] Therefore, we are forced to use a probabilistic timing method similar to that used by market research firms for polling constituents about issues and voting preferences. We intentionally use a clock with a period known to be longer than the operations being timed. During a single operation, this clock will either tick once or not change. The presence or absence of a tick is then a binomial parameter, and can be treated using well-known statistical techniques. We have assumed that measured operations begin at a time that is uncorrelated with the occurrence of clock ticks. To date, our experience has validated this assumption.

To measure a particular operation, we repeat the operation hundreds or thousands of times. We check the clock before and after each operation and total the number of times that a tick occurred. To estimate the time required for the operation, we first divide the number of trials by the number of perceived clock ticks. This gives us the percentage of the clock period that it takes to execute this operation. This percentage is multiplied by the known clock period to give the latency time for this operation.

Since the presence or absence of a tick is a binomial parameter, and we have independence, we can use a standard formula for confidence intervals, and calculate the number of trials necessary to insure a reasonable margin of error. The formula that we use is:

$$n = \frac{\mathit{confidence\ interval}^2}{4(\mathit{margin\ of\ error}^2)}$$

The values in the current tables were computed using a confidence of 95%, and a margin of error of 0.02 for distributed tests and 0.005 for local tests. The confidence interval of 95% is 1.96. That is, we want the resulting value to be within 2 percent of the **true** value with 95% confidence. Using these numbers and the previous formula we calculated that distributed tests require 2401 trials of each operation and local tests require 38,416 trials to insure the desired accuracy.

We have found it necessary to modify some of our tests as we learn more about the behavior of the Camelot system under different conditions. Associated with each table is an explanation of each test and a discussion of any anomalies we noticed. Our goal was to provide statistics that allow the user to closely estimate the average cost of a given sequence of operations. As such, we have attempted to produce times which reflect the expected time, not the minimum time.

The elapsed time metrics that are reported were measured on Camelot Release 1.0(84) and Mach Release 2.5 on IBM RT-APC PCs, Model 125, and a DECstation 5000/200. The IBM RTs had 12 megabytes of memory, and the DECstation 5000 had 24 megabytes of memory. Machines were interconnected on a single 10 megabit/second Ethernet. The elapsed time is reported under conditions of no load. Measurements were made using the `probtest` and `cpa` programs, which are available as part of the Camelot release. In all tests, Camelot used local (raw) logging partitions. The *Forces* and *LogData* metrics have been determined analytically based on our knowledge of Camelot's transaction processing algorithms.

[1]The available clock resolution on our machines is 16 milliseconds, and many Camelot operations execute in a fraction of a millisecond.

Camelot Library Primitive	Elapsed RT	Elapsed DS
Null RPC	1.16	0.41
MIG RPC	1.33	0.43
SERVER_CALL, SERVER_CALL_2, 32/32	2.00	0.82
SERVER_CALL, SERVER_CALL_2, 32/1K	2.46	0.97
SERVER_CALL, SERVER_CALL_2, 32/16K	3.38	0.96

Table 18.1: Local RPC Performance
Elapsed times are in milliseconds.

Camelot Library Primitive	Elapsed RT
Null RPC	12.36
MIG RPC	11.32
SERVER_CALL, SERVER_CALL_2, 32/32	12.37
SERVER_CALL, SERVER_CALL_2, 32/1K	15.15
SERVER_CALL, SERVER_CALL_2, 32/16K	207.

Table 18.2: Distributed RPC Performance
Elapsed times are in milliseconds.

18.2.1 Remote Procedure Calls

RPCs in Camelot are made using the SERVER_CALL and SERVER_CALL_2 primitives. Tables 18.1 and 18.2 describe the performance of these primitives. Times for null and MIG RPCs are reported as base figures. The null RPC time is the amount of time it takes to send a message consisting of only a message header. The MIG RPC time is equivalent to a TA_Begin call. Times for the various server call primitives are reported for requests that are 32 byte arrays, and responses that are either 32 byte arrays, 1024 byte arrays, and 16 kilobyte arrays. The latter are page aligned and passed out-of-line. The measurements primarily test the performance of MIG, Camelot Library's multi-threading code for clients and servers, and Mach. No measurements of WRAP_SERVER_CALL and WRAP_SERVER_CALL_2 have been included, as their performance can be approximated from the performance of SERVER_CALL. In the distributed case, the performance will be slightly better since the Communication Manager does not need to inform the Transaction Manager of the spread of a transaction.

18.2.2 Synchronization Primitives

The performance of the Camelot Library synchronization primitives is described in Table 18.3. Camelot lock primitives were measured by timing the operation on a single lock. Since LOCK_NAME is a simple C expression, we do not report a time for it here. LOCK and UNLOCK were timed by repeatedly locking and unlocking the lock and timing the appropriate operation. The three statistics for LOCK are the costs of locking a free lock, locking a lock where the intra-familial contention is resolved at the server, and locking a lock where the local Transaction Manager is contacted to resolve the contention. The family position indicators described in Section 16.3.5 are used to resolve

Camelot Library Primitive	Elapsed RT	Elapsed DS
LOCK (free)	0.21	0.83
LOCK (server)	0.33	0.40
LOCK (Transaction Manager)	4.97	1.44
UNLOCK	0.18	0.35

Table 18.3: Synchronization Primitives
Elapsed times are in milliseconds.

contention at the server.

Locks which are not immediately granted due to contention were not timed because the time is dependent on when the lock holders release the lock. Similarly, locks not granted due to intra-familial contention that cannot be resolved by the local Transaction Manager were not timed. This might occur in a distributed transaction in which the subtransactions involved are created on different sites. In resolving intra-familial contention, it was assumed that there was only one intra-familial holder.

We believe that the slower times for the DECstation are due to the absence of an atomic read-modify-write instruction, such as a "test-and-set". The effect is more pronounced for obtaining a free lock because it involves a greater number of mutex locking operations than the other LOCK cases.

18.2.3 Transaction Management Primitives

The performance of Camelot transaction primitives is described in this section. Statistics are given for the performance of beginning transactions, committing read-only transactions, and committing modify transactions with a simplex log. Commit costs include all transaction management overhead except that done when the transaction is initiated by a BEGIN_TRANSACTION primitive. In particular, commit costs include the cost of servers joining transactions.

Begin Transaction Primitives

Table 18.4 describes the costs of beginning transactions. BEGIN_TRANSACTION times are measured by repeatedly beginning a transaction, and then ending it with no operations in between. Nested BEGINs are measured at a single level of nesting, with the top-level transaction being committed between tests.

The library obtains TIDs from the Transaction Manager in blocks using the TA_GetTids call. The cost of this call is thus amortized over a number of non-nested BEGIN_TRANSACTION operations. This optimization is not used for nested transactions; the nested BEGIN_TRANSACTION time includes the cost of an RPC to the Transaction Manager to obtain a TID. The BEGIN_TRANSACTION operation for a server-based transaction is faster than its more general counterpart because it does not communicate with the Transaction Manager.

Camelot Library Primitive	Elapsed RT	Elapsed DS
BEGIN_TOP_LEVEL_TRANSACTION BEGIN_TRANSACTION if top-level BEGIN_TOP_LEVEL_TRANSACTION_2 unless server-based	0.61	0.54
BEGIN_TRANSACTION, nested	2.44	0.97
BEGIN_TOP_LEVEL_TRANSACTION_2, server-based	0.39	0.36

Table 18.4: Begin Transaction Primitives
Elapsed times are in milliseconds.

Camelot Library Primitive	Elapsed RT	Elapsed DS	LogData	Forces
END_TOP_LEVEL_TRANSACTION END_TRANSACTION if top-level END_TOP_LEVEL_TRANSACTION_2, local, standard or hybrid-atomic	$2.59 + 2.01s$	$1.21 + 0.64s$	0	0
END_TOP_LEVEL_TRANSACTION_2, local, server-based	0.49	0.60	0	0
END_TOP_LEVEL_TRANSACTION_2, lazy, server-based	0.43	0.67	0	0
END_TRANSACTION nested	2.02	0.89	0	0

Table 18.5: End Transaction Primitives for Local Read-Only Transactions
Elapsed times are in milliseconds. The number of servers is s.

Committing Read-Only Transactions

Tables 18.5 and 18.6 describe the overhead of committing local and distributed read-only transactions, respectively. The protocol used for local transactions is an optimized two-phased protocol. The local tests were run using 1-3 servers. In Table 18.6, n is the number of nodes. The distributed tests were run using 2-4 sites. We did not analysis the performance of more than one server per site.

Note that server-based transactions are strictly local to the server at which they are created. Note also that a nested commit is local in effect, as commit information for distributed nested transactions is not eagerly propagated. We believe the slower times for the DECstation are again due to locking. We are at a loss to explain the anomalous behavior of distributed read-only transactions committed with the non-blocking protocol. The behavior is reproducible with 2-4 sites, and one server on each site.

END_TRANSACTION times are measured by repeatedly beginning a transaction, doing a single read operation, and then ending the transaction. Nested END_TRANSACTIONs are measured at a single level of nesting, with the whole transaction being committed between tests.

Committing Write Transactions

Tables 18.7 and 18.8 describe the overhead of committing local and distributed write transactions, respectively. END_TRANSACTION times are measured by repeatedly beginning a transaction, performing a single write operation, and then ending the transaction. Nested END_TRANSACTIONs

Camelot Library Primitive	Elapsed RT	LogData	Forces
END_TOP_LEVEL_TRANSACTION END_TRANSACTION if top-level END_TOP_LEVEL_TRANSACTION_2, two-phased, standard or hybrid-atomic	$7.6 + 1.7n$	0	0
END_TOP_LEVEL_TRANSACTION END_TRANSACTION if top-level END_TOP_LEVEL_TRANSACTION_2, non-blocking, standard or hybrid-atomic	$17.57 - 1.28n$	0	0

Table 18.6: End Transaction Primitives for Distributed Read-Only Transactions
Elapsed times are in milliseconds. The number of nodes is n.

Camelot Library Primitive	Elapsed RT	Elapsed DS	LogData	Forces
END_TOP_LEVEL_TRANSACTION END_TRANSACTION if top-level END_TOP_LEVEL_TRANSACTION_2, local, standard or hybrid-atomic	$12.66 + 0.84s$	$8.9 + 6.0s$	32	1
END_TOP_LEVEL_TRANSACTION_2, local, server-based	12.53	16.55	32	1
END_TOP_LEVEL_TRANSACTION_2, lazy, server-based	0.64	0.70	32	0
END_TRANSACTION, nested	2.00	0.88	0	0

Table 18.7: End Transaction Primitives for Local Write Transactions
Elapsed times are in milliseconds. The number of servers is s.

Camelot Library Primitive	Elapsed RT	LogData	Forces
END_TOP_LEVEL_TRANSACTION END_TRANSACTION if top-level END_TOP_LEVEL_TRANSACTION_2, two-phased, standard or hybrid-atomic	$25.2 + 11.2n$	Coord: $4(n - 1) + 48$ Sub: $58s_i + 8l_i + 60$	n
END_TOP_LEVEL_TRANSACTION END_TRANSACTION if top-level END_TOP_LEVEL_TRANSACTION_2, non-blocking, standard or hybrid-atomic	$76.7 + 9.9n$	Coord: $24n + 58s_i + 8l_i + 108$ Sub: $24n + 58s_i + 8l_i + 88$	$2n$

Table 18.8: End Transaction Primitives for Distributed Write Transactions
Elapsed times are in milliseconds. The number of servers on the ith node is s_i, the number of write locks held on the ith node is l_i, and the number of nodes is n.

are measured at a single level of nesting, with the whole transaction being committed between tests. Again, local tests were run using 1-3 servers, and distributed tests were run using 2-4 sites.

In Table 18.7, s is the number of servers. In Table 18.8, n is the number of nodes, s_i is the number of servers on the ith node, and l_i is the number of write locks held on the ith node. All of the times in these tables (with the exception of nested transactions), include the time for joining the transaction. This is because servers join a transaction only once, regardless of the number of operations done within the transaction.

We observed a sharp increase in the times for local write transactions on the DECstation at three servers. This accounts for the much larger coefficient on the server term. The non-blocking protocol is much more expensive because it sends an extra round of messages for quorum formation and the messages also contain information about the state of all the sites involved in the transaction. Log records are larger because they also contain site data. An extra log force is required on all sites, as discussed in Section 16.3.3.

18.3 Recoverable Virtual Memory Costs

This section provides performance data on recoverable virtual memory. The relevant primitives are the costs of reading and writing recoverable virtual memory. The parameters that affect the primitives are the number of bytes that are read or written and whether the operation causes paging. Section 18.3.1 presents the cost of non-paging read and write operations. Section 18.3.2 gives the cost of paging read and write operations.

18.3.1 Non-paging Tests

A non-paging test measures the incremental cost to a transaction of reading or writing an additional region that is currently cached in physical memory. The non-paging tests are done by measuring the amount of elapsed time it takes to execute 1000 transactions. A large number of transactions is used because the clock resolution is approximately 16 milliseconds and the incremental cost of reading or writing a region is sub-millisecond.

Each transaction reads or writes x bytes of data either k times or $2k$ times in the same region in recoverable virtual memory. For example, a 32 byte write test would measure the time to execute 1000 transactions where each transaction writes the same 32 byte region 50 times. Call this time $t_{1000.32.50}$. A similar measurement would be done of 1000 transactions that write the same 32 byte region 100 times producing a time $t_{1000.32.100}$. The cost of an incremental write would then be

$$\frac{t_{1000.32.100} - t_{1000,32.50}}{1000(100-50)}.$$

Each entry in the table was calculated by measuring accesses of 4, 32, 128, 256, 512, 1024, 1536, 2048, 2560, 3072, 3584, and 4096 bytes. Regression was then used to produce expressions in Table 18.9 for an access of b bytes.

Since all of the tests are CPU intensive, many measurements are taken and the minimum is used. This reduces the amount of stray processing that is measured during the tests. For write tests, the call to write the log to disk is bypassed so that the transactions will not synchronize with the disk. The cost of incremental transfer time for a log record is measured separately from the CPU time and

Access	Elapsed RT	LogData
REC	$0.016 + 0.000163b$	0
MODIFY, MODIFY_BYTES, NV logging	$0.760 + 0.001561b$	40+b

Table 18.9: Non-paging Recoverable Virtual Memory Access Times
Elapsed times are in milliseconds. The number of bytes modified is *b*.

Operation	Elapsed RT	LogData
32 byte paging read	37	0
32 byte paging write	44	112

Table 18.10: Paging Costs
Elapsed times are in milliseconds.

added back in to produce the numbers in the table. Cases in which regions span page boundaries are not measured.

18.3.2 Paging Tests

The frequency and cost of paging data to and from secondary storage is affected by the quantity of physical memory, the quantity of virtual memory including that devoted to recoverable segments, page access patterns, effects of the periodic writing of hot pages to disk (as part of the checkpoint code), and the use of prefetch, preflush and zero-fill. Therefore, it is not possible to describe paging behavior in very general terms. Server writers will have to determine, or measure, paging behavior for their particular servers and machine configurations.

However, this section can provide an indication of the costs of reading pages from recoverable storage, writing pages to recoverable storage, and pre-fetching, pre-flushing, and zero-filling pages.

On the RT/APC, the average rotational latency is 8.3 milliseconds. The average seek time is 28 milliseconds. The latency for sequential 4096-byte (one kernel page) accesses is 21 milliseconds. Table 18.10 describe the latency for 32 byte paging read and writes. For writes, the log data consists of fetch, modify, and end-write records.

The paging tests were done by measuring the amount of elapsed time it takes to execute 10 transactions. Each transaction reads or writes 32 bytes of data 50 times or 100 times. Call the times t_{50} and t_{100}. Each 32 byte read or write is to a different 4096 byte page. The amount of available memory on the test machine is only 1057 pages so Camelot must cause paging. All disk I/O for the log and backing storage is skipped so that only CPU times were measured. Once the test reached steady state, times were recorded. The times were measured repeatedly and the average was used. The average values for t_{50} and t_{100} are subtracted as follows $\frac{t_{100} - t_{50}}{10(100-50)}$ to compute the incremental cost of a paging read or write operation. The average seek time of 28 milliseconds and a read/write time of 4 milliseconds per 4096 byte page were added to the CPU times to produce the numbers in the table.

18.4 Recovery Costs

Recovery is extremely hard to characterize since it is affected by the number and types of log records written during the period to be recovered. On an IBM RT/APC, the average time to process a record that is not involved in a recovery is approximately 1 millisecond. Processing a record that describes a region involved in this recovery averages 16 milliseconds. Our experience with the Camelot system has shown that node recovery is typically under 2 minutes for even a heavy load. Abort recovery (both nested and non-nested) varies widely based on the number of records and the available physical memory for the Camelot processes. Clock times of 500 milliseconds were seen during good runs, while clock times of up to 2 minutes were seen when the transaction was particularly complex, and the machine had only limited physical memory.

Part IV

The Avalon Language

Chapter 19

A Tutorial Introduction

**Jeannette Wing, Maurice Herlihy,
Stewart Clamen, David Detlefs, Karen Kietzke,
Richard Lerner, and Su-Yuen Ling**

This part of the book presents the Avalon system. Avalon/C++ is a superset of C++ [114], itself an extension of C [59]. C++ is designed to combine advantages of C, such as concise syntax, efficient object code, and portability, with important features of object-oriented programming, such as abstract data types, inheritance, and generic functions. This part of the book assumes the reader has some knowledge of C++ and it freely use its terminology; see Stroustrup [114] for more information on C++.

Avalon's run-time environment relies on Camelot to handle operating-system level details of transaction management, inter-node communication, commit protocols, and automatic crash recovery. Much of Avalon's design has been inspired by Argus [75] and we owe the descriptions of some of Avalon's control structures to the *Argus Reference Manual* [70]. For other papers on Avalon/C++ , please see [25, 49, 50, 123].

This chapter provides a tutorial introduction to the language. It introduces terminology and presents detailed walkthroughs of three simple examples. Chapter 20 is a reference manual for the Avalon extensions to C++. Note that it is only about nine pages long. Chapter 21 describes the library of Avalon built-in classes and the *catalog server*. Chapter 22 presents a list of practical guidelines for novice and expert programmers. The full grammar for Avalon/C++ appears in Appendix D.

19.1 Terminology

An Avalon/C++ system consists of a set of *programs*, each of which is an *application* or a *server*. Servers encapsulate a set of objects and export a set of operations and a set of constructors. Objects may be *stable* or *volatile*; stable objects survive crashes, while volatile objects do not. A server resides at a single physical node, but each node may be home to multiple servers. Applications invoke operations on servers, which may, in turn, invoke operations on other servers. Applications may explicitly create a server at a specified node by calling one of its constructors. Rather than sharing data directly, servers communicate by calling one another's operations. An operation call is a remote procedure call (RPC) with call-by-value transmission of arguments and results.

An Avalon server is very much like a C++ class. Just like a class, a server encapsulates some data, and defines the operations that can be used to manipulate that data. A client invokes an operation on a server object using the same syntax it would use to invoke an operation on a class object. There are two main differences between classes and servers. First, a server supports concurrency: more than one client may invoke operations on a server at the same time. These concurrent operations execute as concurrent threads within the server. The server must be implemented so that this concurrency makes sense. Second, a server's data (if the server is implemented correctly) is *persistent* (i.e., it will survive crashes in a consistent state).

Avalon/C++ includes a variety of primitives for creating transactions in sequence or in parallel, and for aborting and committing transactions. Each transaction is identified with a process, and is the execution of a sequence of operations.

Avalon/C++ provides transaction semantics via *atomic objects.* All objects accessed by transactions must be atomic to ensure their serializability, transaction-consistency, and persistence. Avalon/C++ provides a collection of built-in atomic types, and users may define their own atomic types by inheriting from the built-in ones.

Sometimes it may be too expensive to guarantee atomicity at all levels of a system. Instead it is often useful to implement atomic objects from non-atomic components, called *recoverable objects*; they satisfy certain weak consistency properties in the presence of crashes. Users who define their own atomic types from non-atomic components are responsible for ensuring that their types are indeed atomic.

This rest of chapter describes at length three examples illustrating all the basic features of Avalon/C++. The first example shows how to create, commit, and abort transactions; to invoke operations on servers; and to define and use a simple atomic type derived from the built-in Avalon class `atomic`. The second and third examples illustrate the use of two other built-in classes, `trans_id` and `subatomic`, to show another way Avalon users can define atomic types, and to show what makes Avalon especially different from other (fault-tolerant) distributed programming languages. We hope the reader will see that programming in Avalon/C++ is not much different from ordinary C++ programming.

19.2 Array of Atomic Integers

In this section, we walk through the use and implementation of a simple Avalon server, called "Jill," and client, called "Jack" (so named for historical reasons). The programs described in this section are Avalon reimplementations of the Camelot Library server and application described in Chapter 5. The Jill server encapsulates an array of *atomic integers.* From the client's viewpoint, each of these integers is atomic; they are recovered after a crash to the state observed by the last committed transaction, and they ensure the serializability of the transactions that access them. Since each of the elements of the array is atomic, the array as a whole is also atomic. The elements of the Jill array are initially given the value -1 to represent an uninitialized state, after which the Jill server permits only non-negative values to be written in the array.

An atomic array of integers might be useful as a representation for a conference room reservation system. The elements of the array could represent blocks of time, and writing a value into an element could represent reserving the conference room at that time for the person represented by that value. Or, the array could be used to represent a set of bank accounts, indexed by account numbers. Applications that wished to transfer money from one account to another could do so within a transaction, so that no partial transfers would ever happen. These examples are only meant to be suggestive; in both cases, other representations might be more convenient and/or efficient. Still, they show that even a very simple server such as Jill is not too far removed from real-world applications.

19.2.1 Using Jack and Jill

The Avalon implementations of Jack and Jill are semantically identical to their Camelot Library counterparts. Thus, the sample execution in Section 5.2 is equally applicable to the Camelot Library and Avalon versions of Jack and Jill. The only observable difference between the Avalon and Camelot Library versions is that the command to execute the Avalon version of Jack is `av_jack`, rather than `jack`. With the exception of this detail, however, the typescript in Section 5.2 could just as well have been produced by the Avalon versions of Jack and Jill; all commentary in the Section applies fully to the Avalon versions. If the reader has not read the Section, it is suggested that he do so at this time.

The next two sections describe the declaration and definition of the Jill server, all the way down to the level of the Avalon built-in `atomic_int` type; the following section then describes the Jack application program.

19.2.2 The Jill Server Declaration

A C++ class has a *declaration* and a *definition*. A class declaration is generally put in an include file, so that all files that need to use the class can have access to the necessary information. The class definition (the bodies of the class operations) is put in one or more files, each of which includes the declaration. An Avalon server should be written using the same conventions. Thus, we will first examine Figure 19.1, the include file that declares the Jill server.

The first line of this file includes the file `avalon.h`. All Avalon programs must include this file before all others. The next three statements in the file declare and initialize constants used in the program. We follow the C++ recommendation against using preprocessor macros whenever possible. The first two constants, `INDEX_OUT_OF_BOUNDS` and `ILLEGAL_VALUE`, are used as error codes. The third, `ARRAY_SIZE`, determines the size of the array.

Next, we come to the declaration of the Jill server. This is textually identical to a C++ class declaration, with the keyword `server` substituted for `class`. A Jill server contains one data member, `data`, and four operations, which are the only means of accessing the server's data. A server differs slightly from a class in that all data members of a server must be private. Here, `data` is also declared to be `stable`, which asserts that it is persistent (i.e., will survive crashes). Avalon guarantees persistence of the built-in atomic data type, `atomic_int`; in general, the programmer must correctly implement any user-defined type of `stable` variables to ensure their persistence. Though the Jill server does not, a server could also have data members that are volatile, that is, not stable. Volatile data are often useful for efficiency, but care should be taken to ensure that all important data is stable. For example, a server might represent a database as set of records, and maintain a volatile index that allows operations to look up records based on different fields of

av_jill.h:

```
#include <avalon.h>

// Error return codes from operation procedures.
const int INDEX_OUT_OF_BOUNDS = 1; // Attempt to access a location out of bounds.
const int ILLEGAL_VALUE = 2;       // Attempt to insert a negative number.


// System Constants.
const int ARRAY_SIZE = 1000;       // Number of cells in the array.

server jill {
  stable atomic_int data[ARRAY_SIZE];
  stable atomic_int generation;
 public:
  int read(int index);
  void write(int index, int value);
  jill () : ("av_jill", "localhost", 5);
  void main ();
};
```

Figure 19.1: Declaration of Jill Server

the record. The index would speed up the server during normal operation, but could always be reconstructed after a crash.

The four operations of the Jill server come in two categories: *user operations* and *server operations*. `Read`, `write`, and the constructor, `jill`, are user operations, the ones that clients can invoke. `Read` returns the integer stored at the given index, and `write` writes the given value at the given index. The intent of these should be fairly clear; we will go over their implementations shortly. The constructor is a special user operation invoked to initialize the Jill server. A server will not accept any calls to other user operations until it has received a constructor call, and it will not accept any constructor calls once it has started accepting calls to other user operations. Since all servers implicitly inherit from the `server_root` class, the colon syntax tells the `server_root` constructor where to find the server executable (first argument), what machine to start it on (second argument), and how many chunks of recoverable storage to allocate (third argument). See Section 21.3.1 for a more complete description of the `server_root` constructor. The remaining operation, `main`, is invoked automatically by the server. For implementation reasons, every server must have a `main` operation, even if it has no body. (The definition of `main` serves as a marker, so the Avalon preprocessor can decide where to put the C++ `main` procedure for the server.) If the `main` operation does have a body, it is executed in the background, concurrently with user operations. Another kind of server operation (not shown here), invoked automatically by the system, is an optional `recover` operation. If defined, it is executed whenever the server is started after any crash. A typical `recover` operation might reinitialize volatile data.

atomic_int.h:

```
// Declares the atomic integer class.

#include <avalon.h>

class atomic_int: public atomic {
  int val;
 public:
  int operator=(int rhs);
  operator int();
};
```

atomic_int.av:

```
// Defines the atomic integer class.

#include <avalon.h>

int atomic_int::operator=(int rhs) {
  write_lock();
  pinning () return val = rhs;
}

atomic_int::operator int() {
  read_lock();
  return val;
}
```

Figure 19.2: The `atomic_int` Class

19.2.3 The Jill Server Definition

Jill's Data Member

Jill's data member, `data`, is a `stable` array of `ARRAY_SIZE atomic_ints`. An `atomic_int` is an atomic integer, an integer specially implemented so that it ensures the serializability of transactions that access it, and is recovered after a crash with the value observed by the last committed transaction that accessed it. These properties are quite easy to achieve in Avalon. Figure 19.2 shows the declaration and definition of the `atomic_int` class.

The file `atomic_int.h` declares the `atomic_int` class. This is *derived* from the class `atomic`, which provides operations that are used to make integers appear atomic. In particular, class `atomic` has two operations, `read_lock` and `write_lock`, which can be used in implementing operations of derived classes.

The class `atomic_int` has one data member, an integer called `val`, which holds the value of the atomic integer. We show two operations of `atomic_ints`, both of which are C++ overloaded operators. One is the assignment operator, and the other is the coercion operator that converts an `atomic_int` into an `int`. The assignment operator is the only way to change the value of an `atomic_int`, and the coercion to `int` is the only way of using that value in a program. Thus,

av_jill.av:

```
// The body of the "av\_jill" server.

#include "av_jill.h"

int jill::read(int index) {
  // If index is out of bounds, return an error code.
  if (index < 0 || index >= ARRAY_SIZE) undo (INDEX_OUT_OF_BOUNDS) leave;
  return data[index];
}

void jill::write(int index, int value) {
  // If index is out of bounds, return an error code.
  if (index < 0 || index >= ARRAY_SIZE) undo (INDEX_OUT_OF_BOUNDS) leave;

  // If value is negative, return an error code.
  if (value < 0) undo (ILLEGAL_VALUE) leave;

  data[index] = value;
}

jill::jill() {
  for (int i = 0; i < ARRAY_SIZE; i++) data[i] = -1;
}

void jill::main() {}
```

Figure 19.3: Definition of the Jill Server

these operators mediate all access to the atomic integer.

In the file `atomic_int.av`, we see that the implementations of these operations are quite simple. Taking them in reverse order, we see that the `operator int()` simply calls `read_lock` and returns the current value. The assignment operator gets a write lock on the `atomic_int`, and then, within a `pinning` block, it sets the value to a new value, and returns the new value. The pinning block informs the Camelot system that the change must be logged permanently (i.e., to stable storage) so that in the event of crash recovery, the value of an atomic integer is consistent. Modifications to any atomic object should always be made from within a pinning block. The use of read and write locks guarantees that if a transaction observes the value of an atomic integer, then no other transaction may change it until the observer terminates. (Note that data type induction is needed to really make this guarantee; we can prove that this is true only if these two operators are the only ways of accessing `atomic_ints`.)

Jill's Operations

Now that we understand atomic integers, we can consider the implementation of the operations of the Jill server. Figure 19.3 shows the contents of the file `av_jill.av`, which contains the definitions.

Read takes an index, and returns the value at that index. Read assumes that it is being invoked by a client that is executing within a transaction. If the index is not within the array bounds, read executes the statement:

```
undo (INDEX_OUT_OF_BOUNDS) leave;
```

This aborts the client's transaction. The abort code INDEX_OUT_OF_BOUNDS can be used in an except clause, as we will see when we examine the Jack application. If the index passes this test, then we simply return the value in the data array at the index. Actually, this is a little more subtle than that: the elements of data are atomic_ints, and read returns an int. Thus, the C++ automatic coercion mechanisms call the coercion operator on the indexed element before returning it. The coercion operator gets a read lock on the element before returning its value. Write is very similar. It checks that the index is within the proper range, and that the value to be written is not negative; if so, it assigns the new value to the element. Again, the overloaded assignment operator of atomic_int takes care of getting the write lock on the atomic integer and logging its new value. The important lesson to learn from the Jill server is how the right implementation of atomic_int made it possible to treat atomic_ints almost as if they were regular ints within the bodies of the server's operations.

The constructor, jill, sets all the elements of data to -1, as we specified in the description of Jill. Finally, the server operation main has no body but, as we have explained, every server must have a main operation.

19.2.4 The Jack Application

This section shows the code for the Avalon application, "Jack," which uses a Jill server. Most Avalon applications look very similar to Jack so in subsequent examples, we will omit the application-side code. When Jack starts, it enters a transaction. It then executes user commands until the user enters the command to exit the program. The user may read or write array elements, start nested transactions, and commit or abort transactions. Figure 19.4 shows the first part of the code in av_jack.av.

Like all Avalon programs, av_jack.av starts by including avalon.h. It also includes stream.h and ctype.h from the C++ library, and av_jill.h to get the declaration of the Jill server. After the includes, av_jack.av declares two more constants used as abort codes within this file and declares the two functions defined in this file so that they can be used before they are defined. The next statement declares a global variable of the Jill server type. The client program can invoke operations on this server object just as if it were a class object.

The main procedure prints out an initial message and locates the Jill server. If it cannot find the Jill server, it calls the jill constructor. It then repeatedly calls jill_transaction until the value of quit_flag indicates that the user wants to exit the program. Finally, the print_help procedure prints out a help message.

Now we consider the heart of the Jack application, the jill_transaction function. jill_transaction begins (Figure 19.5) by starting a transaction. It then enters a command loop, in which it remains until the user decides to quit the program, or terminate (commit or abort) the current top-level transaction. It prints out a prompt (which contains the current transaction nesting level, which it is given as an input.) Next, it gets an input command, and

av_jack.av:

```
#include <avalon.h>
#include <stream.h>
#include <ctype.h>
#include "av_jill.h"

// Abort codes.
const int USER_REQUESTED_ABORT = 100;
const int TOP_LEVEL_ABORT = 101;

// Forward declarations.
void jill_transaction(int, int*);
void print_help();

// Global server variable.
jill *jill_srv;


void main() {
  int quit_flag = 0;

  cout << "Looking for jill...\n";
  jill_srv = (jill*) &locate_server ("jill");
  if (jill_srv == NULL){
    cout << "Couldn't find jill.  Starting a new jill...\n";
    jill_srv = new jill;
  }else cout << "Found jill.\n";

  cout << "Type ? for a list of commands.\n";
  while (quit_flag < 2) {
    quit_flag = 0;
    jill_transaction(1, &quit_flag);
    cout << "(Transaction was top level.)\n";
  }
  exit(0);
}

// print_help -- Prints the commands.

void print_help() {
  cout << "\n\
Commands are: \n\
    r   Read array element.\n\
    w   Write array element.\n\
    b   Begin nested transaction.\n\
    c   Commit innermost transaction.\n\
    a   Abort innermost transaction.\n\
    A   Abort top level transaction.\n\
    q   Abort top level transaction and quit program.\n\n";
}
```

Figure 19.4: First Part of the Jack Application

```
// Interactively construct and perform a transaction utilizing the jill
// server.  Can be called recursively to construct nested transactions.

void jill_transaction(int level, int* quit_flag_ptr) {
  start transaction {
    char cmd;

    while (!*quit_flag_ptr) {
      int index = 0;
      int value = 0;

      cout << "Jack[" << level << "] ";
      while(isspace(cmd = getchar()))
        ;

      switch(cmd) {
       case 'r':                // Read an array element
        cout << "Location to read: ";
        cin >> index;
        value = jill_srv->read(index);
        if (value == -1)
          cout << "Location " << index << " is uninitialized.\n";
        else
          cout << "Value at location " << index << " is " << value << ".\n";
        break;

       case 'w':                // Write an array element
        cout << "Location to write: ";
        cin >> index;
        cout << "Value to write: ";
        cin >> value;
        jill_srv->write(index, value);
        cout << "Write succeeded.\n";
        break;

       case 'c':                // Commit this transaction
        leave;

       case 'a':                // Abort this transaction
        undo (USER_REQUESTED_ABORT) leave;

       case 'A':                // Abort top-level transaction
        undo (TOP_LEVEL_ABORT) leave;
        // ...continued...
```

Figure 19.5: Beginning of the `jill_transaction` Function

```
        // ...rest of jill_transaction...
        case 'q':                  // Abort to top level transaction and quit.
         *quit_flag_ptr = 2;
         undo return;

        case 'b':                  // Begin a subtransaction
         jill_transaction(level+1, quit_flag_ptr);
         continue;

        case '?':                  // Print short help message
         print_help();
         break;

        default:
         cout << "Unknown command. Type ? for a list of commands.\n";
       }
     }
     // Quit_flag from nested transaction is non-zero, so we must undo return.
     undo return;
   } except (trans_status) {
    case TOP_LEVEL_ABORT:
     *quit_flag_ptr = 1;
    case USER_REQUESTED_ABORT:
     cout << "Transaction aborted as per request.\n";
     return;
    case INDEX_OUT_OF_BOUNDS:
     cout << "Transaction aborted: Array index out of bounds.\n";
     return;
    case ILLEGAL_VALUE:
     cout << "Transaction aborted:  Attempt to write a negative value.\n";
     return;
    default:
     cout << avalon_abort_code_to_str(trans_status) << "\n";
     return;
   }
   // Otherwise, we committed.
   cout << "Transaction committed.\n";
}
```

Figure 19.6: End of the `jill_transaction` Function

enters a switch statement that processes that input. The 'r' and 'w' commands should be fairly self-explanatory. Note that the read and write operations are invoked on the object denoted by the jill_srv variable exactly as if it were a normal class object. The 'c' command uses the leave statement to commit and exit the current transaction. The 'a' command aborts the innermost transaction, using the undo leave statement. We pass an abort code that indicates that the user aborted the transaction. The 'A' command aborts the current top-level transaction. This is implemented by first aborting the innermost transaction, using a special abort code. We will see in a moment how this code is processed. The 'q' command exits the program. To do this, we set the quit_flag, and exit jill_transaction. We use the special undo return statement to indicate that we not only want to return from the current procedure, but also to abort any transactions started by that procedure. The 'b' command starts a nested transaction by making a recursive call to jill_transaction (with level incremented by one.) An input of '?' causes the help message to be printed, and if the input command is none of these, a message to that effect is printed.

The rest of jill_transaction is shown in Figure 19.6. In this figure is the statement just after the body of the loop that waited for the quit_flag to be set (by a nested transaction.) If we reach here, we do the same thing we did when the user entered a 'q': undo return. The next scope we leave is that of the transaction. This transaction block has an except clause appended to it. An except clause allows access to the abort codes provided in undo leave statements. If a transaction with an except clause aborts, the abort code, if there is one, is assigned to the variable named after the except. The rest of the except statement is exactly like a switch on this value. In jill_transaction, the first two cases handle user-requested aborts. In either case, we print out a message and return. If a top-level abort has been requested, then we set the quit_flag to exit all enclosing jill_transaction calls. The third and fourth cases handle transactions that were aborted by server operations because of improper inputs. They both print an appropriate message and return from jill_transaction. Finally, if the transaction aborted but the code is none of the above, then the abort must have been caused by the underlying system. We can find out why by calling the routine avalon_abort_code_to_string, which takes an integer argument (Section 20.4.6). All arms of the except statement return from jill_transaction, so if we exit the transaction and reach the last line of the procedure, the transaction must have committed. We print a message to that effect.

19.3 FIFO Queue

Let us consider how one would implement an *atomic first-in-first-out (FIFO) queue*. The easiest way to define such a queue is to inherit from atomic. A limitation of this approach is that enq and deq operations would both be classified as writers, permitting little concurrency. Instead, we show how a highly concurrent atomic FIFO queue can be implemented by inheriting from subatomic. Our implementation is interesting for two reasons. First, it supports more concurrency than commutativity-based concurrency control schemes such as two-phase locking. For example, it permits concurrent enq operations, even though enqs do not commute. Second, it supports more concurrency than any locking-based protocol, because it takes advantage of state information. For example, it permits concurrent enq and deq operations while the queue is non-empty.

In order to permit such concurrency it is necessary to provide:

1. A way to determine whether one transaction has committed with respect to another. In

particular, suppose A and B are concurrent transactions:

- If it is known that A has committed with respect to transaction B, then B should be allowed to observe the effects of A's operations. Thus, B need not wait and may proceed.
- If it is not known that A has committed with respect to B, then B must not do anything that depends on A's effects, since A may still commit or abort. B should also not invalidate any results that A may have observed, since B may commit before A. Thus, B might have to wait till A completes.

2. Exclusive access to an object per operation. That is, while transactions may go on concurrently, we need to prevent individual operations from interfering with each other.

Fortunately, Avalon provides the first capability with the class `trans_id`, which gives us a way to test transaction-commit order, and the second with the class `subatomic`, which gives us a way to provide mutual exclusion per object.

In Avalon when a transaction commits, the run-time system assigns it a timestamp generated by a logical clock [60]. Atomic objects are expected to ensure that all transactions are serializable in the order of their commit timestamps, a property called *hybrid atomicity* [120]. This property is automatically ensured by two-phase locking protocols [30], such as that used for the `atomic_ints` in Jill's array. However, additional concurrency can be achieved by taking the timestamp ordering explicitly into account. The `trans_id` class provides operations that permit run-time testing of transaction-commit order, and thus of serialization order. In particular, `trans_id` provides a partial-ordering function <. For transactions with `trans_ids` t1 and t2, if t1 < t2 evaluates to true, then if both transactions commit, t1 is serialized before t2. We say that t1 is "committed with respect to" t2. Note that < induces a partial order on `trans_ids`; as transactions commit they become comparable. Section 21.1.2 describes this type in more detail.

Class `subatomic` provides operations that give transactions exclusive access to objects. Each subatomic object has a short-term lock, similar to a monitor lock, used to ensure that concurrent operations do not interfere with each other. Avalon's special control construct, the `when` statement, is used as a kind of conditional critical region:

```
when ( <TEST> ) {
  <...BODY...>
}
```

The calling process atomically acquires the object's short-term lock, blocks until the condition becomes true (releasing the lock if it is not), and then executes the body. The lock is released after the body is executed. Any changes made to the object while the lock is held will not be backed up to stable storage until sometime after the lock is released. A transaction's changes are guaranteed to be backed up before it commits.

19.3.1 The Queue Representation

Figure 19.7 shows that information about `enq` invocations is recorded in a `struct`. The `item` component is the enqueued item, the `enqr` component is a `trans_id` generated by the enqueuing transaction, and the last component defines a constructor operation for initializing the struct. Information about `deq` invocations is recorded similarly in `deq_rec`'s.

```
struct enq_rec {
  int item;                  // Item enqueued.
  trans_id enqr;             // Who enqueued it.
  enq_rec(int i, trans_id& t) { item = i; enqr = t; }
};

struct deq_rec {
  int item;                 // Item dequeued.
  trans_id enqr;            // Who enqueued it.
  trans_id deqr;            // Who dequeued it.
  deq_rec(int itm, trans_id& en, trans_id& de);
   { item = itm; enqr = en; deqr = de; }
};

class atomic_int_queue : public subatomic {
  deq_stack deqd;           // Stack of deq records.
  enq_heap enqd;            // Heap of enq records.
 public:
  atomic_int_queue() {};    // Create empty queue.
  void enq(int item);       // Enqueue an item.
  int deq();                // Dequeue an item.
  void commit(trans_id&);
  void abort(trans_id&);
  ãtomic_int_queue();
};
```

Figure 19.7: Queue Representation

```
void atomic_int_queue::enq(int item) {
  trans_id tid = trans_id();
  when (deqd.is_empty() || (deqd.top()->enqr < tid))
    enqd.insert(item, tid);
}

int atomic_int_queue::deq() {
  trans_id tid = trans_id();
  when ((deqd.is_empty() || deqd.top()->deqr < tid)
        && enqd.min_exists() && (enqd.get_min()->enqr < tid)) {
    enq_rec* min_er = enqd.delete_min();
    deq_rec dr(*min_er, tid);
    deqd.push(dr);
    return min_er->item;
  }
}
```

Figure 19.8: Queue Operations

The queue is represented as follows: The `deqd` component is a stack of `deq_rec`'s used to undo aborted `deq` operations. The `enqd` component is a *partially ordered heap* of `enq_rec`'s, ordered by their `enq_tid` fields. A partially ordered heap provides operations to enqueue an `enq_rec`, to test whether there exists a unique oldest `enq_rec`, to dequeue it if it exists, and to keep and discard all `enq_rec`'s committed with respect to a particular transaction identifier.

Our implementation satisfies the following representation invariant: First, assuming all enqueued items are distinct, an item is either "enqueued" or "dequeued", but not both: if an `enq_rec` containing `[item, enqr]` is in the `enqd` component, then there is no `deq_rec` containing `[item, enqr, deqr]` in the `deqd` component, and vice-versa. Second, the stack order of two items mirrors both their enqueuing order and their dequeuing order: if `d1` is below `d2` in the `deqd` stack, then `d1→enqr < d2→enqr` and `d1→deqr < d2→deqr`. Finally, any dequeued item must previously have been enqueued: for all `deq_rec`'s `d`, `d→enqr < d→deqr`.

19.3.2 The Queue Operations

`Enq` and `deq` operations (Figure 19.8) may proceed under the following conditions: A transaction A may dequeue an item if (1) the most recent dequeuing transaction is committed with respect to A, and (2) there exists a unique oldest element in the queue whose enqueuing transaction is committed with respect to A. The first condition ensures that A will not have dequeued the wrong item if the earlier dequeuer aborts, and the second condition ensures that there is some element for A to dequeue. Similarly, A may enqueue an item if the last item dequeued was enqueued by a transaction B committed with respect to A. This condition ensures that A will not be serialized before B, violating the FIFO ordering.

Both `enq` and `deq` first obtain a new, unique `trans_id` for the calling transaction. The constructor creates and commits a "dummy" subtransaction, returning the subtransaction's `trans_id` to the calling transaction (i.e., parent). Since this constructor call returns a unique `trans_id`, a parent transaction can thus generate multiple trans_ids ordered in the serialization order of their creation events. We exploit this property here by using this trans_id to tag the current enq (deq) operation.

As in the atomic_int example, the modifications done by enq and deq must be wrapped in a pinning construct to ensure persistence (that is, changes are made to stable storage).

We use the when statement to guard against simultaneous access to the queue object itself. Enq checks whether the item most recently dequeued was enqueued by a transaction committed with respect to the caller. If so, the new trans_id and the new item are inserted in enqd. Otherwise, the transaction releases the short-term lock and tries again later. Deq tests whether the most recent dequeuing transaction has committed with respect to the caller, and whether enqd has a unique oldest item. If the transaction that enqueued this item has committed with respect to the caller, it removes the item from enqd and records it in deqd. Otherwise, the caller releases the short-term lock, suspends execution, and tries again later.

19.3.3 Commit and Abort

Avalon lets programmers define type-specific commit and abort operations for atomic data types inheriting from class subatomic. They each take a trans_id as an argument. The Avalon run-time system automatically calls an object's abort operation whenever a transaction that may have modified the object aborts. Whenever a top-level transaction commits, the system calls the commit operation on all subatomic (and atomic) objects that the transaction (or any of its descendants) may have modified. We make no guarantee about the arrival times of commit operations (i.e., when the run-time system is informed of a transaction's commit). In particular, if T1 commits before T2, the run-time might execute T2's commit before T1's. In addition, the order in which commit (abort) operations for a given transaction are applied to multiple objects is left unspecified.

Figure 19.9 gives the code for the queue's commit and abort operations. When a top-level transaction commits, it discards deq_rec's no longer needed for recovery. The representation invariant ensures that all deq_rec's below the top are also superfluous (they have all committed with respect to the top), and can be discarded. Abort has more work to do. It undoes every operation executed by a transaction committed with respect to the aborting transaction. It interprets deqd as an undo log, popping records for aborted operations, and inserting the items back in enqd. Abort then flushes all items enqueued by the aborted transaction and its descendants.

Notice that commit and abort for the queue example use the descendant operation of trans_id's rather than the $<$ operation. For example, when we are aborting, we want to remove all items enqueued by transactions that we know are aborting (i.e., the aborting transaction and all of its descendants). If we were to use $<$, an item enqueued by a separate top-level transaction that committed before the aborting transaction would be incorrectly deleted.

19.3.4 Enq and Deq Synchronization Revisited

Let us look more carefully at the synchronization conditions on enq and deq. Consider why enq must wait for the enqueuer of the last dequeued item to commit. If it does not wait, then it is possible that a dequeuer may get the wrong head of the queue as a result of the commit of some concurrent enqueue. For example, suppose a transaction A starts two subtransactions A1 and A2. A1 enqueues 5 and commits. A2 does a dequeue (A2 can proceed because A1 has committed with respect to A2),

```
void atomic_int_queue::commit(trans_id& committer) {
  when (TRUE)
    if (!deqd.is_empty() && descendant(deqd.top()->deqr, committer)) {
      deqd.clear();
    }
}

void atomic_int_queue::abort(trans_id& aborter) {
  when (TRUE) {
    while (!deqd.is_empty() && descendant(deqd.top()->deqr, aborter)) {
      deq_rec* d = deqd.pop();
      enqd.insert(d->item, d->enqr);
    }
    enqd.discard(aborter);
  }
}
```

Figure 19.9: Queue's Commit and Abort

gets a 5, but does not yet commit. Now suppose another top-level transaction B starts and tries to enqueue 7. (B and A2 are concurrent.) If B does not wait then it proceeds to put 7 at the head of the queue (A2 has temporarily claimed the 5). If B commits before A (the parent transaction of A1 and A2), then B is serialized before A, implying that A2 should get a 7, not a 5. In short, the FIFO behavior of the queue is violated because B did not wait for A to commit.

The condition on `enq` is sufficient as well. In particular, an enqueuing transaction does not need to wait for the dequeuer of the last dequeued item to commit because in some circumstances it can proceed even if the dequeuer has not finished. For example, suppose transactions A, B, and C are top-level transactions. A enqueues 5 and commits. B dequeues 5, but remains active. If C wants to enqueue, it should be allowed to proceed even though B (the dequeuer of the last dequeued item) has not completed. Here, if B commits, it does not matter whether B commits before or after C; B will correctly see 5 as the head of the queue and C will correctly place 7 as the new head. If B aborts, then C will correctly place 7 after 5, which remains at the head of the queue. Thus, C can proceed without waiting for B to complete because there is no way C can be serialized before A and it does not matter in which order B and C are serialized.

It is easier to see why a dequeuing transaction, B, must wait for the dequeuer, A, of the last dequeued item to be committed with respect B. If B proceeds to dequeue without waiting for A to complete, then it will have dequeued the wrong item if A aborts.

19.4 Atomic Counters

As our final example, suppose we wish to implement an *atomic counter* with operations to increment (`inc`), decrement (`dec`), and test for zero (`is_zero`). This counter could be used to represent a joint checking account: One party might be depositing money at one branch, another party might be withdrawing money from somewhere else, and a third party, perhaps an auditor, might be searching for depleted accounts. This is not quite realistic since one could not find out the exact balance of the

```
class atomic_counter: public atomic {
  nonnegative_int count;
 public:
  atomic_counter()  {pinning() count = 0;} // initialize counter
  void inc();
  void dec();
  bool is_zero();
}

void atomic_counter:: inc() {
  write_lock();
  pinning () count += 1;
}

void atomic_counter:: dec() {
  write_lock();
  pinning () count -= 1;                // will return max of count-1 and 0
}

bool is_zero(); {
  read_lock();
  return (count == 0);
}
```

Figure 19.10: Atomic Counter Derived from Class Atomic

account (there is no read operation), but adding that function would complicate our example.

By deriving from class `atomic`, we can easily implement the atomic counter as shown in Figure 19.10 (Recall that class `atomic` provides `read_lock` and `write_lock` operations.)

The counter is represented by a `nonnegative_int`, a class supporting all the usual arithmetic operations on integers, with the property that its value must be greater than or equal to zero. (The overloaded subtraction operation is a "monus" operation.) Again, one can see that building a new atomic class from class `atomic` is fairly straightforward: before performing its real work, an accessing operation ("reader") should first obtain a read lock; a modifying operation ("writer") should first obtain a write lock and then pin the object.

This implementation, however, does not realize much concurrency. From the abstract viewpoint of our atomic counter, incrementing and decrementing transactions can go on concurrently (`inc` and `dec` are "blind" writes since they do not return any results); moreover, under certain conditions, it should be possible to return a result to `is_zero` even before all incrementing and decrementing transactions have completed. The implementation in Figure 19.10 does not support this degree of concurrency since it is based on standard two-phase read/write locking.

Thus, as for the queue example, we will use `trans_ids` and subatomic objects as an alternative way to build atomic objects.

19.4.1 Counter Representation

Let us walk through the revised representation of the atomic counter by beginning with some auxiliary structures.

`counter_range`

A `counter_range` (Figure 19.11) keeps track of the range of possible values of the counter in order to permit `is_zero` to return, in some cases, before all transactions have completed.

The range of possible values is represented by a "*committed*" value (`committed`), a positive effect (`pos`), and a negative effect (`neg`). `Committed` is the value of the counter constructed from the actual committed value of the counter and any operations that are committed to the top level, but whose commit operations have not yet been called. `Pos` is the maximum amount by which the effects of uncommitted operations included in the `counter_range` could increment the counter. `Neg` represents the maximum amount by which they could decrement the counter. `Neg` may be positive, in which case the operations do not decrease the value of the counter.

The `counter_range` class provides operations that allow a `counter_range` to be constructed from a "*family*" (i.e., a list of operations whose `trans_ids` are committed to the least common ancestor). In Figure 19.12, for example, if `a3` and `a4` are committed and `A`, `a1`, and `a2` are still active, `a2`, `a3`, and `a4` are in the same family. `a2` is included in the family even though it is still active because `a3` and `a4` are committed with respect to it. `A` and `a1` are separate families. Each operation in a family shifts the range computed so far, thus allowing operations within the family to cancel each other out. A `counter_range` may also be constructed from a list of families. In this case, a `counter_range` is constructed for each family in the list. These `counter_ranges` are then combined to increase the total range.

`Counter_range` also provides `is_zero` and `is_not_zero` operations, which may be used by a query to determine the state of the counter. If the state of the counter is known, one of these operations will return `TRUE`. Otherwise, they will both return `FALSE`. These operations take an optional argument which specifies an amount by which to shift the range before doing the test. This argument is used by the `is_zero_work` operation to represent operations that are known to serialize immediately before a query.

`op_seq` and `op_list`

An `op_seq` (Figure 19.13) keeps track of operations that are in the same family.

An `op_list` (Figure 19.13) is used to construct an `op_seq`. It is assumed that each operation added to an `op_list` is in the same family as the other operations in the list and is not serialized before any of the other operations.

An `op_list_list` (Figure 19.14) sorts operations into families. It is assumed that no operation appended to an `op_list_list` is serialized before the any of the other operations already in the list.

Recoverable Sorted Association List and `log_entry`

Our atomic counter will allow concurrency by putting all operations into a log and applying them to the counter at commit time, rather than applying them to the counter at the time they are requested.

```
class counter_range {
  nonnegative_int committed;
  nonnegative_int pos;
  int neg;

public:
  counter_range()                      { init (0); }
  counter_range(op_seq& os)            { init (0); *this+=os; }
  counter_range(int, op_list_list&);
  void init (nonnegative_int c)        { pos = 0; neg = 0; committed = c; }
  bool is_zero (int i = 0)             { return ((int(committed)+int(pos)+i)
                                                   <= 0); }
  bool is_not_zero (int i = 0)         { return ((((neg+i) <= 0) &&
                                                    ((committed+neg+i) > 0)) ||
                                                   (((neg+i) > 0) &&
                                                    ((committed+i) > 0))); }
  counter_range& operator+= (op_seq&);
  counter_range& operator+= (int i)     { pos = pos + i; neg = neg + i;
                                          return *this; }
  counter_range& operator+= (counter_range& cr)
                                        { pos += int(cr.pos);
                                          if (cr.neg < 0) neg += cr.neg;
                                          committed += int(cr.committed);
                                          return *this; }
  counter_range& operator= (counter_range& cr)
    { pos = cr.pos; neg = cr.neg; committed = cr.committed; return *this; }
};

counter_range::counter_range (int i, op_list_list& oll)
{
  init (i);
  if (oll.ol != NULL){
    for (op_list_list *l = &oll; l; l = l->next){
      counter_range cr (*(l->ol->head));
      *this += cr;
    }
  }
}

counter_range& counter_range::operator+= (op_seq& to_add)
{
  for (op_seq* op = &to_add; op; op = op->next_op)
    *this += op->to_dec ? -1 : 1;
  return *this;
}
```

Figure 19.11: `counter_range`

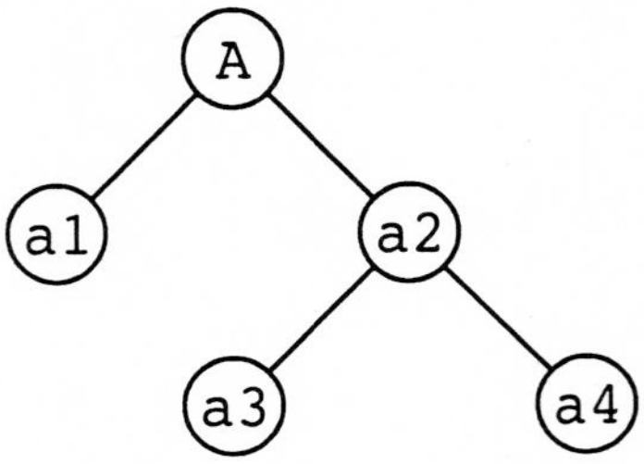

Figure 19.12: Family

```
class op_seq {
  friend class counter_range;
  friend class op_list;
  trans_id id;
  bool to_dec;
  op_seq* next_op;
public:
  op_seq(trans_id& t, bool b) { id = t; to_dec = b; next_op = NULL; }
  op_seq(op_seq& os)          { id = os.id; to_dec = os.to_dec; next_op = os.next_op; }
  ōp_seq()                    { if (next_op != NULL) delete next_op; }
  bool family (op_seq& os) { return both (id, os.id); }
};

class op_list {
  friend class counter_range;
  op_seq* head;
  op_seq* tail;
ublic:
  op_list() { head = tail = NULL; }
  op_list& operator<< (op_seq&);
  ōp_list() { if (head) delete head; }
  bool family (op_seq& os)      { return head->family (os); }
  bool empty ()                 { return (head == NULL); }
  operator op_seq ()            { return *head; }
};

op_list& op_list::operator<< (op_seq& os) {
  if (tail == NULL){
    head = tail = new op_seq (os.id, os.to_dec);
  }else{
    tail->next_op = new op_seq (os.id, os.to_dec);
    tail = tail->next_op;
  }
  return *this;
}
```

Figure 19.13: `op_seq` **and** `op_list`

```
class op_list_list {
  friend class counter_range;
  op_list* ol;
  op_list_list* next;
public:
  op_list_list()  { ol = NULL; next = NULL; }
  õp_list_list() { if (ol != NULL) delete ol; if (next != NULL) delete next; }
  op_list_list& operator<< (op_seq&);
};

op_list_list& op_list_list::operator<< (op_seq& os) {
  op_list_list* prev = NULL;

  if (ol == NULL){
    ol = new op_list;
    *ol << os;
    return *this;
  }
  for (op_list_list* l = this; l; prev = l, l = l->next){
    if (l->ol->family(os)){
      *(l->ol) << os;
      return *this;
    }
  }
  prev->next = new op_list_list;
  *(prev->next) << os;
  return *this;
}
```

Figure 19.14: `op_list_list`

```
class log_entry :public recoverable {
  trans_id id;
  bool zero;

public:
  log_entry(trans_id&, bool);
  bool operator<(log_entry& le)          { return (id < le.id); }
  bool operator<(trans_id& t)            { return (id < t); }
  bool operator>(log_entry& le)          { return (id > le.id); }
  bool operator>(trans_id& t)            { return (id > t); }
  log_entry& operator=(log_entry&);
  operator op_seq ()                     { return op_seq(id, zero); }
  operator trans_id ()                   { return id; }
  operator bool ()                       { return zero; }
};

log_entry::log_entry(trans_id& t, bool z)
{
  pinning () { id = t; zero = z; }
}

log_entry& log_entry::operator=(log_entry& le)
{
  pinning () { id = le.id; zero = le.zero; }
  return *this;
}

boolean_t tid_eq( trans_id& t1,  trans_id& t2)
{ return (t1 == t2); }

boolean_t tid_lt( trans_id& t1,  trans_id& t2)
{ return (t1 < t2); }

typedef log_entry* Plog_entry;

#include "recov_sorted_alist.h"
recov_sorted_alistdeclare(trans_id,Plog_entry,tid_eq,tid_lt);
recov_sorted_alistittrdecl(trans_id,Plog_entry,tid_eq,tid_lt);

typedef recov_sorted_alist(trans_id,Plog_entry,tid_eq,tid_lt) log_t;
typedef recov_sorted_alist_ittr(trans_id,Plog_entry,tid_eq,tid_lt) logittr;

recov_sorted_alistimplement(trans_id,Plog_entry,tid_eq,tid_lt);
recov_sorted_alistittrimpl(trans_id,Plog_entry,tid_eq,tid_lt);
```

Figure 19.15: Counter's Log Entry and Recoverable Sorted Association List

Assume we have defined elsewhere (in `recov_sorted_alist.h`) types for a recoverable sorted association list (`recov_sorted_alist`), parameterized over the tag type (e.g., `trans_id`) and value type (e.g., pointer to `log_entry`) of the pairs to be inserted in the list, an equality function (e.g., on `trans_ids`) used for list insertion, lookup, and removal, and a comparison function (e.g., < on `trans_ids`) used for ordering the elements in the list. Its iterative version, (`recov_sorted_alist_ittr`), similar to that used in the C++ Manual (p. 183 of [114]), provides a method for looping over all elements in the list, guaranteeing that elements are yielded in sorted order. Our list (Figure 19.15) is sorted by `trans_id`'s partial order < so that we can iterate over transactions in commit-time order.

Each `log_entry` has a unique `trans_id` (`id`) for serialization and a `bool` (`zero`) that represents the operation that was done. The value of `zero` can have a couple of different meanings. If the `log_entry` represents a query, `zero` is the result of the query. If the `log_entry` represents an increment or decrement operation, `zero` is `TRUE` if that operation takes the counter value toward zero (i.e., if it is a decrement). `Zero` is `FALSE` if the operation is an increment. We keep these different types of `log_entrys` in different recoverable sorted association lists.

The `atomic_counter` Class

The representation of the `atomic_counter` class is shown in Figure 19.16. We represent the counter by a non-negative integer (`count`), an operation log (`op_log`), which keeps track of `inc` and `dec` operations, and a query log (`query_log`), which keeps track of `is_zero` operations.

The value of `count` is determined by the operations of transactions that have committed to the top level, and whose commit operations have been called.

Implementations of the `inc` and `dec` operations are shown in Figure 19.16. They use the internal auxiliary functions shown in Figure 19.17. The `add_op_to_log` routine first calls the `trans_id` constructor with the value `CURRENT` to obtain the `trans_id` of the calling transaction. It then uses a `when` contstruct to ensure exclusive access to the counter and verifies that the insertion of the operation record is possible by calling `add_op_to_log_work`. The `add_op_to_log_work` routine returns `FALSE` if the operation cannot be added at this time, causing the `when` construct to pause and be reactivated at a later time when the situation changes. When the condition in the `when` statement succeeds, `add_op_to_log` obtains a unique `trans_id` and adds the operation to the `op_log`.

The `add_op_to_log_work` routine identifies active transactions whose view of the counter might be changed by the current operation by looking through the `query_log` for queries that are not currently serialized before the proposed operation. Each query satisfying this condition is redone by the `is_zero_work` function (we will look at this function later). If the result of the query changes, the proposed operation must wait. If the proposed operation does not change any of these queries, it may proceed.

Like `add_op_to_log`, the `is_zero` routine, shown in Figure 19.18, uses a `when` construct. It calls `is_zero_work` to determine whether the state of the counter is known. If state of the counter is known, it obtains a unique `trans_id` and inserts the state of the counter in the `query_log`.

The `is_zero_work` routine, shown in Figure 19.19, determines whether the state of the counter is known, and if so, whether or not the counter is zero. The state of the counter is determined with respect to `is_zero_work`'s first argument, `id`. `Id` is the `trans_id` of the transaction requesting the query, if this query is being done for the first time. It is the unique `trans_id` assigned to the

```
class atomic_counter : public subatomic {
  nonnegative_int count;
  log_t op_log;
  log_t query_log;

  bool is_zero_work(trans_id&, bool&, op_seq* = NULL);
  void add_op_to_log(bool);
  bool add_op_to_log_work(trans_id&, bool);

public:
  atomic_counter();
  void inc();
  void dec();
  bool is_zero();
  void commit(trans_id& t);
  void abort(trans_id& t);
};

atomic_counter::atomic_counter ()
{
  pinning () count = 0;
}

// Add increment operation to log
void atomic_counter::inc()      { add_op_to_log(FALSE); }

// Add decrement operation to log
void atomic_counter::dec()      { add_op_to_log(TRUE); }
```

Figure 19.16: Atomic Counter Derived from Class Subatomic

```
void atomic_counter::add_op_to_log(bool to_dec) {
  // Add (inc/dec) operation to op_log.
  trans_id current_id = trans_id (CURRENT);
  log_entry* entry = NULL;

  when (add_op_to_log_work(current_id, to_dec)) {
    trans_id new_id;
    entry = new log_entry(new_id,to_dec);
    op_log.insert(new_id, entry);
  }
}

bool atomic_counter::add_op_to_log_work(trans_id& id,
                                        bool to_dec) {
  log_entry** entry;

  logittr next_entry(query_log);

  op_seq this_op (id, to_dec);

  // Look for queries that aren't committed wrt. me.
  for (entry = next_entry(); entry; entry = next_entry()) {
    if (!((**entry) < id)){
      bool known, zero = TRUE;
      // Uncommitted wrt. me.  Redo the query and return FALSE if the proposed
      // operation changes the result.
      known = is_zero_work (trans_id(**entry), zero, &this_op);
      if (!known || (zero != bool(**entry))) return FALSE;
    }
  }

  return TRUE;
}
```

Figure 19.17: Counter's `inc` and `dec` Auxiliary Operations

```
bool atomic_counter::is_zero()
{ bool zero = TRUE;
  trans_id current_id = trans_id(CURRENT);

  when (is_zero_work(current_id, zero)) {
    trans_id new_id;
    query_log.insert(new_id, new log_entry(new_id, zero));
    return zero;
  }
}
```

Figure 19.18: Counter's `is_zero` Operation

```
bool atomic_counter::is_zero_work(trans_id& id, bool& zero, op_seq* new_op){
  log_entry** entry;
  logittr next_entry(op_log);
  nonnegative_int committed_value(count);
  int family_value = 0;
  op_list_list other_ops;

  for (entry = next_entry(); entry; entry = next_entry()){
    if ((**entry) < id){
      if (both (trans_id(**entry), id)){
        // A member of this family.
        family_value += (bool(**entry) ? -1 : 1);
      }else if (descendant (trans_id(**entry), id)){
        // A member of this family.
        family_value += (bool(**entry) ? -1 : 1);
      }else{
        // relatively-committed but not a member of this family
        if (trans_id(**entry).done()){
          committed_value += (bool(**entry) ? -1 : 1);
        }else other_ops << op_seq (**entry);
      }
    }else{
      // Ignore operations that are known to serialize after this query.
      if (!((**entry) > id)){
        other_ops << op_seq (**entry);
      }
    }
  }

  // Add the new operation if it was specified.
  if (new_op != NULL) other_ops << *new_op;

  // Do this family's operations guarantee a non-zero value?
  if (family_value > 0){
    zero = FALSE;
    return TRUE;
  }

  // The range without the query's family.
  counter_range unc_range (int(committed_value), other_ops);

  // Can we tell whether or not the counter is zero?
  if (unc_range.is_not_zero(family_value) || unc_range.is_zero(family_value)){
    zero = unc_range.is_zero(family_value);
    return TRUE;
  }
  zero = FALSE;
  return FALSE;
}
```

Figure 19.19: Counter's `is_zero_work` Operation

query, if the query is being redone.

`Is_zero_work` iterates over all `op_log` entries, separating them into 4 groups:

1. Operations that are known to serialize before `id` and that are in `id`'s family (`family_value`).
2. Operations that are committed to the top level (`committed_value`).
3. Operations that are known to serialize after `id`.
4. Operations that do not fit into any of the previous categories (`other_ops`).

When `is_zero_work` is called by `add_op_to_log_work` to redo a query, the operation that is being requested (`new_op`) is specified. Since `add_op_to_log` only redoes queries that are not committed with respect to `new_op`'s parent transaction, `new_op` is included in group 4.

The operations in Group 4 are used to construct a `counter_range` that represents the possible values of the counter. If the low end of the range is bounded below by a positive integer, the value of the counter will be non-zero for all possible orderings of the uncommitted transactions. `Is_zero_work`'s second argument, `zero`, will be set to `FALSE` in this case. If the high end of the range is bounded by zero, the value of the counter will be zero for all possible orderings. `Zero` will be set to `TRUE` in this case. `Is_zero_work` returns `TRUE` if the state of the counter is known, `FALSE` otherwise.

The operations in Group 1 will serialize immediately before the query. Let's examine why this is true. `Is_zero_work` will be called in two cases:

1. A client has requested an increment or decrement and the query is being redone to make sure the proposed operation does not change it.
2. A client has requested a query.

In Case 1, since the query already has a unique `trans_id`, it is impossible for any uncommitted subtransactions of the query's parent transaction to serialize before the query. In Case 2, since `is_zero` holds the short-term lock on the counter, no new operation can come between Group 1 and the query, thus, we only have to worry about uncommitted subtransactions of the query's parent transaction that commit before we obtain a unique `trans_id` for the query. Since the only way to start nested transactions in Avalon/C++ is to use the `start` or `costart` statement, and both of these statements suspend the parent while there are active subtransactions, the fact that a query is being requested implies that the transaction requesting the query does not have any uncommitted subtransactions.

Since we know that the operations in Group 1 will serialize immediately before the query, we may use those operations to shift the range in the appropriate direction when we try to determine the value of the counter. This is accomplished by passing `family_value` to `counter_range`'s `is_zero` and `is_not_zero` functions. Since the minimum value of the counter is zero, if the net effect of the operations in Group 1 is to increment the counter, we know that the counter is non-zero without even looking at the range.

If we manage to obtain the short-term lock between the time a transaction commits and the time its commit operation is called, there will be some operations in Group 2. The operations in this group are applied directly to our copy of the committed value of the counter. This is the correct thing to do, since the commit operation would have applied these operations directly to the committed value if we had waited a little while longer.

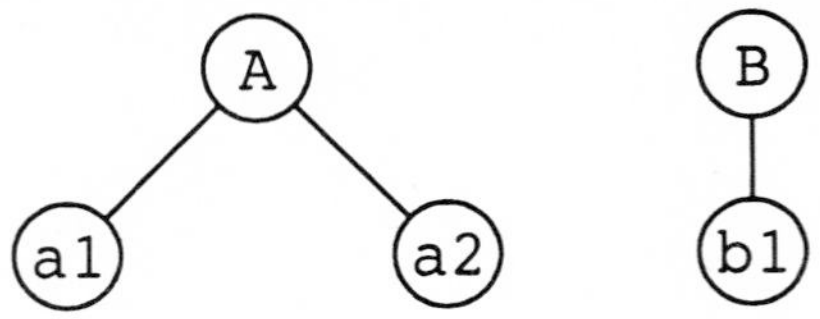

Figure 19.20: Serialization Example

If we are redoing a query, there may be some operations in Group 3. These operations are ignored, since we can be sure that they will never become visible to the query.

The range constructed by `is_zero_work` does not take full advantage of the ordering restrictions imposed on `trans_ids` by the tree structure of transactions (i.e., it assumes a "flat" universe which may be grouped into *families*). For example, suppose `A` and `B` are different top-level transactions (see Figure 19.20). It is impossible for `b1` to be serialized between `a1` and `a2`. More concurrency may be achieved by taking these ordering restrictions into account in all cases, rather than in the single case of operations in the query's family; this is left as an exercise to the reader.

19.4.2 Counter's Commit and Abort

The `commit` operation, shown in Figure 19.21, removes unneeded records from `op_log` and `query_log`. It updates the value of the counter by going through `op_log` in serialization order and applying all operations whose `trans_ids` are committed with respect to the committing transaction to the counter value. These operations are then removed from `op_log`. All queries that satisfy this condition are removed from `query_log`. We need to use the $<$ operator, rather than the `descendant` operation, because we cannot assume anything about the order in which commit operations are executed.

Suppose `A` and `B` are transactions (see Figure 19.22) and the committed value before either transaction commits is 0. Suppose `A` does one `inc` and `B` does one `dec`. If `A` commits, followed by `B`, the counter's committed value after `A`'s `commit` operation is executed should be 1; then after `B` commits, the counter's value changes to 0. However, if we were to execute `B`'s `commit` operation before `A`'s, then `B` would leave the value of the counter unchanged (a `dec` has no effect on the counter if its value is 0 already), and `A` would change it to a final value of 1, which is wrong. By using $<$, the `commit` operation makes sure it installs all changes of transactions that have committed with respect to the committing transaction, not just its descendants.

Unlike the `commit` operation, the `abort` operation, shown in Figure 19.23, only removes operations whose `trans_ids` are descendants of the aborting transaction from `op_log` and `query_log`. It would be incorrect to delete operations done on behalf of a transaction that is not a descendant of the aborting transaction, even if the `trans_ids` associated with those operations are committed with respect to the aborted transaction.

For example, suppose `A` is a top level transaction that has executed some operations before starting a nested transaction, `a1` (see Figure 19.24.) If `a1` aborts, only operations that were executed on `a1`'s behalf should be removed from the logs. Although the operations executed on `A`'s behalf before `a1` started are committed with respect to `a1`, it would be incorrect to remove them from the logs, since `A` might commit.

```
void atomic_counter::commit(trans_id& t)
{ log_entry** entry;

  when(TRUE) {
    {
      logittr next_entry(op_log);
      for (entry = next_entry(); entry; entry = next_entry()) {
        if ((**entry) < t) {
          pinning () {
            count += (bool(**entry) ? -1 : 1);
            op_log.remove(trans_id(**entry));
            delete *entry;
          }
        }
      }
    }
    {
      logittr next_entry(query_log);
      for (entry = next_entry(); entry; entry = next_entry()){
        if ((**entry) < t){
          pinning () {
            query_log.remove (trans_id(**entry));
            delete *entry;
          }
        }
      }
    }
  }
}
```

Figure 19.21: Counter's Commit Operation

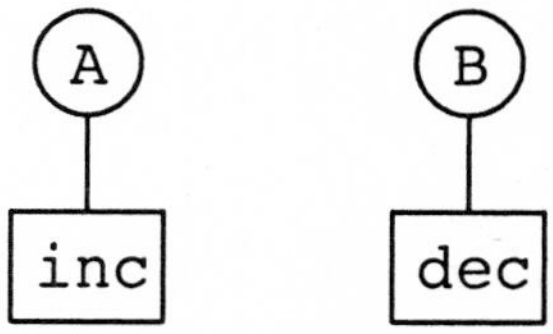

Figure 19.22: Commit Example

```
void atomic_counter::abort(trans_id& t)
{ log_entry** entry;

  when(TRUE) {
    {
      logittr next_entry(op_log);
      for (entry = next_entry(); entry; entry = next_entry()) {
        if (descendant(trans_id(**entry), t)) {
          pinning () {
            op_log.remove(trans_id(**entry));
            delete *entry;
          }
        }
      }
    }
    {
      logittr next_entry(query_log);
      for (entry = next_entry(); entry; entry = next_entry()) {
        if (descendant(trans_id(**entry), t)) {
          pinning () {
            query_log.remove(trans_id(**entry));
            delete *entry;
          }
        }
      }
    }
  }
}
```

Figure 19.23: Counter's Abort Operation

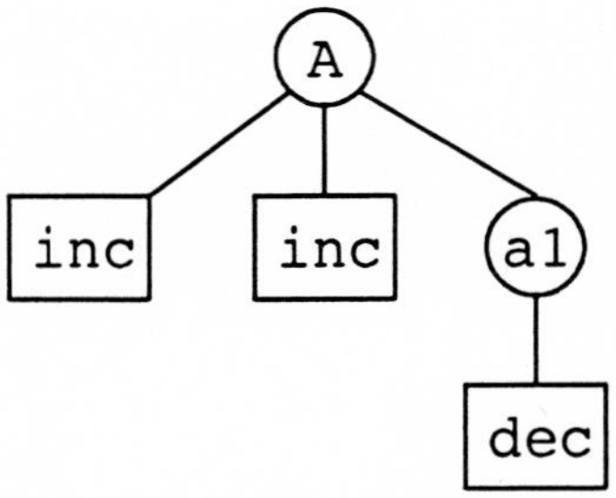

Figure 19.24: Abort Example

Chapter 20

Reference Manual

Jeannette Wing, Maurice Herlihy,
Stewart Clamen, David Detlefs, Karen Kietzke,
Richard Lerner, and Su-Yuen Ling

20.1 Lexical Considerations

Avalon nonterminals are in Roman face. C++ nonterminals are in italics, as in Section 14 of the C++ Reference Manual in [114]. Keywords are in bold typeface. C++ extended BNF is used. For example, *symbol*$_{\text{opt}}$ means an optional *symbol*. A C++ nonterminal followed by ":..." denotes an extension to that nonterminal.

The extended set of keywords is as follows:

```
costart     pinning     stable      transaction     when
except      process     start       undo            whenswitch
leave       server      toplevel    variant
```

20.2 Servers

aggr: ...
    `server`
decl-specifier: ...
    server-specifier
server-specifier:
    class-specifier
sc-specifier: ...
    `stable`

An Avalon server object is an instance of a `server` definition. A server definition, like a C++ class definition, encapsulates a set of objects, and exports to clients a set of operations that manipulate the objects and a set of operations that create and destroy instances of servers. A client invokes an operation on a server by calling a member function of a server object. Creating a new instance of a server causes a new server process to be started. When a server object is deleted, the server is killed.

20.2.1 Defining Servers

A server definition contains the following parts:

- Data declarations: Data declared to be `stable` in the server are restored following a failure. To be restored properly, `stable` data must be derived from one of Avalon's three base classes (Section 20.3): `recoverable`, `atomic` or `subatomic`. All data must be implemented to control concurrent access.

- A mandatory `main`. The `main` member function is executed as a background process when the server is started. This function can be used to provide code that needs to be run independently of the server's other operations. A printer server, for example, could use `main` for the code to run the printer. `Main` must exist, even if empty, because Avalon uses the existence of a `main` implementation to determine that the current compilation is for a server, rather than just for a client.

- An optional `recover` operation, which is executed whenever the server is restarted after a failure.

- Exported (and possibly internal) operations: The exported operations provide the clients the only means of accessing the server's data. Communication between clients and servers is through (hidden) remote procedure call (RPC) with call-by-value transmission of data.

- A nonempty set of constructors: A server's constructor defines the parameters that a client must use when creating a new server and provides code to execute when the server is started. In contrast to constructors for classes, a server's constructor must also specify to the run-time system the parameters needed to start the server process; these parameters are specified in the declaration in a way similar to passing parameters to the constructor of a class's parent (see example below). When a client calls a server's constructor, the specified parameters are passed to the routines that start the server.[1]

Example

Below is a simple server declaration:

```
server simple {
  stable atomic_int val;                   // Protected atomic integer
 public:
  simple(x_string p, x_string n) : (p,n);  // Constructor
  int  get();                              // An exported operation
```

[1]Unlike normal C++ usage, the startup parameters must be in the declaration seen by the client, rather than with the constructor definition. This information is useful only to the client, so it must appear in a place visible to the client, such as the server declaration.

```
    void set(int i);                    // Another exported operation
    void recover();                     // Called upon server recovery
    void main();                        // Background process
};
```

The parameters to the right of the colon in the constructor are passed to the run-time routines that start the server. The first parameter is the name of an executable file; if the full path name is not given, the user's path is used. The second parameter is the name of a node on which to start the server. If the value "localhost" or NULL is given, the local machine is used; otherwise an `x_string` argument such as "wing.avalon.cs.cmu.edu" can be given to start the server on some remote machine.

20.2.2 Using Servers

For an Avalon program to make use of a server, it must first obtain a reference to an instance of the appropriate server. As shown below the client may either create a new server object, starting a new server process:

```
(1)  printserver* p = new printserver(...);         // Start a new printserver
(2)  printserver q (...);
```

or it may, with the Avalon library `locate_server` function (see end of Section 21.3), obtain a reference to an existing server object representing a running server process:

```
(3)  printserver* p = (printserver*) &locate_server(...);
                                  // Locate an existing printserver
```

Calls to `server_root` functions and server constructors should not be used as initializers for global or static variables since the run-time system may be incompletely initialized at the time those variables are initialized.

Once a server instance is found, operations are invoked on the object as for any C++ object:

```
p->spool ("myfile.txt");                      // Invoke an operation
q.spool ("myfile.txt");                       // or this way
```

Since server objects are really just C++ objects with special operations, they can be manipulated in the same manner as other C++ objects. In particular, server objects and references to servers can be passed as parameters to and returned as values from functions.

20.3 Base Classes

There are three base Avalon classes: `recoverable`, `atomic`, and `subatomic`. Users define their own recoverable types by deriving from `recoverable`. They define their own atomic types by deriving from `atomic` or `subatomic`, and are responsible for ensuring that the types they define are indeed atomic. If a type is not atomic then transactions that use objects of that type are not guaranteed to be atomic. We expect most users to derive from class `atomic`, and more experienced (and demanding) users to derive from `subatomic`, especially if more control over the object's synchronization and recovery is desired. We refer the reader to Chapter 22, in particular Section 22.2, for correct usage of base classes, and [123] for a more formal description of their interfaces.

In writing the descriptions of the meanings of a class's member functions, we use the following clauses:

- **modifies**: A list of objects whose values may possibly change as a result of executing the operation.
- **requires**: A pre-condition on any invocation state of the operation. The caller is responsible for ensuring it holds; the implementor may assume it holds at the point of invocation.
- **when**: A condition on the state of the system that must hold before the operation proceeds. This condition is often necessary to give since the state of the system may change between the point of invocation and the actual point of execution of an operation.
- **ensures**: A post-condition on the returning state. The implementor must ensure that it holds; the caller may assume it holds upon return.

In C++, a pointer to the object for which a member function is invoked is a hidden argument to the function. As C++ does, we refer to this implicit argument as `this` in our specifications.

The absence of a **requires** (**when**) clause is the same as the predicate being TRUE. The absence of a **modifies** clause indicates that no changes are made to the values of any object. This specification style and notational conventions are borrowed from Larch [41].

20.3.1 Class Recoverable

Class Definition

```
class recoverable {
 public:
   virtual void pin(int size);
   virtual void unpin(int size);
};
```

Operations

`void pin(int size)`

ensures Subsequent changes to the object will not be recorded to stable storage until a later matching unpin operation. Multiple pins (and their matching unpins) by the same transaction to the same object have no effect. If the object is already pinned by a transaction different from the calling transaction, a run-time error is signaled.

`void unpin(int size)`

requires The calling transaction is currently pinning the object.

modifies The value of the object in stable storage.

ensures If there is exactly one outstanding pin operation, the modifications to the object are logged to stable storage.

The `pin` and `unpin` operations, which should be called in pairs, are used to notify the run-time system that a modification to an object is to be made. In most cases, the integer argument to pin and unpin should be the size of the object being pinned. After a crash, a recoverable object will be restored to a previous state in which it was not pinned. The `pin` and `unpin` operations are usually not called explicitly by programmers; instead, Avalon/C++ provides a special control structure, the `pinning` block (Section 20.4.7), both for syntactic convenience and as a safety measure.

20.3.2 Class Atomic

`Atomic` is a subclass of `recoverable`, specialized to provide two-phase read/write locking and automatic recovery. Objects derived from class `atomic` should be thought of as containing *long-term locks*, to ensure serializability. Each transaction obtains read (write) locks on all objects it accesses (modifies); locks are held until the transaction commits or aborts.

Class Definition

```
class atomic: public recoverable {
 public:
 // pin and unpin are inherited from recoverable.
   virtual void read_lock();
   virtual void write_lock();
}
```

Operations

`void read_lock()`

when No transaction other than the calling transaction has a write lock on the object.

ensures If the calling transaction already has a read lock on the object, there is no effect; otherwise, it obtains a read lock on the object. Many transactions may simultaneously hold read locks on the same object.

`void write_lock()`

when No transaction other than the calling transaction has a read or write lock on the object.

ensures If the calling transaction already has a write lock on the object, there is no effect; otherwise it obtains a write lock on the object, preventing other transactions from gaining any kind of lock on it.

`Read_lock` and `write_lock` suspend the calling transaction until the requested lock can be granted (i.e., until the `when` condition holds); this may involve waiting for other transactions to complete and release their locks.

The run-time system guarantees that for nested transactions, the following rules are obeyed in obtaining read and write locks:

- A child can get a read lock if all transactions holding write locks are ancestors.
- A child can get a write lock if all transactions holding read or write locks are ancestors.
- When a child commits, locks are inherited by parents.
- When a child aborts, locks are discarded.

The run-time system guarantees transaction-consistency of atomic objects, by performing special abort processing that "undoes" the effects of aborted transactions, including those aborted by crashes. Thus, implementors of atomic types derived from `atomic` need not provide explicit commit or abort operations. Finally, persistence is "inherited" from class `recoverable`; its `pin` and `unpin` operations should be used in the same way as described in Section 20.3.1.

20.3.3 Class Subatomic

Like `atomic`, `subatomic` provides the means for objects of its derived classes to ensure atomicity. While `atomic` provides a quick and convenient way to define new atomic objects, `subatomic` provides primitives to give programmers more detailed control over their objects' synchronization and recovery mechanisms. This control can be used to exploit type-specific properties of objects to permit higher levels of concurrency and more efficient recovery.

A subatomic object must synchronize concurrent accesses at two levels: *short-term* synchronization to ensure that concurrently invoked operations are executed in mutual exclusion, and *long-term* synchronization to ensure that the effects of transactions are serializable. For short-term synchronization, each object derived from class `subatomic` should be thought of as containing a *short-term lock*, much like a monitor lock.

Class Definition

```
class subatomic: public recoverable {
 protected:
   void seize();
   void release();
   void pause();
 public:
 // pin and unpin are public, by inheritance from recoverable.
   virtual void commit(trans_id& tid);
   virtual void abort(trans_tid& tid);
}
```

Operations

`void seize()`
when No transaction holds the short-term lock on the object.
ensures The calling transaction obtains the short-term lock on the object.

`void release()`
requires The calling transaction holds the short-term lock.
ensures The calling transaction relinquishes the short-term lock.

`void pause()`
requires The calling transaction holds the short-term lock.
ensures The calling transaction releases the lock, waits for some duration, and reacquires the lock before returning.

The above operations ensure that only one transaction may hold the short-term lock at a time, thus allowing type implementors to ensure that transactions have mutually exclusive access to subatomic objects. These operations are *protected* members of the `subatomic` class: They are not provided to clients of derived classes, since it would not be useful for clients to call them. Like `pin` and `unpin`, the above operations are usually not called explicitly; instead, Avalon/C++ provides special control structures, the `when` and `whenswitch` statements (Section 20.4.8), which automatically seize, release, and pause on the short-term lock.

Since `commit` and `abort` are C++ virtual operations, classes derived from `subatomic` are allowed (and indeed, expected) to reimplement these operations. They each take a reference to a transaction identifier (TID) as an argument. (See the Avalon class `trans_id` of Section 21.1.2.) The typical effects of these operations are specified as follows:

`void` commit(trans_id& tid)
  requires The transaction "tid" has committed.
  ensures Non-idempotent undo information stored for transactions that have committed with respect to "tid" is discarded.

`void` abort(trans_id& tid)
  requires The transaction "tid" has aborted.
  ensures The effects of every transaction that has committed with respect to "tid" are undone.

Commit operations are called for only transactions that commit at the top-level. Whenever a top-level transaction commits (aborts), the Avalon run-time system calls the `commit` (`abort`) operation of all subatomic objects accessed by that transaction or its descendants. `Abort` operations are also called when nested transactions abort. When `commit` or `abort` is called by the system, the most specific implementation for the object will be called. Thus, `subatomic` allows type-specific commit and abort processing, which is useful and often necessary in implementing user-defined atomic types efficiently. Notice that users need not call `commit` and `abort` explicitly; the system automatically calls them when appropriate.

20.4 Control Structures

20.4.1 Start

statement: ...
  `start` trans-body
trans-body:
  trans-tag *statement* except-clause $_{opt}$
trans-tag:
  `toplevel`
  `transaction`

Sequential transactions are created by means of a `start` statement. The `toplevel` qualifier causes the body of the `start` statement to execute as a new top-level (root) transaction. The `transaction` qualifier causes the body to execute as a subtransaction of the current transaction, if there is one; otherwise, it too begins a new top-level transaction. When the body terminates, the transaction either commits or aborts. Normal completion of the body results in a commit of the transaction. Control flow statements (`return`, `leave`, `break`, and `continue`) that transfer control outside the scope of the transaction normally commit it, unless they state otherwise via an `undo` qualifier (Sections 20.4.4, 20.4.3, 20.4.5). The `undo leave` statement can be used to pass an abort code that can be used as a switch value in an `except` clause (Section 20.4.6). `Goto` statements that transfer control outside a transaction are currently not supported. Future versions of Avalon will prohibit such transfers at compile-time; presently, the result of such a statement is undefined.

20.4.2 Costart

statement: ...
    `costart` { coarms }
coarms:
    coarm coarms$_{opt}$
coarm:
    trans-body

Concurrent transactions and processes are created by means of the `costart` statement. The process executing the `costart` is suspended; it resumes after the `costart` is finished. Execution of the `costart` consists of executing all the coarms concurrently. No guarantee is made about order of execution, or of initialization. Each coarm runs as a separate (lightweight) process. The `toplevel` or `transaction` qualifier indicates whether the coarm is a top-level transaction or subtransaction.

A coarm may terminate without terminating the entire `costart` either by normal completion of its body, or by executing a `leave` statement (Section 20.4.3). A coarm may also terminate by transferring control outside the `costart` statement. If an outside transfer occurs, the following steps take place:

1. All containing statements are terminated to the outermost level of the coarm, at which point the coarm becomes the *controlling* coarm.

2. Every other active coarm is terminated (and aborts if declared as a transaction). The controlling coarm is suspended until all other coarms terminate.

3. The controlling coarm commits or aborts.

4. The entire `costart` terminates. Control flow continues outside the `costart` statement.

20.4.3 Leave

statement: ...
    `leave ;`
    `undo` (*expression*)$_{opt}$ `leave ;`

Executing a `leave` statement terminates the (innermost) transaction in which the `leave` occurs. By itself, `leave` commits the transaction, but with the `undo` qualifier, it aborts the transaction. An unqualified `leave` statement must occur textually within the scope of a transaction, or a compile-time error results. An `undo leave` statement need not occur within the textual scope of a transaction, but it must occur within the dynamic scope of one, or a run-time error will occur. The optional integer *expression* in an `undo leave` statement can be used to pass a value that can be used in the `except` clause of the aborted transaction (see section 20.4.6.) The value of the expression must be greater than zero, but less than or equal to the constant `AVALON_SYS_USER_ABORT_MAX`[2], or a run-time error will result. If the expression can be evaluated at compile-time, this restriction will be enforced then.

20.4.4 Return

statement: ...

`undo`$_{opt}$ `return` *expression*$_{opt}$

The `return` statement terminates execution of the containing operation. If no `undo` qualifier is present, then all containing transactions (if any) terminated by this statement are committed. If the `undo` qualifier is present, then all terminated transactions are aborted. When a `return` statement in a coarm causes control to leave the `costart` statement, active sibling coarms are aborted. The `undo` qualifier can only be used within the lexical scope of a transaction, or a compile-time error will result.

20.4.5 Break and Continue

statement: ...

`undo`$_{opt}$ `break;`

`undo`$_{opt}$ `continue;`

Terminating a cycle of a loop (`while`, `do`, `for`), or a `switch` statement may also terminate one or more transactions within the loop or switch. If no `undo` qualifier is present, then all these terminated transactions (if any) are committed. If the `undo` qualifier is present, then all of the terminated transactions are aborted. When a `break` or `continue` in a coarm causes control to leave the `costart` statement, active sibling coarms are aborted. The `undo` qualifier can only be used within the lexical scope of a transaction, or a compile-time error will result.

20.4.6 Except Clauses

except-clause:

`except` (*identifier*)$_{opt}$ *statement*

An `except` clause, which may be appended to a transaction body, is used to handle different cases of an aborting transaction. After a transaction aborts, it allows some case-specific action to be taken. The *statement* in the clause is expected to be one or more `case` statements. If the transaction was aborted as a result of an `undo (`*expression*`) leave` statement, then the value of the integer *expression* (called the *abort code*) is used to determine which of the cases in *statement* are executed, just as in a `switch` statement. The Avalon run-time system may abort the transaction for a variety of other reasons; in this case, the abort code will be an integer greater then `AVALON_SYS_USER_ABORT_MAX`. If the optional *identifier* is present, then an integer variable of that name will be defined to have the value of the abort code within the scope of the `except` clause. The routine `avalon_abort_code_to_string` may be used to translate system abort codes to strings describing the reason for the abort:

---

[2]Currently equal to $(2^{15}) - 1$.

char* avalon_abort_code_to_string(int ac)
ensures The returned string describes the reason for an underlying system-induced abort according to the integer abort code ac.

20.4.7 Pinning

statement: ...
`pinning` (*pinning*$_{\mathrm{opt}}$) *statement*

The `pinning` statement indicates that *statement* may modify *expression*. *Statement* should not contain a server call or anything else that could cause an abort. An abort inside a pinning statement will cause deadlock. *Expression* must evaluate to be the address of a recoverable object (Section 20.3.1); if it is not provided, `this` will be used. All modifications to recoverable objects should be done within `pinning` statements. If a recoverable object is not "pinned" in memory while it is being modified, it may cease to be recoverable and may have other serious consequences on the run-time system. If the object to be pinned is of variable size, then explicit calls to `pin` and `unpin` are necessary; the `pinning` statement cannot be used.

20.4.8 When

statement: ...
`when` (*expression*) *statement*
`whenswitch` (*expression*) *statement*

The `when` statement provides short-term synchronization for operations on `this`, which must be a subatomic object (Section 20.3.3). After a short-term lock on `this` is obtained, *expression* is evaluated; if true, *statement* is executed. If *expression* evaluates to false, execution pauses, temporarily relinquishing the lock, until it becomes true. The short-term lock is released after *statement* is executed.

The `when` statement can also be used to provide *operation consistency* of implementations of operations of subatomic objects. The operations done in a `when` statement are done atomically: either they all happen or none of them happen. If the implementation of a subatomic operation does all of its work in a `when` statement, operation consistency is guaranteed. `When`s can be nested, but the use of more than one (non-nested) `when` statements in the implementation of an operation (e.g., two `when`s in sequence) is strongly discouraged and will void this guarantee.

As its name suggests, the `whenswitch` statement is a combination of the `when` and `switch` statements. *Expression* and *statement* are handled just as they would be in a `switch` statement, with one difference: the `default` action is to pause execution until the value of *expression* equals the value of one of the `cases`. Since the `default` action is provided, it is illegal to include a `default` in *statement*.

20.5 Transmission of Data

Clients and servers communicate through remote procedure call. The arguments and return values of server member functions are passed by value. The only exception is that reference arguments are passed by value-result (i.e., their values are copied back to the client when the server function

Types	Transmissible	Non-Transmissible
C++ Fundamental	int, short int, *long int unsigned int*, char, float, double, enum, references	pointers, other references
Avalon/C++ Fundamental	bool, trans_id, x_string (character strings)	
C++ Derived (!)	servers, arrays, variants, classes (-), structs (-)	unions, functions, classes (+), structs (+)
Avalon/C++ Derived		recoverable, atomic, subatomic

Italics indicates that transmission of that type is not yet supported by the current implementation.
(!) Provided component types and inherited supertypes, if any, are transmissible.
(+) With union or bitfield component types.
(-) With no union or bitfield component types.

Figure 20.1: Transmissible and Non-Transmissible Types

returns). Pointers to objects are not transmissible. Objects of any other C++ or Avalon fundamental type are transmissible. An array, struct, or variant (Section 21.1.4) is transmissible if and only if all its component types are transmissible. Unions cannot be transmitted, since their actual type is not known at compile time. The chart in Figure 20.1 summarizes which types are transmissible and which are not. Future releases of Avalon/C++ are likely to reduce the restrictions on transmissible types, and allow pointer indirection in structures to be transmitted (by copying) between server and client.

In most cases, users can rely on the Avalon/C++ compiler to determine automatically how to transmit a value as an argument to a server function. In the cases where the compiler fails to recognize a type as transmissible, or when the automatically generated transmission functions are inefficient, the user can define his or her own transmission functions as part of the class definition. Section 22.4.2 explains how this can be accomplished, and should be read on a need-to-know basis only.

Chapter 21

Library

**Jeannette Wing, Maurice Herlihy,
Stewart Clamen, David Detlefs, Karen Kietzke,
Richard Lerner, and Su-Yuen Ling**

21.1 Non-atomic Avalon/C++ Types and Type Generators

21.1.1 Bools

Avalon defines a boolean type, `bool`, with exactly two values, `TRUE` and `FALSE`, and the usual C++ operations on booleans: !, &&, | |, ==, !=, and =.

21.1.2 Transaction Identifiers

The Avalon run-time system guarantees that the serialization order of transactions is the order in which they commit. The `trans_id` class defines operations on Avalon transaction identifiers (TIDs) to permit run-time testing of the transaction serialization order. There is a *trans_id server* at each site that keeps track of all the `trans_ids` at that site and handles sending `trans_ids` to other sites that need them.

Class Definition

```
class trans_id {
public:
 trans_id(int = UNIQUE);
 ~trans_id();
 trans_id&  operator=(trans_id& t);
 bool  operator==(trans_id& t);
 bool  operator<(trans_id& t);
 bool  operator>(trans_id& t);
```

```
    bool done();
    friend bool both(trans_id& t1, trans_id& t2);
    friend bool descendant(trans_id& t1, trans_id& t2);
};
```

Operations

trans_id(), trans_id(UNIQUE)
ensures A dummy subtransaction is created and committed and the subtransaction's identifier is returned to the calling transaction. Note that UNIQUE is the default argument to the trans_id constructor.

trans_id(CURRENT)
ensures Returns the trans_id of an operation's calling transaction.

~trans_id()
ensures The trans_id is deleted.

trans_id& `operator=`(trans_id& t)
modifies `this`
ensures `this` becomes identical to *t*.

bool `operator==`(trans_id& t)
ensures *t1* == *t* evaluates to `TRUE` if *t1* and *t* are equivalent; `FALSE`, otherwise. Note that trans_id's created by different operations within the same transaction are not equivalent.

bool `operator<`(trans_id& t)
ensures If $t1 < t$ evaluates to `TRUE`, then if both *t1* and *t* commit to the top level, *t1* serializes before *t*. If the expression evaluates to `FALSE`, either *t1* serializes after *t*, or *t1* and *t* are incomparable.

bool `operator>`(trans_id& t)
ensures If $t1 > t$ evaluates to `TRUE`, then if both *t1* and *t* commit to the top level, *t1* serializes after *t*. If the expression evaluates to `FALSE`, either *t1* serializes before *t*, or *t1* and *t* are incomparable.

bool done()
ensures Returns `TRUE` if `this` is committed to the top level; `FALSE`, otherwise.

bool both(trans_id& t1, trans_id& t2)
ensures Returns `TRUE` if *t1* and *t2* are committed to their least common ancestor; `FALSE`, otherwise.

bool descendant(trans_id& t1, trans_id& t2)
ensures Returns `TRUE` if *t1* is a descendant of *t2*; `FALSE`, otherwise.

21.1.3 x_string: Transmissible Strings

Strings are normally declared in C++ in two subtly different ways: (1) as a fixed array of chars, whose size is known at compile time, and (2) as a character pointer, terminated by a null character, whose size is dynamic. Whereas strings as arrays of characters can be trivially transmitted (Section 20.5), strings as character pointers cannot because pointers are not transmissible. The built-in Avalon/C++ class, `x_string`, provides for transmission of dynamically allocated strings.

Class Definition

```
struct x_string {
 x_string();
 x_string(x_string& s);
 x_string(char* c);
 ~x_string();
 x_string&  operator=(x_string& s);
 x_string&  operator=(char* c);
 operator char*();
 friend ostream&  operator<<(ostream& o, x_string& s);
 friend istream&  operator >>(istream& i, x_string& s);
 friend bool  operator==(x_string& s1, x_string& s2);
 friend bool  operator!=(x_string& s1, x_string& s2);
};
```

Operations

x_string()
  ensures Returns an empty x_string.

x_string (x_string& s)
  ensures Returns an x_string constructed from *s*.

x_string (char* c)
  ensures Returns an x_string constructed from *c*.

~x_string ()
  ensures The x_string is deleted.

x_string& `operator=` (x_string& s)
  modifies `this`
  ensures `this` becomes equivalent to *s*.

x_string& `operator=` (char* c)
  modifies `this`
  ensures `this` becomes equivalent to *c*.

`operator` char*()
  ensures Coerces an x_string into a character array.

ostream& `operator<<` (ostream& o, x_string& s)
  modifies o
  ensures *s* is written to the output stream *o*.

istream& `operator>>` (istream& i, x_string& s)
  modifies i, s
  ensures *s* is read from the input stream *i*.

bool `operator==` (x_string& s1, x_string& s2)
  ensures Returns `TRUE` if *s*1 and *s*2 contain the same characters in the same order; `FALSE` otherwise. Equality is case-sensitive.

bool `operator!=` (x_string& s1, x_string& s2)

ensures Returns `FALSE` if $s1$ and $s2$ contain the same characters in the same order; `TRUE` otherwise.

Example

```
server nameList {
 public:
  add_member(x_string member_name);
  x_string pick_random_member();
};

main() {
  namelist nl;
  char* name = new char;

  nl.add_member("Stewart");
  name = nl.pick_random_member();
}
```

The constructor from `char*` to `x_string` will be automatically called in the case of calls to `nameList::add_member`. The coercion operator will transform into a `char*` the result value of `nameList::pick_random_member`.

21.1.4 Variants

aggr: ...
`variant`
decl-specifier: ...
variant-specifier
variant-specifier:
class-specifier

Avalon/C++ provides an aggregate data type generator, the `variant`, which is declared similarly to a structure or class. An object of variant type can contain a value from a set of types. A variant differs from a standard C++ structure in that it can be only one of its possible subtypes at any given time; it differs from the standard C++ union type in that it is transmissible (i.e., can be sent as an argument to or returned as a result from a server member function).

A variant is a tagged, discriminated union and is made up of two parts, a *tag* and a *value*. The *tag* field specifies which of the possible subtypes is stored in the *value* field, while the *value* field contains some instance of that specified type.

Operations

A variant declaration of the form:

`variant` VT $\{T_1\ V_1; ... ; T_n\ V_n;\}$;

automatically defines the following operations:

VT `operator=` (VT v)

modifies `this`

ensures Copies *v* into `this`. The operational effect is that `this`'s tag field changes to be *v*'s, and `this`'s value field is assigned *v*'s, using the the assignment operator defined on *v*'s type.

bool `operator==` (VT v)

ensures *v*1 == *v* returns `TRUE` if *v*1 and *v* have the same tag, and their values are equal; `FALSE`, otherwise. Two *void* instances of the same variant type are equal.

bool is_void ()

ensures Returns `TRUE` if *this* has no value, and is of the special null-valued `void` type; `FALSE`, otherwise. The `void` type represents the state of a variant instance prior to its first assignment.

and the following operations for each type T_i and tag V_i:

void set_V_i(T_i val)

modifies `this`

ensures Sets the tag of `this` to V_i and its value to val.

T_i value_V_i()

ensures Returns the value of `this` if its tag is V_i; returns a run-time error otherwise.

bool is_V_i()

ensures Returns `TRUE` if the tag of `this` is V_i; `FALSE`, otherwise.

Restrictions

Variants are a special type of class, and can only be declared and defined at the top level (i.e., variants cannot be nested within declarations or definitions of other types, including variants). Variants cannot have member functions.

Example

```
enum PF {FAIL, PASS};
variant grade {
  char  letter;
  short percentage;
  PF    pass_fail;
};
```

In the above example, `grade::set_letter(char c)` would be defined to set the tag of the variant instance to `char`, and its value to `c`, `bool grade::is_letter()` returns `TRUE` if the tag of the variant instance is `char`, and `FALSE` otherwise, and `char grade::value_letter()` returns the `char` value of the instance if it contains a `char`, and produces a run-time error otherwise. Similar functions for `percentage` and `pass_fail` are provided as well.

21.2 Atomic Types

Each C++ fundamental type, `t`, has a derived Avalon atomic type counterpart, `atomic_t`, where `t` currently can be `int`, `char`, or `float`. There is also an Avalon atomic type for booleans, `atomic_bool`, and for (dynamically-sized) strings, `atomic_string` (Section 21.2.1). Each

Avalon atomic type has the same sets of values and operations as its non-atomic counterpart. No atomic type is transmissible.

21.2.1 Atomic Strings

The `atomic_string` class is intended to be used in a manner similar to a `char*`, as used to represent C++ strings. They should be used as components of atomic and subatomic objects to ensure their recoverability. An `atomic_string` can be of arbitrary, varying length.

Class Definition

```
class atomic_string {
 public:
 atomic_string();
 atomic_string(const char* str);
 atomic_string(atomic_string& astr);
 void operator=(const char* str);
 void operator=(const atomic_string& astr);
 operator char*();
 friend bool  operator==(const atomic_string& astr, const char* str);
 friend bool  operator==(const char* str, const atomic_string& astr);
 friend ostream&   operator<<(ostream& s, atomic_string& astr);
};
```

Operations

atomic_string()
  ensures Creates and returns a new, empty atomic_string.

atomic_string(const char* str)
atomic_string(const atomic_string& astr)
  ensures Creates and returns a new atomic_string, initialized with the value of *str (astr)*.

void operator=(const char* str)
void operator=(const atomic_string& astr)
  modifies this
  ensures Assigns *str (astr)* to an atomic_string, adjusting the amount of storage for the string if necessary.

operator char*()
  ensures Coerces an atomic_string into a “standard” C string, char*, allowing atomic_strings to be used in standard C routines.

bool operator==(const atomic_string& astr, const char* str)
bool operator==(const char* str, const atomic_string& astr)
  ensures Returns TRUE if *astr* and *str* contain the same characters in the same order; FALSE, otherwise. Equality is case-sensitive.

ostream& operator<<(ostream& s, atomic_string& astr)
  modifies s

ensures *astr* is written to the output stream *s*.

Restrictions

The `char*` returned by the coercion operator must only be used as a `const char*` (i.e., the contents of the string should not be changed). The returned `char*` is only valid until the next operation on an `atomic_string`. Thus, multiple coercions may return different `char*` addresses.

Example

```
server foo {
  stable atomic_string a_str;
        ...
};

a_str = "Hello";
if (a_str == "Hello") ...
ulstrcmp (a_str, "hello");
```

`a_str` is defined to be an `atomic_string`. When the server is started, `a_str` is created uninitialized. The first statement assigns the value `"Hello"` to `a_str`. The second statement uses the equality operator. The last statement shows a use of an `atomic_string` where a `char*` is expected; this use is only acceptable if the called routine does not attempt to modify the contents of the `char*` generated by the coercion. See 22.2 for other usage guidelines.

21.3 Catalog Server

The *catalog server* [63] is part of the Avalon run-time system. It maintains a mapping of server attributes to unique server names, and services lookup requests.

When a server starts, it must check in its attributes. The required attributes (type name (`TYPE`), unique name (`UNIQUE_NAME`), and node (`NODE`)), are automatically registered when the server starts. If more attributes are desired, the server programmer can add them in the constructor code. For example, a printer server might add the identity of the printer it is servicing.

Example

```
printserver::printserver (...) {
  CatalogS.set_attribute (_avalon_my_cserver_id, "PRINTER", "iron");
};
```

To avoid boot-strapping problems, Avalon ensures that all clients have a reference to the catalog server, which has a fixed unique name, `CatalogS`. `_avalon_my_cserver_id` is the unique ID returned by the catalog server's `check_in` function.

When a client wants to locate a server, the `locate_server` function (see Section 21.3.1.) calls the catalog operation `name` with a list of attributes and returns an object representing the described server.

Class Definition

```
server catalog {
 public:
  int check_in(attr_list alist);
  void remove(int id);
  void set_attributes(int id, attr_list new_alist);
  void set_attribute(int id, x_string attribute, x_string new_value);
  void remove_attribute(int id, x_string attribute);
  attr_list get_attributes(int id);
  x_string get_attribute(int id, x_string attribute);
  int find(attr_list alist);
  x_string name(attr_list alist);
  void main();
};
```

Operations

int check_in(attr_list alist)
  modifies catalog server
  ensures Creates a new entry in the catalog server with the attributes specified in *alist* and returns a unique ID to be later used to examine and modify the attributes of the new entry.

void remove(int id)
  modifies catalog server
  ensures Deletes the entry of the server identified as *id*.

void set_attributes(int id, attr_list new_alist)
  modifies Attributes of *id*
  ensures Replaces the attributed list of the server entry *id* with the new list *alist*.

void set_attribute(int id, x_string attribute, x_string new_value)
  modifies *attribute's* value
  ensures Replaces the value of *attribute* with *new_value* for the server *id* in the catalog server.

void remove_attribute(int id, x_string attribute)
  modifies Attributes of *id*.
  ensures The set of attributes for *id* no longer contains *attribute*.

attr_list get_attributes(int id)
  ensures Returns a list of attributes for the server *id*.

x_string get_attribute(int id, x_string attribute)
  ensures Returns the value associated with *attribute* for the server *id*.

int find(attr_list alist)
  ensures Returns the unique ID of a server whose attributes match *alist*.

x_string name(attr_list alist)
  ensures Returns the value of the *unique name* attribute of a server whose attributes match *alist*.

void main()
  ensures No effect.

21.3.1 server_root

The `server_root` class handles starting, killing, and locating servers. All servers that use the catalog server (this is the default) implicitly inherit from the `server_root` class.

Class Definition

```
class server_root {
public:
 server_root (const char* commandLine,
      const char* hostName,
      u_int n = 1,
      bool autoRestart = TRUE);
  void kill_server (bool no_restart = FALSE);
  friend server_root& locate_server (char* typename,
                    attr_list* atlist = NULL,
                    int retry = 5);
  friend server_root& get_server (char* uniqueServerName);
};
```

Operations

server_root (const char* commandLine, constchar* hostName, u_int n = 1, bool autoRestart = `TRUE`)

ensures Starts and initializes a server on node *hostName*, using the executable file and arguments given by *commandLine*, and allocating *n* (Camelot) chunks of recoverable storage. *autoRestart* specifies whether or not the server is to be automatically restarted when it is killed. If a full path is not specified, the executable file is found on the user's path, and "/../<*local machine name*>" is prepended to the path for remote servers. The server is started on the local machine if *hostName* is `NULL` or "localhost".

`void` kill_server (bool no_restart = `FALSE`)

modifies catalog server

ensures If *no_restart* is `TRUE` or the `autoRestart` argument to the server's constructor was `FALSE`, kills the server and deletes it's entry from the catalog server; restarts the server otherwise.

server_root& locate_server (char* typename, attr_list attrl==`NULL`, int retry = 5)

requires Each instance of a type of server supplies identifying attributes when it is started.

ensures Returns a reference to a server of type *typename* with attribute values that match those in *attrl*, if such a server exists; returns `NULL` otherwise. For multiple instances of a particular type of server, a specific instance may be selected by listing its unique attributes in *attrl*. `locate_server` will make *retry* attempts to contact the catalog server before giving up. If `retry` is zero, `locate_server` will keep trying until it finds the catalog server.

server_root& get_server (char* unique_server_name)

ensures Returns a reference to a server object for the named server, for those cases where the unique name and location are fixed or otherwise known. This is useful for servers that do not use the catalog server.

Note that since `locate_server` is a generic function, the resulting reference must be coerced to the appropriate type when received.

Example

```
attr_list alist;                   // a new attribute list
alist.push ("PRINTER", "iron"); // CMU printers are named after gems and minerals

printserver& ps = (printserver&) locate_server ("printserver", alist);
if (&ps != NULL)                   // check for NULL return value
  ps.spool (filename);
```

This code obtains a reference to the printserver server object for the printer "iron." If such a server exists, it invokes the server's `spool` operation.

Chapter 22

Guidelines for Programmers

**Jeannette Wing, Maurice Herlihy,
Stewart Clamen, David Detlefs, Karen Kietzke,
Richard Lerner, and Su-Yuen Ling**

22.1 Choosing Identifiers

In most ways, Avalon hides the complexity of its underlying mechanisms. When choosing identifiers, however, it must be remembered that Avalon is a preprocessor that generates code for the underlying system, Camelot, which in turn is built on top of Mach. Fortunately between Mach, Camelot, Avalon, C++, and C, some valid identifiers remain.

Here are some guidelines:

1. Do not begin your identifiers with "`_avalon`". Except for names documented in this report, all identifiers inserted into the generated code by Avalon/C++ begin with this string.

2. Do not end your identifiers with "`_t`". All Camelot types end with "`_t`".

3. Do not end your `struct` names with "`_struct`". Again, Camelot uses these.

4. Beware of uppercase identifiers. There are many constants (#`define`, enums, etc.) and macros which use uppercase identifiers.

22.2 Using and Implementing Avalon Types

This section gives some guidelines for correct usage of the two Avalon built-in classes, `atomic` and `recoverable`. The rules outlined here do not represent the only correct usage, but rather, a that which is "guaranteed" to provide correct results. These rules, of course, do not address standard programming practices such as "*Do not free memory twice.*"

In the Avalon programming model, there are three kinds of programmers:

Client programmers: These people write programs that invoke operations on servers. Their job is to ensure that the operations are called correctly. There is only one rule for client programmers to obey: **All server operation invocations must be made within a transaction.**

Type users/Server programmers: These people define servers, and use built-in or user-defined types. Their job is to declare, construct, and invoke operations properly on instances of these types.

Type implementors: These people define new Avalon types, derived from built-in or other user-defined types. Their job is to define and implement the member functions of the type such that, provided it is used correctly, it will exhibit a desired behavior. Note that, when creating a new Avalon type that uses another Avalon type, the programmer is both a type implementor (of the new type) and a type user (of the used type).

In the next four sections, we give rules for users of recoverable types, users of atomic types, implementors of recoverable types, and finally, implementors of atomic types.

22.2.1 Using a Recoverable Type

Allocation: All Avalon types are allocated from *recoverable memory* (a special heap). This is accomplished through an appropriate constructor provided by either the type implementor or generated by Avalon. Care must still be taken, however, not to force allocation of an Avalon type from other than recoverable memory (such as the stack). Thus:

1. Do not declare variables or functions of an Avalon type. Instead, use references or pointers to Avalon types.

2. Do not `new` an array of Avalon objects (e.g., `new` myatomic[10]).[1]

3. Do not coerce a non-Avalon type to an Avalon type either explicitly or implicitly as shown below. The trouble here is that C++ interprets a constructor of one argument as a coercion from the argument's type to the class type. In the example, C++ converts the `char* "string"` to an `atomic_string` reference by creating a temporary variable on the stack of type `atomic_string`.

```
str = (atomic_string)"string";                    // explicit coercion
atomic_string::atomic_string (char* istr) {...} // constructor taking a char* argument
void afunction (atomic_string& s) {...}         // function expecting an Avalon type
afunction ("string");                            // BAD code!
```

Use: All usage of an Avalon type should be through member functions provided by the type.

22.2.2 Using an Atomic Type

Constructing Atomic Objects: When constructing an atomic object it is important that the creating transaction has exclusive access to the location that will hold the new object. Thus:

[1]This restriction should be temporary.

```
class myatomic : public atomic {
  atomic_int* i;
  ...
  void newint (int);
};

void myatomic::newint (int n) {
  (*this).write_lock();
  pinning () i = new atomic_int (n);
}
```

Before creating the new `atomic_int`, the function obtains exclusive access to the variable (`i`) that will hold the address of the object.

Destroying Atomic Objects: Similarly, when destroying an atomic object, the transaction must have exclusive access to all pointers to the object.

```
class myatomic : public atomic {
  atomic_int* i;
  ...
  void deleteint();
};

void myatomic::deleteint() {
  (*this).write_lock();
  delete i;
  pinning () i = 0;
}
```

22.2.3 Implementing Recoverable Types

Constructors and Destructors: Storage for all Avalon types must be allocated from recoverable memory. Avalon takes care of storage allocation and deallocation for types with constructors that do not make assignments to `this`. See the section **Assignment to This** for special rules concerning the proper use of such assignments.

Any initializations made to the object within a constructor must be within a `pinning` block or between `pin` and `unpin` statements (see the section below on **Modifications**).

Contents: Avalon types may be constructed from only the following types:

1. In-line basetypes such as int, char, bool, etc.,
2. In-line Avalon types,
3. Pointers to Avalon types.
4. In-line arrays and structs of the preceding types.

All fields must be either `private` or `protected`.

Modifications: All modifications must be (dynamically) within a `pinning` block or a `pin/unpin` pair. There must be a matching `unpin` called for each `pin` and `unpin` may not be called without a prior call to a matching `pin`.

Coercions: Care should be taken against providing the user with a pointer directly into recoverable memory. All changes to a recoverable object should occur within only the object's member functions. For example, an `atomic_string` may have an `operator char*` function. This function should `malloc` volatile memory to hold the string rather than return a pointer to the array in recoverable memory. Otherwise, the user could modify it outside a `pinning` block with undefined results. Ideally, C++ would let you define an `operator const char*`, but it does not.

Overriding Member Functions: If the type overrides the default `pin` and `unpin` operations, the new implementations must ensure that, if `pinning`, or `pin` and `unpin` are properly called, all changes will be made within calls to `recoverable::pin` and `recoverable::unpin`.

Assignment to This: C++ allows the programmer to manage the allocation of objects through special code in its constructors, particularly assignments to the variable `this`. Using assignments to `this`, the programmer can, for example, implement variable-sized objects, and objects that are allocated from a programmer maintained free memory store. When using an assignment to `this`, however, care must be taken not to interfere with Avalon's managing of the recoverable heap.

In what follows, we will describe the requirements for

- A simple constructor that explicitly allocates its memory,
- Variable-sized objects, and
- Objects that may be either allocated by the constructor or pre-allocated (such as when the object is an in-line part of a struct).

A simple constructor or destructor could look like this:

```
mytype::mytype() {
  int mysize = sizeof(mytype);
  this = (mytype*) REC_MALLOC (mysize);

  pinning() {
    // Initialize the fields of your type.
  }
}

mytype::~mytype() {
  pinning() {
    // Cleanup the fields of your type.
  }

  REC_FREE(this);
  this = 0;
}
```

In the constructor:

- All execution paths must make an assignment to `this`.
- To allocate memory for the object you must use `REC_MALLOC` rather than `new` or `malloc`. If you have reason to allocate another recoverable object, you may (and should) use `new`. For example:

  ```
  this = (mytype*) new atomic_int;
  ```

- You must compute the size correctly (use `sizeof(your_type)` so you include any space needed by the type's ancestors.)

- No member functions (e.g. `pin` and `unpin`) may be called before the assignment to this.

In the destructor:

- `REC_FREE` (rather than `delete` or `free`) must be used to deallocate the memory.

- After deallocation, `this` must be assigned the value 0 so that the ancestor's destructors will not be called.

- No member functions may be called after the deallocation of `this`.

The most common use of an assignment to `this` is to implement variable-sized objects.[2] Any recoverable type for which `sizeof(yourtype)` may return an incorrect value must either call the functions `pin` and `unpin` with the correct size rather than use the `pinning` statement, or override these functions so that they use the correct size, allowing `pinning` to work properly (as shown here).

```
void mytype::pin(int ignore_size) {
  int size = (*this).object_size;
  recoverable::pin(size);
}

void mytype::unpin(int ignore_size) {
  int size = (*this).object_size;
  recoverable::unpin(size);
}
```

These functions ignore the incorrect size which the `pinning` statement uses when it calls `pin` and `unpin` and instead, uses the real size of the object. This particular example assumes that the constructor stores the allocated size in the field `object_size`.

It is important to remember that, with C++, many uses of a type force the allocation of the object's memory prior to calling its constructor. These uses include: (1) construction of a derived type, (2) allocation of an array of objects of this type, and (3) in-line use of the type in a struct. If a type that handles its own allocation (assignment to `this`) is to be used in these situations, the constructor must be written such that:

1. Memory is allocated only if `this` is 0 upon entering.

2. If `this` is not 0, an assignment to `this` is still executed. The statement `this = this;` will suffice.

3. If memory is allocated, the function `(*this).on_heap` is called after the assignment to `this`. This tells the destructor that the memory was allocated and needs to be deallocated.

[2] The last field of a struct is declared as an array of size 1. When you construct an instance of the type, however, you `REC_MALLOC` as much memory as needed for an array of the desired length (plus the initial fixed size portion of the struct and its ancestors). See [114] for examples.

For example:

```
mytype::mytype() {
  if (this == 0) {
    int mysize = sizeof(mytype) + <whateverelse>;
    this = (mytype*) REC_MALLOC (mysize);
    (*this).on_heap();
  }
  else this = this;

  pinning() {
    // Initialize the fields of your type.
  }
}
```

The destructor would then deallocate the memory only if the constructor allocated it:

```
mytype::mytype() {
  pinning() {
    // Cleanup the fields of your type.
  }

  if ((*this).get_heap_bit() == TRUE) {
    REC_FREE (this);
    this = 0;
  }
}
```

The functions `on_heap` and `get_heap_bit` are protected member functions exported by class `recoverable`. (Since these are used only in the rare instances in which programmers wish to pre-allocate objects, they are not described with the other exported functions.) The function `on_heap` simply sets a bit in the object that is checked by the function `get_heap_bit` (returning `TRUE` if it was set and `FALSE` otherwise).

22.2.4 Implementing an Atomic Type

Types derived from class `atomic` should follow the requirements outlined above. In addition, if the type is expected to exhibit atomic behavior (serializability, transaction-consistency, and persistence), the guidelines in this section should be followed.

Contents: Pointer fields in the type should point only to types that are atomic (derived from `atomic` or `subatomic`), or recoverable provided that concurrent access to a recoverable object is protected by an appropriate lock on the containing atomic object.

Modifications:

1. `read_lock` on the object should be called by a member function prior to accessing any data in the object. `write_lock` should be called prior to any modification to the data. Pointers to non-atomic (recoverable) objects should be treated the same as in-line non-atomic objects in that appropriate locks should be obtained on the enclosing atomic object prior to invoking member functions on the object. No locking is required when accessing atomic components (in-line or pointers) since the objects' member functions should acquire the necessary locks.

2. If it is intended that a non-in-line subcomponent of an object be protected through locks on the containing object, the subcomponent should be derived from `recoverable` rather than `atomic` (i.e., the object is persistent but relies on the caller for concurrency control).

Coercions: An atomic object should not be coerced to a non-atomic type.

Overriding Member Functions: If the type overrides the default locking operations, the new implementations must ensure that, if the type user properly calls `read_lock` or `write_lock`, the appropriate calls to `atomic::read_lock` and `atomic::write_lock` are made.

22.3 Constructing an Avalon Program

22.3.1 Server Programs

A server program should be broken into files as follows:

<server>.h declares the server and includes any type definitions required by the server.

<server>.av provides the implementation for each of the server's member functions and any support functions not declared or included in <server>.h.

<other>.{av,o} provides the implementation for any functions declared in <server>.h other than the server's member functions.

A server program should be linked with the following libraries in order:

```
-lmisc -lava -lgen -lcamlib -lswitches -ltermcap \
-lthreads -lcam -lmach -lm -lnode
```

22.3.2 Client Programs

A client program includes the <server>.h file for each server it uses. Avalon ensures that implementations for the server's member functions are included. It is the responsibility of the programmer, however, to include the implementations of any other functions declared in <server>.h and any files it includes. In general, a client program must be linked with all of the .o files for each server it uses *except for <server>.o*. The libraries needed by the server should also be linked with the client program.

22.3.3 Example Templates

```
---- myserver.h ----
#include <avalon.h>  // always first file included.
#include <mytype.h>  // defines types used by the server.

server myserver {
  mytype mt;
 public:
  myserver (...) : (...);
  ms_op1 (...);
```

```
                ms_op2 (...);
            };
```

```
---- myserver.av ----
#include <myserver.h>

int private_utility () {...}

myserver::myserver (...) {...}
myserver::ms_op1 (...) {... private_utility(); ...}
myserver::ms_op2 (...) {...}
```

```
---- myclient.av ----
#include <myserver.h>
...
```

```
---- mytype.av ----
#include <mytype.h>

mytype::mytype(...) {...}
mytype::mt_op1(...) {...}
mytype::mt_op2(...) {...}
```

```
---- server.make ----
acc -o myserver myserver.o mytype.o \
        -lmisc -lava -lgen -lcamlib \
        -lswitches -ltermcap -lthreads
        -lcam -lmach -lm -lnode
```

```
---- client.make ----
acc -o myclient myclient.o mytype.o \
    -lmisc -lava -lgen -lcamlib \
    -lswitches -ltermcap -lthreads \
    -lcam -lmach -lm -lnode
```

The file `myserver.av` provides only the implementations of the server's member functions and the implementation of `private_utility` which is not defined in `myserver.h` and thus, will not be needed by the client. The object file generated for `myserver.av` is linked in with the server program but not the client program.

The file `mytype.av` provides implementations of the other functions defined in `myserver.h` through the `#include <mytype.h>`. Since the client includes this file, it also needs to be linked with `mytype.o`. Finally, both the client and the server need to be linked with the standard set of libraries needed by Avalon.

22.4 For Experts Only

22.4.1 Undo and Destructors

When a transaction is aborted using an `undo leave (return, break, continue)` statement, control may be transferred directly to the textual end of the transaction using the C `longjmp` mechanism. This transfer of control will exit one or more blocks in which automatic variables may have been initialized by a constructor. These variables may be instances of a class that has a destructor, and, if so, this destructor would normally be called on these variables before the block was exited. When a transaction is aborted, however, these variables will not have destructors called for them. (Note that this is a problem shared with any use of the `setjmp/longjmp` mechanism in C++.)

Normally, the constructor and destructor of a class only modify the object on which they are invoked. This may not be a serious problem; the only result of not calling the destructor is that space on the free store is gradually lost. However, some classes are written so that the constructor and destructor modify some external data structures, and rely on the assumption that both the constructor and the destructor will be called for each object to maintain the integrity of those data structures. These kinds of classes would interact badly with `undo` statements that exit multiple blocks, and should probably be avoided. Future versions of Avalon/C++ may attempt to handle this interaction more gracefully.

22.4.2 User-Defined Transmission Functions

Before any class instance can be actually transmitted to another process, it must be translated into a special, built-in class called `_ava_message`. The _ava_message abstract representation is that of a queue. Objects are removed from the queue in the same order in which they were inserted.

Class Definition

```
class _ava_message {
    _ava_message();
    _ava_message&  operator <<(_ava_message& msg);
    _ava_message&  operator <<(_ava_msgfield& msg);
    _ava_message&  operator >>(_ava_message& msg);
    };
```

Operations

_ava_message()
    ensures Creates and returns a new instance of an _ava_message.

_ava_message& `operator`<<(_ava_message& msg)

_ava_message& `operator`<<(_ava_msgfield& msg)
    ensures Appends *msg* to the end of an _ava_message.

_ava_message& `operator`>>(_ava_message& msg)
    ensures Extracts built-in base types from the message instance. Higher-order types are extracted using the class's *_recompose* function (see below) with the message instance as an argument.

To add user-defined transmission to a user-defined class, you must define two class member functions in order to be able to transmit a class instance:

`operator` _ava_message()
    ensures Coerces a class instance into an _ava_message. It will typically need to call the transmission functions on other types. For each class, _ava_message instances are constructed by calling the class's coercion operator. For each built-in fundamental type (int, chars, floats), a special class, *_ava_msgfield*, with overloaded constructors, is provided. Since enumerations are represented in C++ as integer constants, they should be treated as if they were of type *int* for the purpose of transmission.

`void` _recompose(_ava_message& msg)
    modifies `*this` (Obscure, but true.)
    ensures Constructs a new instance of the class and overwrites the old one with the new.

Figure 22.1 gives a sample of transmission functions for a simple class.

22.4.3 Processes

A coarm of a `costart` statement can also be a regular process[3] with no transaction semantics:

coarm: ...
    `process` *statement*

We make no guarantees as to the semantics to processes that run concurrently with transaction coarms, or processes that run within transactions.

22.4.4 Pragmas

pragma:
    `@pragma@` pragma-list
pragma-list:
    prag
    prag , pragma-list
prag:
    identifier
    identifer = value

A pragma[4] is used to convey information to the compiler. Use of pragmas is an appropriate escape mechanism to Camelot features.

For example, Camelot provides two different kinds of logging, *new-value/old-value* and *new-value only* and mechanisms to support various commit protocols. Different combinations are useful depending on the expected length of a transaction. Thus, we allow the user to specify via a pragma whether a newly started transaction will be "short" or "long." The standard default is "medium" and the following combinations are defined for each value:

Short new-value only logging
    blocking commit protocol (e.g., two-phase commit)

Medium new-value/old-value logging
    blocking commit protocol (e.g., two-phase commit)

Long new-value/old-value logging
    non-blocking commit protocol

Default The default value is "Medium."

Notice that the combination of new-value only logging and a non-blocking commit protocol is not permitted.

Other pragma values will be determined to incorporate other meaningful combinations (e.g., to indicate using a "highly optimized" protocol for a local transaction).

---

[3]Support for `processes` has not yet been implemented and will not be soon.
[4]Support for `pragmas` has not yet been implemented and will not be soon.

```
struct address {
  int     number;
  char    street[40];
  char    appt[8];
  char    city[20];
  char    state[3];
  int     zipcode;
};

class personnel {
  char    name[40];
  int     ss_number;
  float   salary;
  enum {WEEKLY, HOURLY, MONTHLY} payroll_type;
  address home_address;

  personnel(istream);                   // For data entry
  personnel(char* new_name, int new_ss, float new_sal, address new_add);
  operator _ava_message();
  void _recompose(_ava_message&);
};

// Definitions of constructors omitted

personnel:: _ava_message() {
  _ava_message msg = new _ava_message();
  int i;

  // this->name
  for (i = 0; i < 40; i++) *msg << _ava_msgfield(name[i]);

  *msg << _ava_msgfield(ss_number);              // this->ss_number
  *msg << _ava_msgfield(salary);                 // this->salary
  *msg << _ava_msgfield((int) payroll_type);     // this->payroll_type
  *msg << _ava_message(home_address);            // this->home_address

  return (*msg);
}

void personnel _recompose(_ava_message& msg) {
  int i;

  for (i = 0; i < 40; i++) msg >> name[i];        // this->name
  msg >> ss_number;                               // this->ss_number
  msg >> salary;                                  // this->salary
 { int temp; msg >>_temp; payroll_type = temp; }  // this->payroll_type
  home_address._recompose(msg);                   // this->home_address
}
```

Figure 22.1: User-defined Transmission Functions

Restrictions

In general, pragmas are only allowed at any place where the syntax rules allow a declaration. Currently, pragmas are treated exactly as comments, and thus, can appear anywhere a comment can appear. No interpretation of pragma values is currently done.

Part V

Advanced Features

Chapter 23

Common Lisp Interface

David B. McDonald

23.1 Introduction

CMU Common Lisp [78] is an implementation of Common Lisp [110] that runs under Mach. Lisp code has been developed to allow CMU Common Lisp to access Camelot servers as a client process. Although this does not allow access to all the features provided by Camelot, it does allow a Lisp process to do transaction processing by accessing Camelot servers.

Lisp provides an interactive style of programming that makes it simple to interact with a Camelot server. With C code, it is necessary to write it, compile it, link it, and run it – probably iterating as bugs are found. This style tends to have a relatively long turn around time. With Lisp code, it is possible to type in Lisp forms and see the results immediately. This provides an environment that leads to faster development of code. Thus Lisp provides a good testbed for developing user interfaces to information stored in Camelot servers.

CMU Common Lisp supports remote procedure call (RPC), allowing Lisp to communicate with other processes. At the simplest level, Lisp can communicate with Camelot data servers directly using the macro `wrap-server-call`. This allows Lisp to read and/or modify information stored in the data server transactionally. For more complicated transaction processing, it is necessary to make RPC calls to the Camelot Transaction Manager, allowing Lisp to begin, end, and kill transactions. The `do-transaction` macro encapsulates the details of the interaction with the Camelot Transaction Manager. The `server-call` macro can be used within the dynamic scope of `do-transaction` to invoke RPC operations by Camelot servers. Nested transactions may be created by executing multiple `do-transaction` calls.

CMU Common Lisp uses Matchmaker [55], an ancestor of MIG, to generate interfaces to various system components, including an eval server which allows one Lisp process to communicate with other local or remote Lisp processes. Matchmaker has been modified to generate client side code for Lisp from Camelot MIG definition files. When the Lisp code generated in this manner is compiled and loaded into the Lisp system, it is possible for Lisp to make calls to any Camelot server. Currently, it is not possible to have Lisp act as a Camelot server, although Matchmaker does support servers written in Lisp.

This chapter describes how CMU Common Lisp interfaces to Camelot servers. This allows the benefits of having a reliable distributed database accessible from Lisp as well as all the advantages of Lisp's highly interactive style of programming. The following section describes the Lisp level support that is necessary to make it easy for a Lisp programmer to make RPCs to Camelot servers. A few examples of clients written in Lisp are presented. The next section describes a simple Camelot server written in C using the Camelot Library and the Portable Common Loops (PCL) implementation of the Common Lisp Object System (CLOS). This allows a Lisp programmer to easily store and retrieve recoverable objects.

23.2 Accessing Camelot Servers from Lisp

In this section, the variables, functions, and macros necessary to interact with Camelot servers are described.

`camelot:*camelot-timeout*` [*Variable*]

`*camelot-timeout*` specifies the default timeout value in seconds to the RPCs made from Lisp to Camelot servers. This value is used if no timeout value is given to `wrap-server-call` or `server-call`, described below. The initial value of `*camelot-timeout*` is 10 seconds.

`camelot:*camelot-clients-pathname*` [*Variable*]

`*camelot-clients-pathname*` specifies where to look when Lisp needs to load interface routines for the client side of Camelot servers.

`camelot:initialize-application` *name* [*Function*]

This function must be called before any invocation of `do-top-level-transaction` or `do-transaction`. It initializes data structures necessary for Lisp to start, end, and kill transactions through Camelot's Transaction Manager. *Name* should be a string and is used as the name of the application while Lisp is performing Camelot transactions. `initialize-application` returns T if Camelot has been successfully initialized, and NIL otherwise.

`camelot:load-camelot-client` *name* [*Function*]

`load-camelot-client` loads the Lisp code necessary to make RPCs to the Camelot server named *name*. If necessary, Matchmaker is run on the MIG interface specification file, the resulting client code is compiled, and loaded into the currently running Lisp process. Once the client side of the interface code has been loaded into the Lisp process, it is possible to make calls to the Camelot server using either of the macros `wrap-server-call` or `server-call`. Load-camelot-client signals an error if it does not successfully load the code to interface to the server.

`camelot:wrap-server-call` *server function-spec* `&optional` *timeout* [*Macro*]

`wrap-server-call` performs an RPC to *server* as specified by *function-spec*. *server* should be a string which is the name of a Camelot server. *Function-spec* should be a list consisting of the following items: a symbol that names the remote procedure to be invoked and the parameters to be passed to this remote procedure. The optional *timeout* value is the number of seconds to wait for the RPC to return before timing out. This value defaults to the value of the symbol `*camelot-timeout*`. `wrap-server-call` cause the operation to be wrapped in a top-level transaction at the server.

`camelot:server-call` *server function-spec* `&optional` *timeout* [*Macro*]
The macro `server-call` is similar to `wrap-server-call` except that it must be dynamically nested inside a `do-transaction` or `do-top-level-transaction` macro. `server-call` performs an operation (RPC) that is part of a Camelot transaction and is not a transaction in and of itself.

`camelot:do-transaction &body` *code* [*Macro*]
The macro `do-transaction` starts a new transaction. If there is currently no transaction outstanding, it starts a new top-level transaction, otherwise it starts a nested transaction. `do-transaction` allows any number of Lisp forms to be specified as the *code* parameter to execute within this transaction. These forms may use `server-call` to have Camelot servers perform operations on behalf of the transaction. Also, local computations can be done on data and `server-call` can be used to write data back to a server. `do-transaction` returns the status of the transaction as its value. This will be 0 when the transaction is committed successfully and non-zero when the transaction has been aborted.

`camelot:do-transaction-2` *trans-type protocol* `&body` *code* [*Macro*]
`do-transaction-2` is similar to `do-transaction` except that it allows the user to specify explicitly the type of the transaction and commit protocol to use. The argument *trans-type* should be one of the transaction types supported by Camelot. The argument *protocol* may be used to specify the protocol type to use for distributed transactions (two-phased or non-blocking). Currently only two-phased commit is implemented.

`camelot:do-top-level-transaction &body` *code* [*Macro*]
The macro `do-top-level-transaction` is similar to `do-transaction` except that it always starts a new top-level transaction.

`camelot:do-top-level-transaction-2` *trans-type protocol* `&body` *code* [*Macro*]
`do-top-level-transaction-2` is similar to `do-transaction-2` except that it always starts a new top-level transaction.

`camelot:abort-transaction` *status* `&optional` *top-level* [*Macro*]
The macro `abort-transaction` can be used to abort a transaction. The *status* argument should be an integer specifying the reason for the abort. If the optional argument *top-level* is non-nil, then the top-level transaction associated with the current transaction is aborted. Otherwise, just the inner-most nested transaction is aborted.

The above variables, macros, and functions provide sufficient functionality for Lisp to interact with Camelot servers. This means that Lisp can access all the services provided by Camelot servers on the same machine or on remote machines. These macros hide much of the low level detail from a Lisp user, allowing the user to concentrate on the structure of the transactions and the operations to be performed within them.

23.3 Examples

This section describes two examples of the Lisp to Camelot interface. The first example is a simple use of the `wrap-server-call` macro to invoke operations on the Jill server, described in Chapter 5, implements an array of 32 bit integers in shared, recoverable storage. The second example shows `do-transaction` and `server-call` used in a more complicated use of the

Jill server.

Jill defines two remote procedures, one to read the value of a cell given its index and the other to write a new value to a cell given its index and the value to write. These RPCs always return a general return code which specifies whether an operation succeeded and if it failed an indication of why it failed. The remote procedure `jill_read` also returns the value of a cell. In C this is handled by passing a pointer to where the result should be stored. Since Common Lisp allows multiple return values, the generated Lisp code returns multiple values directly.

With the above definitions for the Jill server, it is possible to call the macro `wrap-server-call` as follows to access the Jill server:

```
* (camelot:wrap-server-call "jill" (jill:jill_write 10 20))
0
* (camelot:wrap-server-call "jill" (jill:jill_read 10))
0
20
```

The first call tells the Jill server to write the value 20 into the 10th cell of the recoverable array. It returns the value 0 which signifies that the write succeeded. The second call tells the Jill server to read the value of the 10th cell. This call returns two values: 0 which signifies that the read succeeded and 20 which is the value just written into the 10th cell of the array. Note that these macro calls can be typed to the Lisp read-eval-print loop allowing the user to immediately see the results of the macros.

The following example is more complex since it shows the ability of Lisp to create top-level transactions, to create nested transactions, to abort transactions, to abort top-level transactions, and to make calls to the Jill server that supports a simple shared, recoverable array. This example shows how easy it is to write a simple camelot application that allows a user to interact with a camelot server.

```
(in-package "JACK" :use '("CAMELOT" "LISP"))
(defconstant user-requested-abort 100)
(defvar quit-flag nil)

;;; Initialize camelot and call jill-transaction.
(defun jack ()
  (unless (initialize-camelot "jack")
    (error "Failed to initialize Camelot."))
  (setq quit-flag nil)
  (do ((exit nil))
      (exit T)
    (jill-transaction 1)
    (setq exit quit-flag)
    (format t "Transaction was top level.~%")))

;;; Establish a transaction and execute commands from the user,
;;; allowing  the user to read a location of a shared, recoverable
;;; array; to write a location of a shared, recoverable array; to
;;; commit a transaction; to abort the inner most transaction; to
;;; abort the top-level transaction; to quit; or to begin a new
;;;  nested transaction.
```

```
(defun jill-transaction (level)
  (let* ((status
          (do-transaction
           (do ((exit nil))
               (exit 0)
             (format t "Jack [~D]: " level)
             (let ((cmd (do ((c (read-char) (read-char)))
                            ((alpha-char-p c) c))))
               (case cmd
                 (#\r (do-jill-read))
                 (#\w (do-jill-write))
                 (#\c (setq exit t))
                 (#\a (abort-transaction user-requested-abort))
                 (#\A (abort-transaction user-requested-abort t))
                 (#\q (setq quit-flag t)
                      (abort-transaction user-requested-abort t))
                 (#\b (jill-transaction (1+ level)))
                 (T (format t "Unknown command, ~C.~%" cmd))))))))
    (case status
      (0 (format t "Transaction committed.~%"))
      (#.user-requested-abort
       (format t "Transaction aborted as per request.~%"))
      (t (format t "Transaction aborted, status = ~D.~%" status)))))

;;; Read a location of a shared, recoverable array after reading the
;;; location from the user.
(defun do-jill-read ()
  (format t "Location to read: ")
  (let ((index (read))
        (value (server-call "jill" (jill:jill_read index))))
    (if (= value -1)
        (format t "Location ~D is uninitialized.~%" index)
        (format t "Value at location ~D is ~D.~%"
                index value))))

;;; Write a value to a location of a shared, recoverable array after
;;; reading the location and value from the user.
(defun do-jill-write ()
  (format t "Location to write: ")
  (let ((index (read)))
    (format t "Value to write: ")
    (let ((value (read)))
      (server-call "jill" (jill:jill_write index value))
      (format t "Write succeeded.~%"))))
```

The example above should be straightforward, since the Lisp code supporting access to Camelot servers is hiding most of the details from the user. The example is placed in the `jack` package which uses the `lisp` and `camelot` packages. The `camelot` package contains the support code for accessing Camelot servers. A constant, `user-requested-abort`, defines the status code returned when the user requests to abort a transaction. A global variable, `quit-flag`, is defined that is used to tell the `jack` function when to return control to the Lisp read-eval-print loop.

The function `jack` initializes the data structures necessary to access the Camelot Transaction Manager, so that Lisp can create transactions. Then it goes into a loop calling the function `jill-transaction` which starts a top-level transaction.

The function `jill-transaction` is defined which begins a new transaction. It goes into a loop reading characters from the user and performing the appropriate operation. During a transaction, it can read a value from the shared, recoverable array by calling the function `do-jill-read`. It can write a value to a location in the shared, recoverable array by calling `do-jill-write`. It can can commit the current transaction by exiting the loop within the `do-transaction` with a success status code causing the `do-transaction` to do the work necessary to commit the transaction. It can abort the current transaction, or the top-level transaction. It can quit from the `jack` function by aborting the current transaction. Finally, it can create a new, nested transaction by calling `jill-transaction` recursively. It is not necessary to have a call to `do-transaction` lexically nested within a `do-transaction` to create a nested transaction, it only needs to be dynamically in the scope when the program is run.

The two functions `do-jill-read` and `do-jill-write` read input from the user and read a location or write a value to a location of the shared recoverable array, respectively. Note that these functions are called dynamically within the scope of a `do-transaction` allowing the `server-call` macros to perform the correct operations.

23.4 The Lisp Recoverable Object Server

The macros, functions, and variables described above allows a Lisp user to access Camelot data servers. However, Lisp is restricted to using only the operations provided by these data servers. In many cases this may not provide the Lisp user with a sufficiently rich environment to do all he wants with recoverable objects.

One solution to this problem is to create a Lisp library that is completely equivalent to the Camelot Library. Unfortunately, doing this in the current implementation of CMU Common Lisp would be quite difficult. Currently, Lisp only supports a single thread of control, whereas Camelot data servers may use several so that many different transactions can be served at the same time. Also, Lisp uses most of the address space of an IBM RT PC which would restrict the amount of recoverable storage that can be conveniently mapped into the Lisp address space. Also, Lisp does not provide the locking primitives necessary to make sure that multiple transactions see a consistent state of recoverable storage at all times.

Since there is a C library that makes writing Camelot servers convenient, we created a Lisp Recoverable Object (LRO) server in C that could be accessed through Lisp via the mechanisms described in the previous sections. Building on top of this, several CLOS classes and methods were defined allowing the Lisp user simple access to the LRO server in a normal Lisp style. The rest of this section describes the types of objects supported, a macro for defining records, and several functions that allow a Lisp user to manipulate recoverable objects stored in the LRO server.

23.4.1 Lisp Recoverable Object Server Support

The LRO server supports several functions that perform RPCs to the C server written using the Camelot Library. Lisp code calls the above functions to perform all the operations on recoverable objects. The description of these functions assume that they are called using the `server-call` macro described above. This means that they must be within the scope of a transaction.

`lrec:lrec_malloc` *size* [*Function*]

`Lrec_malloc` accepts an integer which should be the size in bytes of a recoverable object to be allocated. If successful, it returns an integer (**recid**) which is the identifier for a recoverable object. This recid is used in other calls so that various operations can be performed on the object associated with the recid. If unsuccessful, the innermost transaction is aborted with a status code specifying the error.

`lrec:lrec_free` *recid* [*Function*]

`Lrec_free` accepts an integer which should be a recid such as returned by lrec_malloc above and frees the storage associated with that recid. It returns no values. In the case of an error, the innermost transaction is aborted with a status code specifying the error.

`lrec:lrec_rec` *recid offset length* [*Function*]

`Lrec_rec` accepts three arguments: a *recid* as returned by `rec_malloc`, an integer offset in bytes into the object, and an integer length in bytes of the data to return. It returns an alien value which contains the data specified in the request. If unsuccessful, it aborts the innermost transaction with a status code specifying the error.

`lrec:lrec_modify` *recid offset length data* [*Function*]

`Lrec_modify` accepts four arguments: a *recid* as returned by `rec_malloc`, an integer offset in bytes into the object, an integer length in bytes of the data to be modified, and an alien value specifying the data to overwrite the current data with. It returns no values. If unsuccessful, it aborts the innermost transaction with a status code specifying the error.

`lrec:lrec_checkin` *name recid* [*Function*]

`Lrec_checkin` accepts a string and a recid as returned by rec_malloc. The recid is associated with the string, so that `rec_lookup` can be used to return the recid given the string. This functionality is provided so that recoverable objects can be referenced more easily from a different Lisp or across invocations of Lisp. It returns no values. If unsuccessful, it aborts the innermost transaction with a status code specifying the error.

`lrec:lrec_lookup` *name* [*Function*]

`Lrec_lookup` accepts *name* which should be a string and returns the recid checked in by `lrec_checkin`. If unsuccessful, it aborts the innermost transaction with a status code specifying the error.

`lrec:lrec_query` *recid* [*Function*]

`Lrec_query` accepts a recid and returns three values: a string which is the name that has been checked in for the object (the null string if the name has not been checked in), an integer specifying the length of the object in bytes, and an integer that is currently not used and should always be 0. If unsuccessful, it aborts the innermost transaction with a status code specifying the error.

23.4.2 Types supported

The Lisp code supports several different types of recoverable objects, as follows:

:integer A signed 32 bit integer. Lisp integers bigger than 32 bits store only the low order 32 bits.

:single-float A signed 32 bit floating point number.

:double-float A signed 64 bit floating point number.

(:string size) A null terminated string with maximum length of **size**. If the keyword **:string** is used, a null terminated string of length specified by the variable `*default-string-size*` is created.

(:vector size subtype) A vector of length **size** whose elements are of type **subtype**. Subtype can be any of the types described here.

(:pointer subtype) A pointer to an object of type **subtype**. Subtype can be any of the types described here.

record A record type is a structure that contains items of any of the types described here. The macro `define-recoverable-record` is used to create information about a record type.

23.4.3 Accessing recoverable objects in Lisp

This section describes a higher level interface that has been built on top of the primitive Lisp Recoverable Object Server interface described in Section 23.4.1. This interface was derived from the Camelot C library interface. Each of the types described in the previous section has an associated CLOS class. An instance of one of these class objects contains information to access the object stored in the Lisp Recoverable Object Server using the primitive interface described above. Methods and setf methods on instances of these classes allow a Lisp programmer to access recoverable objects in a more standard Lisp way.

`lro:rec-malloc` *type* `&optional` *name* [*Function*]

`rec-malloc` allocates an object in the LRO server and returns a CLOS instance that can be used to access the object. *Type* must be given and specifies the type of the object stored in the LRO server so that Lisp can do the correct coercion to or from corresponding Lisp type when the object is referenced. *Type* is one of the types described above. *Name* is optional and if given should be a string that is associated with the object in the LRO server. This name can be used to connect to the object from the same Lisp or a different Lisp in the future (see `rec-connect` below).

`lro:rec-connect` *name type* [*Function*]

`rec-connect` is used to connect to an object already stored in the LRO server. It returns a CLOS instance that can be used to access the object. *Name* should be the name used in the call to `rec-malloc` when the object was first created. *Type* should be the same type used in the call to `rec-malloc` when the object was created. Note that a different type may be specified, but the result is unpredictable since the LRO server does not maintain type information.

`lro:rec-free` *object* [*Function*]

`rec-free` accepts a CLOS instance as returned by `rec-malloc` or `rec-connect` and frees the associated object in the LRO server. All future references to the object will cause the transaction to abort.

`lro:rec` *ro* [*Function*]

`rec` is used to obtain the value of an object stored in the LRO server. It accepts *ro*, which must be a CLOS instance as returned by `rec-malloc` or `rec-connect`, and returns the value stored in the LRO server. The appropriate Lisp object is returned (e.g., an integer for **:integer**, a short-float for **:single-float**, a lisp string for **:string**, etc.). `rec` has an associated setf form that allows Lisp to store a new value into an object stored in the LRO server.

`lro:rec-svref` *ro i* [*Function*]

`rec-svref` is similar to `rec`, except *ro* must be a CLOS instance returned by `rec-malloc` or `rec-connect` where the specified type was a vector. The *i*'th element of the vector is returned. `rec-svref` has an associated setf form that allows Lisp to store a value into a vector stored in the LRO server.

`lro:define-recoverable-record` *name-opts* `&rest` *slots* [*Macro*]

`define-recoverable-record` defines the structure of a record that can be stored in the LRO server. *name-opts* is either a symbol that specifies the name of the record type, or a list of the form (*name* **:conc-name** *cname*). *name* must be a symbol that specifies the name of the record type. If *cname* is specified, it is used to form the symbols for the slot accessor symbols. Otherwise, the symbol specifying the name of the record type is used to form the slot accessor symbols. The slot accessor symbols are formed by appending this symbol followed by a minus sign to the front of the symbol naming a slot. The *slots* should be a list of the form (slot-name slot-type), where slot-name is a symbol and slot-type is one of the types described above. Note that slot-type can be a symbol that names a previously defined recoverable record. `define-recoverable-record` creates a function named `make-<record-name>`, where `<record-name>` is the name of the record. It also creates an accessor function of the form `<record-name>-<slot-name>` for each of the specified slots. Associated with each accessor function is a setf form that allows that field of the record to be set in the LRO server.

23.4.4 Example of the Lisp Recoverable Object Server

Following is a brief example of the use of the LRO server.

```
* (initialize-application "Lisp")
T
* (setq ri (rec-malloc :integer "ri"))
#<RECOVERABLE-INTEGER >
* (setf (rec ri) 5)
5
* (rec ri)
5
* (setf (rec ri)
        (* (rec ri) (rec ri)))
25
* (rec ri)
25
* (setq rs (rec-malloc '(:string 256) "rs"))
#<RECOVERABLE-STRING >
* (setf (rec rs) "A string")
"A string"
* (rec rs)
"A string"
```

```
* (setq rv (rec-malloc '(:vector 100 :single-float) "rvs"))
#<RECOVERABLE-VECTOR >
* (dotimes (i 100) (setf (rec-svref rv i) i))
NIL
* (rec-svref rv 10)
10.0
* (rec-svref rv 80)
80.0
* (define-recoverable-record foo
    (x :integer)
    (y :single-float)
    (s :string))
FOO-X
* (setq rc (make-foo))
#<RECOVERABLE-RECORD >
* (setf (foo-x rc) 10)
10
* (setf (foo-y rc) 5.0)
5.0
* (setf (foo-s rc) "Another string")
"Another string"
* (foo-x rc)
10
* (foo-y rc)
5.0
* (foo-s rc)
"Another string"
*
```

23.5 Summary and Future Work

This chapter has described a CMU Common Lisp interface to Camelot. Although it does not provide access to the full facilities provided by Camelot, it does provide a convenient interface to Camelot servers. This allows application programmers to quickly and efficiently write Lisp code to make RPCs to Camelot servers that provide access to shared, recoverable storage.

Currently, all access to a shared, recoverable segment must be done through RPC calls to a Camelot server that provides this service. This introduces a significant performance penalty since there is a large amount of work and possible network delays to perform an RPC. A future plan is to allow Lisp to have direct access to a shared, recoverable segment thus removing the need to do RPCs to Camelot servers to access such segments. Once this has been implemented, it should be possible for more than one Lisp process to access efficiently a shared, recoverable segment.

Chapter 24

Strongbox

J. D. Tygar
Bennet S. Yee

24.1 Introduction

This chapter discusses the interfaces to *Strongbox*, a library of routines providing security for Camelot. The goals of Strongbox include enabling programs to run in a secure environment while making only minimal assumptions about the security of the operating system kernel and other system components. These programs are called *self-securing*. We have made the use of Strongbox relatively transparent to programmers who write Camelot servers. This allows existing servers to be retrofitted with security and allows programmers to separate security from other concerns. Strongbox provides facilities to protect the privacy of data and the integrity of data from alteration, and to quickly implement a variety of policy decisions about data protection. The current version of Strongbox does not yet address several secondary concerns including *traffic analysis* of data message exchange, communication by adjusting the use of network resources (the *covert channel* problem), or the availability of system components (the *denial of service* problem). Future versions of our work will address these concerns. However, Strongbox can be used in conjunction with any solution to these secondary concerns.

At the core of Strongbox are new routines for authentication and fingerprinting. End-to-end private key encryption protects the privacy and integrity of messages passed between clients, servers, and other system components. The authentication algorithm provides us with support for a capability based protection system. This authentication system differs from previous authentication and key exchange protocols such as Needham-Shroeder [84] in that it can be proved to not leak any information that would allow eavesdroppers to masquerade as either party.

Integrity of data or program text files is checked in Strongbox by using provably secure cryptographic checksums. These checksums, called *fingerprints*, are computed prior to storing data in the file system and are checked when the system retrieves data. Further details about these algorithms and the assumptions we use can be found in Section 24.7

In Section 24.2, we discuss the design goals of Strongbox – the functional goals for the system, the performance goals, and the design constraints. In Section 24.3, we discuss the overall architecture of Strongbox, giving an overview of how Strongbox works. In Section 24.4, we present cookbook-style instructions on how to convert existing, non-secure Camelot clients and servers to use Strongbox, building on the previous `jack` and `jill` examples given in Chapter 5. In Section 24.5, we discuss the design of the secure loader and the white pages server, key components of Strongbox. In Section 24.6, we present the administrative interface provided by Strongbox to manipulate the access control list and to check data integrity. In Section 24.7 we discuss two basic algorithms used to create self-securing programs. In Section 24.8.3, we give performance figures and code size for these algorithms, and discuss issues of booting Strongbox.

24.2 Design Goals

Security is a pressing problem for distributed systems. Distributed systems exchange data between a variety of users over a variety of sites which may be geographically separated. A user who stores important data on processor A must trust not just processor A but also the processors $B, C, D, \ldots$ with which A communicates. The distributed security problem is difficult, and few major distributed systems attempt to address it. In fact, conventional approaches to computer security are so complex that they actually discourage designers from trying to build a secure distributed system. A software engineer who wishes to build a secure distributed data application finds that he must depend on the security of a distributed database which depends on the security of a distributed file system which depends on the security of a distributed operating system kernel, etc. It is hard to make a distributed system work efficiently without considering security issues. Strongbox addresses the issues by supporting self-securing programs which use only minimal assumptions about the security of the underlying kernel.

24.2.1 Functional Goals

The primary functional goals of Strongbox are to guarantee the integrity and privacy of data handled by it. Section 24.3 shows that the architecture of Strongbox protects data from modification or guarantees that data messages will be protected by end-to-end encryption. In Section 24.7 we show that Strongbox's fingerprinting and authentication algorithms do not leak information.

An additional functional goal of Strongbox is to provide Camelot programmers with a security library that can be easily used in a server or client. We do not expect programmers to master the subtleties of a delicate protection mechanism. We have structured our interface to Camelot so that converting an existing client server to be secure requires only a few simple modifications to the program text. In fact, it is so easy to modify clients and servers that it is possible to write an AWK[1] program which takes as input either an insecure server and a list of server subsystems or an insecure client and computes, as output, a secure server or client.

24.2.2 Performance Goals

Security is typically expensive. It is not uncommon for secure versions of operating systems to run an order of magnitude slower than their insecure counterparts. We view this as completely

[1] AWK is the UNIX utility for pattern scanning and processing. [4]

unacceptable for real applications; we demand that the overhead for security, amortized over all computations, should use no more than 5% of the processor cycles. We have strived to make our security routines extremely fast, and we give our performance figures in Section 24.8.3.

Another measure of effectiveness of security code is the size of the code. The smaller the code is, the less likely it is to contain errors and the easier it is to verify, whether by formal or other methods. Since our library isolates simple points of communication, we believe that we have met those goals.

24.2.3 Constraints

It is necessary to make assumptions when building secure facilities. For example, if the system design calls for use of cryptography one must make the assumption that the cryptosystem used can not be deciphered by unauthorized agents. Since cryptosystems can always be broken by non-deterministic agents (which can simply guess the cleartext and the key and verify that the encryption function holds) if we adopt the practice of considering operations in P as tractable and operations in NP as intractable, then showing a secure cryptosystem exists is equivalent to showing P is different from NP, a well known open (and difficult) problem.

In building Strongbox, we made several assumptions. First, we made a complexity assumption that some problem, such as factoring large integers or inverting DES, is intractable. We assumed that our base operating system, Mach, supports protected address spaces, including virtual address spaces stored on a disk. We assumed that the Disk Manager and the secure loader do not reveal authentication information or fingerprint keys to any other agent. We assumed that application programs use our protection scheme uniformly, and do not explicitly bypass protection mechanisms.[2] We assumed that our algorithms were implemented without error, and that the compiler produced correct object code for them.

We did not address issues of denial of service, covert channel analysis, or of leaking information through traffic analysis of messages. Although we have not explicitly addressed these problems, we conjecture that they may be solved by approaches motivated by the self-securing paradigm. For example, Camelot supports fault tolerance, and Strongbox makes that fault tolerance secure. We believe that the security facility on Camelot could be extended to support protection against denial of service attacks. (For some theoretical contributions to these issues, see [48, 92].) In loosely-coupled distributed systems, covert channel analysis may be considerably simplified by assigning to entire processors just a single security classification. Interactions between security levels will take place over the data network, which is a simpler object to examine for covert channels than the entire distributed operating system. We are continuing to explore approaches such as these in ongoing research.

24.3 Strongbox Architecture

Strongbox is implemented by three components: a secure loader, a library of security routines that secure servers and secure clients use, and a white pages server (a repository of essential authentication information). Figure 24.1 shows the components of the Strongbox and their relationships to each other, and to Mach and Camelot.

[2] The current release of Camelot does not in fact satisfy this, since log values are written in unencrypted log files.

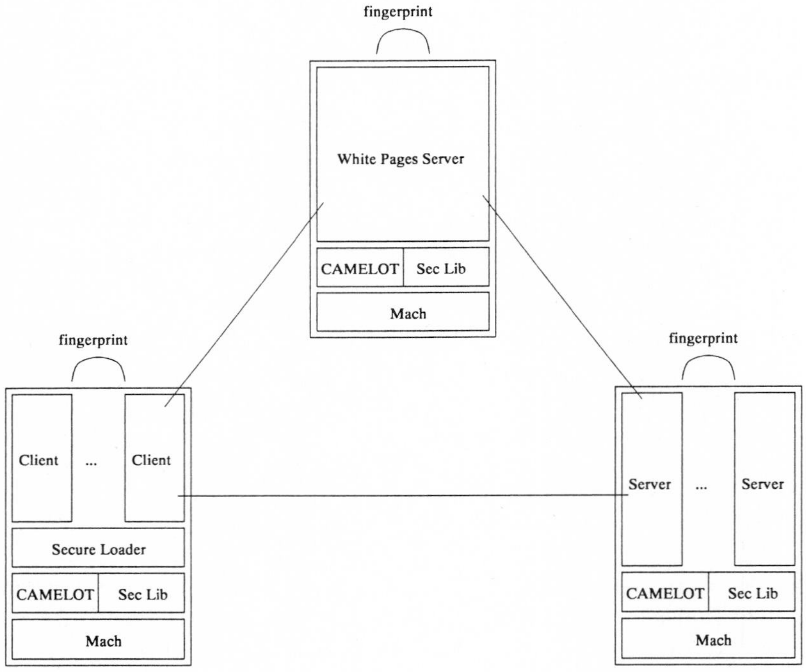

Figure 24.1: Strongbox Architecture

In this figure, we show how Strongbox interacts with Camelot and Mach. Each of the large boxes denote a computer. The client, server, and white pages server is shown as running on different machines; this is not a requirement of Strongbox, however, so they may all reside on the same computer. The lines among the client, server, and white pages server boxes denote communication that may be visible on the communication network. Within each computer, the smaller boxes denote the major software components: the Mach operating system kernel, the basic Camelot servers which uses the Mach services, the Security Library which is used by every secure server or client, the white pages server, the secure loader, and the secure clients and servers. The curved arrows denote the fingerprint operation which verifies that none of the files have been corrupted.

To run a secure task, we access the secure loader. The secure loader first copies the load image of the task into memory, and then verifies that the load image has not been corrupted while it was stored in the file system. The check must be done after the loader reads the image into memory because we do not trust the file system: if we just check the copy of the image in the file, we would be vulnerable to an adversary modifying the image during the timing window between when the loader checks the image and when the loader actually loads it. To do the checking, the secure loader calculates a cryptographic checksum, called a *fingerprint*. After the fingerprint has been verified to be identical to the one computed when the image was last written to the file system, the secure loader initializes the task's address space and starts the task running. We assume that the software development tools are secure against tampering, and that they can be trusted to write out the load image correctly; the software development may be done on a secure, isolated machine or on a machine with tools that have been converted to using Strongbox's fingerprinting. The initialization of the secure task is performed by using Mach's virtual memory primitives to set up the address space and thread control primitives to set up the initial contents of CPU registers.

After the secure task starts running, the secure loader sends it the solution to a randomly generated authentication puzzle which will be used later for authenticating the task to others, and checks in the puzzle (but not the solution) with the white pages server. The secure task has handshaking code as part of its startup sequence which receives the authentication puzzle solution as well as a capability token for accessing the white pages server. Since we know the load image is correct, this startup sequence could not have been tampered with. This communication is completely local to a machine and thus will not appear in any network communication; furthermore, note that the puzzle solution never appears in the file system. (Section 24.7 describes the fingerprinting and authentication algorithms.)

The authentication puzzle/solution pairs are inexpensive to generate; finding a solution when given just the puzzle, however, is extremely difficult (equivalent to factoring a composite number that is the product of two large primes). Checking the validity of a solution is also easy. This work property is analogous to that of password schemes where guessing a randomly generated password is extremely difficult. Unlike conventional password schemes, however, it has the additional benefit that the validity of the puzzle solution can be verified without revealing any information on it (the *zero knowledge* property – see Section 24.7).

For Camelot applications, the secure loader is a separate program that runs directly on Mach. For servers, the secure loader is part of the Disk Manager, which Camelot already uses to load servers. Because the secure loader is incorporated in the Disk Manager, we assume the integrity of the Disk Manager. (See Section 24.8.1 for the discussion on checking the integrity of the secure loader and Disk Manager at boot-time.)

Our protection system is based on capability tokens (capabilities). The capabilities are used as identification tokens which specify the list of operations the holder is allowed to invoke. Most of the time, capabilities are simply used to identify a user in a way that is similar to Andrew tokens [99] – the operations listed under the capability is just those that the user is permitted. In addition, however, they can also be used for *group* identity/membership or for implementing the UNIX real/effective-uid style of access control where applications can have the access rights of multiple parties [20].

The security library routines perform several tasks: they maintain the access control database for the server; they authenticate the identities of the clients and the server; and they maintain the database of capabilities. The protection system uses these capabilities to check access permissions.

The white pages server maintains a list of tasks and the authentication puzzles which identify them. Whenever an agent is to be authenticated, the authenticator asks the white pages server for the authentication puzzle. The white pages server also maintains the fingerprints of the load images for the secure loader.

The white pages server, the secure loader, and Camelot are all started up at boot time before any user tasks can be started. At this time, the secure loader and Camelot generate new authentication puzzles/solutions for themselves, check in the puzzles with the white pages server, and the white pages server registers itself with the Camelot name server. It is possible to substitute a process's name server port so that its port lookups will give erroneous results. Such substitution, however, does not corrupt the servers. To run a client that a server will listen to (i.e., for which servers will find a puzzle when the servers look in the white pages), the client must be started up by the secure loader since the white pages server will accept new entries only from the secure loader.

A typical session is as follows: The client wishes to invoke a remote operation by a server to which it has not authenticated itself. It uses a secure remote procedure call (RPC) handling macro, which attempts the operation. The operation fails, returning `CAP_MECH_PERMISSION_DENIED`, at which point the macro looks up the server's authentication puzzle with the white pages server and authenticates the client and the server identities to each other. At the server side, the protection system also looks up the client's puzzle with the white pages server as part of the authentication. After authentication completes, all traffic between clients and servers are encrypted.

Depending on the security of the paging devices, external memory managers may be used to protect the integrity of memory by fingerprinting pages as they go onto disk and verifying the fingerprint as they come off. To protect against leaking information as well as integrity, encryption is required.

24.3.1 Security Library Architecture

The security library provides client-server authentication, capability-based access to a server, and access control bookkeeping routines used in a server. We have designed the security library such that typical usage is very similar to that of the standard, non-secure Camelot Library.

In the Camelot Library, the `SERVER_CALL` macros handle the transactional bookkeeping for invoking an RPC. For secure communication between the client and the server, the various versions of Camelot's `SERVER_CALL` macros are supplanted by versions that are prefixed by `SEC_`. (For example, `SERVER_CALL` becomes `SEC_SERVER_CALL`.) The `SEC_` macros automatically perform authentication and provide the client with a capability to the server. The capability is used transparently; the client program need not reference it at all. The secure macros automatically re-authenticate after server failure, thereby allowing transparent recovery for most applications.

The client may elect to perform explicit authentication instead of using the automatic authentication provided. This gives the client control over the management of the capabilities: a client may authenticate once as itself and another time as a member of a privileged group. By using versions of the `SERVER_CALL` macros prefixed by `SEC_CAP_`, a client may specify the capability to be used with the server. This gives a client the ability to use the access rights of two or more agents. The details of authenticated `SERVER_CALLS` are described in the following section.

Each server has two databases that are maintained by the protection routines. The first, stored in recoverable storage, contains a mapping from user names to permissions. When a client authenticates successfully, the protection routines construct a new capability based on the permissions in this database. The protection routines return this new capability to the client and also enter it into the second database. The permissions in the first database are changed via special capability management routines the access to which is controlled in the same way as any other RPC. The second database, stored only in virtual memory, maps capabilities to permissions and is consulted each time an RPC request arrives to check that the client has permissions to invoke the requested operation. The authentication RPCs, of course, are exempt from the permissions check. The reason that there are two databases is to minimize the amount of memory leaked due to stale capabilities: since most capabilities never expire, we keep the capabilities in non-recoverable memory to prevent memory leak from capabilities to which references has been lost by all clients. Clients that survive a server crash must reauthenticate in order to regain their privileges.

It is easy to convert an existing non-secure server to be secure because only the initialization code and the argument declarations for the operation procedures are affected. Strongbox provides a separate, high level message demultiplexing procedure that performs the permission check. Decryption is performed here also. The appropriate key is inferred from the capability argument's index field, which is not encrypted. The demultiplexing procedure then hands the messages over to the individual subsystems' (lower level) demultiplexing procedures which unpack the arguments and make the actual server-side procedure call. This service is performed for all RPCs except those in the authentication protocol. By performing the permission check at this point, we eliminate the need to modify the service procedures' body, and reduce the work required to make a server secure.

24.4 Converting Camelot Clients and Servers to be Secure

This section is a cookbook guide to the conversion of Camelot clients and servers to use Strongbox. To illustrate the changes necessary, we will modify the Jack and Jill example given in 5. We first describe the changes to the clients, using Jack as an example, and then the changes to servers, using Jill as an example.

The required changes are minimal and a simple AWK program [4] could be used to automatically convert existing programs. Typically, however, attention should be given to the security policy that is desired and further changes may be necessary.

24.4.1 Changes to Clients

In order to make clients secure, several macros called inside Camelot clients must be replaced by their secure counterparts. These macros are defined in the Camelot include file `strongbox.h`. This file is included in secure servers' header files automatically generated by the Message Interface Generator (MIG). Here are instructions for converting clients to be secure:

1. Non-secure Camelot clients call `INITIALIZE_APPLICATION(`*name*`)` to register the client with the Transaction Manager. `SEC_INITIALIZE_APPLICATION(`*name*`)` replaces this macro in secure clients. This macro initializes the data structures used for authentication and for maintaining a secure channel once authenticated. If the client was not loaded by the secure loader, this macro aborts the execution of the client. For example, to make the Jack application secure, we would replace the code fragment in `jack.c`

```
if(!INITIALIZE_APPLICATION("Jack"))
{
```

```
        printf("Camelot is not running on this node!\n");
        exit(1);
    }
```

by

```
    if(!SEC_INITIALIZE_APPLICATION("Jack"))
    {
        printf("Both Camelot and the White Pages\n");
        printf("server must be running on this node!\n");
        exit(1);
    }
```

2. Non-secure clients call servers using SERVER_CALL, and SERVER_CALL_2. In secure clients the calls are replaced by SEC_SERVER_CALL, and SEC_SERVER_CALL_2. The secure versions of the server call macros perform necessary authentication steps. The first time a client calls a server with one of the secure macros, it looks up in the white pages the entry defining the server's authentication puzzle. (Note that the connection from the client to the white pages is guaranteed to be secure since it is an authenticated connection. The initial puzzle associated with the white pages is loaded into the client by the secure loader.) The macros ARGS and NOARGS pass certain parameters from the client to the server. In secure clients, these macros are replaced by SEC_ARGS and SEC_NOARGS respectively, which also pass secure parameter information such as the capabilities possessed by the client. For example, to make Jack secure, we would replace the code fragments in `jack.c`

```
SERVER_CALL("Jill", jill_read(ARGS index, &value));
    ...
SERVER_CALL("Jill", jill_write(ARGS index, value));
```

by

```
SEC_SERVER_CALL("Jill", jill_read(SEC_ARGS index, &value));
    ...
SEC_SERVER_CALL("Jill", jill_write(SEC_ARGS index, value));
```

24.4.2 Changes to Servers

Converting Camelot servers to be secure is just as simple as the client conversion. Once again we replace server macros with their secure counterparts. We also add some new macros and specify information to specify protected entry points. Here are the modifications necessary to make servers secure:

1. To include appropriate Strongbox macro definitions, in the `.defs` file insert after `#include <camelot.defs>` the line `#include <strongbox.defs>`. The modified RPC definition file should be compiled by MIG with the `-s` flag, i.e., `mig -s jill.defs`.

2. Make the macro call SEC_DECLARATIONS the first entry of the recoverable storage declarations. This allocates storage for Strongbox internal variables.[3] For example, to make Jill secure, we would replace the code fragment in jill_globals.h

```
BEGIN_RECOVERABLE_DECLARATIONS
    struct jill_array_struct
    {
        int data[ARRAY_SIZE];
    } jill_array;
END_RECOVERABLE_DECLARATIONS
```

by

```
BEGIN_RECOVERABLE_DECLARATIONS
    SEC_DECLARATIONS;
    struct jill_array_struct
    {
        int data[ARRAY_SIZE];
    } jill_array;
END_RECOVERABLE_DECLARATIONS
```

3. The security system must know the location of all protected entry points in a server. The macro SEC_SYMTAB(subsys) generates the appropriate information to manage the entry points defined by the MIG subsystem *subsys*. The SEC_SYMTAB(subsys) declarations should all appear consecutively immediately before SEC_INITIALIZE_SERVER, which replaces INITIALIZE_SERVER. The SEC_INITIALIZE_SERVER macro terminates the list of entry points and calls the server initialization code. For example, the Jill server has only one system: "jill", and to make Jill secure, we would replace the code fragment in jill.c

```
INITIALIZE_SERVER(jill_init, FALSE, "Jill");
```

by

```
SEC_SYMTAB(jill);
SEC_INITIALIZE_SERVER(jill_init, FALSE, "sJill");
```

4. The first initialization transaction executed by a server is a special initialization procedure. This procedure is the first argument to INITIALIZE_SERVER. To initialize access control specific Strongbox data, the macro SEC_INIT must be called as part of this initialization procedure. For example, to make Jill secure, we would replace the code fragment in jill.c

```
int jill_init()
BEGIN("jill_init")
    struct jill_array_struct temp;
    int i;
```

[3] SEC_DECLARATIONS also generates some padding between server data and Strongbox data. When programmers modify servers so that new recoverable storage is used, this padding may be adjusted to retain recoverability of previously stored objects. If the size of the recoverable storage is changed, use SEC_DECLARATIONS_PAD(*pad*) where *pad* is the size of the desired padding in words. *pad* typically is SEC_DECLARATIONS_DEFAULT_PADDING - delta, where delta is the change in the size of the recoverable storage. The default value of SEC_DECLARATIONS_DEFAULT_PADDING is 1024 bytes, so this can only accommodate relatively small size changes.

```
    /* Load up a temporary copy of the array with -1's */
    for (i=0; i < ARRAY_SIZE; i++)
        temp.data[i] = -1;

    MODIFY(REC(jill_array), temp);
END
```

by

```
int jill_init()
BEGIN("jill_init")
    struct jill_array_struct temp;
    int i;

    /* Load up a temporary copy of the array with -1's */
    for (i=0; i < ARRAY_SIZE; i++)
        temp.data[i] = -1;

    MODIFY(REC(jill_array), temp);
    SEC_INIT;
END
```

5. In Camelot, the macro START_SERVER causes the server to go into a state in which it may accept requests and process transactions. In the secure version of servers, this macro is replaced by SEC_START_SERVER, which starts the server so that it can only accept secure server calls. If START_SERVER_2 is used, it is replaced with SEC_START_SERVER_2. For example, to make Jill secure, we would replace the code fragment in `jill.c`

```
START_SERVER(jill_server, 10, 0);
```

by

```
SEC_START_SERVER(jill_server, 10, 0);
```

6. In secure servers operation procedures are passed the capability used by the client to access the entry point of the server. This capability can be used for tracing, auditing, and more elaborate protection schemes. It is passed as the first argument, of type `cap_t`, to every operation procedure. For example, to make Jill secure, we would replace the code fragments in `jill.c`

```
void op_jill_read(index, valPtr)
int index, *valPtr;
{
        ...
}

void op_jill_write(index, value)
int index, value;
{
        ...
}
```

by

```
void op_jill_read(cap, index, valPtr)
cap_t       cap;
int index, *valPtr;
{
        ...
}

void op_jill_write(cap, index, value)
cap_t       cap;
int index, value;
{
        ...
}
```

24.5 Secure Loader and White Pages Server

24.5.1 Secure Loader

The secure loader is a trusted server that invokes secure Camelot clients for the user. It loads the executable image and starts the client after checking that the client has not been corrupted. Then, it obtains a random puzzle solution from the white pages for the client when it registers the client with the white pages. It also initializes the client with the puzzle associated with the white pages so the client can make a secure server call to the white pages. At the same time, it also passes a secure random seed to the client's pseudo-random number generator. Finally, it gives a default capability to the client for using the white pages server to perform puzzle lookups. The puzzle solution, the random seed, and the initial capability is sent to the client via a RPC using the *bootstrap* port. Since both the secure loader and the newly started secure client are resident on the same machine, the content of these messages will never be visible on any networks. The Disk Manager plays a corresponding role for servers.

24.5.2 White Pages

As we will discuss in Section 24.7, the security of Strongbox depends on a constant which is the product of two large primes. Successfully breaking Strongbox's authentication routine is algorithmically equivalent to factoring the constant. We have provided a default composite number in the Camelot release. If this value should be changed for a particular installation, a new number can be generated by running the `NewSecrets` program, also included with the Camelot release. `NewSecrets` generates new header files containing a new composite number and secret factors with which Strongbox is built. Of course, binaries compiled with one set of constants are incompatible with those compiled with another set of numbers.

24.6 Interfaces

The key idea here is that every RPC message is prepended with a capability which is checked prior to invoking the operation at the server. The messages are also encrypted, so that somebody listening on the network will not have access to the data (excluding port names).[4] The macros mentioned in Section 24.4 performs the prepending, and the Strongbox demultiplexing procedure transparently performs the access check. The first argument of every operation routine in a secure server is the capability used by the client; the routines may use this argument to perform finer grain access checks.

24.6.1 Client/Server Interfaces

In addition to the normal service remote operations that a server provides, each secure server has other remote procedures that are defined by Strongbox. Strongbox's capability subsystem exports remote operations to perform access control administration such as adding a new user, giving a user the rights to invoke a remote operation, or removing a user's rights. Since the Strongbox's remote operations are treated in the same manner as the service remote operations, an administrator may give administrative privileges to a trusted user as well.

There are currently three remote routines which allow an administrative login to manipulate the access permissions list.

```
void op_CapMech_AddUser(authCap,userName)
        cap_t                           authCap;
        cap_symbolic_user_name_t        userName;
```

`authCap` the invoking user's capability (administrator).
`userName` the symbolic name of the user who is being added.

```
void op_CapMech_Permit(authCap,userName,operation)
        cap_t                           authCap;
        cap_symbolic_user_name_t        userName;
        cap_operation_name_t            operation;
```

`authCap` the invoking user's capability (administrator).
`userName` the symbolic name of the user who is being permitted to invoke the operation.
`operation` the name of the operation which the user `userName` is now allowed to invoke.

---

[4]The prepended capability is in two parts, an index and a secret random number. The index is not encrypted so that the receiver can determine which key to use to decrypt the rest of the message; the random number is encrypted along with the rest of the data, so the capability is not leaked.

```
void op_CapMech_Unpermit(authCap,userName,operation)
        cap_t                                 authCap;
        cap_symbolic_user_name_t              userName;
        cap_operation_name_t                  operation;
```

`authCap` the invoking user's capability (administrator).

`userName` the symbolic name of the user who is being unpermitted to invoke the operation.

`operation` the name of the operation which the user `userName` is now disallowed from invoking.

The operation `CapMech_AddUser` adds a new user; `CapMech_Permit` gives a user permission to invoke the named operation; and `CapMech_Unpermit` removes the user's permission to invoke the operation. Note that these operations are treated in the same fashion as service remote operations, so an administrator may give permission to invoke `CapMech_Unpermit`, for example, to security personnel.

The administrator login is `local1` by default. This should be changed as appropriate for the installation.

24.6.2 White Pages Interface

```
void op_Wp_Fp_Check(cap, fn, data, size, ok)
cap_t              cap;
sec_filename_t     fn;
char               *data;    /* OOL */
vm_offset_t        size;
int                *ok;
```

`cap` the capability of the invoker.

`fn` the name of the file whose data is being checked.

`data` the out-of-line transmitted data which is the contents of the file.

`size` the size of data transmitted.

`ok` the return area for whether the data fingerprints correctly.

This routine allow users to check the fingerprints of data. The argument *data* contains the contents of the file `fn`. The white pages returns in `*ok` a nonzero if the data's fingerprint matches the stored fingerprint.

24.7 Security Algorithms

24.7.1 Zero Knowledge Authentication

Authentication is at the heart of the security system for any loosely-coupled distributed operating system. For notational convenience, we refer to a client denoted *A* and a server denoted *B*. *A* and *B* may reside on different processors. A and B must prove their identities. The problem is made more difficult since A and B must typically accomplish this by exchanging messages over a potentially vulnerable data network. Since messages transmitted over the network may be intercepted by a third party, C, A and B must find a way to prove their identities without revealing information which would allow C to successfully feign an identity as A or as B.

How well do existing authentication methods accomplish this goal? In practice, not very well. For example, Rivest, Shamir, and Adleman proposed an authentication method based on the RSA public-key signature methods [95]. In their protocol, values are encrypted according to a public-key encryption function $E(m) = m^e \bmod n$, where m is a message, e is an encryption key, and n is the product of two large primes p and q. Decryption is accomplished through the function $D(c) = c^d \bmod n$, where c is the ciphertext, d is chosen so that $ed = 1 \bmod (p-1)(q-1)$. It is true there is no published method for quickly decrypting messages given only e and n, and not the factorization of n. However, this method leaks information. For example, Lipton points out that the well known Legendre function L satisfies the relation $L(m, n) = L(E(m), n)$ [68]. Indeed, the problem is much worse than this. Alexi, Chor, Goldreich, and Schnorr recently proved that if an adversary can, $50\% + \epsilon$ of the time, find the low order bit of m given $E(m)$, the adversary can invert arbitrary RSA encryptions [5, 19]. A corollary to this result is that the usual query-response methods for encryption, such as the family of protocols described in [79], an adversary can emulate another agent in the system after engaging in $O((\log n)^2)$ authentications.

Needham and Schroeder have suggested an authentication method which uses private-key cryptographic methods [84]. Needham and Schroeder's work presupposes on a secure key distribution method and a private key cryptosystem. Recent work by Luby and Rackoff suggests that authentication methods depending on DES are vulnerable to a "low-bit" attack similar to the one mentioned above for the RSA cryptosystem [76]. For example, the first author has found a method to subvert the authentication scheme used by the Andrew File System VICE [100], which uses a strategy similar to Needham and Schroeder's.

To give users confidence in a system, we would like to be able to prove that an authentication method does not leak information. Several researchers have independently proposed protocols, termed *zero-knowledge protocols*, which satisfy this constraint given the complexity assumption that P $\neq$ NP [37, 32]. To get a flavor of the type of argument used, we summarize a zero knowledge protocol below for A proving to B that some graph G with n vertices known to both A and B contains a k-clique (that is, a set Q of k vertices such that between every two vertices in Q there exists an edge). (This version of the proof is due to M. Blum.) Let G be a graph with n vertices be known to both A and B. Suppose that A knows a k-clique in G. Since the problem of finding a k-clique in an arbitrary graph is NP-complete, B can not in general find the k-clique. This protocol will allow A to prove to B that G has a k-clique without revealing any information about the vertices in Q.

1. A secretly labels each vertex of G with random unique integer from 1 to n.

2. A prepares $\frac{n(n-1)}{2}$ envelopes labeled uniquely with a pair of integers $\langle i, j \rangle, i < j$. A puts "Yes" in the envelope labeled $\langle i, j \rangle$ if an edge exist between the vertices labeled i and j, and "No" otherwise.

3. A seals the envelopes and presents them to B. B flips a coin and reports its value to A. If it is heads, A must open all the envelopes and show the numbering of the vertices of G. B then verifies that the descriptions are correct. On the other hand, if B gets tails, A must then open

just the envelopes which are labeled $\langle i, j \rangle$ where i and j belong to Q. B then verifies that all envelopes contain "Yes".

4. The above protocol is repeated t times (with an independent random numbering assigned each time in step 1). If A successfully responds to B's queries, the probability that A does know know a proof is 2^{-t}.

It is clear that if A knows a k-clique and correctly follows the above protocol, A will succeed. On the other hand, suppose C is trying to masquerade as A. Since C does not know a k-clique, C has two choices: it can correctly perform step 2 (in which case it is caught whenever B gets tails) or it can put false values in the envelopes (in which case it is caught whenever B gets heads). Hence in each of the t iterations of the protocol the probability that C's ignorance is revealed is 1/2. After t iterations, C will be caught with probability $1 - 2^{-t}$. Finally, notice that B does not get any information about the location of the clique. If B could find information about the clique from the above protocol, it could generate the same information by flipping a coin and generating a random numbering of the graph when it gets heads and a random numbering of a complete graph on k vertices when it gets tails.

Notice that since any problem lying in NP can be reduced to the NP-complete problem k-clique [57], A could use this protocol to prove to B that it had a proof or disproof of, for example, Fermat's Last Theorem. At the end of this protocol, B would be convinced that A did in fact have a proof or disproof without having any idea which way the problem was resolved, much less any idea of the technique used to solve the problem. Certainly, this protocol could be used to generate authentication proofs: A would publish the graph G in a public white pages. To prove its identity, A would give a zero-knowledge proof of the existence of a k-clique in the graph.

In practice, this protocol would not work well. First, A would have to find a graph G in which it was computationally intractable to find a k-clique. While it is true that our complexity hypothesis guarantees that such graphs must exist, most random graphs with k-cliques can have those cliques found through efficient heuristics [34]. Second, A and B would have to develop a good cryptographic scheme for implementing "envelope exchange". For even a modest security level the size of data involved here is on the order of 10^{200} bytes. Using the highest bandwidth transmission techniques available today, execution of this protocol would exceed the time remaining before the heat death of the universe.

24.7.2 Our protocol

In research described in [118], we have developed a family of zero-knowledge protocols which are efficient for real use in applications. Our timing figures are given in Section 24.8.3. Below we give a simplified (and slightly less efficient) version of the protocol.

The protocol we use can depend on one of two complexity assumptions: that factoring large integers can not be done in polynomial time, or that it is hard to invert messages encrypted by random keys under DES. Other similar complexity assumptions may be used instead. The protocol described below depends on the complexity of factoring integers. We recall the following lemma by Rabin [89]: *If there exists a polynomial time algorithm for finding square roots modulo $n = pq$, where p and q are large primes, then we can factor pq in polynomial time.* Rabin observed that we can take a random integer r between 1 and $pq - 1$; check that $\mathrm{GCD}(r, n) \neq 1$ (if this value is p or q, then we have factored n). Calculate $x = r^2 \bmod n$ and find a square root s, so that $s^2 = x = r^2 \bmod n$;

a simple number-theoretic argument demonstrates that x has four square roots modulo n, including r and $-r$. Since r is chosen at random, there is a 50% chance that $s \neq \pm r \bmod n$. If $s = \pm r \bmod n$, then we can pick a new r and repeat the algorithm. If $s \neq \pm r \bmod n$, then it is the case that $\mathrm{GCD}(r + s. n) = p$ or q. Hence finding square roots is equivalent to factoring.

In this protocol, we assume that the system manager publishes a product of two large primes $n = pq$, keeping the factorization secret. This n can be used for all authentication protocols, and no one need ever know its factorization. To initialize its puzzle, A picks a random r and publishes $x = r^2$ in the white pages. A will prove it knows a square root of x without revealing any information about the value.

Here is the protocol:

1. A computes t temporary random values, $v_1. v_2, \ldots, v_t$, where each v_i satisfies $1 \leq v_i \leq pq - 1$. A sends to B the vector $< v_1^2 \bmod n. v_2^2 \bmod n, \ldots, v_t^2 \bmod n >$.

2. B flips t independent coins and send back a vector of t random bits $< b_1, \ldots, b_t >$ to A.

3. For $1 \leq i \leq t$, A computes

$$z_i = \begin{cases} v_i & \text{if } b_i = 0 \\ rv_i \bmod n & \text{otherwise} \end{cases}$$

   A transmits the vector $< z_1. \ldots. z_t >$.

4. B verifies that for $1 \leq i \leq t$, that

$$z_i^2 = \begin{cases} v_i^2 \bmod n & \text{if } b_i = 0 \\ xv_i^2 \bmod n & \text{otherwise} \end{cases}$$

   If the equalities hold, A has authenticated its identity to B with probability $1 - 2^t$.

Once again note that if A knows a value r such that $r^2 = x \bmod n$, then it can easily follow the above protocol. Suppose C is trying to masquerade as A. Since C doesn't know such a value r, it can not know both v_i) and $rv_i \bmod n$, since $r = rv_i(v_i)^{-1} \bmod n$. Finally, all that B sees is a series of random values of the form $< z_i. z_i^2 \bmod n >$. If B could find any information about r from the above protocol, it could do so by generating a set of t random values and squaring them modulo n, and thus factoring n.

The above protocol uses only an expected $3t$ multiplications to generate security of $1 - 2^{-t}$. Our improved protocol uses only expected $1.5t$ multiplications to achieve the same level of security.

24.7.3 Self-securing programs

As mentioned above, our algorithm presumes communication networks which are potentially vulnerable. A and B need to use methods to protect the privacy and integrity of their data. If we extend an authentication algorithm to also support key exchange, A and B can transmit their messages though highly secure private-key encryption methods. We have adapted our algorithms to also perform this operation – A can send a temporary key e_A and B can send a temporary key e_B. Both parties can then use a trusted private key encryption method, such as DES with the key $e = e_A \oplus e_B$, where $\oplus$ is bit-wise exclusive-or. Hence, if A and B have protected address spaces, we can make all messages transmitted in the system public, since no observer can find the encryption key used. Also, sending messages encrypted by the key removes the need to re-authenticated until either party decides to establish a new temporary key. This approach yields a *self-securing program* which requires only a minimal amount of security in our base operating system. See [118] for details of our key-exchange algorithm.

Indeed, our algorithm obviates the need to ever use public key cryptography. If A wishes to transmit a message to B without having shared private key, A can simply authenticate itself to B exchanging a temporary encryption key. All further communications are protected by encryption. The signature functions of public key cryptography can be performed by the fingerprinting algorithm given below.

24.7.4 Fingerprinting

Karp and Rabin introduced an algorithm which computes a *cryptographic checksum* [58]. Their algorithm takes a bit string s of arbitrary length and secret key k of d bits (where $d - 1$ is prime) and returns a *fingerprint* sequence of $d - 1$ bits $\phi_k(s)$. Each key k defines a fingerprint function, and if the keys are chosen with uniform distribution, the family of fingerprint functions ϕ_k can be viewed as a provably good random hash function in the style of [17]. Without the secret key, computing a fingerprint given a string of bits is intractable. On the other hand, if the secret key is known, it is easy to compute the fingerprint.

Given the fingerprint algorithm, the problem of protecting the integrity of data from alteration becomes much simpler. For example, to protect a file F, we could store $< F, \phi_k(F) >$. If an adversary attempts to alter the file by replacing it with F', he will need to calculate $\phi_k(F')$. But since the adversary does not know k, he can not compute the fingerprint of F'. Even if the adversary attempts to find a F' with the same fingerprint $\phi_k(F) = \phi_k(F')$, he will be thwarted, since the problem of finding an input which generates a given fingerprint is intractable without the key value k.

The fingerprinting algorithm views a sequence of bits s as a polynomial $f_s(x)$ over the integers modulo 2. For example, the bit sequence s ="100101001" is taken to be the polynomial $f(x) = x^8 + x^5 + x^3 + 1$. The secret key for this algorithm corresponds to a random irreducible polynomial $g(x)$ of degree $d-1$ over the integers modulo 2. It is extremely easy to generate these polynomials (several approaches are outlined in [91, 90]) and we have implemented two different efficient routines for doing so. Compute $r(x) = f_s(x) \bmod g(x)$. Then $r(x)$ is a polynomial over the integers modulo 2 of degree at most $d - 1$. Both the polynomial $r(x)$ and the key k can be represented as a string of d bits. The bits produced by the algorithm define the ϕ function.

Because this algorithm can be conveniently implemented as a systolic array, a group of researchers led by H. T. Kung chose it to implement in hardware [33]. By using new techniques, we have software implementations of this algorithm which run on the IBM RT/APC in time comparable with the fastest hardware implementation (see Section 24.8.3).

24.8 Special Issues

24.8.1 Booting

Special problems arise when a Camelot system is booted. The boot program must pick up the fingerprint key so that it can validate the authenticity of the Mach kernel, the Disk Manager, the white pages server, and the secure loader; similarly, the white pages server must pick up a random seed for a pseudo-random number generator which it will use for authentication and for generating seeds for secure servers that the secure loader brings up.

In the current version of Strongbox, we omit checking the fingerprints of the core programs and the initial pseudo-random seed is obtained from system statistics such as the last modification time of the `/tmp` directory, the control terminal, the current time, etc. Note that these system statistics are *not* good sources of random numbers: they are used merely for expediency. In future versions, we will address these problems by having the fingerprint values and initial random seed be entered by an operator. There are several ways to insure that the white pages server, secure loader, Disk Manager, and kernel are correct; one of the most straightforward is to make sure that the boot ROM associated with the machine calls a routine which calculates the fingerprint of the secure loader and the operating system kernel before booting those programs. If the fingerprinted values match the correct values, we can be sure that all is well since forging a fingerprint will succeed only 2^{-32} of the time. But how can we insure that the operator entering these values can be trusted? Several solutions to the "trusted operator" problem are possible including physical security measures and password based authentication of operators. Strongbox validates users by requiring them to enter passwords when they initially bringing up the system. Once the secure loader and Disk Manager are running, the system will continue running securely since the secure loader will verify the fingerprint of every server it brings up and will pass it a random seed it can use for its own pseudo-random number generation.

The pseudo-random numbers are used for authentication, key exchange, and puzzle generation. All puzzles other than that of the white pages server are generated as needed. The white pages server's puzzle solution as well as the key exchange secret may be changed for any particular instance of Strongbox, but once fixed they can not be changed. These secrets are present in C header files that are not exported to the user. These files should not be placed on an untrustworthy machine. Similarly, the values are present in the `wp` binary, so that file should also be secret. Currently, we simply assume that this binary is kept on removable media and that the operator removes it after booting Camelot.

24.8.2 Starting Strongbox

This section describes how to start up the current version of Strongbox after Camelot is booted. The start up procedure does not yet address the issues described above; future versions of Strongbox will have a simpler and more automated start up procedure that will be run when the kernel is booted.

After successfully bringing up Camelot, there are some additional steps needed before secure servers and clients can be run. First, the white pages server and the secure loader must be brought up by using the NCA program. Add the two servers using the `as` command, and start them using the `ss` command. The white pages server must be completely up prior to starting the secure loader.

When the white pages server and the secure loader are up, secure servers can be added to the

Node Server's database and started. Secure clients are run via the sec_run interface. The two system clients wp_admin and sec_admin are automatically fingerprinted when the white pages server starts up; other clients must be first fingerprinted. To do this, run the wp_admin program. Use the f (fingerprint) command to fingerprint the secure client, commit the transaction, and now sec_run can be used to execute the client. Note that if the secure server was just initialized, nobody except the administrator will have any access permissions, so sec_admin must be run to give users permissions. Start up sec_admin via sec_run as was done with wp_admin, and give the name of the secure server at the "Server" prompt (this is the name in the SEC_INITIALIZE_SERVER macro). The p (permit) command will prompt for the name of the RPC and the user name to whom permission should be given.

24.8.3 Performance

This section gives timing figures for Strongbox's implementations of authentication and fingerprinting. Our timing figures are for an IBM-RT/APC, which is a RISC machine running at 4 MIPS.

An IBM-RT/APC requires 105 mS to perform (one-way) authentication in addition to the RPC overhead. To perform the authentication, the client invokes two RPCs. The overhead for performing an RPC is approximately 35 msec [108]. We have an efficient software implementation of DES which works at a rate of 220 encryptions per sec.

An IBM-RT/APC achieves a fingerprinting rate of 880 KByte/sec. The fingerprinting routine uses a 65536 (2^{16}) entry table of pre-computed partial residues to achieve this speed.[5] The table contains the value $x^{32}a(x)$ mod $g(x)$ where $a(x)$ is the two byte index considered as a polynomial modulo 2, and $g(x)$ is the irreducible polynomial used (in our implementation, $deg(g(x)) = 31$). The inner loop simply reads data two bytes at a time and uses the value as an index into this table to obtain the partial residue to exclusive-or into a running residue.

A brute force initialization of the 65536-entry table would take considerable time. To initialize the 65536-entry table efficiently, we first compute 256-entry table of partial residues. The 256-entry table contains the residues $x^{32}a(x)$ mod $g(x)$ where $a(x)$ is the byte index considered as a polynomial modulo 2, and $g(x)$ is the irreducible polynomial as before. The larger table is computed from the smaller by indexing into the smaller table first by the upper 8 bits of the larger table index, and then indexing again using the lower 8 bits of the larger table index exclusive-or'ed with the upper 8 bits of the result of the previous look-up. The initialization cost is approximately 1 sec.

In security, smaller code size is desirable since the system is easier to verify and is less likely to contain bugs. The core authentication routines consists of 75 lines of C code not including comments. The fingerprinting code consists of 211 lines of C code not including comments. Our total core routines are relatively small: 248 lines of C code.

Currently, the secure loader fingerprints the entire image of the client program before allowing execution. This has some performance impacts: instead of demand paging from the file and performing page-out to a secure paging device, reading the entire program causes excessive paging/disk activity that might be avoidable (some pages of the program may never be needed). This would mean that any external memory managers must handle page-in requests of program text by checking a per-page fingerprint against a known value given by the white pages server's database.

[5] We also have a less memory intensive version which uses a 256 entry table fingerprints at a rate 710 KByte/sec.

24.9 Conclusions

We have demonstrated that self-securing programs are an effective and efficient solution to the distributed computer security problem. Our approach is aimed at the client-server model, and could be straightforwardly ported to other client-server systems. While we have not attempted to address other models of distributed computation, any system in which various agents communicate or store data may be able to use some of these algorithms. We will continue to improve Strongbox and plan to address solutions to the denial of service problem in future work.

Chapter 25

The Design of the Camelot Distributed Log Facility

Dean S. Daniels

25.1 Introduction

The Camelot distributed log facility is an alternative to the local Log Manager that permits the operation of a Camelot node which does not have enough local disk space (or disk arms) for a stable storage log. This facility is the preferred log implementation for Camelot in a workstation environment.

The distributed log facility operates by sending log records to dedicated log server nodes. Log servers can be used by multiple Camelot clients simultaneously. Reliability is achieved by replicating log records on multiple servers.

25.1.1 Functional Goals

The distributed log facility provides the same functional interface as the local Log Manager, and the two may be used interchangeably.

Distributed logging has cost, reliability, and administrative advantages in some environments. These advantages are particularly applicable in a workstation environment, but they might also apply to multiprocessor systems. Cost advantages can be obtained if expensive logging devices are shared. For example, in a workstation environment, it would be wasteful to dedicate duplexed disks and tapes to each workstation. The cost depends on the cost of server nodes and on the number of clients that can share each server. Reliability can be better for shared facilities, because they can be replicated at multiple locations. Reliability is a critical issue for transaction processing logs, since the log is the basis for all error recovery in the system. With some performance loss, a transaction processing system can tolerate unreliable storage for data, provided that the log is available for failure recovery. Hence, local disk storage can be viewed as a cache for data that resides in the log. It is easier to manage high volumes of log data at a small number of logging nodes, than at all transaction processing nodes. For the workstation environment these administrative advantages are particularly important; log data can be at a physically secure central locations that are more convenient for service personnel.

25.1.2 Performance Goals

The two most important aspects to the performance of the distributed log are the latency of log writes and the number of Camelot nodes that can be supported by each log server. Write latency depends on many factors, including the number of Camelot nodes using each server. Even under the most favorable conditions, it is difficult for writes to a distributed log to be as fast as writes to local logging disks. The cost, reliability, and administrative advantages of distributed logging must be weighed against the performance penalty. Log servers attempt to mitigate this penalty by using privileged mechanisms such as low-level interfaces to network datagrams and I/O to raw disk partitions. Log servers can also use specialized hardware that would be too costly to support on every workstation, such as battery-based uninterruptible power supplies (UPSs). Also, workstation log implementations are likely to suffer disk arm contention if the same disks are used for both data and log storage.

25.1.3 Constraints

The distributed log servers were to be implemented using workstations and UPSs. Like Camelot nodes, log servers run the Mach operating system. The server software runs as a separate Camelot process. No special operating system facilities were added to support either the distributed log servers or the client software on Camelot nodes.

25.2 Architecture

The distributed log facility is intended to be used over a local area network (as illustrated in Figure 25.1) as logging performance would be unacceptable if each log write had to traverse gateways or long distance networks.

The software implementing the client side of the distributed log facility executes as part of the Disk Manager. The client buffers log records from the Disk Manager and sends them to log servers when a message buffer fills or when the Disk Manager forces a log record. The client receives acknowledgments from log servers and maintains state information for the log replication algorithm. When the Disk Manager reads a log record, the client sends a request message to one of the log servers storing the desired log record.

The distributed log facility implements stable log storage by sending each log record to two or more log servers, where the data is stored in non-volatile storage. An alternative would be to send data to a single log server with duplexed disk storage. There are several advantages to replicating log data using multiple log servers. First, server nodes become simpler and less expensive, because they do not need multiple logging disks and controllers. The number of disks and controllers that can be attached to a small server node is often limited, so this consideration can be important in practice. Second, data is less vulnerable to loss or corruption. Separate servers are less likely to have a common failure than a single server with multiple disks. In particular, the distance between log

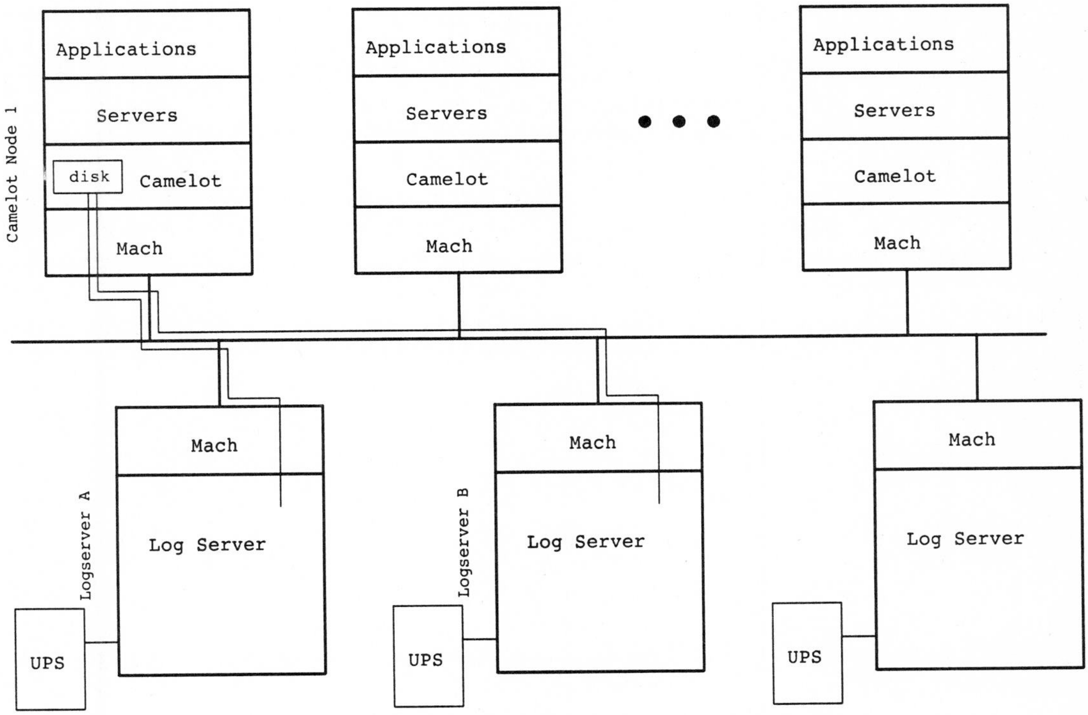

Figure 25.1: A Camelot Network with Log Servers
This shows a collection of Camelot nodes on a local area network, which could be bridged to a long haul network and other Camelot nodes. On the local area network are three log server nodes, ready to accept or provide log data. Camelot Node 1 is shown as using Log Servers A and B actively. Node 1 would begin to use the remaining log server should either Log Server A or B become unavailable.

servers interconnected with local network technology can be much higher than the distance between disks on a single node; hence, log data replicated on multiple servers would survive many disasters that would destroy log data replicated on a single server. Third, the availability of the log is increased both for normal transaction processing and for recovery after client node failures. Any individual server can always be removed from the network for servicing without interrupting normal transaction processing, and in many cases without affecting client node failure recovery. Finally, using multiple servers rather than multiple disks on one server offers more flexibility when configuring a system. Clients can choose the degree of replication of their log data. Normal processing availability may be traded against node recovery availability by varying the parameters to the replicated log algorithm described below.

Because log data storage at each log server need only survive power failures, the main memory used to buffer log data can easily be made non-volatile by attaching a UPS to the server node. The UPS permits log servers to acknowledge log data as soon as it is received (before it is written to disk). This significantly improves the speed of log writes.

Log servers use disks for permanent storage of log data. The disk can be conventional magnetic disks or write-once optical disks. Disk data structures used by the log server are designed for append-only storage. This makes optical disks easier to use and improves the performance of magnetic disk because disk seeks for writing are minimized.

25.3 Algorithms

25.3.1 Replication Algorithms

Log data is replicated using a specialized quorum consensus algorithm [36, 23, 12, 46] that exploits the fact that a replicated log has only a single client. A replicated log uses a collection of M log server nodes, with each client's log record being stored on N of the M log servers. Log servers may store portions of the replicated logs from many clients. Like the available copies replication algorithm [9], this algorithm permits read operations to use only one server. Concurrent access and network partitions are not concerns because a replicated log is accessed by only a single client process.

Unlike other distributed replication algorithms, the log replication algorithm can not depend on an underlying transaction system to insure that operations on different replica are consistently coordinated. The log replication algorithm uses time-ordered unique identifiers to resolve ambiguities that can be caused by the lack of a distributed atomic update mechanism. The generator for time-ordered unique identifiers is itself replicated.

Replicated Unique Identifier Generators

A *replicated identifier generator* is an abstract data type with only one operation: `NewID`, a function which returns a new unique identifier. These identifiers are integers. Identifiers issued by the same generator can be compared with equal and less than operators. Two identifiers are equal only if they are the result of the same `NewID` invocation. One identifier is less than another only if it was the result of an earlier invocation of `NewID`.

The state of the replicated identifier generator is replicated on N *generator state representative* nodes that each store an integer in non-volatile storage.[1] Generator state representatives provide Read and Write operations that are atomic at individual representatives.

The NewID operation first reads the generator state from $\lceil \frac{N+1}{2} \rceil$ representatives. Then, NewID writes a value higher than any read to $\lceil \frac{N}{2} \rceil$ representatives. Any overlapping assignment of reads and writes can be used. Finally, the value written is returned as a new identifier.

Because the set of generator state representatives read by any NewID operation intersects the set of representatives written by all preceding NewID operations that returned values, identifiers returned by a NewID invocation are always greater than those returned by previous invocations. If a crash interrupts a NewID operation, then a value written to too few representatives could be omitted from the sequence of identifiers generated.

The difference between an infinite sequence of unique identifiers generated as described here and a sequence of log sequence numbers generated by the replicated log WriteLog operation described in **Replicated Logs**, below, is that the replicated log ReadLog operation may be used to determine whether the sequence contains a particular integer. Similarly, the scheme described here provides no way to determine the last identifier generated.

Replicated Logs

A replicated log is an instance of an abstract type that is an append-only sequence of records. Records in a replicated log are identified by log sequence numbers (LSNs), which are increasing integers. A replicated log is used by only one transaction processing node, which permits a replication technique that is simpler than those that support multiple clients. The data stored in a log record depends on the precise recovery and transaction management algorithms used by the client node.

There are three major operations on replicated logs, though implementations would have a few others for reasons of efficiency: The WriteLog operation takes a log record as an argument, writes it to the log, and returns the LSN associated with that record. Consecutive calls to WriteLog return increasing LSNs. The WriteLog could be implemented by a LD_Write operation immediately followed by a LD_ForceLsn operation. The ReadLog operation takes an LSN as an argument and returns the corresponding log record. If the argument to ReadLog is an LSN that has not been returned by some preceding WriteLog operation, an exception is signaled. ReadLog is essentially the same as the LD_Read operation. The EndOfLog operation is used to determine the LSN of the most recently written log record. EndOfLog corresponds to the LD_HighStable operation. This simplified description contains no space management operations such as LD_SetReserve or DL_RequestTruncate.

WriteLog operations on a replicated log are implemented by sending log records to N log servers. The single logging process on the client node caches information about what log servers store log records so that each Readlog operation can be implemented with a request to one log server. When a client node is restarted after a crash, it must initialize the cached information. Naturally, the algorithm cannot require the use of an underlying transaction facility. To ensure that any WriteLog operation that was interrupted by the client's crash is performed atomically, this replication technique uses additional fields in log records stored on log servers, as described below, and the client node initialization procedures described in **Replication algorithm**, below.

[1] Append-only storage may be used to implement generator state representatives.

Server 1

LSN	Epoch	Present
1	1	yes
2	1	yes
3	1	yes
3	3	yes
4	3	no
5	3	yes
6	3	yes
7	3	yes
8	3	yes
9	3	yes

Server 2

LSN	Epoch	Present
1	1	yes
2	1	yes
3	1	yes
6	3	yes
7	3	yes

Server 3

LSN	Epoch	Present
3	3	yes
4	3	no
5	3	yes
8	3	yes
9	3	yes

Figure 25.2: Three log server nodes

Log Servers and their Operations

Log servers implement an abstraction used by the replication algorithm to represent individual copies of the replicated log. In addition to the log data and LSN, log records stored on log servers contain an *epoch number* and a boolean *present flag* indicating that the log record is present in the replicated directory. Epochs are non-decreasing integers and all log records written between two client restarts have the same epoch number. If the present flag is false, no log data need be stored. The present flag will be false for some log records that are written as a result of the recovery procedure performed when a client is restarted.

Successive records on a log server are written with non-decreasing LSNs and non-decreasing epoch numbers. A log record is uniquely identified by a $\langle$LSN, Epoch$\rangle$ pair. Log servers group log records into sequences that have the same epoch number and consecutive LSNs. For example, Server 1 in Figure 25.2 contains log records in the intervals $\langle 1, 1\rangle \ldots \langle 3, 1\rangle$ and $\langle 3, 3\rangle \ldots \langle 9, 3\rangle$.

Log servers implement three synchronous operations to support replicated logs.[2] Unlike the `WriteLog` operation on replicated logs, the `ServerWriteLog` operation takes the LSN, epoch number, and present flag for the record as arguments (along with the data). The `ServerReadLog` operation returns the present flag and log record with highest epoch number and the requested LSN. A log server does not respond to `ServerReadLog` requests for records that it does not store, but it must respond to requests for records that are stored, regardless of whether they are marked present or not. The `IntervalList` operation returns the epoch number, low LSN, and high LSN for each consecutive sequence of log records stored for a client node. `IntervalList` is used when restarting a client node.

Replication Algorithm

A replicated log is the set of ⟨LSN,Data⟩ pairs in all log servers such that the log record is marked present and the same LSN does not exist with a higher epoch number. The replication algorithm ensures that the replicated log can be read or written despite the failure of $N-1$ or fewer log servers. The replicated log shown in Figure 25.2 consists of records in the intervals $\langle 1,1\rangle \ldots \langle 2,1\rangle$, $\langle 3,3\rangle$, and $\langle 5,3\rangle \ldots \langle 9,3\rangle$. Each of these records appears on $N = 2$ log servers.

Like other quorum consensus algorithms, the correctness of this algorithm depends on having a non-empty intersection among the quorums used for different operations. That is, if there are M total nodes and the client writes to N of them, with $M > N$, `ReadLog` performed with explicit voting will always require 2 or more `ServerReadLog` operations. Yet M must be greater than N to provide high availability for `WriteLog`. To permit `ReadLog` operations to be executed using a single `ServerReadLog`, this replication algorithm caches enough information on each client node to enable the client to determine which log servers store data needed for a particular `ReadLog` operation.

Client nodes initialize their cached information when they are restarted by receiving the results of `IntervalList` operations from at least $M - N + 1$ log servers. This number guarantees that a merged set of interval lists will contain at least one server storing each log record. In merging the interval lists, only the entries with the highest epoch number for a particular LSN are kept. In effect, this replication algorithm performs the voting needed to achieve quorum consensus for all `ReadLog` operations at client node initialization time. That is, `EndOfLog` operations return the high value in the merged interval list and `ReadLog` operations use the list to determine a server to which to direct a `ServerReadLog` operation. If the requested record is beyond the end of the log or if the log record returned by the `ServerReadLog` operation is marked not present, an exception is signaled.

When initialized, a client must also obtain a new epoch number for use with `ServerWriteLog` operations. This epoch number must be higher than any other epoch number used during the previous operation of this client. **Replicated Unique Identifier Generators**, above, describes a simple method for implementing an increasing unique identifier generator that can be used to assign epoch numbers and is replicated for high availability.

The `WriteLog` operation assigns an LSN by incrementing the highest LSN in the merged interval list and performs `ServerWriteLog` operations on N log servers. If a server has received a log record in the same epoch with an LSN immediately preceding the sequence number of the

[2]The operations are presented in a simplified way here; a more realistic interface that supports error recovery and the blocking of multiple log operations into a single server operation is described in Section 25.3.3.

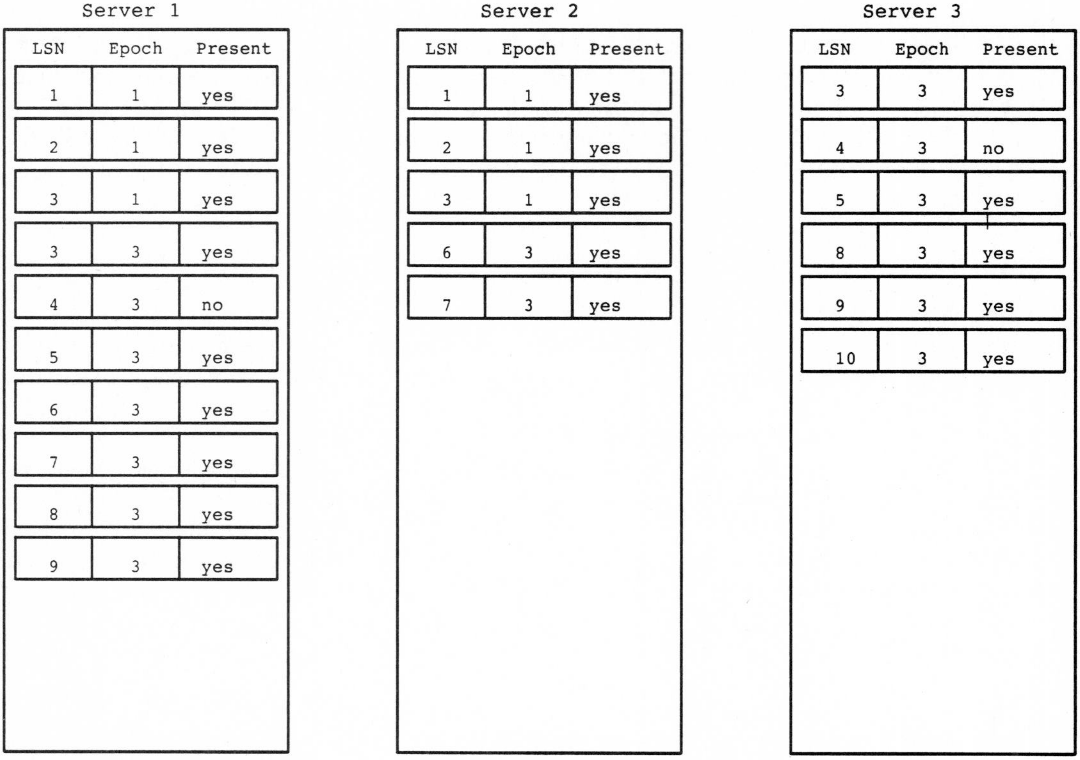

Figure 25.3: A partially written log record

new log record, it extends its current sequence of log records to include the new record; otherwise it creates a new sequence. To prevent large numbers of separate sequences from being created, clients should attempt to perform consecutive writes to the same servers. However, a client can switch servers when necessary.

The `WriteLog` operation is not atomic and a client node crash can cause `ServerWriteLog` operations for some log record to have been performed on fewer than *N* log servers. In such a situation, client initialization might not gather an interval list containing the LSN for the partially written log record. Figure 25.3 shows a replicated log with log record 10 partially written. If Servers 1 and 2 were used for client initialization, then the Recovery Manager would not read log record 10 during recovery, but if Server 3 were included then record 10 would affect recovery.

When a client node is initialized it is necessary to ensure that the log write that was occurring at the time of the crash appears atomic to users of the replicated log. Because log writes are synchronous, there is at most one log record that has been written to fewer than *N* log servers. If such a record exists, the `WriteLog` operation cannot have completed and the transaction processing

Server 1

LSN	Epoch	Present
1	1	yes
2	1	yes
3	1	yes
3	3	yes
4	3	no
5	3	yes
6	3	yes
7	3	yes
8	3	yes
9	3	yes
9	4	yes
10	4	no

Server 2

LSN	Epoch	Present
1	1	yes
2	1	yes
3	1	yes
6	3	yes
7	3	yes
9	4	yes
10	4	no

Server 3

LSN	Epoch	Present
3	3	yes
4	3	no
5	3	yes
8	3	yes
9	3	yes
10	3	yes

Figure 25.4: After crash recovery

node cannot have depended on whether the operation was successfully or unsuccessfully performed. Therefore, the log replication algorithm may report the record as existing or as not existing provided that all reports are consistent.

Since there is doubt concerning only the log record with the highest LSN, it is copied from a log server storing it (using `ServerReadLog` and `ServerWriteLog`) to *N* log servers. The record is copied with the client node's new epoch number. Copying this log record assures that if the last record were partially written, it would subsequently appear in the interval lists of at least *N* log servers. Finally, a log record marked as not present is written to *N* log servers with an LSN one higher than that of the copied record. This final record has an epoch number higher than that of any copy of any partially written record and hence a partially written record with the same LSN will not be kept when interval lists are merged in any subsequent client initialization. Figure 25.4 shows the replicated log from Figure 25.3 after execution of this procedure using Servers 1 and 2.[3]

[3]The careful reader will notice that log record 4 only appears as marked not present in Figures 25.2, 25.3, and 25.4. This resulted from a previous client restart using Servers 1 and 3.

The client initialization procedure is not atomic. A log record can be partially copied, and the log record marked not present can be partially written. However, the procedure is restartable in that the client's Recovery Manager will not act on any log records prior to the completion of the recovery procedure. Once the recovery procedure completes, its effects are persistent.

25.3.2 Log Client/Log Server Communication

There are two separate components to the communication interface between log clients and servers. The low level component is the connection-oriented transport protocol that is used to move messages between client and server nodes. The high level component is the message protocols that are used to implement the distributed log replication algorithms. This section describes both components in bottom up order.

Transport Protocol

The Camelot distributed log facility's transport protocol is used for flow control and multi-packet message delivery only. It does not perform retransmission for error recovery, although it does detect and discard out-of-sequence and duplicate packets. The message level protocols retry after a timeout when messages are discarded because of errors detected by the transport protocol.

The messages transmitted by the transport protocol are called *chains* because they are chains of packet buffers. Routines are provided for putting data in chains and extracting data from chains. An interface for sending a single packet chain without first allocating and packing the chain is also provided.

The transport protocol is layered on the UDP/IP protocol. UDP packets are sent and received using a special packet filter interface that is part of the Mach operating system. The packet filter mechanism allows UDP/IP packets to be sent by sending a Mach message containing the packet to a special kernel port. Packets are received by first passing a port to the kernel in the `NetIPCListen` call [8], together with a packet filter specifying the IP and UDP header field values that the desired packet should contain. The kernel then sends packets received from the net with those header values to the port passed in the `NetIPCListen` call. The transport protocol uses a specially designated UDP port.

Connection initiation uses a timer based subprotocol [119]. Flow control uses a moving window strategy and flow control allocations are on a per packet basis.

25.3.3 Message Protocols

There are eleven different messages that pass from clients to log servers and nine different messages that are sent from log servers to clients. Most of the messages exchanged are treated as remote procedure calls (RPCs) and returns. The major exception to this is the special protocol for log writes described in **WriteLog Subprotocol**, below. A similar protocol is used for the log copying that goes on at client restart time. Messages containing log data have a special format and are packed according to the rules given in **Data Message Packing and ReadLog Buffering**, below.

Data Message Packing and ReadLog Buffering

The `CopyLog`, `WriteLog`, `ForceLog`, and `ReadLogReply` all use the format shown in Figure 25.5. This layout allows the records to be packed into the messages as they are presented (e.g., in log write calls). The offsets array must be assembled and copied into the message just before it is sent. The goal of the message packing policy is to send either a single packet message containing as many records as will fit, or a multi-packet message containing one log record. Less than a full packet of log records may be sent in the case of log forces, copy log operations when the records remaining to be copied total less than a full packet, and read log operations when a log server does not store a full packet of log records contiguous to the requested log record.

The Camelot recovery algorithms do not use forward log scans. All log accesses are either direct by LSN or, as part of a backward log scan. The Camelot log interface (described in Section C.10) supports direct access and backward scans through the `LD_Read` call, which returns the LSN of the preceding log record along with the requested record.

RPC Subprotocols

Most of the messages in the distributed logging protocols are request and response pairs that constitute RPCs executed on log servers. These messages pairs include `ReadEpoch` and `ReadEpochReply`, `WriteEpoch` and `WriteEpochReply`, `RequestIntervals` and `Intervals`, `CopyLog` and `CopyLogReply`, and `InstallCopies` and `InstallCopiesReply` messages. These message pairs are not programmed as synchronous RPCs. Instead, the client sends a request message and then waits in a receive loop until a response is received. The client can process other messages, like `RequestTruncate`, while waiting for a reply. Except for the `ReadLog` and `ReadLogReply` pair, the RPC subprotocol pairs are executed as parallel RPCs that execute simultaneously on different servers.

The log truncation messages, `Truncate` and `RequestTruncate`, are one-way RPCs that are executed on the log client and log server, respectively.

`ReadEpoch/ReadEpochReply` RPCs read the unique identifier generator state from log servers. `ReadEpoch` messages contain a client identifier. `ReadEpochReply` messages contain the epoch number stored at the log server for the client.

`WriteEpoch/WriteEpochReply` RPCs write the unique identifier generator state to log servers. `WriteEpoch` messages contain a client identifier and a new epoch number. The epoch number from the `WriteEpoch` message is contained in `WriteEpochReply` messages.

`RequestIntervals/Intervals` RPCs read interval lists from log servers. A client identifier is contained in `RequestIntervals` messages. `Intervals` messages contain a count, and an array of records containing low and high LSNs, and epoch numbers for each interval of contiguous LSNs that a log server stores for the client.

`ReadLog/ReadLogReply` RPCs read log records from a log server. `ReadLog` messages contain a client identifier, a LSN, and an epoch number. `ReadLogReply` messages contain an epoch number, high and low LSNs and log data. The layout of a `ReadLogReply` message is shown in Figure 25.5.

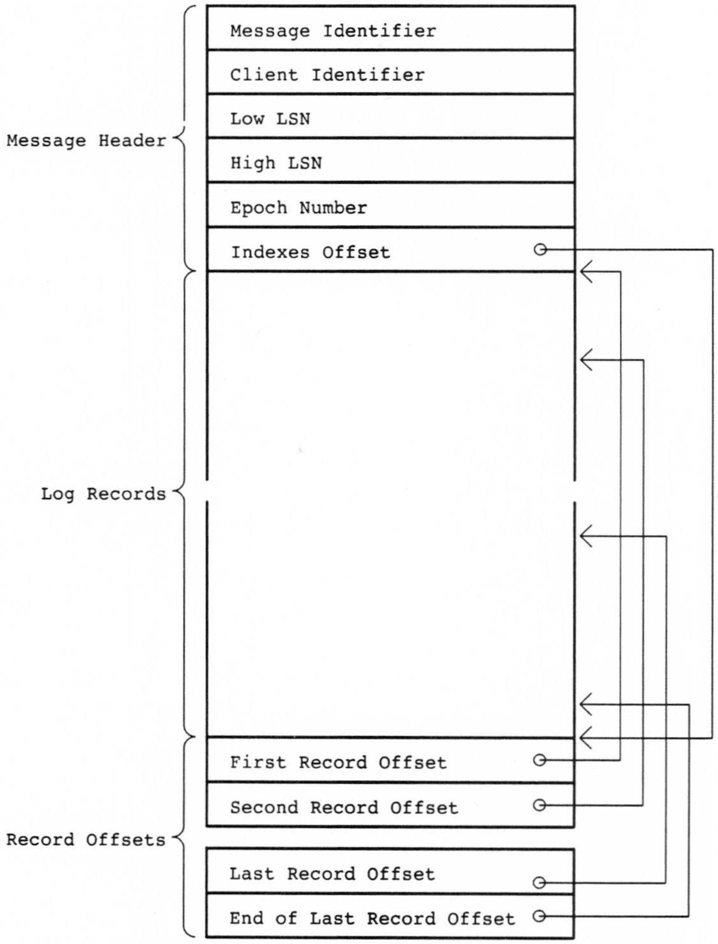

Figure 25.5: Log Data Message Layout

`CopyLog`/`CopyLogReply` RPCs are used to copy log records during client restart (the `CopyLog` subprotocol is described in **CopyLog Subprotocol**, below. `CopyLog` messages contain a client identifier, an epoch number, high and low LSNs, and log data. The layout of a `CopyLog` message is shown in Figure 25.5. `CopyLogReply` messages contain an epoch number, and high and low LSNs.

`InstallCopies`/`InstallCopiesReply` RPCs are used to terminate the copy log subprotocol (described in **CopyLog Subprotocol,** below). number. `InstallCopies` messages contain a client identifier and an epoch number. `InstallCopiesReply` messages contain an epoch number.

`Truncate` messages contain a client identifier and an LSN and are used as one-way RPCs to truncate a client's log at a log server. The message indicates that a log server may discard all records with LSNs less than the LSN contained in the message.

`RequestTruncate` messages are used as one-way RPCs to request that a client truncate its log. These messages ware sent periodically when a log server's free disk space is less than some threshold. The messages contain a target LSN for the client's log truncation.

WriteLog Subprotocol

The `WriteLog` subprotocol supports both streaming of large amounts of log data and fast forces. The subprotocol automatically detects lost messages and establishes state information for the distributed replication algorithm when a client switches log servers.

The `WriteLog` subprotocol uses the following messages that are sent from clients to log servers:

`WriteLog` messages contain a client identifier, an epoch number, high and low LSNs and log data. The layout of a `WriteLog` message is shown in Figure 25.5. The log server sends a `MissingLSNs` message in response to this message if some log records might be missing because of a lost message. Otherwise, the server stores the log data contained in the message and no response is sent.

`ForceLog` messages contain a client identifier, an epoch number, high and log log sequence numbers and log data. The layout of a `ForceLog` message is shown in Figure 25.5. The log server sends a `MissingLSNs` message in response to this message if some log records might be missing because of a lost message. Otherwise, the server stores the log data contained in the message and a `NewHighLSN` message is sent in response.

`NewInterval` messages contain a client identifier, and an LSN. They are sent by a log client in response to a `MissingLsns` message and inform a log server that some (or all) of the log records it regards as missing are stored at other log servers and so the log server should start a new interval of contiguous LSNs. A `NewHighLSN` message or a `MissingLSNs` message is sent in response.

`ForceLSN` messages contain a client identifier and an LSN. The message requests an indication of whether a log server stores a record with an LSN equal to or greater than the LSN in the message. If the log server stores such a record, a NewHighLSN message is sent in response. Otherwise, a MissingLSNs message is sent in response.

The WriteLog subprotocol uses the following messages that are sent from log servers to clients:

NewHighLSN messages are sent in response to ForceLog, ForceLSN, and NewInterval messages. They contain the high non-volatile LSN for at a server for the client they are sent to.

MissingLSNs messages are sent in response to WriteLog, ForceLog, ForceLSN, and NewInterval messages. The messages contain low and high LSN delimiting a range of LSNs that the server believes should be (re)sent to it.

The subprotocol relies on two pieces of state information at a log server. The first is the *high stored LSN*. When a log server restarts (actually when a client first contacts a server) the high stored LSN is set to the highest LSN stored at the server for the client. The high stored LSN is subsequently updated as described below. The second state information is the *high received LSN*. The high received LSN is originally set to the value of the high stored LSN and is updated as described below.

Normally, a log client spools log data to servers using WriteLog messages. WriteLog messages can be sent at any rate without waiting for acknowledgments because the flow control mechanisms in the transport protocol prevent a client from overrunning a log server. Unless a message is lost, a client sends a ForceLog message for one of two reasons. First, the transaction processing system might issue an LD_ForceLsn call with the LSN of a log record that the log client is buffering. Second, while processing an LD_Write call, the log client might detect that it has reached the maximum number of log records that are permitted to be written, but unacknowledged (50 in current implementations of the Camelot distributed log facility). In either case all buffered records are sent in a ForceLog message.

ForceLog messages are (logically) synchronous. After sending a ForceLog message, a client sends no additional messages until a reply is received or a timeout occurs. If a timeout occurs, the client sends a ForceLSN message to any log servers that have not responded. If too many timeouts occur, a log client chooses a new server and sends a ForceLSN message to the new server. A client also sends a ForceLSN message when a LD_ForceLSN call requests the log client to force a log record that has been sent to servers in a WriteLog message but has not been acknowledged by some servers.

Normally, when a log server receives a WriteLog message, the LSNs in the message are contiguous with the high received LSN and the log server simply adds the records to its storage and updates its high stored LSN and high received LSN to be the high LSN in the WriteLog message. A ForceLog message with LSNs that are contiguous with previously received data is processed the same way, and a NewHighLSN message with the new high stored LSN (the high LSN in the ForceLog message) is sent in reply. If a ForceLSN message is received with a LSN that is less than or equal to the high stored LSN for a client, the servers responds with a NewHighLSN message with the high stored LSN for the client.

When a log server receives a WriteLog or ForceLog message with data that is not contiguous with the high stored LSN for a client, or it receives a ForceLSN message for a LSN that is greater than the high stored LSN, the missing log write subprotocol is invoked. First, the log server updates the high received LSN for the client if the high LSN in the `WriteLog` or `ForceLog`, or the LSN in the `ForceLSN` message is greater the high received LSN. Other than updating the high received LSN, data in `WriteLog` and `ForceLog` messages is discarded. The log server then sends a `MissingLSNs` message to the client for the range from one greater than the high stored LSN through the high received LSN for the client.

A `MissingLSNs` message implicitly acknowledges all LSNs less than the low LSNs in its range, and the first thing a log client does when it receives a `MissingLSNs` message is to update its record of what LSNs the server has acknowledged. Next, the log client checks to see whether some or all of the log records that the server is missing have been acknowledged by a write quorum of other log servers. In this case the client sends the log server a `NewInterval` message with the highest LSN acknowledged by a write quorum of log servers. A `NewInterval` message is often sent when a client switches log servers. If a `NewInterval` message is not sent, then the log client sends all or some of the missing log records to the server in a `ForceLog` message. The message packing policy described in **Data Message Packing and ReadLog Buffering**, above, is followed when determining how many of the missing log records to send.

When a log server receives a `NewInterval` message it updates its high stored LSN for the client to be the LSN in the message. If the high received LSN is still greater than the high stored LSN for the client, the log server sends another `MissingLSNs` message. Otherwise, the log server sends a `NewHighLSN` message with the new high stored LSN.

When a log server receives a `ForceLog` message while its high received LSN is greater than its high stored LSN for the client it processes the message in the same way as any normal `ForceLog` message except that a `NewHighLSN` response is sent only if the high received LSN and high stored LSN are equal after processing the `ForceLog` message. Otherwise a `MissingLSNs` message is sent in reply.

CopyLog Subprotocol

The Camelot distributed log facility uses distributed replication for log representation, but modifies the algorithm given in Section 25.3 to allow more than one log record to be buffered or sent to log servers but not acknowledged. This means that during client restart a number of log records must be copied. This copying is done using a special subprotocol involving the `ReadLog`, `ReadLogReply`, `CopyLog`, `CopyLogReply`, `InstallCopies`, and `InstallCopiesReply` messages.

Log records to be copied are obtained from a log server storing them by sending `ReadLog` messages. After enough log records to fill a `CopyLog` message are obtained, a `CopyLog` message is sent to a write quorum of log servers. This process is repeated until all records to be copied have been acknowledged (via `CopyLogReply`) by a write quorum.

The `InstallCopies` message is intended to allow a log server using append-only storage to reduce the overhead of copying records by buffering the index information for many records and then installing that information all at once. This is useful because the order in which records are copied violates the assumptions under which index structures like append-forests are designed. Installing the index data for all copied records at once reduces the overhead.

25.3.4 Log Clients

The distributed Log Manager is the client side of the communication interface described in Section 25.3.2, and implements the logging interface using the distributed log replication algorithm from Section 25.3.1. The log servers to be used by the distributed Log Manager are determined at system configuration time, and when Camelot is started the names of nodes running log servers are passed to the distributed Log Manager as command line parameters.

The distributed Log Manager executes as part of the Disk Manager and exports an interface to both the Disk Manager (for writing the log) and the Recovery Manager (for reading the log). The distributed Log Manager is structured as a single monitor with a single mutex variable, `ldMutex`, controlling access. There is a Disk Manager thread dedicated to servicing RPCs from the Recovery Manager's log interface and processing asynchronous messages (like `RequestTruncate`) from log servers. Routines in the LD interface acquire `ldMutex` at the beginning of their execution (and release `ldMutex` before exiting) whether they are executed by the server loop thread processing RPCs from the Recovery Manager or by other Disk Manager threads calling the interface directly. The server loop thread acquires `ldMutex` before processing messages from log servers.

There are three major software modules in the distributed Log Manager. The lowest level is the transport protocol module that is common to both the log client and log server. The next level is a client state module that encapsulates the state of the higher level logging algorithm for each client. Among other functions the client state module translates transport protocol connection identifiers to server identifiers, reopens transport connections when they fail, lists what LSNs are stored by what servers, and lists records have been sent to servers but not acknowledged. The Log Manager interface module implements all LD routines, and is responsible for log record buffering, message packing, and implementation of the log replication algorithm using the information in the client state module. The Log Manager interface module assigns consecutive LSNs by incrementing an internal high LSN variable, which is initialized during the `LD_OpenLog` call.

The Log Manager interface module maintains two log record buffers. The first is the log tail. It contains the most recently written log records, including all records that have been written but not acknowledged by enough log servers. The tail is used to retransmit log records and as a cache for `LD_Read` calls. It can contain records that have been acknowledged by a write quorum if the tail uses less space than a maximum length that is set when when the log client is compiled. The second buffer maintained by the Log Manager is a cache of the most recently received `ReadLogReply` message. This cache enables some sequential log reads to be satisfied without messages to servers.

25.3.5 Log Server Design

Log server nodes are equipped with large disk partitions dedicated for log data and UPSs to implement non-volatile virtual memory. Mach is the operating system for the servers. The log server is a user level process with special privileges for accessing the logging disk as a raw device and for network access.

This section first describes the thread structure of the log server and then examines the main memory and disk data structures implemented by a log server. Section 25.3.6 explains how uninterruptible power supplies are used to make a log server's virtual memory non-volatile.

Log Server Threads

The log server is a single Mach task with two threads of control to permit the logging disk to be written asynchronously while new log data is being received in the other thread. An additional thread to process log reads was designed but not implemented.

The main log server thread performs all log server functions except for disk writes. These functions include server initialization, transport protocol and higher level message processing, packing received log records into disk buffers, maintenance of index and other main memory structures, locating log data on disk (or in a main memory buffer) when a `ReadLog` message is received, and checkpointing the log server's state to disk during idle times and when a power failure occurs. Log writes are acknowledged as soon as log data is buffered in main memory.

The track writer thread's sole function is to write buffered log data to disk. A separate thread is used for this function so that the synchronous UNIX `write` calls do not delay the main thread while it is receiving log data. Buffers of log data to be written to disk are passed from the main thread to the track writer in a main memory queue. The track writer and main thread synchronize their access to the queue using mutual exclusion semaphores and condition variables.

The log read thread was intended to permit the main thread to continue receiving new log data while the log read thread executed synchronous disk read operations to satisfy a `ReadLog` message. The thread was not included in the log server's initial implementation because of the difficulty of synchronizing the log read thread's activity with other threads and because use of buffering and hints eliminated many disk accesses for reads.

Log Server Data Structures

Disk storage is the only permanent non-volatile storage on a log server. All data necessary for restarting a log server has a disk representation. For client log records, the disk representation is the only one that the log server manipulates. Other information, like the interval lists describing what log records are stored for each client, is normally manipulated in a main memory data structure and is checkpointed[4] to disk when a power failure occurs.

Main Memory Structures

Two main memory data structures are used by log servers. Both structures are hash tables indexed by client identifier and there is some redundancy between the two tables. The first table, called the client information table, is accessed by the log server module that implements the server side of the logging message protocols. There is no disk representation for the client information table. The second table, called the interval lists table, is accessed by the disk storage component of the log server. The interval lists table is written to disk during a server checkpoint.

Figure 25.6 shows a record from the client information table. The table is keyed by the `clientId` field in the record, which is the identifier of a client of the log server. There is an entry in the table for each client that the log server has communicated with since the server was restarted. The `ci` field is the most recently used transport layer connection for the client. The other fields are the high stored and high received LSNs for the client that are used by the logging message protocols.

---

[4]Here, checkpoint is a copy of the main memory structures on disk, not the checkpoints that transaction systems create to bound recovery time.

clientId
ci
highStableLSN
highReceivedLSN

Figure 25.6: Client Information Table Record

clientId
epochNumber
iList

Figure 25.7: Interval Lists Table Record

epochNumber
lowLSN
highLSN
lowBlockAddress
highBlockAddress
nextPointer

Figure 25.8: Interval List Element Record

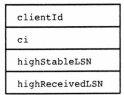

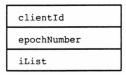

The interval lists table contains an entry for each client that has data stored on a log server. Figure 25.7 shows the record format for the table, which is keyed by the client identifier in the `clientId` field. The `epochNumber` field in the record is the state for the replicated unique identifier generator used by the log replication algorithm. The `ReadEpoch` and `WriteEpoch` messages request access to this value for a client. The `iList` field is the root of the interval list for the client.

An interval list is a singly linked list of records describing the interval records with contiguous LSNs stored for a client. Figure 25.8 shows the record format for an element in the list. Each element in an interval list describes a disjoint interval of contiguous LSNs from `lowLsn` to `highLsn`. All log records in an interval have the same epoch number as given by the `epochNumber` field. The address of the first and last disk blocks containing records from an interval are given in the `lowBlockAddress` and `highBlockAddress` fields. Interval lists are ordered with the higher ranges of LSNs first.

Disk Data Structures

The log server uses disk blocks consisting of many sectors to permit more efficient disk transfers. It is intended that log server disk blocks correspond to tracks on the logging disk, but some disk interfaces do not support this correspondence because disk sectors with adjacent addresses may not be adjacent on disk. In any case, the use of a large block size does amortize the overhead for operating system calls and initiating I/O.

Use of a multi-sector disk block raises the issue of block integrity. All sectors might not be written to disk if a block write is interrupted by a failure. Such an error would not be caught by the sector oriented error detection built into a disk drive. A block checksum could be used to address this problem. The implementation of the Camelot log server does not use checksums, so the Camelot log server is vulnerable to failures during writes.

Each disk block begins with the logical byte address of the block in the (logically) append-only disk space for the log server. Disk blocks are assigned new logical addresses as space is reused. The physical address of a block is its logical address modulo the size of the logging space. Immediately after the block address is a one byte code that determines the type of block. There are five block types. The zero block type code indicates an unused block, so the disk space can be written with zeros to initialize the Log Manager. The other block types are data blocks, data continuation blocks, checkpoint header blocks and checkpoint continuation blocks.

Data and data continuation blocks contain log records from (potentially) multiple clients. The difference between the two block types is that the first record on a data continuation block is the continuation of a record that spans multiple blocks. Data block layouts are designed to allow log records to be copied directly into disk buffers as they are received. Records that are from the same client, have the same epoch number, and have a contiguous range of LSNs may be stored in groups of up to 256. The records in a group share the common group identifier information shown in Figure 25.9. The group identifier layout compresses the LSN information for a set of log records and allows the space for client identifiers, epoch numbers and LSNs to be amortized over many log records. The range of LSNs in a group is indicated in the group identifier by a base LSN and the integer offset of the highest LSN in the group. Immediately following the block type field on data and data continuation blocks is an eight bit count of the number of groups on the block and the sixteen bit offset of the first of the group identifiers.

`clientId`
`epochNumber`
`lowLSN`
`highLSNoffset`

Figure 25.9: Data Block Record Group Identifier Record

The layout of data and data continuation blocks is shown in Figure 25.10. All records are packed contiguously after the block header information. The group identifiers follow records, and the record index information follows the group identifiers. Record index information consists of a record length and the offset in the block of each record. There is a block of index information for each group identifier and the blocks are stored in the same order as the group identifiers. Within a block, the offset information is in LSN order. When a record spans multiple blocks, the length of the record given in the first block is the length of the entire record (the amount of the record stored in the block is found by subtracting its starting offset from the group identifier offset in the disk block header). The length for the first record appearing on a data continuation block is the length of that portion of the record only.

Checkpoint and checkpoint continuation blocks are written when a log server checkpoints itself before shutting down (for example, because of a line power failure, see Section 25.3.6). Checkpoint information consists of one checkpoint block followed by zero or more checkpoint continuation blocks. A checkpoint contains enough information to rebuild the interval list table in main memory. Besides the block type, the headers of checkpoint and checkpoint continuation blocks contain two counts, the count of interval list elements (from the lists for all clients) in the entire checkpoint, and the count of elements on that block (Figure 25.12). The interval list elements, as shown in Figure 25.11, contain the information from the list elements in the interval lists table and in addition each element contains the client identifier and the unique identifier state (`epochNumber` field) from the interval list table header. This redundant structure was chosen because it simplifies the generation and processing of checkpoints. The counts in the checkpoint headers are used to verify that a multi-block checkpoint was completely written.

25.3.6 Uninterruptible Power Supply Operations

The uninterruptible power supplies used for Camelot log servers have a built-in RS232 interface connected to a processor that runs a monitor program. When a log server starts it sends a message to the monitor program. This message contains a log server port to which the monitor program sends a shutdown request message to when the line power to the UPS fails. A log server thread is dedicated to waiting for message on this signal port. When a shutdown message is received, the signal handling thread sets a flag. The flag is noticed by the main log server thread after normal message handling and the log server flushes disk buffers, checkpoints itself, and exits. The monitor program detects the log server shutdown when it receives a port death notification for the signal port. At this point, the monitor program can shut down the UPS if necessary.

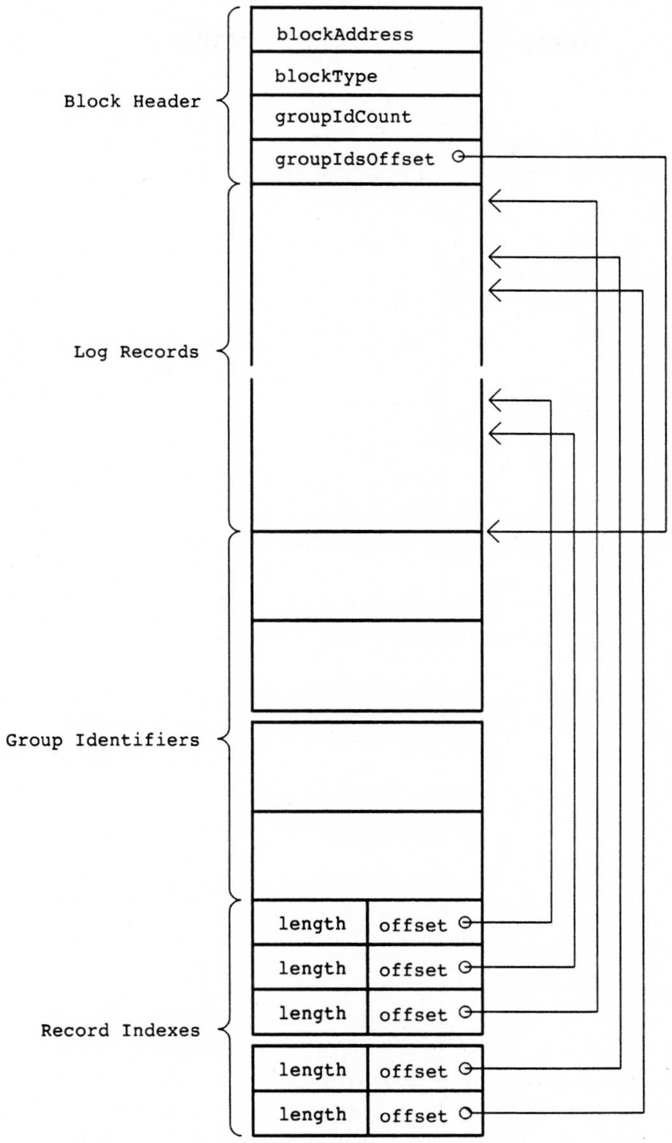

Figure 25.10: Data Block Layout

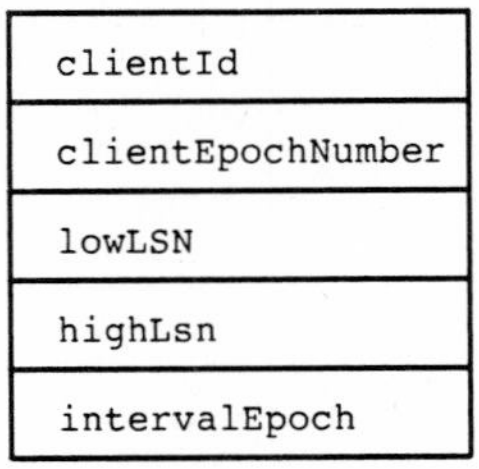

Figure 25.11: Checkpoint Interval List Record

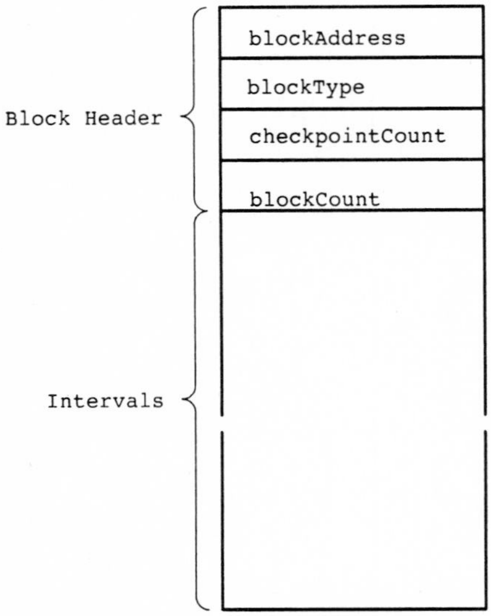

Figure 25.12: Checkpoint Block Layout

25.4 Related Work

Unlike the parallel logging architecture proposed by Agrawal and DeWitt [2, 3], distributed logging is intended to permit multiple transaction processors to share logging disks, rather than to accommodate a high volume of log data generated by a single (multi-processor) transaction processor. Of course, several distributed log servers may operate in parallel in a distributed environment that generates a large volume of log data.

Tandem TXP systems use a form of a distributed log service [13, 14]. This service is based on mirroring, rather than on distributed replication.

25.5 Conclusions

25.5.1 Design Weaknesses

Weaknesses of this design include:

- The replication algorithm as described here does not deal with decay of the non-volatile data in log servers.
- The use of a distributed log precludes commit protocol optimizations by using a common commit coordinator.
- The log space management policy has the drawback of making the availability of the replicated log service dependent on the availability of individual clients.
- The communications protocols use three messages instead of one to recover from the loss of a datagram in some common cases.
- The current implementation does not use multicast.

25.5.2 Future Work

Log Record Splitting and Caching

Log records written by a recovery manager often contain independent redo and undo components. The redo component of a log record must be written stably to the log before transaction commit. The undo component of a log record does not need to be written to the log until just before the pages referenced in the log record are written to non-volatile storage. Frequently transactions commit before the pages they modify are written to non-volatile storage.

If log records are *split* into separate redo and undo components, the volume of logged data may be reduced. Redo components of log records are sent to log servers as they are generated, with the rest of the log data stream. Undo components of log records are *cached* in virtual memory at client nodes. When a transaction commits, the undo components of log records written by the transaction are flushed from the cache. If a page referenced by an undo component of a log record in the cache is scheduled for cleaning, the undo component must be sent to log servers first. If a transaction aborts while the undo components of its log records are in the cache, then the log records are available locally and do not need to be retrieved from a log server.

The performance improvements possible with log record splitting and caching depend on the size of the cache, and on the length of transactions. If transactions are very short, then the fraction of log records that may be split will be small, and splitting will not save much data volume. Very long running transactions will not complete before pages they modify are cleaned, and splitting will also not save data volume. The cached log records will speed up aborts and relieve disk arm movement contention on log servers because log reads will go to the caches at the clients.

Load Assignment

The interface presented in Section 25.3.3 does not contain protocols for assigning clients to log servers. Ideally, clients should distribute their load evenly among log servers so as to minimize response times. If the only technique for detecting overloaded servers is for a client to recognize degraded performance with a short timeout, then clients might change servers too frequently resulting in very long interval lists. If servers shed load by ignoring clients, then clients of failed servers might try one server after another without success. Presumably, simple decentralized strategies for assigning loads fairly can be used. The development of these strategies is likely to be a problem that is very amenable to analytic modeling and simple experimentation.

Security

Any information available from a database can be reconstructed from a recovery log. A log is also the repository of last resort for information that is potentially very valuable. Therefore, the malicious destruction of a recovery log could be very costly. There are two security problems in distributed logging. Both can be solved using established techniques from the literature.

The first problem to be resolved is the unauthorized release of information in a log. An end-to-end encryption mechanism, whereby a client encrypts and decrypts log data with a key known only to the client, can be used to ensure that data can not be read by any other entity. Such a mechanism simplifies the construction of log servers slightly because they do not need to prevent the unauthorized release of log data.

The second problem is authentication of log servers and clients to each other. Proper authentication of servers is necessary to be able to assign responsibility for data. A server that acknowledges receiving log data can incur a (potentially monetary) responsibility for the integrity of the data only if its client can show that the particular server did in fact acknowledge the data. Otherwise the server could claim that the data was acknowledged by an impostor. This authentication can be accomplished with standard encryption-based protocols.

Part VI

Appendices

Appendix A

Debugging

Dean Thompson
Elliot Jaffe

Debugging Camelot application/server pairs is difficult. The unique environment that Camelot provides – client/server interaction with parallelism, transactions, and recoverable storage – is unfamiliar to many Camelot users. It also is not supported well by many existing tools (such as debuggers), and not enough new tools are available.

Don't despair. The transactional model and the simple elegance of the Library interface help a lot. Once you gain some basic familiarity with transactions and the Camelot interface, you will find that most bugs are either errors in your high-level logic (which are fun to debug) or low-level mistakes that have nothing to do with Camelot (not a new problem). Only occasionally will you encounter low-level problems caused by subtle misuse of the Camelot Library primitives. With persistence, and by using the macros and other facilities that we do provide for debugging, you should be able to find your way past any problem.

Be patient. Think about your problems carefully. Be methodical. *Almost every programmer in the world right now is a complete beginner at writing concurrent, transactional code.* Everyone makes many mistakes at first and has a terrible time finding them. Enjoy the new experience, and expect to spend time finding your first few bugs and learning how to write good Camelot code.

A.1 Avoiding Bugs

Camelot is a very good environment for writing correct code. Unfortunately, as things stand now, it is a relatively poor environment for debugging incorrect code. This make it especially important to write Camelot code carefully, with attention to elegance and good design. Try to anticipate problem areas and think about them in advance.

Most new Camelot users make at least two of these basic errors:

- Misunderstanding transactions.
- Incorrect locking.

- Mixing up references to volatile and recoverable storage.
- Forgetting that transactions abort. More specifically:
  - Incorrect use of volatile operations transactions.
  - Incorrect use of I/O in transactions.
  - Incorrect use of mutexes in transactions.

The rest of this section will discuss each of these problem areas in more detail.

A.1.1 Misunderstanding Transactions

This is a tough one. Some Camelot users will have worked extensively with general nested transactions before. Most (including the Camelot implementation team) know what transactions are, and are familiar with their abstract properties, but will at first overlook some of the practical implications. A few examples may help you start thinking about what to look out for.

If an application starts a transaction and never commits it, all work done by the transaction is aborted. This applies to concurrent transactions too. It is true even if the transaction completed all of its operations successfully. Pay some attention to what will happen when a user presses `^C`.

Flow of control is transferred when a transaction aborts. Forgetting this can lead to all sorts of problems. Several paragraphs are devoted to this subject later.

Allowing transactions to communicate with each other can violate serializability. Communication through server calls and correctly locked recoverable storage is guaranteed correct. Letting one transaction write to a file system or a global (non-recoverable) variable and then having another transaction read it can lead to extremely subtle concurrency bugs. Transaction abort can turn the information into a lie, or data flow in the wrong direction may make two transactions non-serializable. Violating the strict transaction model is fine when it leads to improved efficiency without violating the constraints that are appropriate for a particular application or data structure. Every violation, however, deserves a great deal of careful thought.

A.1.2 Incorrect Locking

If recoverable storage is read or modified without being correctly locked, the resulting concurrency bugs can be very subtle. Imagine for example, that a locking error leaves a time window when with very low probability a concurrent transaction can corrupt one pointer in the database. Suppose the pointer will on average be read several days or a week later. Will you ever find this bug? Probably not. Many other equally horrible (but plausible) scenarios can be invented.

To make discussing locks easier, consider an example with two transactions called *A* and *B*. Assume *A* performs some operations on recoverable storage and then quiesces, but does not commit. Now *B* begins performing operations at the same server.

The following rule should almost never be violated: If *A* modifies any data, it must hold sufficient write locks (and *B* should pick up sufficient locks) to prevent *B* from reading the modified bytes. These locks must be held until *A* completes – they cannot be dropped or demoted to read locks. Be careful that *B* cannot avoid whatever write locks are held by using some other access path to the data. If *B* is reading data that *A* has modified and *A* aborts, *B* can see a random mixture of bytes from the old and new values.

The other two traditional read/write locking rules will sometimes be violated for good reasons, but should normally be followed:

- If *A reads* any data, it should hold sufficient read or write locks (and *B* should pick up sufficient locks) to guarantee that *B* will not *write* the data.
- If *A writes* any data, it should hold sufficient read or write locks (and *B* should pick up sufficient locks) to guarantee that *B* will not *write* the data.

These rules are needed to ensure strict serializability between transactions. They can be broken in certain cases where serializability at some level of abstraction is sufficient, and cheaper than strict physical serializability. If you didn't understand what I just said, don't even think about breaking the above rules.

Again, be careful about cases where *B* access the data from a different direction than *A*. You can't afford to lock every byte individually – so be sure you lock some byte(s) that both transactions are guaranteed to encounter.

A.1.3 Mixing Up References to Volatile and Recoverable Storage

One weakness in the Camelot Library coding environment is that recoverable and volatile variables of the same type are indistinguishable at compile time. An integer in recoverable storage and a global or local integer variable look identical to the compiler.

The one mistake in this area that is easy to make and a bit hard to detect is doing a regular assignment to a variable in recoverable storage. The value of the data will be set correctly when the assignment is done, and may stay correct. An abort or server recovery, however, may later leave this value in place when it should have been changed, or may incorrectly change the data back to some old value.

What makes this bug very subtle is `MODIFY` statements are most often left out when assigning to pointer fields in recoverable data structures. If one pointer field is sometimes assigned to, rather than modified, the server may work fine as long as there is no failure. The first abort, or even the hundredth abort, may then corrupt the data structure. This will go undetected until some code tries to follow the pointer, when the server will typically 'seg fault'.

A.1.4 Forgetting that Transactions Abort

Transactions abort. They really do. This means that flow of control may suddenly transfer to the `END_TRANSACTION` of *any* enclosing transaction block. Getting used to this is difficult, and even relatively experienced users may miss some of the practical implications.

If within a transaction block you only manipulate local variables, recoverable storage, and locks, failure behavior will probably follow your mental model well. An abort or crash will completely undo the effects of one or more uncommitted transactions, without affecting any committed ones. If, on the other hand, you do file I/O, terminal I/O, or manipulation of global variables (including mutexes) within a transaction, you must be extremely careful to take the effects of an abort or crash into account. You may need to use the fact that *flow of control can only transfer from within a Camelot Library call.* An abort will never yank you out of your own code. Any time you use a library function or macro, the Library will check for aborts and by transfer control if one has occurred.

Sometimes it is useful to perform operations within the scope of a transaction even though they are not transactional and should not (or cannot) be undone if the transaction aborts. The classic example is locking a mutex. Because servers have multiple threads, any global variables or structures in non-recoverable storage must be protected by either locks or mutexes. Mutexes are faster, but must be used with great care. If you lock a mutex and then make any call to the Camelot Library, an abort may transfer flow of control past the point where the mutex would have been unlocked.

Another example of the same idea would be an application which prints some data and a prompt before each user command. If the user is allowed to perform more than one operation within a transaction, the data and prompt may be printed from within the scope of a transaction. This is fine, as long as no Camelot call (such as `MODIFY`, `LOCK`, or `SERVER_CALL`) is done while the display is in an inconsistent state. The use of any Camelot call gives the Library an opportunity to recognize an abort and transfer flow of control. In our example, this might leave the screen in an inconsistent state.

The situation is a bit different when you want to perform non-transactional operations as part of a transaction, and have them not be done if the transaction aborts. The best way to handle this in an application is usually to not do the non-transactional work until you know the transaction has committed. Within a server, which does not always begin the transaction it participates in, you may have to use a 'commit procedure' or 'abort procedure' to get this effect.

For example, consider an application that keeps a local cache to cut down on the cost of server calls for frequently accessed data. If data written by the application is added to the cache, it would be a serious mistake to add it from within the transaction that does the write. Instead, the application should wait until it knows the write has committed, and then update its cache.

A.2 Tools and Techniques

This section describes some of the techniques that are available for debugging Camelot servers and applications. For the most part, they are familiar debugging techniques modified to suit the new environment.

If you find you have trouble with the debuggers, and need other support beyond what is described in the rest of this section, you may want to try the tracing facilities that we have used in-house to develop our own servers and application. For source code, see the definitions for `BEGIN`, `END`, `RET`, and `RETURN` in the include files or in the Camelot coding standards[116].

A.2.1 Print Statements and their Relatives

`stdin`, `stdout`, and `stderr` do not work properly in Camelot servers. Do not try to use `printf` or other UNIX functions that write to stdout (except see Section A.2.4 below). You can use `fprintf` to a file you have opened, but be careful. Using the current Mach library, concurrent `fprintf` calls from parallel threads within one process may lead to trouble. You would need to use mutexes to be sure only one thread is doing output at a time.

A good solution to the output problem is to use a macro that we are currently exporting to all servers and applications. The macro is called 'DEBUG', and closely resembles a printf. The implementation used by applications sends data to stdout. The implementation used by servers sends the output to the Master Control Program (mcp). The mcp redirects the output to the Camelot output log.

The syntax for this macro looks slightly strange. This is because it takes as one argument the complete, parenthesized argument list for a `sprintf` to a buffer called `msg`. If this seems unclear, the description and examples below should help.

```
DEBUG{n,(msg, format-string, arg, ...));
```

For example:

```
DEBUG(5,(msg,
        'disk: No such transaction: \%s\n',
        Tio_TidToStr(tid)));

DEBUG(10,(msg,
         'tran: TA_Begin called: parentTid=\%s\n',
         Tio_TidToStr(parentTid)));
```

The DEBUG macro generates output only if `camDebugLevel`, a global variable defined in the Camelot object library, is greater than or equal to the parameter **n**. You should set this variable in your server or application initialization routine. Traditionally, we have used a default value of '5' and taken a '-d' switch to set the value anywhere between 1 and 100.

A.2.2 Adb

Camelot servers that crash due to a segmentation violations (segfault), or bus errors, print a short `context` before printing whatever trace information is available. This context information can be used in conjunction with adb to pin down the exact location where the server has died. The program counter (pc), that is provided as part of the context, is the location where the server has died. You can now use adb to find out in what procedure or function the server this location resides. Start adb with the program name as the command line argument. Then type the pc, with a ?X. This will give you the name of the procedure or function that the server died in, along with an offset from the beginning of that procedure or function.[1] Here is a short example of this method.

Server #2, run from the file 'myserver', died. The context said

```
Server 2: C: SEGMENTATION VIOLATION!
Server 2: C: sig=11
Server 2: C: code=0
Server 2: C: sc_pc=0x707bc
...
```

at a prompt, type

[1]on a Sun, the location specified, may be the location just after the error. This is because the pc is incremented before the memory access it made, and it upon the memory access that the server died.

```
%adb myserver
```

adb has no prompt. Now type

```
0x707bc?X
```

Adb will repond with something like:

```
_MyProcedure_Call+0x25c      <machine instruction>
```

From this we know that the server died in the procedure MyProcedure_Call, and that it died at offset 25c from the beginning of that procedure. If you are proficient in the machine language of your hardware, it may be possible for you to translate from the machine instructions that adb gives you into the source code that you wrote. In most cases, this is relatively hard.

A.2.3 Gdb

Mach provides a version of the `gdb` debugger that allows you to attach to a running task and debug it. This version of `gdb` also understands multi-threaded tasks. This is very useful for debugging data servers.

To use `gdb`, start up Camelot and your data server. Run `ps` to find the process ID (PID) of the data server. Start `gdb` with the name of the data server's executable file as the first argument:

```
gdb /usr/joe/myserver
```

Use the `attach` command in `gdb` to attach to the process:

```
attach <PID>
```

Debug the program using normal Mach `gdb` commands. The program has a very good help utility.

A.2.4 Other Debuggers

Previously, we mentioned that there is no stdin or stdout for a server. This makes using a debugger next to impossible. Fortunately, there is a way to run your server in Camelot, and still have a stdin and stdout. First, it is necessary to compile you program with the proper switches for the debugger that you are using. In most cases, this means the `-g` switch. Then, you must start Camelot by hand. Look at the Header printed by the Camelot program. It should have a line that starts with `Command Line:`. Copy that line to a piece of paper. It should be something like:

```
/usr/camelot/pre_aleph/bin/mcp
    l: -p /dev/rsd0b 0 512 16711168
    d:diskllog -p /usr/camelot/log/paging 0 512 2560000 -I
    r:recllog
```

This technique works best in an environment with multiple windows or terminals. In one window, type this command line, with the addition of `-S -i` after `d:diskllog`. The new command line should look like:

```
/usr/camelot/pre_aleph/bin/mcp
    l: -p /dev/rsd0b 0 512 16711168
    d:diskllog -Si -p /usr/camelot/log/paging 0 512 2560000 -I
    r:recllog
```

This command line will not return to the shell. In another window or terminal, start the nca. Now, add your favorite debugger as a server and start it. In the window where you started Camelot, you should get the prompt for your debugger. You can now start your server, and use all of the features of your debugger.

A.2.5 Camelot Signals

Camelot processes understand message based signals. These signals are similar in spirit and function to Unix signals. Camelot Signals are used to print out debugging messages and to set internal variables that control debugging information, checkpoint intervals, timeouts, *etc.* Output generated from Camelot Signals goes into the Camelot system output log (which is in `/tmp/camelot.log`, by default) for servers and Camelot components. Applications print their status reports on the controlling tty.

Each Camelot task allocates a signal handling thread that listens for signal messages that are sent by the `camsignal` program. The `camsignal` program is invoked with the following commandline:

```
Usage: camsignal <pname> [<name> <argument>]*
```

The `<pname>` parameter is the Camelot task you wish to signal either it's PID or its "special" name. Special names are registered for Camelot component task: `tran` for the Transaction Manager, `disk` for the Disk Manager, *etc.*

The `<name>` parameter specifies the signal. All tasks understand the `help` signal. This will cause the task to list to the output log the other signals it accepts. The Camelot Library supports a very nice `systat` command that prints out status of applications and servers. Some signals take integer arguments.

Appendix B

Abort Codes

Joshua J. Bloch

In this appendix, we list the system abort codes that can be returned when a transaction tries to commit (or abort). We divide the abort codes into two groups: true system abort codes, which come from Camelot system tasks; and Library abort codes, which come from the Camelot Library. True system abort codes are prefixed with AC_, while Library abort codes are prefixed with ACC_. Library abort codes are actually *restricted user abort codes.*

B.1 System Abort Codes

- AC_ILLEGAL_ABORT_CODE - The abort was voluntary, but the user passed an abort code outside of the legal range. Note that Camelot Library servers and applications will never cause this abort code. as the Library will intercept the illegal abort code specified by the user and return ACC_ILLEGAL_USER_ABORT_CODE instead.

- AC_COMMIT_FAILED - The commit protocol was unsuccessful, typically because a server voted not to commit the transaction. This code will also be returned if a remote site fails to respond to the Transaction Coordinator, in a distributed transaction.

- AC_SERVER_DIED - A server that was involved in the transaction crashed.

- AC_APPLICATION_DIED - The application that started the transaction is no longer running. (Only servers will receive this code.)

- AC_ANCESTOR_ABORTED - An ancestor of this transaction was aborted, either voluntarily or by the system, causing all of its descendants to abort. This code will rarely be seen by a Camelot Library program, as the library will transfer control beyond the outermost aborted transaction. Occasionally a Library program thread may "notice" a descendant abort before the abort message for the outermost aborting transaction has been processed.

- AC_COMMITTED_CHILD_ABORTED - A child of this transaction that had already committed was aborted (either voluntarily or by the system).

- AC_LONG_RUNNING - The Disk Manager aborted the transaction because it ran too long.
- AC_LWM_MISMATCH - The Communication Manager detected that a site involved in the transaction crashed and restarted.
- AC_SB_TRANS_MISUSE - A server-based transaction attempted to make a remote procedure call (RPC). Note that Camelot Library servers will never cause this abort code, as the Library will catch this error and halt the faulty server, printing an appropriate message in the system log.
- AC_BAD_CAM_DATA - Bad Camelot data was detected by the Communication Manager during an RPC. (Indicates communication error or internal error.)
- AC_NODE_DEATH - A Remote camelot node died during an RPC.

B.2 Library Abort Codes

- ACC_ILLEGAL_USER_ABORT_CODE - The abort was voluntary, but the user passed an abort code outside of the legal range.
- ACC_JOIN_AFTER_ABORT - A server's attempt to join the transaction failed because the transaction had already aborted.
- ACC_SERVER_LOOKUP_FAILED - Attempts to contact a server in order to perform a server call were unsuccessful.
- ACC_SERVER_CALL_TIMEOUT - No response to a server call was received within the designated timeout interval.
- ACC_SERVER_CALL_FAILED - A Communication error occurred when attempting an RPC.
- ACC_FAMILY_TOO_LONG_AT_SERVER - The transaction was aborted by a server because it remained uncommitted for a time longer than the amount specified in the transTimeOut parameter to START_SERVER.
- ACC_MALLOC_OUT_OF_MEMORY - A call to REC_MALLOC (or REC_NEW) failed because there was insufficient memory left on the recoverable heap.
- ACC_OUT_OF_LOCK_SPACES - A call to ALLOC_LOCK_SPACE failed because there were no more lock spaces available.

Appendix C

Camelot Interface Specification

This appendix presents the Camelot component interfaces. Each interface has a two letter name. The first letter represents the component that receives the call, and the second represents the components that makes sends the call. Component names are abbreviated as follows:

- A – application
- C – Communications Manager
- D – Disk Manager
- L – Log Manager
- M – Master Control Program
- N – Node Server
- R – Recovery Manager
- S – data server
- T – Transaction Manager

Each interface is presented in a separate section below.

C.1 AT Interface

This message is sent to an application when a transaction dies for any reason other than being the argument to `TA_Kill`. This means that the message will be sent if another process kills the transaction or one of its ancestors, or if the application kills one of its ancestors. As an optimization, if a top-level transaction is killed, `AT_TransactionHasDied` is NOT sent on behalf of the top-level transaction's descendants.

```
simpleroutine AT_TransactionHasDied(
                atPort           : port_t;
                tid              : cam_tid_t;
                status           : int);
```

`atPort` the port on which the application receives messages from the Transaction Manager.

`tid` the transaction that is dying.
`status` a description of the cause of the abort.

C.2 CA Interface

This call is used by an application to look up a server.

```
routine CA_Lookup(
                caPort              : port_t;
                name                : cam_object_name_t;
                site                : cam_object_name_t;
            OUT port                : port_t);
```

`caPort` is the port that applications use to contact the Communication Manager.
`name` is the server's name.
`site` is the server's site.
`port` is the port of the desired server, which is returned by this call.

C.3 CS Interface

This call is used by servers to enable applications (or other servers) to look it up by its name.

```
routine CS_SignIn(
                csPort              : port_t;
                name                : cam_object_name_t;
                signature           : u_int;
                port                : port_t);
```

`csPort` is the port that servers use to contact the Communication Manager.
`name` is the string name of the server.
`signature` is a value used to prevent others from signing out a server that they didn't sign in.
`port` is the port on which the server may be reached.

This allows a server to remove its port from service. If a data server dies, perhaps because its site went down, then every process using it receives a `PORT_DELETED` notice. If a server calls `CS_SignOut`, its remote clients receive a `PORT_DELETED` notice. Local clients are only notified when the server deallocates the port, either by exiting or explicitly calling `port_deallocate`.

```
routine CS_SignOut(
                csPort              : port_t;
                name                : cam_object_name_t;
                signature           : u_int);
```

`csPort` is the port that servers use to contact the Communication Manager.
`name` is the string name of the server.
`signature` is a value used to prevent others from signing out a server that they didn't sign in.

This call allows a server to look up another server.

```
routine CS_Lookup(
                csPort          : port_t;
                name            : cam_object_name_t;
                site            : cam_object_name_t;
            OUT port            : port_t);
```

`csPort` is the port that servers use to contact the Communication Manager.
`name` is the other server's name.
`site` is the other server's site.
`port` is the port of the desired server, which is returned by this call.

C.4 CT Interface

The Transaction Manger uses this call to register its public service port with the Communication Manager. This port is used by servers and applications to make the `TA_AddApplication` call.

```
routine CT_SignIn(
                ctPort          : port_t;
                tranName        : cam_object_name_t;
                tranPort        : port_t);
```

`ctPort` is the port on which the Communication Manager receives messages from the Disk Manager.
`tranName` is the name to associate with the Transaction Manager's public port.
`tranPort` is the Transaction Manager's public service port.

C.5 DL Interface

When the Log Manager starts running low on space, it uses this call to tell the Disk Manager to truncate the log. Successive calls will cause the Disk Manager to try harder to reduce log space. Eventually, the Disk Manager will start aborting long running transactions, flushing pages, etc.

```
simpleroutine DL_RequestTruncate(
                dlPort          : port_t;
                truncationPoint : cam_lsn_t);
```

`dlPort` is the port on which the Disk Manager receives requests from the Log Manager. Since the Log Manager is now compiled in to the Disk Manager, this parameter is ignored.

`trunctionPoint` is the LSN that the Log Manager would like to become the new truncation point.

C.6 DN Interface

Server startup is requested by the Node Server on behalf of some application. The Disk Manager will start the specified servers and attempt to recover them.

```
routine DN_StartDataServers(
                dnPort          : port_t;
                serverIds       : cam_server_id_list_t);
```

`dnPort` The port on which the Disk Manager receives requests from the Node Server.

`serverIds` A list of data servers to be started.

Since the Disk Manager is the parent of all data servers, the the Node Server must send requests to kill data servers to the Disk Manager.

```
simpleroutine DN_KillDataServer(
                dnPort          : port_t;
                serverId        : cam_server_id_t);
```

`dnPort` The port on which the Disk Manager receives requests from the Node Server.

`serverId` The ID of the server to be killed.

This call is used by the Node Server to find out the state of a server. If the Disk Manager has no record of a server, it will say the server is `CAM_SS_DOWN_CLEAN`.

```
routine DN_GetServerState(
                dnPort          : port_t;
                serverId        : cam_server_id_t;
            OUT state           : cam_server_state_t);
```

`dnPort` The port on which the Disk Manager receives requests from the Node Server.

`serverId` The ID of the server whose state is requested.

`state` The state of the server.

The Node Server uses this call at startup time to give the Disk Manager a port for `ND_` calls, and to give the Disk Manager a list of all servers in the Node Server's database. The Disk Manager does an `ND_GetRestartAdvice()` for each server in the list, showing a transition from `CAM_SS_UNDEFINED` to `CAM_SS_DOWN_CLEAN` or `CAM_SS_DOWN_DIRTY` as appropriate.

```
simpleroutine DN_Initialize(
                dnPort          : port_t;
                ndPort          : port_t;
                serverIds       : cam_server_id_list_t);
```

`dnPort` The port on which the Disk Manager receives requests from the Node Server.
`ndPort` The port on which the Node Server receives requests from the Disk Manager.
`serverIds` The ids of all the servers in the Node Server's database.

This call shuts Camelot down. The Disk Manager will send a shutdown request to the MCP.

```
routine DN_ShutdownCamelot(
                dnPort          : port_t);
```

`dnPort` The port on which the Disk Manager receives requests from the Node Server.

This call allows the Node Server to set the maximum recovery time. Since recovery time is a function of the number of records scanned during recovery, this call takes the maximum number of records we should scan during recovery. This Disk Manager will adjust hot page, long running transaction, and checkpoint criteria based on this number.

```
routine DN_SetRecoveryTime(
                dnPort          : port_t;
                maxRecords      : u_int);
```

`dnPort` The port on which the Disk Manager receives requests from the Node Server.
`maxRecords` The maximum number of records to be scanned during recovery.

This call allows the Node Server to query the Disk Manager about the current checkpoint interval.

```
routine DN_GetCheckpointInterval(
                dnPort          : port_t;
            OUT interval        : u_int);
```

`dnPort` The port on which the Disk Manager receives requests from the Node Server.
`interval` The current checkpoint interval, in records.

This call allows the Node Server to set the chunk size.

```
routine DN_SetChunkSize(
                dnPort          : port_t;
                chunkSizeInBits : u_int);
```

`dnPort` The port on which the Disk Manager receives requests from the Node Server.

`chunkSizeInBits` The chunk size is specified in bits, i.e., the base 2 log of the number of bytes.

This is the first step in deleting a server. The Disk Manager will lock the server record, and return an error if the server is not down.

```
routine DN_DeleteServerPhase1(
                dnPort            : port_t;
                serverId          : cam_server_id_t);
```

`dnPort` The port on which the Disk Manager receives requests from the Node Server.

`serverId` The ID of the server to be deleted.

This is the second and final step in deleting a server. The Disk Manager will spool a server-deletion record that references the specified TID, so that if that transaction's family commits the server will be permanently deleted. The Disk Manager will now drop the lock on the server.

```
routine DN_DeleteServerPhase2(
                dnPort            : port_t;
                serverId          : cam_server_id_t;
                tid               : cam_tid_t);
```

`dnPort` The port on which the Disk Manager receives requests from the Node Server.

`serverId` The ID of the server to be deleted.

`tid` The identifier of the transaction on behalf of which the server is being deleted.

C.7 DR Interface

This call takes a list of TIDs and returns the list of LSNs of the log records that describe changes made on behalf of these transactions. The TIDs must be in the same family.

```
routine DR_GetTranLsns(
                drPort            : port_t;
                tidList           : cam_tid_list_t;
            OUT lsnList           : cam_lsn_list_t;
            OUT readOnlyCnt       : u_int;
            OUT cachePtr          : pointer_t);
```

`drPort` The port on which the Disk Manager receives requests from the Recovery Manager.

`tidList` the list of transactions in which the Recovery Manager is interested.

`lsnList` The list of the LSNs spooled on behalf of this family. The list is in decreasing order (from newest to oldest). The Disk Manager may not truncate these log records until it gets a `DR_DoneWithLsns` message (see below).

`readOnlyCnt` The count of the number of the given transactions that are read-only.

`cachePtr` refers to the data that must be transferred from the version of Log Manager being used by the Disk Manager to the (read-only) version used by the Recovery Manager to make them consistent.

This call takes a list of region pointers (and lengths) and returns a list of all the LSNs (of modify records) that describe changes to the regions' pages since those pages were last written to non-volatile storage. This list will be in descending order with no duplicates. The Disk Manager may not truncate these log records out of the log until it gets a `DR_DoneWithLsns` message (see below).

```
routine DR_GetObjectLsns(
                drPort          : port_t;
                rptrList        : cam_regptr_list_t;
                sizeList        : cam_size_list_t;
            OUT lsnList         : cam_lsn_list_t);
```

`drPort` The port on which the Disk Manager receives requests from the Recovery Manager.

`rptrList` the list of regions in which the Recovery Manager is interested.

`sizeList` the size of the list of regions in the `rptrList`.

`lsnList` The list of the LSNs spooled on behalf of this family. The list is in decreasing order (from newest to oldest). The Disk Manager may not truncate these log records until it gets a DR_DoneWithLsns message (see below).

This call returns the contents of a region from disk, rather than from a log record.

```
routine DR_DataRead(
                drPort          : port_t;
                regptr          : cam_regptr_t;
                size            : u_int;
            OUT data            : pointer_t);
```

`drPort` The port on which the Disk Manager receives requests from the Recovery Manager.

`regptr` The pointer to the beginning of the region.

`size` The size of the region in bytes.

`data` A copy of the contents of the region, returned out of line.

A request from the Recovery Manager to take a checkpoint. This request is given after each node or server recovery pass.

```
routine DR_Checkpoint(
                drPort          : port_t;
                recovered       : cam_server_id_list_t;
                notRecovered    : cam_server_id_list_t);
```

`drPort` The port on which the Disk Manager receives requests from the Recovery Manager.
`recovered` A list of ids of the server that have been recovered.
`notRecovered` A list of ids of the server that have not been recovered.

If a data server does not respond to messages from the Recovery Manager, the Recovery Manager will kill the data server.

```
routine DR_KillDataServer(
                drPort          : port_t;
                serverId        : cam_server_id_t);
```

`drPort` The port on which the Disk Manager receives requests from the Recovery Manager.
`serverId` The ID of the server to be kill.

This call indicates that no recovery thread is currently using an LSN list which contains LSNs less then the given LSN. This call is needed to accomodate a very specific circumstance. During recovery processing, the Disk Manager is still doing forward processing. The Disk Manager may write out pages and truncate the log. Future recovery passes will find needed values on disk, written out, but some currently active recovery threads may already be committed to finding these values in the log.

```
routine DR_DoneWithLsns(
                drPort          : port_t;
                lsn             : cam_lsn_t);
```

`drPort` The port on which the Disk Manager receives requests from the Recovery Manager.
`lsn` The lowest LSN that the Recovery Manager still cares about.

This call allows the Disk Manager to re-build its structures when the Recovery Manager un-does changes on behalf of an aborted or incomplete OVNV transaction. It also writes the undo record on behalf of the Recovery Manager.

```
routine DR_UndoOvnv(
                drPort          : port_t;
                serverId        : cam_server_id_t;
                tid             : cam_tid_t;
```

```
                    regptr          : cam_regptr_t;
                    oldValue        : pointer_t;
                    lsnUndone       : cam_lsn_t);
```

`drPort` The port on which the Disk Manager receives requests from the Recovery Manager.
`serverId` The server whose recoverable storage is being manipulated.
`tid` The identifier of the transaction that is being undone.
`regptr` The point to the region being manipulated.
`oldValue` The old value of the region, sent out of line.
`lsnUndone` The LSN of the log record that is being undone.

This call allows the Disk Manager to create appropriate patch records when the Recovery Manager changes the state of an object.

```
routine DR_Restore(
                    drPort          : port_t;
                    famId           : cam_fam_id_t;
                    regptr          : cam_regptr_t;
                    newValue        : pointer_t);
```

`drPort` The port on which the Disk Manager receives requests from the Recovery Manager.
`famId` The ID of the family on whose behalf the patch will be done.
`regptr` The point to the region being manipulated.
`newValue` The new value of the region, sent out of line.

This call writes the Recovery Manager's abort record for aborted NV transactions.

```
routine DR_AbortNv(
                    drPort          : port_t;
                    tidList         : cam_tid_list_t);
```

`drPort` The port on which the Disk Manager receives requests from the Recovery Manager.
`tidList` The list of TIDs for the new value transactions that are being aborted.

This call allows the Recovery Manager to setup the grid after a crash.

```
routine DR_BackLinkTran(
                    drPort          : port_t;
                    famId           : cam_fam_id_t;
                    lsn             : cam_lsn_t;
                    recordNumber    : u_int;
                    backstopRecord  : boolean_t);
```

`drPort` The port on which the Disk Manager receives requests from the Recovery Manager.
`famId` The ID of the family in which this record will be linked.
`lsn` The LSN of the record to be linked into the grid.
`recordNumber` The number of the record to be linked into the grid.
`backstopRecord` A flag indicating if this a backstopRecord.

This call allows the Recovery Manager to setup the grid after a crash.

```
routine DR_BackLinkPage(
                drPort            : port_t;
                regptr            : cam_regptr_t;
                length            : u_int;
                lsn               : cam_lsn_t;
                recordNumber      : u_int);
```

`drPort` The port on which the Disk Manager receives requests from the Recovery Manager.
`regptr` The pointer to the region that is being linked into the grid.
`length` The length of the region that is being linked into the grid.
`lsn` The LSN of the record to be linked into the grid.
`recordNumber` The number of the record to be linked into the grid.

This call allows the Recovery Manager to setup the grid after a crash.

```
routine DR_BackLinkAbort(
                drPort            : port_t;
                lsn               : cam_lsn_t;
                recordNumber      : u_int);
```

`drPort` The port on which the Disk Manager receives requests from the Recovery Manager.
`lsn` The LSN of the abort record to be linked into the grid.
`recordNumber` The number of the abort record to be linked into the grid.

This call allows the Recovery Manager to write a backstop record.

```
routine DR_Backstop(
                drPort            : port_t;
                tid               : cam_tid_t;
                server            : cam_server_id_t;
                lastOne           : boolean_t;
                backstopDataPtr : pointer_t);
```

`drPort` The port on which the Disk Manager receives requests from the Recovery Manager.
`tid` The identifier of the transaction that is being backstopped.

`server` The ID of the server whose records are copied in this backstop record.

`lastOne` A flag indicating if this is the last backstop record for this transaction.

`backstopDataPtr` That backstop data, sent out of line.

C.8 DS Interface

This call gives the server all the information and capabilities it needs to reference recoverable regions.

```
routine DS_Initialize(
                dsPort          : port_t;
            OUT serverId        : cam_server_id_t;
            OUT recoveryOnly    : boolean_t;
            OUT tsPort          : port_t;
            OUT mPort           : port_t;
            OUT sPort           : port_t
                      = (MSG_TYPE_PORT_ALL, 32);
            OUT sharedMemAddr   : vm_address_t;
            OUT segDescList     : cam_segment_desc_list_t;
            OUT segPortList     : port_array_t);
```

`dsPort` The port on which the Disk Manager receives requests from this server.

`serverId` The ID of this server. This value is informational. For security reasons, data servers never provide IDs in requests to Camelot. The data server's ID is derived from the port in which the request is made. It is conceivable that a data server might use its ID in the NA interface to ask the Node Server to give it information about itself, or to change its resource allocations.

`recoveryOnly` A flag is set to `TRUE` if the server is expected to just recover and exit. Otherwise the server will recover and make itself available for use.

`tsPort` The port used in calls to the Transaction Manager for beginning, joining, and killing transactions.

`mPort` The port used to send debugging information to the MCP.

`sPort` The port used to receive requests from Camelot system components. These requests indicate that transactions have prepared, committed, or aborted. During transaction abort and recovery, these messages describe changes which must be made to recoverable storage. Upon receiving the reply to the `DS_Initialize` message, the data server will get receive and ownership rights on the `sPort`.

`sharedMemAddr` The address of the shared memory queue. This queue is used to efficiently pin regions and spool log records.

`segDescList` A list of this server's segment descriptors.
`segPortList` A list of ports used in the `vm_allocate_pager` call to map recoverable storage into a data server's address space.

The servers uses this call to inform the Disk Manager that it has completed recovery and is about to open for business.

```
routine DS_RecoveryComplete(
                dsPort          : port_t);
```

`dsPort` The port on which the Disk Manager receives requests from this server.

This call is used to "pin" a region in virtual memory (i.e., the Disk Manager will not copy a modified page out to non-volatile storage if it contains any pinned regions).

```
routine DS_PinRegion(
                dsPort          : port_t;
                tid             : cam_tid_t;
                regptr          : cam_regptr_t;
                size            : u_int);
```

`dsPort` The port on which the Disk Manager receives requests from this server.
`tid` The identifier of the transaction pinning this region.
`regptr` The pointer to the region being pinned.
`size` The size of the region being pinned.

This call is used to spool the old and new values of a region to the log. This call will unpin the region.

```
routine DS_LogOldValueNewValue(
                dsPort          : port_t;
                tid             : cam_tid_t;
                regptr          : cam_regptr_t;
                oldValue        : pointer_t;
                newValue        : pointer_t);
```

`dsPort` The port on which the Disk Manager receives requests from this server.
`tid` The identifier of the transaction pinning this region.
`regptr` The pointer to the region being pinned.
`oldValue` The old value of this region, sent out of line.
`newValue` The new value of this region, sent out of line.

This call is used to spool the new value of a region to the log. The region will remained pinned until the transaction commits.

```
routine DS_LogNewValue(
                dsPort          : port_t;
                tid             : cam_tid_t;
                regptr          : cam_regptr_t;
                newValue        : pointer_t);
```

`dsPort` The port on which the Disk Manager receives requests from this server.
`tid` The identifier of the transaction pinning this region.
`regptr` The pointer to the region being pinned.
`newValue` The new value of this region, sent out of line.

This call is used to spool prepare data (e.g., lock tables) to the log. This call is issued by data servers if they have been told to prepare in a `ST_Vote` message.

```
routine DS_Prepare(
                dsPort          : port_t;
                famId           : cam_fam_id_t;
                prepareData     : pointer_t);
```

`dsPort` The port on which the Disk Manager receives requests from this server.
`famId` The ID of the transaction family.
`prepareData` The data to be stored in the prepare record, sent out of line.

This call allows data servers to force commit records for server-based transactions.

```
routine DS_ForceCommit(
                dsPort          : port_t;
                famId           : cam_fam_id_t);
```

`dsPort` The port on which the Disk Manager receives requests from this server.
`famId` The ID of the server-based transaction family.

This call allows data servers to come down 'clean'. All of the server's pages will be written to backing storage, unless they are pinned. If the server is still involved in active transactions, some pages may be pinned.

```
routine DS_FlushAllPages(
                dsPort          : port_t);
```

`dsPort` The port on which the Disk Manager receives requests from this server.

This temporary call allows data servers to restore the state of their recoverable storage after a crash when the external memory management interface is not being used.

```
routine DS_LoadSegment(
                dsPort              : port_t;
                regptr              : cam_regptr_t;
                length              : u_int;
            OUT data                : pointer_t);
```

`dsPort` The port on which the Disk Manager receives requests from this server.
`regptr` The pointer to the region.
`length` The length to the region.
`data` The data on disk, returned out of line.

This call is used to prefetch the pages on which a region resides.

```
routine DS_Prefetch(
                dsPort              : port_t;
                regptr              : cam_regptr_t;
                length              : u_int);
```

`dsPort` The port on which the Disk Manager receives requests from this server.
`regptr` The pointer to the region.
`length` The length to the region.

This call is used to preflush the pages on which a region resides.

```
routine DS_Preflush(
                dsPort              : port_t;
                regptr              : cam_regptr_t;
                length              : u_int);
```

`dsPort` The port on which the Disk Manager receives requests from this server.
`regptr` The pointer to the region.
`length` The length to the region.

This call is used to zerofill the pages on which a region resides.

```
routine DS_ZeroFill(
                dsPort              : port_t;
                regptr              : cam_regptr_t;
                length              : u_int);
```

`dsPort` The port on which the Disk Manager receives requests from this server.
`regptr` The pointer to the region.
`length` The length to the region.

This call is used to spool the current value of a region for debugging purposes.

```
routine DS_LogDebugRecord(
                dsPort          : port_t;
                tid             : cam_tid_t;
                regptr          : cam_regptr_t;
                value           : pointer_t);
```

`dsPort` The port on which the Disk Manager receives requests from this server.
`tid` The identifier of the transaction on behalf of which we are running.
`regptr` The pointer to the region being manipulated.
`value` The value of this region, sent out of line.

C.9 DT Interface

Write records to the log. The short form of this call is provided with fixed sized buffers so that out of line data will not be sent. If the log record or one of the variable length lists does not fit, then the long form of the call should be used. This call is synchronous, because the Transaction Manager needs to know that log records have really been written before it can declare that a transaction has committed.

```
routine DT_SmallLogWrite(
            dtPort          : port_t;
            unused          : u_int;
            dataLength      : u_int;
            data            : cam_short_log_record_t;
            serverCount     : u_int;
            serverList      : cam_short_server_id_list_t;
            completeLength  : u_int;
            completeTrans   : cam_short_tid_list_t);
```

`dtPort` The port on which the Disk Manager receives messages from the Transaction Manager.
`unused` This parameter is ignored.
`dataLength` The length of the data.
`data` The data contains the records, one after another, each record preceded by its length. The length is an aligned `u_int`.
`serverCount` The number of servers in the `serverList`.
`serverList` A list of servers that should have their shared memory queues processed before the data are processed.
`completeLength` The number of TIDs in the `completeList`.
`completeTrans` A list of complete transactions. This list is piggy-backed with these messages so that the Disk Manager can clean its data structures.

Write records to the log. This call is synchronous, because the Transaction Manager needs to know that log records have really been written before it can declare that a transaction has committed.

```
routine DT_LargeLogWrite(
                dtPort          : port_t;
                unsed           : u_int;
                data            : pointer_t;
                serverListPtr   : cam_server_id_list_t;
                completeTrans   : cam_tid_list_t);
```

`dtPort` The port on which the Disk Manager receives messages from the Transaction Manager.

`unused` This parameter is ignored.

`data` The data contains the records, one after another, each record preceded by its length. The length is an aligned `u_int`.

`serverListPtr` A list of servers that should have their shared memory queues processed before the data are processed.

`completeTrans` A list of complete transactions. This list is piggybacked with these messages so that the Disk Manager can clean its data structures.

If ST_Suspend times out, TranMan will kill the data server using this call. At some time in the future, this call may also be made if a data server is caught trying to break security in some way; this is unimplemented.

```
routine DT_KillDataServer(
                dtPort          : port_t;
                serverId        : cam_server_id_t);
```

`dtPort` The port on which the Disk Manager receives messages from the Transaction Manager.

`serverId` The ID of the server to be killed.

C.10 LD Interface

Open the log.

```
routine LD_OpenLog(
                ldPort          : port_t;
                nbrClfsToUse    : u_int;
                readOnly        : boolean_t);
```

`ldPort` The port on which the Log Manager receives messages from the Disk Manager. If the Log Manager is loaded into the Disk Manager, this parameter is `PORT_NULL`.

`nbrClfsToUse` The number of Central Logging Facilities to use.

`readOnly` The Recovery Manager uses this parameter to open the log read-only.

Write a log record. Return as soon as record is buffered.

```
routine LD_Write(
                ldPort              : port_t;
                recPtr              : pointer_t;
                forceWhenFull       : boolean_t;
                newTruncPoint       : cam_lsn_t;
            OUT lsn                 : cam_lsn_t;
            OUT bufferSent          : boolean_t;
            OUT reqTruncPoint       : cam_lsn_t);
```

`ldPort` The port on which the Log Manager receives messages from the Disk Manager. If the Log Manager is loaded into the Disk Manager, this parameter is PORT_NULL.

`recPtr` The pointer to the log record, which is sent out of line.

`forceWhenFull` A flag indicating that a force is to be done when this buffer is full.

`newTruncPoint` The LSN of the new truncation point.

`lsn` The LSN of the newly written log record.

`bufferSent` A flag indicating whether or not this log record caused a buffer to be sent to disk. This does not mean that (all of) this log record was sent to disk.

`reqTruncPoint` The LSN that the Log Manager would like to be the new truncation point.

Immediately force up to LSN. Return when stable to LSN.

```
routine LD_ForceLsn(
                ldPort              : port_t;
                lsn                 : cam_lsn_t);
```

`ldPort` The port on which the Log Manager receives messages from the Disk Manager. If the Log Manager is loaded into the Disk Manager, this parameter is PORT_NULL.

`lsn` The LSN of the log record up to which we force.

Return the current high stable LSN.

```
routine LD_HighStable(
                ldPort              : port_t;
            OUT lsn                 : cam_lsn_t);
```

`ldPort` The port on which the Log Manager receives messages from the Disk Manager. If the Log Manager is loaded into the Disk Manager, this parameter is `PORT_NULL`.
`lsn` The LSN of the most recently written log record that is stable.

Return the current high LSN written.

```
routine LD_HighWritten(
                ldPort              : port_t;
            OUT lsn                 : cam_lsn_t);
```

`ldPort` The port on which the Log Manager receives messages from the Disk Manager. If the Log Manager is loaded into the Disk Manager, this parameter is `PORT_NULL`.
`lsn` The LSN of the most recently written log record.

Read a record given an LSN.

```
routine LD_Read(
                ldPort              : port_t;
                lsn                 : cam_lsn_t;
            OUT prevLsn             : cam_lsn_t;
            OUT recPtr              : pointer_t);
```

`ldPort` The port on which the Log Manager receives messages from the Disk Manager. If the Log Manager is loaded into the Disk Manager, this parameter is `PORT_NULL`.
`lsn` The LSN of the log record we wish to read.
`prevLsn` The LSN of the log record that precedes the one requested.
`recPtr` A pointer to the record, which is returned out of line.

This call instructs the Log Manager to reserve the specifed amount of space in the log. When the amount of used log space approaches the specified minimum, the Log Manager should begin to send `DL_RequestTruncate` messages.

```
routine LD_SetReserve(
                ldPort              : port_t;
                reserveInBytes      : u_int);
```

`ldPort` The port on which the Log Manager receives messages from the Disk Manager. If the Log Manager is loaded into the Disk Manager, this parameter is `PORT_NULL`.
`reserveInBytes` The new reserve limit, in bytes.

This call asks the Log Manager for the size of the logging device.

```
routine LD_GetLogSize(
                ldPort              : port_t;
        OUT     logSize             : u_int);
```

`ldPort` The port on which the Log Manager receives messages from the Disk Manager. In the compiled in version of the Log Manager, this parameter is `PORT_NULL`.

`logSize` The size of the log in bytes.

C.11 MD Interface

The Disk Manager uses this routine to exchange ports with the log component, the Recovery Manager, and the Transaction Manager.

```
routine MD_Initialize(
                mPort           : port_t;
                dlPort          : port_t;
                drPort          : port_t;
                dtPort          : port_t;
            OUT ldPort          : port_t;
            OUT rdPort          : port_t;
            OUT tdPort          : port_t);
```

`mPort` is the port to the Master Control Program.

`dlPort` is the port on which the Disk Manager will receive messages from the Log Manager. Since the Log Manager is now loaded with Disk Manager, `PORT_NULL` should be used for this parameter.

`drPort` is the port on which the Disk Manager will receive messages from the Recovery Manager.

`dtPort` is the port on which the Disk Manager will receive messages from the Transaction Manager.

`ldPort` is the port on which the Log Manager will receive messages from the Disk Manager. Since the Log Manager is now loaded with the Disk Manager, `PORT_NULL` will be returned.

`rdPort` is the port on which the Recovery Manager will receive messages from the Disk Manager.

`tdPort` is the port on which the Transaction Manager will receive messages from the Disk Manager.

The Disk Manager makes this call to get a debugging output port (an `msPort`, for a server that is being started. The server can use this port in the `MX_WriteDebugging` call to send debugging messages back to the MCP.

```
routine MD_AddDataServer(
                mPort           : port_t;
                serverId        : cam_server_id_t;
            OUT msPort          : port_t);
```

`mPort` is the port to the Master Control Program.

`serverId` is the ID of the server.
`msPort` is the port that the server can use to send debugging output.

At the Node Server's request, the Disk Manager will tell the Master Control Program to bring down Camelot.

```
simpleroutine MD_ShutdownCamelot(mPort : port_t);
```

`mPort` is the port to the Master Control Program.

C.12 MR Interface

The Recovery Manager uses this routine to exchange ports with the the Disk Manager and the Transaction Manager.

```
routine MR_Initialize(
                mPort             : port_t;
                rdPort            : port_t;
                rtPort            : port_t;
            OUT drPort            : port_t;
            OUT trPort            : port_t);
```

`mPort` is the port to the MCP.
`rdPort` is the port on which the Recovery Manager will receive messages from the Disk Manager.
`rtPort` is the port on which the Recovery Manager will receive messages from the Transaction Manager.
`drPort` is the port on which the Disk Manager will receive messages from the Recovery Manager.
`trPort` is the port on which the Transaction Manager will receive messages from the Recovery Manager.

C.13 MT Interface

The Transaction Manager uses this routine to exchange ports with the Communications Manager, the Disk Manager, and the Recovery Manager.

```
routine MT_Initialize(
                mPort             : port_t;
                tcPort            : port_t;
                tdPort            : port_t;
                trPort            : port_t;
            OUT ctPort            : port_t;
            OUT dtPort            : port_t;
            OUT rtPort            : port_t);
```

`mPort` is the port to the MCP.

`tcPort` is the port on which the Transaction Manager will receive messages from the Communication Manager. Since the Communication Manager is now loaded with Transaction Manager, `PORT_NULL` should be used for this parameter.

`tdPort` is the port on which the Transaction Manager will receive messages from the Disk Manager.

`trPort` is the port on which the Transaction Manager will receive messages from the Recovery Manager.

`ctPort` is the port on which the Communication Manager will receive messages from the Transaction Manager. Since the Communications Manager is now loaded with Transaction Manager, `PORT_NULL` will be returned.

`dtPort` is the port on which the Disk Manager will receive messages from the Transaction Manager.

`rtPort` is the port on which the Recovery Manager will receive messages from the Transaction Manager.

C.14 MX Interface

This routine is used by call Camelot Processes to send debugging information to the console or a UNIX file. Message are sent to the MCP so that that will be synchronized. The MCP prefaces each debugging message with the identity of the process that send the output (`Disk:`, `Server 1:`, *etc*).

```
simpleroutine MX_WriteDebugging(
                mPort               : port_t;
                str                 : string800);
```

`mPort` is a port to the MCP. Each Camelot process has a different `mPort` so that the MCP will know what prefix to prepend to the debugging message.

`str` is the debugging message.

C.15 NA Interface

This call allows users to log into the Node Server. It takes a password and a user name, and returns a pointer to a transaction ID which is used as a key for all subsequent Node Server operations on behalf of that user. This key is a parameter for most of the other call in this section.

```
camelotroutine NA_Login(
                userName            : user_name_t;
                password            : password_t;
            OUT key                 : cam_tid_t);
```

`userName` The user name of the person logging in.
`password` The password of the user logging in.
`key` A token to identify the caller in subsequent calls.

This call returns a list of the users who are currently logged in. A user may be logged in multiple times. Some operations may not be performed on a user who is logged in.

```
camelotroutine NA_ListLogins(
                    key              : cam_tid_t;
                OUT userNameList     : user_name_list_t);
```

`key` The key identifies the caller.
`userNameList` This is the list of users currently logged in.

This call allows the addition of new users. The privelege of a new user is specified by the privilege parameter. The allowed privilege types are `ADMIN`, `USER`, and `NONE`.

```
camelotroutine NA_AddUser(
                    key              : cam_tid_t;
                    userName         : user_name_t;
                    password         : password_t;
                    privilege        : privilege_t);
```

`key` The key identifies the caller.
`userName` This is the new user name.
`password` This is the password for the new user.
`privilege` The privilege to be allowed to the new user.

This call changes a user's privilege. The caller of this function must be logged in with a user ID which has `ADMIN` privileges to execute this call. Otherwise, anybody could modify their own privileges.

```
camelotroutine NA_SetPrivilege(
                    key              : cam_tid_t;
                    userName         : user_name_t;
                    privilege        : privilege_t);
```

`key` The key identifies the caller.
`userName` The name of the user whose privileges are being changed.
`privilege` The new privilege that the specified user will be permited.

This call changes a user's password. The calling program should make sure that the password has been properly acquired.

```
camelotroutine NA_SetPassword(
                    key              : cam_tid_t;
                    userName         : user_name_t;
                    password         : password_t);
```

`key` The key identifies the caller.
`userName` This is the name of the user whose password is being changed.
`password` This is the new password for the user.

This call allows the deletion of users. You must have ADMIN privileges to call this function, and you can't delete a user who is logged in.

```
camelotroutine NA_DeleteUser(
                key             : cam_tid_t;
                userName        : user_name_t);
```

`key` The key identifies the caller.
`userName` This is the name of the user to be deleted from the system.

This call shows the privileges of a given user. Anybody may make this call.

```
camelotroutine NA_ShowUser(
                key             : cam_tid_t;
                userName        : user_name_t;
            OUT privilege       : privilege_t);
```

`key` The key identifies the caller.
`userName` This the user about whom the information is requested.
`privilege` This is the privilege of the specifed user.

This call returns a list of all users. This is useful when you want to confirm an add user or delete user call made previously.

```
camelotroutine NA_ListUsers(
                key             : cam_tid_t;
            OUT userlist        : user_name_list_t);
```

`key` The key identifies the caller.
`userName` This is the list of the authorized users of Camelot on this system.

This call sets the chunk size on this node. This call must be made when there are no servers in the Node Server's database. The chunksize must be specified in two ways. The first is the size in bytes of each chunk. This is for use by the Node Server. The other is the width of the chunk size in bits, which is effectively the base two log of the of the size in bytes.

```
camelotroutine NA_SetChunkSize(
                key             : cam_tid_t;
                chunkBytes      : u_int;
                chunkBits       : u_int);
```

`key` The key identifies the caller.
`chunkBytes` This is the size, in bytes, of a chunk of recoverable storage.

`chunkBits` This is the base two log of `chunkBytes`.

This call returns the chunk size on this node. Useful when somebody else has been using the system, and you want to know to what the chunk size has been set.

```
camelotroutine NA_ShowChunkSize(
                    key               : cam_tid_t;
                OUT chunkBytes        : u_int);
```

`key` The key identifies the caller.

`chunkBytes` This is the current size, in bytes, of a chunk of recoverable storage.

This call allows the addition of new servers. If the `serverID` parameter is `nullServerId`, the Node Server will pick and return an unused server ID. If the `segmentID` parameter is `nullSegmentId`, the Node Server will pick and return an unused segment ID.

```
camelotroutine NA_AddServer(
                    key               : cam_tid_t;
              INOUT serverID          : cam_server_id_t;
                    owner             : user_name_t;
                    autoRestart       : boolean_t;
                    commandLine       : camelot_string_t;
              INOUT segmentID         : cam_segment_id_t;
                    quotaChunks       : u_int);
```

`key` The key identifies the caller.

`serverID` This is the server identifier that will be assigned to the new server.

`owner` This the name of the user that owns the server.

`autoRestart` This is true if the server should be restarted whenever Camelot is restarted.

`commandLine` This is the command line that will be used to start the server.

`segmentID` This is the segment identifier for the recoverable segment that the server will use.

`quotaChunks` This is the size of the server's recoverable segment in chunks.

This call allows the addition of new segments to existing servers. Segments are deleted by deleting the server.

```
camelotroutine NA_AddSegment(
                    key               : cam_tid_t;
                    serverID          : cam_server_id_t;
              INOUT segmentID         : cam_segment_id_t;
                    quotaChunks       : u_int);
```

`key` The key identifies the caller.
`serverID` This identifies the server that will use the new segment.
`segmentID` This is the segment identifier for the new recoverable segment.
`quotaChunks` This is the size of the recoverable segment in chunks.

This call changes the auto-restart flag, which specifies whether the server is to be brought up at node startup time.

```
camelotroutine NA_SetAutoRestart(
                    key              : cam_tid_t;
                    serverID         : cam_server_id_t;
                    autoRestart      : boolean_t);
```

`key` The key identifies the caller.
`serverID` This identifies the server to be affected.
`autoRestart` This indicates whether or not the server should be restarted when Camelot restarts on this node.

This call changes a server's command line. The command line is the path name along with any switches that must be used to execute the server.

```
camelotroutine NA_SetCommandLine(
                    key              : cam_tid_t;
                    serverID         : cam_server_id_t;
                    commandLine      : camelot_string_t);
```

`key` The key identifies the caller.
`serverID` This identifies the server whose command is to be changed.
`commandLine` The new command to be used to start the server.

This call changes a segment's quota. A quota is the maximum number of chunks in a segment that can be used for a server's recoverable data.

```
camelotroutine NA_SetQuota(
                    key              : cam_tid_t;
                    segmentID        : cam_segment_id_t;
                    quotaChunks      : int);
```

`key` The key identifies the caller.
`segmentID` This identifies the segment whose quota is being changed.
`quotaChunks` This is the new quota, in chunks, for the segment.

This call allows the deletion of servers. A server can only be deleted when it is down.

```
camelotroutine NA_DeleteServer(
                    key              : cam_tid_t;
                    serverID         : cam_server_id_t);
```

`key` The key identifies the caller.
`serverID` The identifier of the server to be deleted.

This call shows information about a server. This includes a list of all segments tied to that server ID, number of chunks used for each segment, the server's command line, whether or not it is scheduled to be automatically restarted at node startup, its owner, and its state.

```
camelotroutine NA_ShowServer(
                    key               : cam_tid_t;
                    serverID          : cam_server_id_t;
                OUT owner             : user_name_t;
                OUT autoRestart       : boolean_t;
                OUT commandLine       : camelot_string_t;
                OUT segDescList       : cam_segment_desc_list_t;
                OUT chunksUsedList    : cam_size_list_t;
                OUT state             : cam_server_state_t);
```

`key` The key identifies the caller.
`serverId` This is the identifier of the server that the caller wants information about.
`owner` The name of user that owns the server.
`autoRestart` This is true, if the server should automatically be restarted when Camelot is restarted.
`commandLine` This is the command used to start the server.
`segDescList` This is an array of descriptors describing the recoverable segments associated with the server.
`chucksUsedList` This array lists the number of chunks used by the server in each of its recoverable segments.
`state` This is the current state of the server.

This call returns a list of all servers on the node. This is a list of ONLY their server ID's. For further information on any individual server, NA_ShowServer must be used.

```
camelotroutine NA_ListServers(
                    key               : cam_tid_t;
                OUT serverlist        : cam_server_id_list_t);
```

`key` The key identifies the caller.
`serverList` This is the ids of the Camelot servers registered with the Node Server.

This command lists the current recovery time. The recovery time is specified by the user in minutes.

```
camelotroutine NA_ListRecTime(
                    key               : cam_tid_t;
          OUT       minutes           : u_int);
```

`key` The key identifies the caller.
`minutes` This is the current maximum time allowed for node recovery. See the description of `NA_SetRecTime` for more information.

This command sets the recovery time. The recovery time is specified by the user in minutes.

```
camelotroutine NA_SetRecTime(
                    key                 : cam_tid_t;
                    minutes             : u_int);
```

`key` The key identifies the caller.
`minutes` This is the maximum duration of node recovery that the user will tolerate. Camelot will calculate how often it needs to write checkpoint records so that it can perform node recovery within this time limit.

This command lists the current restart policy parameters. Servers will not be auto-restarted more than "limit" times every "interval" minutes.

```
camelotroutine NA_ListRestartPolicy(
                    key                 : cam_tid_t;
           OUT      limit               : u_int;
           OUT      interval            : u_int);
```

`key` The key identifies the caller.
`limit` The number of times a server may be restarted during the listed interval.
`interval` This is the length of the restart interval in minutes.

This command sets the restart policy parameters. Servers will not be auto-restarted more than "limit" times every "interval" minutes.

```
camelotroutine NA_SetRestartPolicy(
                    key                 : cam_tid_t;
                    limit               : u_int;
                    interval            : u_int);
```

`key` The key identifies the caller.
`limit` The number of times a server may be restarted during the given interval.
`interval` This is the length of the restart interval in minutes.

This command gets the current checkpoint interval from the Node Server, who gets it from the Disk Manager. The checkpoint interval is computed from the recovery time, but the computation is non-trivial.

```
camelotroutine NA_ListCheckpointInterval(
                    key                 : cam_tid_t;
                OUT interval            : u_int);
```

`key` The key identifies the caller.
`interval` This is the current size of the checkpoint interval in records.

This call tells the Node Server to start a data server. All switches to be used by that server are specified in the command line for that server.

```
camelotroutine NA_StartServers(
                key              : cam_tid_t;
                serverID         : cam_server_id_list_t);
```

`key` The key identifies the caller.
`serverID` The identifier of the server to be started.

This call tells the Node Server to shut down a data server. If the data server is in the `UP` state, the Node Server instructs the Disk Manager to send a terminate signal to the data server.

```
camelotroutine NA_ShutdownServer(
                key              : cam_tid_t;
                serverID         : cam_server_id_t;
                cleanLevel       : clean_level_t);
```

`key` The key identifies the caller.
`serverID` The identifier of the server to be killed.
`cleanLevel` An indication of whether to attempt to shut the server down cleanly, allowing current transactions to finish. This parameter is currently unused.

This call tells the Node Server to shut Camelot down. All system components quietly go to sleep.

```
camelotroutine NA_ShutdownCamelot(key : cam_tid_t);
```

`key` The key identifies the caller.

This call tells the node to return its current uptime in seconds.

```
camelotroutine NA_GetUpTime(
        OUT     upTime : u_int);
```

`upTime` The current uptime in seconds.

C.16 ND Interface

This call is used to allocate a new chunk on the disk. A completely filled in `chunk_loc_record_t` is returned. The `segmentId`, `offsetInChunks` and `reverseAllocate` fields are copied from the in parameters. The values of the `partNumber` and `chunkNumber` fields are chosed by the Node Server. The `sectorsAllocated` field is set to zero.

```
camelotroutine ND_ChunkAllocate(
                  segmentId        : cam_segment_id_t;
                  offsetInChunks   : u_int;
                  reverseAllocate  : boolean_t;
              OUT chunkDesc        : cam_chunk_desc_t);
```

`segmentId` The ID of the segment to which we are allocating.
`offsetInChucks` The offset within the segment.
`reverseAllocate` A flag indicating that allocation should take place from the top of the segment down.
`chuckDesc` The new chunk descriptor.

This call is used to allocate more sectors in a chunk. To reduce the number of calls to `ND_ChunkAllocate`, the Disk Manager may use the `chunkForPart` to indicate that a pre-allocated chunk should be returned.

```
camelotroutine ND_ChunkUpdate(
                  chunkDesc        : cam_chunk_desc_t;
                  chunkForPart     : u_int;
              OUT chunkNumber      : u_int);
```

`chunkDesc` A valid chunk descriptor that contains a new value for the `sectorsAllocated` field. Valid `chunk_desc_t`'s are returned by `ND_ChunkAllocate` or are constructed using a `chunkNumber` parameter returned by a previous call to `ND_ChunkUpdate`.
`chunkForPart` A parameter to request a pre-allocated chunk for the specified disk partition. If zero is specified, no pre-allocation will be done.
`chunkNumber` The pre-allocated chunk number.

This call is used to delete chunks. The Disk Manager uses this call to implement zero-fill. This interface is somewhat awkward, but it allows the Disk Manager to atomically delete a range of whole chunks and change the allocation of two other chunks. The only use the Disk Manager makes of this call is to use `chunk1` and `chunk2` to delete portions of chunks at the beginning and end of a range if a non-multiple of chunks is zer-filled.

```
camelotroutine ND_ChunkDelete(
                  segmentId        : cam_segment_id_t;
                  offsetInChunks   : u_int;
                  lengthInChunks   : u_int;
                  chunk1           : cam_chunk_desc_t;
                  chunk2           : cam_chunk_desc_t);
```

`segmentId` The ID of the segment from which we are deleting.
`offsetInChucks` The offset within the segment.
`lengthInChunks` The size of the deletion.

`chunk1` A chunk descriptor we also wish to update.
`chunk2` A chunk descriptor we also wish to update.

This call is used to ask the Node Server for advice when a server transitions to a new down state, or when the Node Server has requested that the server be started. The Node Server is consulted on this because its recoverable database contains all relevant information about the server and about any variable parameters needed to implement the restart policy.

```
camelotroutine ND_GetRestartAdvice(
                   serverId          : cam_server_id_t;
                   atYourRequest     : boolean_t;
                   oldState          : cam_server_state_t;
                   newState          : cam_server_state_t;
               OUT shouldRestart     : boolean_t;
               OUT recoveryOnly      : boolean_t;
               OUT commandLine       : pointer_t;
               OUT segDescList       : cam_segment_desc_list_t;
               OUT chunkDescList     : cam_chunk_desc_list_t);
```

`serverId` The ID of the server about which we inquire.
`atYourRequest` A flag that, if `TRUE`, means the Node Server has already requested the server be started and should supply the necessary information. If the `atYourRequest` flag is `FALSE`, it means the server has transitioned to a new down state, and the Node Server has the option of restarting it. The Disk Manager describes the transition, and is told whether to restart the server.
`oldState` The previous state of the data server.
`newState` The new state of the data server.
`shouldRestart` A boolean specifying whether the server should be restarted at all.
`recoveryOnly` A boolean specifying whether the server should just run recovery and exit or should actually stay up. Not meaningful if `shouldRestart` is `FALSE`.
`commandLine` The command line that should be executed to start the server. Not meaningful if `shouldRestart` is `FALSE`.
`segDescList` A list of segment descriptors for the server. Not meaningful if `shouldRestart` is `FALSE`.
`chunkDescList` A list of disk mappings for the server. Not meaningful if `shouldRestart` is `FALSE`.

This call is used by the Disk Manager to report recovery statistics to the Node Server each time recovery is done.

```
camelotroutine ND_RecoveryStats(
                   numRecords        : u_int;
                   numMsecs          : u_int);
```

`numRecords` The number of records processed in the last recovery pass.
`numMsecs` The number of milliseconds of elapsed time used to do the last recovery pass.

C.17 RD Interface

The Disk Manager requests that the recovery manager backstop a new-value transaction. Backstopping is done so that a prepared new-value transaction can be copied forward in the log.

```
routine RD_Backstop(
                rdPort              : port_t;
                tid                 : cam_tid_t);
```

`rdPort` the port on which the Recovery Manager receives messages from the Disk Manager
`tid` the identifier of the new-value transaction.

Server recovery is first requested by the Node Server, since that is where the information about servers and recoverable segments is kept. But the Node Server sends his request to the Disk Manager, since that is where the list of `srPorts` is kept. The Disk Manager then uses this call to tell the Recovery Manager to do the work.

```
routine RD_RecoverServers(
                rdPort              : port_t;
                serverIDs           : cam_server_id_list_t;
                segDescList         : cam_segment_desc_list_t;
                srPorts             : port_array_t;
                highRecNbr          : u_int;
                cachePtr            : pointer_t =
                ^ array [] of (MSG_TYPE_CHAR, 8, dealloc);
            OUT nbrRecordsProcessed : u_int;
            OUT milliseconds        : u_int);
```

`rdPort` the port on which the Recovery Manager receives messages from the Disk Manager.
`serverIds` the list of servers of be recovered.
`segDescList` is the list of segments used by the servers being recovered.
`srPorts` is the list of ports to be used by the Recovery Manager to perform recovery.
`highRecNbr` is the record number assigned (internally by the Disk Manager) to the last record currently in the log. As the Recovery Manager reads the log, it decrements this record number so that when it back-links old records into the grid, it can indicate to the Disk Manager exactly how far back they are in the log. The Disk Manager uses this information to control page flush (and potentially other) strategies.

`cachePtr` refers to the data that must be transferred from the version of Log Manager being used by the Disk Manager to the (read-only) version used by the Recovery Manager to make them consistent.

`nbrRecordsProcessed` and `milliseconds` are given to the Node Server by the Disk Manager for use in setting parameters that will affect recovery time.

The Disk Manager may request recovery of pages or segments for media recovery. Tell RecMan to recover certain pages.

```
routine RD_RecoverPages(
            rdPort          : port_t;
            pageIDs         : cam_segment_id_list_t;
            offsets         : cam_offset_list_t);
```

`rdPort` the port on which the Recovery Manager receives messages from the Disk Manager.

`pageIDs` The ids of the pages to be recovered.

`offsets` The lengths of the pages to be recovered.

Tell Recovery Manager to recover certain segments.

```
routine RD_RecoverSegment(
            rdPort          : port_t;
            segmentList     : cam_segment_id_list_t);
```

`rdPort` the port on which the Recovery Manager receives messages from the Disk Manager.

`segmentList` The list of segments to recover.

If the Disk Manager should notice that a server is down, it can purge all data structures for that server (including dirty pages) only if subsequent checkpoint records list the dead server in the `NRList`. To eliminate the possibility of a race condition, the Disk Manager uses the `RD_ServerDied` call.

```
routine RD_ServerDied(
            rdPort          : port_t;
            deadServer      : cam_server_id_t);
```

`rdPort` the port on which the Recovery Manager receives messages from the Disk Manager.

`deadServer` the ID of the dead server.

If the Disk Manager is using an external Log Manager, it needs to give the Recovery Manager a port to it so the Recovery Manager can read log records. If the Disk Manager is using an internal Log Manager, it still needs to make this call because the Recovery Manager uses it as an indication that the log has been initialized and may be safely opened.

The Disk Manager must make this call AFTER LD_OpenLog(), because the Recovery Manager assumes that once this call has been received it may safely open its own interface to the log.

```
routine RD_SetLoggerPort(
                rdPort              : port_t;
                ldPort              : port_t);
```

`rdPort` the port on which the Recovery Manager receives messages from the Disk Manager.
`ldPort` the Log Manager port.

C.18 RT Interface

This call tells the Recovery Manager to abort the specified transactions. It is synchronous, so that the Transaction Manager may know when data restoration is finished.

```
routine RT_Abort(
                rtPort              : port_t;
                tidArray            : cam_tid_list_t);
```

`rtPort` is the port on which the Recovery Manager receives messages from the Transaction Manager.
`tidArray` is a list of transactions to abort. As an optimization, if a top-level transaction aborts, it is not necessary to send a list of all of its descendants.

C.19 SR Interface

When the Recovery Manager determines that a region needs to be restored it sends this message (or `SR_RestoreBatch()`, below) to the data server. The data server pins the specified region using the `DS_PinRegion()` call and writes the specified value into the region. The Recovery and Disk Managers will handle the unpinning. This call should really be `ST_RestoreRegion`.

```
routine SR_RestoreObject(
                sPort               : port_t;
                regptr              : cam_regptr_t;
                value               : pointer_t);
```

`regptr` A pointer to the region being restored.
`value` The value to restore to region, sent out of line.

This is equivalent to one or more `SR_RestoreObject()` calls. The data server should pin each region and assign the specified value as described in the `SR_RestoreObject()` call.

```
routine SR_RestoreBatch(
                sPort               : port_t;
                dataPtr             : pointer_t);
```

`sPort` The port on which a data server receives requests from Camelot components.
`data` The data sent contains one or more occurrences of: `cam_reg_ptr` region pointer, `u_int` length, data filled to next `int` word.

When a distributed transaction begins to commit, all data servers (that are not on the coordinator's site) will spool prepare data (e.g., lock tables) to the log. This call is used to give data servers back the data they stored in the `DS_Prepare` call (e.g., so that can restore locks).

```
routine SR_RePrepare(
                sPort               : port_t;
                famId               : cam_fam_id_t;
                prepareData         : pointer_t);
```

`sPort` The port on which a data server receives requests from Camelot components.
`famId` The ID of the transaction prepared family.
`prepareData` The data written in the `DS_Prepare` call.

The Recovery Manager uses this call to tell the server that its recoverable storage has been restored to a transaction consistent state. The server can now look at its recoverable storage, initialize the storage if necessary, publish its name, and begin to service requests.

```
simpleroutine SR_RecoveryComplete(
                sPort               : port_t);
```

`sPort` The port on which a data server receives requests from Camelot components.

C.20 ST Interface

This call instructs servers to suspend and then vote on the transaction.

```
routine ST_Vote(
                sPort               : port_t;
                famId               : cam_fam_id_t;
                timestamp           : cam_timestamp_t;
                prepare             : boolean_t;
            OUT result              : cam_vote_t);
```

`sPort` is the port on which the server receives messages from the Transaction Manager.
`famId` is identifier of the transaction family.
`timestamp` is the commit timestamp.
`prepare` if TRUE, the server should log its locks before responding. This will be the case only at subordinate sites.

`result` is the server's vote.

Inform the server that the transaction is committed.

```
simpleroutine ST_Commit(
                sPort           : port_t;
                famId           : cam_fam_id_t);
```

`sPort` is the port on which the server receives messages from the Transaction Manager.
`famId` is the identifier of the family that committed.

Inform a server that voted read-only dependent that the local log was forced. This call does not indicate the outcome of the transaction.

```
simpleroutine ST_Done(
                sPort           : port_t;
                famId           : cam_fam_id_t);
```

`sPort` is the port on which the server receives messages from the Transaction Manager.
`famId` is the identifier of the family that completed.

Inform the server that the transaction is aborted. This call is used if a transaction aborts or a family fails to commit. This means that a server must expect this call after an ST_Suspend for a transaction or an ST_Vote for a family.

```
simpleroutine ST_Abort(
                sPort           : port_t;
                tid             : cam_tid_t);
```

`sPort` is the port on which the server receives messages from the Transaction Manager.
`tid` is the identifier of the transaction that aborted.

This call instructs servers to stop serving a transaction which is being aborted. A server must not respond to the call until it is certain that no threads will operate on behalf of this transaction ever again. This includes reading or modifying recoverable storage. If a tree of transactions is aborting, an ST_Suspend will be sent for each one.

```
routine ST_Suspend(
                sPort           : port_t;
                tid             : cam_tid_t;
                status          : int);
```

`sPort` is the port on which the server receives messages from the Transaction Manager.
`tid` is the identifier of the transaction being aborted.
`status` is a code for the cause of the abort.

C.21 TA Interface

This call is used to begin a transaction.

```
routine TA_Begin(
                taPort          : port_t;
                parentTid       : cam_tid_t;
                transType       : cam_transaction_type_t;
            OUT newTid          : cam_tid_t);
```

`taPort` is the port returned by the `TA_AddApplication` call.

`parentTid` specifies whether to start a top-level or nested transaction. When it is all 0's (`CAM_NULL_TID`), a new top-level transaction is begun. If it already exists, a nested transaction is begun as its child.

`transType` specifies what kind of transaction to begin. The six possibilities are the cross product of the commit class (standard, hybrid atomic, or server-based), and the logging method (new value or old value/new value). Nested transactions are automatically coerced to the parent's type if the `transType` does not match.

`newTid` is an out parameter containing the TID of the new transaction.

This call is used to commit a transaction. The return code is `CAM_ER_SUCCESS` if commit succeeds, commit fails, or if the transaction already aborted. For any other outcome (such as bad arguments), the return code is `AC_ILLEGAL_ABORT_CODE`. In this case, calling `TA_End` again with the correct arguments will commit the transaction.

```
routine TA_End(
                taPort          : port_t;
                tid             : cam_tid_t;
                protocolType    : cam_protocol_type_t;
            OUT timestamp       : cam_timestamp_t;
            OUT status          : int);
```

`taPort` from the `TA_AddApplication` call. This port must be the same as the port of the caller of `TA_Begin`.

`tid` is the TID of the transaction to be committed. All of its children must be committed or aborted at the time of this call.

`protocolType` is the type of commit protocol to be used, either two-phase or non-blocking.

`timestamp` is the commit timestamp. This is returned non-null for hybrid atomic transactions.

`status` indicates whether the transaction committed successfully. It is 0 if the transaction committed, and `CAM_AC_COMMIT_FAILED` if the commit failed. If there were uncompleted nested transactions at the time of the call, it contains `CAM_ER_ACTIVE_CHILDREN`. If the transaction was already aborted, it contains the abort code.

This call is used to abort a transaction. The input parameters are:

```
routine TA_Kill(
                taPort              : port_t;
                tid                 : cam_tid_t;
                status              : int);
```

`taPort` from the `TA_AddApplication` call.
`tid` is the identifier of the transaction to be aborted.
`status` is the abort code describing the cause of the abort.

Before using transaction management services, an application calls `TA_AddApplication` to register itself with the TranMan. If the application name is invalid, `SERV_FAILURE` is returned and the out parameters are meaningless.

```
routine TA_AddApplication(
                tPort               : port_t;
                atPort              : port_t;
                applName            : camelot_string_t;
            OUT applicationID       : cam_application_id_t;
            OUT taPort              : port_t);
```

`tPort` is a special port registered at the name server (under the name `TranPort`) by the Transaction Manager. The Transaction Manager listens only for `TA_AddApplication` calls on this port.
`atPort` is the port to which messages in the AT interface will be sent.
`applName` is a string containing the name of the application.
`applicationID` is an integer unique among applications at this site.
`taPort` is the port to which the application should send its future `TA_` calls.

An application calls `TA_GetTids` to begin one or more transactions. This call behaves like `TA_Begin`, except there is one extra parameter–`numRequested`, or the number of TIDs (transactions) requested.

Along with a return code, this call returns the number of TIDs granted in `numRequested`, and a list of those TIDs in `newTidArray`. If too many TIDs are requested (this is controlled by the parameter `CAM_MAX_TID_ARRAY_SIZE`), then the return code is `CAM_ER_TOO_MANY_TIDS` and `newTidArray` contains a list of `CAM_MAX_TID_ARRAY_SIZE` null TIDs.

```
routine TA_GetTids(
                taPort              : port_t;
                parentTid           : cam_tid_t;
                transType           : cam_transaction_type_t;
                numRequested        : u_int;
            OUT newTidArray         : cam_tid_array_t);
```

`taPort` The port returned from the `TA_AddApplication` call.

`parentTid` The identifier of the parent of the new transactions.
`transType` The type of transaction to begin.
`numRequested` The number of TIDs requested.
`newTidArray` An array of new TIDs, returned out-of-line.

This call returns the current timestamp value. A timestamp has a clock value as its high bits, and a node ID as its low bits.

```
routine TA_GetTimeStamp(
                taPort              : port_t;
            OUT timestamp           : cam_timestamp_t);
```

`tsPort` is the port on which the Transaction Manager receives calls from servers.
`timestamp` is the current timestamp.

C.22 TC Interface

The Communication Manager calls `TC_SendingRequest` to notify the Transaction Manager that it is about to forward a transactional RPC to a remote site.

```
routine TC_SendingRequest(
                tcPort              : port_t;
                tid                 : cam_tid_t;
                remoteSite          : cam_node_id_t;
            OUT piggyBackData       : cam_data_t);
```

`tcPort` is the port on which the Transaction Manager receives messages from the Communication Manager.
`tid` is the transaction that is spreading.
`remoteSite` is the site to which the transaction is spreading.
`piggyBackData` is data that the Transaction Manager wants sent to the Transaction Manager on the remote site.

The Communication Manager calls `TC_ReceivedRequest` to notify the Transaction Manager that it has received a transactional RPC from a remote site.

```
routine TC_ReceivedRequest(
                tcPort              : port_t;
                tid                 : cam_tid_t;
                piggyBackData       : cam_data_t);
```

`tcPort` is the port on which the Transaction Manager receives messages from the Communication Manager.
`tid` is the transaction that encloses this server call.

`piggyBackData` is the data that the remote Transaction Manager piggy-backed on this message.

The Communication Manager calls `TC_SendingReply` to notify the Transaction Manager that it is about to reply to a transactional RPC.

```
routine TC_SendingReply(
                tcPort              : port_t;
                tid                 : cam_tid_t;
            OUT piggyBackData       : cam_data_t);
```

`tcPort` is the port on which the Transaction Manager receives messages from the Communication Manager.
`tid` is the transaction that encloses this server call.
`piggyBackData` is data that the Transaction Manager wants sent to the Transaction Manager on the remote site.

The Communication Manager calls `TC_ReceivedReply` to notify the Transaction Manager that it has received the reply to a transactional RPC.

```
routine TC_ReceivedReply(
                tcPort              : port_t;
                tid                 : cam_tid_t;
                piggyBackData       : cam_data_t);
```

`tcPort` is the port on which the Transaction Manager receives messages from the Communication Manager.
`tid` is the transaction that encloses this server call.
`remoteSite` is the site to which the transaction is spreading.
`piggyBackData` is the data that the remote Transaction Manager piggy-backed on this message.

C.23 TD Interface

The Disk Manager uses this call to request that the Transaction Manager produce data to be written into the next checkpoint record. This call is done asynchronously on the Disk Manager side; therefore stale data may be written into the checkpoint record. We must always take care to ensure that this is ok.

```
routine TD_Checkpoint(
                tdPort              : port_t;
            OUT data                : pointer_t);
```

`tdPort` is the port on which the Transaction Manager receives messages from the Disk Manager.

`data` is the data the Transaction Manager wishes to place in the checkpoint record.

This is the call the Disk Manager uses to inform the Transaction Manager that a server is being started. Both the Disk Manager and the Transaction Manager set the server's state to "recovering" at this point.

```
routine TD_AddDataServer(
                tdPort            : port_t;
                serverId          : cam_server_id_t;
                sendPort          : port_t;
            OUT rcvPort           : port_t);
```

`tdPort` is the port on which the Transaction Manager receives messages from the Disk Manager.
`serverId` is the permanent ID of the server.
`sendPort` is the port to which Transaction Manager sends messages to servers.
`rcvPort` is the port to which the server sends messages to the Transaction Manager.

The Disk Manager makes this call when a data server comes up. This is the point at which the Disk Manager and the Transaction Manager set the server's state to "up".

```
routine TD_DataServerUp(
                tdPort            : port_t;
                serverId          : cam_server_id_t);
```

`tdPort` is the port on which the Transaction Manager receives messages from the Disk Manager.
`serverId` represents the server that is coming up.

The Disk Manager calls TD_Kill for long-running transactions. This call is used only for top-level transactions. Return codes are the same as those for TA_Kill.

```
routine TD_Kill(
                tdPort            : port_t;
                tid               : cam_tid_t;
                status            : int);
```

`tdPort` is the port on which the Transaction Manager receives messages from the Disk Manager.
`tid` is the transaction the Disk Manager wants to abort.
`status` is a code for the reason for the abort.

This call is used by the Disk Manager to ask the Transaction Manager to produce a new prepare record for some transaction that is already prepared. If in fact the transaction is no longer prepared, the Transaction Manager will return zero bytes of data. This call is used by the Disk Manager when copying log records forward for a prepared transaction that is impeding log truncation.

```
routine TD_ProduceNewPrepareRecord(
                tdPort            : port_t;
                tid               : cam_tid_t;
            OUT preparePtrPtr     : pointer_t);
```

`tdPort` is the port on which the Transaction Manager receives messages from the Disk Manager.
`tid` is the prepared transaction.
`preparePtrPtr` is the address of a pointer to the prepare record.

After a data server dies, the Disk Manager uses this call to inform the Transaction Manager, and to be sure all active transactions in which the server was involved are aborted. This call does not return until RT_Abort has finished for each transaction that will be aborted.

```
routine TD_CleanupServerDeath(
                tdPort            : port_t;
                serverId          : cam_server_id_t;
            OUT preparedTrans     : cam_tid_list_t);
```

`tdPort` is the port on which the Transaction Manager receives messages from the Disk Manager.
`serverId` is the server that died.
`preparedTrans` is the list of prepared transactions with which this server is involved.

C.24 TR Interface

This call is used during recovery. The RecMan gives log records previously written on behalf of the TranMan back to the TranMan. This is how the TranMan is able to recover the state of transactions. The call must be able to accommodate log records of unbounded size.

```
routine TR_ReplayLog(
                trPort            : port_t;
                data              : pointer_t);
```

`trPort` is the port on which the Transaction Manager receives messages from the Recovery Manager.
`data` is a pointer to the log records.

C.25 TS Interface

This call is used by a server to join a transaction. If the server has already joined this transaction, the return code is `CAM_ER_ALREADY_JOINED`.

```
routine TS_Join(
                tsPort            : port_t;
                tid               : cam_tid_t);
```

`tsPort` is the port on which the Transaction Manager receives calls from servers.

`tid` is the identifier of the transaction that the caller wants to join.

A data server calls this routine to discover if the locks nominally held by one transaction can be broken and given to another transaction. The parameters are:

```
routine TS_IsLockInheritable(
                tsPort            : port_t;
                holdingTrans      : cam_tid_t;
                requestingTrans   : cam_tid_t;
           OUT  answer            : boolean_t);
```

`tsPort` is the Transaction Manager's port for the server.

`holdingTrans` is the transaction that is the nominal holder.

`requestingTrans` is the transaction requesting the lock.

`answer` indicates whether or not the lock may be inherited. It will be true if the requestor and the holder are committed up to their least common ancestor, or if the holder cannot be found.

A data server calls this routine to wait until such time as the locks held by one transaction can be broken and given to another. The wait may be forever – for example, the holder may be deadlocked with another transaction. If the waiting transaction aborts, the call returns with code CAM_ER_WAITING_TRANS_ABORTED.

```
routine TS_WaitBeforeInheritingLock(
                tsPort           : port_t;
                holdingTrans     : cam_tid_t;
                requestingTrans: cam_tid_t);
```

`tsPort` is the Transaction Manager's port for the server.

`holdingTrans` is the transaction that is the nominal holder.

`requestingTrans` is the transaction requesting the lock.

Appendix D

Avalon Grammar

The language this grammar defines is a strict superset of that presented in Section 14 of the Reference Manual in [114].

D.1 Expressions

expression:
  term
  expression binary-operator expression
  expression ? *expression* : *expression*
  expression-list
expression-list:
  expression
  expression-list , *expression*
term:
  primary-expression
  unary-operator term
  term ++
  term −−
  `sizeof` *expression*
  `sizeof` (*type-name*)
  (*type-name*) *expression*
  simple-type-name (*expression-list*)
  `new` *type-name* $initializer_{opt}$
  `new` (*type-name*)
  `delete` *expression*
  `delete` [*expression*] *expression*

primary-expression:
  id
  :: *identifier*
  constant
  string
  `this`
  (*expression*)
  primary-expression[*expression*]
  primary-expression ($expression\text{-}list_{opt}$)
  primary-expression . *id*
  primary-expression − > *id*
id:
  identifier
  operator-function-name
  typedef-name :: *identifier*
  typedef-name :: *operator-function-name*
operator:
  unary-operator
  binary-operator
  special-operator
  free-store-operator

Binary operators have precedence decreasing as indicated:

binary-operator: **one of**
    * / %
    + -
    << >>
    < >
    == !=
    &
    ^
    |
    &&
    ||
    assignment-operator
assignment-operator: **one of**
    = += -= *= /= %=
    ^= &= |= >>= <<=
unary-operator: **one of**
    * & + − ~ ! ++ −−
special-operator: **one of**
    () []

free-store-operator: **one of**
    `new` `delete`
type-name:
    decl-specifiers abstract-decl
abstract-decl:
    empty
    * *abstract-decl*
    abstract-decl (*argument-declaration-list*)
    abstract-decl [*constant-expression*$_{opt}$]
simple-type-name:
    typedef-name
    `char`
    `short`
    `int`
    `long`
    `unsigned`
    `float`
    `double`
    `void`
typedef-name:
    identifier

D.2 Declarations

declaration:
    decl-specifiers$_{opt}$ *declarator-list*$_{opt}$;
    name-declaration
    asm-declaration
    pragma
name-declaration:
    aggr identifier ;
    `enum` *identifier* ;
aggr:
    `class`
    `struct`
    `union`
    `server`
    `variant`
asm-declaration:
    `asm` *(string)* ;
pragma:
    `@pragma@` pragma-list
pragma-list:
    prag
    prag , pragma-list

prag:
    identifier
    identifer = value
decl-specifiers:
    decl-specifier decl-specifiers$_{opt}$
decl-specifier:
    sc-specifier
    type-specifier
    fct-specifier
    `friend`
    `typedef`
    server-specifier
    variant-specifier
type-specifier:
    simple-type-name
    class-specifier
    enum-specifier
    elaborated-type-specifier
    `const`

sc-specifier:
    `auto`
    `extern`
    `register`
    `static`
    `stable`
fct-specifier:
    `inline`
    `overload`
    `virtual`
server-specifier:
    class-specifier
variant-specifier:
    class-specifier
elaborated-type-specifier:
    key typedef-name
    key identifier
key:
    `class`
    `struct`
    `union`
    `enum`
    `server`
    `variant`
declarator-list:
    init-declarator
    init-declarator , declarator-list
init-declarator:
    declarator initializer$_{opt}$
declarator:
    dname
    (*declarator*)
    * `const` $_{opt}$ *declarator*
    & `const` $_{opt}$ *declarator*
    declarator (*argument-declaration-list*)
    declarator [*constant-expression*$_{opt}$]
dname:
    simple-dname
    typedef-name :: simple-dname
simple-dname:
    identifier
    typedef-name
    ~ *typedef-name*
    operator-function-name
    conversion-function-name
operator-function-name:
    `operator` *operator*
conversion-function-name:
    `operator` *type*

argument-declaration-list:
    arg-declaration-list$_{opt}$ ... $_{opt}$
arg-declaration-list:
    arg-declaration-list , argument-declaration
    argument-declaration
argument-declaration:
    decl-specifiers declarator
    decl-specifiers declarator = expression
    decl-specifiers abstract-decl
    decl-specifiers abstract-decl = expression
class-specifier:
    class-head { *member-list*$_{opt}$ }
class-head:
    aggr identifier$_{opt}$
    aggr identifier : `public` $_{opt}$ *typedef-name*
member-list:
    member-declaration member-list$_{opt}$
member-declaration:
    decl-specifiers$_{opt}$ *member-decl initializer*$_{opt}$;
    function-definition ;$_{opt}$
    decl-specifiers$_{opt}$ *fct-decl base-initializer*$_{opt}$
    `private:`
    `protected:`
    `public:`
member-decl:
    declarator
    identifier$_{opt}$ *: constant-expression*
initializer:
    = *expression*
    = { *initializer-list* }
    = { *initializer-list* , }
    (*expression-list*)
initializer-list:
    expression
    initializer-list , initializer-list
    { *initializer-list* }
enum-specifier:
    `enum` *identifier*$_{opt}$ { *enum-list* }
enum-list:
    enumerator
    enum-list , enumerator
enumerator:
    identifier
    identifier = constant-expression

D.3 Statements

compound-statement:
{ *statement-list*$_{opt}$ }
statement-list:
statement
statement statement-list
statement:
declaration
compound-statement
expression$_{opt}$;
`if` (*expression*) *statement*
`if` (*expression*) *statement*
`else` *statement*
`while` (*expression*) *statement*
`do` *statement* `while` (*expression*) ;
`for` (*statement expression*$_{opt}$; *expression*$_{opt}$)
statement
`switch` (*expression*) *statement*
`case` *constant-expression* : *statement*
`default` : *statement*
`undo`$_{opt}$ `break` ;
`undo`$_{opt}$ `continue` ;
`goto` *identifier ;*
identifier : statement
`start` trans-body
`costart` { coarms }
`leave` ;
`undo` (*expression*)$_{opt}$ `leave` ;
`undo`$_{opt}$ `return` *expression*$_{opt}$
`pinning` (*expression*$_{opt}$) *statement*
`when` (*expression*) *statement*
`whenswitch` (*expression*) *statement*
pragma

trans-body:
trans-tag *statement* except-clause$_{opt}$
trans-tag:
`toplevel`
`transaction`
coarms:
coarm coarms$_{opt}$
coarm:
trans-body
`process` *statement*
except-clause:
`except` (*identifier*)$_{opt}$ *statement*

D.4 External Definitions

program:
external-definition
external-definition program
external-definition:
function-definition
declaration
function-definition:
decl-specifiers$_{opt}$ *fct-decl*
base-initializer$_{opt}$ *fct-body*
fct-decl:
declarator (*argument-declaration-list*)

fct-body:
compound-statement
base-initializer:
: member-initializer-list
member-initializer-list:
member-initializer
member-initializer , member-initializer-list
member-initializer:
identifier$_{opt}$ (*argument-list*$_{opt}$)

Bibliography

[1] G. M. Adelson-Velskiĭ and E. M. Landis. An Algorithm for the Organization of Information. *Soviet Mathmatics*, 3(5):1259–1262, September 1962. Translated from Russian *Doklady, Akademiĭ Nauk SSSR* 146(2):263-266.

[2] Rakesh Agrawal. A Parallel Logging Algorithm for Multiprocessor Database Machines. In *Proceedings of the Fourth International Workshop on Database Machines*, pages 256–276, March 1985.

[3] Rakesh Agrawal and David J. DeWitt. Recovery Architectures for Multiprocessor Database Machines. In *Proceedings of ACM-SIGMOD 1985 International Conference on Management of Data*, pages 132–145, May 1985.

[4] Alfred Aho, Brian Kernighan, and Peter Weinberger. *The AWK Language*. Addison-Wesley, 1987.

[5] W. Alexi, B. Chor, O. Goldreich, and C. P. Schnorr. RSA and Rabin Functions: Certain Parts are as Hard as the Whole. *SIAM Journal on Computing*, 17(2), April 1988.

[6] Anonymous, et al. A Measure of Transaction Processing Power. *Datamation*, 31(7), April 1985. Also available as Technical Report TR 85.2, Tandem Corporation, Cupertino, California, January 1985.

[7] Emmanuel A. Arnould, François J. Bitz, Eric C. Cooper, H. T. Kung, Robert D. Sansom, and Peter A. Steenkiste. The Design of Nectar: A Network Backplane for Heterogeneous Multicomputers. In *Proceedings of the Third International Conference on Architectural Support for Programming Languages and Operating Systems (ASPLOS-III)*, pages 205–216, April 1989. Also available as Technical Report CMU-CS-89-101, Carnegie Mellon University, January 1989.

[8] Robert V. Baron, David L. Black, William Bolosky, Jonathan Chew, David B. Golub, Richard F. Rashid, Avadis Tevanian, Jr., and Michael Wayne Young. Mach Kernel Interface Manual. Department of Computer Science, Carnegie Mellon University, Pittsburgh, Pennsylvania, February 1987.

[9] P. Bernstein and N. Goodman. An Algorithm for Concurrency Control and Recovery in Replicated Distributed Databases. *ACM Transactions on Database Systems*, 9(4):596–615, December 1984.

[10] David L. Black, David B. Golub, Richard F. Rashid, Avadis Tevanian, Jr., and Michael Wayne Young. The Mach Exception Handling Facility. Technical Report CMU-CS-88-129, Carnegie Mellon University, April 1988.

[11] Joshua J. Bloch. *A Practical Approach to Replication of Abstract Data Objects*. PhD thesis, Carnegie Mellon University, May 1990. Also available as Technical Report CMU-CS-90-133, Carnegie Mellon University, May 1990.

[12] Joshua J. Bloch, Dean S. Daniels, and Alfred Z. Spector. A Weighted Voting Algorithm for Replicated Directories. *JACM*, 34(4), October 1987. Also available as Technical Report CMU-CS-86-132, Carnegie Mellon University, July 1986.

[13] Andrea J. Borr. Transaction Monitoring in Encompass (TM): Reliable Distributed Transaction Processing. In *Proceedings of the Very Large Database Conference*, pages 155–165, September 1981.

[14] Andrea J. Borr. Robustness to Croach in a Distributed Database: A Non Shared-Memory Multi-Processor Approach. In *Proceedings of the Very Large Database Conference*, pages 445–453, August 1984.

[15] Richard S. Brice and Stephen W. Sherman. An Extension of the Performance of a Database Manager in a Virtual Memory System using Partially Locked Virtual Buffers. *ACM Transactions on Database Systems*, 2(2):196–207, June 1976.

[16] Mark R. Brown, Karen N. Kolling, and Edward A. Taft. The Alpine File System. *ACM Trans. on Computer Systems*, 3(4):261–293, November 1985.

[17] J. Carter and M. Wegman. Universal Classes of Hash Functions. In *Proceedings of the Seventeenth IEEE Foundations of Computer Science*, pages 106–112, May 1976.

[18] Albert Chang and Mark F. Mergen. 801 Storage: Architecture and Programming. *ACM Transactions on Computer Systems*, 6(1):28–50, February 1988.

[19] Ben-Zion Chor. *Two Issues in Public Key Cryptography: RSA Bit Security and a New Knapsack Type System*. ACM Distiguished Dissertations. MIT Press, 1986.

[20] Computer Systems Research Group, Computer Science Division, Department of Electrical Engineering and Computer Science, University of California, Berkeley, California 94720. *UNIX Programmer's Reference Manual (PRM)*, April 1986.

[21] Eric C. Cooper and Richard P. Draves. C Threads. Technical Report CMU-CS-88-154, Carnegie Mellon University, June 1988.

[22] Dean S. Daniels. *Distributed Logging for Transaction Processing*. PhD thesis, Carnegie Mellon University, December 1988. Also available as Technical Report CMU-CS-89-114, Carnegie Mellon University, August 1988.

[23] Dean S. Daniels and Alfred Z. Spector. An Algorithm for Replicated Directories. In *Proceedings of the Second Annual Symposium on Principles of Distributed Computing*, pages 104–113. ACM, August 1983. Also available in *Operating Systems Review*, 20(1):24-43, January 1986.

[24] Dean S. Daniels, Alfred Z. Spector, and Dean Thompson. Distributed Logging for Transaction Processing. In *Sigmod '87 Proceedings*. ACM, May 1987. Also available as Technical Report CMU-CS-86-106, Carnegie Mellon University, June 1986.

[25] David Detlefs, Maurice P. Herlihy, and Jeannette M. Wing. Inheritance of Synchronization/Recovery Properties in Avalon/C++. *Computer*, 21(12), December 1988.

[26] Dan Duchamp. *Transaction Management*. PhD thesis, Carnegie Mellon University, June 1989. Also available as Technical Report CMU-CS-88-192, Carnegie Mellon University, June 1989.

[27] Wolfgang Effelsberg and Theo Haerder. Principles of Database Buffer Management. *ACM Transactions on Database Systems*, 9(4):560–595, December 1984.

[28] Jeffrey L. Eppinger. *Virtual Memory Management for Transaction Processing Systems*. PhD thesis, Carnegie Mellon University, February 1989. Also available as Technical Report CMU-CS-89-115, Carnegie Mellon University, February 1989.

[29] Jeffrey L. Eppinger and Alfred Z. Spector. Virtual Memory Management for Recoverable Objects in the TABS Prototype. Technical Report CMU-CS-85-163, Carnegie Mellon University, December 1985.

[30] K. P. Eswaran, James N. Gray, Raymond A. Lorie, and Irving L. Traiger. The Notions of Consistency and Predicate Locks in a Database System. *Communications of the ACM*, 19(11):624–633, November 1976.

[31] D. DeWitt et. al. Implementation Techniques for Main Memory Database Systems. In *Proceedings of ACM SIGMOD '84*, pages 1–8, May 1984.

[32] Uriel Feige, Amos Fiat, and Adi Shamir. Zero Knowledge Proofs of Identity. In *Proceedings of the Nineteenth ACM Symposium on Theory of Computing*, pages 210–217, May 1987.

[33] A. L. Fisher, H. T. Kung, L. M. Monier, and Y. Dohi. Architecture of the PSC: a Programmable Systolic Chip. *Journal of VLSI and Computer Systems*, 1(2):153–169, 1984.

[34] A. M. Frieze. Parallel Algorithms for Finding Hamilton Cycles in Random Graphs. *Information Processing Letters*, 25:111–117, 1987.

[35] D. Gawlick and D. Kinkade. Varieties of Concurrency Control in IMS/VS Fast Path. *IEEE Database Engineering*, June 1985.

[36] David K. Gifford. Weighted Voting for Replicated Data. In *Proceedings of the Seventh Symposium on Operating System Principles*, pages 150–162. ACM, December 1979.

[37] Shafi Goldwasser, Silvio Micali, and Charles Rackoff. The Knowledge Complexity of Interactive Proof Systems. In *Proceedings of the Seventeenth Annual ACM Symposium on Theory of Computing*, pages 291–304, May 1985.

[38] James N. Gray. Notes on Database Operating Systems. In R. Bayer and R. M. Graham and G. Seegmüller, editor, *Operating Systems - An Advanced Course*, volume 60 of *Lecture Notes in Computer Science*, pages 393–481. Springer-Verlag, 1978. Also available as Technical Report RJ2188, IBM Research Laboratory, San Jose, California, 1978.

[39] James N. Gray. A Transaction Model. Technical Report RJ2895, IBM Research Laboratory, San Jose, California, August 1980.

[40] Mach Networking Group. Network Server Design. Department of Computer Science, Carnegie Mellon University, Pittsburgh, Pennsylvania, February 1988.

[41] J. V. Guttag, J. J. Horning, and J. M. Wing. Larch in Five Easy Pieces. Technical Report 5, DEC Systems Research Center, July 1985.

[42] Roger Haskin, Yoni Malachi, Wayne Sawdon, and Gregory Chan. Recovery Management in QuickSilver. *ACM Transactions on Computer Systems*, 6(1):82–108, February 1988.

[43] Andrew B. Hastings. Distributed Lock Management in a Transaction Processing Environment. Technical Report CMU-CS-89-152, Carnegie Mellon University, May 1989.

[44] Pat Helland. Transaction Monitoring Facility. *Database Engineering*, 8(2):9–18, June 1985.

[45] Pat Helland, Harald Sammer, Jim Lyon, Richard Carr, Phil Garrett, and Andreas Reuter. Group Commit Timers and High Volume Transaction Systems. Presented at the Second International Workshop on High Performance Transaction Systems, Asilomar, September 1987.

[46] Maurice P. Herlihy. General Quorum Consensus: A Replication Method for Abstract Data Types. Technical Report CMU-CS-84-164, Carnegie Mellon University, December 1984.

[47] Maurice P. Herlihy. A Quorum-Consensus Replication Method for Abstract Data Types. *ACM Transactions on Computer Systems*, 4(1), February 1986.

[48] Maurice P. Herlihy and J. D. Tygar. How to Make Replicated Data Secure. In *Advances in Cryptology, CRYPTO-87*. Springer-Verlag, August 1987.

[49] Maurice P. Herlihy and Jeannette M. Wing. Avalon: Language Support for Reliable Distributed Systems. In *Proceedings of the Seventeenth International Symposium on Fault-Tolerant Computing*. IEEE, July 1987.

[50] Maurice P. Herlihy and Jeannette M. Wing. Reasoning About Atomic Objects. In *Proceedings of the Symposium on Real-Time and Fault-Tolerant Systems*, Warwick, England, September 1988. Also available as Technical Report CMU-CS-87-176, Carnegie Mellon University.

[51] C. A. R. Hoare. Monitors: An Operating System Structuring Concept. *Communications of the ACM*, 17(10):549–557, October 1974.

[52] IBM Corporation. *Customer Information Control System/Virtual Storage, Introduction to Program Logic*, sc33-0067-1 edition, June 1978.

[53] IBM Corporation, World Trade Systems Center, San Jose, CA. *IMS Version 1 Release 1.5 Fast Path Feature Description and Design Guide*, 1979.

[54] Michael B. Jones, Richard P. Draves, and Mary R. Thompson. MIG - The Mach Interface Generator. Mach Group Document, 1987.

[55] Michael B. Jones, Richard F. Rashid, and Mary R. Thompson. Accent: A Communication Oriented Network Operating System Kernel. In *Proceedings of the Twelfth Annual Symposium on Principles of Programming Languages*, pages 225–235. ACM, 1985.

[56] Michael B. Jones, Richard F. Rashid, and Mary R. Thompson. Matchmaker: An Interface Specification Language for Distributed Processing. In *Proceedings of the Twelfth Annual Symposium on Principles of Programming Languages*, pages 225–235. ACM, January 1985.

[57] R. M. Karp. Reducibility among Combinatorial Problems. In R. E. Miller and J. W. Thatcher, editors, *Complexity of Computer Computations*, pages 85–103. Plenum Press, New York, 1972.

[58] Richard M. Karp and Michael O. Rabin. Efficient Randomized Pattern-Matching Algorithms. Technical Report TR-31-81, Aiken Laboratory, Harvard University, December 1981.

[59] Brian Kernighan and Dennis Ritchie. *The C Programming Language.* Prentice-Hall, 1978.

[60] Leslie Lamport. Time, Clocks, and the Ordering of Events in a Distributed System. *Communications of the ACM*, 21(7):558–565, July 1978.

[61] Butler W. Lampson. Atomic Transactions. In G. Goos and J. Hartmanis, editors, *Distributed Systems - Architecture and Implementation: An Advanced Course*, volume 105 of *Lecture Notes in Computer Science*, chapter 11, pages 246–265. Springer-Verlag, 1981.

[62] Butler W. Lampson and David D. Redell. Experience with Processes and Monitors in Mesa. *Communications of the ACM*, 23(2):105–117, February 1980.

[63] Richard Allen Lerner. Reliable Servers: Design and Implementation in Avalon/C++. In *Proceedings International Symposium on Databases in Parallel and Distributed Systems*, pages 13–21, Austin, TX, December 1988. IEEE. Also available as Technical Report CMU-CS-88-177, Carnegie Mellon University, September 1988.

[64] Kai Li and Paul Hudak. Memory Coherence in Shared Virtual Memory Systems. In *Proceedings of the Fifth Annual ACM Symposium on Principles of Distributed Computing*, pages 229–239. ACM, August 1986.

[65] Bruce Lindsay, John McPherson, and Hamid Pirahesh. A Data Management Extension Architecture. In *Proceedings of ACM SIGMOD '87*, pages 220–226. ACM, May 1987.

[66] Bruce G. Lindsay, Laura M. Haas, C. Mohan, Paul F. Wilms, and Robert A. Yost. Computation and Communication in R*: A Distributed Database Manager. *ACM Transactions on Computer Systems*, 2(1):24–38, February 1984.

[67] Bruce G. Lindsay, et al. Notes on Distributed Databases. Technical Report RJ2571, IBM Research Laboratory, San Jose, California, July 1979. Also appears in Droffen and Poole (editors), *Distributed Databases*, Cambridge University Press, 1980.

[68] R. Lipton. Personal communication.

[69] B. Liskov, D. Curtis, P. Johnson, and R. Scheifler. Implementation of Argus. In *Proceedings of the Eleventh Symposium on Operating System Principles*, pages 111–122. ACM, November 1987.

[70] B. Liskov, M. Day, M. Herlihy, P. Johnson, G. Leavens, R. Scheifler, and W. Weihl. Argus Reference Manual. Technical Report TR-400, MIT Laboratory for Computer Science, Cambridge, MA, November 1987.

[71] B. Liskov, A. Snyder, R.Atkinson, and C. Schaffert. Abstraction Mechanisms in CLU. *Communications of the ACM*, 20(8), August 1977.

[72] Barbara H. Liskov. Overview of the Argus Language and System. Programming Methodology Group Memo 40, MIT Laboratory for Computer Science, February 1984.

[73] Barbara H. Liskov. Progress Report of the Programming Methodology Group. In *MIT LCS Progress Report*, volume 21, pages 142–176. MIT Press, June 1984.

[74] Barbara H. Liskov, Robert Scheifler, Edward Walker, and William Weihl. Orphan Detection. Programming Methodology Group Memo 53, Laboratory for Computer Science, Massachusetts Institute for Technology, February 1987.

[75] Barbara H. Liskov and Robert W. Scheifler. Guardians and Actions: Linguistic Support for Robust, Distributed Programs. *ACM Transactions on Programming Languages and Systems*, 5(3):381–404, July 1983.

[76] Michael Luby and Charles Rackoff. Pseudo-random Permutation Generators and Cryptographic Composition. In *Proceedings of the Eighteenth ACM Symp. on Theory of Computing*, pages 356–363, May 1986.

[77] R. L. Mattson, J. Gecsei, D. R. Slutz, and I. L. Traiger. Evaluation Techniques for Storage Hierarchies. *IBM Systems Journal*, 9(2):78–117, 1970.

[78] David McDonald, Scott Fahlman, and Alfred Spector. An Efficient Common Lisp for the IBM RT PC. In *IBM Academic Information Systems University AEP Conference*, pages 556–580, June 1987. Also available as Technical Report CMU-CS-87-134, Carnegie Mellon University, July 1987.

[79] C. Meyer and S. Matyas. *Cryptography*. Wiley, 1982.

[80] C. Mohan, D. Haderle, B. Lindsay, H. Pirahesh, and P. Schwarz. Aries: A Transaction Recovery Method Supporting Fine-granularity Locking and Partial Rollbacks Using Write-ahead Logging. Technical Report RJ6649, IBM Almaden Research Center, January 1989.

[81] C. Mohan and B. Lindsay. Efficient Commit Protocols for the Tree of Processes Model of Distributed Transactions. In *Proceedings of the Second Annual Symposium on Principles of Distributed Computing*, pages 76–88. ACM, August 1983.

[82] J. Eliot B. Moss. *Nested Transactions: An Approach to Reliable Distributed Computing.* MIT Press, 1985.

[83] E. T. Mueller, J. D. Moore, and G. J. Popek. A Nested Transaction Mechanism for LOCUS. In *Proceedings of the Ninth Symposium on Operating Systems Principles*, pages 71–89, October 1983.

[84] Roger M. Needham and Michael D. Schroeder. Using Encryption for Authentication in Large Networks of Computers. *Communications of the ACM*, 21(12):993–999, December 1978. Also available as Technical Report, CSL-78-4, Xerox Research Center, Palo Alto, CA.

[85] R. J. Peterson and J. P. Strickland. LOG Write-Ahead Protocols and IMS/VS Logging. In *Proceedings of the Second ACM SIGACT-SIGMOD Symposium on Principles of Database Systems*, pages 216–243. ACM, March 1983.

[86] Jonathan B. Postel. Internetwork Protocol Approaches. In Paul E. Green, Jr., editor, *Computer Network Architectures and Protocols*, chapter 18, pages 511–526. Plenum Press, 1982.

[87] C. Pu. Personal communication.

[88] C. Pu. *Replication and Nested Transactions in the Eden Distributed System.* PhD thesis, Univ. of Washington, 1986.

[89] Michael Rabin. Digitalized Signatures and Public-Key Functions as Intractable as Factorization. Technical Report TR-212, MIT Laboratory for Computer Science, January 1979.

[90] Michael Rabin. Fingerprinting by Random Polynomials. Technical Report TR-81-15, Aiken Laboratory, Harvard University, May 1981.

[91] Michael O. Rabin. Probabilistic Algorithms in Finite Fields. *SIAM Journal on Computing*, 9:273–280, 1980.

[92] Michael O. Rabin. Efficient Dispersal of Information for Security and Fault Tolerance. Technical Report TR-02-87, Aiken Laboratory, Harvard Univerisity, April 1987.

[93] Richard F. Rashid. Threads of a New System. *Unix Review*, 4(8):37–49, August 1986.

[94] David P. Reed. *Naming and Synchronization in a Decentralized Computer System.* PhD thesis, MIT, September 1978.

[95] R. Rivest, A. Shamir, and L. Adleman. A Method for Obtaining Digital Signatures and Public-Key Cryptosystems. *Communications of the ACM*, 21(2):120–126, February 1978.

[96] Paul Rovner, Roy Levin, and John Wick. On Extending Modula-2 for Building Large, Integrated Systems. Technical Report 3, DEC Systems Research Center, January 1985.

[97] Giovanni Maria Sacco and Mario Schkolnick. Buffer Management in Relational Database Systems. *ACM Transactions on Database Systems*, 11(4):473–498, December 1986.

[98] Robert Daniell Sansom. *Building a Secure Distributed Computer System*. PhD thesis, Carnegie Mellon University, May 1988. Also available as Technical Report CMU-CS-88-141, Carnegie Mellon University, May 1988.

[99] M. Satyanarayanan. Integrating Security in a Large Distributed Environment. Technical Report CMU-CS-87-179, Carnegie Mellon University, November 1987.

[100] M. Satyanarayanan, John H. Howard, David A. Nichols, Robert N. Sidebotham, Alfred Z. Spector, and Michael J. West. The ITC Distributed File System: Principles and Design. In *Proceedings of the Tenth Symposium on Operating System Principles*, pages 35–50. ACM, December 1985. Also available as Technical Report CMU-ITC-039, Carnegie Mellon University, April 1985.

[101] Peter M. Schwarz. *Transactions on Typed Objects*. PhD thesis, Carnegie Mellon University, December 1984. Also available as Technical Report CMU-CS-84-166, Carnegie Mellon University, December 1984.

[102] Peter M. Schwarz and Alfred Z. Spector. Synchronizing Shared Abstract Types. *ACM Transactions on Computer Systems*, 2(3):223–250, August 1984. Also available in Stanley Zdonik and David Maier (editors), Readings in Object-Oriented Databases. Morgan Kaufmann, 1988. Also available as Technical Report CMU-CS-83-163, Carnegie Mellon University, November 1983.

[103] Stephen W. Sherman and Richard S. Brice. Performance of a Database Manager in a Virtual Memory System. *ACM Transactions on Database Systems*, 1(4):317–343, December 1976.

[104] M. D. Skeen. *Crash Recovery in a Distributed Database System*. PhD thesis, University of California, Berkeley, May 1982.

[105] Alfred Z. Spector, Jacob Butcher, Dean S. Daniels, Daniel J. Duchamp, Jeffrey L. Eppinger, Charles E. Fineman, Abdelsalam Heddaya, and Peter M. Schwarz. Support for Distributed Transactions in the TABS Prototype. *IEEE Transactions on Software Engineering*, SE-11(6):520–530, June 1985. Also available in Proceedings of the Fourth Symposium on Reliability in Distributed Software and Database Systems, Silver Springs, Maryland, IEEE, October, 1984 and as Technical Report CMU-CS-84-132, Carnegie Mellon University, July 1984.

[106] Alfred Z. Spector, Dean S. Daniels, Daniel J. Duchamp, Jeffrey L. Eppinger, and Randy Pausch. Distributed Transactions for Reliable Systems. In *Proceedings of the Tenth Symposium on Operating System Principles*, pages 127–146. ACM, December 1985. Also available in Concurrency Control and Reliability in Distributed Systems, Bharat K. Bhargava, ed., pp. 214-249, Van Nostrand Reinhold Company, New York, and as Technical Report CMU-CS-85-117, Carnegie Mellon University, September 1985.

[107] Alfred Z. Spector and Peter M. Schwarz. Transactions: A Construct for Reliable Distributed Computing. *Operating Systems Review*, 17(2):18–35, April 1983. Also available as Technical Report CMU-CS-82-143, Carnegie Mellon University, January 1983.

[108] Alfred Z. Spector, Dean Thompson, Randy Pausch, Jeffrey L. Eppinger, Richard Draves, Dan Duchamp, Dean S. Daniels, and Joshua J. Bloch. Camelot: A Distributed Transaction Facility for Mach and the Internet - An Interim Report. Technical Report CMU-CS-87-129, CMU, June 1987.

[109] Lindsey L. Spratt. The Transaction Resolution Journal: Extending the Before Journal. *Operating Systems Review*, 19(3):55–62, July 1985.

[110] Guy L. Steele, Jr. *Common Lisp: The Language*. Digital Press, 1984.

[111] Michael Stonebraker. Operating System Support for Database Management. *Communications of the ACM*, 24(7):412–418, July 1981.

[112] Michael Stonebraker. Virtual Memory Transaction Management. *Operating Systems Review*, 18(2):8–16, April 1984.

[113] Michael Stonebraker and Larry Rowe. The Design of POSTGRES. In *Proceedings of ACM SIGMOD '86*, pages 189–222. ACM, May 1987.

[114] B. Stroustrup. *The C++ Programming Language*. Addison-Wesley, Reading, Massachusetts, 1986.

[115] Tandem. *NonStop SQL Benchmark Workbook*, 84160 edition, March 1987.

[116] Dean Thompson. Coding Standards for Camelot. Camelot Working Memo 1, June 1986.

[117] Irving L. Traiger. Virtual Memory Management for Database Systems. *Operating Systems Review*, 16(4):26–48, October 1982. Also available as Technical Report RJ3489, IBM Research Laboratory, San Jose, California, May 1982.

[118] J. D. Tygar and Bennet S. Yee. Strongbox: A System for Self-Securing Programs. In Rachard F. Rashid, editor, *Carnegie Mellon Computer Science: A 25-Year Commemorative*. Addison-Wesley, Reading, Massachusetts, 1991.

[119] R. W. Watson. IPC Interface and End-To-End Protocols. In B. W. Lampson, editor, *Distributed Systems - Architecture and Implementation: An Advanced Course*, volume 105 of *Lecture Notes in Computer Science*, chapter 7, pages 140–174. Springer-Verlag, 1981.

[120] William E. Weihl. *Specification and Implementation of Atomic Data Types*. PhD thesis, MIT, March 1984.

[121] Matthew J. Weinstein, Thomas W. Page, Jr., Brian K. Livezey, and Gerald J. Popek. Transactions and Synchronization in a Distributed Operating System. In *Proceedings of the Tenth Symposium on Operating System Principles*, pages 115–126. ACM, December 1985.

[122] R. Williams, et al. R*: An Overview of the Architecture. Technical Report RJ3325, IBM Research Laboratory, San Jose, California, December 1981.

[123] J. M. Wing. Using Larch to Specify Avalon/C++ Objects. *IEEE Transactions on Software Engineering*, pages 1076–1088, September 1990.

[124] Michael Wayne Young, Avadis Tevanian, Jr., Richard F. Rashid, David B. Golub, Jeffrey L. Eppinger, Jonathan Chew, William Bolosky, David L. Black, and Robert V. Baron. The Duality of Memory and Communication in the Implementation of a Multiprocessor Operating System. In *Proceedings of the Eleventh Symposium on Operating System Principles*, pages 63–76. ACM, November 1987.

Index

B

C

D

E

F

G

H

I

J

M

N

O

P

Q

R

S

T

U